Macroeconomics
Theory & Applications

Robert Lester

Australia • Brazil • Canada • Mexico • Singapore • United Kingdom • United States

Macroeconomics: Theory and Applications, 1e
Robert Lester

SVP, Higher Education Product Management: Cheryl Costantini

VP, Product Management, Learning Experiences: Thais Alencar

Product Director: Joe Sabatino

Sr. Product Portfolio Manager: Chris Rader

Product Assistant: Autumn Lala-Sonora

Learning Designer: Sarah Huber

Senior Content Manager: Colleen A Farmer

Digital Project Manager: Judy Kwan

In-House Subject Matter Experts: Eugenia Belova, Andrew DeJong

Executive Product Marketing Manager: John Carey

IP Analyst: Rida Syed

IP Project Manager: Anjali Kambli

Production Service: Lumina Datamatics Ltd.

Designer: Erin Griffin

Cover and Interior Image Sources: Andriy Onufriyenko / Getty Images

Copyright © 2024 Cengage Learning, Inc. ALL RIGHTS RESERVED.

No part of this work covered by the copyright herein may be reproduced or distributed in any form or by any means, except as permitted by U.S. copyright law, without the prior written permission of the copyright owner.

Unless otherwise noted, all content is Copyright © Cengage Learning, Inc.

> For product information and technology assistance, contact us at
> **Cengage Customer & Sales Support, 1-800-354-9706 or support.cengage.com.**
>
> For permission to use material from this text or product, submit all requests online at **www.copyright.com**.

Library of Congress Control Number: 2023909710

Student Edition:
ISBN: 978-0-357-90177-9

Loose-leaf Edition:
ISBN: 978-0-357-90178-6

Cengage
200 Pier 4 Boulevard
Boston, MA 02210
USA

Cengage is a leading provider of customized learning solutions with employees residing in nearly 40 different countries and sales in more than 125 countries around the world. Find your local representative at: **www.cengage.com**.

To learn more about Cengage platforms and services, register or access your online learning solution, or purchase materials for your course, visit **www.cengage.com**.

Printed in the United States of America
Print Number: 01   Print Year: 2023

Dedication

To Mom, Dad, and Gordie

About the Author

Robert Lester is an associate professor of economics at Colby College in Waterville, Maine. Prior to joining Colby in 2015, he earned his PhD at the University of Notre Dame and a bachelor's degree at the University of Montana. He teaches classes in principles and intermediate macroeconomics and economic growth. He is the coauthor along with Julio Garín (Claremont McKenna College) and Eric Sims (University of Notre Dame) of the opensource textbook, Intermediate Macroeconomics.

Professor Lester's research is in applied macroeconomics with a particular focus in monetary policy and labor markets. His research has appeared in academic journals such as the *Review of Economics and Statistics*, *European Economic Review*, and *Journal of Money, Credit, and Banking*. He and Seth Neumuller (Wellesley College) cofounded the Workshop on Economic Dynamics in 2020 which brings together macroeconomists from the Northeast for an annual research conference.

Brief Contents

Preface xiii

Part 1 Growth

Chapter 1 Defining and Measuring GDP 1
Chapter 2 Production Functions 27
Chapter 3 The Solow Model of Economic Growth 48
Chapter 4 Explaining Total Factor Productivity 74

Part 2 Classical Theory

Chapter 5 Money, Prices, and Nominal Interest Rates 100
Chapter 6 Saving, Investment, and the Real Interest Rate 124
Chapter 7 International Trade and the Macroeconomy 157
Chapter 8 Labor Markets 183
Chapter 9 Government Spending and the Macroeconomy 215

Part 3 Business Cycles

Chapter 10 Introduction to Business Cycles 248
Chapter 11 The IS–MP Model 265
Chapter 12 The IS–MP–AS Model 293
Chapter 13 IS–MP–AS in the Open Economy 326

Part 4 Banking and Financial Markets

Chapter 14 Banking and the Macroeconomy 355
Chapter 15 Bonds, Stocks, and Monetary Policy 375

Mathematical Appendix 398
Solutions to Odd-Numbered Problems 405
Glossary 450
Index 454

Contents

Preface   xiii

Part 1   Growth

Chapter 1   **Defining and Measuring GDP   1**

1-1 Defining GDP   2
Application 1.1: Valuing Nonmarket Work   3
1-2 Calculating GDP   5
   1-2a The Value-Added Approach   6
   1-2b The Income Approach   6
   1-2c The Expenditure Approach   8
1-3 Separating Changes in Prices and Quantities in the Measure of GDP   13
   1-3a Tracking Price Changes Within a Country: The GDP Deflator   14
   1-3b Tracking Price Changes Across Countries: Purchasing Power Parity   16
1-4 Getting the Most Out of GDP Data   17
   1-4a The Facts of GDP per Capita   18
   1-4b The Connection Between GDP per Capita and Living Standards   20
Application 1.2: Inequality and GDP   22
Chapter Summary   24
Key Terms   24
Review Questions   24
Problems   24

Chapter 2   **Production Functions   27**

2-1 Production Functions   27
   2-1a The Aggregate Production Function   27
   2-1b The Shape of the Aggregate Production Function   28
2-2 Supply and Demand in the Capital and Labor Markets   30
   2-2a The Supply of Labor and Capital   31
   2-2b The Demand for Capital and Labor   32
   2-2c Combining Supply and Demand   34
Application 2.1: How Does Immigration Affect Wages?   37
2-3 Using the Production Function to Understand Cross-Country Income Differences   38
   2-3a Cobb–Douglas Production Function   38
   2-3b Putting the Cobb–Douglas Production Function to Work   39
Application 2.2: Measuring Factor Shares   42

Contents   vii

Chapter Summary 43
Key Terms 43
Review Questions 44
Problems 44

Chapter 3   The Solow Model of Economic Growth 48

3-1 The Solow Model of Economic Growth 48
   3-1a Basic Ingredients of the Solow Model 49
   3-1b Graphically Characterizing the Model 52
   3-1c Algebraically Solving the Model 53
3-2 Predictions of the Solow Model 54
   3-2a An Increase in the Savings Rate 54
   3-2b An Increase in the Population Growth Rate 56
   3-2c An Increase in TFP 56
   3-2d Putting It All Together 57
Application 3.1: Fiscal Policy in the Solow Model 59
3-3 Dynamic Efficiency and the Macroeconomy 60
3-4 Taking the Solow Model to the Data 62
   3-4a The Long-Run Predictions of the Solow Model 62
   3-4b Transition Dynamics in the Model and Data 65
   3-4c Summarizing the Performance of the Solow Model
   in Explaining the Data 68
Application 3.2: Growth and Climate Change 68
Chapter Summary 69
Key Terms 70
Review Questions 70
Problems 70

Chapter 4   Explaining Total Factor Productivity 74

4-1 Why Are Cross-Country TFP Differences So Big? 74
   4-1a Reviewing Cross-Country TFP Differences 75
   4-1b Misallocation Theories of TFP 76
Application 4.1: Real-World Distortions 78
   4-1c Financial Constraints and TFP 79
4-2 Growth Accounting 82
   4-2a The Growth Accounting Framework 82
   4-2b Growth Accounting in Action 83
4-3 The Romer Model of Endogenous Growth 85
   4-3a A Macroeconomic Impossibility Theorem 85
   4-3b Preliminaries of the Endogenous Growth Model 86
   4-3c Solving the Endogenous Growth Model 88
Application 4.2: Are Ideas Getting Harder to Find? 90
   4-3d Analyzing the Model Graphically 92
Chapter Summary 95
Key Terms 95
Review Questions 95
Problems 96

Part 2   Classical Theory

Chapter 5   Money, Prices, and Nominal Interest Rates 100

5-1 Measuring the Economy's Price Level 101
   5-1a The Consumer Price Index 101
   5-1b Practical Challenges to Calculating the CPI 102
   5-1c The CPI versus the GDP Deflator 104

viii   Contents

Application 5.1: Have Wages Increased?   106

5-2 Defining, Measuring, and Analyzing Money   107
5-2a The Roles of Money   107

Application 5.2: Is Bitcoin Money?   109

5-2b Measuring the Money Supply   109
5-2c The Quantity Theory of Money   111

5-3 The Costs of Inflation   113
5-3a Inflation Is a Tax   113
5-3b Inflation Imposes Shoe Leather Costs   113
5-3c Unexpected Inflation Redistributes Income   114
5-3d Inflation Distorts Relative Prices   115

5-4 The Supply of Money, the Demand for Money, and Nominal Interest Rate Determination   116
5-4a The Supply and Demand of Money   116
5-4b Graphical Derivation of the Equilibrium Nominal Interest Rate   117

Chapter Summary   119
Key Terms   120
Review Questions   120
Problems   120

Chapter 6   Saving, Investment, and the Real Interest Rate   124

6-1 Real Interest Rates and Nominal Interest Rates   125
6-1a The Fisher Equation   125

6-2 Consumption-Savings Decisions   127
6-2a Budget Constraints   127
6-2b Preferences for Current and Future Consumption   131
6-2c Characterizing the Optimal Consumption Bundle   135
6-2d The Consumption Function   140

Application 6.1: The Retirement Puzzle   141

6-3 A Model of Investment   143
6-4 Determination of the Equilibrium Real Interest Rate   144
6-4a Government Spending, Private Savings, and Public Savings   145
6-4b Graphical Determination of the Equilibrium Real Interest Rate   145
6-4c Comparative Statics in the Savings–Investment Model   146

Application 6.2: What Explains Declining Real Interest Rates?   149

Chapter Summary   151
Key Terms   151
Review Questions   152
Problems   152

Chapter 7   International Trade and the Macroeconomy   157

7-1 Exchange Rates   157
7-1a Calculating Nominal Exchange Rates   158
7-1b From Nominal to Real Exchange Rates   158
7-1c When Is the Law of One Price Actually a Law?   160

7-2 The Economist's Case for Free Trade (with Caveats)   160
7-2a The Ricardian Model   161
7-2b Ricardian Model with Comparative Advantage   164
7-2c The Limits to Free Trade   165

7-3 Accounting for Imports and Exports in the GDP Equation   166

Contents   ix

Application 7.1: The China Shock   167
    7-3a Imports, Exports, and the Flow of Capital   169
Application 7.2: The U.S. Trade Deficit   170
    7-3b Real Interest Rate Determination in the Open
        Economy   172
    7-3c Comparative Statics in the Open-Economy Savings–
        Investment Model   173
Chapter Summary   178
Key Terms   178
Questions for Review   178
Problems   179

Chapter 8   Labor Markets   183

8-1 The Data of the Labor Market   183
    8-1a National Trends of the Extensive and Intensive Margins of
    the Labor Market   185
    8-1b Labor Market Trends by Demographic Group   187
8-2 Labor–Leisure Model   190
    8-2a Budget Constraint and Preferences   190
    8-2b Optimization and Comparative Statics   194
    8-2c Labor Force Participation and the Reservation Wage   198
    8-2d Algebraically Solving for the Optimal Quantities of Labor,
    Leisure, and the Reservation Wage   199
Application 8.1: Labor Force Participation and the Quality of Leisure
Goods   201
8-3 A Model of Unemployment   202
    8-3a Worker and Firm Behavior   203
    8-3b Deriving the Equilibrium   203
    8-3c Graphically Characterizing the Equilibrium   205
Application 8.2: Indicators of Labor Market Utilization   208
Chapter Summary   210
Key Terms   210
Review Questions   210
Problems   210

Chapter 9   Government Spending and the Macroeconomy   215

9-1 A Primer on Government Spending and Revenue   215
    9-1a The Categories of Government Spending   216
    9-1b The Sources of Government Revenue   219
9-2 Taxation in the Consumption–Savings Model   221
    9-2a Incorporating Taxes in the Lifetime Budget Constraint   221
    9-2b Analyzing the Effects of Tax Changes on Consumption and
    Savings   224
**9-3 The Method of Government Financing and Macroeconomic
Outcomes   227**
    9-3a The Government's Intertemporal Budget Constraint   227
    9-3b The Ricardian Equivalence Theorem   228
    9-3c Deficit Financing in the Savings–Investment Model   230
Application 9.1: Consumption Responses from Stimulus Checks   233
9-4 The Sustainability of U.S. Government Debt   234
    9-4a The Government's Budget Constraint over the Very Long
    Run   234
    9-4b Forecasting Government Revenue and Expenditure   236

x Contents

9-4c Is It Possible to Grow Out of the Debt Problem? 237
9-4d Fiscal and Monetary Interactions with the Government's
Debt 239
Application 9.2: The End of Four Big Inflations 240
Chapter Summary 242
Key Terms 242
Questions for Review 243
Problems 243

Part 3 Business Cycles

Chapter 10 Introduction to Business Cycles 248

10-1 Measuring Business Cycles 249
10-1a Measuring the Trend 251
10-1b The Stylized Facts of Business Cycles 253
10-1c Trend GDP Is Not the Same Thing as Potential GDP 257
10-2 Real Business Cycle Theory 257
10-2a Total Factor Productivity as a Source of Business Cycle
Variation 259
10-2b Critiques of the RBC Model 260
10-2c What Does the RBC Model Teach Us? 261
Application 10.1: The Welfare Costs of Business Cycles 262
Chapter Summary 262
Key Terms 263
Questions for Review 263
Problems 263

Chapter 11 The IS–MP Model 265

11-1 The IS Curve 265
11-1a The Components of the IS Curve 266
11-1b Deriving the IS Curve Graphically 268
11-2 The Monetary Policy Rule 269
11-2a The MP Curve 270
11-2b Interest Rate Rules Versus Money Supply Rules 273
Application 11.1: Rules Versus Discretion and the Taylor Rule 275
**11-3 Solving for Output and the Real Interest Rate in the IS–MP
Model 276**
11-3a Comparative Statics 277
11-3b Solving the IS–MP Model Algebraically 281
11-3c The IS–MP Model and the Great Recession 281
Application 11.2: Do Changes in Monetary Policy Affect
Inequality? 286
Chapter Summary 288
Key Terms 289
Questions for Review 289
Problems 289

Chapter 12 The IS–MP–AS Model 293

12-1 The Aggregate Supply Curve 293
12-1a Completely Flexible Prices and Wages 294
12-1b Sticky Nominal Wages 298
Application 12.1: Measuring Inflation Expectations 303
12-1c Alternatives to the Wage-Contracting Model 305

Contents **xi**

12-2 The IS–MP–AS Model 306
12-2a Graphing the IS–MP–AS Model 307
12-2b Comparative Statics in the IS–MP–AS Model 310
12-2c Does the IS–MP–AS Model Explain Business Cycle Facts? 315

Application 12.2: Inflation Targeting Is a Good Idea: What Should the Target Be? 318

Chapter Summary 320
Key Terms 320
Questions for Review 320
Problems 320

Chapter 13 IS–MP–AS in the Open Economy 326

13-1 The Open Economy IS–MP–AS model 327
13-1a The Open Economy IS Curve 327
13-1b The MP Curve and Determination of Real Exchange Rates 329
13-1c The Complete IS–MP–AS Diagram 332

13-2 Comparative Statics in the Open-Economy IS–MP–AS Model 333
13-2a Shift in the IS Curve 333
13-2b Shift in the AS Curve 335
13-2c Changes to r_t^w and Q_t 337

13-3 Exchange Rate Regimes 340
13-3a Benefits and Disadvantages of Fixed Exchange Rates 340

Application 13.1: Speculative Attacks 341

13-3b Exchange Rate Targeting in IS–MP–AS Model 343
13-3c Capital Controls and the Impossible Trinity 346
13-3d Currency Unions 347

Application 13.2: The Free Silver Movement 349

Chapter Summary 349
Key Terms 350
Questions for Review 350
Problems 350

Part 4 Banking and Financial Markets

Chapter 14 Banking and the Macroeconomy 355

14-1 Why Do Banks Exist? 356
14-1a Maturity Transformation 356
14-1b Diversification of Risk 357
14-1c Adverse Selection and Screening 358
14-1d Moral Hazard and Monitoring 360

14-2 The Bank's Balance Sheet 361
14-2a Assets and Liabilities of a Bank 361
14-2b Balance Sheet Concepts 363

14-3 Bank Risks, Runs, and Regulations 366
14-3a Liquidity Versus Solvency Risk 366

Application 14.1: Bank Failures and the Case of Silicon Valley Bank 368

14-3b Bank Runs 369
14-3c Bank Regulation and Policy 369

Application 14.2: Too Big to Fail 370

xii Contents

Chapter Summary 371
Key Terms 372
Questions for Review 372
Problems 372

Chapter 15   Bonds, Stocks, and Monetary Policy   375

15-1 Bond Prices and Interest Rates   375
  15-1a Bonds: Definitions, Types, and Pricing   376
  15-1b The Term Structure   379
Application 15.1: Does an Inverted Yield Curve Predict Recessions?   383
  15-1c The Risk Structure of Interest Rates   384
  15-1d Monetary Policy and the Term and Risk Structure of Interest Rates   385
15-2 The Stock Market and Monetary Policy   387
  15-2a Pricing Stocks   387
  15-2b Stock Market Performance and Valuation   389
  15-2c Monetary Policy and the Value of the Stock Market   392
Application 15.2: Bubble Watching in the U.S. Housing Market   393
Chapter Summary   395
Key Terms   395
Questions for Review   395
Problems   396

Mathematical Appendix   398

Solutions to Odd-Numbered Problems   405

Glossary   450

Index   454

Preface

About this book

This is a book on intermediate macroeconomics, and is intended for students who have taken principles of macroeconomics. There are no additional mathematical or economic prerequisites beyond the principles course, but students should be comfortable analyzing problems graphically and algebraically.

The first goal of this book is to deepen students' understanding of the macroeconomy beyond what was learned at the principles level. Specifically, it seeks to partly close the gap between a student's understanding of macroeconomics today and the way macroeconomics is practiced by professional economists in academia and in policy institutions such as the Federal Reserve.

Modern macroeconomics is built on microeconomic foundations, that is, individuals and firms acting purposefully in maximizing some objective. Solid microeconomic foundations ensure that relationships derived between aggregate macroeconomic variables are consistent with the deliberate decisions made by individual economic actors. This is why microeconomic foundations are appealing to professional economists. As such, the book emphasizes microeconomic behavior from the very start.

Using these microeconomic foundations, the book presents a number of modern models used by academic macroeconomists and policy makers. Examples of these models include the dynamic consumption-savings model and the search-and-matching model of unemployment. Microeconomic foundations are also critical to the models of financial markets and asset pricing discussed in the last section of the textbook.

A drawback of microeconomic foundations is that it typically takes a lot of mathematical analysis to derive results. Anticipating this, the second goal of the book is to maximize its accessibility. Calculus is not a prerequisite, and the infrequent uses of calculus are relegated to footnotes. The text relies on functional forms that are straightforward to work with and include step-by-step derivations of each result. All graphs are clearly labeled, and the captions thoroughly describe what is going on in each figure. A mathematical appendix included at the end of the book reviews the natural log function, growth rates, and summary statistics. Thus, the book intends to maximize accessibility without sacrificing microeconomic fundamentals.

Finally, because macroeconomics is a practical discipline, the third goal is for this book to be policy relevant. The models discussed can be used to analyze fiscal and monetary policy. Again, microeconomic fundamentals are key to understanding how individuals and firms react to policy changes. The Federal Reserve, for instance, needs to estimate how businesses change their investment and hiring decisions in response to a change in the nominal interest rate. Or, to take another example, the federal government needs to estimate how individuals change their consumption and savings decisions in response to a change in taxes. The book applies macroeconomic models to specific macroeconomic policies throughout.

Beyond the use of microeconomic fundamentals, the state of the macroeconomics discipline has recently moved in new directions. First is the use of data in motivating and evaluating models. Thirty years ago, it wasn't uncommon for an entire edition of an academic macroeconomics journal to be void of serious data analysis. That is no longer the case. Datasets are more prolific and easier to access today than they ever have been. Macroeconomists use the datasets to test existing theories and to develop new ones.

Motivated by this trend in the discipline, the textbook frequently invokes data from a variety of sources including the Penn World Tables, the Bureau of Economic Analysis, and the Bureau of Labor Statistics. When possible, the data is directly downloaded from the Federal Reserve Economic Data (FRED) from the Federal Reserve Bank of Saint Louis. There are also data exercises available through MindTap that correspond to each chapter. These exercises give students hands-on experience with using real world economic data by allowing them to learn, practice, and explore the FRED.

A second trend in the discipline, not unrelated to the proliferation of data, is a focus on distributional issues. Decades ago, when the only easy to come by data involved aggregate economic variables, macroeconomic models were focused on aggregate economic outcomes. Things are different today. For example, instead of only focusing on how monetary policy affects aggregate consumption, macroeconomic researchers might be interested in how monetary policy affects the consumption of people of different ages or people across the wealth distribution. The ease of accessing data makes answering these sorts of questions possible.

While the models in this book exclusively analyze the behavior of a representative decision maker, they can be used as the foundation for further study into the connection between macroeconomics and inequality. As a motivation for such further study, the book discusses economic inequality in some applications. For instance, Chapter 1 discusses the relationship between GDP and inequality across countries. Chapter 7 discusses the impacts of international trade on inequality. Another application in Chapter 11 looks at the relationship between the Federal Reserve's interest rate changes and income and consumption inequality. More generally, each chapter presents applications which are concise, but offer a closer look at a particular area of macroeconomic research.

Organization of this Book

The book is organized into four sections: growth, classical theory, business cycles, and banking and financial markets. The aim is to provide students with a comprehensive summary of the macroeconomics discipline. Rather than putting all the data concepts into the first chapter or two, each data concept is included in the chapter where it is most relevant. So, labor market topics are included in the labor market chapter and the comparison of various price deflators is included in the chapter on money and prices. By introducing the theory alongside the data, the aim is for students to be able to make connections between the two as easily as possible.

1. Growth

The book begins with four chapters on economic growth and living standards. Chapter 1 covers the definition and measurement of GDP, as well as some of the stylized facts of economic growth and living standards across countries. It also includes a section on the correlation between GDP per capita and variables measuring standard of living across countries.

Chapter 2 introduces students to the aggregate production function. Following convention, output is produced with labor and capital. It reviews the standard assumptions macroeconomists make about production functions and then graphically derives the factor demand curves. The Cobb-Douglas production function appears in the last section of Chapter 2, which shows how it can be used to decompose differences in GDP per capita into differences in inputs versus differences in total factor productivity. From this, students learn that most of the variation in GDP per capita is explained by differences in TFP.

Having covered the Cobb-Douglas production function, chapters 3 and 4 discuss theories of economic growth. Chapter 3 develops the Solow model and shows what the model predicts about income convergence across countries. A key result from the Solow model is that long-run growth only comes through growth in TFP.

Given that TFP explains both the variation in living standards across countries at any point in time and also the long-run growth in GDP per capita, it is critical to understand where differences in TFP come from. This is covered in Chapter 4. Economists have recently turned to theories of misallocation to explain cross-country TFP differences at a point in time, which is covered in the first half of Chapter 4. To the best of my knowledge, no other intermediate macroeconomics book covers this material. The second half of Chapter 4 covers the Romer endogenous growth model which explains why TFP grows over time.

2. Classical Theory

The next section of the book covers a collection of topics that can broadly be grouped under classical theory, meaning that prices are free to instantaneously adjust. Chapter 5 discusses how economists measure price changes in the economy and the economic role and measurement of money. Students learn the quantity theory of money and derive the relationship between the growth of an economy's money supply and its inflation rate. The chapter also includes a model of money supply and demand in which the supply of money is taken to be exogenous, and the nominal interest rate is determined in equilibrium.

Chapter 6 picks up with the connection between the nominal interest rate, real interest rate, and inflation rate. Because the real interest rate is relevant for consumption and investment decisions, the chapter builds microfounded models of consumption and investment behavior. Students derive predictions about how consumption responds to changes in current income, future income, and the real interest rate within the context of a two-period consumption-savings model. Additionally, investment is a consequence of a forward-looking firm's profit maximization decisions. The analysis shows that investment is a negative function of the real interest rate. Using these theories of consumption and investment behavior, the chapter derives the economy's savings supply and investment demand curves. The intersection of these curves determines the economy's real interest rate.

A shortcoming of the savings and investment model in Chapter 6 is that there is no international sector. Chapter 7 fills this void. The chapter starts by distinguishing between real and nominal exchange rates and showing how both are calculated. Next, it discusses the Ricardian model of trade and shows how all countries, at least in aggregate, can gain from trade. Recent research on the distributional impacts of trade shows that the "at least in aggregate" qualifier is important, and students learn about the current state of knowledge on trade and inequality. Building on the preceding parts of the chapter, the last section shows how the international sector fits into the savings supply and investment demand model.

Chapter 8 continues to focus on the decisions of individual households by analyzing the choice of how much to work. After reviewing concepts like the unemployment and labor force participation rates and looking at the data, the chapter derives the optimal choices of leisure and consumption in the one-period labor-leisure model. Because participation in the labor force isn't universal, the chapter derives the reservation wage under which people optimally decide to stay out of the labor force. Students can use the labor-leisure model to analyze how hours worked and labor market participation are affected by wage and non-wage income.

Although the labor-leisure model is useful in analyzing the choice of the optimal quantity of work hours, it cannot address unemployment. Motivated by this, the last section of Chapter 8 introduces students to a search and matching model in which matches between workers and firms are determined by the vacancies posted by firms. Matching is random and not all vacancies are filled. The result is that unemployment occurs in equilibrium. After deriving the model's equilibrium, the chapter graphically analyzes how changes in exogenous variables such as the level of unemployment benefits affect the equilibrium unemployment rate.

Up to this point in the book, the government sector operates exogenously in the background. Chapter 9 is devoted to a deeper discussion of taxes and government spending. The chapter begins by documenting stylized facts about the government sector in the American economy. It then moves onto showing how taxes affect the optimal choice of consumption and savings in the two-period model. Next, the chapter discusses the government's lifetime budget constraint and uses it to discuss the sustainability of the government's debt. The chapter concludes with the connection between monetary and fiscal policy.

By the end of this section, students will understand the microeconomic determinants of consumption, savings, investment, and labor force decisions. Although the equilibrium real interest rate is determined in the savings supply and investment demand model, the level of GDP is taken to be exogenous. Over the longer run, GDP is determined by the factors affecting the Solow model in Chapter 3 which are independent of the economy's nominal variables, such as the inflation rate, and monetary policy. Over the short-run, however, GDP and nominal variables are functions of each other. Section 3 discusses the connection between real and nominal variables over the business cycle.

3. Business Cycles

The business cycle is the variation of an economy's GDP around its trend. Chapter 10 begins by discussing business cycle measurement, as well as some of the stylized facts of business cycles. Students are introduced to the real business cycle model which says that business cycles are the efficient response to short-run changes in TFP. The purpose of introducing the real business cycle model is two-fold. First, it connects business cycles with the models of economic growth from Section 1. Second, to the extent the real business cycle fails at explaining business cycles, it is still useful for economic policy. The reason is that the real business cycle predicts an economy's efficient level of GDP at any point in time which, in principle, policy makers can compare to actual GDP and adjust policy accordingly.

Chapters 11 and 12 analyze business cycles through the lens of the IS-MP-AS model. Expected inflation is exogenously fixed in the short run, so monetary policy effectively controls the real interest rate. Given a real interest rate, output is demand determined. Given a level of output, the aggregate supply (AS) curve determines the economy's inflation rate. These chapters discuss the role of expectations, the optimal choices of monetary policy, and the extent to which the model matches the business cycle facts.

Chapter 13 shows how to extend the IS-MP-AS model into an open-economy setting where the real exchange rate and level of net exports are endogenous variables. The chapter discusses the tradeoffs between fixed and floating exchange rate regimes and allowing the free movement of capital versus regulating it.

The Fed's decision to change interest rates affects the economy in the short run. However, the interest rate the Fed targets is the overnight rate banks borrow and lend to each other. How do changes in that overnight rate affect interest rates households and firms borrow at and banks lend at? Taking a step back, what explains the existence of banks in the first place? The last section of the book deals with these questions.

4. Banking and Financial Markets

Chapter 14 explains the role banks play in connecting savers with investors. Specifically, banks engage in maturity transformation, diversify risk, and limit problems associated with asymmetric information. The chapter introduces students to the bank's balance sheet and some of the key concepts in the balance sheet and measures of bank profitability. The chapter also discusses bank runs and policies designed to limit bank runs without encouraging excessive risk taking by banks.

Chapter 15 covers the pricing of bonds and stocks and how these prices are influenced by monetary policy. Critical to the analysis is the asset pricing equation which equates the price of an asset (such as a bond or a stock) to the present discounted value of its future payments. The basic asset pricing equation can be used to determine the prices of bonds and stocks. Using the bond-pricing equation, the chapter discusses theories about the term structure and risk structure of interest rates. The chapter shows how the Fed's management of the short-term, risk-free interest rate affects the interest rate on longer-duration and riskier debt. More recently, the Fed has taken a more aggressive approach in managing the risk and term structure by purchasing longer-duration and riskier debt. The chapter discusses these developments.

Having developed a model for pricing individual stocks, the next question is whether an individual stock or the entire stock market can be overvalued given its fundamentals. In other words, we want to know under what circumstances it's possible to get a bubble. The chapter discusses bubbles and the tradeoffs monetary policy makers face in detecting and deflating bubbles.

After reading this section students should have a more thorough understanding of the banking sector and how the Fed affects interest rates that are relevant to the decisions of individuals and firms. The material in this section can be used as the foundation for an upper-level course in money and banking.

Features of Text

Learning economics, especially at the intermediate level, requires consistent practice. There are many practice resources available to students within the book and online. This section describes them.

1. Knowledge checks – Each chapter contains several knowledge checks which review the content of each section. Worked solutions to these knowledge checks are provided at the end of each chapter, so that students can compare their work to the solutions.

2. Questions for review and problems – Each chapter concludes with at least five questions for review which test student's knowledge of the material in the chapter. These questions are typically in a short answer format. The end-of-chapter problems are more analytical and use graphical and algebraic analysis to better understand the models in each chapter. Answers to the odd-numbered questions for review and problems are available in the back of the book. A full set of solutions for the questions for review and problems is available to instructors in the instructor's manual.that review the material. The solutions to test bank questions are available to instructors.

3. Applications – Most chapters include two applications which discuss some economic data or recent research on a relevant topic. For instance, an application in Chapter 4 discusses recent research asking whether ideas are getting harder to find. Chapter 12, meanwhile, includes an application that discusses how to measure inflation expectations. To the extent possible, the text tries to make the applications policy relevant and bring in current events.

4. Instructor's manual and PowerPoint slides – The instructor's manual, authored by Dr. Carrie B. Lee (Florida State University) contains chapter summaries, key terms, and additional problems. Every chapter also has a set of PowerPoint slides.

5. Model-building videos – Each chapter includes a video which presents the key model discussed in each chapter and covers its assumptions, equations, equilibrium conditions, and comparative statics.

6. MindTap resources – Students who purchase the MindTap package get access to additional practice problems and data applications.

Acknowledgements

This book would not have been possible without the advice and support of my colleagues. I owe a special thanks to Julio Garín at Claremont McKenna College and Eric Sims at the University of Notre Dame. Julio, Eric, and I wrote a textbook several years ago that we have adapted through the years. The textbook grew out of Eric's very detailed intermediate macroeconomics notes. The process of writing the book with Julio and Eric surely influenced the ideas I brought to the current work. More generally, much of what

I know about economic pedagogy comes from Eric and Julio and I'm grateful to have them as friends and coauthors.

The book benefited from the comments and suggested revisions from Dr. Byunghee Choi at Lebanon Valley College, Dr. Scott W. Hagerty at Northeastern Illinois University, and Dr. Carrie B. Lee at Florida State University. Their advice significantly improved the final product. Dr. Lee is also responsible for the Instructor's Manual and PowerPoint slides. Eugenia Belova and Andrew DeJong, the subject matter experts at Cengage, also provided useful feedback. Eugenia and Andrew developed the online assessment which is critically important for student learning. The MindTap digital content as a whole is a result of a collective work by Cengage's Economic Product Team led by Chris Rader, Portfolio Product Manager. Sarah Huber, the Learning Designer, helped shape the product from a pedagogical standpoint. And Colleen Farmer, the Senior Content Manager, ensured that the textbook moves along each stage of revision until the book's completion.

Finally, I'm thankful for my colleagues and students at Colby College. I'm essentially allowed to teach whatever I want; however I want to teach it. This autonomy has allowed me to experiment with different content and techniques. My senior macroeconomist colleagues, Michael Donihue and David Findlay, have provided invaluable mentorship and were great resources when I had questions on the book. My students are hardworking and eager to learn. They make teaching economics an unambiguous delight.

Chapter 1

Defining and Measuring GDP

Learning Objectives

1.1   Calculate GDP using the income, expenditure, and value-added approaches.

1.2   Distinguish between real and nominal GDP and calculate the GDP deflator.

1.3   Explain the concept of purchasing power parity and how that affects measured cross-country income differences.

1.4   List the stylized facts of economic growth.

1.5   Critically evaluate GDP per person as an accurate measure of living standards.

Comparing the United States of 150 years ago to the United States of today shows unfathomable differences. Transportation was mostly by train or ship, with cars and airplanes still decades away. Most households didn't have plumbing, and access to clean water was still an issue. The average length of the workweek was 60 hours, which doesn't include time spent on chores around the house. Communication was mostly by handwritten letters, as Alexander Graham Bell was still a few years away from patenting the telephone. Life expectancy at childbirth was less than 50 years old, and many infants didn't survive past their first birthday.

Can the differences between then and now be incapsulated in a single number? As far back as the 18th century, the U.S. government has published the *Statistical Abstract of the United States*. The *Abstract* recorded output in select manufacturing industries, agricultural commodities, and construction projects. However, it was not until the Great Depression of the 1930s that the U.S. government felt an urgent need to see a comprehensive picture of how the economy was doing. A general perception was that something had been going terribly wrong, but the leaders of the country had a poor understanding of the economic forces that moved their nation. The U.S. Department of Commerce asked a group of economists at the National Bureau of Economic Research in New York, led by Nobel laureate Simon Kuznets, to develop a set of national economic accounts. In 1937, the Kuznets group published their research, titled *National Income, 1929–1935*. Building off this research, economists developed the national income and product accounts (NIPA), which measure the sources of income and expenditure for the entire national economy.

An important component of the accounts is gross domestic product (GDP). GDP measures the total value of goods and services produced in the United States. An accurate measurement of GDP allows policymakers to organize complex and chaotic real-world data and helps develop optimal policies to improve a country's economic activity.

From the very beginning, however, economists warned of the imperfection of GDP: maximizing economic output is not equivalent to maximizing the quality of life for a country's citizens. To take a simple example, a technique that increases the production of textiles but poisons rivers with lethal chemicals would increase GDP but reduce overall welfare. Kuznets had always emphasized that GDP is simply a measure of a nation's economic activity and cannot be used to measure the nation's welfare. Still, the method presented by the Kuznets team was a giant step forward, as GDP yields valuable insights about our economy in both a domestic and global context.

2 **Part 1** Growth

This chapter discusses how income is measured within a country and over time. Dividing GDP by the population gives a measure of average income per person. Just because income per person is well measured doesn't necessarily mean that it informs us about the quality of life for a country's citizens. The end of this chapter discusses several quality-of-life variables and shows how each of them is correlated with income per person.

Finally, this chapter sets the tone for what comes in the rest of the book. Measurement is important for macroeconomists. It informs us of what our theories get right and what they get wrong. Most of the textbook is devoted to macroeconomic theory, but accurate measurement is vital to evaluating the success of any theory.

1-1 Defining GDP

Gross domestic product (GDP)

The current dollar value of all final goods and services produced in a country in a year.

Gross domestic product (GDP) is the current dollar value of all final goods and services produced in a country in a year. In essence, GDP is a comprehensive measure of everything produced within a country. Because we will be referring to GDP throughout the book, it is worthwhile to spend some time on each part of the definition.

1. **Current dollar value:** The U.S. economy produces many thousands of unique goods and services. Having one objective metric of production requires the value of haircuts to be denominated in the same units as the value of automobiles. The universal unit both in the United States and abroad is currency. In the United States, the currency is the dollar. Every good or service produced in the United States has a dollar value, and GDP is the sum of the current dollar value of everything produced.

   Here is an example: If the economy produced 2 billion haircuts that each cost $20 and 20 million cars that each cost $20,000, then total production was $440 billion (=$20 times 2 billion haircuts plus $20,000 times 20 million cars).

   The word *current* means that GDP is calculated using the current year's prices. In the last example, calculating GDP in 2023 requires using 2023 prices for haircuts and cars. This means that GDP can rise because a greater quantity of goods and services are produced or because prices of goods and services increase.

2. **Of all final:** Imagine that an economy produces ice cream cones. The ice cream shop purchases 1,000 cones at $1 and then sells the cones with ice cream for $4 each. It is tempting to say that GDP increases by the sum of the value of all the individual cones ($1,000) and the value of all the ice cream cones ($4,000), for a total of $5,000. But that isn't quite right. The reason is that the $4 value of each ice cream cone already includes the $1 it costs to purchase each cone. Including the total value of the ice cream cones and the cones themselves would be double counting. The cones are an example of an **intermediate good**: a good that is not ready for consumption or investment. Calculating GDP requires that we omit intermediate goods so as to avoid double counting.

Intermediate good

A good that is not yet ready for final consumption or investment.

3. **Goods and services:** *Goods* are things that are tangible, such as food, cars, and pet supplies. *Services* are not tangible and include things like haircuts, medical care, and airplane rides. GDP includes all goods and services.

4. **Produced:** GDP measures production, not sales. Sometimes production and sales are identical, but not all the time. For instance, if you buy a brand-new hand-crafted coffee table, that counts in GDP. But if you turn around and sell the coffee table on Etsy, that does not count in GDP. There are two sales in this example— the manufacturer sold you the coffee table and you sold the coffee table to some-one else—but there is only one coffee table produced. Thus, the dollar value of the first transaction counts in GDP, but not the second.

   Ideally, GDP would be a comprehensive measure of production; however, in practice, some goods and services produced are omitted from GDP. These products are excluded because no transaction is recorded. Perhaps the biggest

Chapter 1 Defining and Measuring GDP   **3**

omission is the value of childcare. The "production" of childcare is a service and should therefore be counted in GDP. If a parent sends their child to daycare, GDP increases by the amount the parent spends on the daycare. On the other hand, if the parent stays home with the child themselves, then there is no transaction, so nothing gets added to GDP. Economists have attempted to estimate the value of these "home-produced" goods and services, and that research is the subject of Application 1.1.

5. **In a country:** For a good or service to count toward U.S. GDP, it has to be produced in the United States. So, if General Motors (a company headquartered in America) makes a car in Detroit, Michigan, that counts in GDP. If a GM plant in Mexico makes a car, that counts in Mexico's GDP, not in the United States' GDP. The same goes for services. If an American citizen gives a paid economics lecture in Boston, that counts toward U.S. GDP. If the same lecture is given in Beijing, China, then any payment counts toward Chinese GDP.

6. **In a year:** If you walk into a car dealership in January or February, you are likely to see new cars of this year's model as well as the inventory from last year. If you decide to purchase a car that was manufactured this year, that counts in GDP. If you purchase a car that was manufactured last year, that doesn't count in GDP. Remember, the goal is to measure *production*, not *sales*. A car that was produced in 2022 is counted in 2022's GDP even if it doesn't get sold until 2023.

This rule of counting production when it is produced, not when it is sold, has an important nuance. There is often a service attached to the sale of a good, even if the good was produced in the past. For example, when someone buys an existing home with the help of a realtor, the realtor gets a commission. The commission counts in GDP because the realtor's services were produced in the current year. The sale of the house does not, because the house was produced in the past. The same goes for a financial transaction. If you call a financial adviser to buy some shares of a stock, the adviser's commission is included in GDP. The sale of the stock itself is not, because nothing was produced.

✓ Knowledge Check 1-1

Explain why each of the following are or are not included in GDP.

1. You sell your 10-year-old house by yourself.
2. You sell your 10-year-old house by hiring a realtor.
3. You buy a brand-new house.
4. You buy a brick of imported French cheese at the supermarket.
5. You buy a brick of Wisconsin-produced cheese at the supermarket.

——————————————————— Answers are at the end of the chapter.

Application 1.1

Valuing Nonmarket Work

Some goods and services are produced outside the market. A parent staying home to provide childcare is one such example. Since there is no transaction for this service, the care that the parent provides does not get counted in GDP. As another example, if you hire a lawncare company to mow your lawn, that service will be counted in GDP.

But if you mow the lawn yourself, there is no transaction, and nothing gets counted in GDP. In both cases, the lawn gets mowed, so it is somewhat arbitrary that only one case gets counted in GDP. A more comprehensive measure of national output would measure all production activities regardless of whether they were produced on the market.

■ Continues

Application 1.1 (Continued)

Fortunately, economists have developed methods for incorporating the value of nonmarket work into a measure of national output.

Before estimating the value of nonmarket work, we need to know how much time people spend on those activities. The American Time Use Survey (ATUS) collects data on how Americans use their time. Specifically, the ATUS asks survey respondents how they spent every minute of the previous day. The ATUS includes a category for time spent caring for children in the household under age 18, as well as several other categories of nonmarket work. These include:

1. Household activities, such as cleaning, laundry, food preparation and cleanup, and lawn and garden care.

2. Household management activities, such as financial management, interior and exterior maintenance and repair, animal and pet care, and vehicle maintenance.

3. Purchasing goods and services, which includes grocery shopping and other consumer goods.

Broadly speaking, these three types of activities and childcare are referred to as "home production" because the time is spent on maintaining and caring for the household or the household members. Figure 1.1 shows the trends in home production for men and women over the age of 18 between 2011 and 2019. Women spend close to 27 hours per week on home production activities in total, while men spend closer to 17 hours per week. To put this in perspective, women average about 21 hours per week on market work, whereas men average about 28 hours per week. Thus, the time spent on nonmarket work is significant.

The next step is to place a value on these nonmarket hours. The key question is how much would each of these services cost if they were completed by professionals? So, if mowing your lawn takes half an hour and a landscaper earns $25 per hour, then the value of mowing the lawn by yourself is $12.50 ($=0.5 \times \$25$). In theory, you could make this calculation for every single home production activity. One problem with this approach is that you might not be as skilled as the professionals you would otherwise hire to do the housework and maintenance. Take an activity like plumbing. A skilled plumber can easily run $100 per hour. If I spend 10 hours trying to fix my leaking sink and (inevitably) make it worse because I can't follow the YouTube instructions to save my life, does it really make sense to value my toil at $1,000 ($=10 \times \$100$)? Probably not.

As an alternative, and to simplify the estimation, all home production activity can be valued at the median wage of maids and household cleaners. This will provide a lower bound on the value of home production, because these workers have low compensation on average. The median hourly wage for workers in this occupation category was $13.84 in 2021.[2] Americans over the age of 18 average about 3.2 hours per day on home production activities, including childcare. This amounts to 1,168 hours per year per person. The annual value of this time therefore is about $16,165. There are about 258 million people over the age of 18 in the United States. Thus, the total value of home production is $4.2 trillion ($=258$ million $\times$ $16,165$). GDP is about 25 trillion dollars, so incorporating the value of home production activities raises GDP by about 17 percent.

The estimate of $4.2 trillion is a large number and, if anything, represents a lower bound, as median wages of household cleaners are quite low. At the same time, the value of home production as a fraction of GDP decreased over the last 50 years. This is primarily due to more women entering the labor force and spending less time on home production.

Figure 1.1 The weekly hours spent on home production (including and excluding child care for men and women) from the year 2011 to 2019.

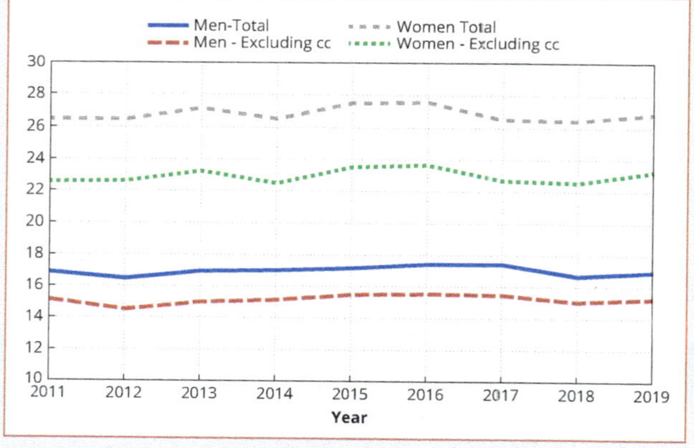

Source: American Time Use Survey.

[2]This statistic is from the Occupational Wage and Employment Statistics database collected by the Bureau of Labor Statistics.

1-2 Calculating GDP

One approach to calculating GDP is to use the definition directly. That is, sum together the current dollar value of all final goods and services produced in a country in a year. Mathematically, if the economy produces N final products (which includes both goods and services) indexed by $i = 1, 2, \ldots, N - 1, N$, then GDP is

$$GDP = \sum_{i=1}^{N} p_i y_i, \qquad (1)$$

where y_i is the quantity of product i and p_i is the price of product i. While the output for every good and service produced in the United States isn't publicly available, GDP estimates at the industry level are. Each business establishment in the United States is classified into an industry according to the North American Industry Classification System (NAICS) and then GDP is calculated at the industry level.

To see how this works, Figure 1.2 shows the GDPs of three industries as a fraction of total GDP. Between 1997 and 2021, the share of total GDP attributed to manufacturing fell from 16 percent to about 11 percent and the share attributed to education and health care rose about 1.5 percentage points. Construction's share, meanwhile, stayed constant at about 4 percent of GDP.

The NAICS system covers industries at a much more disaggregated level than what's reported here. For instance, one type of sub-industry contained in manufacturing is "animal food manufacturing." Within that, there is a sub-sub-industry, "dog and cat food manufacturing." Every broad industry classification can be disaggregated like this. Taken together, the NAICS system provides a comprehensive picture of every industry's contribution to GDP.

From the point of view of data collection, it is difficult to classify what fraction of production falls into final goods and what falls into intermediate goods. For instance, take tires. When you buy newly produced tires to install on your car, the tires count as a final good.

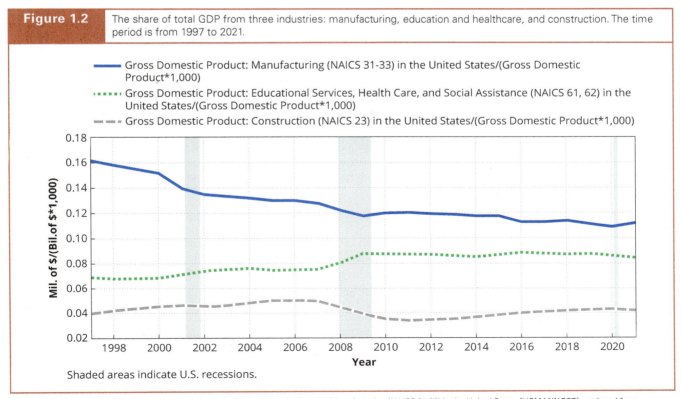

Figure 1.2 The share of total GDP from three industries: manufacturing, education and healthcare, and construction. The time period is from 1997 to 2021.

Shaded areas indicate U.S. recessions.

Source: BEA and FRED, U.S. Bureau of Economic Analysis, Gross Domestic Product: Manufacturing (NAICS 31-33) in the United States [USMANNGSP], retrieved from FRED, Federal Reserve Bank of St. Louis; https://fred.stlouisfed.org/series/USMANNGSP, July 29, 2022.

6 **Part 1** Growth

But when General Motors buys a set of tires to put on a truck they are building, the tires count as an intermediate good and the truck counts as the final good. Faced with the reality of distinguishing intermediate from final goods, it is impractical to use Equation (1) to calculate GDP. There are three ways economists and statisticians compute GDP in practice.

1-2a The Value-Added Approach

The value-added approach to calculating GDP sums the increase in value associated with each step of production. Let's return to the last example of GM buying tires to attach to a new truck. Suppose the tires cost $600 and the truck sells for $30,600. The final good produced is the truck, not the tires. GDP should increase by $30,600. But from the point of view of the person collecting the economics statistics, it isn't known which tires are sold to consumers and which ones are sold as intermediate goods. The value-added approach comes in useful for this.

Table 1.1 shows how this approach works. Suppose Goodyear Tires produces four sets of tires. Three of the sets are sold to consumers and one set is sold to General Motors (GM). The gross output is the total value each business earns for selling its product. Goodyear sold four pairs of tires, so gross output equals $2,400. By assumption, Goodyear uses no intermediate inputs. The value added from tire production is equal to $2,400. GM buys a set of tires for $600, installs them on the new truck, and sells the truck for $30,600. But $600 of that sales price represents the value of the tires. Thus, GM's value added in producing the truck is $30,000 (=$30,600 − $600). GDP for the entire economy is the sum of each business's value added: $30,000 + $2,400 = $32,400.

In practice, government economists and statisticians measure the value of gross output and intermediate inputs for each industry according to their NAICS classification and then infer value added by subtracting intermediate inputs from gross output. The sum of value added for each industry equals GDP for the entire economy.

1-2b The Income Approach

Every final good and service requires inputs in order to produce them. The income approach to calculating GDP sums the total payments going to each input. Manufacturing a car requires a physical factory; various machines and tools; intermediate inputs, such as tires and steering wheels; workers to assemble the car; and managers to supervise the production process. None of these inputs are freely provided. Workers and managers get paid wages, using a physical factory requires a big purchase up front or paying rent to the factory owner, and the owners of the firm want to earn a profit. The income approach sums together all of the income going to various inputs to arrive at GDP.

Because every dollar of revenue is divided between profit and payments to the inputs that produce GDP, calculating GDP using the income approach gives an equivalent answer to calculating GDP using the value-added approach. Thus, the first part of the GDP identity is established:

$$\text{Total value added} \equiv \text{Total income.}$$

The $\equiv$ sign indicates an *identity*. An identity is an equation that always holds true regardless of the numbers. Because the income approach adds together all forms of income, the total is often referred to as **gross national income (GNI)**. Again, absent accounting discrepancies, GDP should equal GNI.

Gross national income (GNI)
The sum of all forms of income earned by a nation's citizens.

Table 1.1	An Example of Calculating Value Added	
	Goodyear	**GM**
Gross output	$600 × 4 = $2,400	$30,600
Intermeciate inputs	$0	$600
Value added	$2,400	$30,000

The income approach is implemented in practice by statistical agencies like the Bureau of Economic Analysis (BEA) in the United States. The BEA classifies income into several major categories.[1]

1. Compensation to employees – This includes wage and salary income to all private and public employees. It also includes employer-provided benefits like health insurance.

2. Taxes on production and imports less subsidies – The tax you are most likely familiar with is the state sales tax, which is a tax applied when a good or service is sold. It is generally applied to all products. An excise tax is a tax applied to a specific good or service. Cigarettes, for example, face an excise tax. Subsidies are payments by the government to private businesses. Note that subsidies are subtracted rather than added to the GDP calculation. The reason is that the subsidy to the business will eventually be realized as income for some other factor of production. Perhaps the firm uses the subsidy for an employee bonus (an increase in employee compensation). Subtracting the subsidy avoids double counting.

3. Consumption of fixed capital – As businesses use their machines, equipment, and physical operating spaces, the value of these **capital goods** declines. The consumption of fixed capital measures **depreciation**, or the decline in value of capital goods associated with physical deterioration and obsolescence. To take one example, think of a desktop computer. The value of the computer can decline because of repeated use (physical deterioration) or because a superior model is introduced (obsolescence).

> **Capital good**
> A machine, piece of equipment, or physical operating space used by a business.
>
> **Depreciation**
> The decline in value of capital goods associated with physical deterioration and obsolescence.

4. Net operating surplus – After subtracting employee compensation, taxes less subsidies, and the consumption of fixed capital from a firm's value added, what's left over is net operating surplus.

    This sounds a little like "profit," but there are a couple of important distinctions. First, net operating surplus subtracts neither interest payments nor rent payment from revenue. That means if a business is borrowing to finance its equipment or is paying rent to the factory owner, neither of those costs are deducted from net operating surplus. But explicit costs are not the only relevant economic costs. If a business owns its factory and its capital stock, using the capital or the factory is still not "free." The reason is that they carry an opportunity cost. Remember from principles of economics that an opportunity cost of using a resource (say the factory) is the price of the best alternative. If the business owns the factory but could rent it for $50,000 per month to another business, the opportunity cost of operating the factory is $50,000. A correct derivation of economic profit would subtract this $50,000 opportunity cost from revenue.

    In practice, measuring opportunity costs to obtain precise estimates of economic profit is quite difficult. Things get even more complicated when you think about nontangible capital like software and patents. Economists have made some progress in measuring pure economic profit, but the general takeaway is that net operating surplus should *not* be interpreted as economic profit.

In summary then, the equation for GNI is:

$$\text{GNI} = \text{Employee compensation}$$
$$+ \text{ Taxes on production and imports less subsidies}$$
$$+ \text{ Consumption of fixed capital}$$
$$+ \text{ Net operating surplus.} \tag{2}$$

Figure 1.3 shows how the share of each component of GNI has evolved over time. The biggest component to GNI is compensation to employees, which accounts for about

---

[1]The BEA assembles the *National Income and Product Accounts Handbook* and makes it freely available on its website, https://www.bea.gov/resources/methodologies/nipa-handbook. I use their definitions throughout this section.

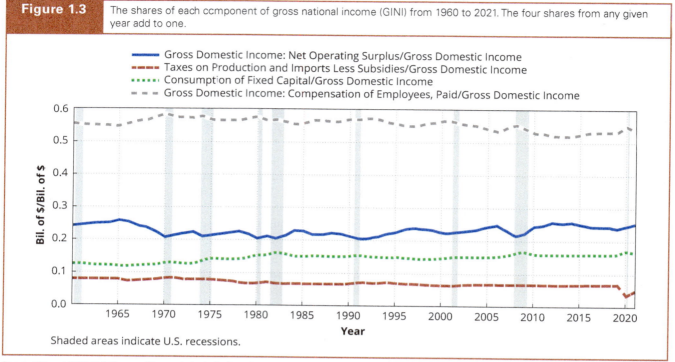

Figure 1.3 The shares of each component of gross national income (GINI) from 1960 to 2021. The four shares from any given year add to one.

Source: BEA and FRED, U.S. Bureau of Economic Analysis, Gross Domestic Income: Net Operating Surplus [GDINOS], retrieved from FRED, Federal Reserve Bank of St. Louis; https://fred.stlouisfed.org/series/GDINOS, July 29, 2022.

55 percent on average. Net operating surplus is the next largest, averaging about 23 percent of GNI on average. The shares of consumption of fixed capital and taxes on production and imports less subsidies are the smallest, averaging about 15 percent and 7 percent.

These shares have stayed relatively constant over time. The share of employee compensation, for instance, has never been less than 50 percent but never more than 60 percent. At the same time, there have been substantial changes in how employees are compensated. The BEA divides employee compensation into two categories: i) wage and salary income, which includes monetary compensation to employees as well as bonuses and tips; and ii) supplements to wages and salaries, which includes employer contributions to pension funds, employer-provided health insurance, and government-sponsored social insurance like Social Security. Figure 1.4 shows how these forms of compensation have evolved over time.

In 1947, wage and salary income made up about 94 percent of total compensation. This share has decreased over the ensuing decades to about 80 percent today. The trend has been primarily driven by an increase in the costs of health insurance and that employers today are more likely to provide health insurance than in the past. The Social Security tax rate also increased from less than 2 percent in 1947 to 6.2 percent today. Taken together, employees now receive a greater share of their income in employer-provided benefits.

1-2c The Expenditure Approach

The expenditure approach to calculating GDP uses the fact that everything that is produced in a year is either sold or goes into inventory. Moreover, since we discussed in the last section that total production always equals total income, we can finalize the accounting identity:

$$\text{Total value added} \equiv \text{Total income} \equiv \text{Total expenditure}. \tag{3}$$

Despite its simplicity, Equation (3) has powerful implications. It says we can look at GDP from the perspective of how income is earned, or how expenditure is allocated, or the total production of (final) goods and services across industries.

Figure 1.4

The trends in employee compensation evolve over time. The two components to employee compensation are (1) wages and salaries and (2) supplements to wages and salaries.

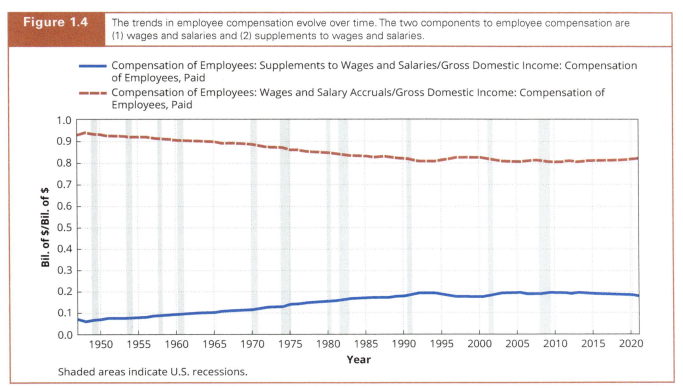

Shaded areas indicate U.S. recessions.

Source: BEA and FRED, U.S. Bureau of Economic Analysis, Compensation of employees: Supplements to wages and salaries [A038RC1Q027SBEA], retrieved from FRED, Federal Reserve Bank of St. Louis; https://fred.stlouisfed.org/series/A038RC1Q027SBEA, July 29, 2022.

The expenditure side of GDP accounting has several big components that we discuss in turn.

1. Consumption includes the purchase of all **durable goods**, nondurable goods, and services intended for final use. A good is durable if it physically persists despite being used. If you buy a pizza, it has some value. Once you eat it though, it's gone. On the other hand, if you buy a car (perhaps to deliver pizzas with), you can use the car day after day until it's not drivable. The car is a durable good; the pizza is a nondurable good. Many times, the distinction between durable and nondurable isn't so clear-cut. A pair of blue jeans has some durability but likely won't last for more than a couple years. The BEA classifies a good as durable if it has an average useful life of more than three years. Table 1.2 shows the distribution of consumption expenditures in 2021.

2. Private investment includes the addition to and replacement of the stock of assets to the economy by private businesses and households. Private investment is often referred to simply as "investment," with the understanding that government investment is part of a different category. Investment is composed of several different categories.

    a. *Residential fixed investment* includes investment in residential structures and equipment. The biggest part of residential fixed investment is the construction of new single-family and multifamily houses. But it also includes additions

Durable good
A good that physically persists despite being used. The BEA defines a durable good as a good with an average useful life of at least three years.

Table 1.2 — Consumption Expenditures (in Billions) for 2021

Nondurable Goods	$3,455.2
Durable Goods	$2,026.2
Services	$10,260.1
Total	**$15,741.6**

Source: BEA.

Part 1 Growth

Table 1.3	Investment (in Billions) for 2021
Nonresidential fixed investment	$3,053.7
Residential fixed investment	$1,086.1
Change in inventories	−$19.9
Total	$4,120.0

Source: BEA.

and improvements to existing houses. So, if you remodel your kitchen, those expenses would be captured in residential fixed investment.

   b. *Nonresidential fixed investment* includes investment in nonresidential structures, equipment, and intellectual property rights. Nonresidential structures would include things like factories and healthcare facilities. Computers, delivery trucks, and construction tools would all be included in equipment. Finally, intellectual property rights includes research and development, newly developed software, and what the BEA calls "entertainment originals." Entertainment originals include investment in movies, TV shows, books, and music.

   c. *Change in private inventories* is a measure of the change in the physical volume of goods stored as inventory. The change in inventories can be positive or negative. To see how this works, suppose a business starts the year with an inventory of 100 smartphones valued at $1,000 each. If it ends the year with 120 smartphones in its inventory, then the value of the change in inventories is $20,000 ($100 × 120 − $100 × 100). If the business were to end the year with 80 smartphones in its inventory, the change in inventory would be −$20,000 ($100 × 80 − $100 × 100). Table 1.3 shows the distribution of investment spending in 2021.

3. Government spending includes the consumption and investment of final goods by the government at the federal, state, and local levels. Government consumption includes things like public school spending and national defense. Government investment includes the addition to and replacement of assets owned by the government. To make this concrete, when a state or local government builds a new elementary school, that is an example of investment. When the same government compensates the teachers at the school, that is an example of consumption.

Transfer payment
Moving money or resources from one person to another without anything being produced.

Importantly, government **transfer payments**, moving money from one person in the economy to another, are not included in GDP. The reason for not including transfer payments is because nothing is produced. For instance, a large part of the federal budget goes toward Social Security spending. But because Social Security is just a transfer from workers who are taxed to retirees, nothing is produced, and so it is not included in GDP.

Table 1.4 shows the breakdown of government spending at the federal level and state and local levels. You might be surprised that federal spending makes up less

Table 1.4	Government Spending (in Billions) for 2021
Federal	
Consumption	$1,205.0
Investment	$360.0
State and Local	
Consumption	$2,045.4
Investment	$442.3
Total	$4,052.7

Source: BEA.

Figure 1.5 The distribution of federal government spending in 2020.

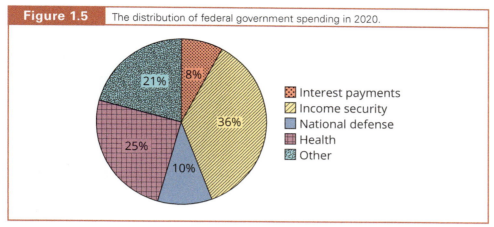

Source: BEA Table 3.16.

than 50 percent of total government consumption and investment. The key to understanding this is that the federal government spends money on a lot of things that do not count toward GDP.

Figure 1.5 shows the distribution of *total* federal government expenditure. More than one-third of the federal government's expenses, or close to 2.5 trillion dollars, go toward income security programs. This includes payments on Social Security, unemployment insurance, and other forms of supplemental income support, such as Temporary Assistance for Needy Families and the Supplemental Nutrition Assistance Program. Another sizeable part of the federal budget that does not contribute to GDP is interest payments on the federal debt. Interest payments amounted to approximately 534 billion dollars in 2020, or 8 percent of total expenditures. With both interest rates and the level of federal debt on the rise, this percentage is likely to increase in the future.

4. Exports minus imports – In the U.S. context, an export is a good or service produced in the United States and sold abroad. According to the definition of GDP, the value of any product produced in the United States is counted in GDP. An import is a good or service produced abroad and sold in the United States. Why subtract the value of imports from GDP? The reason is to avoid counting the value of a product produced abroad in U.S. GDP. For instance, if you live in the United States and buy a car produced in South Korea, durable consumption expenditure goes up. But GDP is a measure of domestic production, so your purchase of the Korean car should not count toward GDP. Since durable consumption goes up by the value of the car, subtracting the value of the import from GDP is the only way to get the accounting correct.

Figure 1.6 shows how net exports, or exports minus imports, have evolved over time in the United States. Before the 1980s, the value of net exports was small. Sometimes it was above zero (exports exceeded imports), and other times it was below zero (imports exceeded exports). Over the past 40 years though, imports have consistently exceeded exports and the gap has grown over time. We return to the implications of this fact later in the book.

In summary, GDP can be calculated by summing the total expenditure of final goods and services in the economy. The GDP expenditure equation is

GDP = Consumption + Investment + Government Spending + Exports − Imports. (4)

Figure 1.7 shows how expenditure shares have changed since 1960 in the United States. The shares have stayed relatively constant over time. Investment has been a bit less than 20 percent of GDP for most of the time. Consumption's share has increased from 61 percent to 68 percent, while government's share has decreased from just over 20 percent in 1960 to just under 20 percent by 2020. Finally, the share of net exports has decreased (grown more negative) over time.

12 Part 1 Growth

Figure 1.6 Net exports, or exports minus imports, from 1947 to 2021.

Shaded areas indicate U.S. recessions.

Source: BEA and FRED Suggested Citation: U.S. Bureau of Economic Analysis, Net Exports of Goods and Services [NETEXP], retrieved from FRED, Federal Reserve Bank of St. Louis; https://fred.stlouisfed.org/series/NETEXP, August 1, 2022.

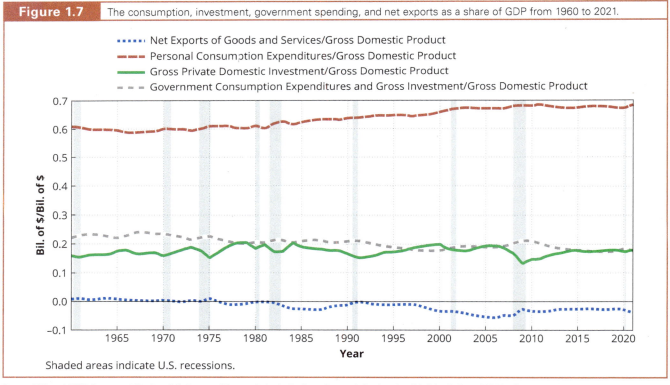

Figure 1.7 The consumption, investment, government spending, and net exports as a share of GDP from 1960 to 2021.

Shaded areas indicate U.S. recessions.

Source: BEA and FRED Suggested Citation: U.S. Bureau of Economic Analysis, Gross Domestic Product: Implicit Price Deflator [GDPDEF], retrieved from FRED, Federal Reserve Bank of St. Louis; https://fred.stlouisfed.org/series/GDPDEF, August 5, 2022.

These facts are interesting in and of themselves, but we cannot infer anything about economic welfare from them. That is, we cannot say whether consumption increasing as a share of GDP is a good or bad thing without an economic model that helps us interpret these facts. Later chapters in this section deal with models of economic growth, and business cycle models are covered in Section 3.

Table 1.5 summarizes the three approaches to calculating GDP.

Chapter 1 Defining and Measuring GDP **13**

Table 1.5	Summarizing the Three Ways of Calculating GDP	
Value-added approach	**Income approach**	**Expenditure approach**
Gross output − Intermediate inputs	Employee compensation + Taxes on production and imports less subsidies + Consumption of fixed capital + Net operating surplus	Consumption + Investment + Government Spending + Net Exports
= Value added	= Income	= Expenditure

✓ Knowledge Check 1-2

Suppose you have the following economic data (in billions). Fill in the blanks of the Table 1.6.

Table 1.6	Example of Calculating GDP Using the Expenditure Approach
Consumption	$13,432
Durable consumption	$4,312
Nondurable consumption	$2,762
Consumption of services	?
Investment	$4,621
Nonresidential fixed investment	$3,000
Residential fixed investment	?
Government Spending	$7,240
Government consumption	$2,252
Government investment	?
Transfer payments	$4,900
Net Exports	−$1,090
GDP	?

Answers are at the end of the chapter.

1-3 Separating Changes in Prices and Quantities in the Measure of GDP

Earlier in the chapter, we noted that GDP can increase because the production of goods and services rises or because of an increase in prices. Formally, GDP is the sum of all final goods and services produced in the economy, or recalling equation (1),

$$GDP = \sum_{i=1}^{N} p_i y_i, \tag{1}$$

where y_i is the quantity of each good or service and p_i is the price of each good or service. GDP can increase because the quantities of goods and services increase or because prices increase. If we are interested in an economy's productive capacity and living standards of its inhabitants, it makes sense to measure these margins separately. Moreover, identical goods and services often sell for different prices in different countries. Accurately accounting for differences in living standards across countries requires using the same prices for identical goods and services across countries. We first address how to deal with price changes over time within a country and then address how to deal with price differences across countries.

14 **Part 1** Growth

1-3a Tracking Price Changes Within a Country: The GDP Deflator

Imagine an economy that produces only apples. In 2021, the economy produced 1,000 bushels of apples, and each bushel sold for $10. GDP equaled $10,000 ($=\$10 \times 1,000$). In 2022, the economy produced 1,500 bushels and sold them for $20, so that GDP equaled $30,000 ($=\$20 \times 1,500$). Thus, GDP grew 200 percent between 2021 and 2022. Some of that increase in GDP represents an increase in the quantity of bushels, and some represents an increase in price. The percent change in price and quantity is respectively given by

$$\% \text{ change in price} = \frac{\$20 - \$10}{\$10} \times 100\% = 100\%,$$

$$\% \text{ change in quantity} = \frac{1,500 - 1,000}{1,000} \times 100\% = 50\%.$$

Nominal GDP
A country's GDP calculated using current-year prices.

Real GDP
A country's GDP calculated using constant prices.

Thus, the economy's output of apples increased by 50 percent. More generally, **nominal GDP** is a country's GDP calculated using current-year prices. **Real GDP** is a country's GDP calculated using constant prices. The choice of what year to calculate prices is called the base year. Table 1.7 shows how to do this. Nominal GDP for each year is shown in the second column and matches the calculation in the previous paragraph. The third column computes real GDP using 2021 as the base year. Real and nominal GDPs are the same in 2021, but real GDP is half of nominal GDP in 2022. This is due to the price of apples doubling between the years. Similarly, real and nominal GDP are the same in 2022 when 2022 is the base year, whereas 2021's real GDP is double its nominal GDP.

A couple of observations might jump out to you. First, the percent change in real GDP equals the percent change in the quantity of apples. This is why economists use changes in real GDP to measure changes in the economy's productive capacity. Second, the percent change in real GDP is independent of the base year. This is not the case in economies that produce more than one product (i.e., every economy in the world).

Turning to the case of multiple products, now suppose that the economy produces both apples and bananas. Some hypothetical data are given in Table 1.8. Nominal GDP is calculated in each year using current-year prices. Between 2021 and 2022, nominal GDP rose by $29,200, a growth rate of 112 percent.

Next, let us calculate real GDP using 2021 as base year:

$$RGDP_{2021} = p_{apples,21}q_{apples,21} + p_{bananas,21}q_{bananas,21}$$

$$= \$10 \times 1,000 + \$4 \times 4,000 = \$26,000.$$

Table 1.7	Computing Nominal and Real GDP with One Good		
	Nominal GDP	**Real GDP using 2021 prices**	**Real GDP using 2022 prices**
2021	$10 × 1,000 = $10,000	$10 × 1,000 = $10,000	$20 × 1,000 = $20,000
2022	$20 × 1,500 = $30,000	$10 × 1,500 = $15,000	$20 × 1,500 = $30,000

Table 1.8	Computing Nominal and Real GDP with Two Goods				
	Apple price	**Quantity of apples**	**Banana price**	**Quantity of bananas**	**Nominal GDP**
2021	$10	1,000	$4	4,000	$10 × 1,000 + $4 × 4,000 = $26,000
2022	$20	1,500	$6	4,200	$20 × 1,500 + $6 × 4,200 = $55,200

As expected, real GDP equals nominal GDP in the base year. To calculate real GDP in 2022 using 2021 as the base year, use 2021 prices and 2022 quantities:

$$RGDP_{2022} = p_{apples,21}q_{apples,22} + p_{bananas,21}q_{bananas,22}$$

$$= \$10 \times 1{,}500 + \$4 \times 4{,}200 = \$31{,}800.$$

The growth rate in real GDP is

$$RGDP\ growth = \frac{RGDP_{2022} - RGDP_{2021}}{RGDP_{2021}} \times 100\%$$

$$= \frac{\$31{,}800 - \$26{,}000}{\$26{,}000} \times 100\% = 22.3\%.$$

The growth rate in real GDP is much smaller than the growth rate of nominal GDP. This, again, is due to the fact that prices rose for both apples and bananas between 2021 and 2022.

We can calculate the change in the overall price level by comparing real GDP (RGDP) to nominal GDP (NGDP) in 2022. Formally, the **GDP deflator** is defined as

$$GDP\ deflator = \frac{NGDP}{RGDP} \times 100. \qquad (4)$$

GDP deflator
A country's nominal GDP divided by its real GDP.

By definition, the GDP deflator is 100 in the base year. In the current example, the GDP deflator in 2022 is

$$GDP\ deflator_{2022} = \frac{NGDP_{2022}}{RGDP_{2022}} \times 100$$

$$= \frac{p_{apples,22}q_{apples,22} + p_{bananas,22}q_{bananas,22}}{p_{apples,21}q_{apples,22} + p_{bananas,21}q_{bananas,22}} \times 100$$

$$= \frac{\$55{,}200}{\$31{,}800} \times 100 = 173.58.$$

The GDP deflator is 173.58 in 2022, meaning that the GDP deflator rose 73.58 percent in 2022. The reason why we can interpret this as an increase in the general price level can be explained by the middle line of the previous equation. The quantities are the same in the numerator and denominator, but the prices change. Thus, the GDP deflator is the quantity-weighted average change in prices between two consecutive years. **Inflation** is an increase in the general price level. This means that the economy's inflation rate according to the GDP deflator was 73.58 percent.

Inflation
An increase in the average price level.

This logic applies to time periods longer than two years as well. Table 1.9 shows hypothetical data from 2020, 2021, and 2022. The base year is 2021. Between 2020 and 2021, the GDP deflator rose 1.2 percent; similarly, between 2021 and 2022, the GDP deflator rose 2.5 percent. As you will see in next knowledge check, the choice of base year affects the quantitative results.

Figure 1.8 shows the U.S. inflation rate as implied by the GDP deflator. The inflation rate was nearly 10 percent in the late 1970s and early 1980s before steadily decreasing to the 2 to 4 percent range from the mid-1980s to 2008. The inflation rate plummeted for a few years after 2008 but crept up again in the wake of the Covid-19 pandemic. A lot of the economic history in this paragraph will be explored at later points in the book.

Table 1.9	Calculating the GDP Deflator and Inflation Rate			
Year	**NGDP**	**RGDP**	**GDP deflator**	**Inflation rate**
2020	$56,500	$57,200	98.8	
2021	$58,000	$58,000	100	1.2%
2022	$62,000	$60,500	102.5	2.5%

Figure 1.8 The annual percent change in the GDP price deflator between 1948 and 2021.

Shaded areas indicate U.S. recessions.

Source: BEA and FRED.

1-3b Tracking Price Changes Across Countries: Purchasing Power Parity

The McDonald's franchise has establishments in countries all over the world. People in different continents can enjoy their most iconic sandwich, the Big Mac. If a Big Mac cost $6 in the United States and 90 pesos in Mexico, would it be correct to conclude that the Big Mac is more expensive in Mexico? No. The reason is because the units are different. A correct comparison requires that you know how many pesos exchange for a dollar. As this book is being written, 1 U.S. dollar exchanges for about 20 Mexican pesos. That means $6 is worth 120 pesos. Thus, based on the information in the example above, the Big Mac would in fact be cheaper in Mexico than the United States.

This example was not selected at random. The *Economist* magazine has been calculating the "Big Mac index" since 1986 to illustrate differences in purchasing power across countries.[3] The index documents the cost of a Big Mac across countries after adjusting for local exchange rates. Figure 1.9 shows that there is, in fact, substantial variation in the cost of the Big Mac across the world. In general, a Big Mac is more expensive in developed countries and less expensive in developing countries.

The Big Mac is a useful indicator of differences in purchasing power across countries because it is completely standardized. That is, the Big Mac is identical in Beijing, China, and Waterville, Maine, and everywhere else across the world. This cannot be said about all other goods and services. For instance, is a haircut more expensive in the United States than in China, after adjusting for exchange rates, because of differences in the purchasing power of the two currencies or because the average quality of haircuts is higher in the United States? While differences in quality do impact prices of identical-looking goods and services, there is a consensus among economists that currencies differ in their purchasing power. Moreover, goods and services tend to be less expensive in developing countries.

We return to the connection between exchange rates, purchasing power, and development later in the textbook. The important idea here is that one U.S. dollar buys less in the United States than that same dollar in developing countries. The implication is that only

---

[3] https://www.economist.com/big-mac-index.

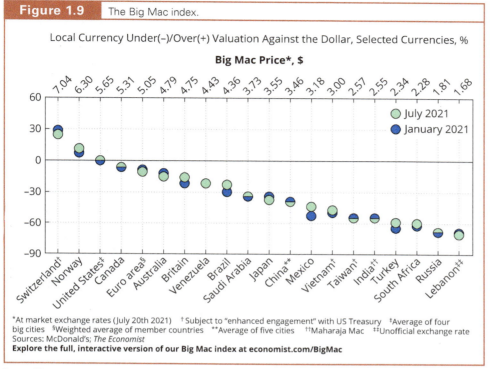

Figure 1.9 The Big Mac index.

Source: BEA and FRED.

correcting for market exchange rates will overstate the differences in GDPs between the United States and developing countries. Returning to the dollar/peso example from earlier, because a dollar buys less of an identical good or service in the United States than in Mexico, the difference in U.S.–Mexico GDP will be overstated. The United States will look richer relative to Mexico than it really is. To correct for this, economists use **purchasing power parity (PPP) exchange rates**, which correct for differences in price levels across countries.

The economic implication here is that you should use purchasing power parity exchange rates when comparing GDPs across countries. Differences in PPP-adjusted output per worker reflect differences in the productive capacity of countries rather than differences in prices. A practical implication is that vacations in developing countries are less expensive than vacations in developed countries.

Purchasing power parity exchange rate
Exchange rate that corrects for differences in price levels across countries.

✓ Knowledge Check 1-3

Return to the economic data in Table 1.8. Calculate real GDP and the GDP deflator for both years using 2022 as a base year. Is your answer affected by the choice of the base year?

Answers are at the end of the chapter.

1-4 Getting the Most Out of GDP Data

Many of the economic models in this book deal with the determination of GDP in the short run and long run. If you look at the business and economics section of any newspaper, chances are you will see articles discussing GDP. Just because we have good data on GDP doesn't mean that it is useful. GDP, however, is highly correlated with many quality-of-life variables across countries. This section discusses some of the evidence.

GDP per capita
GDP divided by a country's population.

GDP per worker
GDP divided by a country's workforce.

First, it is necessary to make one modification. You learned in the last section that it's a good idea to compare GDPs in PPP-adjusted dollars. Even after correcting for differences in purchasing power, a densely populated country like India (population 1.4 billion) has a higher GDP than a smaller country like Ireland (population 5 million). But the average income of Irish citizens exceeds that of citizens of India. An informative measure of income or output also corrects for differences in population. **GDP per capita** is GDP divided by a country's population. This can be interpreted as income per person. Likewise, **GDP per worker** is GDP divided by a country's workforce. GDP per worker will always be higher than GDP per capita because not everyone works. GDP per worker is almost perfectly positively correlated with GDP per capita, so in practice, the two measures can be used interchangeably. Strictly speaking, however, we will use GDP per capita for comparing living standards across countries and GDP per worker for comparing differences in productive capacity across countries.

1-4a The Facts of GDP per Capita

This section discusses some of the facts of GDP per person across time and countries.

Fact 1: There is huge variation in GDP per capita across countries. Figure 1.10 shows the distribution of GDP per capita in 2019. More than one-third of the countries in the world have a GDP per capita of less than $10,000 or less than one-sixth of the level of U.S. GDP per capita (about $62,500). Fourteen countries had a GDP per capita of less than $2,000 per year. The average person in a country like the Democratic Republic of the Congo, with a GDP per capita of about $1,000, earns less income in a year than the average American does in one week.

Fact 2: There is huge variation in the growth rate of GDP per capita over time. Table 1.10 shows GDP per capita over close to two centuries across a number of countries. There are several observations from this data. First, even countries that are well off by today's

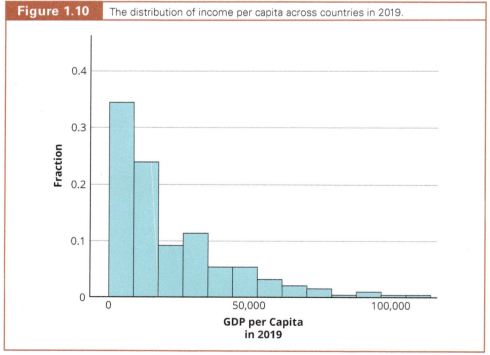

Figure 1.10 The distribution of income per capita across countries in 2019.

Source: PWT 10.0.

Table 1.10	Data is from the Maddison Project Database			
Country	1820	1920	2018	Factor increase 1820–2018
United States	$2,674	$10,153	$55,535	19.77
United Kingdom	$3,306	$7,017	$38,058	10.51
Argentina	$1,591	$5,536	$18,556	10.66
Chile	$824	$4,428	$22,105	25.82
Japan	$1,317	$2,974	$38,674	28.37
China	$882	$994	$13,102	13.85

Source: Groningen Growth and Development Centre.

standards started off quite poor 200 years ago. The level of income per capita in the United States in 1820 was roughly where Ethiopia is today. Second, the increase in GDP per capita in these countries over the last 200 years was significant. U.S. income rose by a factor of nearly 20, or 2,000 percent! Finally, and getting back to the stylized fact, there is huge variation in cumulative growth rates through time. Japan grew by a factor of almost 30, whereas the UK grew by a factor of 10.

Fact 3: There were growth miracles over the past 70 years. The 28-fold increase in Japanese income between 1820 and 2018 may seem impressive, but income per capita in Singapore grew from less than $3,000 in 1960 to $84,500 in 2018, or about a 3,000 percent increase. GDP per capita for Singapore, South Korea, Hong Kong, and Thailand are shown in Figure 1.11. South Korea's income per capita rose from about $1,200 to about $42,000 over the same time period. Hong Kong and Thailand similarly experienced fast rates of growth. Understanding the success of these countries has been a priority for economists and policy makers around the world.

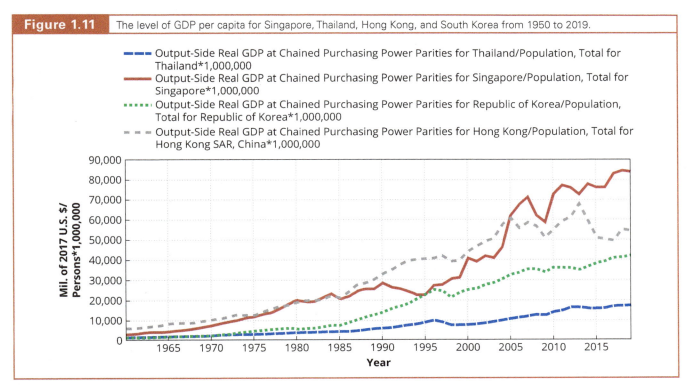

Figure 1.11 The level of GDP per capita for Singapore, Thailand, Hong Kong, and South Korea from 1950 to 2019.

Source: PWT 9.0 and Saint Louis FRED.

Table 1.11	The Rule of 70		
Growth rate	**Today**	**70 years**	**140 years**
1%	$10,000	$20,068	$40,271
2%	$10,000	$39,996	$159,965
3%	$10,000	$79,178	$626,919

Before leaving this section, it is important to emphasize that small changes in *annual* growth rates have big effects on *cumulative* growth rates over many years. A way to frame the question is the following: How does a one percentage point increase in the growth rate of per capita GDP impact long-run GDP per capita? Table 1.11 shows the results where a hypothetical country starts with income per capita equal to $10,000 and the "long run" is defined as either 70 or 140 years. With a 2 percent growth rate, income per capita quadruples in 70 years and increases 16-fold in 140 years. If the growth rate is 3 percent per year, income per capita increases by a factor of 63 in 140 years. Thus, a one percentage point increase in the growth rate doubles income per capita over a horizon of 70 years and quadruples it over 140 years.

The 70-year intervals were not chosen at random. In fact, economists have what is called the **rule of 70**, which tells you how long it takes an economy to double its income per capita.

Rule of 70

An equation used to determine how long it takes an economy to double its income per capita.

Mathematically, the rule can be derived as follows. Let y be income per capita and g be the growth rate. We want to solve for the number of years it takes the economy to double its per capita income. Formally, we want to find the t that solves

$$2y = y\,(1 + g)^t.$$

The right-hand side of the equation is the initial level of income per capita multiplied by the cumulative exponential growth factor, $(1 + g)^t$. Canceling y on both sides and taking natural logarithms gives

$$\ln(2) = \ln(1 + g)^t$$
$$= t \ln(1 + g).$$

The value of $\ln(2)$ is about equal to 0.7 and $\ln(1 + g) \approx g$ for values of g less than 0.1. Applying these approximations gives

$$0.7 = tg.$$

It follows that

$$time\ to\ double = \frac{0.70}{g}. \tag{5}$$

You can see this rule in action in Table 1.11. Income per capita doubles in 70 years when the growth rate is 1 percent, whereas it doubles twice when the growth rate is 2 percent.

The lesson is that small changes in growth rates have very large effects over long horizons. Seventy years is about the length of two generations, i.e., between you and your grandparents. If economic policy makers could somehow raise the growth rate of per capita income by even a little bit, it would have profound implications on income in the long run.

1-4b The Connection Between GDP per Capita and Living Standards

Referring to the measure of a nation's output, Robert F. Kennedy once remarked, "it measures everything in short, except that which makes life worthwhile."[4] Kennedy was right that GDP doesn't measure the quality of a country's education or its healthcare

---

[4]The full speech can be found here: https://www.jfklibrary.org/learn/about-jfk/the-kennedy-family/robert-f-kennedy/robert-f-kennedy-speeches/remarks-at-the-university-of-kansas-march-18-1968.

system. Not to mention that it doesn't measure the strength of our relationships with family and friends. Is GDP totally disconnected with these variables, or even worse, negatively correlated with them? Not everything that is relevant, of course, can be quantified. How would we measure the "strength of our friendships," for instance? But there is good international data on other quality-of-life measures. We can see how these variables correlate with GDP per capita.

The World Development Indicators compiled by the World Bank is a great source of quality-of-life data for many different countries. We will look at how four variables in particular correlate with the natural log of GDP per capita (in PPP dollars).[5]

1. Life expectancy – The number of years a person expects to live in any country.
2. Infant mortality rate – The number of deaths of infants younger than one year of age per 1,000 births.
3. Consumption per capita – The total amount of consumption as measured in the national accounts divided by total population.
4. CO_2 emissions per capita – The number of tons per capita of carbon dioxide emissions for a country divided by total population.

The left panel of Figure 1.12 shows the relationship between GDP per capita and the infant mortality rate. There is a strong negative relationship between the two variables. In the poorest countries, more than 5 percent of infants die before their first birthday. The rate is well below 1 percent in countries with the highest levels of income per capita. The right panel shows the relationship between GDP per capita and life expectancy. There is a strong positive relationship. People born in the richest countries expect to live 20 years longer than people born in the poorest countries.

The left panel on Figure 1.13 shows the relationship between consumption per capita (also in natural logs) and GDP per capita. These variables are strongly positively correlated. Intuitively, people living in countries with higher incomes also consume more. The right panel of Figure 1.13 shows the relationship between per capita CO_2 emissions and GDP per capita. Here the relationship is also clear. Richer countries emit more carbon dioxide into the atmosphere.

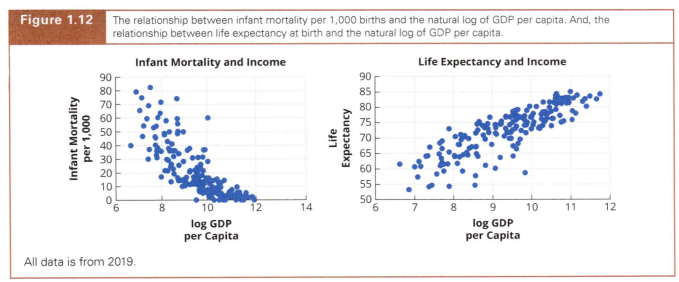

Figure 1.12 The relationship between infant mortality per 1,000 births and the natural log of GDP per capita. And, the relationship between life expectancy at birth and the natural log of GDP per capita.

All data is from 2019.

Source: World Bank's World Development Indicators.

---

[5]Using the natural log makes the data easier to visualize. Nothing is qualitatively affected by this choice.

Figure 1.13

The relationship between the natural log of consumption per capita and the natural log of GDP per capita. And, the relationship between tons of CO_2 emissions per capita and the natural log of GDP per capita.

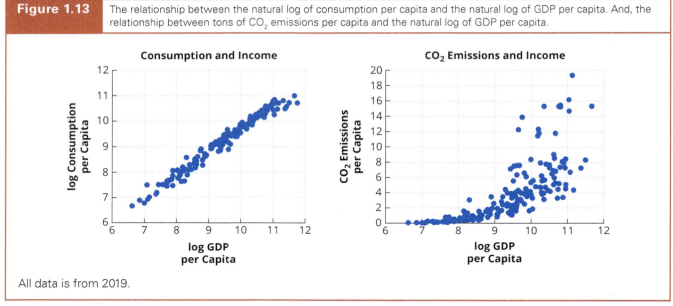

All data is from 2019.

Source: World Bank's World Development Indicators.

In summary, people in rich countries expect to live longer and consume more but also emit more carbon into the atmosphere. In terms of other variables not reported here, literacy rates and education levels are highly positively correlated with GDP per capita. The prevalence of food insecurity and measures of absolute poverty (living under $2 a day) are much rarer in rich countries. Overall, the available evidence shows that the quality and quantity of life are higher in rich countries. Thus, while GDP per capita may not be a perfect measure of well-being, it is a good proxy for it. The next application discusses the relationship between the level of GDP per capita and its distribution across the population.

Application 1.2

Inequality and GDP

Imagine two economies, each with 100 people. In the first economy, each person earns $100,000 per year. In the second economy, one person earns $10 million per year and the other 99 earn nothing. Per capita income is $100,000 in both economies. Which society would you rather live in? In the second economy, you have a 1 percent chance of earning a huge income, but a 99 percent chance of effectively starving. Most people faced with this gamble would prefer earning $100,000 per year with certainty.

This points to a potential shortcoming of using GDP per capita as a stand-in for living standards. GDP per capita measures *average* income. It tells you nothing about the distribution of income across the citizens of a country. As the last example showed, two economies can have the same average income, but vastly different distributions of income. What is the connection between income inequality and GDP per capita across countries? Is a certain level of inequality necessary for achieving economic development?

Figure 1.14 shows the relationship between consumption inequality on the vertical axis and GDP per person relative to the United States on the horizontal axis. Consumption inequality is measured as the standard deviation of the natural log of consumption within a country.[6] Qualitatively, inequality increases the higher a country is on the vertical axis. Consumption inequality is closely tied to income inequality across countries and consumption is a better measure of economic welfare anyway. Countries to the left of 1 on the horizontal axis are poorer than the United States. A number of 0.5 on the horizontal axis, for

[6] Recall from the mathematical appendix that the standard deviation is a measure of the variation of a variable.

■ Continues

Application 1.2 (Continued)

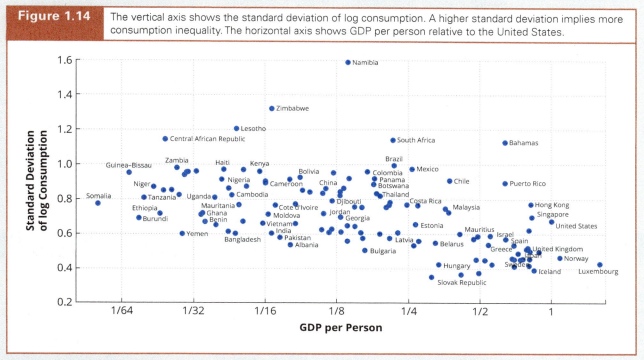

Figure 1.14 The vertical axis shows the standard deviation of log consumption. A higher standard deviation implies more consumption inequality. The horizontal axis shows GDP per person relative to the United States.

Source: Jones and Klenow (2010), https://economics.sas.upenn.edu/sites/default/files/filevault/event_papers/moneymacro09152010.pdf

instance, would mean that GDP per capita is 50 percent of the U.S. level.

By and large, there is a negative correlation between GDP per capita and inequality. Richer countries tend to have less inequality in consumption than poor countries. However, there is a lot of variation. The United States and Norway have roughly the same level of GDP per capita, but consumption inequality is much higher in the United States. The variation is even bigger among less developed nations. Consumption inequality is twice as high in Zimbabwe than Vietnam, even though GDP per capita is similar in both countries.

Why might two countries have different levels of inequality despite having the same GDP per capita? Government taxes and transfers certainly play a role. The Nordic countries and Western Europe have much higher levels of taxes and more generous social safety nets compared to the United States. Higher levels of taxes reduce the incentive to work and invest which limits incomes at the top end. Additionally, a higher level of government transfer payments, perhaps in the form of payments to socioeconomically disadvantaged individuals and families, puts a floor on the minimum levels of consumption and income. The net effect of these policies reduces inequality.

Finally, is some degree of inequality necessary for economic development? Yes. To see why, think of an extreme case. Suppose a country has complete income equality. In this country, income is completely independent of work effort. The person who takes two jobs earns just as much as the person who plays video games all day. This is hardly an ideal system for achieving economic development, as no one will have an incentive to work. Why spend time on a manufacturing floor when you can earn the same income playing *Call of Duty* all day? Hence, a country that promotes complete equality will not achieve economic growth.

The logic presented in this example suggests that some level of inequality is necessary for economic development. It doesn't say what the right level of inequality is. Could the United States, for instance, implement a European-style welfare system and achieve the same level of income per capita? Or would reducing tax rates on high-income earners unleash a flood of investment and work effort, thereby promoting economic growth? These are hotly debated topics in economic policy, and we will return to some of them in later chapters of the book.

24   **Part 1** Growth

Chapter Summary

- Gross domestic product is the dollar value of all final goods and services produced in a country in a year.

- There are three approaches to calculating GDP: the value-added approach, the income approach, and the expenditure approach. Because the total value added of production equals total income and total expenditure, all three approaches give the same answer theoretically. In practice, there are small statistical discrepancies.

- The income approach divides income into i) wage and salary income, ii) taxes on production and imports less subsidies, iii) consumption of fixed capital, and iv) net operating surplus.

- The expenditure approach divides income into i) private consumption, ii) private investment, iii) government consumption and investment, and iv) net exports.

- Real GDP measures how the quantity of goods and services produced changes from year to year holding prices fixed.

- Accurately comparing GDP across countries requires adjusting for differences in purchasing power. Purchasing power parity exchange rates correct for differences in prices of the same goods and services across countries.

- There is wide variation in the level of GDP per capita across countries today and wide variation in cross-country GDP growth rates over the last 200 years.

- GDP per capita is positively correlated with life expectancy and other quality-of-life measures, making it an adequate, but not perfect, proxy for measuring well-being in a country.

Key Terms

Gross domestic product (GDP), 2
Intermediate good, 2
Gross national income (GNI), 6
Capital good, 7
Depreciation, 7
Durable good, 9
Transfer payment, 10
Nominal GDP, 14

Real GDP, 14
GDP deflator, 15
Inflation, 15
Purchasing power parity exchange rate, 17
GDP per capita, 18
GDP per worker, 18
Rule of 70, 20

Review Questions

1. Consider two alternatives: you take your car to the car wash or wash the car in your driveway. Do either, neither, or both of these alternatives contribute to GDP? Explain.

2. Suppose Americans decide to work 10 fewer hours per week and use that time instead for charitable endeavors. What happens to GDP?

3. Suppose nominal GDP grew by 12 percent last year. Provide two reasons why this cannot be interpreted as a 12 percent increase in the purchasing power of the average citizen.

4. Explain why imports are subtracted from the GDP expenditure calculation.

5. Is real GDP per capita a good measure of living standards? Explain.

Problems

1.1 Consider the following economic data.

Year	Price of avocados	Quantity of avocados	Price of bell peppers	Quantity of bell peppers
2021	$0.90	2,500	$1.40	3,000
2022	$1.05	2,750	$1.45	3,400
2023	$1.20	2,800	$1.70	3,600

  a. Calculate nominal GDP, real GDP, and the GDP deflator using 2022 as the base year.

  b. Compute the percent change in nominal GDP, real GDP, and the GDP deflator between 2021 and 2022.

  c. Assuming the population level stayed constant in all three years, did economic well-being rise by more in 2022 or 2023? Explain.

1.2 Suppose you have the following economic data. Assume one pound of peaches goes into each pie. Also assume there are no taxes or subsidies on production.

	Peaches (in pounds)	Peach pies
Price per unit	$2	$12
Quantity sold to final users	2,000	1,000
Quantity sold as intermediate goods	1,000	0
Wages	$4,000	$6,000
Consumption of fixed capital	$500	$1,000
Net operating surplus	?	?

Fill in the missing values in the table and calculate GDP.

Chapter 1 Defining and Measuring GDP   **25**

1.3 When a realtor helps with a property transaction, they are compensated by taking a certain percentage of the sales price of the property.

	Quantity (in thousands)	Average price (in thousands)	Realtor fees
New residential houses	25	$400	2%
old residential houses	150	$250	5%
New factories	20	$1,500	1%
Old factories	30	$800	2%

Calculate the increase in GDP due to the sales of new and old houses and factories. Which of these sales get counted as residential fixed investment and which get counted as nonresidential fixed investment?

1.4 The following economic data shows the income of someone in the 10th percentile and at the median. The parameter E is between 0 and 1 and can be interpreted as a coefficient of equality. An E close to 1 implies that the country has very equal incomes. The income distribution becomes more unequal the further E is below 1.

	2023	2033	2043	2053
10th percentile	E × $60,000			
Median	$60,000			

a. Suppose that income grows at 3 percent per year and $E = 0.5$. Fill in the rest of the table.

b. Suppose income grows at 1 percent per year and $E = 0.9$. Fill in the rest of the table.

c. In which society would you prefer to live in 2053 if you were in the 10th percentile of the income distribution?

d. Derive the year in which a person in the 10th percentile living in the economy of part a has the same income as a person in the 10th percentile living in the economy of part b.

1.5 GDP deflators can be calculated for various industries as well as for the entire economy. Consider the following economic data from 2022 and 2023. Gross output, intermediate inputs, and value added are in billions.

Construction	2022	2023
Gross output	$712	$760
Intermediate inputs	$204	$226
Value added	?	?
Industry deflator	105	107
Manufacturing		
Gross output	$1,240	$1,310
Intermediate inputs	?	?
Value added	$980	$1,002
Industry deflator	103	99

a. Fill in the missing values of the table.

b. If the economy only consists of these two sectors, compute real GDP for both years.

✓ Knowledge Check 1-1 Answer

Selling the 10-year-old house by yourself does not add anything to GDP, but if you pay a realtor to sell the house, the realtor fees are included in GDP. The reason is that the realtor provides a service, and the current dollar value of that service is included in GDP. The value of the 10-year-old house is *not* included in GDP. It was included in the GDP calculation 10 years ago. If you buy a new house, the value of the house is included in GDP because it was produced in the current year.

The brick of French cheese isn't included in U.S. GDP because it was produced in France. The brick of Wisconsin cheese is included in GDP because Wisconsin is in the United States.

✓ Knowledge Check 1-2 Answer

We will approach this from top to bottom. Total consumption is the sum of durable consumption, nondurable consumption, and the consumption of services. The consumption of services is $13,432 − $4,312 − $2,762 = $6,358.

Investment is the sum of residential fixed investment and nonresidential fixed investment. Residential fixed investment is $4,621 − $3,000 = $1,621.

Government spending is the sum of government consumption and government investment. Transfer payments are not included. Government investment is $7,240 − $2,252 = $4,988.

GDP is the sum of private consumption, private investment, government spending, and next exports. Using the numbers in the table, GDP is $13,432 + $4,621 + $7,240 − $1,090 = $24,203.

The table with these values is shown below.

Consumption	$13,432
Durable consumption	$4,312
Nondurable consumption	$2,762
Consumption of services	$6,358
Investment	$4,621
Nonresidential fixed investment	$3,000
Residential fixed investment	$1,621
Government Spending	$7,240
Government consumption	$2,252
Government investment	$4,988
Transfer payments	$4,900
Net Exports	−$1,090
GDP	$24,203

✓ Knowledge Check 1-3 Answer

The table is repeated below.

	Apple price	Quantity of apples	Banana price	Quantity of bananas	Nominal GDP
2021	$10	1,000	$4	4,000	$10 × 1,000 + $4 × 4,000 = $26,000
2022	$20	1,500	$6	4,200	$20 × 1,500 + $6 × 4,200 = $55,200

If the base year is 2022, then real GDP in 2022 is equal to nominal GDP and the GDP deflator equals 100. Real GDP in 2021 is

$$RGDP_{2021} = p_{apples,22} q_{apples,21} + p_{bananas,22} q_{bananas,21}$$
$$= \$20 \times 1{,}000 + \$6 \times \$4{,}000 = \$44{,}000.$$

The GDP deflator is

$$\frac{\$26{,}000}{\$44{,}000} \times 100 = 59.1.$$

The growth rate in real GDP between 2021 and 2022 is 25.5 percent. Recall that real GDP growth was 22.3 percent when using 2021 as a base year. Thus, the choice of base year makes a difference.

Chapter 2 Production Functions

Learning Objectives

2.1 Define a production function.

2.2 Distinguish between an individual-level production function and an aggregate production function.

2.3 Explain the common properties of production functions.

2.4 Graphically derive the demand curves for capital and labor and determine their prices.

2.5 Graphically depict changes to the supply and demand curves for capital and labor.

2.6 Decompose the sources of cross-country income differences into inputs and productivity.

Every business has techniques for combining labor, raw materials, and other inputs into output that it can sell to consumers. For instance, a bakery might combine the labor of bakers with raw materials like butter and sugar and ovens and baking utensils to produce cookies. The cookies are ultimately sold to consumers. Macroeconomists take this same idea but apply it to the aggregate economy. In this chapter, you will learn how economists think about production, how capital and labor markets affect production, and what these teach us about cross-country income differences.

2-1 Production Functions

As you saw in Chapter 1, countries differ substantially in their levels of income per capita. The first step toward making sense of these differences is understanding how GDP per capita is produced. A **production function** turns inputs into output. Here is an example. Think of a bakery that specializes in baking cookies. The output in this case would be the cookies. How are the cookies produced? Using ovens, bakers, and such materials as sugar, butter, and chocolate chips. These are the inputs. The production function tells us how the inputs are transformed into output. Perhaps with four pounds of butter, 12 cups of chocolate chips, and 8 cups of sugar, a baker can produce 24 dozen cookies in an hour.

Entire economies produce more than just cookies, of course, and that can make things more complicated. Imagine separate production functions for the production of cookies, haircuts, airplanes, and smart phones. Fortunately, macroeconomists have simplified how to think about production at the level of an entire economy.

2-1a The Aggregate Production Function

The **aggregate production function** takes the total number of workers and the total quantity of **capital** as the inputs to produce GDP as the output. The first thing that often comes to most people's minds when they hear *capital* is money. Economists are different.

Production function
A mathematical function that describes how inputs are turned into output.

Aggregate production function
A production function describing the entire economy.

Capital
The structures, equipment, and intellectual property that go into producing output.

28 **Part 1** Growth

For an economist, capital includes structures like warehouses and buildings, equipment like tractors and computers, and intellectual property products like research and development and software. The aggregate production function vastly simplifies macroeconomic analysis while still providing insight about differences in GDP across countries.

The aggregate production function can be represented mathematically as:

$$Y = AF(K, L).$$

Here, Y is output or GDP, F is a mathematical function that takes capital and labor, K and L respectively, as its inputs, and A is **total factor productivity (TFP)**. TFP captures how efficiently an economy uses capital and labor in producing output.

It is easiest to understand TFP by way of example. Imagine two bakeries where bakers use ovens to make cookies. In one bakery, each baker performs all the tasks. That is, each baker measures the ingredients, stirs them together, and puts the cookie dough in the oven. In the other bakery, the bakers form an assembly line in which each baker specializes in one task. As modern management theory can attest, production is higher on an assembly line where each worker is responsible for a single duty. Thus, despite having the exact same inputs, the bakeries produce a different quantity of cookies. The difference is captured in the TFP term.

Similar to the level of individual bakeries, aggregate economies differ in how efficiently they use inputs. TFP captures these efficiency differences. Sometimes you will hear TFP referred to as "technology" (like a nickname). When you hear the word *technology*, you might think about cell phone apps, software, and functional MRI machines. But the economist's definition of technology is anything that allows firms, and thus aggregate economies, to increase production with a given level of inputs. Indeed, the assembly line can be thought of as a type of technology for producing cars.

> **Total factor productivity (TFP)**
>
> A term that describes how efficiently inputs are used in producing output.

2-1b The Shape of the Aggregate Production Function

The function $AF(K, L)$ is very general. Economists commonly make four assumptions about the production function.

1. **Both capital and labor are required for production:** The first assumption says that producing output requires positive quantities of capital and labor. To see why this makes sense, return to the example of the bakery. If a bakery has multiple ovens (the capital) but no bakers (the labor), then no cookies are produced. That is, the ovens aren't going to bake cookies without any baker there to operate them. At the same time, bakers cannot produce cookies without ovens. What is true at the level of an individual bakery is also true in the aggregate economy. An economy with all capital and no labor, or vice-versa, will produce no output. Mathematically, this is represented as

$$AF(K, 0) = AF(0, L) = 0.$$

2. **Output is increasing in both capital and labor:** The second assumption says that holding TFP and capital fixed, a bigger labor force increases output. It also says that holding TFP and labor fixed, more capital increases output. A bakery with more bakers or more ovens will produce more cookies. This assumption is depicted in Figure 2.1. The left panel shows that output is increasing in labor (holding fixed capital and TFP), and the right panel shows that output is increasing in capital (holding fixed labor and TFP). The **marginal product of labor** is the amount output changes per unit change of labor. Similarly, the **marginal product of capital** is the amount output changes per unit change of capital. Another way of stating assumption two is that the marginal product of both inputs is positive.

3. **Diminishing marginal products of capital and labor:** This assumption says that the increase in output per unit change in labor decreases as labor increases.

> **Marginal product of labor**
>
> The amount that output changes per unit change of labor.
>
> **Marginal product of capital**
>
> The amount that output changes per unit change of capital.

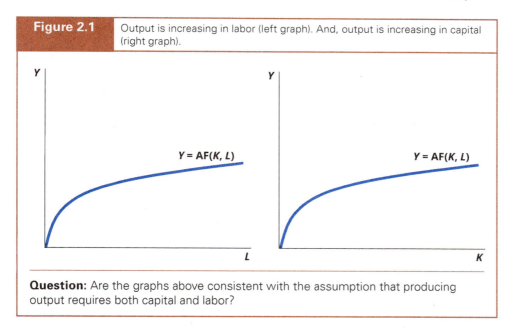

Figure 2.1 Output is increasing in labor (left graph). And, output is increasing in capital (right graph).

Question: Are the graphs above consistent with the assumption that producing output requires both capital and labor?

To wrap your head around this, go back to the bakery. Suppose a bakery starts with 10 ovens and no bakers. Once the bakery hires the first baker, production goes from 0 to 24 dozen cookies per hour. Hence, the marginal product of the first baker is 24 dozen cookies. Adding another baker leaving the number of ovens the same might increase production to 30 dozen cookies per hour, as one baker can stir the ingredients and the other can operate the ovens. Hence, the marginal product of the second baker is six dozen cookies, which is lower than the first baker. Intuitively, the second baker has a lower marginal product than the first baker not because they are any less capable, but because bakers must share the same ovens and utensils. The assumption of diminishing marginal products says that the marginal product of each subsequent baker is lower than the last one. The diminishing marginal products of capital and labor are graphically depicted in Figure 2.2. Focusing on the left panel, you see that the change in output moving from L_1 to L_2 is bigger than the change in output moving from L_2 to L_3. Similarly, the right panel shows that the change in output moving from K_1 to K_2 is bigger than the change in output moving from K_2 to K_3.

4. **Output is constant returns to scale in capital and labor:** The final assumption has to do with **returns to scale**. Returns to scale refers to how output changes when both inputs are scaled up by the same amount. If capital and labor each doubled and output only rose 50 percent, the production function would have decreasing returns to scale. If output instead rose 150 percent, the production function would have increasing returns to scale. If output exactly doubles, there are constant returns to scale. Mathematically, this is represented as

$$AF(2K, 2L) = 2AF(K, L).$$

At the level of the aggregate economy, constant returns to scale is the most reasonable assumption. To see why, imagine replicating all the inputs on Earth. All the land, labor, capital, raw materials, and so on are exactly doubled. This, in essence, just gives us a second Earth that will produce just as much output as the first Earth. This replication argument is why the constant returns to scale assumption is plausible at the aggregate level.

Returns to scale
The factor by which output increases when all inputs double.

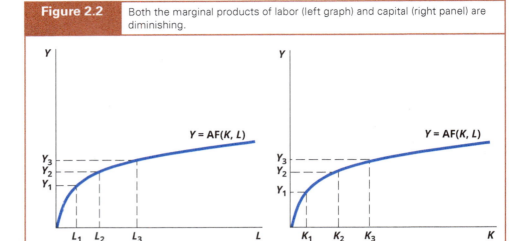

Figure 2.2 Both the marginal products of labor (left graph) and capital (right panel) are diminishing.

The panel on the left shows how output changes with labor. The change in output moving from L_1 to L_2 is bigger than the change in output moving from L_2 to L_3. The panel on the right shows how output changes with capital. The change in output moving from K_1 to K_2 is bigger than the change in output moving from K_2 to K_3.

Question: How would these graphs change if the marginal products of capital and labor were increasing?

Knowledge Check 2-1

Consider the following data in the table below:

L	K	Y	MPL
1	10	4	X
2	10	7	
3	10	9	
4	10	10	
5	10	10.5	
6	10	10.75	

Fill in the missing values. Is the marginal product of labor positive? Is it diminishing?

———————————— Answers are at the end of the chapter.

Knowledge Check 2-2

Can you think of four real-world examples where each of the four assumptions about the production function are violated?

———————————— Answers are at the end of the chapter.

2-2 Supply and Demand in the Capital and Labor Markets

Given a certain quantity of capital and labor and a level of TFP, the production function tells you how much output is produced. Although this is helpful, it leaves a lot to be desired. For instance, economists want to know where the quantities of capital, labor, and

TFP come from. They also want to know how prices of capital and labor are determined. This section takes a first step towards answering these questions.

There are two types of actors in this economy which should be familiar to you from your principles of microeconomics class. **Firms** demand capital and labor to produce output. **Households** supply capital and labor to firms. Because the analysis is at the aggregate level, we assume that all firms are exactly the same and that all households are exactly the same. This allows you to focus on the behavior of one firm, defined as the **representative firm**, and one household, defined as the **representative household**.

2-2a The Supply of Labor and Capital

You will discover the economic mechanisms driving the supply of capital and labor later in this book. We make a simplifying assumption in this chapter, namely that the supply of both inputs is perfectly inelastic. The supply of an input is perfectly inelastic if the quantity supplied does not change with the price. The price at which households supply their labor is the **wage rate**, or w. The price at which households supply capital is the **rental rate**, or r. The supply curves for labor and capital are depicted in Figure 2.3. The household is endowed with $\bar{L}$ units of labor and $\bar{K}$ units of capital. The labor and capital supply curves are given by L^S and K^S respectively. Since the household supplies labor and capital inelastically, $L^S = \bar{L}$ and $K^S = \bar{K}^S$.

Before moving on to the demand side of the market, there is one issue that needs to be addressed. The supply of labor is intuitive. Everyone has 24 hours in a day, and they decide how much they want to work at a given wage rate. Again, the microeconomics of labor supply is discussed later in the book, but there is no conceptual mystery as to what is going on. The supply of capital is less straightforward. Capital is defined as structures, equipment, and intellectual property. What does it mean for households to "own" the capital stock and "rent" the capital stock to firms? This is just a simplifying assumption made for analytic convenience. In the real world, households decide how much to save, and firms take these savings and turn them into investment goods like buildings and machinery. Later in the book, you will learn about the economic mechanisms driving the supply of savings.

Firm
A unit that hires capital and labor to produce output.

Household
A unit that supplies capital and labor and consumes output.

Representative firm
The stand-in firm for the entire economy.

Representative household
The stand-in household for the entire economy.

Wage rate
The price at which households supply their labor.

Rental rate
The price at which households supply their capital.

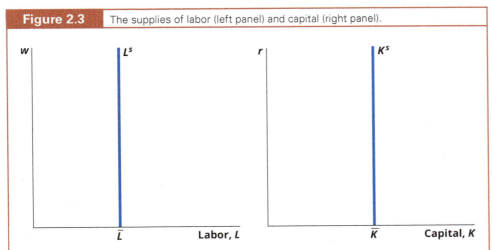

Figure 2.3 The supplies of labor (left panel) and capital (right panel).

The plot on the left shows the supply of labor, L^S. Because labor supply is perfectly inelastic and households are endowed with $\bar{L}$ units of labor, labor supply equals $\bar{L}$. Similarly, the right panel shows the supply of capital, K^S. Because capital supply is perfectly inelastic and households are endowed with $\bar{K}$ units of capital, the quantity of capital supplied is $\bar{K}$.

Question: How does the labor supply curve change if labor supply depends positively on the wage rate?

2-2b The Demand for Capital and Labor

We assume that there are many identical firms producing with the same production function. Since all firms are identical, they will make identical decisions. Therefore, we can focus on the decisions of a "representative firm" that uses the aggregate production function. The firm hires labor from households. Each unit of labor costs w, so the firm's total labor cost is wL. Similarly, each unit of capital costs r, so the firm's total capital cost is rK. The firm uses the labor and capital it hires to produce output using the aggregate production function, $Y = AF(K, L)$. Total revenue equals the quantity of output produced multiplied by the price per unit of output. As a simplifying assumption, assume that the price per unit of output is equal to one. This implies that total revenue is equal to total production, $Y = AF(K, L)$. Profit is defined as the difference between revenue and costs. Mathematically,

$$Profit = AF(K, L) - wL - rK.$$

The goal of the firm is to choose capital and labor to maximize profit. Although we focus on the behavior of a representative firm, it is important to remember that there are many identical firms in the market, which means no one firm has control over the prices of capital and labor. In other words, the representative firm operates in a perfectly competitive market.

How does the firm make decisions over how much of each input to hire? It is easiest to understand through an example. To keep things simple, let's assume that the firm uses labor as its only factor of production. The logic is the same in the two-factor case. Start by assuming $w = 2$. Table 2.1 shows some illustrative economic data. Starting in the first row, when the firm hires 10 units of labor, it produces 40 units of output. Its wage bill is $20 = 2 \times 10$; profit is the difference between output and labor costs, or 20.

If the firm hires one additional unit of labor, it is assumed that output rises to 45. Since the 11th unit of labor increased output by 5, the MPL of the 11th unit is 5. The total wage bill is $2 \times 11 = 22$ and profit is $45 - 22 = 23$. Thus, moving from the 10th unit of labor to the 11th unit of labor increased profit by 3. Since profits increase, it is optimal for the firm to hire the 11th unit of labor.

If the firm hires one more unit of labor, output rises to 47, implying that the MPL of the 12th unit is 2. The wage bill is 24, and profits are 23. Thus, there is no change in profit moving between the 11th and 12th units.

The last row of the table shows that profits decline if the firm hires a 13th unit of labor. Since the firm wants to maximize profit, hiring the 13th unit of labor would not be optimal.

It comes down to 11 units of labor versus 12 units of labor. How do we decide what is optimal? In this example, both are optimal. This is a result of labor changing in discrete units, i.e., moving from integer to integer. In general, the change in profits from an additional unit of labor is

$$\Delta Profit = MPL - w.$$

The MPL is the change in revenue from hiring one more worker, while w is the change in total cost from hiring one more worker. The difference between them is the change in profit. If $MPL > w$, then it makes sense to hire one more unit of labor because profit increases. If $MPL < w$, it wouldn't make sense to hire one more unit of labor because profit decreases. It's only where $MPL = w$ that the firm cannot make any improvement by increasing or decreasing the amount of labor. Thus, the optimal quantity of labor is always found where $MPL = w$. That is $L = 12$ in Table 2.1.

Now suppose the wage decreases to 1. Table 2.2 shows the same analysis we just did for Table 2.1. Given our result that profit maximizing firms hire until the point $MPL = w$, you

Table 2.1	Optimal Hiring Decisions ($w = 2$)				
L	Y	MPL	wL	Profit	ΔProfit
10	40	X	20	20	X
11	45	5	22	23	3
12	**47**	**2**	**24**	**23**	**0**
13	48	1	26	22	−1

Table 2.2	Optimal Hiring Decisions ($w = 1$)				
L	Y	MPL	wL	Profit	ΔProfit
10	40	X	10	30	X
11	45	5	11	34	4
12	47	2	12	35	1
13	48	1	13	35	0

shouldn't be surprised that the optimal amount of labor increases, in this case to 13. Consequently, a decrease in the wage leads to the firm hiring more units of labor. Another way of saying this is that a decrease in the wage increases the firm's *quantity demanded of labor*.

This example shows why we might expect the firm's labor demand curve to be sloping downward. But a conclusion with more generality requires that we go back to the profit maximizing rule, $w = MPL$. If the wage goes up, the MPL must also go up. But because the MPL is diminishing, that means the quantity of labor hired must go down. Thus, an increase in the wage reduces the quantity of labor demanded.

If the wage goes down, the MPL must also go down. Since the MPL is diminishing, that means the quantity of labor hired must go up. So, a decrease in the wage increases the quantity of labor demanded. Combining these results shows that the labor demand curve is downward sloping.

The capital stock was held fixed in this example, but in reality, the firm makes decisions over capital and labor simultaneously. The same intuition that applies for labor also applies for capital. If the marginal product of capital (MPK) exceeds the rental rate, then the firm will find it optimal to hire more capital. If the MPK is less than the rental rate, then the firm finds it optimal to hire less capital. Consequently, the profit maximizing firm finds it optimal to hire capital up until the point where

$$MPK = r.$$

Figure 2.4 shows how to graphically derive the demand curves for labor and capital. The left panel shows the derivation of the demand for labor. At w_1, the firm finds it optimal to

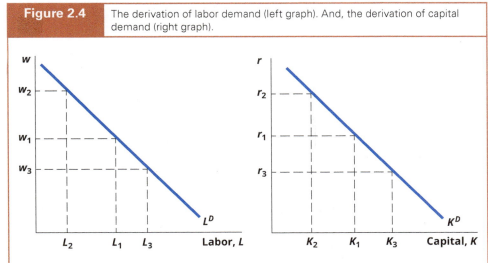

Figure 2.4 The derivation of labor demand (left graph). And, the derivation of capital demand (right graph).

The plot on the left shows the derivation of labor demand. As w increases from w_1 to w_2, the firm finds it optimal to hire less labor. As w decreases from w_1 to w_3, the firm finds it optimal to hire more labor. The plot on the right shows the derivation of capital demand. As r increases from r_1 to r_2, the firm finds it optimal to hire less capital. As r decreases from r_1 to r_3, the firm finds it optimal to hire more capital.

Question: How would an increase in TFP affect labor and capital demand?

hire L_1 units of labor. If the wage increases to w_2, then the rule of profit maximization says that the MPL also increases. Since the MPL is diminishing in labor, the firm finds it optimal to hire less labor at w_2. Similarly, if the wage decreases from w_1 to w_3, then the marginal product of labor would go down, implying that the firm hires more labor. Consequently, the labor demand curve slopes downward. This is an intuitive result that should be familiar to you from principles of economics. As the price of a good rises, less of it is purchased.

The right panel of Figure 2.4 shows the derivation of the demand for capital. At r_1 the firm finds it optimal to hire K_1 units of capital. When the rental rate rises to r_2, the profit maximization rule implies that MPK rises, which means the capital stock falls to K_2. Similarly, if the rental rate falls from r_1 to r_3, then the MPK also falls, which means the capital stock rises to K_3. Thus, the demand for capital is sloping downward.

You might notice something peculiar about the demand curves for capital and labor. At every point on both curves, the firm is optimizing. That is MPL = w and MPK = r. That means that the demand curve for labor is equivalent to the MPL at every single level of labor and the demand curve for capital is equivalent to the MPK at every single level of capital. Thus, anything that changes the MPL or MPK will also shift the demand curves. For instance, because an increase in TFP raises the marginal products of capital and labor, their respective demand curves would also shift.

In summary, the demand curves for capital and labor are derived from the profit-maximizing behavior of firms. The optimal rule is to hire labor up to the point where the marginal product of labor equals the wage rate and hire capital up to the point where marginal product of capital equals the rental rate. The quantity of labor demanded varies inversely with the wage rate, and the quantity demanded of capital varies inversely with the rental rate.

2-2c Combining Supply and Demand

Having derived the demand curves, it is now possible to discuss equilibrium price determination. Figure 2.5 shows the equilibrium in the labor market.

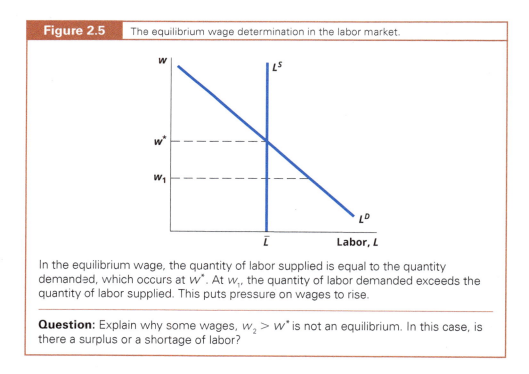

Figure 2.5 The equilibrium wage determination in the labor market.

In the equilibrium wage, the quantity of labor supplied is equal to the quantity demanded, which occurs at w^*. At w_1, the quantity of labor demanded exceeds the quantity of labor supplied. This puts pressure on wages to rise.

Question: Explain why some wages, $w_2 > w^*$ is not an equilibrium. In this case, is there a surplus or a shortage of labor?

The labor demand curve shows the quantity of labor demanded at every wage. The equilibrium quantity of labor is completely pinned down by the supply curve. Since the assumption is that the household supplies its entire labor endowment inelastically, the equilibrium quantity of labor is $\bar{L}$. The equilibrium wage is a wage at which the quantity of labor demanded equals $\bar{L}$. You can see this occurs on the graph at w^*.

Would you expect that labor demand equals labor supply in the real world? In a later chapter, you will learn a model that features unemployment, but the assumption that labor demand equals labor supply is not an unrealistic one, especially over the long run. To see why, suppose the wage is w_1. At w_1, the quantity of labor demanded exceeds $\bar{L}$. Because of this labor shortage, firms compete against one another to secure workers for their own firm, which, as a result, raises wages. As wages rise, the quantity of labor demanded falls until the quantity demanded equals the quantity supplied. Applying this logic, economists usually assume in their analysis that market equilibrium is a good predictor of behavior in real-world markets.

Next, using Figure 2.6, consider an increase in TFP from A_0 to A_1. The labor demand curve at the initial level of TFP is $L^D(A_0)$. An increase in TFP increases the marginal product of labor at every level of labor. Intuitively, an increase in TFP makes each worker more efficient at producing output. Using this higher level of technology, firms are willing to hire more labor at any given wage than when producing with A_0. This shifts the labor demand curve to the right, shown by $L^D(A_1)$. The new equilibrium wage w_1^* reflects that the marginal product of labor at $\bar{L}$ is indeed higher. Thus, an increase in TFP raises wages.

Next, suppose that a change in immigration policy expands the labor force from $\bar{L}_0$ to $\bar{L}_1$. Figure 2.7 shows the increase in the labor supply curve from L_0^S to L_1^S. As the quantity of labor supplied increases, the marginal product of labor decreases until a new equilibrium is reached at w_1^*. Consequently, an increase in the labor force reduces wages. This is an intuitive result and may explain why discourse around immigration is so heated. Should American workers worry that immigration reduces wages? As you will see from Application 2.1 on page 37, the reality is more complicated.

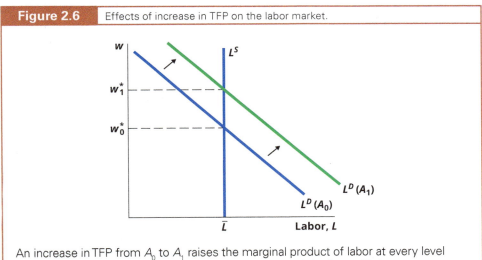

Figure 2.6 Effects of increase in TFP on the labor market.

An increase in TFP from A_0 to A_1 raises the marginal product of labor at every level of labor, which shifts the demand curve up and to the right. In equilibrium, wages increase from w_0^* to w_1^*.

Question: Can you think of an example where technological progress reduces the demand for labor? Is this consistent with the production function assumed in this chapter?

Figure 2.7 — An increase in the supply of labor.

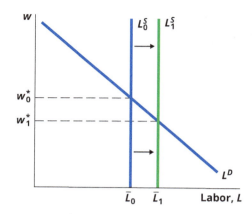

An increase in the number of workers in the economy shifts the labor supply curve from $\bar{L}_0$ to $\bar{L}_1$. The increase in labor reduces the marginal product of labor until the new equilibrium wage is reached, at w_1^*.

Question: Given this increase in the labor force, would wages change by more or less if the demand curve for labor were very elastic?

✓ Knowledge Check 2-3

Suppose the demand curve for labor is given by

$$L^d = \frac{A_t}{w}.$$

Labor supply is given by

$$L^S = \bar{L},$$

where $\bar{L}$ is the exogenous size of the labor force. Solve for the equilibrium wage and verify that it is increasing in A_t and decreasing in $\bar{L}$. Also, fill in the remaining values of this table.

A_t	$\bar{L}$	w
100	10	
250	10	
250	50	
300	50	

————————————— Answers are at the end of the chapter.

✓ Knowledge Check 2-4

Graphically depict equilibrium in the capital market. How does an increase in TFP affect the equilibrium rental rate?

————————————— Answers are at the end of the chapter.

Application 2.1

How Does Immigration Affect Wages?

The simple labor supply and demand model from the previous section predicts that wages decrease in response to an increase in immigration. The result is intuitive and could influence how policymakers and the public perceive the effects of immigration on wages. However, the problem is that in the case of immigration, the simple model makes inaccurate predictions.

Figure 2.8 shows the empirical results of 27 research papers from 1982–2013 assessing the effects of immigrants on the wages of native workers. The figure summarizes the results from various papers that study the impact of a one percentage point increase in immigration on the wages of native workers, grouping them by the magnitude of their findings. The biggest fraction, comprising nearly half the papers, contains the interval [−0.1, 0.1]. This means that a one percentage point increase in immigration changes native wages between −0.1 and 0.1 percent. Looking at the other fractions in the pie chart, you see that most of these papers predict that immigration has either a zero or positive effect on wages.

Why is the baseline model so far off here? Here are several prominent explanations proposed by empirical research:

1. **Immigrants and natives specialize in different tasks:** Not all jobs are created the same. Some, like a car salesperson, require very good language skills. Others, like an auto mechanic, require physical dexterity. Following an influx of immigrants, native workers tend to specialize in jobs that are communication intensive.[1] Since immigrants and native workers specialize in different tasks, an increase in immigrants leads to a small change in the wages of natives.

2. **The capital stock is not fixed:** In the static model of labor supply and demand, workers bring their labor, and that's the end of the story. In the real world, workers not only provide their labor but also save a fraction of their income that then gets turned into capital. The increase in the capital stock increases the marginal product of labor and wages.

3. **Immigration increases the educational attainment of the native-born population:** A particular concern in the United States context is that an influx in immigration will lower the wages of less-educated Americans. Research shows that a one percentage point increase in immigrants increases the probability that native workers complete high school by 0.3 percentage points. It's possible that the increase in immigration gives native workers an additional incentive to complete high school.[2] The reason is that immigrants entering the United States tend to have either very low levels or very high levels of educational attainment compared to native workers. Anticipating the increase in competition if they drop out of high school, native-born students are more likely to stick it out through their degree.

Despite its shortcomings in predicting the effects of immigrants on wages, the baseline labor supply and demand model is still useful. Indeed, the second explanation fits right into the supply and demand framework as long as you think about the supply and demand curves changing over time, rather than a "once and for all" shift. If new workers save and increase the capital stock, the labor demand curve shifts to the right over time, thus raising wages. Distinguishing between labor markets for workers with different levels of educational attainment, meanwhile, can rationalize the third explanation. An increase in the supply of immigrants with low educational attainment causes native students to stay in school, reducing the future supply of less-educated workers, thereby raising the wages of the least educated group.

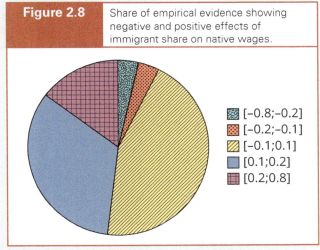

Figure 2.8 Share of empirical evidence showing negative and positive effects of immigrant share on native wages.

- [−0.8;−0.2]
- [−0.2;−0.1]
- [−0.1;0.1]
- [0.1;0.2]
- [0.2;0.8]

Source: https://wol.iza.org/articles/do-immigrant-workers-depress-the-wages-of-native-workers/long

---

[1] Peri, Giovanni and Chad Sparber. 2009. "Task Specialization, Immigration, and Wages." *American Economic Journal: Applied Economics,* 1(3): 135–169.
[2] Hunt, Jennifer. 2017 "The Impact of Immigration on the Educational Attainment of Natives." *Journal of Human Resources,* 52(4): 1060–1118.

2-3 Using the Production Function to Understand Cross-Country Income Differences

The output of the aggregate production function is GDP and the inputs are capital and labor. The efficiency at which an economy makes use of its inputs is TFP. Therefore, cross-country income differences must come from differences in inputs, differences in TFP, or a mix of both. Economists use the production function to decompose the fraction of output differences due to inputs and the remainder that is due to TFP.

2-3a Cobb–Douglas Production Function

So far in this chapter you only know a few general assumptions about the aggregate production function, $Y = AF(K, L)$. Accounting for cross-country income differences requires stronger assumptions about the production function. An aggregate production function commonly used in economic research is the Cobb–Douglas production function. Pioneered by economist Charles Cobb and Senator Paul Douglas in the first half of the 20th century[3],

$$Y = AK^a L^{1-a},$$

where a is a parameter between 0 and 1. The closer a is to one, the more sensitive output is to capital. Output is more sensitive to labor when a is close to 0. The appropriate choice of a is discussed later in Application 2.2. This production function satisfies all four assumptions from 2-1b. For instance, if the economy has no capital, then $Y = A \times 0 \times L^{1-a} = 0$, and likewise for labor. To verify the constant returns to scale assumption is satisfied, double both capital and labor:

$$A(2K)^a (2L)^{1-a} = A2^a 2^{1-a} K^a L^{1-a} = 2AK^a L^{1-a}.$$

As shown formally in the previous equation, doubling both capital and labor exactly doubles output. For any choice of a, you can verify that output is increasing in capital and labor and that their marginal products are diminishing.[4]

One obvious reason some countries produce more than others is that they have bigger populations. For example, it's no surprise that China (population 1.43 billion) produces more than Finland (population 5.53 million). As you learned in Chapter 1, the relevant metric for discussing living standards is GDP per person. To correct for these differences in population and derive a measure of production that is a better indicator of living standards, divide both sides of the production function by the number of workers, L. Mathematically, this is given by

$$y = \frac{Y}{L}$$

$$= A\frac{K^a L^{1-a}}{L}$$

$$= A\frac{K^a L^{1-a}}{L^a L^{1-a}}$$

$$= Ak^a,$$

where $k = \dfrac{K}{L}$ is capital per worker. Output per worker can go up because either capital per worker increases or because the existing capital is used more efficiently. This production function provides a way of decomposing cross-country income differences into differences in capital per worker and differences in TFP.

---

[3]Cobb, Charles W. and Paul H. Douglas. 1928. "A Theory of Production." *American Economic Review, 18*(1): 139–165.
[4]Or, if you are familiar with calculus, you can show these using partial derivatives.

2-3b Putting the Cobb–Douglas Production Function to Work

The Penn World Table contains data on GDP, capital, and population (as well as a host of other variables) for 183 countries from 1950 to 2019. Figure 2.9 shows the strong positive relationship between capital per worker and output per worker. Unsurprisingly, countries that produce more output per worker also have higher levels of capital per worker.

Unlike capital and GDP, TFP is not measured. Instead, TFP is inferred from the production function and the data on capital and GDP.

Using the Cobb–Douglas production function gives

$$A = \frac{y}{k^a}.$$

From a measurement standpoint then, you can think of TFP as all the differences in output per worker not explained by differences in capital per worker. For reasons discussed in Application 2.2, a choice of $a = 1/3$ is appropriate. The relationship between TFP and GDP per worker is shown in Figure 2.10.

Just like the relationship between capital per worker and output per worker, TFP and output per worker are positively related. To summarize, countries that produce high levels of output per worker have greater levels of capital per worker and are also more efficient at using the capital.

The next step is to figure out what percentage of differences in GDP per worker is explained by differences in capital per worker versus differences in TFP. To accomplish this, we compare actual GDP per worker to a hypothetical GDP per worker, y_{hyp}, where TFP is equalized across countries. Mathematically, this is given by

$$y = Ak^{1/3},$$
$$y_{hyp} = \overline{A}k^{1/3}.$$

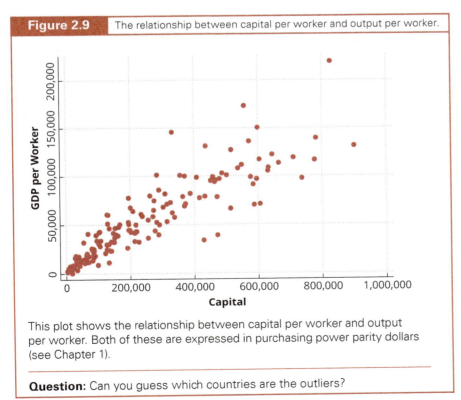

Figure 2.9 The relationship between capital per worker and output per worker.

This plot shows the relationship between capital per worker and output per worker. Both of these are expressed in purchasing power parity dollars (see Chapter 1).

Question: Can you guess which countries are the outliers?

Source: Penn World Tables 10.0.

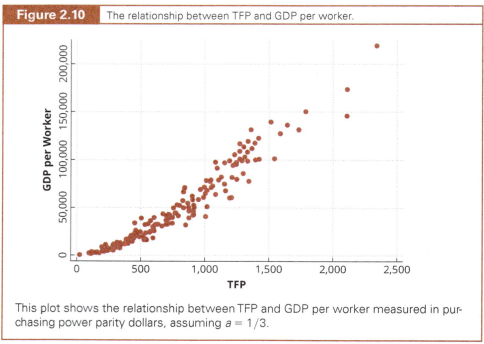

Figure 2.10 The relationship between TFP and GDP per worker.

This plot shows the relationship between TFP and GDP per worker measured in purchasing power parity dollars, assuming $a = 1/3$.

Source: Penn World Tables 10.0.

The second equation holds TFP fixed across countries so that the only source of variation is capital per worker. There are a few different ways of separating the contribution of capital from that of TFPs. One of the more straightforward approaches is to look at the ratio of income per worker at the 90th percentile to the 10th percentile for y and y_{hyp}. A country is at the 90th percentile of output per worker if 90 percent of countries in the data have lower levels of output per worker. The 10th percentile is defined analogously. In 2019, the 90–10 ratio was about 17.5 so the country at the 90th percentile produces about 17.5 as much as the country in the 10th percentile. Define "capital's share" as the 90–10 ratio for y_{hyp} divided by the 90–10 ratio for y. Mathematically, this is given by

$$\text{capital share} = \frac{y_{hyp}^{90}/y_{hyp}^{10}}{y^{90}/y^{10}}.$$

The higher is this ratio, the higher is capital's share. The capital share in 2019 was 19.1 percent. Or, equivalently, differences in TFP explained close to 81 percent of the variance in output per worker across countries in 2019. Over the next two chapters, you will learn models that explain differences in the rates of capital accumulation and TFP growth across countries.

Before leaving this section, it is worthwhile to consider the economics behind these results. Recall that calculating TFP requires a choice of a. Figure 2.11 shows two production functions: one with $a = 1/3$ and the other with $a = 2/3$. Each production function has $A = 1$. For a given level of capital per worker, the production function with the higher a produces more output. Intuitively, a production function with a higher a has a higher marginal product of capital at every point and runs into diminishing returns much more slowly than the production function with lower a. Another way to think about it is that capital is more important in producing output the higher is a.

How does this influence capital's share of the variance in output per worker? As you might expect, as a increases, the share explained by capital also increases. The table below shows the results of varying a.

Just as expected, as a gets bigger, capital becomes more important in explaining differences in output per worker across countries. Application 2.2 discusses how economists choose an appropriate a and how it might be changing over time.

a	Capital's share of variance in output per worker
$a = 1/3$	19.1%
$a = 1/2$	35.1%
$a = 2/3$	64.4%
$a = 3/4$	87.2%

Figure 2.11 Two production functions.

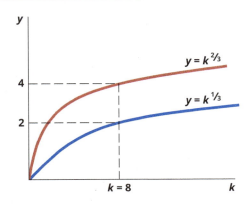

There are two production functions written in per worker terms. The blue line assumes $a = 1/3$, and the red line assumes $a = 2/3$. Both production functions have the same level of TFP, $A = 1$. With the same level of capital, the production function with $a = 2/3$ produces more output.

Question: Draw a production function with $a = 1$. Which of the four assumptions are violated?

Source: Penn World Tables 10.0.

✓ Knowledge Check 2-5

Suppose the aggregate production function is Cobb–Douglas:

$$Y = AK^a L^{1-a}.$$

Assume $a = 1/3$ and fill in the rest of the table.

		A = 1	A = 2
L	K	Y	Y
100	100		
200	100		
300	100		
100	200		
100	300		

Answers are at the end of the chapter.

✓ Knowledge Check 2-6

What economic factors might affect a country's rate of capital accumulation?

Answers are at the end of the chapter.

Application 2.2

Measuring Factor Shares

A convenient feature of the Cobb–Douglas production function is that a in the production function maps to something measurable in the data. Recall from Chapter 1 that the income approach to calculating GDP splits income into distinctive categories like labor earnings, profit, earnings from rent, etc. The Cobb–Douglas aggregate production function assumes there are only three potential sources of income: labor earnings, income derived from renting capital, and profit.

In particular, starting with $Y = AK^a L^{1-a}$ and assuming that markets are perfectly competitive implies that the fraction of income going to labor is a constant, $1 - a$, and capital's share of income is a. As a consequence of perfect competition, no income is left over for economic profit.

This leads to a testable implication. If the aggregate production function is well described by the Cobb–Douglas function and markets are perfectly competitive, then the share of income going to labor and capital should be stable over time. GDP and its sources are measured by the Bureau of Economic Analysis's National Income and Product Accounts. Since labor income is more easily measured than capital income, it is more straightforward to look at the share of labor income. Labor's share of income is also included in the Penn World Tables, which were used in the last section. Figure 2.12 shows the trend in labor's share of income for the United States.

Labor's share of income was relatively stable until the mid-1970s at about 0.64. This is why something close to $a = 1/3$ is appropriate. The labor share dropped until the mid-1980s and then rose until the end of the century. Since 2000, there has been a sustained decrease in labor's share. Economists Brent Neiman and Loukas Karabarbounis (2014) show that labor's share of income declined across most of the industrialized world staring in the 1980s, although the exact timing and quantitative magnitudes of the decline are different across countries.[5] What might explain the decline in the labor share in the 21st century? Empirical research offers the following hypotheses:

1. One argument is that the Cobb–Douglas production function does not accurately model the aggregate production function. Using advanced statistical techniques, some researchers have estimated that labor and capital are more substitutable than implied by Cobb–Douglas.[6] As information technology advanced over the past 30 years, the price of capital fell, which

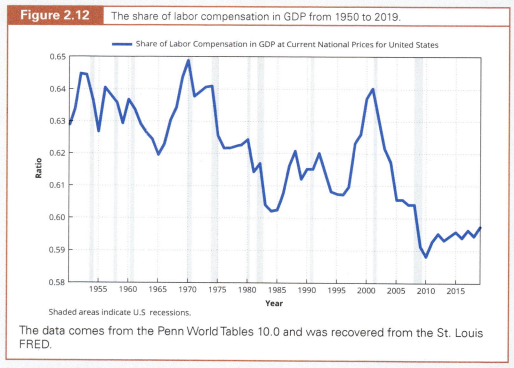

Figure 2.12 The share of labor compensation in GDP from 1950 to 2019.

Shaded areas indicate U.S recessions.

The data comes from the Penn World Tables 10.0 and was recovered from the St. Louis FRED.

Source: St. Louis FRED.

■ Continues

Chapter 2 Production Functions **43**

Application 2.2 (Continued)

led firms to substitute toward capital and away from labor. Since the quantity of capital increased faster than the decrease in the price of capital, labor's share of income decreased and capital's share of income increased.

2. Another hypothesis is that sales have concentrated to "superstar" firms. The leading example of a superstar firm is Amazon, which has replaced everything from bookstores to toy stores and, more recently, grocery stores. Amazon provides consumers with easy delivery of a wide range of products. A key fact about these superstar firms is that they have higher profits and lower labor shares compared to smaller firms. Using detailed firm-level data in the United States and internationally, a team of economists has shown that market shares across industries have gravitated to these superstar firms.[7] The change in composition of

sales partly explains the decline in the labor share of income.

Although product market concentration has increased and the labor share decreased since 2000, it does not mean people are worse off. In general, it is a good thing if resources are allocated to more productive firms even if these firms make more profit. If, on the other hand, the increase in profit and product market concentration was caused by entry barriers like licensing and different forms of regulation, consumers would be hurt.

It is generally accepted by now that the labor share has declined across most of the world and across most industries within countries. Untangling the competing theories of the declining labor share, however, is an ongoing area of research.

[5]Karabarbounis, Loukas and Brent Neiman. 2014. "The Global Decline of the Labor Share." *Quarterly Journal of Economics, 129*(1): 61–103.
[6]This is what Karabarbounis and Neiman found.
[7]Autor, David, David Dorn, Lawrence Katz, Christina Patterson, and John Van Reenen. 2020. "The Fall of the Labor Share and the Rise of Superstar Firms." *Quarterly Journal of Economics, 135*(2): 645–709.

Chapter Summary

- A production function describes how inputs are transformed into output. The aggregate production function combines a country's labor, capital, and TFP to produce output.

- Four common assumptions of the aggregate production function are: i) production requires both labor and capital, ii) the marginal products of capital and labor are always positive, iii) the marginal products of capital and labor are diminishing, and iv) the production function is constant returns to scale in capital and labor.

- The demand curves for capital and labor are implicitly given by their respective marginal products.

- The prices of capital and labor are determined through the interaction of demand and supply. This chapter assumes that the supply of each factor is perfectly inelastic.

- The Cobb–Douglas aggregate production function is commonly used in applied economic research and is used in this chapter to understand cross-country differences in GDP per worker.

- Cross-country differences in GDP per worker can be divided between differences due to capital per worker and differences due to TFP. Penn World Table data from 2019 shows that differences in capital per worker explained about 15 percent of the variation in GDP per worker.

Key Terms

Production function, 27
Aggregate production function, 27
Capital, 27
Total factor productivity (TFP), 28
Marginal product of labor, 28
Marginal product of capital, 28
Returns to scale, 29

Firm, 31
Household, 31
Representative firm, 31
Representative household, 31
Wage rate, 31
Rental rate, 31

44 **Part 1** Growth

Review Questions

1. Explain how TFP is different from the inputs in a production function.

2. If a production function is constant returns to scale, doubling all the inputs exactly doubles output. Under what circumstances does this mean the production function cannot have diminishing marginal products?

3. Do differences in TFP or capital per worker explain most of the variation in cross-country income?

4. What are profits equal to in the model of perfect competition? How would your answer change if there were imperfect competition?

5. Intuitively explain why the demand curves for labor and capital slope down.

Problems

2.1 For each of the following production functions, list which (if any) of the four assumptions from Section 2-1b are violated.

   a. $Y = L + K$

   b. $Y = KL$

   c. $Y = \min [K, L]$ where, for example, $Y = \min [3, 4] = 3$

2.2 Suppose you have the following Cobb–Doulas production function:

$$Y = AK^a L^{1-a}.$$

Assume $a = 1/3$.

   a. Assume that K = 2. Fill out the rest of this table (you will need a calculator).

L	A = 1		A = 2	
	Y	MPL	Y	MPL
1				
2				
3				
4				

Is the marginal product of labor positive or negative? Is it increasing or decreasing in L? How does an increase in A affect the MPL and the demand curve for labor?

   b. Assume that L = 2. Fill out the rest of this table.

K	A = 1		A = 2	
	Y	MPK	Y	MPK
1				
2				
3				
4				

Is the marginal product of capital positive or negative? Is it increasing or decreasing in K? How does an increase in A affect the MPK and the demand curve for capital?

2.3 Depict how each of the following changes affects the level of wages or the rental rate.

   a. A plague kills 25 percent of a country's population.

   b. A new regulation makes it less efficient for firms to hire capital and labor.

   c. Congress implements a law that taxes revenue at rate $0 < t < 1$. The revenue for the firm is now $(1 - t) AF (K, L)$.

   d. Congress implements a law that taxes profit at rate $0 < t < 1$.

2.4 Between 1975 and 2019 the U.S. population grew by about 100 million people. At the same time, wages for the median worker were stagnant. How can you explain this using the tools of labor supply and demand model?

2.5 Suppose the aggregate production function is given by

$$Y = AK^a(hL)^{1-a},$$

where L is the number of workers and h is the hours worked per worker in a year. The average U.S. worker in 2019, for instance, worked close to 1,800 hours over the course of the year.

   a. Algebraically transform this production function into per-worker form.

   b. The Penn World Tables discussed in Section 2.3 have data on h for each country. Since the PWT also has data on GDP, capital, and the number of workers, do you have enough information to infer TFP? If so, use the production function to solve for TFP as a function of these variables.

   c. Output per worker and hours per worker are negatively correlated across countries. That is, workers in richer countries tend to work less than workers in poorer countries. Would this make TFP differences across countries bigger or smaller compared to the production function that omitted hours per worker (discussed in Section 2.3b)?

Knowledge Check 2-1 Answer

The marginal product of labor is the amount output changes per unit change of an input. Moving from 1 unit of labor to 2 units of labor increases output from 4 to 7, so the MPL is 3. Moving from 2 units of labor to 3 units of labor increases output from 7 to 9, so the MPL is 2. Moving from 3 units of labor to 4 units of labor increases output from 9 to 10, so the MPL is 1. Moving from 4 units of labor to 5 units of labor increases output from 10 to 10.5, so the MPL is 0.5. Moving from 5 units of labor to 6 units of labor increases output from 10.5 to 10.75, so the MPL is 0.25.

L	K	Y	MPL
1	10	4	X
2	10	7	3
3	10	9	2
4	10	10	1
5	10	10.5	0.5
6	10	10.75	0.25

The marginal product of labor decreases as labor increases.

 Knowledge Check 2-2 Answer

Your answers will obviously be different, but here are four examples.

1. Teaching an in-person class only requires labor. Teaching is the service that is being produced and, in this case, it only requires one input. This violates the first assumption.

2. Returning to the baking example, moving from one baker in a kitchen with one oven to 1,000 bakers in the same kitchen could actually decrease cookie output. The bakers wouldn't be physically able to move around in the kitchen to produce cookies. This violates the second assumption.

3. In the baking example, imagine that there are two bakers in the kitchen who can combine ingredients, but don't know how to operate the oven. The number of cookies produced is zero. If a third baker who knows how to operate the oven is added, cookie production increases. Output increases by more in moving from the second to the third baker than moving from the first to the second. This violates the third assumption.

4. Suppose that developing a pharmaceutical drug takes the effort of 1,000 of a laboratory's employees. But after the drug is developed, it only takes one employee to manufacture 1,000 units of the drug. In other words, it takes 1,000 employees to develop the first unit and 1/1000 employee to develop all subsequent units. This is an example of increasing returns to scale and it violates the fourth assumption.

Knowledge Check 2-3 Answer

Imposing that labor supply equals labor demand gives

$$\bar{L} = \frac{A_t}{w}.$$

Solving for w gives

$$w = \frac{A_t}{\bar{L}}.$$

TFP is in the numerator, so wages are increasing in TFP. The labor force is in the denominator. An increase in the labor force therefore reduces wages. These results are consistent with the discussion in the previous section. The wage column of the table can be filled in by substituting particular values of TFP and the labor force into the previous equation.

A_t	$\bar{L}$	w
100	10	10
250	10	25
250	50	5
300	50	6

Knowledge Check 2-4 Answer

The demand for capital is downwards sloping. The supply is perfectly inelastic. The equilibrium rental rate is determined by the intersection of supply and demand. This is shown in Figure 2.13. An increase in TFP shifts the capital demand curve to the right. The equilibrium rental rate increases from r_0^* to r_1^*.

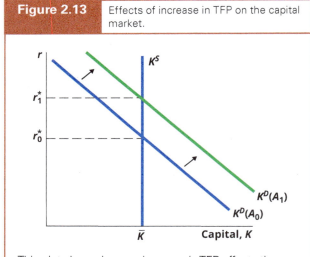

Figure 2.13 Effects of increase in TFP on the capital market.

This plot shows how an increase in TFP affects the capital market. An increase in TFP from A_0 to A_1 raises the marginal product of labor at every level of capital which shifts the demand curve up and to the right. In equilibrium, the rental rate increases from r_0^* to r_1^*.

✓ Knowledge Check 2-5 Answer

The missing values of the table can be filled in by substituting for the particular values of labor, capital, and TFP into the production function. For instance, when $A_t = 1$ and $L_t = K_t = 100$, you get

$$Y = AK^a L^{1-a} = 100^{1/3} \times 100^{2/3} = 100.$$

The rest of the table can be filled out exactly like this.

		A = 1	A = 2
L	K	Y	Y
100	100	100	200
200	100	158.74	317.48
300	100	208	416
100	200	126	252
100	300	144.25	288.5

There are three observations from this table. First, output is increasing in both capital and labor. This is exactly what we would expect given our assumptions in Section 1. Second, an increase in TFP, holding fixed the quantities of labor and capital, increases output. This is exactly aligned with the analysis in Section 2.2. Finally, the marginal products of capital and labor are diminishing. Going from 100 to 200 workers adds more to output than going from 200 to 300 workers. The same is true for capital.

✓ Knowledge Check 2-6 Answer

As an open-ended question, there isn't only one right answer. But we can come up with some educated guesses. One factor might be a country's savings rate. Countries that save a greater fraction of their income can invest in more capital. Another factor might be the degree to which a country's government protects private property rights. With insecure property rights, owners of capital aren't able to protect their investments. Foreseeing this possibility in advance, people will rationally choose to not accumulate as much capital.

Chapter 3

The Solow Model of Economic Growth

Learning Objectives

3.1 Explain the variables, parameters, and key equations of the Solow model.

3.2 Graphically depict the equilibrium in the Solow model.

3.3 Algebraically solve for the steady state.

3.4 Predict the effects of changes in parameters and exogenous variables within the Solow model.

3.5 Identify the conditions under which the economy is dynamically inefficient.

3.6 Use the Solow model to forecast the growth performance of countries.

By the close of the 1940s, the American economy was becoming the center of the economic world. World War II had decimated the capital stocks and infrastructure in Japan and Europe. Production of everything from agricultural goods to manufacturing goods was low. Food shortages in some parts of Europe became a serious issue. But then, seemingly out of nowhere, these economies took off. Over the next two decades, Japan, the UK, and many countries in continental Europe experienced rapid rates of economic growth.

Some of this economic growth can be attributed to the United States' sending Europe foreign aid through the Marshall Plan. Ambitious as the plan was for its time, no economy received more than several billion dollars, and Japan didn't receive any aid. So, what exactly explains the takeoff growth of these economies?

This chapter introduces you to the Solow model of economic growth. The Solow model explicitly shows how capital accumulates through time and is therefore particularly helpful at answering such questions as what happened to these economies after World War II. Moreover, the model can speak to why all countries don't experience high rates of growth after a war. With a few equations and parameters, you will be able to forecast where an economy is going.

3-1 The Solow Model of Economic Growth

You learned in the previous chapter how capital and labor are transformed into output. Given fixed quantities of capital and labor, you were able to compute the quantity of GDP produced and solve for the factor prices. Although this was a useful starting place, the model in the last chapter was static. Thinking about economic growth—that is, how GDP and GDP per worker change over time—requires us to consider how the quantity of capital and labor change over time. The Solow model of economic growth does just that.[1] The Solow model is the backbone of essentially all models of economic growth used by economists. In fact, the model is so influential that the inventor of the model, Robert Solow, received the Nobel Prize in 1987 for his contributions to the field of economic growth.

---

[1] Robert, Solow. 1956. "A Contribution to the Theory of Economic Growth." *Quarterly Journal of Economics, 70*(1): 65–94.

Chapter 3 The Solow Model of Economic Growth **49**

In the Solow model, new capital, or investment, is created by individuals in the economy saving some fraction of their income. If investment exceeds the amount of capital that is worn out in the production process, then the capital stock grows and the economy produces more output. It is the balancing act between the addition of new capital and the destruction of old capital that determines if the economy is growing or shrinking over time.

3-1a Basic Ingredients of the Solow Model

There are three key equations in the Solow model. You are familiar with the first one. It is the Cobb–Douglas aggregate production function,

$$Y_t = A_t K_t^a L_t^{1-a}. \tag{1}$$

Here, Y_t is output, or GDP, L_t is the number of workers, and K_t is the capital stock. The variable a, where $0 < a < 1$, is a parameter and A_t is total factor productivity (TFP). The only small difference compared to what you saw in the previous chapter is the t subscript, which denotes the current time period. That is, if we wrote this production function for 2023, then $t = 2023$. If we wrote the production function for the prior year, then $t = 2022$, and so on. It is important to keep track of the time period because the model is dynamic.

The next equation describes population growth. To keep things simple, assume that the population grows at constant rate $n > 0$ so that

$$L_{t+1} = (1 + n)L_t. \tag{2}$$

The population next year is this year's population times one plus the population growth rate. For instance, if the population this year is 100 million ($L_t = 100$ million) and the annual population growth rate is 2 percent ($n = 0.02$), then the population next year will be $(1 + 0.02)100 = 102$ million. Population in two years will be $(1 + 0.02) \times 102 = 104.04$. This bit of algebra shows that population increases more between year 2 and year 3 than between year 1 and year 2. This is a natural consequence of exponential growth. A constant population growth rate implies ever larger increases in the population through time.

If the capital stock is fixed, a continually expanding labor force drives down the marginal product of labor and wages. However, the capital stock is not fixed in the Solow model. What factors determine how capital changes over time? Imagine that an industrial farm has 100 tractors at the start of the year. Over the course of the year, the farm owners invest in 12 new tractors. At the same time, the 10 oldest tractors break down to a point they are no longer functional. Translating this story into math, K_t is 100 tractors. Since the 12 new tractors exceeds the 10 broken tractors by two, K_{t+1} is 102. The 12 new tractors are classified as **investment**. The 10 broken tractors are classified as depreciated capital. This example can be generalized by the equation

$$K_{t+1} = (1 - d)K_t + I_t, \tag{3}$$

where $0 < d < 1$ is the **depreciation rate**. The capital stock next year (K_{t+1}) is equal to the capital stock this year that remains after depreciation, $(1 - d)K_t$, plus investment, I_t. If $I_t > dK_t$, then the capital stock increases. If the reverse inequality holds, then the capital stock decreases. If investment exactly equals depreciated capital, then the capital stock does not change.

To close out the model, we need to know where investment comes from. Just as in the real world, investment in the Solow model comes from savings set aside by households. The Solow model assumes that a constant fraction, s, of income is saved each period. Assuming all savings is transformed into investment,

$$I_t = sY_t. \tag{4}$$

Investment
New capital created by the fraction of household income used as savings.

Depreciation rate
The rate at which capital that is used up during the course of production.

50 Part 1 Growth

Table 3.1	Summary of the Solow Model		
Endogenous variables		**Exogenous variables**	**Parameters**
Y_t, K_{t+1}, I_t		L_t, A	s, n, d, a

Key equations:

1. $Y_t = A_t K_t^a L_t^{1-a}$ (production function)

2. $L_{t+1} = (1 + n)L_t$ (population)

3. $K_{t+1} = (1 - d)K_t + I_t$ (capital accumulation)

4. $I_t = sY_t$ (Investment rule)

This table describes the variables, parameters, and key equations of the Solow model.

That is, investment equals the savings rate times GDP. The fraction of output that is not invested is consumed so that GDP is divided entirely between consumption and investment.

Table 3.1 summarizes the variables and key equations of the model. Because this will come up again in the book, it is worthwhile to review the difference between endogenous variables, exogenous variables, and parameters. A variable is something that can be represented by a number and can change. An endogenous variable is a variable that is solved for within the model, while an exogenous variable is determined outside the model. A parameter is a fixed constant that governs the mathematical relationships between the variables. In experimenting with the model, we may wish to consider one-time changes in parameters, but (by assumption) they do not evolve over time. As a rule of thumb, both types of variables have time subscripts, but parameters do not.

The endogenous variables in the model are Y_t, K_{t+1}, and I_t. Output and investment have time t subscripts, and capital has a time $t + 1$ subscript. The reason is that K_t was determined by the accumulation equation in the prior period, $t - 1$. The exogenous variables are population and TFP given respectively by A_t and L_t. The parameters are s (the savings rate), n (the population growth rate), d (the depreciation rate), and a (the curvature parameter on the production function).

The next step is to put the endogenous variables, Y_t and K_{t+1}, in per-worker terms. This transformation makes the model easier to solve, and per-worker variables are more relevant for understanding a country's productive capacity and well-being of its population. Define $y_t = \dfrac{Y_t}{L_t}$ as output per worker and $k_{t+1} = \dfrac{K_{t+1}}{L_{t+1}}$ as capital per worker. Output per worker is solved for by dividing both sides of the Cobb–Doulas production function by L_t:

$$y_t = \frac{A_t K_t^a L_t^{1-a}}{L_t}$$

$$= \frac{A_t K_t^a L_t^{1-a}}{L_t^a L_t^{1-a}}$$

$$= A_t k_t^a. \tag{5}$$

You can see from Equation (5) that the curvature parameter, a, determines how quickly the economy runs into diminishing productivity of capital. If a is close to 1, then the per-worker production function is almost linear in capital. This means that it takes a lot of capital before diminishing marginal productivity sets it. On the other hand, if a is close to 0, then diminishing marginal productivity sets in faster. Figure 3.1 shows two per-worker production functions, both with $A_t = 1$. The marginal product of capital is higher at every level of capital when a is bigger.

Figure 3.1 Two per-worker production functions with different curvature parameters.

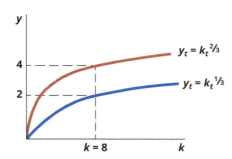

There are two production functions written in per-worker terms. The blue line assumes $a = 1/3$, and the red line assumes $a = 2/3$. Both production functions have the same level of TFP, $A_t = 1$. With the same level of capital, the production function with $a = 2/3$ produces more output.

Question: Draw a production function with $a = 1$. Is the marginal product of capital diminishing?

Next, divide both sides of the capital accumulation equation by L_t and use the mathematical trick that $\frac{L_{t+1}}{L_{t+1}} = 1$:

$$\frac{K_{t+1}}{L_t} = (1-d)\frac{K_t}{L_t} + s\frac{Y_t}{L_t}$$

$$\Leftrightarrow \frac{K_{t+1}}{L_t}\frac{L_{t+1}}{L_{t+1}} = (1-d)k_t + sy_t$$

$$\Leftrightarrow k_{t+1}(1+n) = (1-d)k_t + sy_t$$

$$\Leftrightarrow k_{t+1} = \frac{1}{1+n}[(1-d)k_t + sy_t]. \tag{6}$$

The second step multiplies the left-hand side by $1 = \frac{L_{t+1}}{L_{t+1}}$ and the third step uses the fact that $\frac{L_{t+1}}{L_t} = 1 + n$. Equation (6) describes the evolution of the per-worker capital stock over time. Together with the per-worker production function, these equations trace the dynamics of output and capital per worker for every single period in the model. The reason why the right-hand side of the accumulation equation is divided by $1 + n$ is because the existing capital stock gets spread more thinly the more people are in the economy. Another way to think about it is if the aggregate capital stock, K_t, is fixed, then the per-worker capital stock gets smaller and smaller with time as more workers enter the economy.

✓ Knowledge Check 3-1

Assuming $d = 0.1$, $s = 0.2$, $n = 0.01$, $A_t = 1$, and $a = 1/3$, complete the rest of the table.

Time period (t)	k_t	sy_t	$(1-d)k_t$	k_{t+1}	$k_{t+1} - k_t$
0	2				
1					
2					
3					
4					

Answers are at the end of the chapter.

What happens to the change in capital over time. That is, does the difference $k_{t+1} - k_t$ get bigger or smaller as t increases?

3-1b Graphically Characterizing the Model

If the goal is to solve for the economy's capital stock and GDP in every time period, how many variables do we have to solve for? The answer is infinitely many. Because time goes on forever, there is a (future) capital stock and level of GDP to solve for in every period. This, needless to say, is impractical. Fortunately, there is a better way to approach this problem.

Balanced growth path
A situation in which all of an economy's variables are growing at a constant, although not necessarily the same, rate.

Steady state
A situation in which an economic variable is not growing or shrinking over time.

A **balanced growth path** (BGP) occurs when all variables are growing at a constant, although not necessarily the same, rate. A **steady state** is a particular case of a balanced growth path where the variables don't grow at all. These concepts suggest how to solve the model. First, one must determine if a steady state or BGP exists. If it does, we can characterize the behavior of the economy in steady state, as well as away from steady state.

If a steady-state level of capital per worker exists, then $k_{t+1} = k_t = k_{ss}$. Substituting the production function into the accumulation equation gives

$$k_{t+1} = \frac{1}{1+n}[(1-d)k_t + sy_t]$$
$$= \frac{1}{1+n}[(1-d)k_t + sA_t k_t^a]. \quad (7)$$

Now draw k_{t+1} as a function of k_t and also the 45-degree line which tells us all the points where $k_{t+1} = k_t$. This is shown in Figure 3.2. When $k_t = 0$ then $k_{t+1} = 0$. As k_t increases, k_{t+1} increases. Intuitively, holding all else constant, the bigger the capital stock this year, the bigger the capital stock next year. Since $a < 1$, the accumulation line is concave, or bowed out away from the origin. Moreover, you can convince yourself that the marginal product of capital per worker gets very close to zero the bigger is k_t. This means that as k_t gets really big, the slope of the accumulation line is $\frac{1-d}{1+n} < 1$. Since the 45-degree line has a slope of 1 for all levels of capital, we can be sure that the accumulation line eventually crosses the 45-degree line exactly once.

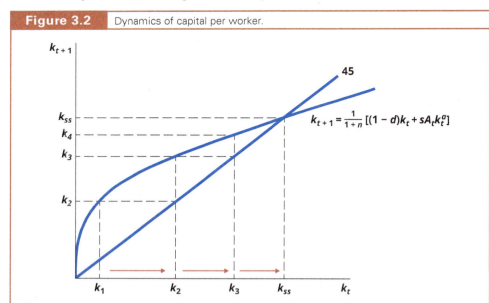

Figure 3.2 Dynamics of capital per worker.

Starting at k_1 in the first year, the accumulation equation implies a capital level of k_2 next year. Tracing that over to the 45-degree line gives the capital stock in year 2, k_2. Tracing up to the accumulation equation shows that the capital stock is k_3 in the third year. Repeating this process shows that the capital per worker converges to k^{ss}.

Question: Starting at $k_1 > k^{ss}$, show that the economy converges to the steady-state level of capital per worker.

If capital per worker is at its steady state, then it won't move absent a change in an exogenous variable or a parameter. But what if the economy starts outside of its steady state? To answer this, return to the same graph and start with a capital stock lower than k_{ss}. In year $t = 1$, the economy starts at k_1. Given a level of capital per worker of k_1 in the first year, the accumulation equation tells you how much capital will be available in year $t = 2$. Graphically, you find this by tracing up from k_1 to the accumulation line. Doing so yields a capital stock next year of $k_{t+1} = k_2$. Recalling that the 45-degree line contains all the points where $k_{t+1} = k_t$, you can trace over to the 45-degree line to find a capital per worker of $k_t = k_2$ in $t = 2$. Note that the capital stock has increased between years 1 and 2. Repeating this step, you can find the capital stock in the next year by tracing up to the accumulation line starting from $k_t = k_2$. This gives $k_{t+1} = k_3$. Trace over to the 45-degree line to find $k_t = k_3$ in year 3. Again, the capital stock grew between years 2 and 3. The pattern now is clear. If the economy starts with a level of capital per worker below the steady state, then capital per worker increases over time. As an exercise, you can show that the economy likewise converges to the steady state if it starts with $k_1 > k_{ss}$.

The economic intuition behind the convergence to the steady state is revealing. At a low capital stock like $k_1 < k_{ss}$, the marginal product of capital is high and the amount of depreciated capital, dk_1, is low. Thus, investment exceeds depreciation and the per-worker capital stock grows. As this continues to happen, the marginal product of capital declines and the amount of depreciated capital increases until the economy arrives at steady state. The logic goes in reverse if $k_1 > k_{ss}$. There, the marginal product of capital is relatively small, and the amount of depreciated capital is big. Depreciated capital exceeds investment, decreasing the per-worker capital stock. This continues until the economy converges to k_{ss}.

In summary, the economy has a unique steady-state level of per-worker capital stock. If the per-worker capital stock starts above or below the steady state, the economy converges to the steady state over time. There are two points before moving on. First, convergence does not happen instantaneously. The time period in the model is a year, and it takes several years for the economy to get close to the steady state. The length of time this takes in reality depends on how far the economy is from steady state and on parameter values like the savings rate, s, and population growth rate, n. Second, the biggest movement in the capital stock happens between years 1 and 2. The subsequent changes in the capital stock get smaller with time. The intuition again is that the difference between investment and depreciated capital gets smaller over time as the economy converges. This has the real-world implication that the further an economy is away from its steady state, the faster it will grow. We compare this prediction to the data later in the chapter.

3-1c Algebraically Solving the Model

In the previous section, you saw that the economy converges to a steady-state capital stock, k^{ss}. Using the equations of the model, it is possible to solve for the steady-state level of capital per worker. Start with the accumulation equation

$$k_{t+1} = \frac{1}{1+n}[(1-d)k_t + sA_t k_t^a].$$

Next, impose a steady-state level of capital per worker $k_{t+1} = k_t = k_{ss}$. This gives

$$k_{ss} = \frac{1}{1+n}[(1-d)k_{ss} + sA_t k_{ss}^a].$$

Now solve for k_{ss}:

$$k_{ss} = \frac{1}{1+n}[(1-d)k_{ss} + sA_t k_{ss}^a]$$

$$\Leftrightarrow (1+n)k_{ss} = (1-d)k_{ss} + sA_t k_{ss}^a$$

$$\Leftrightarrow (d+n)k_{ss} = sA_t k_{ss}^a$$

54   Part 1 Growth

$$\Leftrightarrow k_{ss}^{1-a} = \frac{sA_t}{d+n}$$

$$\Leftrightarrow k_{ss} = \left(\frac{sA_t}{d+n}\right)^{\frac{1}{1-a}}. \tag{8}$$

Steady-state output per worker can be found by substituting steady-state capital per worker into the production function:

$$y_{ss} = A_t k_{ss}^a$$

$$= A_t \left(\frac{sA_t}{d+n}\right)^{\frac{a}{1-a}}. \tag{9}$$

Some of the predictions of the model can be directly observed from these equations. An economy's GDP per worker increases with the savings rate and TFP and decreases with the population growth rate and depreciation rate. The intuition for these results is discussed in the next section.

Finally, since the per-worker capital stock and output per worker have steady states, total GDP and the aggregate capital stock will not. Recall that

$$K_t = k_t L_t,$$

$$Y_t = y_t L_t.$$

Since the labor force grows at a constant rate, n, total GDP and the aggregate capital stock also grow at rate n when the per-worker variables are in steady state. This is an example of a balanced growth path. All variables are growing at a constant rate, but not necessarily the *same* rate.

> ✓ **Knowledge Check 3-2**
>
> Assume $d = 0.1$, $s = 0.2$, $n = 0.01$, $A_t = 1$, and $a = 1/3$. Calculate steady-state capital, output, consumption, and investment all in per-worker terms.
>
> ——————————————————————————— Answers are at the end of the chapter.

3-2 Predictions of the Solow Model

The Solow model makes a number of predictions about cross-country income differences that can be compared to the data. As you saw in the previous section, a country's level of GDP per worker is affected by the rates of savings, population growth, and depreciation, as well as the level of TFP. You can infer from these equations how the long-run economic performance of a country is affected by these parameters. To get a better understanding of the economic intuition driving these results, it is best to build on the graphical analysis of Section 3-1b.

3-2a An Increase in the Savings Rate

To start, consider a one-time increase in the savings rate, s. From the capital accumulation equation, $k_{t+1} = \frac{1}{1+n}[(1-d)k_t + sA_t k_t^a]$, you see that an increase in s increases k_{t+1} for every level of k_t. This implies that the capital accumulation line shifts up. Figure 3.3 shows the results. The economy starts at a steady-state level of capital per worker, k_0^{ss}. When the savings rate increases from s_0 to s_1, investment increases, which shifts the capital accumulation line up. As soon as the shift occurs, the economy is displaced from steady state. Because the accumulation line shifts up, you know that k_0^{ss} is below the new level of steady-state capital per worker. Therefore, the economy accumulates capital over time, with

Figure 3.3 Effects of an increase in the savings rate.

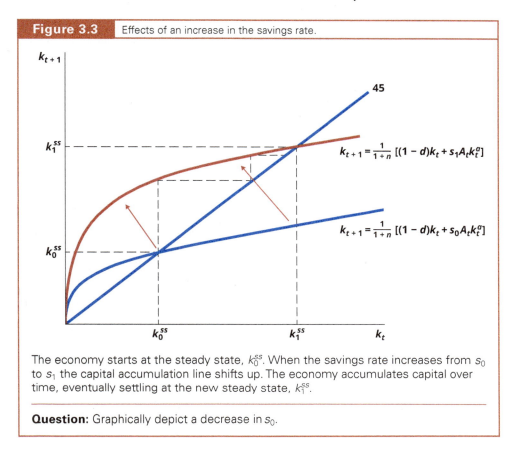

The economy starts at the steady state, k_0^{ss}. When the savings rate increases from s_0 to s_1 the capital accumulation line shifts up. The economy accumulates capital over time, eventually settling at the new steady state, k_1^{ss}.

Question: Graphically depict a decrease in s_0.

---

the dynamics between steady states shown by the dots, and eventually settles at a new steady state, k_1^{ss}.

It may be easier to understand the transition between steady states following a change to one of the model parameters by plotting the transition dynamics of capital per worker and output per worker. These are shown in Figure 3.4. The figure shows that the savings rate increases at t_0. The rise in the savings rate implies that investment increases while depreciated capital stays fixed, which increases the capital stock over time. Note there is no immediate jump in the capital stock. That is k_t stays fixed, but k_{t+1} increases. As time goes on, the economy converges to the new higher steady state, k_1^{ss}.

Figure 3.4 Time paths of capital and output per-worker following an increase in the savings rate.

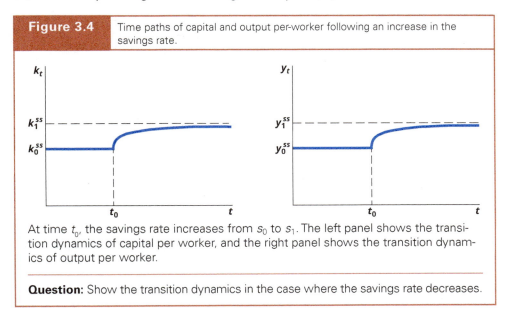

At time t_0, the savings rate increases from s_0 to s_1. The left panel shows the transition dynamics of capital per worker, and the right panel shows the transition dynamics of output per worker.

Question: Show the transition dynamics in the case where the savings rate decreases.

The panel on the right-hand side of Figure 3.4 shows the transition dynamics of output per worker. Recall from Equation (5) that output per worker is $y_t = A_t k_t^a$. Output per worker is only a function of capital per worker and TFP. Since TFP stays fixed by assumption, output per worker inherits qualitatively identical transition dynamics as capital per worker. In summary, a rise in the savings rate increases the levels of capital per worker and output per worker in the long run, but the transition dynamics take time to play out.

3-2b An Increase in the Population Growth Rate

Next, consider an increase in the population growth rate, n. Looking at the capital accumulation equation shows that an increase in n decreases k_{t+1} for every k_t. Intuitively, an increase in the population growth rate spreads the existing (total) capital stock among more workers in the next year. Thus, the capital accumulation line shifts down. This is shown in Figure 3.5. This is essentially the mirror image of an increase in the savings rate. The transition dynamics for capital and output per worker follow the same transition dynamics as in Figure 3.4, but in the opposite direction. In fact, you can see from the algebra that in steady state, $sy^{ss} = (d + n)k^{ss}$. This says that steady-state investment equals depreciated capital plus the fraction of the capital stock that goes to the bigger population in the next year. To be in steady state, the economy must invest enough to offset depreciation and supply the future generation of incoming workers with capital. Thus, there is a symmetry between depreciation and population growth. Whereas capital is actually destroyed through depreciation, capital is effectively destroyed by population growth because the existing capital stock has to be spread across more workers.

3-2c An Increase in TFP

Finally, consider a one-time increase in A_t. From the capital accumulation equation, $k_{t+1} = \dfrac{1}{1+n}[dk_t + sA_t k_t^a]$, you see that an increase in A_t increases k_{t+1} for every level of k_t. This implies an upward shift in the capital accumulation line. Figure 3.6 shows the

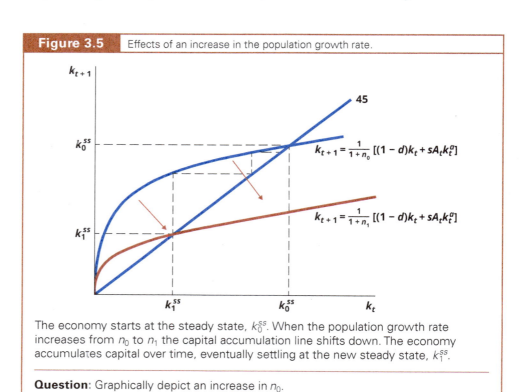

Figure 3.5 Effects of an increase in the population growth rate.

The economy starts at the steady state, k_0^{ss}. When the population growth rate increases from n_0 to n_1 the capital accumulation line shifts down. The economy accumulates capital over time, eventually settling at the new steady state, k_1^{ss}.

Question: Graphically depict an increase in n_0.

Figure 3.6 Effects of an increase in TFP.

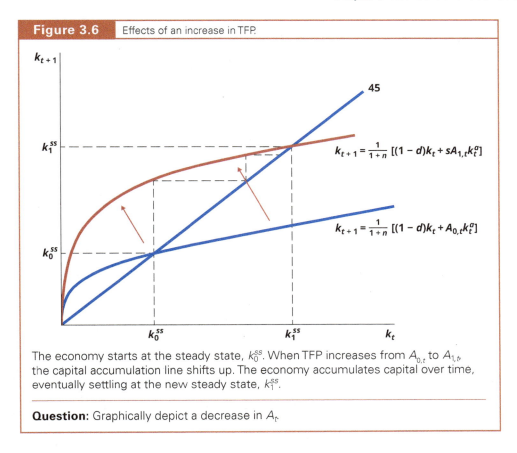

The economy starts at the steady state, k_0^{ss}. When TFP increases from $A_{0,t}$ to $A_{1,t}$, the capital accumulation line shifts up. The economy accumulates capital over time, eventually settling at the new steady state, k_1^{ss}.

Question: Graphically depict a decrease in A_t.

---

results. The economy starts at a steady-state level of capital per worker, k_0^{ss}. When TFP increases from $A_{0,t}$ to $A_{1,t}$ the capital accumulation line shifts up. The intuition is that higher TFP raises output and because investment is constant fraction of output, investment goes up too. Because investment exceeds depreciated capital, the economy accumulates more capital, eventually settling at a new steady state of k_1^{ss}.

Figure 3.7 shows the transition dynamics of capital per worker and output per worker. Assume the increase in A_t occurs at t_0. The panel on the left shows the dynamics of capital per worker. The dynamics are qualitatively identical to the case of an increase in the savings rate. The rise in TFP increases capital per worker in the next period, k_{t+1}, while leaving capital per worker in the current period unchanged. Eventually the economy converges to a higher level of capital per worker.

The panel on the right shows the dynamics of output per worker. The rise in A_t immediately makes production more efficient, increasing output per worker even though capital per worker hasn't changed. This is reflected by the jump in output per worker. After the initial jump, output per worker inherits the transition dynamics of capital per worker, increasing over time and eventually settling at a new steady state, y_1^{ss}.

3-2d Putting It All Together

In summary, the Solow model predicts that high savings rates and levels of TFP and low population growth rates cause countries to have higher levels of output per worker. These predictions are tested in the next section. At this point, though, you might be a bit puzzled. The title of this chapter is "The Solow **Growth** Model" (emphasis added), and yet you have learned that the economy converges to a balanced growth path in which output per worker stays constant. But you saw in Chapter 1 that, at least in the United States,

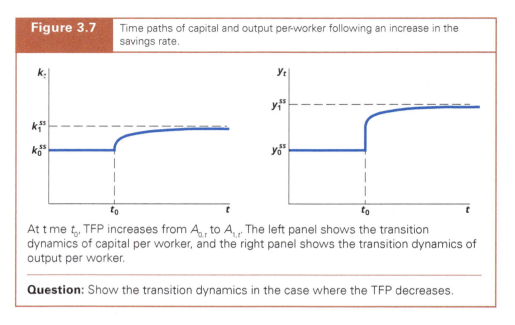

Figure 3.7 Time paths of capital and output per-worker following an increase in the savings rate.

At time t_0, TFP increases from $A_{0,t}$ to $A_{1,t}$. The left panel shows the transition dynamics of capital per worker, and the right panel shows the transition dynamics of output per worker.

Question: Show the transition dynamics in the case where the TFP decreases.

GDP per capita consistently grows year after year. How can the Solow model be reconciled with this fact?

There are two candidates for raising output per worker: increase the savings rate or increase TFP. Since a one-time increase in either of these eventually causes the economy to return to steady state, the only way to get sustained growth in output per worker is through continuous increases in s or A_t. Remember though that s is the savings *rate*—the fraction of income that is saved. An $s = 0.8$, for instance, means households save 80 percent of their income and consume 20 percent. The household cannot save more than 100 percent of its income, which means that s is capped at one. Logically then, sustained growth in income per capita cannot be caused through increases in the savings rate. Moreover, once the savings rate hits 100 percent, there is no output left over for consumption. Of course, this would be undesirable from the household's perspective.

Unlike the savings rate, there is no upper-bound on TFP. Indeed, in many aspects of life, technology has continually advanced over the last several hundred years. To take one example: you can get a 64-gigabyte flash drive for under $10 today. An iMac in 1998, meanwhile, had a 4-gigabyte hard drive and sold for a retail price of over $1,000. And while this example might be extreme, it is not exceptional. TFP growth has averaged 1.5 percent per year in the United States over the past half century. Sustained TFP growth in the Solow model means that the economy produces more with the same inputs year after year and that the capital accumulation line continually shifts upward. Higher levels of TFP give rise to higher levels of investment, which is turned into capital and used to produce output.

The lesson is that sustained TFP growth is the only variable that delivers sustained output per capita growth in the Solow model. This is only partly satisfying, though, since TFP is an exogenous variable in the Solow model. You will learn a model of endogenous TFP in Chapter 4.

The version of the model we have analyzed so far does not include a role for the government sector. Application 3.1 analyzes how income taxes affect output per capital in both the short and long run.

Knowledge Check 3-3

What does the capital accumulation line look like if $a = 1$? Will a one-time increase in the savings rate affect the long-run growth rate of capital per worker?

Answers are at the end of the chapter.

Chapter 3 The Solow Model of Economic Growth   **59**

Application 3.1

Fiscal Policy in the Solow Model

The baseline Solow model doesn't include the government sector. There is no role for taxes or government spending or any sort of regulation. Real-world debates over tax policy and government infrastructure plans heavily focus on their contribution to economic growth. This application focuses on tax policy.

Consider taxes first. Suppose that income is taxed at rate $0 < x < 1$. In not having a government sector at all, the version of the Solow model we covered so far implicitly assumes $x = 0$. How does the income tax change the principal equations of the model? Income available to consumption and investment is $(1 - x)Y_t$. You can think of the xY_t raised in taxes as going to something like military expenditure, which doesn't enter the model. The production function tells us how much output is created for given amounts of capital, labor, and TFP, and is therefore not directly affected by taxes. How about the accumulation equation? It is still given by

$$K_{t+1} = I_t + (1 - d)K_t$$

But since only a fraction, $(1 - x)$, of income is available for investment, the accumulation equation becomes

$$K_{t+1} = s(1 - x)Y_t + (1 - d)k_t$$
$$= s(1 - x)A_t K_t^a L_t^{1-a} + (1 - d)K_t$$

To make things a bit simpler, assume that $n = 0$ and $L_t = 1$ so that output is the same as output per capita in perpetuity. Under these assumptions, impose the steady state in the accumulation equation and solve for steady-state capital:

$$K_{ss} = s(1 - x)A_t K_{ss}^a + (1 - d)K_{ss}$$
$$\Leftrightarrow dK_{ss} = sA_t(1 - x)K_{ss}^a$$
$$\Leftrightarrow K_{ss} = \left(\frac{s(1 - x)A_t}{d}\right)^{\frac{1}{1-a}}.$$

This is very similar to steady-state capital (per worker) in Equation (8), but capital per worker with taxes is strictly lower than without taxes because $1 - x < 1$. Intuitively, some of the economic pie goes to the government, which reduces overall investment. Since investment is smaller, the steady-state capital stock decreases. Steady-state output is

$$Y_{ss} = A_t \left(\frac{s(1 - x)A_t}{d}\right)^{\frac{a}{1-a}}.$$

From this equation, you can see that the steady-state level of output decreases with taxes. Smaller levels of capital mean smaller levels of output.

When politicians debate the effects of cutting the income tax rate, they tend to focus on what those cuts will do to economic growth. Indeed, the 2017 Tax Cuts and Jobs Act passed by Congress and signed by President Trump was advertised as a policy that would spur economic growth. Are these claims accurate? We can answer this using the model.

There is more than one income tax rate in the real world. Tax rates depend on the type of income and the income level of the tax payer. For the purposes of this example, let's simply assume $x = 0.2$. Then, government's share of output is 20 percent, which is roughly in line with the data. Assume $A_t = 1$, $s = 0.2$, $d = 0.1$, and $a = 1/3$. Steady-state output is

$$Y_{ss} = \left(\frac{0.2(1 - 0.2)}{0.1}\right)^{\frac{1}{2}} = 1.265.$$

Imagine that the tax rate decreases to 0.1. What happens to economic growth? The capital stock in the next year is given by

$$K_{t+1} = s(1 - x)K_t^a + (1 - d)K_t$$
$$= 0.2(1 - 0.1)2.024^{1/3} + (1 - 0.1)2.024$$
$$= 2.049.$$

Output next year is given by

$$Y_t = K_t^a = 2.049^{1/3} = 1.270.$$

Thus, growth rate in output the first year after the tax cut is 0.41 percent. The tax cut increases the growth rate of output by a little less than half of one percent. Table 3.2 shows the levels of output and the growth rate of output over a six-year horizon.

Table 3.2	Time Path of GDP Following a Decrease in the Tax Rate	
Time	Y_t	**Growth rate**
0	1.265	
1	1.270	0.41%
2	1.275	0.38%
3	1.280	0.36%
4	1.284	0.33%
5	1.288	0.31%
6	1.291	0.28%

Output continues to grow over time, but, as the economy converges to a new steady state, the growth rate slows down. Eventually, the economy settles at a new steady-state output level of 1.34.

■Continues

Application 3.1 (Continued)

So, do tax cuts increase growth? In the short run, yes. In the long run, no. What can we say about the magnitudes? Trend growth in output per capita has been about one percent a year, so, from that perspective, the increase in growth in the first year is fairly large. There are a couple of caveats though. First, cutting the average tax rate in half would be a massive tax cut, much bigger than anything in the Tax Cuts and Jobs Act. Second, even the most politically conservative policymakers would concede that some government spending is productive. If productive government spending went down in response to this large decrease in tax rates, the output gains would be more limited.

On net, the Solow model predicts that the long-run levels of output and capital rise when taxes decrease.

Getting to those new long-run levels takes time, though, and the temporary increases in growth rates won't be that big. Consequently, cutting taxes may or may not be a good idea; however, the Solow model tells us that tax cuts shouldn't be justified by their effects on short-run economic growth.

In addition to collecting taxes, the government spends resources that contribute to output. Government infrastructure projects, such as building roads and bridges, add to the economy's capital stock. The Solow model can be extended to include stocks of private and public capital. In that environment, sustained infrastructure investment increases steady-state output per worker.

3-3 Dynamic Efficiency and the Macroeconomy

Imagine a worker who gets paid at the beginning of the month and has to decide how to allocate their paycheck over the month. The only source of expenditure for the worker is food. If the worker puts the entire paycheck in the bank, there is the potential to earn a lot of interest, but the worker will have nothing to eat today. Alternatively, if the worker consumes the entire paycheck today, starvation looms in the next 29 days. Faced with the undesirability of these two extremes, the worker will choose to save some but not all of the paycheck today.

The logic for the aggregate economy is similar. You have seen that steady-state output per worker depends positively on the savings rate. Households don't care about GDP, per se, but rather consumption. A natural question then is what savings rate maximizes long-run consumption per worker,

$$c^{ss} = (1 - s)y^{ss}.$$

A savings rate of 1 would maximize steady-state output per worker, but at the expense of devoting all income to investment. Thus, a savings rate of 1 would maximize long-run output per worker, but minimize long-run consumption per worker. On the other hand, a savings rate of 0 would imply that all income goes toward consumption. While consumption would be high initially, the capital stock would eventually be depleted to 0. Thus, a savings rate of 0 also minimizes long-run consumption per worker. The conclusion, therefore, is that the savings rate that maximizes long-run consumption per worker must lie between 0 and 1. A higher savings rate increases the capital stock and output, which, all else equal, increases future consumption. On the other hand, a higher savings rate reduces the fraction of income that gets consumed today. The **golden-rule savings rate** balances these two effects, thereby maximizing steady-state consumption per worker.

Golden-rule savings rate
The savings rate that maximizes long-run consumption.

The intuition for the golden-rule savings rate is shown in Figure 3.8. The figure plots steady-state output per worker and investment per worker as a function of capital per worker. Recall that in steady state, the quantity of investment exactly offsets the amount of capital that depreciates plus the amount that goes to the economy's new workers. The difference between output and investment is consumption. This means that when the difference between the two lines is maximized, then consumption per worker is also

Figure 3.8 Steady state output, consumption, and investment per worker as a function of capital per worker.

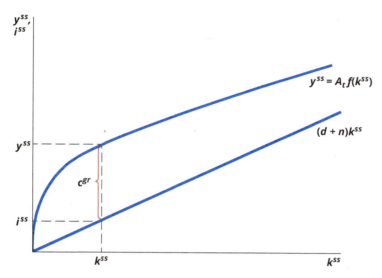

The line bowed out to the origin is the production function, which shows steady-state output per worker as a function of steady-state capital per worker. The linear line shows steady-state investment. The difference between the two lines is steady-state consumption per worker. c^{gr} is the maximum level of long-run consumption per worker. This is defined as the golden-rule level of consumption.

Question: How would an increase in d affect the plot?

---

maximized. Visually analyzing Figure 3.8 shows that this maximum occurs when the slopes of the two lines are equal. That is, the slope of the production function equals $(d + n)$. The savings rate that achieves this maximum is s^{gr}—the golden-rule savings rate.

If $s < s^{gr}$, then long-run consumption would increase with a higher savings rate. That would also imply, however, that current generations would have to sacrifice by saving more and consuming less today in order to maximize the consumption of future generations of workers. Thus, there is a conflict between the well-being of those workers alive today versus those yet to be born.

On the other hand, if $s > s^{gr}$, there is no intergenerational tradeoff. Reducing the savings rate to the golden-rule level would increase the consumption of the workers in every generation. Essentially, the higher fraction of output consumed more than offsets the decrease in output resulting from the lower capital stock. A situation in which $s > s^{gr}$ is **dynamically inefficient**, as every generation could be made better off through a reduction in the savings rate.

Although the savings rate is taken as given in the Solow model, in reality it is affected by economic policies, such as taxes and regulation. Policymakers, therefore, might want to know how their economy's savings rate compares to the golden-rule savings rate. Notice that s^{gr} equates the slope of the production function with $(d + n)$ and, in general, there may be no analytic solution. In the case of the Cobb–Douglas production function, though, the math works out to where $s^{gr} = a$, where a is the production function parameter on capital. In Chapter 2, you learned that economists estimate a to be about 1/3. Thus, if the savings rate is above 1/3, then the economy is dynamically inefficient. If the savings rate is below 1/3, then the consumption of future generations could go up at the expense of consumption of current generations. To recap:

If $s = 1/3$, steady state level of consumption is maximized;

If $s > 1/3$, savings could be reduced and consumption increased for every generation;

If $s < 1/3$, long-run consumption can increase if current generations saves more.

Dynamic inefficiency
A situation in which an economy's savings rate is above the golden-rule savings rate.

Figure 3.9 The savings rates for Japan, the United States, and China.

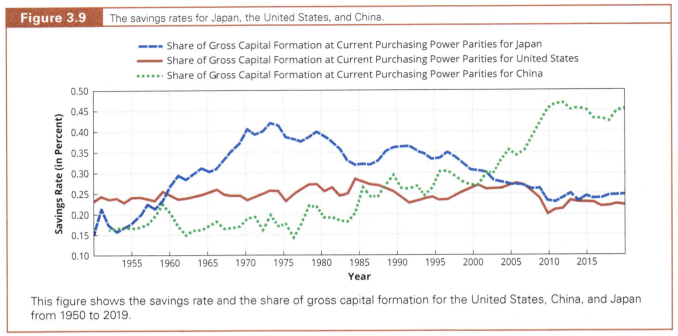

This figure shows the savings rate and the share of gross capital formation for the United States, China, and Japan from 1950 to 2019.

Source: Saint Louis FRED and the Penn World Table 9.0.

Some, but not all, countries display dynamic inefficiency. The savings rates for Japan, the United States, and China are shown in Figure 3.9. The savings rate in the United States consistently hovers at about 0.25, implying no dynamic inefficiency. Both China and Japan, on the other hand, experience periods where the savings rate exceeds 1/3. Indeed, China's savings rate since 2003 has exceeded this level. China's rising savings rate between 2000 and 2010 occurred in tandem with a 9 percent growth rate in output per capita. Despite this remarkable rate of economic growth, the Solow model predicts that Chinese citizens of current and future generations could enjoy higher levels of consumption if savings rates were reduced. This example shows that the Solow model makes concrete predictions on how to improve social welfare in the real world.

✓ Knowledge Check 3-4

Suppose an economy initially sits in steady state with the following parameters: $s = 0.2$, $d = 0.1$, $n = 0.01$, $a = 1/3$, and $A_t = 1$. Then the economy permanently raises its savings rate to $s = 0.3$. Does long-run consumption per worker increase or decrease? How about consumption per worker in the short run? Calculate steady-state consumption per worker under the old and new savings rates.

Answers are at the end of the chapter.

3-4 Taking the Solow Model to the Data

As you read in the previous section, the Solow model makes a number of predictions about long-run income differences across countries. More subtly, the model makes predictions about the growth performances of countries outside their balanced growth paths. This section uses data on GDP per worker to test both predictions in turn.

3-4a The Long-Run Predictions of the Solow Model

The Solow model predicts that richer countries will have higher savings rates, lower population growth rates, and higher levels of TFP. The Penn World Table 10.0 has data on all of these variables, which can be used to test the predictions of the model. There are 183 countries in the data; we look specifically at data from 2019.

Chapter 3 The Solow Model of Economic Growth   63

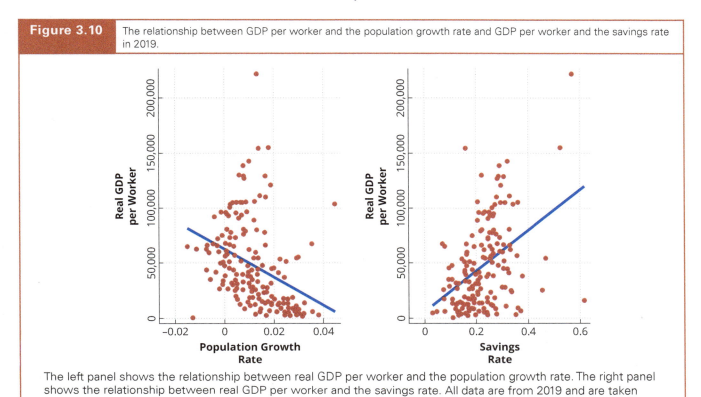

Figure 3.10 The relationship between GDP per worker and the population growth rate and GDP per worker and the savings rate in 2019.

The left panel shows the relationship between real GDP per worker and the population growth rate. The right panel shows the relationship between real GDP per worker and the savings rate. All data are from 2019 and are taken from the Penn World Table 10.0.

Source: PWT 10.0.

Figure 3.10 contains the results. The left panel shows a negative relationship between a country's population growth rate and its real GDP per worker. The right panel, meanwhile, shows that the savings rate and real GDP per worker are positively correlated. Qualitatively speaking, the Solow model gets these predictions exactly right.

The level of each country's TFP can be inferred from the production function and data on GDP per worker and capital per worker. Recall that with the Cobb–Douglas production function, $y_t = A_t k_t^a$. The level of TFP for each country in 2019 can be solved by rearranging this equation:

$$A_{2019} = \frac{y_{2019}}{k_{2019}^a}.$$

The relationship between TFP and real GDP per worker is shown in Figure 3.11. The model predicts that these variables are positively correlated, and this is supported by the strong positive correlation in the data. Again, the Solow model makes the right prediction qualitatively.

The Solow model correctly predicts the correlations between GDP per worker and several economic variables. But can anything be said about the *quantitative* predictions? That is, given the differences in GDP per worker that exist in the data, can we attribute some proportion of these differences to TFP, some of the differences to savings rates, and so on? The answer is yes.

The equation for steady-state output per worker is given by

$$y^{ss} = A_t \left(\frac{sA_t}{d+n} \right)^{\frac{a}{1-a}}.$$

You can use this equation to analyze relative income per worker differences between two countries. The first thing to note is that realistic differences in the population growth rate will not meaningfully affect relative incomes. The reason is that population growth is between about 0 and 3 percent for most countries. However, the depreciation rate is usually much higher, at about 10 percent. Thus, the denominator, $d + n$, won't move around too

Figure 3.11 The relationship between real GDP per worker and TFP in 2019.

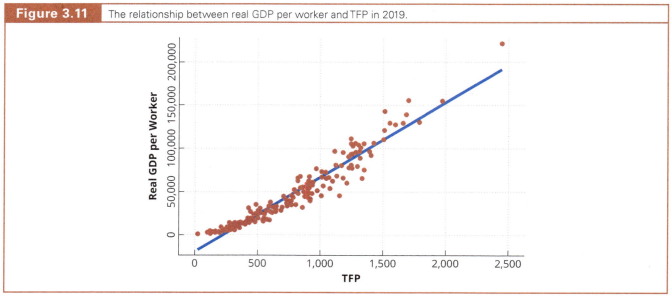

Source: PWT 10.0.

much for realistic differences in n. This means that differences in long-run income per capita are coming from differences in savings rates or differences in TFP.

You can compare the predicted steady-state differences in income between any two countries. To take just one example, let's compare the economies of the United States and Egypt. Assuming identical $d + n$ in both countries, the difference in relative long-run income per capita in the United States and Egypt can be written as

$$\frac{y_{US}}{y_{EG}} = \left(\frac{A_{US}}{A_{EG}}\right)^{\frac{1}{1-a}}\left(\frac{s_{US}}{s_{EG}}\right)^{\frac{a}{1-a}}.$$

The left-hand side is the difference in relative income per capita. In 2019, U.S. output per worker was $130,107 and output per worker in Egypt was $45,183. Thus, the relative difference was about 2.88. Some share of this difference will be attributed to differences in TFP, the first fraction on the right-hand side, and the rest is attributed to differences in savings rates, the second term on the right-hand side. The savings rates in 2019 for the United States and Egypt, respectively, were 22 percent and 9.5 percent. This means that the savings rate was 2.33 times higher in the United States than in Egypt. If $a = 0.5$, then $\frac{a}{1-a} = 1$, so differences in the savings rates would explain $\frac{2.33}{2.88} = 0.81$, or 81 percent of the difference between income per worker in the United States and income per worker in Egypt. But, you've already learned that a is closer to 1/3. This means that $\frac{a}{1-a} = 0.5$. With the correct choice of a, differences in savings rates explain only 53 percent of the differences in GDP per worker.

Variation in the data on saving rates explains an even smaller proportion of the differences in income per worker between countries at the very top of the world income distribution and those at the very bottom. For instance, if a 10-fold income gap were to be explained entirely by differences in savings rates, there would need to be a 100-fold difference in savings rates, as $100^{0.5} = 10$. The savings rates of high-income countries are typically between 0.2 and 0.4. Explaining the gaps between high and low-income countries through differences in savings rates would require the savings rates in low-income countries to be essentially 0. A quick glance at the right panel of Figure 3.10 shows that this isn't true in the data. Moreover, because these quantitative results are similar in years before 2019, these results aren't driven by 2019 being a special year where economies are far off from their balanced growth paths. The conclusion is that TFP explains most of the variation in long-run income per capita.

3-4b Transition Dynamics in the Model and Data

The Solow model makes the following prediction: if countries have identical parameters and TFP then they will converge to the same level of income per capita in the long run. Thus, observed differences in income per capita are either due to countries being temporarily off their steady states or differences in TFP or parameters. You can visualize this graphically.

In the left panel of Figure 3.12, economies A and B have the same production function and exogenous variables and parameters, but Economy B finds itself below steady state. Absent a change in exogenous variables and parameters, the model predicts that Economy A stays in steady state. In Economy B, meanwhile, investment exceeds depreciation and capital accumulates until arriving at the same steady state. Thus, the model under these circumstances predicts that income differences are only temporary.

Alternatively, the right panel shows a case where income differences are caused by the economies having different accumulation lines. This could be because of differences in savings rates, population growth rates, or levels of TFP. In this scenario, absent a change in any of the exogenous variables, Economy B is permanently poorer than Economy A. Thus, the model under these circumstances predicts that income differences persist even in the long run.

As alluded to in the chapter's introduction, an interesting historical case study of convergence occurred after World War II. Because the battles were primarily fought in Japan and Europe, the capital stocks in those economies suffered greater destruction compared to the capital stock in the United States. Figure 3.13 shows the large convergence in incomes per capita after the war. In 1960, Japan's income per capita was less than 30 percent of the U.S. level and Germany's was about half. Over the next three decades, both economies rebuilt their capital stocks and closed the gap relative to the United States. By 1990, Japan and Germany had close to 75 percent of U.S. income per capita.

Since 1990, there has been no convergence in income per capita. Indeed, by 2019, the income gaps were a bit wider than 30 years prior. The reason is that the economies were

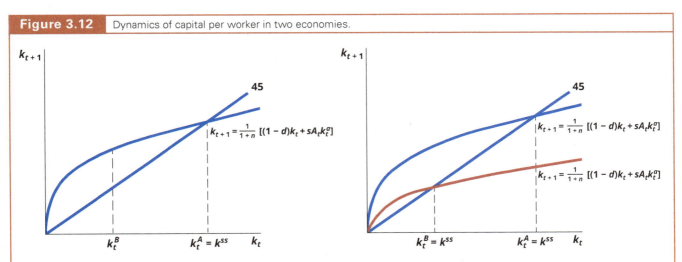

Figure 3.12 Dynamics of capital per worker in two economies.

The panel on the left shows two economies with the same exogenous variables. Economy A is in steady state and Economy B is below steady state. Economy B is predicted to catch up to Economy A. The panel on the right shows two economies with different steady states. Economy B, absent a change in exogenous variables, is permanently poorer than Economy A.

Question: If the economies in the left panel have exactly the same production function, but Economy A has more capital than Economy B where are the returns to capital the highest? **Hint:** Think about the marginal product of capital.

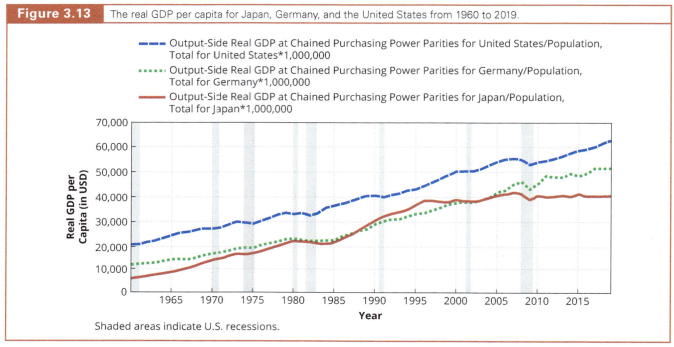

Figure 3.13 The real GDP per capita for Japan, Germany, and the United States from 1960 to 2019.

Shaded areas indicate U.S. recessions.

Source: Saint Louis FRED and PWT 9.0.

Unconditional convergence
A prediction that all countries will eventually have the same levels of real GDP per worker regardless of any differences in exogenous variables or parameters.

Conditional convergence
A prediction that all countries with identical savings rates, population growth rates, and levels of TFP will eventually have the same level of real GDP per worker.

converging to different steady states. Germany has about 10 percent lower TFP than the United States while Japan's is about 35 percent lower. Thus, in the same case study, you have an example where there was a period of catch-up growth but ultimately the economies converged to different steady states.

Although the comparison between Germany, Japan, and the United States shows how to apply the Solow model to the data, you might be wondering how the model performs more generally. For this, we will look at all 168 countries in the Penn World Table. The view that countries will converge to a common level of income per capita is called **unconditional convergence**. The Solow model, on the other hand, predicts **conditional convergence**, which is the view that countries will converge to a common level of income per capita only if they have the same exogenous variables and parameters. You have already seen that countries differ in their levels of TFP and savings rates, so finding unconditional convergence in the data would be evidence against the model.

Figure 3.14 plots cumulative real GDP per worker growth between 1970 and 2019 for 168 countries on the vertical axis and their initial real GDP per worker on the horizontal axis. If the unconditional convergence hypothesis were correct, countries with low initial levels of income per capita would grow faster than countries with high initial levels of income per capita. The figure shows only a slight negative correlation, which indicates that some initially poor countries catch up to rich countries, but there is a lot of variation in the data. The lack of convergence is actually evidence in favor of the Solow model, as countries with different parameters converge to different steady states. In other words, the Solow model predicts that two countries will converge if and only if they have the same underlying parameters.

Here is an example. Suppose country A starts with an initial level of income per worker that is 50 percent of the income per worker in country B. This can be expressed mathematically as

$$\frac{y_{A,0}}{y_{B,0}} = 0.5.$$

The initial level of income, denoted by a time subscript of 0, is 50 percent lower in country A than country B. The question is whether this income gap will narrow, widen, or stay the same over time. If the gap narrows, these countries converge. To determine how the income

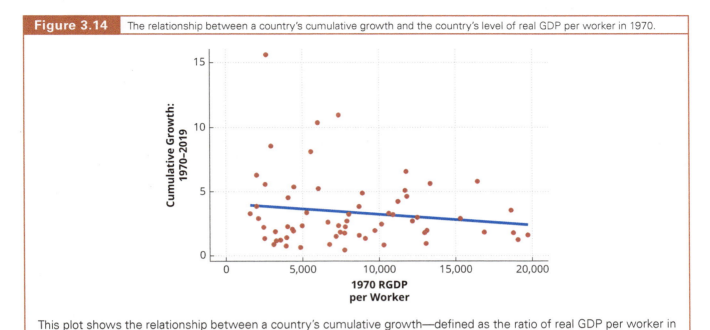

Figure 3.14 The relationship between a country's cumulative growth and the country's level of real GDP per worker in 1970.

This plot shows the relationship between a country's cumulative growth—defined as the ratio of real GDP per worker in 2019 divided by real GDP per worker in 1970—and the country's level of real GDP per worker in 1970.

Source: PWT 10.0.

gap will evolve, we can compare the initial levels of income to the long-run levels of income per worker. To make the calculation easier, assume (like we did in the Egypt and United States example above) that the population growth rate and depreciation rate are the same across countries. Under these assumptions, the ratio of long-run income in country A to country B is

$$\frac{y_A^{ss}}{y_B^{ss}} = \left(\frac{A_A}{A_B}\right)^{\frac{1}{1-a}} \left(\frac{S_A}{S_B}\right)^{\frac{a}{1-a}}. \tag{10}$$

Assuming $a = 1/3$, we can predict how long-run income differences compare to short-run income differences. Table 3.3 shows the results from three different experiments. In the first row, the countries are assumed to have the same savings rates and TFPs. The model predicts that in the long run, the countries will have identical levels of output per worker. This is an example of convergence. The second row shows the case where the initial income ratio simply equals the steady-state income ratio so the income gap neither widens nor narrows. Finally, the third row shows an example where the differences in savings rates and TFPs imply that the income gap widens over time.

These were just three examples. You can use the steady state output per worker equation to predict the evolution of long-run income differences for any set of parameters. Combining this theory with the data in the Penn World Table makes the Solow model very useful in forecasting long-run income differences.

Table 3.3 Long-run Predictions of GDP per Worker as a Function of Savings Rates and TFP

Initial income ratio	Savings rates	TFP	Steady-state ratio	Convergence?
	$s_A = 0.2, s_B = 0.2$	$A_A = 1, A_B = 1$	1	Yes
$\frac{y_{A,0}}{y_{B,0}} = 0.5$	$s_A = 0.2, s_B = 0.2$	$A_A = 0.63, A_B = 1$	0.5	No
	$s_A = 0.1, s_B = 0.2$	$A_A = 0.63, A_B = 1$	0.35	No

3-4c Summarizing the Performance of the Solow Model in Explaining the Data

The Solow model predicts that countries with higher savings rates, lower population growth rates, and higher levels of TFP will have higher levels of income per capita. This is confirmed by the data. The Solow model also predicts that because savings rates, population growth rates, and levels of TFP differ in the data, then low-income countries will not catch up to high-income countries in so far as their low levels of income are caused by low levels of TFP or low savings rates. If countries have identical savings rates, population growth rates, and TFP levels, the Solow model predicts that they will converge to the same level of income per capita in the long run. Finally, a quantitative evaluation of the Solow model attributes most of the long-run differences in income per capita to differences in TFP rather than differences in population growth or savings rates. A major limitation of the Solow model is that TFP is exogenous, or determined outside the model. This begs the question of what determines TFP. This is reserved for Chapter 4.

Before wrapping up the chapter, it's worthwhile to discuss one other long-run concern: climate change and, specifically, the relationship between economic growth and climate change. This is the topic of Application 3.2.

Knowledge Check 3-5

Suppose Country A is in steady state and Country B's capital per worker is 10 percent below steady state. Country B has 85 percent of the TFP level of Country A, but the countries are otherwise identical. What can you say about the relative growth performances and long-run relative incomes of the two economies?

Answers are at the end of the chapter.

Application 3.2

Growth and Climate Change

The aggregate production function we have considered thus far omits environmental factors as inputs for production. When you think about it, though, there are many products, especially agricultural commodities, that critically depend on environmental factors. Just a few degrees warmer or cooler or just a little more or less rain per year can totally change the varieties and quantities of crops grown in a particular climate. At the same time, the production of many manufacturing and agricultural goods emit waste into the atmosphere, which affects the climate. Thus, the interaction between economic growth and climate change is complicated.

A little microeconomics is helpful for analyzing the problem of climate change. When you drive a traditional gas-consuming vehicle, you pay for the gas at the pump but not for the very slight degradation to the environment and air quality coming from your use of gasoline. In other words, the social cost of fuel consumption is higher than the private cost. When the social cost of any activity exceeds its private cost, economists predict that society gets too much of it. The very slight degradation of the environment coming from my or your driving becomes very large once it's aggregated across an entire economy. Moreover, as mentioned in the last paragraph, the production of many agricultural and manufacturing goods further pollutes the economy.

William Nordhaus won the 2018 Nobel Prize in economics for his work on the environment and economic growth. The principle environmental damage his work focused on was that coming from carbon dioxide (CO_2) emissions. Nordhaus and his coauthors developed economic models that account for the interaction between economic growth and environmental quality. Figure 3.15, taken from Nordhaus's prize lecture, shows the climate "circular flow" diagram.[2]

Starting in the top-left square, economic growth that entails fuel-consuming activities, such as driving, flying, cooking, and heating, leads to rising CO_2 levels. Rising CO_2 levels in turn lead to climate change manifested in rising temperatures and sea levels. Climate change affects crop

---

[2]Nordhaus, William. 2018. "Climate Change: The Ultimate Challenge for Economics." Prize Lecture, Yale University, December 8, 2018.

Continues

Application 3.2 (Continued)

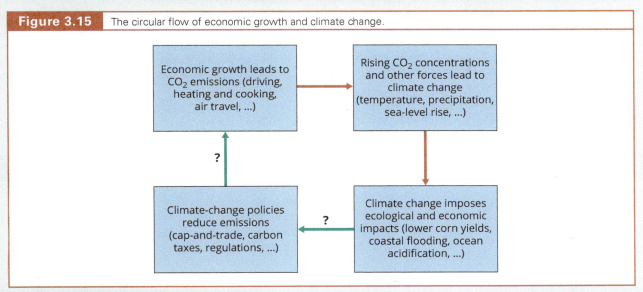

Figure 3.15 The circular flow of economic growth and climate change.

Source: https://www.nobelprize.org/uploads/2018/10/nordhaus-lecture.pdf

production and standards of living across the globe. For instance, if climate change leads to more severe weather events like hurricanes, people in coastal communities will bear the cost. Finally, climate change policies, such as emissions caps or carbon taxes, can reduce emissions, but, like all taxes and regulations, could also affect economic growth. Notice that two of the arrows have question marks. That's because those links do not yet exist, as there are no international agreements limiting the global emissions of CO_2.

The economic approach to reducing CO_2 emissions balances the benefits of lowering emissions, such as better air quality, lower temperatures, and more predictable weather patterns, with the costs of lowering emissions, namely in the form of higher fuel prices. The fact that reducing emissions entails both costs and benefits means that while the optimal price of carbon is higher than it is today, it isn't so high as to imply 100 percent abatement.

In his lecture, Nordhaus summarizes some of the key findings of what effective carbon-reducing policies would look like. First, policies should raise the price of carbon as soon as possible; the carbon price should rise over time as individuals and firms adapt to the rising cost of energy. Second, the policies should aim for maximum participation and a uniform price of carbon across all economic sectors and countries. If carbon is cheaper in some parts of the world than others, then carbon-intensive production could just migrate to countries where carbon is cheap. While higher prices of fuel may reduce GDP in the short run, these guidelines have the potential to lower the risk of climate disasters and improve environmental quality at the lowest cost to economic growth.

The economics of climate change remains an active area of research as policymakers around the world look to solutions for global warming. There are a number of interesting challenges that these policymakers must confront, including how to best forecast the rise in global temperatures under various policies and how to get broad support across all countries. Needless to say, the stakes of getting the right answers are high.

Chapter Summary

- The Solow model of economic growth uses a production function, an equation for population growth, and an equation describing the accumulation of capital to predict the short-run and long-run economic performance of economies.
- The key endogenous variables in the Solow model are GDP, Y_t, investment, I_t, and next period's capital stock, K_{t+1} where the subscript t denotes time. The exogenous variables are the population, L_t, and TFP, A_t. The parameters in the Solow model are the depreciation rate, savings rate, population growth rate, and curvature of the production function given by s, n, d, and a, respectively.
- Absent a change in parameters and exogenous variables, the Solow model shows that all countries converge to a balanced growth path in the long run, implying that capital per worker and income per worker are eventually constant.

70 **Part 1** Growth

- The only way to get sustained growth in the Solow model is to have continuous growth in TFP, which is supported by the data.
- An economy maximizes its long-run consumption by setting the savings rate equal to the golden-rule savings rate. If the economy is saving more than the golden-rule level, all current and future generations could be made better off by reducing the savings rate. If the economy is saving less than the golden-rule level, it is possible to make future generations better-off, but at the expense of the current generation.
- The Solow model predicts that countries with higher savings rates, lower population growth rates, and higher levels of TFP

will have higher levels of income per capita. All of these predictions are supported by the data.

- The Solow model predicts that countries below their steady states will grow faster than countries at or near their steady states. This is supported by the data.
- A quantitative evaluation of the Solow model shows that most of the persistent differences in real GDP per worker are attributed to TFP rather than differences in population growth rates or savings rates.

Key Terms

Investment, 49
Depreciation rate, 49
Balanced growth path, 52
Steady state, 52

Golden-rule savings rate, 60
Dynamic inefficiency, 61
Unconditional convergence, 66
Conditional convergence, 66

Review Questions

1. Argue that $k_t = 0$ is a steady state in the Solow model. Do you think it is a realistic outcome given the dynamics of the model? Explain.

2. What intergenerational tradeoffs exist if an economy is saving less than the golden-rule savings rate? Why don't these tradeoffs exist if the economy is saving more than the golden-rule level?

3. Explain why one-time increases in the savings rate and level of TFP lead to permanently higher levels in GDP per worker but not to permanently higher growth rates in GDP per worker.

4. What is the only source of sustainable long-run growth in the Solow model?

5. Explain the difference between unconditional and conditional convergence. Which does the Solow model predict? Which is supported by the data?

Problems

3.1 Suppose you have an economy with a production function and capital accumulation equation given respectively by

$$Y_t = A_t K_t^a L_t^{1-a},$$

$$K_{t+1} = (1 - d)K_t + sY_t.$$

Assume the labor force grows at rate $n > 0$.

a. Convert the production function and capital accumulation equation into per-worker terms.

b. Graph the per-worker capital accumulation equation and show that the economy converges to a steady state, $k^{ss} > 0$.

c. Show the effects on the capital accumulation line of a one-time permanent increase in the depreciation rate, d. Also plot the transition dynamics of capital per worker and output per worker.

d. Algebraically solve for the steady state of output per worker, y^{ss}, and capital per worker, k^{ss}. Solve for numeric

values of these variables if $a = 1/3$, $s = 0.2$, $A_t = 1$, $d = 0.1$, and $n = 0.01$.

e. If d increases to 0.15, by what percent does output per worker fall in the long run?

3.2 Suppose you have an economy with a production function and capital accumulation equation given respectively by

$$Y_t = A_t K_t^a L_t^{1-a},$$

$$K_{t+1} = (1 - d)K_t + sY_t.$$

Assume $a = 1/3$, $s = 0.2$, $d = 0.1$, $A_t = 1$, and $n = 0.02$.

a. Solve for steady-state output per worker and capital per worker.

b. Suppose the economy starts with a level of capital $k_1 = 0.5$. Fill out the following table:

Chapter 3 The Solow Model of Economic Growth　　**71**

Year	k_t	y_t	$i_t = sy_t$	$(d+n)k_t$	$i_t - (d+n)k_t$
1	0.5				
2					
3					
4					
5					

Summarize your findings about the dynamics in this economy. Is it consistent with the qualitative analysis discussed in the chapter?

a. Start at $k_1 = k^{ss}$ and assume the level of TFP doubles from 1 to 2. Fill out the table in part b under these new assumptions. Summarize your findings.

3.3 Suppose you have an economy with a Cobb–Douglas aggregate production function with $a = 1/3$.

a. What is the golden-rule savings rate for this economy?

b. Suppose the economy starts in a steady state with $s = 0.2$ and then it experiences a one-time permanent change in its savings rate to 0.3. Draw the transition dynamics of consumption per worker.

c. Suppose the economy starts in a steady state with $s = 0.4$ and then experiences a one-time permanent change in its savings rate to 0.5. Draw the transition dynamics of consumption per worker.

d. Based on your answers to parts b and c, should economic policy always look to increase a country's savings rate?

3.4 Assume an economy has a standard production function and capital accumulation equation. The economy is hit with a hurricane.

a. Assume that half of the capital stock is destroyed by the hurricane, but no one dies. Show how this affects the capital accumulation graph. Also plot the transition dynamics of output per worker and capital per worker.

b. Alternatively, assume that the hurricane destroys none of the capital stock but half of the population dies. Show how this affects the capital accumulation graph. Also plot the transition dynamics of output per worker and capital per worker.

3.5 Suppose an economy has the following Cobb–Douglas aggregate production function:

$$Y_t = A_t K_t^a (h_t L_t)^{1-a}$$

where h_t is the economy's human capital. You can think of human capital as the knowledge workers attain through experience and education. The capital accumulation equation is standard and population grows at rate n.

a. Convert the production function and capital accumulation equation into per-worker terms.

b. Algebraically solve for steady-state output per worker and capital per worker.

c. How does a one-time increase in h_t affect output per worker in the long run?

d. Human capital is a function of an economy's education level. In particular, economists conventionally write the function as an exponential function,

$$h_t = e^{bu_t}.$$

Here, u_t is the number of years of education for an average person in the economy and $b > 0$ is a parameter that represents the quality of a country's schooling. Describe two ways economic policy makers can increase an economy's human capital. What are the tradeoffs associated with each?

✓ Knowledge Check 3-1 Answer

We will cover the first row together. Recalling Equation (5), the per-worker production function is

$$y_t = A_t k_t^a.$$

Using the value of a and A_t, we have

$$y_t = k_t^{1/3}.$$

Evaluating this equation at $t = 0$ gives

$$y_0 = 2^{1/3} = 1.260.$$

This means

$$sy_0 = 0.2(1.26) = 0.252.$$

Likewise, the amount of depreciated capital is

$$(1 - d)k_0 = (1 - 0.1) \times 2 = 1.8.$$

Recalling Equation (6), the capital accumulation equation in per-worker terms is given by

$$k_{t+1} = \frac{1}{1+n}[(1-d)k_t + sy_t].$$

72 **Part 1** Growth

We can plug in the particular values based on the work above.

$$k_1 = \frac{1}{1+n}[(1-d)k_t + sy_t]$$

$$= \frac{1}{1+0.01}[1.8 + 0.252]$$

$$= 2.032.$$

Thus, the per-worker capital stock is growing. Using the steps laid out above, you can fill in the rest of the table. For your reference, the solutions are shown below. The change in capital, $k_{t+1} - k_t$ gets smaller over time. This is consistent with the qualitative analysis in Section 3-1b.

Time period (t)	k_t	sy_t	$(1-d)k_t$	k_{t+1}	$k_{t+1} - k_t$
0	2	0.252	1.80	2.032	0.032
1	2.03	0.253	1.829	2.061	0.030
2	2.061	0.255	1.855	2.089	0.027
3	2.089	0.256	1.880	2.114	0.026
4	2.114	0.257	1.903	2.138	0.024

✓ Knowledge Check 3-2 Answer

Equation (8) shows that steady-state capital per worker is

$$k_{ss} = \left(\frac{sA_t}{d+n}\right)^{\frac{1}{1-a}}.$$

Substituting in the parameter values gives

$$k_{ss} = \left(\frac{0.2}{0.1+0.01}\right)^{\frac{1}{1-1/3}} = 2.452.$$

Steady-state output per worker is

$$y_{ss} = k_{ss}^{1/3} = 1.35.$$

Recall that output is divided between consumption and investment. From Equation (4), you know that investment is a constant fraction, s, of output. This means that the remaining fraction of output, $1-s$, goes to consumption. The per-worker steady states are

$$i_{ss} = sy_{ss} = 0.27,$$

$$c_{ss} = (1-s)y_{ss} = 1.08.$$

✓ Knowledge Check 3-3 Answer

If $a = 1$, then the production function in per-worker terms is

$$y_t = A_t k_t.$$

The capital accumulation equation in per-worker terms is

$$k_{t+1} = \frac{1}{1+n}[(1-d)k_t + sA_t k_t].$$

Chapter 3 The Solow Model of Economic Growth · **73**

Factoring the k_t from the equation gives

$$k_{t+1} = \frac{1 - d + sA_t}{1 + n} k_t.$$

The result is a linear equation. To make things easier to read, let $b = \dfrac{1 - d + sA_t}{1 + n}$.

The accumulation equation is then $k_{t+1} = bk_t$. Consider three cases. If $b = 1$, then $k_{t+1} = k_t$. This implies that whatever level of capital the economy starts with is the steady state. If the economy were to experience an exogenous increase or decrease in the capital stock, it would go to a new steady state. If $b < 1$, k_{t+1} is smaller than k_t and k_{t+2} is smaller than k_{t+1} and so on. Continued iteration of this equation implies that the per-worker capital stock converges to 0. If $b > 1$ then the logic is reversed. The per-worker capital stock gets bigger and bigger over time even if TFP is constant. You can use this analysis to investigate a one-time increase in the savings rate.

This example shows the importance of the diminishing marginal returns to capital assumption. There is strong empirical evidence for diminishing returns of capital at the level of the aggregate economy. Chapter 2 discusses some of the evidence.

✓ Knowledge Check 3-4 Answer

Since $s < a$, consumption is below its golden-rule level. The increase in the savings rate decreases consumption initially, as a greater fraction of income goes toward investment. In the long run, however, consumption increases.

Steady-state consumption per worker is

$$c_{ss} = (1 - s)y_{ss}$$

$$= (1 - s)\left(\frac{s}{n + d}\right)^{\frac{a}{1 - a}}$$

$$= (1 - s)\left(\frac{s}{0.11}\right)^{1/2}.$$

When $s = 0.2$, $c_{ss} = 1.08$. When $s = 0.3$, $c_{ss} = 1.77$. Just as predicted, steady-state consumption increases with the savings rate.

✓ Knowledge Check 3-5 Answer

Since Country A is in steady state, income per worker will stay constant. Since Country B is below steady state, capital per worker will increase over time, implying a positive rate of growth for output per worker. As Country B converges to steady state, growth in output per worker will slow down and eventually fall to 0. Since Country B has a lower level of TFP than Country A, and assuming the other parameters are identical in the two countries, Country B will have a lower income than Country A in the long run. Indeed, assuming $a = 1/3$ and using Equation (10), the income of Country B relative to Country A is

$$\frac{y_B}{y_A} = \left(\frac{A_B}{A_A}\right)^{\frac{1}{1 - a}} = 0.85^{1.5} = 0.78.$$

Thus, long-run output per worker is 22 percent lower in Country B.

Chapter 4

Explaining Total Factor Productivity

Learning Objectives

4.1 Discuss theories explaining TFP differences across countries at a given point in time.

4.2 Perform a growth accounting exercise on any country.

4.3 Explain what distinguishes ideas from other types of economic inputs.

4.4 Algebraically solve for the balanced growth path in the endogenous growth model.

4.5 Graphically depict comparative static exercises in the Romer model.

Total factor productivity
A term that describes how efficiently inputs are used in producing output.

The world only has only so much land, water, and raw materials. The law of conservation of mass from physics and chemistry tells us that matter can neither be created nor destroyed.[1] It can only be rearranged. The implication, economically speaking, is that growth in income per person has to come from new and better ways of organizing resources. In other words, economic growth comes from more efficient ways of combining inputs into output. You may recall that this is our definition of **total factor productivity (TFP)**.

There are many ways to think about TFP in reality. In the technology sector, scientists are able to pack more memory into a computer year after year. Computers themselves stay the same size or even get smaller, but researchers continue to develop new methods for maximizing memory. Likewise, farmers implement new types of fertilizers to increase the yield on their crops. The quantity of labor and amount of money farm owners spend on fertilizer may stay the same, but output increases. Finally, the retail sector is full of productivity-enhancing innovations, including "just-in-time" inventory, which leverages computer technology to track inventories and minimize waste across businesses. Inventory management was key to the success of Walmart in the 1990s and Amazon today. These micro-level innovations are important for macro-level growth.

You've already seen that TFP is important for determining cross-country income differences. This chapter first proposes some theories about why these TFP differences exist at a point in time across countries. Then it goes on to explain the sources of TFP growth over time. We will explore where these new ideas for rearranging inputs come from and how, if at all, economic policy can affect the growth rate of TFP.

4-1 Why Are Cross-Country TFP Differences So Big?

In Chapter 2, you learned that differences in GDP per worker can be attributed to either differences in inputs or differences in TFP. Our accounting exercise showed that most of the differences come from TFP. In this section, you will learn about some of the leading economic theories that attempt to explain the differences in TFP across countries.

---

[1]Paul Romer made a similar argument in https://www.econlib.org/library/Enc1/EconomicGrowth.html.

4-1a Reviewing Cross-Country TFP Differences

The standard Cobb–Douglas production function with capital and labor as inputs is

$$Y_t = A_t K_t^a L_t^{1-a}, \tag{1}$$

where K_t is capital, L_t is labor, or the number of workers employed, and A_t is TFP. Using observable data on GDP, capital, and employment from the Penn World Table, you can infer TFP by rearranging the production function:

$$A_t = \frac{Y_t}{K_t^a L_t^{1-a}}. \tag{2}$$

Figure 4.1 shows the distribution of TFP relative to the United States in 2019. This figure shows that a large proportion of countries don't have even half the level of TFP as the United States. Indeed, over one-third of the countries in the data have less than a quarter of the level of TFP as the United States.

Figure 4.2 shows that the dispersion in TFP has not gotten much smaller over time. Specifically, the figure shows the ratio of TFP of a country at the 90th percentile versus TFP of a country at the 10th percentile.[2] The ratio hasn't gotten smaller than 5 and has gone up to as high as 7.5 over the last 40 years. Thus, in 2019, a country like the Netherlands, near the 90th percentile, had a TFP close to five times as high as a country like Nepal, near the 10th percentile.

You might wonder whether these large TFP differences are evidence against the Solow model. The answer is subtle. On one hand, the Solow model predicts that countries will converge to the same levels of income per worker conditional on having the same TFP levels and parameters. If countries converged to the same levels of income despite having large

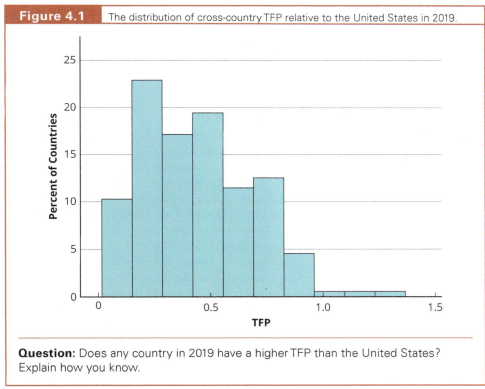

Figure 4.1 The distribution of cross-country TFP relative to the United States in 2019.

Question: Does any country in 2019 have a higher TFP than the United States? Explain how you know.

Source: PWT 10.0.

---

[2] If a country is at the 90th percentile of TFP, 90 percent of countries in the data have a lower level of TFP.

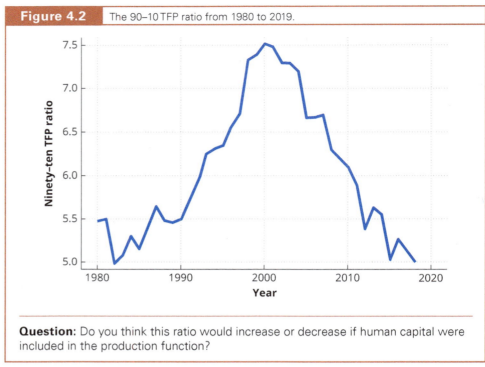

Figure 4.2 The 90–10 TFP ratio from 1980 to 2019.

Question: Do you think this ratio would increase or decrease if human capital were included in the production function?

Source: PWT 10.0.

TFP differences, the Solow model would be directly contradicted. Large TFP differences in and of themselves are not evidence against the Solow model. On the other hand, since differences in TFP explain most of the variation in income per worker across countries, the fact that the Solow model takes TFP as exogenous means the model is leaving a big piece of the story unexplained. Fortunately, economists have recently developed theories that help us understand TFP differences across countries.

4-1b Misallocation Theories of TFP

Up to this point, we have assumed that all firms are identical, or, equivalently, that there is one representative firm. In the real world, firms are different along a number of dimensions, including TFP. Think about the retail sector in the United States. On one end of the distribution, there are small "mom-and-pop" stores that might do all their accounting and inventory control by hand. On the other end of the distribution, you have Amazon, who manages its inventory using sophisticated computer programs and transportation between a large number of massive warehouses. To be more specific, imagine an economy that has three firms with TFPs ranging from lowest to highest, or $A_1 < A_2 < A_3$. With the exception of these different levels of TFP, these production functions are the same. Recall from Chapter 2 that a property of the Cobb–Douglas production function is that the marginal products of capital and labor increase with TFP. This is reflected graphically by firms with higher TFPs having labor and capital demand curves further out to the right. The left panel of Figure 4.3 shows the results in the case of labor.

An implication is that for any given wage, firms with higher levels of TFP should be bigger. Intuitively, the economy maximizes efficiency when more productive and efficient firms operate at a larger scale. The economy depicted in the left panel is free of any economic **distortions**. A distortion is anything that reduces economic efficiency. Distortions may include taxes and subsidies imposed by the government, monopoly power held by firms, or an externality like pollution.

The right panel of Figure 4.3 depicts an economy with distortions—in the form of taxes and subsidies. In this case, the least efficient firm with a TFP level of A_1 is subsidized at rate s. For every $1 the firm earns in revenue, it collects $1(1 + s)$ after the subsidy.

Distortion
Anything that reduces economic efficiency. Examples include taxes and subsidies imposed by the government, monopoly power held by firms, and externalities like pollution.

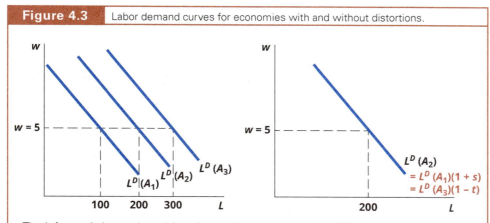

Figure 4.3 Labor demand curves for economies with and without distortions.

The left panel shows three labor demand curves indexed by TFP. At any given wage, firms with higher levels of TFP find it optimal to employ greater quantities of labor. The plot on the right shows a case where the least productive firm receives a subsidy of s and the most productive firm gets taxed at rate t.

Question: What is each firm's marginal product of labor when $w = 5$ in the left panel?

Since the subsidy increases revenue for every unit sold, the firm's demand for labor shifts to the right. As drawn in the right panel of Figure 4.3, the subsidy is just high enough to make the demand for labor of the least productive firm equal to the demand for labor of the firm with a TFP level of A_2. Similarly, if the most productive firm is taxed at rate t, then it collects $\$1(1-t)$ for every $1 earned in revenue. This has the effect of shifting the labor demand curve to the left. As drawn in the right panel of Figure 4.3, the tax is just high enough to make the demand for labor of the most productive firm equal to the demand for labor of the firm with a TFP level of A_2. On net then, rather than more productive firms being bigger, they are all the same size.

To put this in terms of actual numbers, imagine there are 600 workers in an economy and 600 units of capital (perhaps machines or tractors). Each firm has a Cobb–Douglas production function,

$$Y_i = A_i K_i^a L_i^{1-a},$$

where $i = 1, 2,$ or 3. Since there are no intermediate goods, GDP for the entire economy is the sum of output produced by the three firms:

$$\begin{aligned} \text{GDP} &= Y_1 + Y_2 + Y_3 \\ &= A_1 K_1^a L_1^{1-a} + A_2 K_2^a L_2^{1-a} + A_3 K_3^a L_3^{1-a}. \end{aligned}$$

Assuming $A_1 = 10$, $A_2 = 20$, and $A_3 = 30$, we can solve for GDP under different allocations of capital and labor across firms. Table 4.1 shows the results. The first set of columns show the results when more efficient firms are bigger than less efficient firms. GDP in this economy is the total output of the three firms, or 14,000. Aggregate TFP is computed using Equation (2).

Table 4.1 TFP and Output in Economies with and without Distortions

	Without distortions			With distortions		
	K	L	Y	K	L	Y
Firm 1	100	100	1,000	200	200	2,000
Firm 2	200	200	4,000	200	200	4,000
Firm 3	300	300	9,000	200	200	6,000
Total	600	600	14,000	600	600	12,000
Aggregate TFP	$A = \dfrac{\text{GDP}}{K^a L^{1-a}}$		23.3			20

The results for the economy with distortions are shown in the last three columns. The subsidies to the unproductive firm and taxes on the productive firm imply that all three firms are of equal size. The economy's GDP and TFP both decrease by about 14 percent. The reason is that the economy with distortions doesn't allow for more productive firms to be bigger than less productive firms. The result is a less efficient economy and a lower level of GDP.

The lesson is that two economies can have identical quantities of resources and each economy can have the same share of productive and unproductive firms, but GDP per worker can be different. The reason is that the distribution of capital and labor matters. Economies with higher levels of GDP per worker tend to allocate more resources to productive firms, whereas productive firms in economies with lower levels of GDP per worker find it harder to scale up.

Application 4.1 analyzes the quantitative effects of real-world distortions in China, India, and the United States.

Application 4.1

Real-World Distortions

Over the past 15 years or so, economists have explored the extent to which misallocation contributes to differences in TFP and GDP per capita. In an important paper, Chang-Tai Hsieh and Peter Klenow measured misallocation across manufacturing firms in China, India, and the United States.[3]

Figure 4.4 shows the distribution of firm size across countries. Looking at each scale, it is the relative numbers that are important. Moving from 8 to 64 means comparing one firm to another that is 8 times as big. The authors compare the actual firm-size distribution to the efficient firm-size distribution, where the latter is computed assuming that there are no distortions. Just as the theory predicted in the previous section, economic distortions compress the distribution of firm size across countries. The authors calculate that moving from the actual to the efficient firm size distribution would increase TFP between 87 to 115 percent in China and 100 to 128 percent in India.

What specific policies contribute to these underlying distortions? In the case of China, Hsieh and Klenow focused on state-owned enterprises (SOEs). The idea is that inefficient businesses may nevertheless be propped up by the government and insulated from competition. Evidence across three surveys in 1998, 2001, and 2005 suggests that while SOEs had lower productivities than other firms in the first two surveys, the difference largely evaporated by 2005. The share of SOEs declined from 29 percent to 8 percent over this seven-year stretch. Consequently, inefficiently big SOEs explain a quantitatively significant

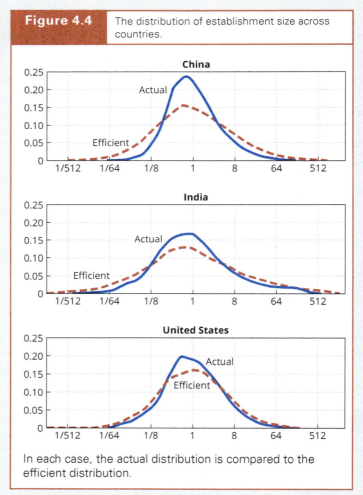

Figure 4.4 The distribution of establishment size across countries.

In each case, the actual distribution is compared to the efficient distribution.

Source: Hsieh and Klenow (2009), QJE.

[3]Hsieh, Chang-Tai and Peter Klenow. 2009. "Misallocation and Manufacturing TFP in China and India." *Quarterly Journal of Economics, 124*(4): 1403–1448.

Continues

Chapter 4 Explaining Total Factor Productivity **79**

Application 4.1 (Continued)

fraction of misallocation in China in the early years, but not the misallocation that remained in 2005.

In the case of India, from its independence in 1947 until the 1980s, the Indian government heavily regulated its private sector. Some of the regulations included subsidies and preferential access to credit for small firms and severe constraints on expansion by large firms.[4] Many Indian industries also faced licensing requirements. Beginning in the 1980s and continuing over the next two decades, the Indian government removed many of these regulations. Hsieh and Klenow showed that industries with firm-size regulations had higher rates of misallocation, but the effects of licensure were less clear. The Indian government removed licensing requirements for about 40 percent of industries in 1985 and another 42 percent of industries in 1991. There is no evidence that deregulation reduced misallocation on average. Still, firms that continued to face size limits experienced higher rates of misallocation than the deregulated firms.

Economic research is still ongoing in this subject. Understanding the causes of misallocation and how each form of misallocation quantitatively affects TFP is very important for explaining cross-country income differences.

[4]For a discussion, see Kochhar, Kalpana, Utsav Kumar, Raghuram Rajan, Arvind Subramanian, and Ioannis Tokatlidis. 2006. "India's Pattern of Development: What Happened, What Follows?" *Journal of Monetary Economics, 53*(5): 981–1019.

4-1c Financial Constraints and TFP

One reason poor economies allocate fewer resources to productive firms is that some of these highly productive firms may be owned by individuals with low wealth. Here is the idea. One purpose of a **financial intermediary**, such as a bank, is to match people who want to save with people to want to borrow. In the context of entrepreneurship, business owners or potential business owners have the ideas but may have no wealth; highly wealthy individuals or institutions have the wealth but not the ideas. In the United States and other advanced economies, aspiring entrepreneurs can present their ideas to a bank with the hope of obtaining a loan or they can pitch their idea to a venture capital firm with the hope that the firm might invest in the project. The bank or venture capital firm is the intermediary in this case. They determine which projects are likely to earn a profit.

Financial intermediary
An institution that matches people who want to save with people who want to borrow.

In the absence of effective financial intermediation, prospective business owners either have to find lenders or investors by themselves or rely on their personal wealth to finance their venture. Finding lenders and investors on a case-by-case basis is difficult for two reasons. First, it is very inefficient. Every time a potential investor is pitched an idea they would have to investigate the prospects of the idea themselves. And just because someone is rich, doesn't necessarily put them in a good position to personally judge the profitability of a business venture. Likewise, from the entrepreneur's perspective, depending on the size of the project, they may have to convince five or ten investors that the project is worthwhile, rather than one bank. This would be very time-consuming.

The second reason is that contract enforcement tends to be weaker in poor countries than rich countries. For example, suppose a business owner takes out a loan for $1,000 and promises to pay it back one year from now. The lender must have some assurance that the borrower will repay the loan. Detailed laws of contract enforcement and bankruptcy regulate these types of contracts in rich countries, but these laws tend to be much less developed and enforced in poor countries. This means that investors will be less likely to finance projects in poor countries where there is no guarantee that the borrower will be obligated to repay. For these reasons, personal wealth is much more important for financing business ventures in poor countries.

How does this implication affect TFP? Similar to Section 4-1b, imagine that every individual in the economy is endowed with an idea where each idea is modeled as a level of TFP, A_i. Good ideas are modeled as high values of TFP, and bad ideas are modeled as low values of TFP. Individuals are also endowed with a level of wealth, a_i. Each individual decides to work at a business or start their own business. Starting a business requires funding, though, and individuals can obtain this funding by using their own wealth or borrowing or some combination of the two. Total TFP in the economy is just a size-weighted average of TFPs of the businesses in operation. If an individual goes to work, their TFP does not count toward the aggregate because their idea is left unimplemented.

The efficient solution to this problem is that all individuals with high TFPs start a business regardless of their level of individual wealth. This is shown in the left panel of Figure 4.5. TFP is on the horizontal axis, and individual wealth is on the vertical axis. All individuals with TFPs above a threshold, $\overline{A}$, should operate a business, and all individuals with $A_i < \overline{A}$ should be workers. The intuition is that one's wealth does not determine the quality of one's idea. Aggregate TFP is a function of individual TFPs, not wealth. Thus, in an efficiently operating economy, the wealth distribution is irrelevant in determining who starts a business. Wealthy people with bad ideas can simply invest their resources into good business ideas. And people with good ideas but low wealth can borrow from an intermediary to start a business.

In the real world, and especially in developing economies, the wealth distribution does affect who starts a business. More wealthy individuals can start a business without relying on financial intermediation and less wealthy individuals don't always have access to well-functioning intermediaries. This situation is graphically depicted in the right panel of Figure 4.5. Now there isn't a unique cutoff for who starts a business. Rather, for every level of TFP, A_i, there is a cutoff wealth level, $\overline{a}$, above which the individual opens a business and below which the individual goes to work. As a result, some ideas that are above the threshold $\overline{A}$ end up not getting financed because of imperfect financial markets. Specifically, all individuals to the right of $\overline{A}$ but below the red line would end up being workers in the economy with imperfect intermediation but would have been business owners in the efficient economy. The reason again is that, despite having a good idea, they cannot obtain sufficient financing to start a business and they don't have enough wealth to start the business itself.

There are many factors that contribute to underdeveloped financial markets in less developed economies. One, as previously mentioned, is a lack of contract enforcement. If lenders know there is limited legal recourse for requiring repayment by the borrower, the lender will demand more collateral upfront. Then, if a borrower defaults, either because the project falls through or because they abscond with the funds, the lender is at least left with something.

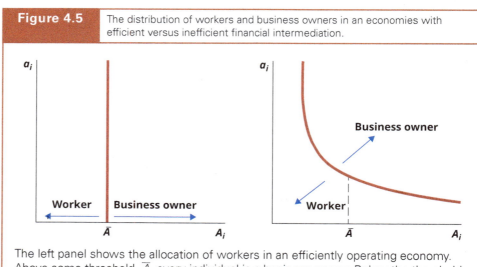

Figure 4.5 The distribution of workers and business owners in an economies with efficient versus inefficient financial intermediation.

The left panel shows the allocation of workers in an efficiently operating economy. Above some threshold, $\overline{A}$, every individual is a business owner. Below the threshold, every individual is a worker. The right panel depicts an economy where business ownership is a function of wealth. All the individuals to the northeast of the red line are business owners. All the individuals to the southwest are workers.

Question: Which workers in the right panel would have been business owners in the left panel? Label this on the graph.

Chapter 4 Explaining Total Factor Productivity   **81**

Another potential reason is that property rights tend to be less established in poor countries. This means that a borrower who hypothetically obtains lending from an intermediary has to take steps to minimize the risk of expropriation. For instance, maybe a farmer in a country with less secure property rights installs a video camera on their farm or hires an employee to guard the harvested crops. These actions, though perhaps necessary, divert resources away from productive activities (e.g., growing crops) to unproductive activities. Lenders will naturally be more reluctant to provide funding when a large part of the investment goes toward unproductive activities. Moreover, if property rights are insecure, entrepreneurs cannot use the value of the property as collateral for loans. This will naturally lower the scale of operation for businesses in developing countries.

Finally, in countries with underdeveloped financial markets, information disclosure about the prospects of potential business ventures is more limited compared to countries with developed financial markets. In the United States, lenders can (and do) ask for income tax forms, profit and loss statements, business plans, and other forms of documentation from potential borrowers. This information helps determine how likely the borrower is to repay. If the lender does not have this documentation, there is **asymmetric information** between the borrower and lender. Asymmetric information refers to a situation when one party in a transaction is in possession of more information than the other. In our context, the borrower has more information than the lender. Because the lender knows they are missing some critical information, they will be less willing to lend or only lend at higher interest rates. This again means that people with good ideas for business ventures, but a small stock of personal wealth, are less likely to obtain funding.

No economy has perfect financial markets, so personal wealth will always impact who starts a business to some degree. The theory presented here suggests that if poor countries have less developed financial markets (and they do, at least on average), then aggregate TFP levels will be adversely affected.

Asymmetric information
A situation in which two people are engaged in a transaction and one person knows more than the other person.

✔ Knowledge Check 4-1

Suppose there are three potential entrepreneurs in a country, each with a different level of TFP, A_i. Each potential entrepreneur also has a level of wealth given by a_i.

A_i	a_i
30	0
20	50
10	100

Suppose there are 300 workers in the economy and that the fraction of the labor force going to each entrepreneur is given by l_i, with $0 < l_i < 1$. Aggregate TFP is therefore given by

$$A = \sum_{i=1}^{3} A_i l_i.$$

Calculate aggregate TFP based on three different labor allocations.

1. Labor is divided equally among the entrepreneurs.
2. Labor is allocated in proportion to individual TFP.
3. Labor is split 50–50 between the two entrepreneurs with positive levels of wealth.

How is aggregate TFP affected by the labor allocation? Explain the economic intuition of this result.

—————————————————————— Answers are at the end of the chapter.

82 **Part 1** Growth

> ✓ **Knowledge Check 4-2**
>
> The theory of misallocation in Section 4-1b was static; that is, there was no time component. Do you think an identical pattern of taxes and subsidies would increase or decrease income differences in a model with capital accumulation relative to the static model? Explain.
>
> ———————————————————————— Answers are at the end of the chapter.

4-2 Growth Accounting

A key result of our analysis of the Solow model in Chapter 3 was that if the Solow model is to explain growth in GDP per worker over the long run, it must come from TFP growth. The intuition is that while changes in other parameters, such as the savings rate, affect the level of GDP per worker, the savings rate can only go so high. TFP, however, is unbounded. The procedure of dividing GDP growth into the share that is attributable to TFP versus what is attributed to all other factors is called **growth accounting**. This section explains the growth accounting framework and then uses it to account for growth in the United States and several advanced economies.

Growth accounting
The procedure of dividing GDP growth into the share that is attributable to TFP and what is attributed to all other factors.

4-2a The Growth Accounting Framework

The growth accounting procedure starts by returning to the Cobb–Douglas production function, Equation (1):

$$Y_t = A_t K_t^a L_t^{1-a}.$$

We are interested in the growth rate of output per worker. To transform Equation (1) into per worker terms, divide it by L_t:

$$y_t = \frac{Y_t}{L_t}$$

$$= \frac{A_t K_t^a L_t^{1-a}}{L_t}$$

$$= \frac{A_t K_t^a L_t^{1-a}}{L_t^a L_t^{1-a}}$$

$$= A_t k_t^a. \tag{3}$$

Here, y_t is output per worker and k_t is capital per worker. It would be tempting from here to divide the growth rate in output per worker into a TFP component, A_t, and a capital per worker component, k_t^a. This would actually understate the importance of TFP in the growth rate of output per worker. Here is why. Suppose there is a one-time increase in TFP. That increases output per worker on impact, but also increases capital per worker over time through the capital accumulation equation. Thus, some of the credit given to capital per worker is misattributed.

To properly account for growth, we can rewrite Equation (2) in terms of the capital to output ratio. To start with, divide both sides of Equation (3) by y_t^a:

$$y_t^{1-a} = \frac{A_t k_t^a}{y_t^a}$$

$$= A_t \left(\frac{k_t}{y_t}\right)^a.$$

Next, raise both sides to the $\dfrac{1}{1-a}$ power. This gives

Chapter 4 Explaining Total Factor Productivity **83**

$$y_t = A_t^{\frac{1}{1-a}} \left(\frac{k_t}{y_t}\right)^{\frac{a}{1-a}}. \tag{4}$$

As you will show in the next knowledge check, the capital to output ratio is independent of TFP along a balanced growth path. In particular, along a balanced growth path,

$$\frac{k_t}{y_t} = \frac{s}{n+d}.$$

Increases in the savings rate will increase capital relative to output in the long run. Equation (4) then properly accounts for the roles of TFP and changes in the capital to output ratio. For ease of interpretation Equation (4) can be rewritten as

$$y_t = \widetilde{A}_t \widetilde{k}_t, \tag{5}$$

where $\widetilde{A}_t = A_t^{\frac{1}{1-a}}$ and $\widetilde{k}_t = \left(\frac{k_t}{y_t}\right)^{\frac{a}{1-a}}$. Output per worker equals the product of a TFP component and a capital to output component. Recall, from Mathematical Appendix the rule that the growth rate of a product is the sum of growth rates.[5] The growth rate of output per worker, $g_{y,t}$, in period t is

$$g_{y,t} = g_{A,t} + g_{k,t}. \tag{6}$$

Here, $g_{A,t}$ is the growth rate of $\widetilde{A}_t$ and $g_{k,t}$ is the growth rate of $\widetilde{k}_t$. Using Equation (6), we can decompose the growth rate of output per worker into its TFP component and capital-to-output component in any given year for any given country.

4-2b Growth Accounting in Action

The growth accounting framework can be used for any country over any time period. In this section, we account for growth in Japan, the United States, France, and Australia from 1950 to 2019. Figure 4.6 shows that these countries, while rich from a global perspective, have experienced significantly different patterns of growth in output per worker.

The United States has had the highest level of output per worker for the entire time period. Japan, meanwhile, converged nearly to parity with Australia and France in the mid-1990s before stagnating for the next 20 years. France started off with about half the GDP per worker as Australia but converged by the 1970s.

Table 4.2 shows the results of the growth accounting exercise. The top row for each country shows the average annual growth in GDP per worker by decade. The bottom row shows the average annual TFP growth by decade. The first thing to notice is that the growth rates of GDP per worker in the table largely support the visual analysis in Figure 4.6. Japan grew quickly before stagnating, France converged to Australia by the 1970s, and the growth rates for the United States have been somewhere in the middle of the other countries. The second thing to notice is the growth rate of GDP per worker was fastest in the first two decades and has slowed down across all countries since 2000. Finally, as predicted by the Solow model, TFP growth accounts for most of the growth in GDP per capita across countries, ranging from a low of 54 percent in Japan to a high of 106 percent in the United States. This number is bigger than 100 percent in the United States because the average TFP growth rate exceeded the average growth rate in output per worker. This means that the capital to output ratio decreased in the United States over this time period. The share is the lowest in Japan. This makes sense especially in the 1970s, as the Japanese savings rate rose from about 27 percent to about 40 percent.

---

[5]Specifically, if you have a function $Z_t = X_t Y_t$, where Z_t, X_t, and Y_t are all variables, then the growth rate between two adjacent periods, t and $t - 1$, is approximated by $g_{z,t} = g_{x,t} + g_{y,t}$.

84 Part 1 Growth

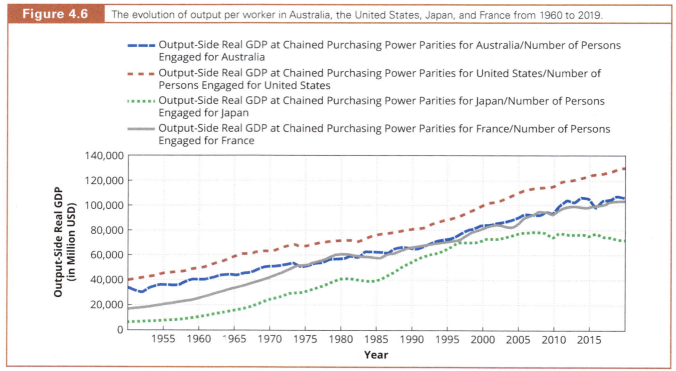

Figure 4.6 The evolution of output per worker in Australia, the United States, Japan, and France from 1960 to 2019.

Source: PWT 9.0 and FRED.

Table 4.2 Averages of Growth in GDP per Worker and TFP by Decade

	1960–69	1970–79	1980–89	1990–99	2000–09	2010–19	TFP Share
Australia	2.6	1.2	1.7	2.3	1.4	1.5	94.7
	3.2	1.0	1.5	1.8	1.8	1.0	
France	5.1	3.9	0.9	2.1	1.4	1.1	82.0
	5.2	3.7	1.3	2.7	−0.2	0.4	
Japan	8.3	5.5	3.0	2.9	0.4	−0.3	54.2
	7.8	3.6	3.4	1.4	−0.2	0.4	
United States	2.7	1.2	1.2	2.0	1.5	1.3	106.3
	3.1	1.3	1.3	2.4	1.2	1.7	

Each country contains two rows of data. The top row of each pair shows the average annual growth rate of GDP per worker in each decade. The bottom row of each pair shows the average annual TFP growth rate in each decade. The last column shows the percentage of GDP growth explained by TFP growth.

The results from the growth accounting exercise present a catch-22 for the Solow model. Going in its favor, the Solow model predicts that any sustained growth in GDP per worker must come from TFP growth. That is exactly what we see in the case of these four countries and is supported by the data more generally. On the other hand, the Solow model does not provide a theory of TFP growth. This is where we turn next.

Chapter 4 Explaining Total Factor Productivity   85

> **✓ Knowledge Check 4-3**
>
> Start with the per-worker capital accumulation equation from Chapter 3:
>
> $$k_{t+1} = \frac{1}{1+n}[sy_t + (1-d)k_t].$$
>
> Using this equation, prove that the steady-state capital-to-output ratio equals $\frac{s}{n+d}$. Calculate the capital-to-output ratio assuming $n + d = 0.10$ and for three different values of s: 0.1, 0.2, 0.3. How does an increase in TFP affect the capital-to-output ratio in steady state? Compare this to the immediate effect on the capital-to-output ratio of a one-time increase in TFP. What explains the difference?
>
> ———————————————————————————————— Answers are at the end of the chapter.

4-3 The Romer Model of Endogenous Growth

The Romer model of endogenous growth was developed in a series of papers by economist Paul Romer, a co-recipient of the 2018 Nobel Prize in economics.[6,7] Fundamentally, you can think of the Romer model as a model of **ideas**. A new idea has the potential to increase output for any given input. In other words, a new idea raises or at least has the potential to raise TFP. Throughout this section, TFP and ideas are referred to interchangeably. We will first discuss the microeconomic foundations of Romer's ideas and then move on to a formal model.

Idea
Anything that has the potential to increase output for any given level of inputs.

4-3a A Macroeconomic Impossibility Theorem

Romer's model of economic growth depends on two uncontroversial, but perhaps nonobvious, observations. As you will see, these two observations lead to a striking conclusion.

1. **Ideas are nonrival.** A **rival good** is one in which one person's use of the good diminishes the potential of other people to use the good. For example, a cookie is a rival good. If I eat a cookie, that is one fewer cookie for you to eat. The cookie recipe, however, is nonrival. My use of the recipe in no way impedes your use of the recipe. The cookie recipe is an idea. This lesson applies more generally. Ideas are nonrival, while the other inputs to production, most notably labor and capital, are rival. One more worker in a factory is one fewer worker available to harvest crops. One more computer allocated to a biotechnology firm is one fewer computer for a doctor's office.

   Rival good
   A good characterized by the property that one person's use of it diminishes the potential of other people to use the good.

2. **Output is constant returns to scale in rival inputs.** This is our standard assumption on the aggregate production function. The conceptual argument goes as follows. Imagine that we doubled all the rival inputs on planet Earth. That would of course include the labor and capital, but you could also include land, raw materials, and so on. Then we would just have another Earth. Doubling the rival inputs exactly doubles output.

   But if the stock of ideas were to double along with all the rival inputs, then output would more than double. Not only would we have twice as much land, labor, and capital, but we would have more ideas to use on *both* planets because ideas are nonrival. Thus, while output is constant returns to scale in rival inputs, output is increasing returns to scale if one includes ideas as an input.

---

[6]See for instance: Romer, Paul. 1990. Endogenous Technological Change. *Journal of Political Economy*, 98(5): 1002–1037.

[7]Romer shared the prize with William Nordhaus, who was discussed in Chapter 2.

This distinction between constant and increasing returns can be demonstrated by the standard Cobb–Douglas production function,

$$Y = AK^a L^{1-a}.$$

The rival inputs are capital and labor. Doubling capital and labor gives

$$A(2K)^a(2L)^{1-a} = A2^a 2^{1-a} K^a L^{1-a} = 2AK^a L^{1-a}.$$

Output is constant returns to scale in rival inputs. Doubling capital, labor, and TFP gives

$$2A(2K)^a(2L)^{1-a} = 2A2^a 2^{1-a} K^a L^{1-a} = 4AK^a L^{1-a}.$$

Doubling TFP, capital, and labor quadruples output. Thus, output is increasing returns to scale once TFP, or the stock of ideas, is included as an input.

Combining these two observations leads to a surprising result: either perfect competition is impossible or people invent ideas for free. The logic here is that a perfectly competitive representative firm pays capital and labor their marginal products. If the production function is constant returns to scale in rival inputs (observation 2), then the compensation to labor plus the compensation to capital equals total revenue.[8] This implies that there is no remaining revenue to compensate the production of ideas.

Is it plausible that people produce ideas without the expectation of being compensated? It is certainly true that there are individual cases of this. Computer programmers, for instance, have produced open source software like Python and R. On the other hand, many ideas are protected by intellectual property rights. Even the most common types of Software, e.g., Microsoft Office, are patented. Pharmaceutical companies develop lifesaving medicines but get to provide them as a monopoly for a while. Authors and musicians may produce some free books and music, but a lot of it is copyrighted. In sum, it is not plausible that most ideas are created by inventors with no expectation of compensation.

Romer concluded that the only realistic way of making sense of the two observations is to jettison the assumption of perfect competition. His mathematical model of growth and imperfect competition is beyond the scope of this book, but we cover the macroeconomic basics in the next section.

4-3b Preliminaries of the Endogenous Growth Model

The endogenous growth model has two sectors: A research sector that produces ideas, and an output-producing sector. Ideas are first produced and then used along with other inputs to produce GDP. The labor force is divided between the two sectors. In terms of an equation, this is given by

$$L_t = L_{Y,t} + L_{R,t}, \tag{7}$$

where $L_{Y,t}$ is labor allocated to the output sector and $L_{R,t}$ is labor allocated to the research sector. You can think of $L_{R,t}$ as scientists. Almost always, the research- and output-producing sectors exist within the same industry. The Covid-19 vaccines manufactured by Moderna and Pfizer were the product of thousands of hours spent researching mRNA. Likewise, workers who manufacture electric cars and scientists who develop longer-lasting and more efficient batteries often work in the same company.

---

[8]This is a result called Euler's theorem, from calculus. The theorem says that a constant returns to scale production function, $A_t F(K_t, L_t)$, can be written as

$$A_t F(K_t, L_t) = A_t F_K(K_t, L_t) K_t + A_t F_L(K_t, L_t) L_t$$

where F_K and F_L are the derivatives of the production function with respect to capital and labor, respectively. These derivatives are also equal to the marginal products of each input. Since a profit-maximizing firm equates factor prices to marginal products, the equation above can be written as

$$A_t F(K_t, L_t) = A_t F_K(K_t, L_t) K_t + A_t F_L(K_t, L_t) L_t = r_t K_t + w_t L_t.$$

Since the left-hand side is total revenue and the right-hand side is total cost, profit equals zero.

The fraction of the labor force allocated to the research sector is given exogenously by s_R, where $0 < s_R < 1$. That means the total number of researchers is given by

$$L_{R,t} = s_R L_t. \tag{8}$$

Just as in the Solow model, the labor force grows exogenously at rate $n > 0$:

$$L_{t+1} = L_t(1 + n). \tag{9}$$

To simplify things, assume that GDP is produced with labor as the only input into the production function. The production function in the output-producing sector is

$$Y_t = A_t L_{y,t}. \tag{10}$$

Note that this violates our assumption of diminishing marginal productivity. Adding one worker always increases output by A_t. This assumption needs to be violated because the only rival input is labor and it is important, for reasons discussed in the last section, that output be constant returns to scale in rival inputs. The entire analysis could be reworked to include capital accumulation and a traditional Cobb–Douglas production function, but that would make things much more complicated and not provide anything especially insightful.

Finally, the idea accumulation equation is given by

$$A_{t+1} - A_t = L_{R,t} A_t^b. \tag{11}$$

The left-hand side is the change in the stock of ideas between periods t and $t + 1$. The right-hand side is the total number of ideas produced in period t. The number of ideas is increasing in the number of scientists. Intuitively, if more scientists are looking to invent ideas, more ideas will end up being invented. Idea production also depends on A_t itself. It isn't clear if a larger stock of ideas should make subsequent invention easier or more difficult. On the one hand, if the easiest and best ideas are thought of first, then a bigger stock of ideas could make future discovery more difficult. This is the case mathematically if $b < 0$. On the other hand, some ideas possibly open the door for many other ideas to be discovered. For example, Newton's invention of calculus blazed the path for discoveries in fields like physics and astronomy. If $b > 0$, then idea production gets easier as the stock of ideas increases. The takeaway is that the production of new ideas is a positive function of b.

The model is summarized in Table 4.3. One thing to note is that the stock of ideas in period t, A_t is already known at the beginning of the period, so A_{t+1} is an unknown variable from the perspective of period t.

Just as in the Solow model, it is usually impossible to solve for the entire time path of all the variables. Instead, we will derive the balanced growth path using some math and then graphically characterize deviations from the balanced growth path.

Table 4.3	Description of the Romer Model	
Endogenous variables	**Exogenous variables**	**Parameters**
$Y_t, A_{t+1}, L_{y,t}, L_{R,t}$	L_t	s_R, b, n

Key equations:

1. $L_t = L_{Y,t} + L_{R,t}$ (Allocation of labor, Eq (7))

2. $L_{R,t} = s_R L_t$ (Number of workers in the research sector, Eq (8))

3. $L_{t+1} = L_t(1 + n)$ (Population growth equation, Eq (9))

4. $Y_t = A_t L_{y,t}$ (Production function in output-producing sector, Eq (10))

5. $A_{t+1} - A_t = L_{R,t} A_t^b$ (Idea accumulation equation, Eq (11))

4-3c Solving the Endogenous Growth Model

To begin the derivation of the balanced growth path, divide each side of the idea accumulation equation by A_t,

$$\frac{A_{t+1} - A_t}{A_t} = \frac{L_{R,t}}{A_t^{1-b}}. \tag{12}$$

The left-hand side of Equation (12) is the growth rate of TFP. If the economy is on a balanced growth path, all growth rates are constant. Call this time-invariant growth rate g_a. For the TFP growth rate to be constant, the numerator and denominator on the right-hand side need to be growing at the same rate. Recall that the number of researchers is given by the equation

$$L_{R,t} = s_R L_t.$$

By assumption, s_R is a fixed constant and the total population grows at rate n. This means $L_{R,t}$ also grows at rate n. Intuitively, an increase in the share of the labor force allocated to research increases the number of researchers but does not affect the growth rate of the number of researchers.

The Mathematical appendix shows that the growth rate of a variable raised to an exponent is just the exponent times the growth rate of the variable.[9] Thus, the growth rate of A_t^{1-b} is $(1 - b)g_{A,t}$. For the denominator to be growing, rather than shrinking, restricts $b < 1$. The balanced growth path requires $(1 - b)g_A = n$ or

$$g_A = \frac{n}{1 - b}. \tag{13}$$

The growth rate of TFP is the growth rate of population discounted by $1 - b$. The intuition is this. A higher population growth rate implies a higher growth rate in the number of scientists. The more scientists there are, the more ideas get created. From Equation (12), an increase in the number of ideas lowers the growth rate of idea accumulation all else equal. Thus, the number of scientists must continually grow in order to get sustained TFP growth. The closer b is to 1, the more new ideas build off old ideas and the higher the growth rate in TFP. As b gets smaller, new ideas get harder to find and the TFP growth gets smaller.

Perhaps a more elegant way of saying it (i.e., without math) is this. Since ideas are nonrival, more ideas for one person means more ideas for everyone. Increasing the number of scientists increases the number of ideas, whereas increasing the growth rate in the number of scientists increases the growth rate in the number of ideas.

One final note on Equations (12) and (13) needs to be mentioned. The value of the parameter b seems like a small technical issue, but it actually profoundly impacts the interpretation of the model. Strictly speaking, economists call the model in this section "semi-endogenous growth." These models were developed by Jones (1995) among others.[10] The big difference between "semi-endogenous" and the earlier models of endogenous growth is the value of b. Earlier models, including Romer's, wrote the idea accumulation equation as

$$\frac{A_{t+1} - A_t}{A_t} = c L_{R,t}$$

where $c > 0$ is a constant. This specification of the idea accumulation equation is consistent with $b = 1$ and implies that the growth rate of TFP is independent of the level of TFP and that a permanent increase in the number of scientists permanently raises the growth rate of TFP. Thus, under this specification, TFP growth should be accelerating over time as the research sector grows.

The primary justification for using the semi-endogenous growth model is that Equation (13) is better supported by the data. Jones (1995) presents evidence that despite a massive increase in the number of scientists in the United States and other advanced economies, U.S. TFP growth has been relatively stable. Figure 4.7 shows one of the figures

---

[9] In particular, the growth rate of $X_t^a = a g_{x,t}$ where $g_{x,t}$ is the growth rate of X_t between $t - 1$ and t.

[10] Jones, Charles I. 1995. "R&D-Based Models of Economic Growth." *Journal of Political Economy*, 103(4): 759–784.

Figure 4.7 US TFP growth and the number of scientists and engineers.

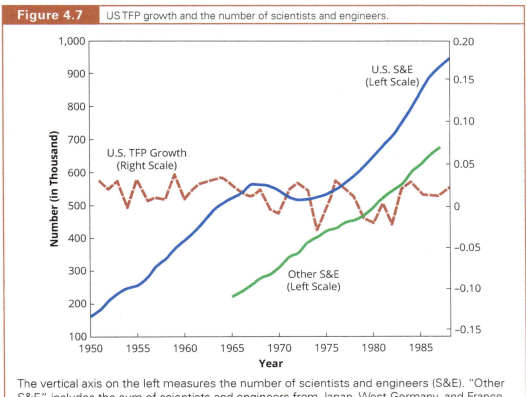

The vertical axis on the left measures the number of scientists and engineers (S&E). "Other S&E" includes the sum of scientists and engineers from Japan, West Germany, and France. The vertical axis on the right measures U.S. TFP growth.

Source: Jones (1995), "R&D-Based Models of Economic Growth."

from his paper. U.S. TFP growth is measured on the right axis, and the number of scientists and engineers (S&E) is measured on this left axis. Although the figure is bit outdated, the empirical results have not changed over the ensuing decades. If anything, as you will see in Application 4.2, ideas have gotten harder to find in more recent history.

Returning to model's equations, the only remaining variable to solve for in the model is GDP or GDP per worker. Recall that GDP is produced with the production function

$$Y_t = A_t L_{y,t}.$$

To put this into per-worker terms, divide both sides by L_t and recall that $L_{y,t} = (1 - s_R)L_t$. Formally, this equation is given by

$$y_t = \frac{Y_t}{L_t}$$
$$= \frac{A_t L_{y,t}}{L_t}$$
$$= A_t(1 - s_R). \tag{14}$$

There are two implications of this equation. First, there is a tradeoff between allocating more workers to the research sector versus allocating more workers to the output-producing sector. Doing the former increases s_R which, over time, will increase TFP. On the other hand, an increase in s_R implies that fewer workers are using the ideas to produce output. Doing the latter decreases s_R, which instantaneously increases output per worker but at the expense of a slower rate of idea creation. There is a similarity between the golden-rule savings rate in the Solow model and the optimal s_R in the endogenous growth model. If $s_R = 1$, then idea creation is

Application 4.2

Are Ideas Getting Harder to Find?

The Romer model shows that ideas are the key to economic growth. There is no iron law that says that the rate at which scientists invent new ideas is constant. Perhaps it's the case that all the easily discoverable ideas, or "low-hanging fruit," have already been discovered. The scientists of the 19th century gave us the steam engine. The scientists of the 20th century gave us the Polio vaccine. Is all that's left over for scientists of the 21st century is to find better alternatives to Grubhub? In a 2020 paper, a team of researchers lead by Stanford University's Nick Bloom asks if ideas are getting harder to find.[11] Their analytic framework starts with an equation similar to Equation (12) in the last section. Namely,

$$\frac{A_{t+1} - A_t}{A_t} = \alpha L_{R,t} \qquad (15)$$

The left-hand side is TFP growth. The right-hand side is the product of α, which they call research productivity, and the number of researchers, $L_{R,t}$. Their paper tests if research productivity is constant at the level of the aggregate economy as well as in individual sectors.

The model of endogenous TFP covered in the last section predicts that research productivity, at least at the aggregate level, is **not** constant. Comparing Equation (15) to Equation (12) shows that they are identical if $\alpha = A_t^{b-1}$. As long as b is less than one, research productivity falls over time. Figure 4.7 showed that while TFP growth has stayed roughly constant, the number of researchers has increased substantially. This implies that research productivity is falling at the level of the aggregate economy. Bloom et al. update the data through 2014 and find the same result.

The authors emphasize that looking at aggregate research productivity may be misleading. Here is the logic. The number of products in the economy has expanded over time. Perhaps the economy's scientists are simply divided between researching for more products as time goes on. In this case, it's possible that research productivity falls at the aggregate level but is constant at the level of individual products.

Here is an example. Imagine an economy that only produces corn. All the scientists in the economy are devoted to deriving new and better ideas for harvesting corn. Suppose that the idea production function for corn features constant research productivity, i.e., α is constant in Equation (15), and that the number of current scientists supports a growth rate of ideas equal to 2 percent. Thus, if the number of scientists double, the growth rate of ideas will increase to 4 percent. Since corn is the only good produced in the economy, the idea growth rate for the entire economy increases from 2 percent to 4 percent.

Instead of devoting twice as many scientists to researching ideas about corn, imagine that the economy starts to produce green beans in addition to corn. The idea production functions for corn and green beans are identical, and all the new scientists work toward finding ideas about green beans. Then, idea growth in the green bean and corn sectors, as well as the aggregate economy, will be 2 percent. Despite doubling the number of scientists, the aggregate growth rate of ideas stays the same. It looks like the research productivity in aggregate is falling, but what is really going on is the number of products is expanding with the number of scientists, so that the number of scientists per product stays constant. Bloom and his coauthors recognized that understanding the true nature of research productivity requires looking at individual products.

The conceptual challenge to investigating research productivity at the product level is quantifying "idea output," or TFP growth, and "idea input," or the number of researchers. The authors are able to quantify these variables for a number of products in the technology, agriculture, and health sectors and find that research productivity has been decreasing across all sectors, albeit at different rates.

To take one example, Figure 4.8 shows their findings in the agricultural sector. TFP is not measured at the level of individual crops because it is difficult to allocate individual inputs to individual crops. To see this, imagine a farmer owns 10 tractors (the capital stock) and plants cotton and soybeans. What fraction of the capital should be allocated to cotton versus soybeans? Even with very careful measurement, this would be a difficult question to answer. As an alternative, the authors use the growth rate of the yield per acre as their measure of "idea output." They use R&D expenditure related to different crops deflated by the wages of high-skilled workers as their measure of "idea input." Conceptually, R&D expenditure is the product of the number of scientists employed times the wage paid to each scientist. Dividing total expenditure by the wage for high-skilled workers, a proxy for the wages for scientists, recovers the effective number of scientists.

---

[11] Bloom, Nicholas, Charles I. Jones, John Van Reenen, and Michael Webb. 2020. "Are Ideas Getting Harder to Find?" *American Economic Review, 110*(4): 1104–1144.

■ Continues

Application 4.2 (Continued)

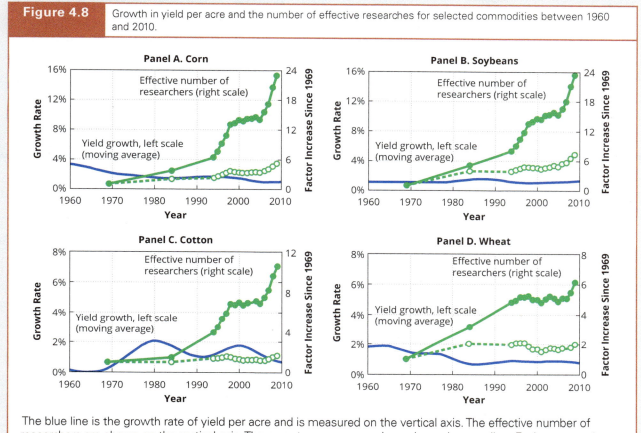

Figure 4.8 Growth in yield per acre and the number of effective researches for selected commodities between 1960 and 2010.

The blue line is the growth rate of yield per acre and is measured on the vertical axis. The effective number of researchers are shown on the vertical axis. There are two measures shown by each green line. Each measure is normalized to one in 1969.

Source: Bloom et al. (2020). "Are Ideas Getting Harder to Find?"

The authors use two different measures of R&D expenditure for each crop, but idea input is increasing for all crops regardless of how it is measured. The effective number of researchers in corn, for instance, rose by a factor of at least 6 and as much as 24 between 1969 and 2014. This implies an average annual decrease in research productivity of between 6.2 and 9.9 percent. This finding generalizes across the other crops as well. The authors conclude that research productivity is falling at the level of individual crops and in the agriculture sector as a whole.

Bloom et al. also look at case studies from medicine and technology and find very similar results. Thus, it doesn't matter if one looks at the aggregate economy or at the level of individual products, research productivity is declining everywhere.

The findings of this paper support the "semi-endogenous" growth model discussed in this chapter. Indeed, the semi-endogenous growth model predicts that research productivity decreases over time. The only way to offset the declines in research productivity and sustain constant TFP growth is through a growing population.

An interesting policy implication emerges from this model. If policymakers want to increase technological advancement over the long run, then population growth should be encouraged. Encouraging population growth cuts against modern-day alarmism that the planet's population is approaching an unsustainable level. While a greater number of people walking on Earth means more mouths to feed, more houses to heat, and more brains to teach, it also means more ideas to enjoy. Yes, a larger population requires greater production of food, but some members of that larger population may think of new methods for genetically engineering crops. On net, production per capita could very well increase. And, indeed, for most of the world's history it has.

Continues

92 **Part 1** Growth

> ### Application 4.2 (Continued)
>
> Concerns over Earth's population are not new. In 1968, Stanford biologist Paul Ehrlich wrote the infamously titled book, *The Population Bomb*. Ehrlich argued that food production would not keep up with Earth's growing population. He advocated steps to reduce population growth to zero, or even make it negative. The empirical evidence accumulated over the next several decades did not support Ehrlich's prediction. Food production outpaced the growth in the world's population. This is not to say that there are no valid concerns with greater population levels. In particular, the consumption of nonrenewable resources coupled with the increasing prevalence of climate change are very real threats. But again, more people means more scientists thinking of solutions to climate change. The net effect of a bigger population on the environment depends on how the greater rate of idea discovery balances with more people consuming nonrenewable resources.

maximized, but there are no workers to produce output. If $s_R = 0$, then the creation of new ideas stops. Neither extreme is optimal, so the ideal value of s_R must lie somewhere in the middle.

The second implication is that output per worker grows at the same rate as TFP. This is true even when the economy is not on a balanced growth path. Since TFP growth is a positive function of population growth, an increase in population growth also increases the growth rate of GDP per capita. You may recall from the Solow model that an increase in the population growth rate lowers the level of capital per worker. While it is true that a higher n spreads the capital stock over more workers, the growth effects coming from a higher n exceed any effects coming from the dilution of the capital stock.

4-3d Analyzing the Model Graphically

To understand how the economy responds to changes in parameters, it is best to analyze the model graphically. To simplify things, assume that $b = 0$ so that the idea accumulation equation can be written as

$$\frac{A_{t+1} - A_t}{A_t} = \frac{s_R L_t}{A_t}. \tag{15}$$

Figure 4.9 graphs Equation (15). TFP growth is increasing in the population to TFP ratio at rate s_R, which is the slope of the function. Along a balanced growth path, TFP growth equals population growth, n. The population to TFP ratio consistent with a balanced growth path is denoted with a "BG" superscript. If the economy starts with an $\frac{L_t}{A_t} > \left(\frac{L_t}{A_t}\right)^{BG}$, then the TFP growth rate exceeds the population growth rate, or $g_{A,t} > n$. This means that A_t grows faster than L_t. Over time, the ratio $\frac{L_t}{A_t}$ drops and the economy returns to the BGP. A symmetric argument applies if $\frac{L_t}{A_t} < \left(\frac{L_t}{A_t}\right)^{BG}$.

Just as in the Solow model, we want to understand how changes in the parameters affect the dynamics of the model. Consider first an increase in the population growth rate. This is shown in Figure 4.10. This shifts the BGP line from n_0 to n_1. The growth rate of the population initially exceeds the growth rate of TFP. Eventually, the economy settles at a new and higher ratio of labor to TFP with a higher growth rate in both variables.

Suppose instead there is a permanent increase in the share of workers in the research sector, s_R. The results are shown in Figure 4.11. An increase in s_R from $s_{R,0}$ to $s_{R,1}$ shifts the TFP growth line to the left and immediately increases TFP growth. Since the growth rate of TFP exceeds the growth rate of the population, $\frac{L_t}{A_t}$ gets smaller over time and the TFP

Figure 4.9 — TFP growth as a function of the labor-to-TFP ratio.

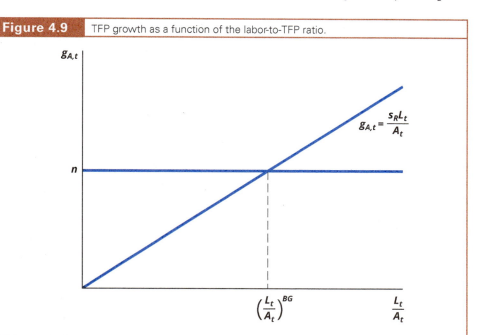

This graph shows how TFP growth is affected by the number of scientists relative to the level of TFP. On a balanced growth path, TFP grows at rate n. The ratio of labor to TFP consistent with the balanced growth path is denoted with a superscript "BG."

Question: What happens to the labor to TFP ratio if the economy starts to the left of the balanced growth path?

Figure 4.10 — The effects of a higher population growth rate on TFP growth.

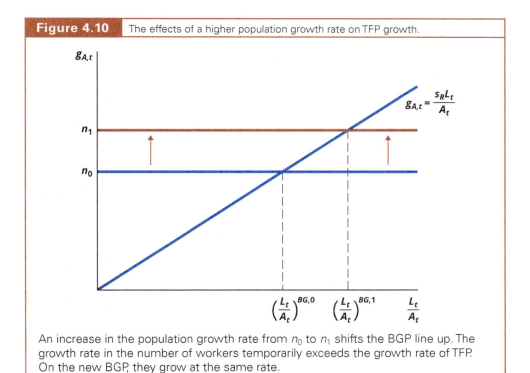

An increase in the population growth rate from n_0 to n_1 shifts the BGP line up. The growth rate in the number of workers temporarily exceeds the growth rate of TFP. On the new BGP, they grow at the same rate.

Question: Draw the time path of the growth rate of output per worker.

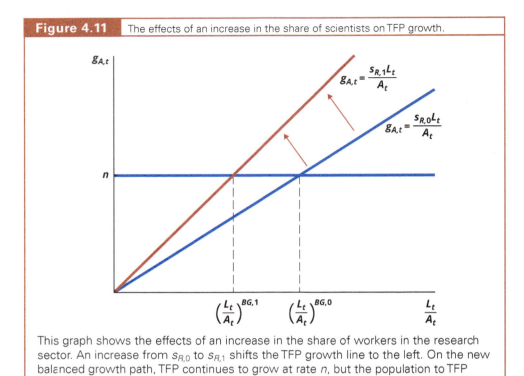

Figure 4.11 The effects of an increase in the share of scientists on TFP growth.

This graph shows the effects of an increase in the share of workers in the research sector. An increase from $s_{R,0}$ to $s_{R,1}$ shifts the TFP growth line to the left. On the new balanced growth path, TFP continues to grow at rate n, but the population to TFP ratio decreases.

Question: Graphically depict a decrease in s_R.

growth rate goes down until it reaches n. Once the TFP growth rate equals n, the population to TFP ratio is at a constant, albeit higher, level. Intuitively, the increase in the share of research scientists increases the number of ideas created. But, as the stock of ideas grows over time, TFP growth falls back to n.

The s_R parameter is of keen interest to economic policymakers. Indeed, there are many programs at the K–12 and college levels that encourage adolescents and young adults to pursue careers in science, technology, engineering, and mathematics, generally referred to as STEM fields. The implication of the model is that encouraging more workers to go into STEM fields will increase the number of new ideas, but not increase the long-run growth rate of idea accumulation. This implication, in and of itself, cannot say whether allocating a greater share of the labor force to STEM fields would be beneficial. If one of these additional scientists discovered the cure for cancer, that would be a profound contribution to humanity, even if the discovery did not lead to new ideas. In other words, economic welfare can be improved by any one idea even if the long-run growth rate doesn't change.

✓ Knowledge Check 4-4

Suppose the idea accumulation equation is given by

$$\frac{A_{t+1} - A_t}{A_t} = \frac{s_R L_t}{A_t}.$$

Assume population grows at rate $n = 0.01$ and $s_R = 0.02$. At $t = 1$, $A_t = 1{,}980$. At $t = 3$, s_R increases to 0.3. Fill in the remainder of the table. Clearly distinguish when the economy is on the balanced growth path.

Continues

Time (t)	L_t	$S_R L_t$	A_t	A_{t+1}	$g_{a,t}$
1	1,000		1,980		
2					
3					
4					

Answers are at the end of the chapter.

Chapter Summary

- Differences in TFP explains most of the cross-country variation in GDP per worker.

- One explanation for these TFP differences is that countries may subsidize or otherwise support inefficient firms and tax or impose regulations on their most efficient firms. These subsidies, taxes, and regulations can distort the allocation of capital and labor across firms. These distortions tend to be quantitatively bigger in developing countries.

- Another explanation for TFP differences is inefficient financial markets. In the absence of well-functioning financial intermediaries, individuals have to rely on their personal wealth to finance their business ideas. In this context, people with good ideas but low levels of wealth don't get to start their businesses or operate on an inefficiently small scale. This lowers TFP in aggregate.

- The concept of growth accounting decomposes growth in output per worker into a part that is explained by changes in the capital to output ratio and a part that is explained by changes in TFP.

- Growth in GDP per worker is mostly explained by TFP growth. This is true in the vast majority of countries over long periods of time.

- In thinking about TFP growth over time, it is most natural to relate TFP to the stock of an economy's ideas.

- If one assumes that ideas are nonrival and that the aggregate production function has constant returns to scale in rival inputs, then perfect competition is unsustainable.

- In a model of endogenous TFP growth, the growth rate of TFP on a balanced growth path is proportional to the population growth rate.

- The difference between "endogenous" and "semi-endogenous" growth models is that the former predicts constant research productivity. The data clearly shows that research productivity is declining. This is true at the level of the aggregate economy and for many individual products.

Key Terms

Total factor productivity, 74
Distortion, 76
Financial intermediary, 79
Asymmetric information, 81

Growth accounting, 82
Idea, 85
Rival good, 85

Review Questions

1. What distinguishes an idea from other economic inputs?
2. Explain how inefficiencies in financial intermediation lead to lower levels of TFP.
3. Why is the capital-to-output ratio instead of capital by itself included in growth accounting exercises?

4. Why does an increase in the population growth rate lead to an increase in the growth rate of TFP? Do you think this is true in all countries? Explain.
5. Compare and contrast the traditional "endogenous" growth model to the "semi-endogenous" growth model.

96 **Part 1** Growth

Problems

4.1 Suppose the aggregate production function is

$$Y_t = A_t K_t^a (e_t P_t)^{1-a},$$

where P_t is the adult population and e_t is the fraction of the adult population that is employed. The number of employed people is $L_t = e_t P_t$.

a. Define output per capita as $y_t = \dfrac{Y_t}{P_t}$. Show that you can write output per capita as

$$y_t = A_t^{\frac{1}{1-a}} \left(\frac{K_t}{Y_t}\right)^{\frac{a}{1-a}} e_t.$$

b. Using the same change of variables as in Equation (5), show that the growth in output per capita is

$$g_y = g_a + g_k + g_e,$$

where g_y is the growth rate of output per capita, g_a is the growth rate of the TFP component, g_k is the growth of the capital to output ratio component, and g_e is the growth rate of the employment rate.

c. Between 1950 and 1990, the employment rate in the United States rose from about 57 percent to 63 percent as more married women entered the labor force. Would omitting the employment rate from the growth accounting equation, raise or lower the contribution attributed to TFP? Explain.

4.2 One problem faced in poor countries is that the most efficient firms are not big enough and inefficient firms are too big. This question investigates the reverse. Namely, can high-TFP firms be too big?

Suppose two firms operate with identical Cobb–Douglas production functions,

$$Y_i = A_i K_i^a L_i^{1-a}.$$

Assume $A_1 = 10$ and $A_2 = 20$. There are 200 total units of labor in the economy and 200 units of capital.

a. Calculate GDP if the capital and labor are divided equally between the firms.

b. Calculate GDP if 75 percent of the capital and labor is allocated to firm 2. Explain the economic intuition of your results.

c. Calculate GDP if 90 percent of the capital and labor is allocated to firm 2. Explain the economic intuition of your results. Can you guess the GDP-maximizing allocation of capital and labor?

d. Suppose the firm-level production function is

$$Y_i = A_i^{1-v} (K_i^a L_i^{1-a})^v$$

where v is a "returns to scale parameter." The logic is that at the level of an individual firm, A_i can be interpreted as managerial quality, which is just another input like capital and labor.

Prove that output at the firm level is constant returns to scale in all three inputs.

e. Redo parts a–c using the modified Cobb–Douglas production function in part d. Explain why it is not optimal for all the inputs to be allocated to firm 2.

4.3 An alternative endogenous growth model is to assume that new ideas are created by R&D spending and not by scientists. The concept is that the economy allocates some GDP to consumption and the rest of it to R&D spending, perhaps on lab equipment. The production function is

$$Y_t = A_t L_t.$$

Assume that population grows at rate $n > 0$. The idea accumulation equation is

$$A_{t+1} - A_t = A_t^b R_t.$$

The economy allocates a constant fraction, s_R, to R&D spending so $R_t = s_R Y_t$.

a. Calculate TFP growth at any point in time.

b. What parameter restriction must be placed on b for a balanced growth path to exist?

c. Assume $b = -1$. Calculate the growth rate of TFP and output per worker on a balanced growth path.

d. Suppose there is a one-time permanent increase in s_R. Describe what happens to the stock of ideas and the growth rate of ideas in the short run and the long run. Hint: You might want to use something like Figure 4.11.

4.4 A slight modification to the idea accumulation equation presented in Section 4.4 is:

$$A_{t+1} - A_t = L_{R,t}^z A_t^b,$$

where $0 < z \le 1$. The accumulation equation in Section 4.4—Equation (11)—is just a special case of this equation when $z = 1$. The idea of allowing z to be less than 1 is that there may be diminishing marginal productivity to researchers. Assume $b < 1$.

a. Derive the growth rate of TFP on a balanced growth path. What happens to the growth rate as z approaches 1? What happens to the growth rate as z approaches 0?

b. Assume $b = 0$ and $z = 1$. Graphically analyze a permanent decrease in the population growth rate. Summarize the short- and long-run effects on TFP and output per capita.

4.5 Suppose the U.S. government considers a massive one-time expansion in high-skilled immigration, with particular emphasis on foreign workers with a graduate degree in a STEM field. You are going to analyze this in the endogenous growth model.

a. What variable does this policy affect?

b. Suppose the idea accumulation equation is identical to Section 3, namely,

$$A_{t+1} - A_t = L_{R,t} A_t^b.$$

Graphically analyze the effects of this policy. What are the short- and long-run implications on the stock of ideas and idea growth?

c. Suppose instead that the idea accumulation equation is

$$A_{t+1} - A_t = L_{R,t} A_t.$$

What are the short- and long-run implications of this policy on the stock of ideas and idea growth?

Knowledge Check 4-1 Answer

First, suppose that labor is divided equally among entrepreneurs. Then $l_i = 1/3$ for each entrepreneur. Aggregate TFP is given by

$$A = \sum_{i=1}^{3} A_i l_i$$
$$= 30(1/3) + 20(1/3) + 10(1/3)$$
$$= 20.$$

Turn to the second allocation, where labor is allocated in proportion to TFP. The first entrepreneur has 1.5 times the TFP of the second entrepreneur and 3 times the TFP of the third entrepreneur. Thus, the labor allocation can be found by solving the following system of equations:

$$l_1 = 1.5 l_2,$$
$$l_1 = 3 l_3,$$
$$l_1 + l_2 + l_3 = 1.$$

Substituting the first two equations into the third gives

$$3 l_3 + 2 l_3 + l_3 = 1.$$

Solving gives $l_3 = 1/6$. This means $l_1 = 1/2$ and $l_2 = 1/3$. Aggregate TFP is given by

$$A = \sum_{i=1}^{3} A_i l_i$$
$$= 30(1/2) + 20(1/3) + 10(1/6)$$
$$= 23.3.$$

Finally, if labor is divided equally amongst the entrepreneurs with positive wealth then

$$A = 20\left(\frac{1}{2}\right) + 10\left(\frac{1}{2}\right) = 15.$$

Aggregate TFP is the highest when labor is allocated in proportion to individual-level TFPs. This is consistent with what we saw in the last section. Aggregate TFP goes up when a greater fraction of resources is allocated highly productive firms and entrepreneurs. Aggregate TFP is the lowest when the most productive entrepreneur doesn't get to operate a business. Since the most talented person in this example also has the lowest wealth, this allocation could be rationalized in an economy afflicted with imperfect financial markets.

Knowledge Check 4-2 Answer

In the economy without distortions, the level of output is higher. Higher levels of output lead to higher levels of investment, which, over time, increase the capital stock. Thus, distortions in a dynamic economy are more costly than distortions in a static economy.

Knowledge Check 4-3 Answer

Imposing the steady state gives

$$k_{ss} = \frac{1}{1+n}[sy_{ss} + (1-d)k_{ss}].$$

Multiplying both sides by $1 + n$ gives

$$k_{ss}(1+n) = sy_{ss} + (1-d)k_{ss}.$$

Next, group the terms involving k_{ss}:

$$k_{ss}(d+n) = sy_{ss}.$$

Finally, rearrange terms to get

$$\frac{k_{ss}}{y_{ss}} = \frac{s}{d+n}.$$

Evaluating this ratio when $n + d = 0.10$ and $s = 0.1$ gives

$$\frac{k_{ss}}{y_{ss}} = \frac{0.1}{0.1} = 1.$$

Evaluating when $s = 0.2$ gives

$$\frac{k_{ss}}{y_{ss}} = \frac{0.2}{0.1} = 2.$$

Evaluating when $s = 0.3$ gives

$$\frac{k_{ss}}{y_{ss}} = \frac{0.3}{0.1} = 3.$$

From this, you can see that the capital-to-output ratio is proportional to the savings rate.

The capital-to-output ratio is independent of TFP in steady state. However, as you saw in Chapter 3, a one-time increase in TFP increases output per worker on impact, but capital per worker doesn't change instantaneously. This means that a one-time increase in TFP lowers the capital-to-output ratio on impact. Over time, capital per worker grows faster than output per worker and the economy converges back to the steady-state ratio.

Knowledge Check 4-4 Answer

The key to answering this question is to use the accumulation equation. Notice that the accumulation equation can be written as

$$A_{t+1} = A_t + s_R L_t.$$

Given that $s_R = 0.02$, the number of researchers is given by

$$s_R L_t = 0.02(1{,}000) = 20.$$

Then it follows that $A_{t+1} = 1{,}980 + 20 = 2{,}000$. The growth rate is given by

$$g_{a,t} = \frac{A_{t+1} - A_t}{A_t} = \frac{2{,}020 - 2{,}000}{2{,}000} = 0.01.$$

Continues

Time (t)	L_t	$s_R L_t$	A_t	A_{t+1}	$g_{a,t}$
1	1,000	20	2,000	2,020	0.01
2	1,010	20.2	2,020	2,040.2	0.01
3	1,020.1	30.6	2,040.2	2,070.8	0.015
4	1,030.3	30.9	2,070.8	2,101.7	0.0149

Since L_t grows at 1 percent per year, $L_2 = (1 + n)L_1 = (1 + 0.01)1,000 = 1,010$. The number of researchers is given by

$$s_R L_t = 0.02(1,010) = 20.2.$$

It follows, that $A_{t+1} = 2,020.2$ and the growth rate is 1 percent. Since the growth rate is constant between periods 1 and 2, the economy is on a BGP.

In $t = 3$, $L_3 = (1 + n)L_2 = (1 + 0.01)1,010 = 1,020.1$. In $t = 3$, the fraction of researchers rises to $s_R = 0.03$. The number of researchers is

$$s_R L_t = 0.03(1,020.1) = 30.6.$$

It follows that $A_{t+1} = 2,070.8$ and the growth rate is 1.5 percent. The economy is now off the balanced growth path. If you do the same calculations for $t = 4$, you find that $g_{a,t} = 0.0149$. Over time, the TFP growth rate settles back to 0.01.

Chapter 5
Money, Prices, and Nominal Interest Rates

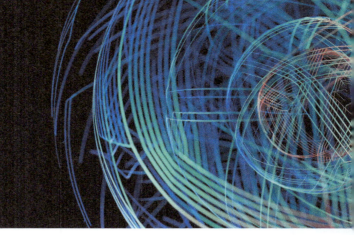

Learning Objectives

5.1 Identify different methods of computing the economy's average price level and inflation rate.

5.2 Explain the three roles of money.

5.3 Distinguish between the different ways of measuring the economy's money supply.

5.4 Derive the relationship between the growth rate of money supply and the inflation rate.

5.5 Analyze the money supply and demand model.

5.6 Discuss the costs of inflation.

As the First World War was declared in 1914, dozens of countries had to choose the way in which to finance their military expenditures. Many countries, like the United States and France, chose to finance the war through taxation. Others, like Germany, chose to borrow from banks and the general population, convinced the loans could be paid back after winning the war.[1]

As you probably know from history class, Germany lost the war and the Treaty of Versailles signed in 1919 compelled the Central Powers—primarily, Germany—to pay reparations to the Allied Powers (France, the United Kingdom, Russia, Italy, Japan, and the United States) to cover damages caused during the war. The debt combined with reparations left Germany in a desperate position. Faced with both these burdens, the German government financed its debts by printing currency. This was a temporary stop gap at best. While about five German marks traded for one U.S. dollar in 1914, by 1923, one U.S. dollar traded for one trillion marks.

The rapid growth of the money supply not only caused inflation but ultimately resulted in hyperinflation, a situation in which prices increase uncontrollably. The effects of hyperinflation can be devastating. In the early 1920s, German citizens took wheelbarrows full of currency to buy a loaf of bread. Citizens who held their wealth in currency or in simple checking accounts saw their life savings almost instantly destroyed. Businesses could not keep up with the constantly changing prices. Hyperinflation, in short, destroyed the German economy.

The case of Germany in the 1910s shows how a certain monetary policy may destroy a country's economy. This chapter investigates the connection between money supply, inflation, and interest rates. You will see that the German example, although extreme, is consistent with economic theory.

---

[1]This example is drawn from https://www.pbs.org/wgbh/commandingheights/shared/minitext/ess_german hyperinflation.html.

5-1 Measuring the Economy's Price Level

Every month, the Bureau of Labor Statistics (BLS) releases a real-time measure of the U.S. economy's **inflation rate**, or the percent change in the average level of prices. While this might sound intuitive, the economy consists of millions of distinct goods and services. How do statistical agencies like the BLS calculate the average level of prices? In what follows, we discuss several of the most popular methods for computing average prices and the inflation rate.

Inflation rate
The percent change in the average level of prices.

5-1a The Consumer Price Index

The BLS computes the **consumer price index (CPI)** every month. The CPI measures the cost of a basket of goods and services purchased by urban consumers. The price of this basket of goods and services is determined in two steps. First, the BLS uses actual purchasing habits of U.S. consumers in urban areas to determine which goods and services should go into the basket. These purchasing habits are also used to determine the weights each good and service should receive. For example, if the average U.S. consumer in urban areas spends $2,000 per month on housing, $1,000 on food and beverages, and $1,000 on transportation, then housing would receive a weight of 50 percent and food and transportation would each receive a weight of 25 percent. Obviously, consumers spend their incomes on many more types of goods and services than these three items. While allocating spending over a greater number of goods and services complicates the analysis, there is no difference conceptually. Also, throughout the chapter, we will use quantity weights as opposed to share weights. This makes the CPI slightly easier to calculate and doesn't qualitatively affect the results.

Consumer price index
The average price of a basket of goods and services purchased by urban consumers.

In the second step, CPI data collectors obtain prices of about 80,000 goods and services by visiting approximately 26,000 retail stores in 87 urban areas. In the context of the previous example, if two components of transportation were oil changes and gasoline, then data collectors would go to various auto shops and gas stations across urban areas in the United States to obtain prices on oil changes and gasoline. Then the data collectors would return to the retail stores either monthly or bimonthly to update the prices.

Finally, with the weights and prices of goods and services determined, the BLS computes the CPI. Formally, the CPI is the ratio of the basket price in current year prices relative to the basket price in base year prices, multiplied by 100. Table 5.1 shows how this works in a simplified economy. To keep things simple, let's focus on two food staples: apples and eggs. The table supposes the average consumer purchases two pounds of apples and three dozen eggs per month.

Because 2022 is the base year, the CPI in 2022 is 100 by construction. The CPI in 2023 is

$$
\begin{aligned}
\text{CPI}_{2023} &= \frac{q_{\text{apple,22}}P_{\text{apple,23}} + q_{\text{egg,22}}P_{\text{egg,23}}}{q_{\text{apple,22}}P_{\text{apple,22}} + q_{\text{egg,22}}P_{\text{egg,22}}} \times 100 \\
&= \frac{2 \times \$2.50 + 3 \times \$4.10}{2 \times \$2 + 3 \times \$4} \times 100 \\
&= \frac{\$17.30}{\$16} \times 100 = 108.13.
\end{aligned}
$$

Table 5.1	Prices and Quantities for Eggs and Apples			
Year	**Apples**		**Eggs**	
	Quantity (pounds)	**Price (dollars per pound)**	**Quantity (dozens)**	**Price (dollars per dozen)**
2022	2	$2	3	$4
2023	1.75	$2.50	3.25	$4.10
2024	2.25	$2.60	3.5	$4.25

Because the CPI is 100 in 2022, the inflation rate between 2022 and 2023 is 8.13 percent. Also note that the price of eggs rose 2.5 percent between 2022 and 2023, while the price of apples rose 25 percent. Because the average consumer spends a greater fraction of their income on eggs, the economy's overall inflation rate is closer to the increase in egg prices.

Next, calculate the CPI in 2024. Continuing to use the quantities from 2022 as the consumption basket, the CPI in 2024 is

$$
\begin{aligned}
\text{CPI}_{2024} &= \frac{q_{\text{apple,22}}P_{\text{apple,24}} + q_{\text{egg,22}}P_{\text{egg,24}}}{q_{\text{apple,22}}P_{\text{apple,22}} + q_{\text{egg,22}}P_{\text{egg,22}}} \times 100 \\
&= \frac{2 \times \$2.60 + 3 \times \$4.25}{2 \times \$2 + 3 \times \$4} \times 100 \\
&= \frac{\$17.75}{\$16} \times 100 = 110.94.
\end{aligned}
$$

This inflation rate is the rate of growth between the CPI in 2024 and 2023, or 2.60 percent. Note that the inflation rate is different than the percentage point change in the CPI between 2024 and 2023, or $110.94 - 108.13 = 2.83$. The lesson here applies more broadly. A change in percentage points is different than the percent change.

5-1b Practical Challenges to Calculating the CPI

The CPI attempts to measure changes in the average level of prices paid by urban consumers. In practice, it faces at least two major challenges.

Recall that the weights in the CPI are constructed using actual spending data by U.S. consumers in urban areas. The base year is the year in which the weights are collected. The weights (and the base year) are updated every two years so that the index captures the evolving spending habits of U.S. consumers. Fixing the weights over the two-year intervals introduces a potential problem that is best illustrated through an example. Suppose a consumer purchases an equal quantity of beef and tofu. Both products are equally weighted in the CPI. Suppose that next year, there is a disruption in the supply chain that reduces the supply of beef by 50 percent and the price skyrockets. Responding to the increase in the price of beef, consumers buy more tofu and less beef. The substitution of tofu for beef changes the composition of the consumption basket such that the price of the new basket (with the lower quantities of beef) increases by less than the fixed-weight basket. The change in price of the fixed-weight basket overstates inflation. Not accounting for the tendency of consumers to substitute away from expensive goods toward cheaper goods increases the CPI. This is called **substitution bias**.

Substitution bias
The error that results from the CPI not accounting for the tendency of consumers to substitute away from expensive goods toward cheaper goods.

The BLS is aware of substitution bias and has taken steps to correct it. The most common correction is to use a chain-weighting technique. To see chain weighting in action, consider the hypothetical economic data in Table 5.2.

The traditional CPI without chain weighting is

$$
\begin{aligned}
\text{CPI}_{2023} &= \frac{q_{\text{beef,22}}P_{\text{beef,23}} + q_{\text{tofu,22}}P_{\text{tofu,23}}}{q_{\text{beef,22}}P_{\text{beef,22}} + q_{\text{tofu,22}}P_{\text{tofu,22}}} \times 100 \\
&= \frac{500 \times \$10 + 500 \times \$3}{500 \times \$5 + 500 \times \$3} \times 100 = 162.5.
\end{aligned}
$$

Table 5.2	Quantities and Prices for Beef and Tofu				
Year	Beef			Tofu	
	Quantity (pounds)	Price (dollars per pound)		Quantity (pounds)	Price (dollars per pound)
2022	500	$5		500	$3
2023	300	$10		700	$3

We conclude that inflation was 62.5 percent between 2022 and 2023. The chain-weighting technique computes an additional measure of the change in the basket price by using 2023 for the weights. Specifically, we have

$$\widetilde{CPI}_{2023} = \frac{q_{beef,23}p_{beef,23} + q_{tofu,23}p_{tofu,23}}{q_{beef,23}p_{beef,22} + q_{tofu,23}p_{tofu,22}} \times 100$$

$$= \frac{300 \times \$10 + 700 \times \$3}{300 \times \$5 + 700 \times \$3} \times 100 = 141.67.$$

Using 2023 quantities implies an inflation rate of 41.67 percent. Chain-weighted CPI is the geometric average of these, or

$$CPI_{CW,2023} = \widetilde{CPI}_{2023}^{0.5} CPI_{2023}^{0.5}$$
$$= 141.67^{0.5} 162.5^{0.5}$$
$$= 151.73.$$

Inflation according to the chain-weighted CPI is 51.73 percent. The chain-weighting approach results in a lower inflation rate because it accounts for consumers substituting away from beef. The chain-weighted CPI more accurately captures the true increase in the price of the consumption basket. In general, chain weighting lowers the inflation rate because it dampens the effect of substitution bias.

The BLS has computed the chain-weighted CPI since 1999. Figure 5.1 compares the year-over-year changes in the chain-weighted CPI to the traditional CPI. The two series closely track each other, but chain-weighted inflation is consistently lower than inflation in the regular CPI. On average, chain weighting reduces the inflation rate by 0.3 percentage points.

Although chain weighting reduces substitution bias, it faces a practical challenge. The weights in the CPI are constructed from the buying habits of U.S. consumers in urban areas. The expenditure data, however, is not collected in real time. The practical implication is that the chain-weighted CPI has to estimate expenditure shares and then revise the measure of inflation for up to two years. These time lags can create difficulties for real-time policy decisions.

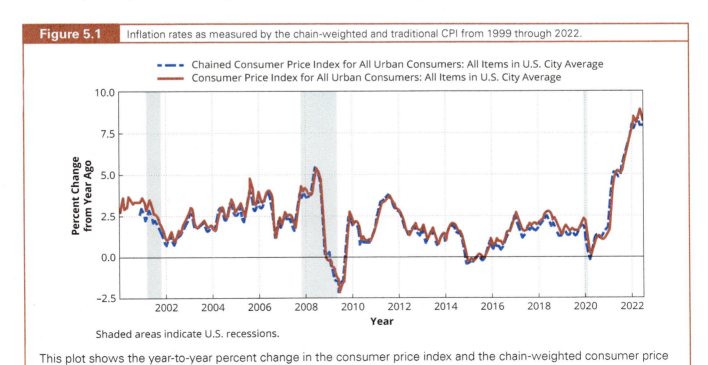

Figure 5.1 Inflation rates as measured by the chain-weighted and traditional CPI from 1999 through 2022.

Shaded areas indicate U.S. recessions.

This plot shows the year-to-year percent change in the consumer price index and the chain-weighted consumer price index between 2000 and 2022.

Source: St Louis FRED and BLS.

The second challenge to calculating the CPI is that not all goods and services stay in the market forever. Imagine a BLS data collector records the price of an iPhone every month at the Apple store. In January through May, the statistician records the price of the latest iPhone model. Suppose that in June, Apple replaces the old iPhone with a new model that comes with a 10 percent higher price tag. Is it correct to say that the price of phones went up 10 percent? The new model surely has more memory, better image quality, and other superior features compared to the old model. Yes, the price of the iPhone went up 10 percent, but the quality of the iPhone improved as well. Simply saying that the price of the iPhone increased by 10 percent would overstate inflation.

The BLS incorporates the value of quality improvements by estimating the value of each component of a product and then adjusting the price of the new product accordingly. For example, if the price of the new iPhone is $100 higher than the old iPhone, but the added memory of the new model is worth $50, then the quality-adjusted price of the iPhone increases by only $50. Adjusting for quality differences is easier for the iPhone than other goods and services. For instance, if a restaurant raises its menu prices after switching to organic vegetables, then, unless the data collector is especially trained to look at ingredient quality, the higher prices won't be correctly attributed to superior vegetables.

5-1c The CPI versus the GDP Deflator

In addition to the CPI, there are other ways to measure changes in prices. Perhaps the most common alternative is the GDP deflator, which you saw in Chapter 1. There are a number of conceptual differences between the CPI and the GDP deflator. First, the GDP deflator incorporates the value of all goods and services included in GDP, whereas the CPI includes goods and services purchased by consumers. Consequently, the price of investment goods appears in the GDP deflator, but not the CPI; whereas the price of imports consumed by individuals in the United States appears in the CPI, but not the GDP deflator. Since the price of investment goods, especially computers and software, has not risen as quickly as the price of consumer goods, inflation implied by the GDP deflator will be lower than the CPI.

Another difference between the CPI and the GDP deflator is that the CPI weights each product with fixed expenditure shares that are updated every two years, whereas the GDP deflator uses fixed prices across years and allows quantities to vary.

We can examine the consequences to the differences in weighting by returning to the beef and tofu example in Table 5.2 (repeated here for reference).

Nominal GDP in 2023 is

$$NGDP_{23} = q_{beef,23}p_{beef,23} + q_{tofu,23}p_{tofu,23}$$
$$= 300 \times \$10 + 700 \times \$3 = \$5,100.$$

Using 2022 as a base year, real GDP in 2023 is

$$RGDP_{23} = q_{beef,23}p_{beef,22} + q_{tofu,23}p_{tofu,22}$$
$$= 300 \times \$5 + 700 \times \$3 = \$3,600.$$

The GDP deflator is the ratio of nominal GDP to real GDP:

$$Deflator_{23} = \frac{NGDP_{23}}{RGDP_{23}} \times 100$$
$$= \frac{\$5,100}{\$3,600} \times 100$$
$$= 141.67.$$

Table 5.2					
Year	Beef			Tofu	
	Quantity (pounds)	Price (dollars per pound)		Quantity (pounds)	Price (dollars per pound)
2022	500	$5		500	$3
2023	300	$10		700	$3

Figure 5.2 Inflation rates as measured by the CPI and GDP deflator form 1960 through 2021.

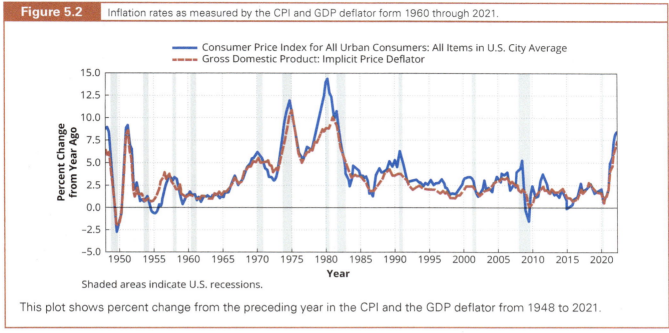

Shaded areas indicate U.S. recessions.

This plot shows percent change from the preceding year in the CPI and the GDP deflator from 1948 to 2021.

Source: St Louis FRED and BLS.

The inflation rate implied by the GDP deflator is therefore 41.67 percent, which is lower than the 62.5 percent implied by the CPI. The reason again is that the CPI does not incorporate the response of consumers to the higher prices. You should also note that the equation for the GDP deflator is identical to the equation for the CPI when 2023 quantities are used as the base year. This won't be true in general, as the deflator and the CPI measure inflation over a different set of goods and services.

As Figure 5.2 shows, the deviations between the CPI and GDP deflator can be quite substantial. In the 1980s, for instance, the growth rate in the CPI exceeded the growth rate in the deflator by close to six percentage points. The difference has gotten smaller over time and chain weighting the CPI and the GDP deflator reduces the difference even more.

In practice, the most appropriate measure of inflation depends on the question being asked. If you are concerned about price changes faced by the average urban American consumer, then the chain-weighted CPI is the best choice. If you are concerned about price changes across all goods and services produced in the United States, then the deflator is the right way to go.

Application 5.1 shows the difference the choice of price index can make when interpreting economic data.

✓ Knowledge Check 5-1

Consider the following economic data from 2022 and 2023. The economy produces apples and tractors domestically and imports cheese from France.

	Apples Quantity (pounds)	Apples Price (dollars per pound)	French cheese Quantity (pounds)	French cheese Price (dollars per pound)	Tractors Quantity	Tractors Price
2022	1,000	$2	500	$8	10	$4,000
2023	1,250	$2.50	300	$12	15	$3,800

Calculate the inflation rate from the GDP deflator and CPI using 2022 as the base year. Also, calculate the inflation rate using the chain-weighted CPI.

Answers are at the end of the chapter.

Application 5.1

Have Wages Increased?

Are workers paid more today than they were 40 years ago? You would think that would be a straightforward question to answer. And if we were only concerned about nominal earnings, or earnings expressed in current dollars, then the answer, as Figure 5.3 shows, would be a resounding yes. The earnings of the median worker in the United States rose from less than $300 per week in 1979 to nearly $1,000 by 2021.

The increase in nominal earnings, however, does not tell us if workers are better off today compared to 40 years ago. The reason is that prices of goods and services have also increased. If wages double, but the cost of living triples, workers are worse off. To get a better sense of the change in the purchasing power of earnings, we need to look at real earnings. Real earnings are the ratio of nominal earnings to a price index. If nominal earnings rise faster than the price index, then the purchasing power of workers increases.

Economic researchers and policymakers commonly look at two price indexes. One is the CPI, which was discussed in the last section. Another is the personal consumption expenditures (PCE) price index published by the Bureau of Economic Analysis. The PCE is actually the Federal Reserve's preferred measure of prices. The CPI differs from the PCE in a number of ways. First, the PCE is a chain-weighted index with a construction similar to the GDP deflator. This reduces the effects of substitution bias in the PCE. Second, the weights in the CPI come from household surveys, while the PCE weights come from surveys of US businesses. Because the response rate is higher for businesses than households, the prices found in the PCE may be more representative of the entire economy. Finally, the coverage is different. The CPI includes goods and services directly purchased by consumers in urban areas, whereas the PCE includes purchases made for consumers by third parties. Employer-provided health insurance premiums are an example of this. In total, the PCE has a broader scope than the CPI.[2]

Figure 5.4 compares the cumulative growth in real earnings from using the PCE and CPI as the price index. According to the CPI, real earnings fell between 1979 and 2000. Earnings did not consistently grow until about 2015. The PCE, on the other hand, shows consistent growth in real earnings. According to the PCE, real earnings were about 20 percent higher in 2015 than in 1979, whereas they did not grow at all over this time frame according to the CPI.

Consequently, the question of whether workers are better off today than 40 years ago does not have a simple answer. Although the CPI may be superior for obtaining real-time data, the PCE is better at dealing with substitution bias and incorporating goods and services purchased by all consumers, not just those in major metro areas.

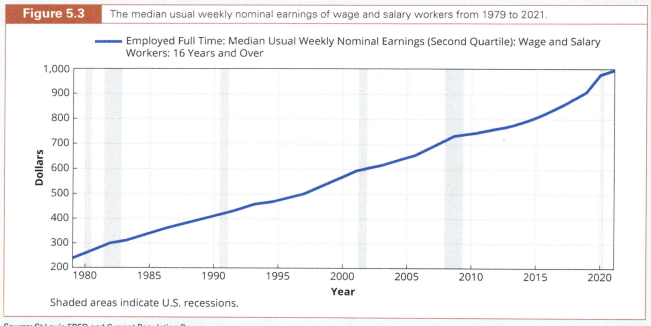

Figure 5.3 The median usual weekly nominal earnings of wage and salary workers from 1979 to 2021.

Shaded areas indicate U.S. recessions.

Source: St Louis FRED and Current Population Survey.

[2] A more detailed explanations of the differences can be found here: https://www.bea.gov/system/files/papers/P2007-4.pdf.

■ Continues

Application 5.1 (Continued)

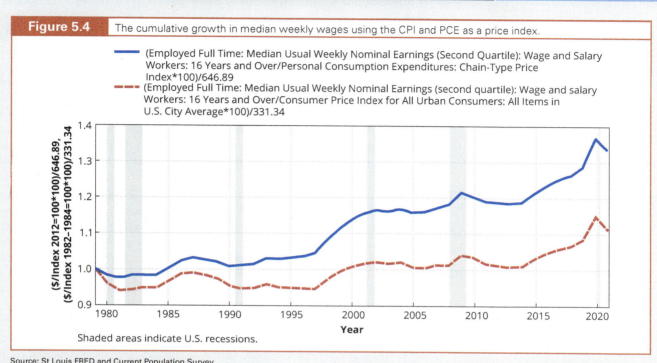

Figure 5.4 The cumulative growth in median weekly wages using the CPI and PCE as a price index.

Shaded areas indicate U.S. recessions.

Source: St Louis FRED and Current Population Survey.

5-2 Defining, Measuring, and Analyzing Money

We usually think about money as the currency in our wallets or the balance in our checking accounts. But for people in German POW camps during World War II, exchanging with these conventional forms of money was out of the question. The economics of exchange in POW camps was eloquently explained by economist R. A. Radford's article "The Economic Organisation of a P.O.W. Camp."[3] During the war, Red Cross volunteers provided prisoners with basic provisions, including biscuits, milk, chocolate, and cigarettes. Although the prisoners couldn't exchange with the usual forms of money, they could exchange the provisions themselves. Over time, cigarettes emerged as a de facto currency because they were easy to store and divide. Even nonsmokers valued cigarettes because they could be traded for other food items. Soon the prices of items were quoted in terms of cigarettes. The price of a chocolate bar, for instance, may have been two cigarettes. Prices could fluctuate based on the preferences of the current prisoners.

Despite the impressive sophistication of the POW economy, exchange in modern economies is even easier. We basically take it for granted that everyone agrees on an acceptable form of currency and that the currency is universally accepted. But what are the roles of money? What makes some forms of money preferable to other forms of money?

5-2a The Roles of Money

Money is an asset that can be exchanged for goods and services. In everyday life, we might make purchases with physical currency in our wallets or by swiping our debit cards. We will think about what money is by focusing on the roles of money. Traditionally, economists have enumerated three functions for money:

---
[3]Radford, R. A. 1945. "The Economic Organisation of a P.O.W. Camp." *Economica*, 12(48): 189–201.

108   Part 2 Classical Theory

Store of value
An asset that preserves at least some of its value over time.

Unit of account
Anything that can be used to quote the prices of goods and services.

Medium of exchange
Anything that can be used to trade for goods and services.

1. Money is a **store of value**, meaning that it preserves at least some of its value over time. This allows people to store their wealth in money. The existence of inflation implies that the value of a given quantity of money declines over time.

2. Money is a **unit of account**, which means the prices of goods and services can be quoted in terms of money. A consistent unit of account vastly simplifies economic calculations. When you go to a grocery store, the price of everything is quoted in dollars. One pound of green beans might cost 2 dollars, and a pound of fresh basil might cost 12 dollars. If the grocery store manager wanted to confuse everybody, the price of a pound of basil could be quoted as six pounds of green beans, which is equivalent to the price of 12 dollars. However, it would be really inconvenient to think about the price of basil in terms of green beans or the price of a candy bar in terms of toilet paper. Quoting all prices in terms of money solves this calculation problem.

3. Money is a **medium of exchange**, meaning that one can trade money for goods and services. Of course, goods and services can be directly exchanged for other goods and services. This is called a *barter economy* and it is usually very inefficient. To see why, think about an example. Suppose you grow corn, and your friend grows apples. If you want some apples and your friend wants some corn, the two of you can figure out fair terms of exchange. But say you want apples and your friend hates corn and only eats zucchini. Then, you need to find someone who harvests zucchini and wants to trade zucchini for corn.

    This three-good example is relatively complicated—now, imagine doing it for any one of thousands of goods and services that are traded in the economy. Searching for trading partners would consume a significant amount of time that could otherwise be spent on production or leisure. Money solves this problem. In the example above, you could purchase apples with money from your corn-hating friend who could then use the money to purchase zucchini or some other garden staple.

Commodity money
A type of money with intrinsic value.

Fiat money
A type of money with no intrinsic value.

Historically, there have been two forms of money. The cigarettes cited at the beginning of this section are an example of **commodity money**. Other common forms of commodity money include salt, livestock, and precious metals. This form of money has intrinsic value. Cigarettes can be smoked, livestock can be eaten, and precious metals can be displayed. Modern economies like the United States' rely on **fiat money**, which has no intrinsic value. Rather, fiat money is valuable because the government declares it to be valuable and people believe it.

Commodity money has some serious problems. First, commodity prices fluctuate based on supply and demand for the particular commodity. If there is a gold rush, the price of everything quoted in gold will increase. The variation in prices creates confusion among market participants. Second, some commodities do not store well. Avocados, to the frustration of many grocery shoppers, only retain their value for a short amount of time, so it would be difficult to use them as a reliable form of currency. Third, many types of commodities vary in quality. Perhaps the livestock at one farm is of a higher quality than the livestock at a neighboring farm. This makes it difficult to value goods and services in terms of livestock. Lastly, some forms of commodity money may be imperfectly divisible. If chickens are the form of commodity money, it would be difficult to exchange one-quarter pound of chicken legs for a pack of gum.

Fiat money solves these problems but comes with some of its own. Fiat money retains its value insofar as people believe that other people (and the government) will accept it. Also, because governments usually control the supply of fiat money, they may find it advantageous to print more money to pay off their debts. Even in countries with low rates of money growth, this is an implicit tax on citizens who hold money. In countries with high rates of money growth, such as Germany in the 1920s, fiat systems can totally collapse. On net, however, modern economies have found it beneficial to use fiat money systems.

Recently, cryptocurrencies such as Bitcoin have gained in popularity. Application 5.2 evaluates the characteristics of these cryptocurrencies.

Chapter 5 Money, Prices, and Nominal Interest Rates

Application 5.2

Is Bitcoin Money?

Bitcoin is a form of digital currency that started in 2009. Since that time, Bitcoin has grown in popularity among investors. But can Bitcoin, and other forms of cryptocurrencies, function well as money? Could a cryptocurrency ever come to replace the U.S. dollar?

First, a little background. Bitcoin is the most popular type of cryptocurrency or currency based in cryptology, or the science of encryption. When anyone starts a Bitcoin account, they receive an anonymized and unique private key from which they can send and receive Bitcoin. Although people in the United States mostly transact with digital money, such as using a debit card, cryptocurrencies are distinct because the records aren't recorded at any financial institution. There is a public ledger of all Bitcoin transactions, but only the user's Bitcoin address is displayed in the ledger. The public ledger prevents double spending but keeps transactions functionally anonymous. Unlike the supply of traditional fiat currencies, the supply of cryptocurrency is decentralized, meaning that it is not controlled by a government or central bank. Instead, the supply of Bitcoin increases through users solving cryptographic puzzles. This is called *mining*.

Does Bitcoin satisfy the criteria of money? Anyone can invest in Bitcoin, making it a store of value. But Bitcoin's short history shows that it is an unstable store of value. In May 2021, one Bitcoin traded for nearly $60,000. A month later, the price decreased to about $35,000. This is equivalent to approximately 64,000 percent annualized rate of inflation. There have been other times where the value of Bitcoin increased tremendously. This volatility may make Bitcoin a good speculative investment, but it is not a risk-free way to store wealth. Consequently, Bitcoin cannot be viewed as a reliable store of value.

Although it's virtually unheard of to see grocery store prices quoted in Bitcoin, it would be perfectly feasible to do so. At the time this book is being written, the price of an avocado is about $1 and one unit of Bitcoin costs $19,133. The grocery store could simply say that one avocado costs 1/19,133 units of Bitcoin. Perhaps customers would get used to it if every grocery store quoted prices in Bitcoin, but that convention is far from established. Moreover, the costs to businesses associated with constantly updating prices could be prohibitive. Thus, cryptocurrencies cannot currently be viewed as a commonly accepted unit of account.

This brings us to the third point: assessing Bitcoin's ability to serve as a medium of exchange. While Bitcoin's acceptance among U.S. retailers is fairly novel, that may be changing. A 2022 report by the consulting firm Deloitte estimated that 75 percent of retailers plan on accepting cryptocurrency over the next five years.[5] Bitcoin's anonymity also appeals to users who wish to transact in private. Still, it is unlikely that in five years the general public will buy cryptocurrencies to be used in routine transactions.

In summary, Bitcoin, to some degree, satisfies each of the three criteria defining money. Bitcoin was the first established cryptocurrency. Since 2009, several rival cryptocurrencies have emerged, such as Ethereum and Tether. Although it is not obvious that any of them will outperform traditional currency and demand deposits, the adoption of cryptocurrencies will likely continue to increase. Their increased prevalence presents potential challenges to central banks in measuring and managing the money supply. You can see this in the way the monetary aggregates are constructed in the United States. Neither M1 nor M2 includes digital currency. If these currencies become more popular in transacting, then traditional measures of the money supply will become less informative to the Fed when they are making monetary policy decisions.

[5]The report is here: https://www2.deloitte.com/content/dam/Deloitte/us/Documents/technology/us-cons-merchant-getting-ready-for-crypto.pdf.

5-2b Measuring the Money Supply

You might think that one could add all the money circulating in the economy to get a measure of the money supply. It turns out, however, that measuring the money supply isn't a simple task. People routinely transact through electronic payment methods, and these aren't tangible like the paper currency in your wallet. Since funds in your checking account satisfy the three necessary roles of money—medium of exchange, unit of account, and store of value—it often makes sense to include them in the definition of the money supply.

Accordingly, the most restrictive definition of the money supply only includes currency. Currency is the paper money and coins circulating in the economy at any given time. M1 includes currency and the funds in checking accounts, often referred to as demand deposits. As of June 2022, there was about $2.5 trillion of currency circulating in the United States, and M1 was about $20.5 trillion. This implies that the quantity of checkable deposits approximately equaled $18 trillion.

We can be broader still. In addition to transacting with debit cards, people frequently move funds from their savings account to their checking account. Even if you can't directly transact from your savings account, you can quickly transfer funds between accounts from your phone. M2 is M1 plus savings deposits, certificates of deposit, and money market mutual funds, which are financial instruments against which checks can be written. M2 was about $21.67 trillion in June 2022, implying that there is a little more than $1 trillion in savings accounts and money market mutual funds.

What distinguishes these definitions of money supply is the **liquidity** of the assets that are included. Liquidity refers to the ease with which assets can be used in exchange. By definition, currency is the most liquid asset since it is "payable for all debts public and private" (which is written on all forms of U.S. currency). Demand deposits can usually be used directly in transactions and are otherwise quickly converted to currency, making them only a little less liquid. Savings deposits and money market mutual funds are even less liquid since they often cannot be used directly in transactions.

Figure 5.5 shows the trends in the quantity of currency, M1, and M2 from 1959 to 2022. All three series have trended up over time, with a particularly large spike in M1 during 2020. The spike in M1 was caused by the Federal Reserve expanding the money supply at the start of the Covid-19 pandemic. The figure also shows that the difference between M1 and M2 significantly shrank during 2020. This was a consequence of the Fed's removing a banking regulation that required banks to allow no more than six transfers per month between a person's savings account and their checking account.[4] After this regulation was removed, banks were free to report savings accounts as a demand deposit or a "transaction account" in the language of the regulation. Evidently, most banks chose to relabel savings accounts after this regulation was removed. Economically speaking, banks and depositors now see savings accounts and demand deposits as nearly indistinguishable.

Liquidity
The ease with which assets can be used in exchange.

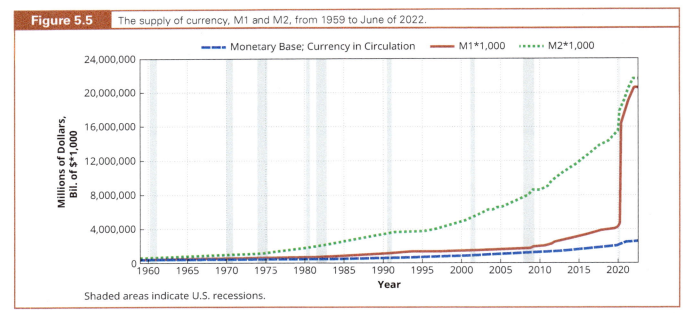

Figure 5.5 The supply of currency, M1 and M2, from 1959 to June of 2022.

Shaded areas indicate U.S. recessions.

Source: St Louis FRED and Federal Reserve Board of Governors.

5-2c The Quantity Theory of Money

We have discussed money in this section and prices in the previous one. How are the two connected? That's exactly what the quantity theory of money is designed to address. The quantity theory starts with the equation

$$M_t V_t = P_t Y_t. \tag{1}$$

Starting with the right-hand side of this equation, P_t is the price level and Y_t is the level of real GDP. The product of the price level and real GDP is nominal GDP. On the left-hand side, M_t is the money supply, and V_t is the velocity of money. The **velocity** of money is the number of times the average unit of money is used in a transaction. To take a simple example, suppose a \$100 bill is used to purchase five dozen doughnuts from a local baker. Then the baker spends the \$100 bill at the dentist. Nominal GDP in this example is \$200. The money supply is \$100 and velocity is equal to two since the \$100 bill was used twice.

Velocity
The number of times the average unit of money turns over.

The quantity equation is actually an identity. An identity is an equation that always holds. If one of the variables change, then the value of another variable has to change to preserve the equality. The quantity equation tells us the connection between the money supply and the price level. Holding velocity and real GDP constant, an increase in the supply of money increases the price level.

Is it realistic to think that real GDP and velocity are not affected by changes in money supply? Before John Maynard Keynes authored *The General Theory of Employment, Interest, and Money* during the heights of the Great Depression, most economists subscribed to the **classical dichotomy**. The classical dichotomy states that real variables are determined independently of nominal variables. Since velocity and real GDP are real variables, the classical dichotomy implies that both variables are determined independently of the money supply.

Classical dichotomy
A theory that predicts that real variables are determined independently of nominal variables.

A lot has happened in the 86 years since Keynes's book was published. In particular, the general consensus among macroeconomists is that the classical dichotomy is a good approximation in the long run, but not in the short run. We return to the subject of how money supply might influence real GDP over the short run in Section 3 of the textbook. For now, let's proceed under the assumption the classical dichotomy is a good representation of the economy in the long run.

It is easier to analyze the long-run consequences of the money supply on the price level by restating the quantity Equation (1) in terms of growth rates. Recall the rule, also discussed in the Mathematical Appendix, that the growth rate of a product is the sum of the growth rates. Applying this rule to both sides of Equation (1) gives

$$g_{m,t} + g_{v,t} = \pi_t + g_{y,t}. \tag{2}$$

In words, the growth rate of the money supply, $g_{m,t}$, plus the growth rate of velocity, $g_{v,t}$, equals inflation, π_t plus the growth rate of real GDP, $g_{y,t}$. Moreover, if the growth rate of velocity is constant, then Equation (2) delivers a clear prediction for inflation. Imposing $g_v = 0$ gives

$$\pi_t = g_{m,t} - g_{y,t}. \tag{2'}$$

Inflation equals the growth rate of the money supply minus the growth rate of real GDP. Over the long run, the growth rate of real GDP is determined by factors discussed in Section 1 of the book that are, consistent with the classical dichotomy, independent of the level or growth rate of the money supply. According to the quantity theory (with constant velocity), inflation occurs when growth in the money supply exceeds real GDP growth.

---

[4]More information can be found here: https://fredblog.stlouisfed.org/2021/01/whats-behind-the-recent-surge-in-the-m1-money-supply/.

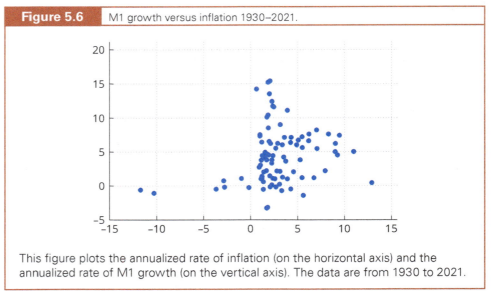

Figure 5.6 M1 growth versus inflation 1930–2021.

This figure plots the annualized rate of inflation (on the horizontal axis) and the annualized rate of M1 growth (on the vertical axis). The data are from 1930 to 2021.

Source: St Louis FRED. BEA, and Federal Reserve Board of Governors.

How well does the quantity theory explain the data? Figure 5.6 shows the relationship between growth in the money supply (measured as M1) and inflation in the United States, where each dot represents a year. The scatter plot shows a positive, albeit weak, relationship with a correlation coefficient at about 0.2. Evidently, the quantity theory explains only some of the variation in the data.

The quantity theory can also be analyzed across countries. Figure 5.7 plots the average rate of inflation from 2012 to 2020 against the average rate of money supply growth for all available countries. The variables are highly correlated with a correlation coefficient of about 0.8.

The evidence presented above can be summarized as follows. There is a high correlation between inflation and the growth rate of the money supply on average and over long periods of time. However, over short horizons, the growth rates of money supply, inflation, real GDP, and even velocity aren't constant, which produces a smaller correlation between inflation and money supply growth in the short run.

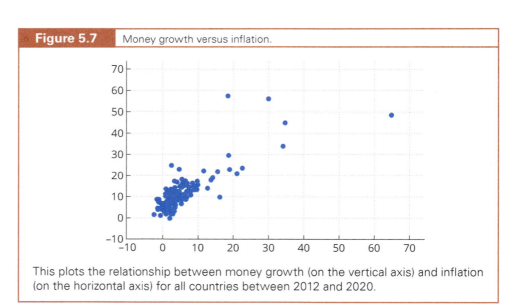

Figure 5.7 Money growth versus inflation.

This plots the relationship between money growth (on the vertical axis) and inflation (on the horizontal axis) for all countries between 2012 and 2020.

Source: WDI.

Chapter 5 Money, Prices, and Nominal Interest Rates **113**

✓ Knowledge Check 5-2

Using Equation (2), fill in the missing values in the table below.

$g_{m,t}$	$g_{v,t}$	$g_{y,t}$	π_t
3%	0%	1%	
	2%	6%	4%
	4%	−2%	−3%
5%	2%		6%
7%		4%	4%

Answers are at the end of the chapter.

5-3 The Costs of Inflation

You now know how to measure inflation and have learned a theory on the origins of inflation. But why spend the time studying inflation at all? Does inflation entail social costs? In the case of the German hyperinflation discussed in the chapter's opener, the costs of inflation are very transparent. High and accelerating rates of inflation made it impossible to plan financially over any time horizon. The currency that people held one day was worthless the next day. Hyperinflation, in short, can destroy an economy. More moderate rates of inflation still have social costs, but they aren't quite as obvious or damaging to the economy.

5-3a Inflation Is a Tax

If you start the year with $100 in a checking account and the inflation rate is 5 percent, you have $95 of purchasing power by year's end. In other words, the wealth in your checking account lost 5 percent of its value. This example holds more generally. Inflation erodes the value of currency and demand deposits and therefore acts as an implicit tax. Unlike the taxes you pay on your wage or capital income, the IRS doesn't collect the inflation tax. Instead, inflation chips away at wealth stored in non-interest-bearing investments.

Who collects the revenue from the inflation tax? The government usually. In some countries the government controls the central bank and can directly finance its spending by printing money. In countries like the United States, the central bank is independent of the federal government. However, the Fed can create money and use it to purchase bonds issued by the government. If the increase in money supply causes inflation, then the real value of the government's debt decreases.

5-3b Inflation Imposes Shoe Leather Costs

Before the advent of debit cards, if people wanted cash, they'd have to physically go the bank to make a withdrawal. If you happened to live in an economy with high inflation during these times, you would want to balance the convenience of making transactions with cash or a check versus protecting the value of your wealth. More wealth stored in currency or a checking account meant more convenience but also a higher inflation tax. People balanced this trade-off by making frequent trips to the bank to transfer money from their interest-bearing savings accounts to non-interest-bearing checking accounts. If people walked to the bank to make these transactions, they would wear their shoes out. Hence the name, "shoe leather costs."

In modern times, inflation doesn't wear out our shoes, but it still entails time costs. Instead of physically going to a bank, people can digitally transfer money between their checking account and whatever interest-bearing securities they own. These transfers sometimes incur fees and can take days to process. The time and money associated with these transfers

Figure 5.8 German currency being prepared for burning.

Albert Harlingue/Roger Viollet/Getty Images

are costs of inflation. These costs are quite large in countries with hyperinflation, as discussed in the chapter's introduction. Simply buying a loaf of bread in the 1920s in Germany required citizens to accurately forecast the change in prices for that day. Leftover cash from earlier in the week was worthless and, as Figure 5.8 shows, used as kindling to start fires.

5-3c Unexpected Inflation Redistributes Income

Professional athletes often sign multiyear contracts worth a fixed nominal amount of money. LeBron James, for instance, signed a two-year $85 million-dollar contract in 2022 that pays $41 million in the first year and $44 million in the second. The first thing that should jump out at you is that it is much more lucrative to be a star professional athlete than an economist. But the more important thing is that the real value of LeBron's contract depends on what happens to prices. If the price level doubles in the second year of his contract, the real value of LeBron's year-two salary is only $22 million. The purchasing power of LeBron's salary is conditional on the future value of the price level.

More generally, any fixed nominal contract is susceptible to inflation risk. If you agree to an annual salary in January expecting inflation to be 2 percent over the next 12 months and it ends up being 4 percent, you lose and your employer wins. If inflation happens to be 1 percent, you win, and your employer loses.

Unexpected inflation also helps debtors at the expense of lenders. Imagine a homebuyer takes out a mortgage at a 5 percent nominal interest rate, expecting inflation to be 2 percent. If inflation happens to be 10 percent, then the borrower compensates the lender with dollars that are less valuable than anticipated. Thus, inflation that is higher than anticipated helps borrowers and hurts lenders. This logic also holds in reverse. Inflation that is lower than anticipated helps lenders at the expense of borrowers. In the previous example, if actual inflation were 1 percent, then the borrower compensates the lender with dollars that are more valuable than anticipated.

One way to deal with unexpected inflation is to make real-value contracts instead of nominal contracts. In the example of wage negotiation, perhaps you and your employer agree to link your monthly wage to the CPI. If the CPI increases 2 percent in one month, then your monthly salary goes up by 2 percent. You could imagine mortgage contracts working in a similar way.

Chapter 5 Money, Prices, and Nominal Interest Rates 115

There are real-world examples of real-valued contracts. Treasury inflation-protected securities (TIPS) are a type of bond issued by the U.S. government, the principal value of which is linked to the CPI. Social security benefits increase with inflation and a number of states index their minimum wages to the CPI. At the same time, real-valued employment contracts are less common. Perhaps this is because inflation, at least in recent history, has been relatively low in the US. It could also be due to employees really hating the idea of a nominal wage cut in the event of deflation.

5-3d Inflation Distorts Relative Prices

Food trucks are popular attractions in city parks. Imagine a city park with a food truck selling pad Thai on the north end of the park and another food truck selling hot dogs on the south end. Ordinarily, a plate of pad Thai sells for $16, and a hot dog sells for $2. The relative price of a plate of pad Thai is eight hot dogs. But imagine the monetary policymaker expands the money supply in such a way as to double the general price level. The owner of the hot dog food truck brings a marker and changes the price of hot dogs on the menu to $4. If the owner of the pad Thai food truck doesn't bring a marker, or is otherwise unaware of the increase in the general price level, pad Thai prices stay at $16. Now a plate of pad Thai sells for four hot dogs. Despite no change in the economic fundamentals, inflation reduces the price of pad Thai relative to hot dogs. Since consumers respond to relative prices, it follows that the demand for the products will also change.

This example is simple but has broad implications. First, information doesn't spread equally across decision makers in the economy. Many businesses have large analytic departments that predict how changes in macroeconomic variables will affect the demand for their products and the cost of their inputs. Gathering this information and making these predictions isn't free. And some businesses might invest more in information acquisition than others. Given the information lag of some businesses, a change in the aggregate price level will have asymmetric effects across businesses.

Another observation is that businesses, by and large, do not continuously update their product prices. Even if firms knew the aggregate price level was going to increase by 1 percent, it may not make sense to mark all their prices up by 1 percent. The reason is that updating prices consumes resources. Think about all the price tags at Home Depot or Lowes. Yes, individual prices get regularly updated, but changing the price of every product whenever inflation jumps up or down by a little bit, would be a huge drain on productivity. These big stores will allow the relative price of their products to change to avoid the big fixed cost of updating their prices.

✓ Knowledge Check 5-3

Suppose an employer and employee are negotiating a three-year contract. They both expect the inflation rate to be 2 percent per year. Compute the real wage in all three years for three different scenarios: their expectations are correct (column 4), the actual inflation rate is 1 percent (column 5), and the actual inflation rate is 4 percent (column 6). In the scenarios where the actual inflation rate differs from the expected inflation rate, explain who wins and who loses.

	Nominal wage	Expected price deflator	Expected real wage	Actual real wage 1	Actual real wage 2
			$\pi = 2\%$	$\pi = 1\%$	$\pi = 4\%$
Year 1	$100,000	100			
Year 2	$105,000	102			
Year 3	$110,025	104.04			

Answers are at the end of the chapter.

5-4 The Supply of Money, the Demand for Money, and Nominal Interest Rate Determination

Nominal interest rate
the percentage return in dollars one gets from investing.

Federal funds rate
The nominal interest rate banks charge each other for overnight loans.

Recall from principles of macroeconomics that a **nominal interest rate** is the percentage return in dollars one gets from investing. If you put a dollar in a savings account that pays a 5 percent interest rate per year, then by the end of the year, you have $1.05. Interest rates hit all-time lows in the aftermath of the Great Recession of 2007–2009. Figure 5.9 shows that the **federal funds rate**, which is the nominal interest rate banks charge each other for overnight lending, was effectively zero from 2010 to 2016. An implication of near-zero interest rates is that it is essentially free to store your wealth in cash rather than an interest-bearing investment. Every dollar you hold in your wallet could have instead been invested into a bond, or some other financial instrument, that earns interest. But if interest rates are zero, then there is no incentive for you to move wealth out of your wallet or checking account and into something that pays interest. This section analyzes the connection between money supply, money demand, and interest rates.

5-4a The Supply and Demand of Money

The federal funds rate shown in Figure 5.9 is the primary interest rate that the Federal Reserve targets when making monetary policy decisions. The central bank's balance sheet and policy tools are discussed in detail in Chapter 15, but for now we consider a simplified version of monetary policy.

The Fed primarily controls the money supply by the interest rate it pays on reserves. Unlike the federal funds rate, which is determined in the market, the interest rate on bank reserves is directly set by the Fed. When the Fed lowers the interest rate on reserves, banks find it optimal to decrease reserves and increase lending. This expands the overall money supply. Symmetric logic implies that an increase in the interest rate on reserves reduces the money supply.

The demand for money can be motivated as follows. Whether it be in the form of paper currency, debit cards, or Venmo, people find it optimal to use money in making some transactions. Importantly, the amount of money that one wishes to hold depends on the price

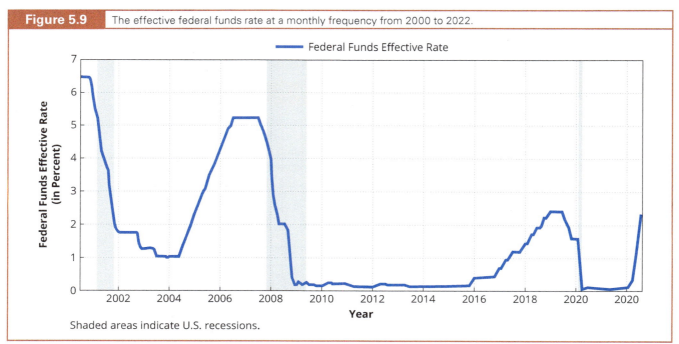

Figure 5.9 The effective federal funds rate at a monthly frequency from 2000 to 2022.

Shaded areas indicate U.S. recessions.

Source: St Louis FRED and Federal Reserve Board of Governors.

level in the economy. If the price level is high, a given quantity of money buys fewer goods and services. Thus, people make decisions over the quantity of real money balances or $\frac{M}{P}$, where P is the economy's price level.

The demand for real money balances is a function of the nominal interest rate and one's level of real income. The reason why money demand depends on the nominal interest rate was mentioned above. The nominal rate is effectively the opportunity cost of holding money. One additional dollar in your checking account is one less dollar in an interest-bearing investment. If the nominal rate increases, holding money becomes costlier in terms of foregone interest. Money demand also depends on real income. If income increases, then people will want to make more transactions and more transactions require more money. Thus, the money demand function can be summarized as

$$\frac{M}{P} = M^d(i, Y), \tag{3}$$

where i is the nominal interest rate, Y is the level of real income, and $M^d(i, Y)$ is a function that depends negatively on i and positively on Y.

Money supply is exogenously set by the Fed, so

$$M^s = \overline{M} \tag{4}$$

where $\overline{M}$ represents a fixed quantity of money. To keep things as simple as possible, assume that real income and the price level are exogenous variables. The model is summarized in Table 5.3.

5-4b Graphical Derivation of the Equilibrium Nominal Interest Rate

Now that we have established where the supply and demand for money comes from, the goal is to understand how a change in money supply affects the nominal rate. To that end, we can graph the supply and demand of money with real money balances on the horizontal axis and the nominal interest rate on the vertical axis. Figure 5.10 shows how this works. The supply of money is fixed and exogenous, but the demand for money is downward sloping in the nominal interest rate. The equilibrium nominal interest rate, i^*, is determined where money supply intersects with money demand.

Start by considering an increase in the money supply from M_0 to M_1. This is shown in Figure 5.11. The increase in money supply shifts the supply of real money balances to the right. At the initial equilibrium nominal interest rate, i_0^*, people want to hold M_0 units of money, not M_1. The only way to convince people to hold the greater stock of money is for the opportunity cost of holding money, the nominal interest rate, to decline. Thus, in equilibrium, nominal interest rates decline. We now have derived the connection between money supply and nominal interest rates. If the Fed wants to target a lower nominal interest rate, they must increase the money supply.

Suppose instead that real income increases. With higher levels of income, people demand higher levels of real money balances. This shifts the money demand curve to the right, as shown in Figure 5.12. Since the money supply is fixed, equilibrium requires that the nominal interest rate must increase. The equilibrium nominal interest rate rises from i_0^* to i_1^*.

Table 5.3	Summary of the Money Supply and Demand Model	
Endogenous variables		**Exogenous variables**
i		**M, P, Y**

Key equations:

1. $\dfrac{M}{P} = M^d(i, Y)$ (Money demand equation)

2. $M^s = \overline{M}$ (Money supply equation)

Figure 5.10 The equilibrium nominal rate occurs where the supply and demand curve intersect.

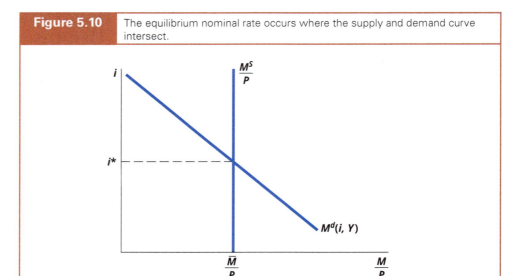

This plot shows how the equilibrium nominal interest rate is determined. The demand for real money balances depends negatively on the nominal interest rate. The supply of real money balances is independent of the nominal interest rate.

Figure 5.11 The effects of an increase in money supply.

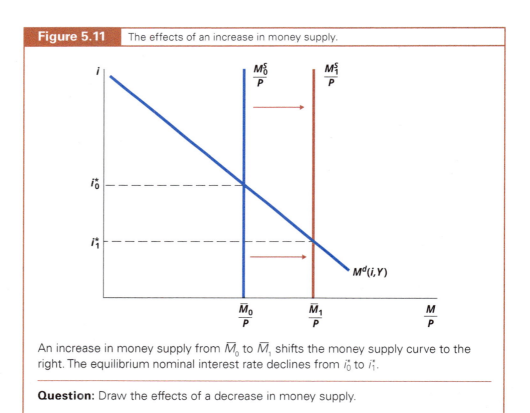

An increase in money supply from $\bar{M}_0$ to $\bar{M}_1$ shifts the money supply curve to the right. The equilibrium nominal interest rate declines from i_0^* to i_1^*.

Question: Draw the effects of a decrease in money supply.

Figure 5.12 The effects of an increase in real income.

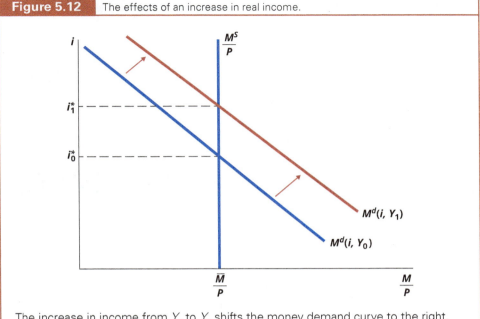

The increase in income from Y_0 to Y_1 shifts the money demand curve to the right. The nominal interest rate increases from i_0^* to i_1^*.

Question: How would the central bank change the money supply to keep the interest rate constant at i_0^*?

✓ Knowledge Check 5-4

Suppose that earned interest is taxed at rate t, making the after-tax return on investment income $(1 - t)i$. Show how the introduction of this tax affects the equilibrium nominal interest rate.

Answers are at the end of the chapter.

Chapter Summary

- The change in the economy's average price level is called the inflation rate. Two of the most common measures of inflation are the consumer price index (CPI) and GDP deflator.

- Because the CPI uses a fixed basket of goods and services to measure inflation, it does not account for consumer's substitution away from more expensive products. This is called substitution bias. Chain-weighting reduces the magnitude of substitution bias.

- Money is an asset that serves as a unit of account, store of value, and medium of exchange.

- Modern economies use fiat money, which has no intrinsic value. Fiat money is valuable because the government declares it to be valuable and people believe that it will be accepted. Economies historically relied on commodity money, such as gold or silver, which has intrinsic value.

- There are different ways of measuring the economy's money supply, with each definition broadening in what it includes as money. Currency includes physical coins and bills only. M1 includes demand deposits plus currency. M2 is M1 plus savings deposits and money market funds.

- The quantity theory of money builds off the identity that nominal GDP equals the amount of money circulating in the economy multiplied by velocity, or the number of times the average unit of money turns over. If velocity is constant, the economy's inflation rate equals the growth rate of the money supply minus GDP growth.

- The supply of money is set by the central bank. The demand for money depends positively on real income and negatively on the nominal interest rate.

- The equilibrium nominal interest rate is determined by the intersection of money supply and demand. The equilibrium nominal rate is a positive function of real income and a negative function of the money supply.

- There are several costs to inflation: inflation is a tax, inflation imposes shoe leather costs, inflation redistributes income, and inflation distorts relative prices.

120 **Part 2** Classical Theory

Key Terms

Inflation rate, 101
Consumer price index, 101
Substitution bias, 102
Store of value, 108
Unit of account, 108
Medium of exchange, 108
Commodity money, 108

Fiat money, 108
Liquidity, 110
Velocity, 111
Classical dichotomy, 111
Nominal interest rate, 116
Federal funds rate, 116

Review Questions

1. Describe some of the shortcomings of the CPI.

2. How is a barter economy different from an economy with money? Which system is more efficient?

3. What are the strengths and weaknesses of a fiat money system?

4. Explain the distinction between currency, M1, and M2. How did this distinction change after 2020?

5. What are the costs of inflation?

6. Why is money demand defined over real money balances as opposed to nominal money balances?

Problems

5.1 Suppose an economy produces tomatoes and X-ray machines. Consumers import sauerkraut from Germany.

Year	Tomatoes (in pounds)		German sauerkraut (in pounds)		X-ray machines	
	Quantity	Price	Quantity	Price	Quantity	Price
2022	8,000	$3	6,000	$4	10	$4,000
2023	10,000	$3.25	5,500	$7	12	$3,800
2024	11,000	$3.40	6,000	$5	13	$3,700

a. Compute the economy's inflation rate for 2023 and 2024 using the CPI and 2022 as a base year.

b. Compute the economy's inflation rate for 2023 and 2024 using the CPI and 2023 as a base year. Does the choice of the base year make a difference?

c. Compute the economy's inflation rate for 2023 and 2024 using the GDP deflator and 2022 as a base year. Does using the GDP deflator make a difference?

5.2 Suppose an economy produces pumpkin pies and smart phones. The data for 2022 and 2023 are shown below.

Year	Pumpkin pie		Smart phones	
	Quantity	Price	Quantity	Price
2022	10,000	$10	100	$1,000
2023	12,000	$12	125	$1,100

a. Calculate the economy's inflation rate using the CPI and 2022 as the base year.

b. Suppose that the smart phone manufacturer introduced a new model of phone in 2023. The new model has 512 gigabytes of storage, whereas the previous model had only 256 gigabytes of storage. They are otherwise identical. Researchers at the BLS know that people are willing to

pay $0.25 for every additional gigabyte of storage. What is the quality-adjusted price of smart phones in 2023?

c. Redo part a, but now with the quality-adjusted price of iPhones. How does accounting for changes in quality affect the economy's inflation rate?

5.3 Consider the money demand equation:

$$\frac{M}{P} = Yi^{-b},$$

where $b > 0$.

a. Show that this equation is identical to the quantity equation of money, Equation (1) in the text, if velocity is equal to i^b.

b. How does velocity depend on the nominal interest rate? Explain the economic intuition for this.

5.4 Suppose the money supply equation is given by:

$$M^s = \overline{M}.$$

The money demand equation is given by:

$$\frac{M}{P} = M^d(i, Y).$$

Chapter 5 Money, Prices, and Nominal Interest Rates　**121**

a. How does the money demand function depend on the nominal interest rate and real income? Explain the economic intuition for each of these.

b. Graphically depict the determination of the equilibrium nominal interest rate.

c. Graphically show how an increase in the price level affects the nominal interest rate. Explain the economic intuition.

d. The demand for money increases when there is more uncertainty in the financial system. For instance, if investors are pessimistic about the stock market, they will sell stocks and hold money. Suppose f is an exogenous variable indexing the uncertainty in financial markets. The money demand function is now

$$\frac{M}{P} = M^d(i, Y, f).$$

How does an increase in f affect money demand and the nominal interest rate?

5.5 Section 5.3d discussed why some firms do not immediately adjust their prices in response to a change in the aggregate price level. Economists have studied this formally using menu-cost models. The idea behind the menu-cost model is that there are fixed costs to updating prices. In a literal sense, there are costs to reprinting menus (even if an employee has to update the website and QR code). This question walks through a simple menu-cost model.

a. Suppose profit for a firm is given by

$$profit = N(p - c).$$

Here, N is the number of units sold, p is the price per unit, and c is the cost per unit. Under what condition does the firm make a positive profit?

b. Now suppose the economy's inflation rate is $\pi > 0$. The firm does not have control over its costs, which adjust automatically with inflation, but it does set its price. If the firm chooses to update its price, it must pay a fixed cost of F. This is the menu cost. If the firm chooses not to update its price, profit is given by

$$profit = N(p - c(1 + \pi)).$$

If the firm chooses to update its price, profit is given by

$$profit = N(p(1 + \pi) - c(1 + \pi)) - F.$$

Derive a condition under which the firm chooses to update its price. How does it depend on $N, \pi, p, c,$ and F? Comment on the economic intuition.

c. At any given time, some firms will find it optimal to raise their prices and others will find it optimal to wait. What will happen to the demand for the firms that don't update their prices?

✓ Knowledge Check 5-1 Answer

The first thing to note is that the French cheese will not be included in the GDP deflator because it wasn't produced in the United States. Tractors will not be included in the CPI because they aren't a consumer good.

Let's start by calculating the GDP deflator. Nominal GDP in 2023 is

$$NGDP_{23} = q_{apples,23}p_{apples,23} + q_{tractors,23}p_{tractors,23}$$
$$= 1{,}250 \times \$2.50 + 15 \times \$3{,}800$$
$$= \$60{,}125.$$

Real GDP using 2022 as the base year is

$$RGDP_{23} = q_{apples,22}p_{apples,23} + q_{tractors,22}p_{tractors,23}$$
$$= 1{,}250 \times \$2 + 15 \times \$4{,}000$$
$$= \$62{,}500.$$

The GDP deflator is the ratio of nominal GDP to real GDP:

$$Deflator_{23} = \frac{NGDP_{23}}{RGDP_{23}} \times 100$$
$$= \frac{\$60{,}125}{\$62{,}125} \times 100$$
$$= 96.2.$$

The deflator implied inflation rate is -3.8 percent.

The CPI using 2022 as the base year is

$$CPI_{23} = \frac{q_{apples,23}p_{apples,22} + q_{cheese,23}p_{cheese,22}}{q_{apples,22}p_{apples,22} + q_{cheese,22}p_{cheese,22}} \times 100$$

$$= \frac{1{,}000 \times \$2.50 + 500 \times \$12}{1{,}000 \times \$2 + 500 \times \$8} \times 100$$

$$= 170.$$

Thus, the inflation rate implied by the CPI is 70 percent.

Finally, to compute chain-weighted CPI, we first have to calculate the CPI using 2023 as the base year.

$$\widetilde{CPI}_{23} = \frac{q_{apples,23}p_{apples,23} + q_{cheese,23}p_{cheese,23}}{q_{apples,22}p_{apples,23} + q_{cheese,22}p_{cheese,23}} \times 100$$

$$= \frac{1{,}250 \times \$2.50 + 300 \times \$12}{1{,}250 \times \$2 + 300 \times \$8} \times 100$$

$$= 137.25.$$

Taking the geometric average of the two CPIs, chain-weighted CPI is

$$CPI_{CW,2023} = \widetilde{CPI}_{2023}^{0.5} CPI_{2023}^{0.5}$$

$$= 137.25^{0.5} 170^{0.5}$$

$$= 152.75.$$

The inflation rate implied by the chain-weighted CPI is 52.75 percent. This is a lower inflation rate than the CPI without chain weighting. Chain-weighted CPI accounts for consumers reducing their demand for French cheese due to the price increase.

✓ Knowledge Check 5-2 Answer

Equation (2) is

$$g_{m,t} + g_{v,t} = \pi_t + g_{y,t}.$$

Each row of the table provides three values. You can use this equation to solve for the fourth. For instance, in the first row, you have

$$3\% + 0\% = \pi_t + 1\%.$$

Solving for inflation gives $\pi_t = 2\%$. Following this procedure for the rest of this table gives

$g_{m,t}$	$g_{v,t}$	$g_{y,t}$	π_t
3%	0%	1%	2%
8%	2%	6%	4%
−9%	4%	−2%	−3%
5%	2%	1%	6%
7%	1%	4%	4%

✓ Knowledge Check 5-3 Answer

If actual inflation matches expectations, then the expected real wage is the nominal wage divided by the price deflator multiplied by 100. We need to construct the price deflator in the other two cases. When inflation is 1 percent, the deflator in Year 2 is 100 × 1.01 = 101. In Year 3, the deflator is 101 × 1.01 = 102.01. The real wage is the ratio of the nominal wage and the price deflator. When inflation is 4 percent, the deflator is Year 2 is 100 × 1.04 = 104 and the deflator in Year 3 is 108.16. The real wage is the ratio of the nominal wage and the price deflator. The real wage figures are shown below.

	Nominal wage	Expected price deflator	Expected real wage	Actual real wage 1 $\pi = 1\%$	Actual real wage 2 $\pi = 4\%$
Year 1	$100,000	100	$100,000	$100,000	$100,000
Year 2	$105,000	102	$102,941	$103,960	$100,961
Year 3	$110,025	104.04	$105,753	$107,875	$101,724

When inflation is lower than expected, the employee wins and the employer loses. When inflation is higher than expected, the employee loses and the employer wins.

✓ Knowledge Check 5-4 Answer

A tax on interest income lowers the opportunity cost of holding money. This shifts the money demand curve to the right. In equilibrium, the pre-tax nominal rate rises. This is shown in Figure 5.13.

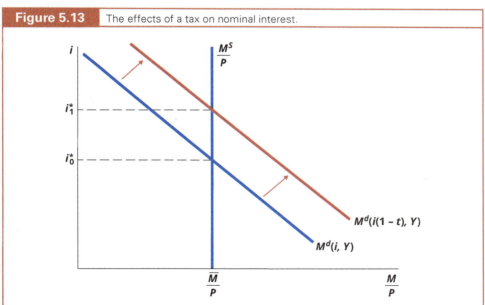

Figure 5.13 The effects of a tax on nominal interest.

The introduction of the tax shifts the money demand curve to the right. In equilibrium, the nominal interest rate rises from i_0^* to i_1^*.

Chapter 6

Saving, Investment, and the Real Interest Rate

Learning Objectives

6.1 Explain the connection between nominal interest rates, real interest rates, and inflation.

6.2 Accurately draw and label budget constraints and indifference curves.

6.3 Solve for the optimal quantities of current and future consumption.

6.4 Explain how changes to exogenous variables affect consumption.

6.5 Qualitatively derive the investment demand curve.

6.6 Graphically depict the equilibrium real interest rate in the savings and investment model.

Living as a college student isn't always luxurious, especially if you live on campus. Living spaces tend to be cramped, and the food can leave you craving McDonalds. At the same time, if you're reading this textbook, you will hopefully find college worth the investment. This is understandable, as college graduates earn a sizeable wage premium. Moreover, your current level of consumption, including tuition, food, rent, and transportation, likely exceeds your current income. Thinking many decades down the road, the same can be said for retirement. During retirement your income goes to close to zero, but it's not as if you stop consuming.

Economists have developed models of consumption and savings to think about these issues. A key insight is that people smooth their consumption over their lifecycle. So, while income is very low during college, high during years in the labor force, and low again in retirement, consumption is relatively smooth. Forward-looking individuals anticipate predictable events like education and retirement and adjust their consumption and savings plans accordingly. True, not all changes in income are predictable, and consumption adjusts in response to those changes. This chapter introduces you to the way economists formalize these ideas.

In addition to income, interest rates play a critical role in consumption-savings decisions. The returns to saving are higher when interest rates increase. Interest rates also affect the investment decisions of firms and business owners. When interest rates are high, borrowing for new investments is expensive. By combining the demand for investment and the supply of savings, we can think about equilibrium real interest rates. You will learn how to graphically derive equilibrium interest rates in this chapter, as well as the factors that affect equilibrium.

6-1 Real Interest Rates and Nominal Interest Rates

Let's say you are thinking about depositing some money into a savings account. By depositing $100 today, you will receive $105 one year from now. Is this a good investment? Let's say prices rise by 5 percent over the course of the year. Then your $105 can really only purchase $100 worth of goods and services in terms of today's prices. If prices stay constant, then you can afford 5 percent more goods and services next year. The same nominal return of $5 yields a different real return in these two circumstances. Whether or not a $5 return is a good or a bad investment depends on what happens to the price level.

As you learned in the chapter on money, prices, and nominal interest rates, the nominal interest rate is the rate of return in terms of dollars. The **real interest rate** reflects the purchasing power value of the interest paid on investment. Intuitively, the real interest rate is the return on an investment in terms of goods and services. If, as in the last example, the nominal interest rate is 5 percent and prices stay constant, then the real interest rate is also 5 percent. If prices increase by 5 percent, then you have no more purchasing power at the end of the year than you did at the beginning of the year.

Real interest rate
The rate of return in terms of goods and services.

Rational households and firms use the real interest rate in making their economic decisions. Calculating the real interest rate requires knowledge of the nominal interest rate and a forecast of how the price level will change. The next section shows the connection between the three variables.

6-1a The Fisher Equation

Let's generalize the example of the $100 deposit decision. If a person invests P_t dollars at the beginning of the year and earns a nominal interest rate of i_t, the person ends the year with $P_t(1 + i_t)$ dollars. If the price level is P_{t+1} the next year, the return in constant purchasing power terms, i.e., the real interest rate, is

$$1 + r_t = \frac{(1 + i_t)}{P_{t+1}^e} P_t. \tag{1}$$

The price level in $t + 1$ is unknown from the perspective of year t and therefore has an "e" superscript to denote an expectation. Since P_{t+1}/P_t is one plus the growth rate of prices, or inflation, we can write Equation (1) as

$$1 + r_t = \frac{(1 + i_t)}{(1 + \pi_{t+1}^e)}, \tag{1'}$$

where π_{t+1}^e is the expected inflation rate. As long as the nominal interest rate and expected inflation rate are sufficiently small, Equation (1') can be approximated as

$$r_t = i_t - \pi_{t+1}^e. \tag{2}$$

The real interest rate is the difference between the nominal interest rate and the expected inflation rate. This is known as the **Fisher equation**, named after economist Irving Fisher (1867–1947). Intuitively, the Fisher equation says that when you save one dollar, the nominal interest rate you earn compensates you for expected inflation and for delaying consumption for a year. The real interest rate in Equation (2) is sometimes referred to as the *ex-ante real interest rate*, because it is the real interest rate that prevails before inflation in $t + 1$ is realized. The *ex-post real interest rate* is the real interest rate that is computed after inflation in $t + 1$ is realized, or $r_t = i_t - \pi_{t+1}$. For example, if the nominal interest rate is 6 percent and expected inflation is 3 percent, then the ex-ante real interest rate is 3 percent. If inflation turns out to be 5 percent, then the ex-post real interest rate is $6 - 5 = 1$ percent.

Fisher equation
An equation that shows that the real interest rate equals the nominal interest rate minus expected inflation.

The Fisher equation makes some interesting predictions that can be compared to the data. Recall that the classical dichotomy introduced in Chapter 5 says that real variables are determined independently of nominal variables. It was argued in the last chapter that the classical dichotomy is a good approximation of the economy in the long run. In the context of the Fisher equation, the classical dichotomy theorizes that the real interest rate is independent of the nominal rate and expected inflation. We might furthermore expect that over long time horizons, expected inflation is approximately equal to actual inflation. The logic is that economic forecasters might get expected inflation wrong in any given month or year but will eventually update their expectations to minimize mistakes. Thus, we can write a version of Equation (2) that we expect to hold in the long run,

$$i = \bar{r} + \pi. \tag{2'}$$

The bar over the real interest rate, $\bar{r}$, indicates that it is determined independently of nominal factors in the long run. Equation (2') says that a one percentage point increase in an economy's long-run inflation rate should translate into a one percentage point increase in the nominal interest rate.

Figure 6.1 shows the relationship between the five-year moving average of the inflation rate as measured by the annual percent growth in the GDP deflator and the federal funds rate from 1960 to 2016 in the United States. A moving average is a technique used to extract the long-run component of a data series. So, the 1960 observation for inflation is really the average inflation rate from 1955 to 1965. The 1961 observation for inflation is the average inflation rate from 1956 to 1966 and so on.

There is a strong positive relationship between the nominal rate and inflation. When the inflation rate rises, the nominal rate also rises. The correlation coefficient is about 0.83, which is very high. This lends strong support for the long-run view of the classical dichotomy. Also, observe that from about 2010 onward, the inflation rate has exceeded the nominal rate, which implies that the real interest rate has been negative over this time. We return to the topic of negative real interest rates later in the chapter.

We can also examine the Fisher equation from a cross-country perspective. Figure 6.2 shows the relationship between inflation rates and nominal interest rates for 149 countries from 2005 to 2019. Again, there is a strong positive relationship between the nominal rates and inflation, with a correlation coefficient of about 0.8.

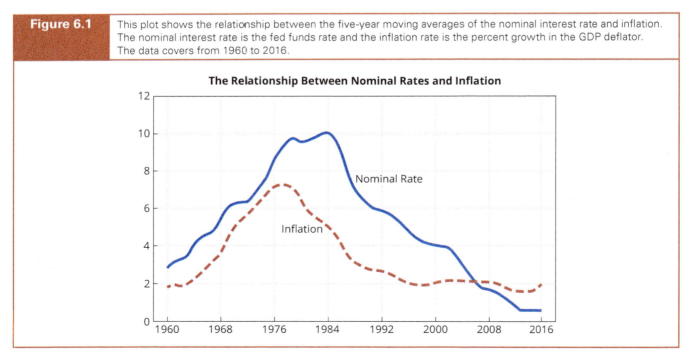

Figure 6.1 This plot shows the relationship between the five-year moving averages of the nominal interest rate and inflation. The nominal interest rate is the fed funds rate and the inflation rate is the percent growth in the GDP deflator. The data covers from 1960 to 2016.

Source: FRED.

Figure 6.2

Relationship between a country's inflation rate, as measured by the GDP price deflator, and the nominal interest rate, as measured by the deposit rate. Each data point is an average from 2005 to 2019.

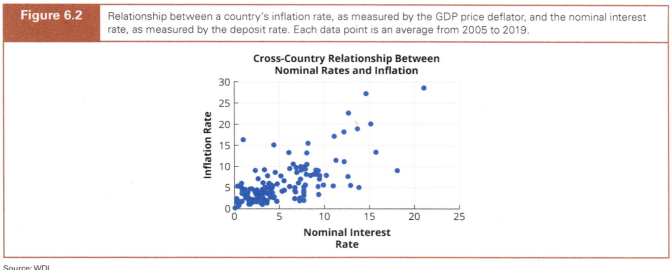

Source: WDI.

Having established the relationship between nominal interest rates, real interest rates, and expected inflation, the rest of this chapter discusses how the real interest rate affects the consumption-savings decisions of households and the investment decisions of firms.

✓ Knowledge Check 6-1

Suppose a home buyer, anticipating a 2 percent inflation rate, takes out a mortgage with a 5 percent nominal interest rate. What is the real interest rate of the mortgage? If the inflation rate turns out to be 5 percent, what is the ex-post real interest rate, i.e., the real interest rate after future inflation has been realized? Does the unexpected inflation help the home buyer or the lender?

— Answers are at the end of the chapter.

6-2 Consumption-Savings Decisions

Chances are you are reading this textbook in a college-level macroeconomics class. One of the reasons you are attending college is to increase your earnings potential in the future. This may entail borrowing in the present to earn a higher income in the future. Some of that borrowing not only finances your tuition and textbooks but also goes toward your living expenses, such as rent and food. That is, despite earning no income or very little income, you are still consuming. Borrowing in the present is economically justified because of the promise of a higher income stream in the future. When a student graduates from college, they can pay back their debt and start saving for retirement.

The foundations of modern consumption-savings theory in macroeconomics are very similar to this microeconomic example. Individuals anticipate their future income stream to the best of their abilities and then make consumption and savings decisions in light of those expectations. The remainder of this section covers the details of a model of consumption and savings. Because the decisions of how much to save and consume occur through time, the model is intertemporal. That means the model must cover a time frame longer than one time period. In the interest of ease of exposition, we will focus primarily on the simplest intertemporal model, the two period case.

6-2a Budget Constraints

We assume that an individual lives for two periods, t and $t + 1$. You can think of these periods as years, but really, they could be anything, e.g., months, decades. The individual earns an income of Y_t in period t and an income of Y_{t+1} in period $t + 1$. In period t, the person

128 **Part 2** Classical Theory

decides how much of their income to consume and how much to save. Formally, this can be written in terms of a budget constraint,

$$C_t + S_t = Y_t. \tag{3}$$

Here, C_t is consumption and S_t is savings. Since a person might find it optimal to borrow in the first period (like our college student in the section's introduction), it is possible for S_t to be less than zero. So, if $S_t > 0$, then the individual is saving. If $S_t < 0$, then the individual is borrowing. Recall that the real interest rate on borrowing and saving is r_t. As discussed in the first section, it is the real interest rate that is relevant for consumption and savings decisions.

The budget constraint in period $t + 1$ is

$$C_{t+1} = Y_{t+1} + S_t(1 + r_t). \tag{4}$$

Equation (4) says that second period consumption is the sum of second period income, first period savings, and interest income from savings, $S_t r_t$. If the individual borrowed in the first period, then $S_t r_t < 0$ is what the individual pays in interest.

Notice that S_t appears in both budget constraints. The problem can be simplified by combining Equations (3) and (4) to eliminate S_t. Solving for S_t in Equation (4) gives

$$S_t = \frac{C_{t+1} - Y_{t+1}}{1 + r_t}.$$

Substituting this into Equation (3) gives

$$C_t + S_t = Y_t$$

$$\Leftrightarrow C_t + \frac{C_{t+1} - Y_{t+1}}{1 + r_t} = Y_t$$

$$\Leftrightarrow C_t + \frac{C_{t+1}}{1 + r_t} = Y_t + \frac{Y_{t+1}}{1 + r_t}. \tag{5}$$

Present discounted value
The denomination of future goods and services in terms of present goods and services.

Equation (5) is called the *intertemporal budget constraint*. It links current and future consumption to current and future income. The left-hand side is consumption in period t plus the **present discounted value** of consumption in period $t + 1$. The present discounted value denominates $t + 1$ consumption in terms of period t prices. This might seem counterintuitive at first, as prices haven't been mentioned. Think about the individual's consumption-saving decision from the perspective of period t. Consuming one additional unit means saving one less unit. That one unit of saving in period t could have purchased $(1 + r_t)$ units of period $t + 1$ consumption. Therefore, the price of one unit of period t consumption is $(1 + r_t)$ units of period $t + 1$ consumption. Dividing, or discounting, C_{t+1} by $1 + r_t$ states current and future consumption in terms of the same prices. By similar logic, the right-hand side of Equation (5) can be interpreted as the present discounted value of lifetime income.

Figure 6.3 depicts the budget constraint graphically. Period t consumption is plotted on the horizontal axis and $t + 1$ consumption is plotted on the vertical axis. If the individual consumes only in the first period, then from Equation (5), $C_t = Y_t + \frac{Y_{t+1}}{1 + r_t}$. Intuitively, the individual can consume all of their income today plus the present discounted value of their future income. In this case, the person would borrow $\frac{Y_{t+1}}{1 + r_t}$ in period t and repay $(1 + r_t)S_t = (1 + r_t)\frac{Y_{t+1}}{1 + r_t} = Y_{t+1}$ in period $t + 1$. Alternatively, if the individual only consumes in the future, then income in period t is saved and has a future value of $(1 + r_t)Y_t$ in period $t + 1$. That means the total value of resources for period $t + 1$ consumption is $Y_t + (1 + r_t)Y_{t+1}$. Since additional unit of period t consumption means forgoing $(1 + r_t)$ units of period $t + 1$ consumption, the slope of the budget line is $-(1 + r_t)$. In summary, the budget line shows all feasible pairs of C_t and C_{t+1} given current income, future income, and the real interest rate.

Figure 6.3

Consumption in period *t* is plotted on the horizontal axis and consumption in period *t*+1 is plotted on the vertical axis. The slope of the budget line is $-(1 + r_t)$.

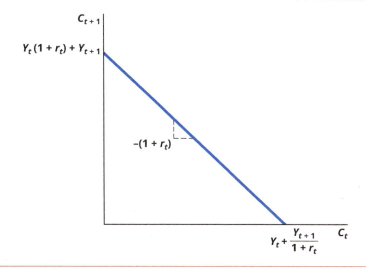

Question: Label the point on the budget constraint where savings equals zero.

The budget line shifts in response to changes in income or the real interest rate. Figure 6.4 shows an increase in current period income from $Y_{0,t}$ to $Y_{1,t}$. The horizontal intercept shifts to the right, and the vertical intercept shifts up. Because the price of one unit of current consumption is still $1 + r_t$ units of future consumption, the new budget line has the same slope as the original. With the higher level of lifetime income, the individual can afford more current and future consumption. Applying the same logic, an increase in future income is conceptually identical to the increase in current income.

Figure 6.4

An increase in period *t* income from $Y_{0,t}$ to $Y_{1,t}$ shifts the budget constraint to the right. The new budget constraint has the same slope as the original budget constraint.

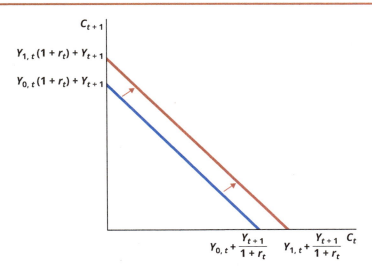

Question: Graphically depict a decrease in current-period income.

> **Figure 6.5** An increase in the real interest rate from $r_{0,t}$ to $r_{1,t}$ pivots the budget constraint clockwise. The horizontal intercept shifts in and the vertical intercept shifts up. The new budget constraint is steeper than the original.

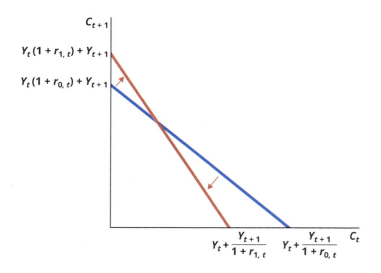

Question: Graphically depict a decrease in the real interest rate.

Figure 6.5 shows an increase in the real interest rate. Since the price of period t consumption is $1 + r_t$ units of future consumption, an increase in the real interest rate raises the price of current consumption. Another way to view it is that one additional unit of period $t + 1$ consumption means forgoing $\frac{1}{1 + r_t}$ units of period t consumption. So, an increase in $1 + r_t$ lowers the price of future consumption. In other words, an increase in the real interest rate simultaneously raises the returns to savings and raises the costs of borrowing. This is graphically depicted by the budget line rotating clockwise. The horizontal intercept shifts in and the vertical intercept shifts up.

Analyzing Figure 6.5, it isn't clear whether the individual has more or fewer resources after the increase in the real interest rate. Notice that the new and old budget line intersect at one point. That is, there is exactly one consumption bundle that is feasible under both interest rates. That point must be where the individual neither saves nor borrows, or $C_t = Y_t$ and $C_{t+1} = Y_{t+1}$. If the original (C_t, C_{t+1}) pair was to the northwest of the intersection point, then $C_t < Y_t$, meaning that the person was saving before the real interest rate increased. Since $r_t S_t$ is the return on savings, an increase in the real interest rate expands lifetime resources for savers. On the other hand, if the original (C_t, C_{t+1}) pair was to the southeast of the intersection point, then $C_t > Y_t$ meaning the person was borrowing before the real rate increased. Since $-r_t S_t$ is the cost of borrowing, an increase in the real interest rate reduces the lifetime resources of borrowers.

✓ Knowledge Check 6-2

Suppose $Y_t = 10$, $Y_{t+1} = 20$, and $r_t = 0.05$. Fill in the missing values of the table.

C_t	C_{t+1}	S_t
	20	
7		
	25	
		2
12		

Answers are at the end of the chapter.

6-2b Preferences for Current and Future Consumption

The last section derived feasible current and future consumption pairs given the real interest rate and a person's lifetime income. We have not discussed how a person values consumption today versus consumption in the future. For that, we need to understand the individual's preferences. Many economic models make assumptions about people's preferences in the context of preferring one type of a good or service over another. For example, one can prefer ice cream over biscuits or trips to a movie theater to watching TV at home. In this chapter, however, we will introduce the concept of intertemporal preferences, when the choice is not between products but the time when a product is consumed, such as a scoop of ice cream today versus the same scoop of ice cream tomorrow. Economists use the term **utility** to describe one's overall level of happiness. Within the context of the two-period consumption problem, the individual's lifetime utility function is a mathematical relationship between consumption over the two periods, which can be written as

$$U = u(C_t) + \beta u(C_{t+1}). \tag{6}$$

Utility
A term used to describe a consumer's overall level of happiness.

Lifetime utility is the sum of the utility from consumption today, $u(C_t)$, and the utility from consumption tomorrow, $\beta u(C_{t+1})$. The parameter β, sometimes referred to as the subjective discount rate, is between zero and one. The idea is that, from the perspective of today, future utility isn't worth as much as current utility all else equal. For example, if a person can eat some amount of ice cream today and the same amount of ice cream one year from now, the future ice cream provides less utility as long as $\beta < 1$. If $\beta = 1$, then the person is perfectly patient and future ice cream provides the same utility as current ice cream. Judging from data and experience, people are not perfectly patient, which justifies $\beta < 1$.

The utility function is an ordinal measure of well-being, not a cardinal one. This means that if one consumption allocation gives a person eight units of utility, which maybe we call *utils*, and another allocation gives a person nine utils, we can say that the second allocation is preferred. However, we can't say that the second allocation raises lifetime well-being by one util. The reason is that the utility function is completely subjective: your version of a util is certainly different from another person's definition of a util.

In general, we will put two conditions on the utility functions we use for consumption-savings problems. The first condition is that utility is increasing in consumption. Intuitively, the more you consume, the greater your well-being. The amount utility changes in response to a small change in consumption is called **marginal utility**. Briefly stated, the first condition says that marginal utility is always positive. This is obviously a simplifying assumption that, in reality, doesn't hold at all times for all goods. For example, the first bite of ice cream raises my utility, but the 100th bite might make me sick, thus lowering overall utility. Nevertheless, the simplifying assumption is useful in most problems.

Marginal utility
The increase in utility that comes with a small increase in consumption.

The second condition is that marginal utility does not increase with consumption. Intuitively, the marginal utility from the first bite of ice cream is quite high. The marginal utility from the second bite is still positive, but not as high as the first bite. The marginal utility of the third bite is lower still. This logic, while not universal, is applicable to the consumption of many goods and services.

Figure 6.6 draws a sample utility function that satisfies the two conditions. Utility is increasing in C_t (condition 1) at a decreasing rate (condition 2). The marginal utility of consumption is the rate utility changes with consumption. Geometrically, this is the slope of the utility function. The marginal utility gained from going from $C_{0,t}$ to $C_{1,t}$ is

$$MU_{1,0} = \frac{u(C_{1,t}) - u(C_{0,t})}{C_{1,t} - C_{0,t}}.$$

Consider a standard utility function, $u = \sqrt{C_t}$. Table 6.1 shows the utility and marginal utility for different levels of consumption. Moving from one to two units of consumption increases utility by 0.41 utils whereas moving from two to three units raises utility by only 0.32 utils. Thus, marginal utility is positive, but diminishing. This means that the square root utility function satisfies the two conditions discussed earlier in this section.

132 **Part 2** Classical Theory

Figure 6.6	Period t utility as a function of period t consumption. The utility function is increasing in consumption at a decreasing rate.

Question: How would the above plot change if the marginal utility were constant?

Table 6.1	Utility and Marginal Utility	
C_t	$u(C_t)$	**MU**
1	1	X
2	1.41	0.41
3	1.73	0.32
4	2	0.27

Indifference curve

All pairs of current and future consumption, (C_t, C_{t+1}), that provide the same level of utility.

Now that you have some understanding of the per-period utility function, we want to know how individuals evaluate different pairs of C_t and C_{t+1}. An **indifference curve** is all C_t and C_{t+1} pairs that give the same level of lifetime utility. Figure 6.7 plots two indifference curves. The blue line labeled U_0 contains all the (C_t, C_{t+1}) pairs that give a certain level of utility, U_0. Because utility is increasing in consumption, if the person consumes more in period t, staying on U_0 requires that the person consume less in period $t + 1$. This implies that indifference curves are downward sloping. For instance, if the individual is initially at the allocation $(C_{0,t}, C_{0,t+1})$, increasing period t consumption to $C_{1,t}$ requires that period $t + 1$ consumption decrease to $C_{1,t+1}$.

The higher the level of utility, the further the indifference curve lies to the northeast away from the origin. At any given level of C_t on U_0, the individual can enjoy that same level of period t consumption and even more C_{t+1} on U_1. So, the consumption bundles on U_1 give a higher level of utility than the consumption bundles on U_0.

As just discussed, positive marginal utility of consumption implies that the indifference curves slope downward. The fact that marginal utility is diminishing implies that the indifference curves are bowed into the origin. Another way of thinking about this is that individuals prefer a balanced mix of consumption today and tomorrow compared to an extreme one way or the other. Figure 6.8 illustrates this point using a standard indifference curve. At points A and B, the individual's total lifetime consumption is 10. Point C provides the same level of utility, but a lower level of lifetime consumption of 8.

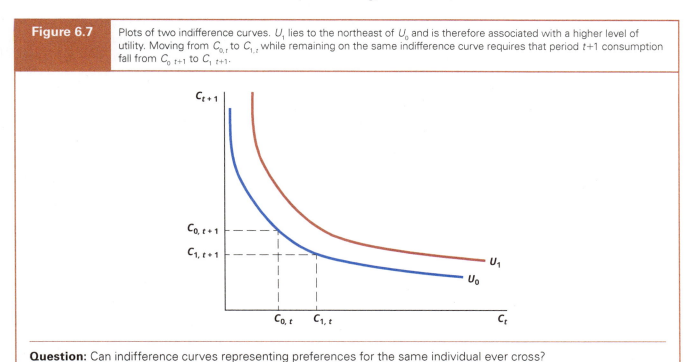

Figure 6.7 Plots of two indifference curves. U_1 lies to the northeast of U_0 and is therefore associated with a higher level of utility. Moving from $C_{0,t}$ to $C_{1,t}$ while remaining on the same indifference curve requires that period $t+1$ consumption fall from $C_{0,t+1}$ to $C_{1,t+1}$.

Question: Can indifference curves representing preferences for the same individual ever cross?

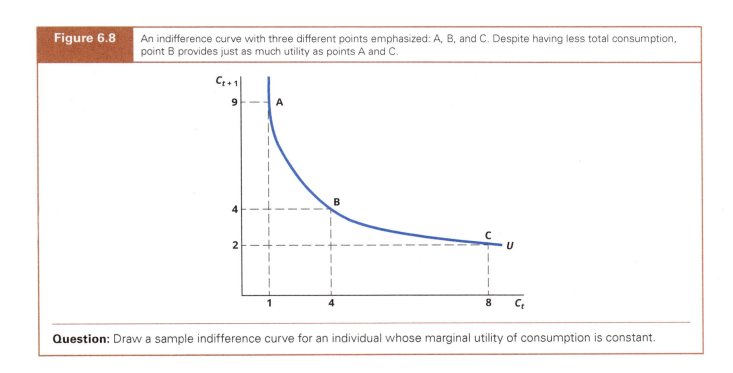

Figure 6.8 An indifference curve with three different points emphasized: A, B, and C. Despite having less total consumption, point B provides just as much utility as points A and C.

Question: Draw a sample indifference curve for an individual whose marginal utility of consumption is constant.

The preference for a balanced mix of present and future consumption is fairly straightforward. In terms of food, most people would prefer to eat a pizza today and a pizza tomorrow rather than two pizzas on the same day. Or, in terms of entertainment, most people would prefer to watch one *Lord of the Rings* movie today and one next week

Marginal rate of substitution
The quantity of future consumption, C_{t+1}, the individual must give up for one additional unit of current consumption, C_t, to stay on the same indifference curve.

rather than getting through both movies in a single session.[1] The individual's willingness to substitute consumption in the present for consumption in the future is formalized by the **marginal rate of substitution** (MRS). The MRS of C_t for C_{t+1} is the quantity of C_{t+1} the individual must give up for one additional unit of C_t to stay on the same indifference curve.[2]

Figure 6.9 shows that, for standard indifference curves, the MRS declines with C_t. If the individual starts with a low level of C_t such as $C_{0,t}$, they would be willing to give up a lot of C_{t+1} for one more unit of C_t. The exact amount is $\Delta C_{0, t+1}$. On the other hand, if the individual starts with a high level of C_t such as $C_{1,t}$, they would be willing to give up only a little of C_{t+1} for one more unit of C_t. The exact amount is $\Delta C_{1, t+1}$. As C_t increases, the amount of C_{t+1} the individual would forgo for one additional unit of C_t declines. This is a direct consequence of a diminishing marginal utility of consumption. When C_t is small relative to C_{t+1}, the marginal utility of consumption in the present is higher than the marginal utility of consumption in the future. Therefore, the individual would be willing to sacrifice more C_{t+1} for C_t. As consumption in the present increases, the marginal utility of C_t declines as does the marginal rate of substitution.

Figure 6.9 The amount of C_{t+1} the consumer is willing to give up for one more unit of C_t while staying on the same indifference curve diminishes in C_t. Moving from $C_{1,t}$ to $C_{1, t+1}$ requires that the consumer forgo $\Delta C_{1, t+1}$. Moving from $C_{2,t}$ to $C_{2, t+1}$ requires that the consumer forgo $\Delta C_{2, t+1}$.

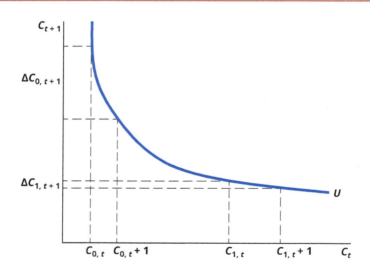

Question: Does the marginal rate of substitution decline if the marginal utility of consumption is constant?

---

[1] It is true that some people prefer *Lord of the Rings* marathons. Their preferences are not well described by these indifference curves.

[2] You can derive the MRS with calculus. The lifetime utility function is

$$U = u(C_t) + \beta u(C_{t+1}).$$

The total derivative is

$$dU = u'(C_t)dC_t + \beta u'(C_{t+1})dC_{t+1}.$$

Setting $dU = 0$ and solving for the slope of the indifference curve gives

$$\frac{dC_{t+1}}{dC_t} = \frac{u'(C_t)}{\beta u'(C_{t+1})}.$$

Knowledge Check 6-3

Perhaps the most common utility function in macroeconomics is the logarithmic function, $u(C_t) = \ln(C_t)$. Lifetime utility is

$$U = \ln(C_t) + \beta \ln(C_{t+1}).$$

It turns out the marginal rate of substitution for this lifetime utility function is $\dfrac{C_{t+1}}{\beta C_t}$, which is diminishing in C_t. Consider two sample indifference curves, one with $U = 10$ and another with $U = 12$. Complete the rest of the table assuming $\beta = 0.95$.

\multicolumn{3}{c}{$U = 10$}	\multicolumn{3}{c}{$U = 12$}
C_t	C_{t+1}	MRS	C_t	C_{t+1}	MRS
400			600		
300			500		
200			400		
100			300		

Answers are at the end of the chapter.

6-2c Characterizing the Optimal Consumption Bundle

The individual's lifetime budget constraint tells us all the affordable pairs of C_t and C_{t+1}. And the individual's preferences tell us how the individual subjectively values different bundles of C_t and C_{t+1}. Given the individual's budget constraint and indifference curves associated with their utility function, we can depict the optimal choice of C_t and C_{t+1} graphically.

First, let's think about some choices that aren't optimal. Figure 6.10 shows four points on a plot with a budget line and indifference curve. At point A, the individual can purchase more consumption in the present and the future thereby raising overall utility. Thus, point A can't be an optimal choice. Point D, meanwhile, lies outside of the budget constraint, which means it isn't feasible. Thus, the optimal consumption pair must lie on the budget constraint.

Figure 6.10 A budget line and indifference curve with four points of emphasis: A, B, C, and D. Point A is not optimal because the consumer could purchase more present and future consumption. Point D is infeasible. The MRS exceeds $1 + r_t$ at point B and $1 + r_t$ exceeds the MRS at point C, making neither point optimal.

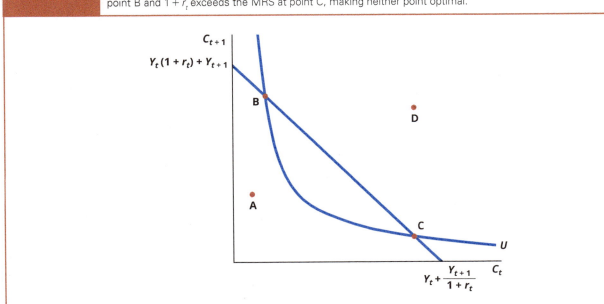

Next, consider point B. At point B, the indifference curve is steeper than the budget line. The slope of the budget line is the opportunity cost of one additional unit of consumption in the present, or $1 + r_t$. The slope of the indifference curve is the MRS or the quantity of C_{t+1} the individual is willing to trade for one more unit of C_t. At point B, the quantity of C_{t+1} the individual is willing to trade for one more unit of C_t is greater than $1 + r_t$. In other words, the rate at which the consumer is subjectively willing to trade future consumption for one additional unit of present consumption exceeds the rate at which the market trades future consumption for one more unit of present consumption. Therefore, the utility maximizing individual will choose to consume more C_t and less C_{t+1} compared to a point like B. This logic can be generalized for any point where $\text{MRS} > 1 + r_t$.

But the logic goes in reverse as well. At point C, $1 + r_t$ exceeds the MRS. The individual is consuming too much in the present and too little in the future. Overall utility can be raised by reducing consumption in the present, thereby driving up the MRS. This is true for any consumption bundle where $\text{MRS} < 1 + r_t$.

From these last two insights, we infer that at the optimal consumption bundle, $\text{MRS} = 1 + r_t$. The rate at which the market trades C_t for C_{t+1} equals the rate at which the individual subjectively trades off C_t for C_{t+1}. Graphically, the optimal point is characterized by the indifference curve being tangent to the budget line. This is shown in Figure 6.11. At the tangency point, the indifference curve just touches the budget line, and the optimal consumption bundle is denoted by (C_t^*, C_{t+1}^*).

We can use the graphical framework to work through comparative static exercises. Consider an increase in current-period income, ΔY_t. One option is for the individual to consume all of this additional income today. This is reflected in the graphical depiction of the budget constraint by shifting the horizontal intercept by ΔY_t. Alternatively, if the individual were to save the entire increase in current-period income, that would leave $(1 + r_t)\Delta Y_t$ for consumption in the next period. Thus, the vertical intercept shifts up by $(1 + r_t)\Delta Y_t$. The results are shown in Figure 6.12. Because the intertemporal price of consumption hasn't changed, the new budget line has the same slope as the initial budget line. The additional income increases the individual's utility, which is reflected by the higher indifference curve. The end result is that the individual consumes more in both periods.

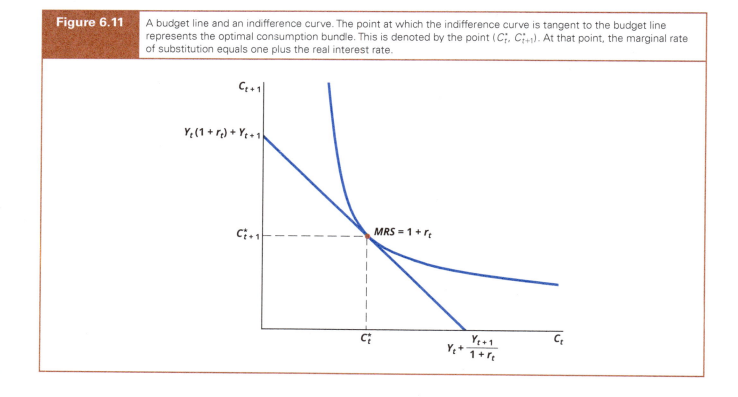

Figure 6.11 A budget line and an indifference curve. The point at which the indifference curve is tangent to the budget line represents the optimal consumption bundle. This is denoted by the point (C_t^*, C_{t+1}^*). At that point, the marginal rate of substitution equals one plus the real interest rate.

Figure 6.12

An increase in current-period income by ΔY_t. This induces a parallel shift in the budget constraint to the right. The optimal consumption bundle moves from $(C_{0,t}^*, C_{0,t+1}^*)$ to $(C_{1,t}^*, C_{1,t+1}^*)$.

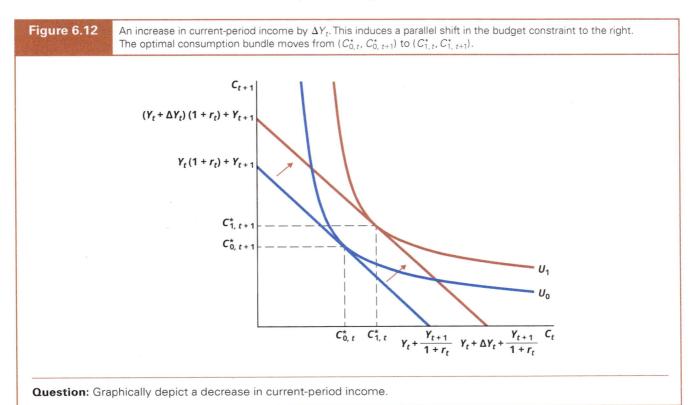

Question: Graphically depict a decrease in current-period income.

The change in the optimal quantities of consumption coming from a change in income that leaves prices constant is called the **income effect**. An increase in Y_t only has an income effect because the intertemporal price of consumption stays the same. Since the individual gets utility from consumption in both periods, we say that an increase in Y_t has a positive income effect.

Figure 6.12 shows that consumption in both periods increases when current-period income increases. This means that savings, S_t, must also rise. The intuition is that because the individual prefers to balance their consumption bundle, an increase in current-period income is divided between multiple periods. The marginal propensity to consume (MPC) out of current income is how much current-period consumption rises per dollar increase in current-period income. Our analysis shows that the MPC is between zero and one.

Next consider an increase in future income given by ΔY_{t+1}. This is shown in Figure 6.13. The increase in future income shifts the vertical intercept up by ΔY_{t+1}. If the person wanted to consume any of the future period's gain in the present, they must borrow. The maximum amount period t consumption could increase is the present discounted value of the increase in income, or $\frac{\Delta Y_{t+1}}{1+r_t}$. Thus, the horizontal intercept shifts out by $\frac{\Delta Y_{t+1}}{1+r_t}$. Because the real interest rate hasn't changed, the new budget line has the same slope as the initial one. The increase in future income has a positive income effect which increases consumption in both periods.

Because C_t rises, it must be the case that the consumer borrows more (or saves less) in period t. Intuitively, the individual wants to smooth consumption and is forward looking. An increase in future income leads the individual to bring some of that income forward by way of borrowing.

In the real world, the ability of individuals to borrow against increases in future income is limited by imperfect financial markets. That is, even if you knew the exact dollar value that comes with your next promotion in five years, it would be difficult to convince

Income effect
The change in the optimal quantities of consumption coming from a change in income that leaves prices constant.

Figure 6.13 An increase in current-period income by ΔY_{t+1}. This induces a parallel shift in the budget constraint to the right. The optimal consumption bundle moves from $(C^*_{0,t}, C^*_{0,t+1})$ to $(C^*_{1,t}, C^*_{1,t+1})$.

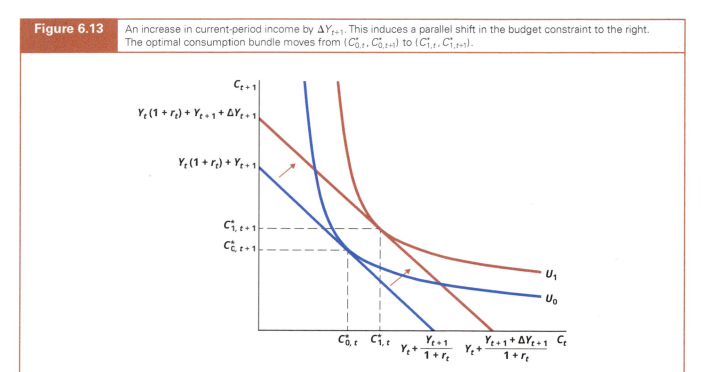

Question: Graphically depict a decrease in current-period income.

the bank to lend you the present discounted value of the raise today. The bank has no idea if you are being truthful or even if you plan on being at the job next year. These information asymmetries limit how much consumers can bring future income into the present.

At the same time, borrowing like this does, to some degree, exist in the real world. If you're reading this textbook, a tangible example to you might be student loans. Students take out loans to finance their higher education expenditures with the expectation that going to college will raise their lifetime incomes. Private banks and governments only provide these loans because they have the same expectations as the students. Another example is how job offers work. If you are fortunate enough to receive a job offer during your senior year, the consumption-savings model predicts that you will increase consumption before you begin to be paid your salary. Occasionally, the purchases will be substantial. Some car dealerships, for instance, will let you finance a car if you can provide proof of your future salary.

Changes in current or future income do not affect the intertemporal price of consumption and therefore only have income effects. A change in the real interest rate does affect the intertemporal price of consumption. Consider an increase in r_t. Because one unit of period t consumption costs $1 + r_t$ units of future consumption, an increase in the real rate increases the relative price of consumption today. As Figure 6.14 shows, the budget constraint steepens. The horizontal intercept shifts in and the vertical intercept shifts up. The initial budget line intersects with the new budget line at the endowment point where there is neither borrowing nor saving. That is, the one point that is feasible under the initial r_t and the new one is the point where consumption equals income in both periods. The new tangency point shows that current-period consumption decreases and future consumption increases.

Compared to a change in income, the change in the real interest rate is obviously more complicated from a geometric perspective, as both the intercepts and the slope change. It is also more complicated from an economic perspective. An increase in the real interest rate affects the optimal quantities of consumption through an income effect and

Figure 6.14

The effects of an increase in the real interest rate. An increase in the real rate from $r_{1,t}$ to $r_{2,t}$ pivots the budget constraint clockwise. The optimal consumption bundle shifts from $(C_{0,t}^*, C_{1,t}^*)$ to $(C_{0,t+1}^*, C_{1,t+1}^*)$.

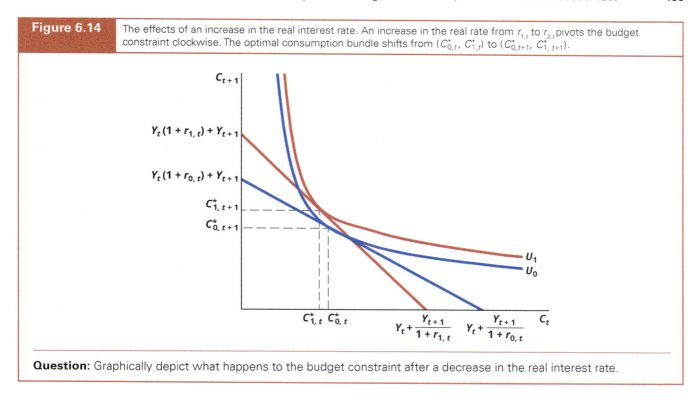

Question: Graphically depict what happens to the budget constraint after a decrease in the real interest rate.

---

a **substitution effect**. The substitution effect is the change in the optimal quantities of consumption resulting from a change in the relative price leaving the level of utility fixed. Intuitively, the substitution effect asks what happens to consumption when the relative price changes ignoring the fact that income also changed. Because an increase in the real interest rate makes period t consumption more expensive and period $t+1$ consumption cheaper, the substitution effect is negative for period t consumption and positive for period $t+1$ consumption. Equivalently, an increase in the real interest rate increases the return on saving and increases the cost of borrowing.

At the initial tangency point in Figure 6.14, the optimal level of period t consumption is less than Y_t implying that the individual is initially a saver. The increase in the real rate raises the return on savings which implies a positive income effect for consumption in both periods. In terms of the graph, the new budget line lies outside of the initial budget line in the region that the individual is a saver.

Table 6.2 summarizes the results of the real interest rate change. The increase in interest income pushes consumption up in both periods. The substitution effect is negative for consumption in the present, which is now relatively more expensive, and positive for consumption in the future, which is now relatively cheaper. On net, the direction of the change for period t consumption is ambiguous, while period $t+1$ consumption unambiguously increases.

Substitution effect
The change in the optimal quantities of consumption resulting from a change in the relative price, leaving the level of utility fixed.

Table 6.2 Effects of a Real Interest Rate Increase on Savers

	C_t	C_{t+1}
Income effect	+	+
Substitution effect	−	+
Net effect	?	+

140 **Part 2** Classical Theory

Since period t decreases in Figure 6.14, we infer that the substitution effect is bigger than the income effect. Sometimes we say that the "substitution effect dominates." This is true of most empirically plausible utility functions and, unless otherwise stated, will be the operating assumption throughout the book.

> ### ✓ Knowledge Check 6-4
>
> Suppose the real interest rate increases and the individual is initially a borrower. Discuss the income and substitution effects and summarize your results in a table similar to Table 6.2.
>
> ───────────────────────────────── Answers are at the end of the chapter.

6-2d The Consumption Function

Last section's graphical characterization of the optimal consumption bundle demonstrated how consumption is affected by current income, future income, and the real interest rate. The consumption function expresses current-period consumption as a function of the exogenous variables, Y_t, Y_{t+1}, and r_t. Mathematically, the consumption function is given by

$$C_t = C(Y_t, Y_{t+1}, r_t). \tag{7}$$

Consumption depends positively on Y_t and Y_{t+1} and, maintaining the assumption that the substitution effect dominates, negatively on r_t.

The abstract representation of the consumption function in Equation (7) is useful, but it's also instructive to analyze the consumption functions that emerge from particular utility functions. Consider the utility function, $u(C_t) = \ln(C_t)$. Lifetime utility is given by

$$U = \ln(C_t) + \beta \ln(C_{t+1}).$$

Recall that for the natural log utility function, the marginal rate of substitution is $\dfrac{C_{t+1}}{\beta C_t}$. At an optimal point, the MRS equals the slope of the budget constraint, or

$$1 + r_t = \frac{C_{t+1}}{\beta C_t}.$$

This equation contains two unknown variables: C_t and C_{t+1}. We can solve for C_{t+1} in terms of C_t by multiplying both sides by βC_t, or

$$C_{t+1} = C_t \beta (1 + r_t).$$

If the rate at which the individual discounts future utility, β, equals the rate at which the market discounts future goods, $\dfrac{1}{1 + r_t}$, then consumption is equal across periods, or consumption is "perfectly smoothed." Next, combine the last equation with the lifetime budget constraint:

$$C_t + \frac{C_{t+1}}{1 + r_t} = Y_t + \frac{Y_{t+1}}{1 + r_t}$$

$$\Leftrightarrow C_t + \frac{C_t \beta (1 + r_t)}{1 + r_t} = Y_t + \frac{Y_{t+1}}{1 + r_t}$$

$$\Leftrightarrow C_t(1 + \beta) = Y_t + \frac{Y_{t+1}}{1 + r_t}$$

$$\Leftrightarrow C_t = \frac{1}{1 + \beta}\left[Y_t + \frac{Y_{t+1}}{1 + r_t}\right].$$

This last line is the consumption function. Consumption in period t depends positively on current and future income and negatively on the real interest rate. That is, when current or future income goes up, consumption goes up. When the real interest rate goes up, consumption goes down. The bracketed part of the consumption function is the present discounted value of lifetime income. Thus, consumption is a constant fraction, $\frac{1}{1+\beta}$, of lifetime income. If the individual is perfectly patient, then future utility is not discounted, meaning $\beta = 1$. In that case, the individual consumes exactly half of the present discounted value of lifetime income today. If the individual doesn't care at all about the future and is perfectly impatient, then $\beta = 0$ and the individual consumes the entirety of lifetime income in the present. This would also hold true if the time horizon were longer than two periods. If $\beta = 0$, the individual only cares about the present and the optimal response is to maximize current-period consumption.

The consumption function summarizes a number of implications from the consumption-savings model. First, consumption is a function of lifetime income, rather than only current income. This is a consequence of the forward-looking nature of the utility maximization problem. Although in reality consumers will not know the future with certainty, the model predicts that they use all available information when making decisions. The second implication is that consumption responds more to permanent changes in income (i.e., both Y_t and Y_{t+1} going up) than to transitory changes in income. The distinction between permanent and temporary changes in income becomes very important when discussing tax policy. Policymakers might cut taxes during a recession in the hopes that such a cut will stimulate consumption. Our results suggest that the response in consumption will depend on the permanence of the tax cut. The third significant implication is that, everything else equal, individuals want to smooth consumption across time. Again, the properties of standard utility functions lead individuals to select balanced bundles of consumption.

The final implication is that consumption only responds to unpredictable changes to income. This is a subtle but important point. Think about a seasonal worker who is paid for landscaping nine months of the year and doesn't receive income for three months of the year. Since this schedule is completely anticipated, the worker's consumption should not be any higher in the working months. Generalizing a bit, an individual's consumption should not decrease at retirement since retirement is a predictable event.

Knowledge Check 6-5

Go back to the consumption function

$$C_t = \frac{1}{1+\beta}\left[Y_t + \frac{Y_{t+1}}{1+r_t}\right].$$

Derive the optimal quantity of savings. Under what conditions are savings negative? How is the quantity of savings affected by the real interest rate?

Answers are at the end of the chapter.

Application 6.1

The Retirement Puzzle

A consistent finding in economic research is that expenditure on food drops as soon as people retire. While the exact estimates of the amount vary, the finding on average is that food expenditure drops by about 10 percent. Taken at face value, this would seem to contradict an important prediction of the consumption-savings model, namely that individuals smooth their consumption. Moreover, retirement isn't a "surprise" event, so it is something that forward-looking individuals should plan for. Does this finding contradict the lifecycle model?

To answer this question, we have to be very careful about distinguishing consumption from expenditure. Yes, food consumption is a function of expenditure, but expenditure isn't the only input to consumption. For example, suppose you want to consume a pizza. One way to do this is to go to the store and buy the pizza dough, sauce,

■ Continues

Application 6.1 (Continued)

and toppings and make the pizza yourself. Maybe that costs $10. Another way is to call your local pizza joint and order a pizza delivered to your door. Maybe that costs $20. Despite having different levels of expenditure, the two pizzas might have identical caloric and nutritional content. This means that the consumption value of the pizzas would be the same.

The pizza example emphasizes what economists mean when we talk about the cost of something. The cost of ordering a pizza for delivery is pretty straightforward, but the cost of making one yourself is subtler. If making the pizza yourself requires shopping for half an hour and preparing and baking it requires another half an hour, you are giving up an hour of your time. If you make $20 per hour at a job, then the cost of making the pizza yourself is $30—$10 for the ingredients plus $20 for the forgone hour of work. In this case, the takeout pizza would actually be cheaper.

In general, food consumption is a function of food expenditure and time spent on shopping and preparation. The opportunity cost of time varies by individual. High wage earners have a high opportunity cost of time, so we would expect them to eat out more. On the other hand, retired people have no labor market earnings and therefore do not forgo wages by spending time on shopping and food production. All else equal, we would expect retirees to spend more time on these activities and this would, to some extent, reduce the inferred consumption gap between retirees and younger people.

Economists Mark Aguiar and Erik Hurst tested this hypothesis using data from the Continuing Survey of Food Intake of Individuals.[3] The survey tracks food expenditures as well as the quantity and quality of food consumed. As Figure 6.15 shows, Aguiar and Hurst found that while food expenditures are 17 percent lower for retired individuals, time spent on preparation is 53 percent higher. Taken together, they found that food consumption hardly moves at all in retirement.

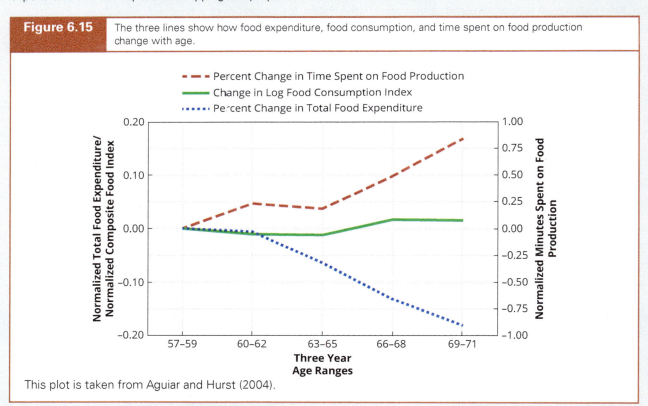

Figure 6.15 The three lines show how food expenditure, food consumption, and time spent on food production change with age.

This plot is taken from Aguiar and Hurst (2004).

Source: https://www.nber.org/system/files/working_papers/w10307/w10307.pdf.

This example shows that we must be careful in distinguishing expenditure from consumption. A meal, a clean house, and a freshly washed car are all functions of expenditure and time. Just because one's expenditures on these items change over time does not mean they aren't smoothing consumption.

---

[3] Aguiar, Mark and Erik Hurst. 2005. "Consumption Versus Expenditure." *Journal of Political Economy*, 113(5): 919–948.

Chapter 6 Saving, Investment, and the Real Interest Rate **143**

6-3 A Model of Investment

The investment decisions of business owners also depend on the real interest rate. The costs of financing the purchase of computers, new software, or warehouses all depend on the real interest rate. This is obviously true if the business purchases these capital goods by borrowing, as borrowing requires paying fixed interest payments. It is less obvious, but still true, when the business owner pays for the investment without borrowing at all.

To see why, think about a business owner who has $10,000 to invest. One option is to use the $10,000 to buy new software. Another option is to put the $10,000 in the bank (or some other risk-free investment) and earn a real return of r_t. As r_t increases, the opportunity cost of buying the software goes up.

Formally, suppose that the business owner is considering investing k_t units of capital into the business. The marginal product of capital (MPK), first defined in Chapter 2, is the amount output increases per unit increase in capital. One unit of capital invested in period t increases output in the next period by MPK_{t+1}. So, the total increase in next period's output is $k_t MPK_{t+1}$. Moreover, the new addition of capital does not simply disappear at the end of period $t + 1$. Rather, some fraction of the new capital gets worn out through the process of using it. Computers eventually break and tractors eventually rust. The fraction of capital that is worn out through use is called the *depreciation rate* and is denoted by d. By the end of period $t + 1$, dk_t of the investment is destroyed and $(1 - d)k_t$ remains. The overall return to investing (ROI) k_t units of capital is

$$ROI = k_t MPK_{t+1} + (1 - d)k_t.$$

Just as in Chapter 2, define total factor productivity (TFP) as the overall efficiency the economy makes use of its inputs. When TFP increases, the economy produces more with any given amount of capital. That is, the marginal product of capital is increasing in TFP. Mathematically, TFP in period t is denoted by A_t. We can write the MPK in period $t + 1$ as a function of future TFP, or

$$ROI = k_t MPK(A_{t+1}) + (1 - d)k_t.$$

Finally, in the real world, investment in new structures and equipment isn't seamless. Relative to depositing money into a savings account, investing in new capital entails risk. Investments in new software often don't raise productivity as anticipated. Sometimes newly constructed buildings stay vacant. We capture the risk entailed in investing in new capital with the term $f_t k_t$. You can think of $f_t \geq 0$ as the **risk premium**, or the added risk of investing in capital relative to the return from a savings account. Thus, the risk-adjusted return on investment is given by

$$ROI = k_t MPK(A_{t+1}) + (1 - d)k_t - f_t k_t. \tag{8}$$

Risk premium
The added risk of investing in capital relative to the return from a savings account.

If the business owner invests k_t in a savings account instead of purchasing new capital, the total amount of resources in period $t + 1$ is $(1 + r_t)k_t$. Rational, profit-maximizing business owners will invest where the return is the highest. If

$$1 + r_t > MPK(A_{t+1}) + (1 - d) - f_t,$$

then it is optimal to invest in the savings account. If all business owners are making the identical decision, then the increase in savings will put downwards pressure on the real interest rate. Alternatively, if the inequality is reversed, then all business owners will invest in new capital, which will, in aggregate, decrease the marginal product of capital. In either case, the economic mechanisms at work drive the risk-free return to equal the risk-adjusted return. In equilibrium it must be the case that

$$r_t = MPK(A_{t+1}) - (d + f_t). \tag{9}$$

The risk-free real interest rate equals the marginal product of capital adjusted for depreciation and risk. We will assume that the depreciation rate stays constant and disregard it in the subsequent analysis.

We can use Equation (9) to intuit an investment decision rule for business owners. A higher r_t raises the return to bank deposits and reduces the demand for investment in new capital.

144 **Part 2** Classical Theory

Likewise, a higher f_t increases the risk on new investment projects and lowers the demand for new capital. Finally, a higher A_{t+1} increases the productivity of new capital and therefore raises the demand for new capital. The investment demand rule can therefore be written as

$$I_t = I(r_t + f_t, A_{t+1}). \tag{10}$$

Investment demand is a negative function of $r_t + f_t$ and positive function of A_{t+1}. An important aspect of this rule is that investment decisions are forward looking. Current-period productivity does not enter into the firm's decision to invest in new capital. The reason is that the new capital isn't used until the next period. This makes intuitive sense. Returning to the software example, a business may decide to invest in new software in 2023, but by the time the new software is delivered, installed, and the employees are trained, it will be 2024.

Finally, it is worth reiterating that investment demand by businesses can be financed through borrowing or through the retained earnings of business owners. Borrowing entails paying risk-adjusted interest, $r_t + f_t$, to the bank, but investing through retained earnings carries the same risk-adjusted opportunity cost of $r_t + f_t$. For ease of exposition, we assume that businesses borrow to finance new investment.

> ✔️ **Knowledge Check 6-6**
>
> Suppose that the demand for investment is a linear function:
>
> $$I_t = A_{t+1} - a(r_t + f_t),$$
>
> where $a > 0$ is the sensitivity of investment demand to the real interest rate. Complete the rest of this table assuming $a = 200$. How do changes in A_{t+1} and f_t affect the investment demand curve? Explain the economic intuition of these changes.
>
> | r_t | I_t | | |
> |---|---|---|---|
> | | Case 1:
$A_{t+1} = 20$, $f_t = 0.02$ | Case 2:
$A_{t+1} = 40$, $f_t = 0.02$ | Case 3:
$A_{t+1} = 20$, $f_t = 0.04$ |
> | 0.01 | | | |
> | 0.02 | | | |
> | 0.03 | | | |
> | 0.04 | | | |
>
> ———————————————— Answers are at the end of the chapter.

6-4 Determination of the Equilibrium Real Interest Rate

The consumption and savings decisions of individuals depend on the real interest rate. The demand for investment by firms also depends on the real interest rate. In this section, we analyze how these forces work together to determine the real interest rate in equilibrium.

Recall from Chapter 1, that the GDP expenditure equation is

$$Y_t = C_t + I_t + G_t + NX_t, \tag{11}$$

where Y_t is GDP, C_t is consumption, I_t, is investment, G_t is government expenditure, and NX_t is net exports. We discussed consumption and investment earlier in this chapter. Chapter 7 discusses the determination of net exports. For now, we assume a closed economy, or $NX_t = 0$. Under this assumption, Equation (11) can be written as

$$Y_t = C_t + I_t + G_t. \tag{11'}$$

Chapter 9 discusses the inputs of government expenditure in some detail, but for now we assume that it is given exogenously, $G_t > 0$. Even when government spending is exogenous, it affects the model in important ways. This is discussed in the next section.

Chapter 6 Saving, Investment, and the Real Interest Rate **145**

6-4a Government Spending, Private Savings, and Public Savings

Every year, the government makes expenditures and collects resources in the form of taxes. If taxes exceed expenditures, the government runs a budget surplus. In this case, the government adds to the savings of the domestic economy. If expenditures exceed taxes, the government runs a budget deficit. In this case, the government reduces the savings of the domestic economy.

Define T_t as current-period taxes. Adding and subtracting T_t from the right-hand side of Equation (11′):

$$Y_t = C_t + I_t + G_t + T_t - T_t$$

$$\Leftrightarrow (Y_t - C_t - T_t) + (T_t - G_t) = I_t. \tag{12}$$

The term $Y_t - C_t - T_t$ is private savings, or GDP minus aggregate consumption and taxes. Similarly, the term $T_t - G_t$ is public savings. If $T_t > G_t$, then the government runs a budget surplus and public savings is positive. The right-hand side is investment. Equation (12) says that investment equals the sum of private savings and public savings.

The consumption and investment demand functions can be substituted into Equation (12) to determine the equilibrium real interest rate. Before doing that, however, the consumption function must be modified. The consumption function given in Equation (8) is

$$C_t = C(Y_t, Y_{t+1}, r_t).$$

Consumption depends on current income, future income, and the real interest rate. With the introduction of government spending and taxes, the consumption rule changes. In particular, since the government imposes taxes on individuals and households, consumption depends on **disposable income**, or income minus taxes. Modifying the consumption function gives

Disposable income
Income minus taxes.

$$C_t = C(Y_t - T_t, Y_{t+1} - T_{t+1}, r_t). \tag{13}$$

Consumption depends on current and future disposable income and the real interest rate.

Substituting the modified consumption function and investment demand function into Equation (12) gives

$$(Y_t - C(Y_t - T_t, Y_{t+1} - T_{t+1}, r_t) - T_t) + (T_t - G_t) = I(r_t + f_t, A_{t+1}). \tag{14}$$

The left-hand side is the total supply of savings, which is a positive function of the real interest rate. The right-hand side is the demand for investment, which is a negative function of the real interest rate. Although Equation (14) looks complicated, we can depict savings and investment in a straightforward supply and demand diagram.

6-4b Graphical Determination of the Equilibrium Real Interest Rate

We will make one simplifying assumption to Equation (14) and that is to assume the government runs a balanced budget. In Chapter 9, we will discuss an economic rationale that justifies this assumption even if the government in reality runs a surplus or deficit. Equation (14) can be written as

$$Y_t - C(Y_t - G_t, Y_{t+1} - G_{t+1}, r_t) - G_t = I(r_t + f_t, A_{t+1}), \tag{15}$$

where G_{t+1} is government expenditure in period $t + 1$. Total savings in the economy is

$$S_t = Y_t - C(Y_t - G_t, Y_{t+1} - G_{t+1}, r_t) - G_t. \tag{16}$$

In equilibrium, savings equals investment. There are two endogenous variables, $S_t(I_t)$ and r_t. There are six exogenous variables: Y_t, Y_{t+1}, G_t, G_{t+1}, A_{t+1}, and f_t. The model is summarized in Table 6.3.

Table 6.3	Summary of the Savings–Investment Model
Endogenous Variables	**Exogenous Variables**
S_t/I_t and r_t	$Y_t, Y_{t+1}, G_t, G_{t+1}, A_{t+1}$, and f_t
Key Equations:	
1. $I_t = I(r_t + f_t, A_{t+1})$	(Investment demand (Eq 10))
2. $S_t = Y_t - C(Y_t - G_t, Y_{t+1} - G_{t+1}, r_t) - G_t$	(Savings supply Eq (16))

Figure 6.16 The savings supply and investment demand curves. The economy is in equilibrium when savings supply equals investment demand. The equilibrium real interest rate is r_t^* and the equilibrium quantity of investment (which is also the equilibrium quantity of savings) is I_t^*.

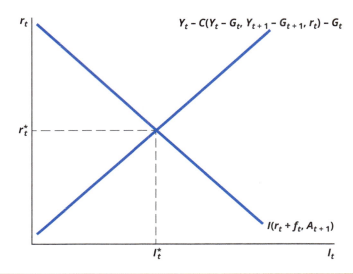

Question: What happens to the slope of the investment demand curve if investment is more sensitive to the real interest rate?

Investment demand is a downward sloping function of r_t and savings supply is an upward sloping function of r_t. Figure 6.16 graphically depicts the supply of and demand for savings. The investment demand curve and savings supply curve intersect at the equilibrium real interest rate, r_t^*.

6-4c Comparative Statics in the Savings–Investment Model

Starting with the supply and demand diagram in Figure 6.15, suppose that income today, Y_t, increases. All else equal, an increase in income raises the quantity of savings. However, consumption also increases, so the change in $Y_t - C_t - G_t$ at first appears ambiguous. Recall from Section 6.2 that the marginal propensity to consume out of current disposable income is less than one. That is, when period t income increases, utility-maximizing individuals smooth consumption by consuming some of the added income today and saving the rest for the future. The result is that the supply of savings increases. This is shown in Figure 6.17. The rightward shift in the supply of savings increases the equilibrium quantity of investment and decreases the equilibrium real interest rate.

Next, suppose that the government increases expenditures in period t. The immediate effect of an increase in expenditures is to decrease the economy's savings. On the other hand, an increase in expenditures reduces disposable income and utility-maximizing individuals respond by reducing consumption. Can we determine what happens to $Y_t - C_t - G_t$? Yes.

Figure 6.17 | The effect of an increase in current-period income. An increase in Y_t from $Y_{0,t}$ to $Y_{1,t}$ shifts the supply of savings to the right. In equilibrium, the real interest rate drops from $r^*_{0,t}$ to $r^*_{1,t}$ and investment increases from $I^*_{0,t}$ to $I^*_{1,t}$.

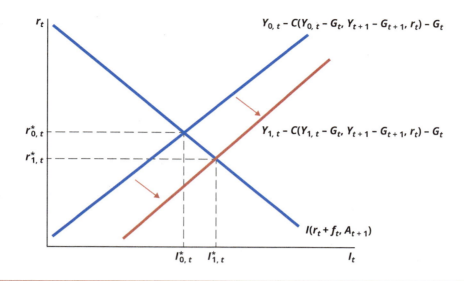

Question: Show the effects of a decrease in current-period income.

The logic is similar to the previous comparative static. Individuals smooth the loss of period t disposable income over both periods. This means that the increase in government expenditures is matched less than one-for-one with a decrease in consumption. The result is that aggregate savings decline. This is shown in Figure 6.18. The equilibrium real interest rate increases and the equilibrium quantity of investment declines.

Figure 6.18 | The effect of an increase in current-period government expenditures. An increase in G_t from $G_{0,t}$ to $G_{1,t}$ shifts the supply of savings to the left. In equilibrium, the real interest rate increases from $r^*_{0,t}$ to $r^*_{1,t}$ and investment decreases from $I^*_{0,t}$ to $I^*_{1,t}$.

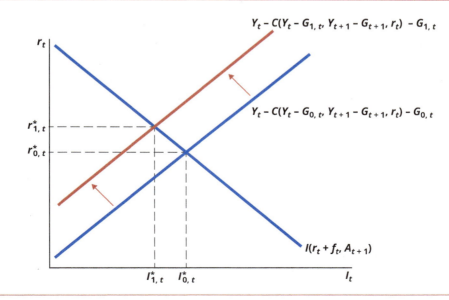

Question: Show the effects of a decrease in current-period government expenditures.

Crowding out
The reduction in investment by private firms that occurs when additional government spending raises real interest rates.

You might recall the concept of **crowding out** from your principles of macroeconomics class. The idea is that an increase in government expenditure raises real interest rates and reduces, or *crowds out*, investment by private businesses. This is consistent with the results in Figure 6.17. Government spending reduces private investment even if the expenditure is financed entirely by taxes. These results alone don't tell us if greater levels of government expenditure are desirable. Answering that question requires knowing how the expenditure is allocated and how individuals in the economy evaluate different types of government expenditure, e.g., roads and schools. Some of these details are discussed in Chapter 9.

Figure 6.19 shows the effects of an increase in future TFP, A_{t+1}. A higher level of future productivity implies a higher return to the investment of new capital. This causes firms to increase their demand for investment at any given real interest rate. The investment demand curve shifts to the right. At the same time, the increase in future productivity also raises future income, Y_{t+1}. Forward-looking individuals will want to smooth their consumption by bringing some of this increase in future income into the present. Consumption goes up and the savings supply curve shifts to the left. The decrease in savings supply and the increase in investment demand work together to push the equilibrium real interest rate up. The change in the equilibrium quantity of investment is ambiguous and depends on the relative magnitudes of the two shifts. As drawn, equilibrium investment stays the same.

The savings–investment model is a useful first step in determining real interest rates. Table 6.4 summarizes the effects of changes in all the exogenous variables on the equilibrium real interest rate and investment. The consumption and investment demand functions will be critical in later chapters of the book. On the other hand, the model is simplified along a number of dimensions. Perhaps the most critical of these is assuming that GDP is exogenous. In the real world, a shock that affects desired consumption or investment also

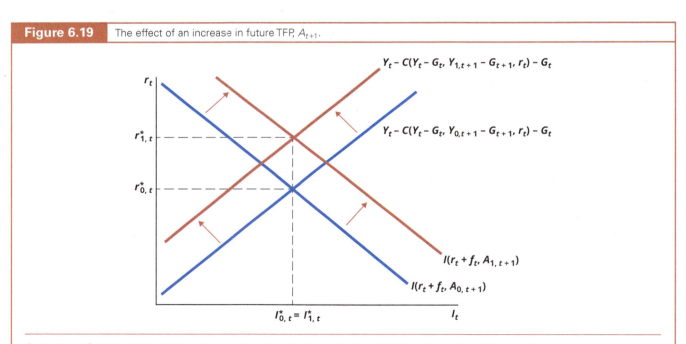

Figure 6.19 The effect of an increase in future TFP, A_{t+1}.

Question: Graphically depict an increase in A_{t+1} that results in equilibrium investment increasing.

Note: An increase in A_{t+1} from $A_{0,\,t+1}$ to $A_{1,\,t+1}$ shifts investment demand to the right. Since an increase in future TFP also raises future income from $Y_{0,\,t+1}$ to $Y_{1,\,t+1}$ savings supply shifts to the left. In equilibrium, the real interest rate increases from $r^*_{0,t}$ to $r^*_{1,t}$. The change in equilibrium investment is ambiguous. As drawn, there is no change in equilibrium investment.

Table 6.4	Summary of Comparative Statics in the Savings/Investment Model	
Increase in:	Δr_t	$\Delta I_t, \Delta S_t$
Y_t	−	+
Y_{t+1}	+	−
A_{t+1}	+	?
G_t	+	−
G_{t+1}	−	+
f_t	−	−

affects output. The chapters in Section 3 of the book deal with the simultaneous determination of interest rates (real and nominal), the inflation rate, and GDP.

Knowledge Check 6-7

Graphically depict a decrease in G_{t+1}. Discuss the economic intuition of your results.

Answers are at the end of the chapter.

Application 6.2

What Explains Declining Real Interest Rates?

As you have learned throughout the chapter, the real interest rate is what is important for saving and investment decisions. Recall that the real interest rate equals the nominal rate minus expected inflation, or $r_t = i_t - \pi^e_{t+1}$. Data on the nominal interest rate is easy to obtain. The one-year Treasury rate on U.S. government bonds, for instance, is a good measure of the risk-free nominal interest rate. Inflation expectations are measured through surveys of households, businesses, and professional forecasters. Using some of this data, the Federal Reserve Bank of Cleveland constructs a measure of the real interest rate. The data is shown in Figure 6.20.

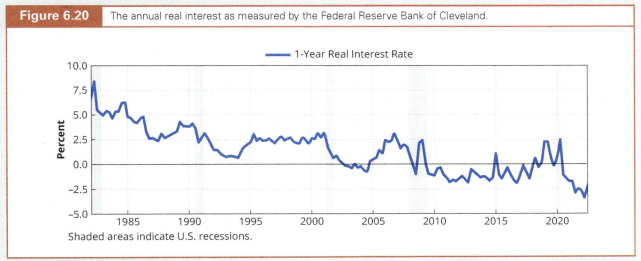

Figure 6.20 The annual real interest as measured by the Federal Reserve Bank of Cleveland.

Shaded areas indicate U.S. recessions.

Source: Here FRED and Cleveland Fed.

■ Continues

Application 6.2 (Continued)

Prior to 2007, the real interest rate usually hovered between 2.5 and 5 percent. Since 2007, the real rate has been negative more often than not. While the data after 2007 is an anomaly, it's not uncommon for the real rate to temporarily be negative. Central banks like the Federal Reserve cut interest rates during recessions. If the nominal rate comes down faster than expected inflation, the real rate can go negative. We see that right after the 2001 recession. During the Great Recession of 2007 through 2009, the Fed reduced nominal rates to zero and left them there until 2016. What is distinctive about the Great Recession and its aftermath is how long the real rate stayed negative. It's becoming clearer that low and perhaps negative real rates are persisting because of structural factors in the economy rather than recessionary ones. Moreover, the real rate has consistently trended down since the 1980s. Can we use the model of the last section to explain the trends?[4]

One factor that may contribute to the trend is low rates of productivity growth. Figure 6.21 shows that annual TFP growth has surpassed 1 percent only one time since 2005. In our model, low TFP growth is represented by a low value of A_{t+1} relative to A_t. If firms expect low TFP growth to persist into the future, then investment demand will shift to the left. Since low values of A_{t+1} also translate into lower values of future income, or Y_{t+1}, the model predicts that individuals will reduce current consumption. This shifts the supply of savings to the right and further lowers real interest rates.

Another factor that could contribute to lower real interest rates is an aging population. Figure 6.22 shows that the fraction of the U.S. population aged 55 and over hovered at about 20 percent as late as 2000 but over the past 20 years, has steadily increased to close to 30 percent. As people expect to live longer, they will save more and that will push real interest rates down. While our two-period model of consumption doesn't explicitly address variable lifespans, we may think that longer life expectancies will increase people's patience in the present. This would be reflected by a higher value of β, which would in turn increase the supply of savings and lower the real interest rate. Furthermore, to the extent older people are expecting to exit the labor force, future GDP, Y_{t+1}, will be lower and that will also decrease the real rate.

Finally, there may be an international dimension to declining real interest rates. As countries like China industrialized in the 1990s and 2000s, their savings rates rose. Between 2000 and 2010, the Chinese savings rate rose from 27 percent to 47 percent. A sizeable fraction of that savings made its way to the United States. The savings and investment model will be extended to include imports, exports, and capital flows in Chapter 7, but for now it's easy to imagine that increased savings from China shifted the U.S. supply of savings to the right and that this further reduced the real interest rate.

While the U.S. population will continue aging, the future of productivity growth and savings rates in other economies are far less clear. If all three trends continue as they have been, negative real interest rates are likely here to stay.

Figure 6.21 TFP growth in the United States from 1980 to 2017.

Shaded areas indicate U.S. recessions.

Source: FRED and PWT (https://fred.stlouisfed.org/series/RTFPNAUSA632NRUG#).

[4] Interested readers can consult Williams, John C. 2017. "Three Questions on R-Star." *FRBSF Economic Letter 2017–05.*

Continues

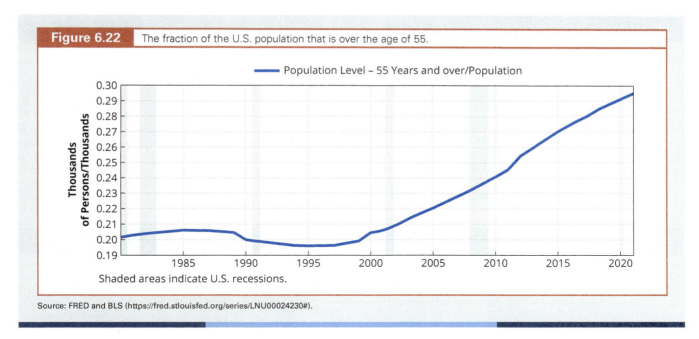

Figure 6.22 The fraction of the U.S. population that is over the age of 55.

Source: FRED and BLS (https://fred.stlouisfed.org/series/LNU00024230#).

Chapter Summary

- The nominal interest rate is the rate of return in terms of dollars. The real interest rate is the rate of return in terms of goods and services.

- Saving and borrowing decisions are determined by the real, not the nominal, interest rate. The two interest rates are linked through the Fisher equation, which says that the real rate equals the nominal rate minus expected inflation.

- Individuals choose how much to consume and save by maximizing their lifetime utility, subject to their present discounted value lifetime budget constraint.

- The consumption function that emerges from the utility maximization problem is a function of current income, future income, and the real interest rate. A general feature of the optimization problem is that individuals smooth consumption across periods.

- Changes in either current or future income only have income effects in that they do not affect the relative price of consumption between periods. An increase in either current-period or future-period income raises consumption today.

- A change in the real interest rate has a substitution effect in that it affects the relative price of consumption between periods. A change in the real rate also has an income effect on borrowers and lenders. Since income and substitution effects sometimes move in the opposite direction, it is not always possible to determine what happens to current and future consumption. We assume that the substitution effect dominates.

- Consumption is more responsive to permanent changes in income compared to temporary ones. Also, according to the model, consumption should only respond to unanticipated changes in income.

- The investment demand of firms is a positive function of future TFP and a negative function of the risk-adjusted real interest rate.

- The equilibrium real interest rate is determined by the consumption-savings decisions of individuals and the investment decisions of firms. Changes in current or future income, the risk adjustment factor, future TFP, or current or future government expenditure all affect the equilibrium real interest rate and the equilibrium quantities of saving and investment.

Key Terms

Real interest rate, 125
Fisher equation, 125
Present discounted value, 128
Utility, 131
Marginal utility, 131
Indifference curve, 132

Marginal rate of substitution, 134
Income effect, 137
Substitution effect, 139
Risk premium, 143
Disposable income, 145
Crowding out, 148

152 **Part 2** Classical Theory

Review Questions

1. Suppose person A's income decreases because they retire from the labor force. Person B's income decreases because they unexpectedly lose their job and enter unemployment. What will happen to the consumption levels of A and B?

2. Commentators often mention that a drop in the stock market has a "negative wealth effect," by which they mean the drop will cause current consumption to decrease. Why would a drop in the value of stock portfolios, which affects future income, affect consumption in the present? Will consumption drop more for workers closer to retirement or further away from it?

3. How is the income effect coming from an increase in the real interest rate different for borrowers and savers?

4. Why do firms' investment decisions depend on future productivity rather than current productivity?

5. Suppose people come to expect government expenditures to increase in the future. How does that affect the equilibrium real interest rate and quantity of investment? Describe the economic intuition.

Problems

6.1 Suppose a person has sequential budget constraints given by

$$C_t + S_t = Y_t,$$

$$C_{t+1} = Y_{t+1} + S_t(1 + r_t).$$

a. Algebraically derive the lifetime budget constraint.

b. Graphically depict the lifetime budget constraint. Make sure you label the intercepts and slope.

c. In reality, borrowers often pay a higher rate of interest than savers receive. This can be formalized by assuming $r_b > r_s$, where r_b is the real interest rate paid by borrowers and r_s is the real interest rate received by lenders. Graphically show how this affects the budget constraint. Clearly label the point at which the person is neither a borrower nor a saver.

6.2 Suppose a person has sequential budget constraints given by

$$C_t + S_t = Y_t - T_t,$$
$$C_{t+1} = Y_{t+1} - T_{t+1} + S_t(1 + r_t),$$

where T_t is a tax in period t and T_{t+1} is a tax in period $t + 1$.

a. Combine the budget constraints to show that the present discounted value of lifetime consumption equals the present discounted value of lifetime income minus the present discounted value of lifetime taxes.

b. Suppose the government is considering an increase in taxes. In particular, they are thinking about either increasing T_t by 10 or T_{t+1} by 12. If $r_t = 0.1$, in which period would the consumer prefer the tax increase? Why?

c. How will your answer to part b change if $r_t = 0.2$? What is the economic intuition here?

d. Assuming that the consumer has indifference curves with standard properties, graphically depict the optimal quantities of consumption. Show how an increase in taxes affects the optimal quantities.

e. Discuss the role of the income and substitution effects in your results for part d.

6.3 Suppose a person has a marginal rate of substitution of $\dfrac{C_{t+1}}{\beta C_t}$ and a standard lifetime budget constraint.

a. Derive the period t consumption function.

b. Assume $\beta = 0.9, Y_t = 5$ and $Y_{t+1} = 10$. Solve for the optimal quantity of period t consumption. Is the person a saver or a borrower?

c. Derive the marginal propensity of consumption if Y_t increases from 5 to 6. How can you tell that the person is smoothing consumption across time?

d. Suppose the person is not allowed to borrow. Formally, $C_t \leq Y_t$. Show how this changes the graphical representation of the lifetime budget constraint.

e. If $\beta = 0.9, Y_t = 5$, and $Y_{t+1} = 10$, argue that the optimal quantity of consumption you solved for in part b is no longer feasible. What is the new optimal level of consumption?

f. Derive the marginal propensity of consumption if Y_t increases from 5 to 6. Is the person smoothing consumption? What explains the difference with part c?

g. Economic researchers have found that the marginal propensity to consume out of one-time tax cuts is highest for people who face borrowing constraints. Are your results in part f consistent with this?

6.4 Consider the savings–investment model. The savings and investment equations are given respectively by

$$S_t = Y_t - C(Y_t - G_t, Y_{t+1} - G_{t+1}, r_t) - G_t,$$
$$I_t = I(r_t + f_t, A_{t+1}).$$

a. Explain the economic meaning of the exogenous variable, f_t.

b. Show graphically how an increase in f_t affects the equilibrium real interest rate and level of investment.

6.5 Consider a quantitative version of the last question. The savings supply equation is given by

$$S_t = Y_t - (a_1(Y_t - G_t) + a_2(Y_{t+1} - G_{t+1}) - a_3 r_t) - G_t,$$

Chapter 6 Saving, Investment, and the Real Interest Rate — 153

where a_1, a_2, and a_3 are positive constants. The investment demand equation is given by

$$I_t = b_1 A_{t+1} - b_2(r_t + f_t)$$

where b_1 and b_2 are positive constants.

a. How is the slope of the savings supply curve affected by a_1? How is the slope of the investment demand curve affected by b_2?

b. Solve for the equilibrium real interest rate.

c. How does the equilibrium real interest rate react in response to a one percentage point increase in f_t?

✓ Knowledge Check 6-1 Answer

If the nominal rate is 5 percent and expected inflation is 2 percent, then the real interest rate is 3 percent. If the inflation rate turns out to be 5 percent, the ex-post real interest rate is 0 percent. The home buyer is helped by unexpected inflation because the loan is being repaid with less valuable dollars.

✓ Knowledge Check 6-2 Answer

1. If $C_{t+1} = Y_{t+1} = 20$, then $C_t = 10$ and $S_t = 0$.

2. If $C_t = 7$ and $C_t + S_t = 10$, then $S_t = 3$. Then use the future budget constraint: $C_{t+1} = Y_{t+1} + (1 + r_t)S_t = 20 + (1 + 0.05)3 = 23.15$.

3. If $C_{t+1} = 25$ and $C_{t+1} = 20 + (1 + r_t)S_t$, then $S_t = 4.76$. Using the first period's budget constraint, $C_t + S_t = 10$, which implies $C_t = 5.24$.

4. If $S_t = 2$ and $C_t + S_t = 10$, then $C_t = 8$. Then use the future budget constraint: $C_{t+1} = Y_{t+1} + (1 + r_t)S_t = 20 + (1 + 0.05)2 = 22.10$.

5. If $C_t = 12$ and $C_t + S_t = 10$, then $S_t = -2$. Then use the future budget constraint: $C_{t+1} = Y_{t+1} + (1 + r_t)S_t = 20 - (1 + 0.05)2 = 17.9$.

C_t	C_{t+1}	S_t
10	20	0
7	23.15	3
5.24	25	4.76
8	22.10	2
12	17.9	−2

✓ Knowledge Check 6-3 Answer

Given a value of C_t and U, we can solve the lifetime utility function for C_{t+1}. Starting with $U = 10$ gives

$$10 = \ln(C_t) + 0.95 \ln(C_{t+1})$$

$$\Leftrightarrow 10 - \ln(C_t) = 0.95 \ln(C_{t+1})$$

$$\Leftrightarrow \frac{10 - \ln(C_t)}{0.95} = \ln(C_{t+1})$$

$$\Leftrightarrow exp\left(\frac{10 - \ln(C_t)}{0.95}\right) = C_{t+1},$$

where "exp" is the exponential function. We can solve for C_{t+1} by plugging in particular values of C_t. When C_t equals 400,

$$C_{t+1} = \exp\left(\frac{10 - \ln(400)}{0.95}\right) = 68.0.$$

The marginal rate of substitution is

$$MRS = \frac{C_{t+1}}{\beta C_t} = \frac{68.0}{(0.95)400} = 0.18.$$

The MRS says that the consumer is willing to give up 0.18 units of C_{t+1} for one more unit of C_t while remaining on the same indifference curve. Alternatively, if the individual moves to the higher indifference curve of $U = 12$ and consumes $C_t = 600$ in period t, then

$$C_{t+1} = \exp\left(\frac{12 - \ln(600)}{0.95}\right) = 364.3.$$

Using the values of C_t and C_{t+1}, we can obtain the marginal rate of substitution:

$$MRS = \frac{C_{t+1}}{\beta C_t} = \frac{364.3}{(0.95)600} = 0.64.$$

The results for the remainder of the rows are shown below.

	U = 10			U = 12	
C_t	C_{t+1}	MRS	C_t	C_{t+1}	MRS
400	68.0	0.18	600	364.3	0.64
300	92.1	0.32	500	441.4	0.93
200	141.1	0.74	400	558.2	1.47
100	292.6	3.08	300	755.7	2.65

As C_t decreases, C_{t+1} must increase to stay on the same indifference curve.

Knowledge Check 6-4 Answer

The fact that the individual is a borrower does not affect the substitution effect. Period t consumption is more expensive, and period $t + 1$ consumption is cheaper. The fact that the individual is a borrower means that the cost of borrowing goes up, so the income effect is negative for consumption in the present and future. Since income and substitution effects move in the same way for period t, C_t unambiguously declines. Income and substitution effects move in the opposite way for C_{t+1}, so the change is ambiguous.

Effects of a Real Interest Rate Increase on Borrowers

	C_t	C_{t+1}
Income effect	−	−
Substitution effect	−	+
Net effect	−	?

Knowledge Check 6-5 Answer

The period t budget constraint is

$$C_t + S_t = Y_t.$$

Substitute the consumption function into the budget constraint and solve for S_t.

$$\frac{1}{1+\beta}\left[Y_t + \frac{Y_{t+1}}{1+r_t}\right] + S_t = Y_t$$

$$\Leftrightarrow Y_t + \frac{Y_{t+1}}{1+r_t} + (1+\beta)S_t = (1+\beta)Y_t$$

$$\Leftrightarrow (1+\beta)S_t = \beta Y_t - \frac{Y_{t+1}}{1+r_t}$$

$$\Leftrightarrow S_t = \frac{1}{1+\beta}\left[\beta Y_t - \frac{Y_{t+1}}{1+r_t}\right]$$

If $\beta Y_t < \frac{Y_{t+1}}{1+r_t}$ then the individual borrows. Intuitively, if future income is sufficiently big relative to current income, then the individual will borrow. Also, observe that savings is an increasing function of the real interest rate. An increase in the real rate makes savings more attractive.

 Knowledge Check 6-6 Answer

We can complete the rest of the table by substituting in the particular values of r_t, f_t, and A_{t+1} into the investment demand equation. Doing so yields

r_t	I_t		
	Case 1: $A_{t+1} = 20$, $f_t = 0.02$	Case 2: $A_{t+1} = 40$, $f_t = 0.02$	Case 3: $A_{t+1} = 20$, $f_t = 0.04$
0.01	14	34	10
0.02	12	32	8
0.03	10	30	6
0.04	8	28	4

Investment demand is downward sloping in r_t. An increase in A_{t+1} shifts investment demand to the right. Higher future productivity raises the return to investment. Firms respond by increasing their desired level of investment at every real interest rate. An increase in f_t raises the cost of capital. Firms respond by reducing their demand for investment at every real interest rate. The investment demand curve shifts to the left.

 Knowledge Check 6-7 Answer

A decrease in G_{t+1} means that future disposable income increases, which causes individuals to consume more today. Since current-period output hasn't changed, the only way to finance the greater level of consumption is to save less. This shifts the supply of savings to the left. In equilibrium, the real interest rate rises and the equilibrium quantity of investment falls. This is shown in Figure 6.23.

Figure 6.23 The effect of a decrease in future government expenditures. An increase in G_{t+1} from $G_{0,t+1}$ to $G_{1,t+1}$ shifts the supply of savings to the left. In equilibrium, the real interest rate increases from $r^*_{0,t}$ to $r^*_{1,t}$ and investment decreases from $I^*_{0,t}$ to $I^*_{1,t}$.

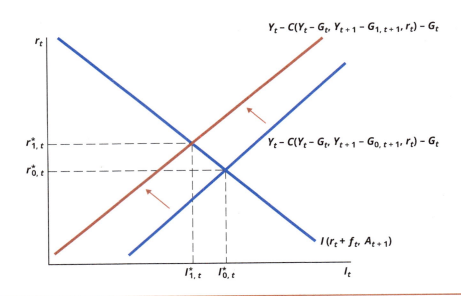

Chapter 7

International Trade and the Macroeconomy

Learning Objectives

7.1 Calculate real and nominal exchange rates between two countries.

7.2 Explain the economic case for free trade and the caveats that go into that argument.

7.3 Explain the connection between the balance of trade and capital flows.

7.4 Show how including foreign trade affects the savings and investment model.

Before reading this chapter, check the tags on your clothes. Chances are, you are wearing something produced in another country. Even countries with retail stores exclusively in the United States produce some of their products abroad. The U.S. company L.L. Bean, for instance, has most of their retail stores in New England, but the Bean slippers I'm wearing are made in Malaysia. The car you drive, the coffee you drink, and the computer on which you type may have been entirely or partly produced in another country. Undeniably, international trade influences our everyday lives. This chapter demonstrates that international trade also has an impact on the macroeconomy.

In the last chapter, you learned how real interest rates, savings, and investment are determined. But the entirety of that analysis was in a closed economy, that is an economy without international trade. The real world contains significant flows of goods, services, and capital across countries. As such, the international dimension of the economy will influence the determination of macroeconomic variables.

International macroeconomics also has important policy implications. We routinely hear about the effects of the trade deficit and the role international trade plays in "shipping jobs overseas." Is minimizing the trade deficit desirable? Do the benefits of international trade outweigh the costs? These are questions explored in this chapter.

7-1 Exchange Rates

Returning to the L.L. Bean slippers example in the introduction, suppose that you find a pair of slippers for $50 in the United States. Then, while traveling in Germany a week later, you find an identical pair of slippers for 40 euros. Are the slippers a better deal in Germany or the United States? To begin to answer that question, you need to know the rate at which euros are traded for dollars. The rate at which one currency is traded for another currency is called a **nominal exchange rate**. This is the rate you commonly see in newspapers or finance websites like exchange-rates.org. We discuss how to calculate nominal exchange rates below.

Nominal exchange rate
The rate at which two currencies trade for each other.

157

7-1a Calculating Nominal Exchange Rates

At the time this book is being written, 0.95 euros exchange for \$1. The dollar-to-euro exchange rate, e, is therefore

$$e = 0.95 \, \frac{euro}{\$}.$$

This nominal exchange rate is 0.95 euros per \$1. If the nominal exchange rate increases, a given dollar purchases more euros. So if the nominal exchange rate rises to 1.05, \$1 can be traded for 1.05 euros. In this case, the U.S. dollar has *appreciated,* or increased in value, relative to the euro. The euro, on the other hand, *depreciated,* or became weaker relative to the dollar. To see this, note that the euro-to-dollar exchange rate is simply the reciprocal of the dollar-to-euro exchange rate, or

$$e = 1.05 \, \frac{\$}{euro}.$$

When the dollar-to-euro exchange rate increases to 1.05, the euro-to-dollar exchange rate decreases to 0.95. Thus, when the dollar appreciates relative to the euro, the euro depreciates relative to the dollar. Table 7.1 shows how the dollar trades relative to other global currencies as of December 2022.

Table 7.1	Nominal Exchange Rates
Dollar to	**Nominal exchange rate**
Euro	0.95
Japanese yen	134.32
Pound sterling	0.81
Chinese yuan	7.02
Mexican peso	19.39

✓ Knowledge Check 7-1

Using the information in Table 7.1, calculate the euro-to-yen and yuan-to-peso exchange rates.

——————————————————————————— Answers are at the end of the chapter.

7-1b From Nominal to Real Exchange Rates

Converting one currency to another is a useful first step in comparing the prices of goods and services across countries. But it is not the end of the story. To see this, let's continue with the slipper example. The fact that the dollar-to-euro exchange rate is 0.95 does not tell you whether slippers are cheaper in Germany or the United States. To make that comparison, we need to combine information on the nominal exchange rate with relative prices across countries.

If the slippers in the United States cost \$50 and the dollar-to-euro exchange rate is 0.95, then the price of U.S. slippers in terms of euros is

$$\$50 \times 0.95 \, \frac{euro}{\$} = 47.5 \; euros.$$

Real exchange rate
The rate at which goods and services in one country trade for goods and services in another country.

Since the price of slippers in Germany is 40 euros, we conclude that the slippers are cheaper in Germany. The lesson is you are better off buying the slippers on your vacation to Germany.

More generally, economists and travelers are interested in the **real exchange rate**, or the rate at which goods and services rather than currencies in one country trade for

Chapter 7 International Trade and the Macroeconomy   **159**

goods and services in another country. The real exchange rate, ε, between the dollar and the euro is

$$\varepsilon = \frac{P_{US}}{P_{Eu}} e, \tag{1}$$

where P_{US} is the price of a good or service in the United States, expressed in dollars, and P_{Eu} is the price of the same good or service in Germany, expressed in euros. In the slipper example, the real exchange rate is 1.1875, meaning that one pair of U.S. slippers trades for 1.1875 slippers in Germany. Why does this make sense? A pair of slippers in the United States sells for \$50. But \$50 is worth $\$50 \times 0.95 = 47.5$ euros. So, 47.5 euros buys you $47.5/40 = 1.1875$ pairs of slippers. Thus, slippers are about 18 percent more expensive in the United States compared to Germany.

Of course, there is nothing special about slippers. We could compute the real exchange rate for any good or service. To take another example, suppose that the price of a Mercedes sedan is \$45,000 in the United States and 40,000 euros in Germany. If the dollar-to-euro exchange rate continues to be 0.95, then the real exchange rate is

$$\varepsilon = \frac{\$45,000}{40,000 \; euros} \times 0.95 \; \frac{euro}{\$}$$
$$= 1.069.$$

So, a Mercedes in the United States is about 7 percent more expensive than in Germany.

Calculating the real exchange rate across one good, however, does not allow us to see whether goods and services in the United States are more or less expensive relative to the rest of the world. To do this, economists depart from an item-by-item comparison and calculate the real exchange rate for a basket of goods and services, similar to the consumer price index, across countries. An increase, or appreciation, in the real exchange rate implies that goods and services in the United States get more expensive relative to the rest of the world. This makes imports cheaper and exports more expensive. Accordingly, net exports go down. Thus, net exports are a negative function of the real exchange rate. Before moving on, you may wonder why the real exchange rate (either of a specific good or an entire index) would not be equal to one everywhere. That is, why would an identical product not trade for the same price in all countries? If a good or service is tradable across countries, you would expect profit maximizing entrepreneurs to move goods and services from countries where they have the lowest price to countries where they have the highest price. If a box of Cap'n Crunch cereal[1] sells for a higher price in Canada than in the United States, you would expect the Quaker Oats company (the producer of Cap'n Crunch) to direct more units of new production to Canada and fewer to the United States. The higher supply of Cap'n Crunch in Canada would drive the Canadian price down, while the lower supply in the United States would drive American prices up. Through this process of **arbitrage**, or exploitation of price differences across countries, the price of any good or service is equalized across countries. The economic logic of arbitrage is powerful, but arbitrage also has its limits. These limits are discussed in the next section.

Arbitrage
The process of exploiting cross-country price differences of an identical product.

✓ Knowledge Check 7-2

Suppose that the price of a Lego set is \$100 in the United States. Letting P_F denote the price of the Lego set in a foreign country, complete the rest of the table. Where is the Lego set the cheapest?

Country	e	P_F	ε
Germany	0.9 euros	80 euros	
Mexico	25 pesos	2,000 pesos	
Japan	140 yen	32,000 yen	

Answers are at the end of the chapter.

---

[1]We are of course talking about Peanut Butter Cap'n Crunch, which is unquestionably superior to either the original or Crunch Berries.

Law of one price
The theory that identical goods and services should trade for the same price, regardless of the location.

7-1c When Is the Law of One Price Actually a Law?

The **law of one price** says that an identical good or service must sell at the same price, regardless of location. Consider crude oil (the key input in gasoline production), which is a standardized commodity, so we don't need to think about quality differences. In 2022, gas prices ranged from about $1 in some Middle Eastern countries to over $7 in Western Europe. One reason for the price differential is transportation costs. Countries that produce gasoline do not need to pay shipping costs to have it imported. The price of gasoline in Kuwait is relatively low because they produce (and export) a lot of petroleum.

A second reason that gasoline prices differ is that countries levy different taxes on it. The government in the Netherlands charges more than $3 per gallon in taxes, whereas Canada's government charges less than $1.[2] It's no surprise that gasoline costs more in the Netherlands than in Canada.

If prices differ even on a commodity like gasoline, they will differ to an even greater extent on goods and services with varying qualities. Thus, while the law of one price has an appealing logic, the real world is a lot more complicated.

7-2 The Economist's Case for Free Trade (with Caveats)

Modern economies are increasingly interconnected. Figure 7.1 shows that, at a global level, total trade (imports plus exports) as a share of GDP increased from less than 30 percent in 1970 to more than 60 percent by 2010. Given this reality, it is reasonable to ask if cross-country trade is a net positive.

More than likely, you learned the benefits of free trade in your principles of economics class. To begin with, it's helpful to think about trade on a smaller scale than a country. Imagine life in a small village of, say, 100 people. One approach to economic production is complete self-sufficiency. Each person plants and harvests their own crops, sews their own clothes, and builds their own houses. This lifestyle may seem idyllic, but people in

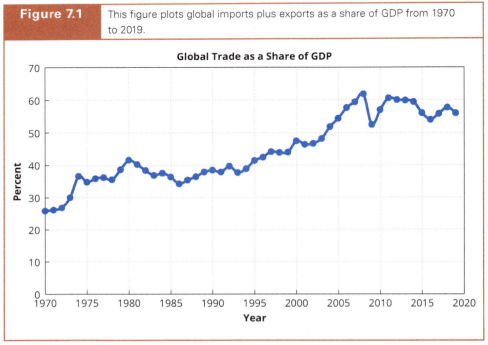

Figure 7.1 This figure plots global imports plus exports as a share of GDP from 1970 to 2019.

Source: WDI.

---
[2]https://afdc.energy.gov/data/10327

Chapter 7 International Trade and the Macroeconomy **161**

this village would undoubtedly be poor. The time it takes for each villager to do *everything* means that no villager develops their skills in any one thing. Because villagers likely differ in their talents, preferences, and endowments of land, economic life can be improved with trade. The person living on the most fertile plot of land could spend all their time growing crops. The person with the most dexterity could make clothing and boots. The most creative person could provide sketch comedy for the village and so on. Collectively, the village would produce more output per person through specialization.

Now imagine that there is a second village just a few miles away. Even better! Now each village can further specialize in what they are relatively good at. Moreover, some things produced in one village might be totally unattainable in the other village. For instance, if one of them borders an ocean, then they can provide fresh seafood to the landlocked village.[3]

What is true among villages is essentially true across countries. They gain from free trade. In other words, the logic applied at the level of the village does not suffer the fallacy of composition when scaled up to a national level. True, things are more complicated at that trans-national level, given that countries differ in their currencies, tariff and quota policies, and subsidies to domestic industries. But the underlying logic in favor of trade is still compelling. Essentially, countries differ in their productivity levels, preferences, and endowments of land and natural resources. Given these differences, there are gains to trade among nations. The next section describes a model that focuses on the differences in productivity levels.

7-2a The Ricardian Model

Named after 18th-century economist David Ricardo, the Ricardian model of trade is one way to think about trade across countries. In the most simplified version of the model, two countries produce two goods using labor as the only input into production. Critically, the countries differ in their productivities for producing each good.

The model is easiest to see through an example. Suppose two countries, A and B, each have 1,000 workers. People in both economies enjoy consuming ice cream and tofu. Workers can be allocated to either the ice cream–producing industry or the tofu industry. In country A, a worker can produce two pints of ice cream or one pound of tofu. Thus, in country A, the opportunity cost of one pound of tofu is two pints of ice cream. In country B, a worker can produce one pint of ice cream or two pounds of tofu. In country B, the opportunity cost of one pound of tofu is one-half pint of ice cream. Since workers in country A are more productive at producing ice cream than workers in country B, we say that workers in country A have an **absolute advantage** in producing ice cream. Similarly, country B's workers have an absolute advantage in producing tofu.

The **production possibilities frontier (PPF)** shows all the combinations of tofu and ice cream that are attainable given each country's labor force and technology levels. Country A can produce 1,000 pounds of tofu if it commits its entire workforce to tofu production or 2,000 pints of ice cream if it commits its entire workforce to ice cream production. One additional pound of tofu comes at the cost of two pints of ice cream. Consequently, the relative price of a pound of tofu is two pints of ice cream. It is the reverse in country B—an additional pound of tofu comes at the cost of one-half pint of ice cream, meaning that the relative price of tofu is one-half pint of ice cream. Figure 7.2 shows the PPFs for each country.

We start the analysis by assuming the countries are in **autarky**, or a situation where they do not trade with each other. Assume that each country devotes half of its labor force to producing tofu and the other half to producing ice cream. This makes sense as long as people in both countries want to consume both tofu and ice cream. Table 7.2 shows the allocations of labor, production, and consumption in each country. Half of the 1,000 workers in country A produce 500 pounds of tofu in total. The other half of the workforce produces 1,000 pints of ice cream. Since there is no trade between the countries, total production of tofu in country A equals total consumption of tofu. Similarly, total production of ice cream in country A equals total consumption of ice cream. The same logic applies to country B.

Absolute advantage
The good or service that an economy produces more efficiently than another economy.

Production possibilities frontier (PPF)
A graph showing all the combinations of two goods produced in a country given its technology levels and the size of its labor force.

Autarky
A situation in which no countries trade with each other.

---
[3]The reference to L.L. Bean and seafood betrays the author's New England location.

162 Part 2 Classical Theory

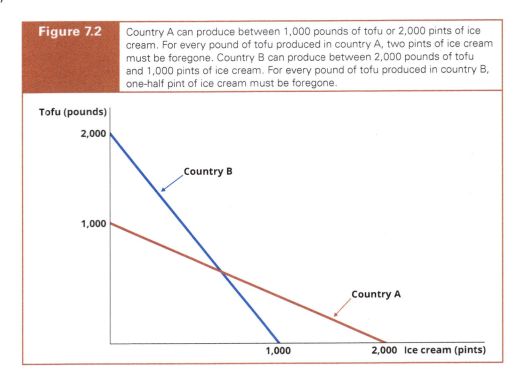

Figure 7.2 Country A can produce between 1,000 pounds of tofu or 2,000 pints of ice cream. For every pound of tofu produced in country A, two pints of ice cream must be foregone. Country B can produce between 2,000 pounds of tofu and 1,000 pints of ice cream. For every pound of tofu produced in country B, one-half pint of ice cream must be foregone.

The last row of Table 7.2 shows that the two countries collectively produce 1,500 pints of ice cream and 1,500 pounds of tofu.

Table 7.2 Allocations in Autarky

	L_{tofu}	L_{ice}	Y_{tofu}	Y_{ice}	C_{tofu}	C_{ice}
A	500	500	500	1,000	500	1,000
B	500	500	1,000	500	1,000	500
A+B	1,000	1,000	1,500	1,500	1,500	1,500

Would countries A and B benefit from opening to trade? Yes. Country A is more productive in producing ice cream and country B is more productive in producing tofu. As Table 7.3a shows, if country A completely specializes in the production of ice cream and country B completely specializes in the production of tofu, the global output of each good increases relative to autarky. Thus, free trade maximizes global GDP.

Table 7.3a Allocations with Free Trade

	L_{tofu}	L_{ice}	Y_{tofu}	Y_{ice}	C_{tofu}	C_{ice}
A	0	1,000	0	2,000	?	?
B	1,000	0	2,000	0	?	?
A+B	1,000	1,000	2,000	2,000	2,000	2,000

It's great that free trade maximizes global GDP, but we want to know if the people in each country are better off under free trade. To see if this is the case, remember that the cost of producing one pound of tofu in country A is two pints of ice cream. It follows that people in country A won't pay more than two pints of ice cream to purchase a pound of tofu from country B. By similar logic, country B won't sell a pound of tofu for less than half a pint of ice cream. Thus, any price of tofu between half a pint and two pints of ice cream makes both countries better off. The **terms of trade** are a country's export price divided by its import price. Better terms of trade for one country necessarily mean worse terms of trade for the other country.

Terms of trade
A country's export price divided by its import price.

Let's say the price for one pound of tofu happens to be one pint of ice cream, meaning that the terms of trade are one for both countries.[4] Then, each country has the same GDP. If people continue to spend half their income on tofu and half on ice cream, then 1,000 pounds of tofu and 1,000 pounds of ice cream are consumed in both countries. The rest of Table 7.3b is shown below.

Table 7.3b	Allocations with Free Trade (Relative Price Equals One)					
	L_{tofu}	L_{ice}	Y_{tofu}	Y_{ice}	C_{tofu}	C_{ice}
A	0	1,000	0	2,000	1,000	1,000
B	1,000	0	2,000	0	1,000	1,000
A+B	1,000	1,000	2,000	2,000	2,000	2,000

People in country A gain in moving from autarky to free trade because their ice cream consumption stays the same, but their tofu consumption increases. People in country B gain because their ice cream consumption increases, but their tofu consumption stays the same.

To gain some economic intuition for the results, Figure 7.3 compares autarky to free trade from country A's perspective. In autarky, country A can consume one more pound of tofu by foregoing two pints of ice cream. With free trade, it can consume one more pound of tofu by foregoing only one pint of ice cream. In other words, in moving to free trade, it's as if country A expanded its production possibilities frontier. However, it hasn't: the underlying technologies are still the same. What's changed is that production no longer has to equal consumption. Country A specializes in what it is good at producing (ice cream) and exports some of it in exchange for importing tofu. Country B does the reverse.

Despite leaving the levels of technology and the labor forced constant, both countries raise their consumptions by opening up to trade. These gains from trade occur because

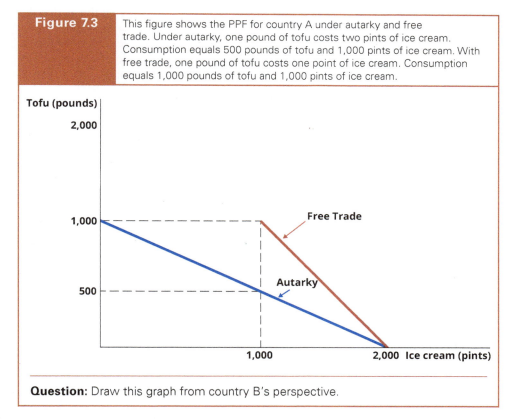

Figure 7.3 This figure shows the PPF for country A under autarky and free trade. Under autarky, one pound of tofu costs two pints of ice cream. Consumption equals 500 pounds of tofu and 1,000 pints of ice cream. With free trade, one pound of tofu costs one point of ice cream. Consumption equals 1,000 pounds of tofu and 1,000 pints of ice cream.

Question: Draw this graph from country B's perspective.

---

[4]This will indeed be the case if there are no shipping costs or tariffs.

164 **Part 2** Classical Theory

countries can specialize in the product they are most productive at producing. What happens when a country is less productive at producing all goods and services relative to another country? Many developing nations, for instance, have lower levels of labor productivity across all products. Are there still gains from trade?

> ✓ **Knowledge Check 7-3**
>
> Referring to the last example, suppose the world price of tofu is 1.25 pints of ice cream. Assuming people in country A continue to spend half their budget on ice cream, fill out a new version of Table 7.3. Explain how the increase in the price of tofu affects the distribution of the gains from trade.
>
> ———— Answers are at the end of the chapter.

7-2b Ricardian Model with Comparative Advantage

As an All-Pro–caliber athlete, Patrick Mahomes can probably mow a lawn faster than any yard-care expert in the Kansas City area. And yet Mahomes still finds it optimal to play football on Sundays rather than mow his lawn. Mahomes' productivity advantage in football is much higher than his productivity advantage in lawn mowing. Although the person mowing Mahomes' lawn may take twice as long as Mahomes himself, their passer rating in an NFL game would likely be many, many times worse than Mahomes'. Mahomes might be the best lawn mower in all of Missouri, but because he makes millions of dollars in an NFL season, his opportunity cost of mowing his lawn is extraordinarily high.

Comparative advantage
The good or service that an economy produces at a lower opportunity cost than another economy.

Just like Patrick Mahomes, nations specialize in their **comparative advantage**, or what they have the lowest opportunity cost of producing. Even if one country is better than another country at producing absolutely everything, there are still likely to be gains from trade.

To see how this works, return to the tofu and ice cream example. Suppose that a worker in country B can produce two pounds of tofu or three pints of ice cream. In autarky, the price of a pound of tofu is 1.5 pints of ice cream. Another way of saying this is that the opportunity cost of one pound of tofu is 1.5 pints of ice cream. A worker in country A can produce one pound of tofu or two pints of ice cream, so the price, or opportunity cost, of one pound of tofu is two pints of ice cream. Table 7.4 shows the allocations in autarky assuming both countries divide their labor force evenly across the sectors.

Table 7.4	Allocations in Autarky					
	L_{tofu}	L_{ice}	Y_{tofu}	Y_{ice}	C_{tofu}	C_{ice}
A	500	500	500	1,000	500	1,000
B	500	500	1,000	1,500	1,000	1,500
A+B	1,000	1,000	1,500	2,500	1,500	2,500

Now let's move to free trade. Since the opportunity cost of producing tofu is higher in country A, it will specialize in producing ice cream. That is, country A has a comparative advantage in producing ice cream. The 1,000 workers in country A collectively produce 2,000 pints of ice cream. Suppose 800 workers in country B produce tofu and 200 produce ice cream. It's necessary for country B to allocate some of its workers to ice cream so that the global production of ice cream doesn't fall. The resulting quantities are shown in Table 7.5.

Table 7.5	Allocations with Free Trade (Relative Price Equals 1.6)					
	L_{tofu}	L_{ice}	Y_{tofu}	Y_{ice}	C_{tofu}	C_{ice}
A	0	1,000	0	2,000	600	1,000
B	800	200	1,600	600	1,000	1,600
A+B	1,000	1,000	1,600	2,600	1,600	2,600

Chapter 7 International Trade and the Macroeconomy

Because the price of tofu in autarky is 1.5 in country B and 2 in country A, the terms of trade must fall somewhere in between. If the export price happens to be 1.6, then country A can export 1,000 pints of ice cream in exchange for $1{,}000/1.6 = 600$ pounds of tofu. Relative to autarky, country A increases its consumption of tofu and leaves constant its consumption of ice cream. Country B increases its consumption of ice cream and leaves constant its consumption of tofu. Both countries gain from trade.

Even though country A is less efficient at producing ice cream and tofu, its comparative advantage is in ice cream. By specializing in producing ice cream, country A can export some of its ice cream in exchange for tofu. In the end, both countries are better off. This lesson has real-world implications. By specializing in the goods and services for which they have a comparative advantage, low-productivity countries gain from trading with high-productivity countries, and vice versa.

> ### ✓ Knowledge Check 7-4
>
> Redo Table 7.5 assuming the price of tofu is 1.8 pints of ice cream. Continue to assume country A exports 1,000 pints of ice cream. How does the higher price of tofu affect the distribution of the gains from trade?
>
> Answers are at the end of the chapter.

7-2c The Limits to Free Trade

The conclusion that countries gain from trade inferred from the stylized examples we reviewed in this chapter can be expanded to contexts with many products and many countries. Yet, in reality, international trade is encumbered by all sorts of government policies. Are governments getting it wrong, or does the case for free trade need to be qualified? Yes.

We can say with a high degree of certainty that global GDP per capita would increase if all trade barriers were eliminated. On the other hand, there may be costs associated with cross-country trade that are not captured in the Ricardian model. Here are a few:

1. **Complete specialization is risky:** In the last example, country A completely specialized in ice cream. If an extreme weather event wipes out soy bean production in country B, then people in country A just have a lot of dessert to eat. Therefore, it may be optimal for a country to produce at least a little bit of everything to avoid a potentially very large downside risk. The choice of words "may be" is intentional. Presumably, country A could purchase tofu from some other country than B. The argument against complete specialization may imply that a country seeks multiple trading partners rather than producing a particular good itself.

2. **Possibility of bottlenecks:** The Ricardian model makes the simplifying assumption that each good is produced entirely in one country. In reality, many products are made of inputs produced from all over the world. For instance, even though General Motors and Ford assemble cars in America, they import microchips for the cars from Southeast Asian countries. When these countries shut down during the Covid-19 pandemic, global automakers were suddenly deprived of microchips. It didn't matter if there were 10,000 new cars ready to be put on the lot. Without microchips, the cars couldn't operate.

   In theory, the Ricardian model extends to trade in intermediate goods. Each country can specialize in the intermediate goods for which it has a comparative advantage. In practice, this leaves vulnerable the production of the final product. If a car is made of 30 essential inputs produced in 30 different countries, all it takes is for something to go wrong in one of those countries to disrupt the entire chain of production. The experience of the pandemic has caused economic policymakers to compare the efficiency gains of specialization to the downside risks of bottlenecks.

3. Infant industries: In the early years of the United States, Alexander Hamilton argued that some industries, particularly in manufacturing, should be supported by the government and sheltered from foreign competition. His idea was that manufacturing industries in the United States faced high fixed costs of production because they were just getting started. If they were to match their international competitors' prices, they would earn a loss. Anticipating this, potential entrepreneurs would never start a manufacturing business. By subsidizing the businesses and placing tariffs on foreign competitors, these infant industries could recoup their start-up costs and eventually be competitive with international businesses on a level playing field.

Although the infant industry argument is logically valid, it faces a number of practical challenges. First, it assumes that the government can pick winners more accurately than lenders in financial markets. If these high-fixed-cost industries would eventually turn a profit that more than compensates for the initial protection, then banks or other investors would be willing to finance these projects. This is perhaps less true in 18th-century America or developing nations today, which don't have the same depth and sophistication of financial markets as developed countries like the United States do.

A related challenge is that political actors, unlike investors, are not motivated by profit and loss. Rather, the politician's job is to please their constituency and retain power. The consequences of this objective may be to allocate public funds to industries that please voters but don't offer the highest return. Moreover, once tariffs against foreign competitors are in place, they may be politically difficult to remove. Despite being well past infant stage, the U.S. steel industry, for instance, has benefited from tariffs during Democratic and Republican presidential administrations from the 20th century through today.

4. Trade has reallocation effects: Workers in the Ricardian model freely move between industries when a country opens to trade. In reality, workers accumulate occupation-specific skills that don't easily transfer to other jobs. Car manufacturers don't suddenly become software engineers. Learning the skills needed to succeed in a new industry takes time, commitment, and may involve a painful unemployment spell. Even after transferring to a new industry, nothing guarantees that a worker will earn the same salary in the new job. At the same time, people whose jobs aren't affected by trade only gain from the cheaper products imported from abroad. Economists have long recognized that trade has distributionary effects. Saying that "all countries gain from trade" is a shorthand that speaks more to the average rather than every single person. But economists also traditionally thought that any reallocation effects to trade would be temporary as workers sort themselves into new industries. New research has challenged this assumption.

7-3 Accounting for Imports and Exports in the GDP Equation

The previous section showed that, in theory, all countries can gain from trade. In reality, the United States imports and exports approximately 1 trillion dollars in a year. So it is important to include an international dimension to our models. Next, you will learn how the international sector changes the savings–investment model of Chapter 6.

First, it is useful to remind yourself why imports are subtracted from the GDP equation. Recall that gross domestic product (GDP) measures goods and services produced *within a country* in a year. Using the expenditure method, GDP is given by

$$Y = C + I + G + X - M, \tag{2}$$

Application 7.1

The China Shock

It's long been recognized that trade can harm particular types of workers. The most common hypothetical is a nation like the United States, whose workers are relatively highly skilled, trading with a developing country, whose workers are relatively less skilled. In this framework, the United States would specialize in products produced with high-skilled labor and export them to less-developed countries. This in turn would widen the income gap between high-skilled and low-skilled workers in the United States.

Until the past 10 years or so, there were two reasons why economists have downplayed the potential effects of trade on inequality. First, for several decades following World War II, the hypothetical above was just that—a hypothetical. The biggest trading partners for the United States were comparably skilled and developed nations like Canada and those in Western Europe. Second, despite the United States' expanding trade relations with East Asian and Latin American countries, particularly Mexico, in the 1980s and 1990s, economists found that widening income inequality was a consequence of technological advancement that favored high-skilled workers.

China's emergence as an economic superpower changed the global economic landscape. From 1990 to 2010, China more than quadrupled its share of value added in global manufacturing. As Figure 7.4 shows, by 2012, nearly 25 percent of the world's manufacturing output was produced in China. Today, China is the United States' third leading trade partner (behind Canada and Mexico). The rise in Chinese manufacturing exports has massively disrupted local labor markets in the United States that historically specialized in manufacturing.

Economists studying the effects of Chinese trade on local labor markets group U.S. counties into commuting zones (CZs). Each county in the United States is placed into exactly one CZ, and each CZ functions as a "local labor market." For instance, many people in Cumberland County in Maine commute to Kennebec County for their jobs. These counties are therefore grouped into the same CZ. Altogether, there are just over 700 CZs in the United States.

Exposure to trade with China varied widely across CZs. Figure 7.5 shows that the Midwest and parts of the South were the most exposed to Chinese imports. This comes as no surprise, given that these areas specialized more heavily in manufacturing (think about the automobile industry in Detroit). Economic researchers have shown that the CZs most exposed to trade with China see a large increase in their unemployment and large reductions in

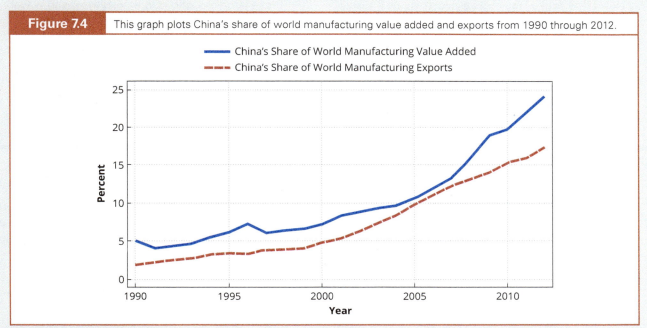

Figure 7.4 This graph plots China's share of world manufacturing value added and exports from 1990 through 2012.

Source: Autor, David, David Dorn, and Gordon Hanson. 2016. "The China Shock: Learning from Labor-Market Adjustment to Large Changes in Trade." *Annual Review of Economics*, 8: 205–240.

[5]Autor, David, David Dorn, and Gordon Hanson. 2016. "The China Shock: Learning from Labor-Market Adjustment to Large Changes in Trade." *Annual Review of Economics*, 8: 205–240.

■ Continues

Application 7.1 (Continued)

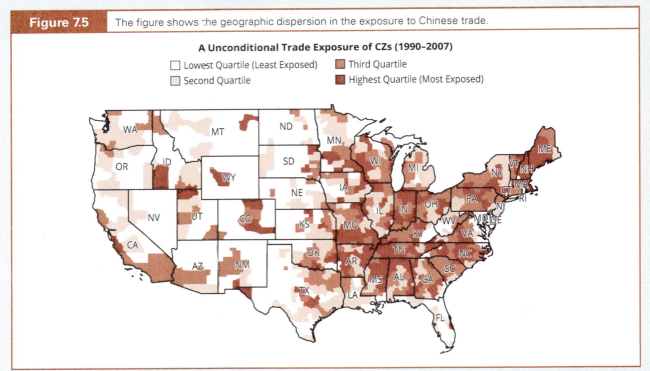

Figure 7.5 The figure shows the geographic dispersion in the exposure to Chinese trade.

Source: Autor, David, David Dorn, and Gordon Hanson. 2016. "The China Shock: Learning from Labor-Market Adjustment to Large Changes in Trade." *Annual Review of Economics*, 8: 205–240.

their average wages.[5] You might expect that workers would migrate in response to these labor market changes. Counterintuitively, this is not what the data show. Areas with high trade exposure did not see big decreases in their population. One potential reason for low levels of migration is that moving is very costly. Another potential reason is that displaced workers often do not want to leave their friends and family by moving to a new state.

These large reductions in employment and wages imply that there are significant adjustment costs associated with trade and that the short-run gains to trade are much lower than the long-run gains when displaced workers can relocate to other sectors. Somewhat depressingly, the research cited above shows that the reductions in employment persist for more than a decade, meaning that the transition to the long run could take a long time.

where Y is GDP, C is consumption, I is investment, G is government spending, X is exports, and M is imports. Each expenditure component is the sum of consumption goods and services produced domestically and those produced abroad. Let the "D" and "F" superscripts denote domestic and foreign respectively. Then, we can write

$$C = C^D + C^F,$$
$$I = I^D + I^F,$$
$$G = G^D + G^F.$$

Substituting these into Equation (1) gives

$$Y = C^D + C^F + I^D + I^F + G^D + G^F + X - M$$
$$= C^D + I^D + G^D + X - M + (C^F + I^F + G^F).$$

Chapter 7 International Trade and the Macroeconomy **169**

Note that the last term in parentheses, $(C^F + I^F + G^F)$, is exactly equal to imports. That is, a country's imports are equal to the goods and services purchased from abroad by private consumers, private firms, or the government. Since GDP measures domestic production, imports need to be subtracted from the expenditure equation and exports need to be added to it to accurately account for GDP. For shorthand, we often write Equation (2) as

$$Y = C + I + G + NX, \qquad (2')$$

where NX is referred to as **net exports**, or exports minus imports.

Net exports
Exports minus imports.

7-3a Imports, Exports, and the Flow of Capital

International trade is a never-ending process. In building economic models, economists make a number of simplifying assumptions. One such simplification is an assumption that trade is conducted in rounds, or periods. So at the end of each period, we can calculate who is gaining from an international transaction and how much. To begin our study of exports, imports, and the flow of capital, let us consider trade between the United States and Mexico, which lasts only one round, or one period. Suppose the United States exports $100 billion worth of corn to Mexico. As a result, the United States receives about 1.9 trillion pesos (since the nominal exchange rate is about 19 pesos per dollar). Since this is a one-period scenario, U.S. citizens will want to spend all of the pesos on goods and services produced in Mexico. It would not make any sense to keep any pesos unspent. So, the 1.9 trillion in pesos will go back to Mexico in exchange for 1.9 trillion pesos worth of Mexican goods and services, say cars.

To summarize, the United States exported $100 billion in corn to Mexico and imported $100 billion in cars. Mexico imported 1.9 trillion pesos worth of corn and exported 1.9 trillion pesos worth of cars. Net exports are equal to zero for both countries.

This example is extremely simple, but it's also insightful. In a world with one period, all trade is balanced, i.e., the value of exports equals the value of imports. A **trade deficit** occurs when imports exceed exports, and a **trade surplus** occurs when exports exceed imports. The one-period example shows why trade surpluses and deficits tend to correct themselves in the long run. If the United States sends $100 billion worth of wheat to Mexico in exchange for 1.9 trillion pesos and things temporarily stop there, the United States runs a trade surplus with Mexico and Mexico runs a trade deficit with the United States. But eventually, the United States will want to spend those 1.9 trillion pesos on something. Thus, in some later period, we would expect to see the United States import 1.9 trillion pesos worth of Mexican goods and services. The United States' initial trade surplus would then be corrected by a trade deficit, and Mexico's deficit would be corrected by a surplus.

Trade deficit
A situation in which imports exceed exports.

Trade surplus
A situation in which exports exceed imports.

Of course, holders of pesos in the United States probably wouldn't stuff them under a mattress. Instead, they would deposit them in one of Mexico's banks or perhaps invest in a Mexican company or purchase a bond issued by the Mexican government. In this case, the United States effectively adds to the stock of Mexican savings.

Generalizing this last example, rewrite Equation (2') as

$$I = Y - C - G - NX.$$

Adding and subtracting taxes, T, from the right-hand side gives

$$I = (Y - C - T) + (T - G) - NX. \qquad (3)$$

This equation says that investment is the sum of private domestic savings, $(Y - C - T)$, public domestic savings, $(T - G)$, and the negative of net exports, $-NX$. If domestic investment exceeds domestic savings, then the "savings gap" is financed from capital flowing into the country from abroad. Conversely, if domestic savings exceeds domestic investment, then some of that domestic savings flows abroad. Letting S^D equal the sum of private and public domestic saving, $(Y - C - T) + (T - G)$, Table 7.6 summarizes the three possibilities.

Table 7.6	Summarizing Savings and Investment in the Open Economy			
Savings and investment	Net exports	Balance of trade	Capital flow
$S^D > I$	$NX > 0$	Trade surplus	Capital outflow
$S^D < I$	$NX < 0$	Trade deficit	Capital inflow
$S^D = I$	$NX = 0$	Balanced trade	Neither capital inflow nor outflow

Countries that run a trade deficit have investment in excess of savings. This means that, on net, foreign investment in domestic stocks, bonds, and other sorts of financial instruments exceeds capital flowing from the domestic country to the rest of the world. Consequently, a country's trade deficit could be a symptom of its citizens not wanting to save enough or its investment opportunities being exceptionally promising. In other words, a trade deficit (or a trade surplus for that matter) is neither inherently good or bad. To make that determination, one needs to know more about a country's saving and investment opportunities.

Application 7.2

The U.S. Trade Deficit

The United States has run a trade deficit every year since 1980. And, as Figure 7.6 shows, the deficit has been persistently high by historical standards since 2000. As the last section mentioned, trade deficits are neither inherently good nor bad. On the one hand, a trade deficit can be a sign of promising investment opportunities in a country. On the other hand, deficits could signal a paucity of domestic savings. Since a country's income is a positive function of its savings rate, a trade deficit could be a symptom of a deeper problem.[6]

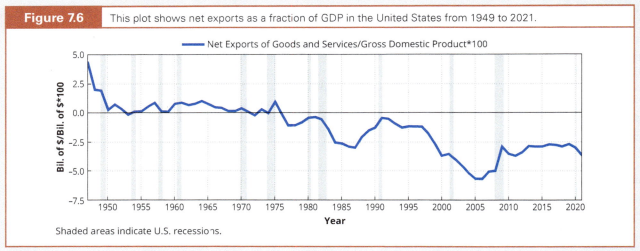

Figure 7.6 This plot shows net exports as a fraction of GDP in the United States from 1949 to 2021.

Shaded areas indicate U.S. recessions.

Source: FRED.

Figure 7.7 shows the personal savings rate and the federal government deficit as a percentage of GDP. The personal savings rate declined from about 10 percent in 1980 to about 5 percent in the early 2000s, although it shot up during the Covid-19 pandemic. The federal deficit is the difference between federal taxes and spending. While you will learn more about taxes, spending, and the deficit in Chapter 9, the important thing to note here is that the deficit as a share of GDP was between 0 and 5 percent between 1980 and 2006 and has generally been much higher since then. Taken together, the data suggests that the sum of private and public savings (as a share of GDP) has declined since the 1980s.

[6] Since a country's objective is to maximize consumption, not income, a higher savings rate might not always be welfare improving. For a more thorough discussion of this, see Chapter 3.

■ Continues

Application 7.2 (Continued)

Figure 7.7 This plot shows the personal savings rate and federal government deficit (as a fraction of GDP) in the United States from 1959 through 2021.

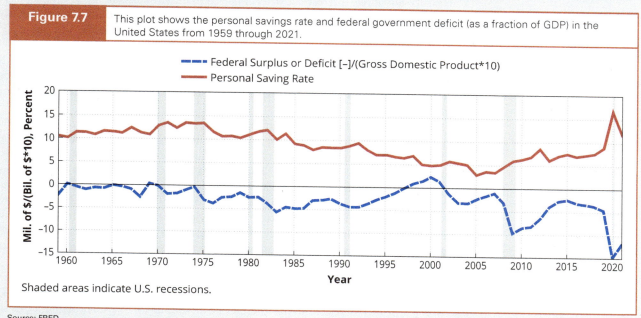

Shaded areas indicate U.S. recessions.

Source: FRED.

Figure 7.8 This plot shows the return on investment, measured as the marginal product of capital net of depreciation, in the United States from 1959 through 2021.

Shaded areas indicate U.S. recessions.

Source: FRED.

Figure 7.8 shows the marginal product of capital net of depreciation which, as Chapter 6 showed, is a measure of the return on investment of capital. The return on investment increased between 1980 and 2000 but has declined since then. To the extent that return on investment was higher in the United States than the rest of the world, some of the trade deficit between 1980 and 2000 can plausibly be attributed to good investment opportunities in the United States. This is not the case after 2000, though.

Finally, it is important to recognize that the trade balance between the United States and the rest of the world depends on what is happening in the United States but also in the rest of the world. With over 1 billion citizens, China's economic development has been particularly important. China's savings rate rose approximately 20 percentage points between 1990 and 2010. Some of that savings was funneled into the domestic economy, but a lot of it went to the United States. The incoming savings from China put upward pressure on the U.S. trade deficit.

7-3b Real Interest Rate Determination in the Open Economy

You learned about real interest rate determination in the closed economy in Chapter 6. The model can be extended to the open economy. The consumption and investment functions are identical to what was derived in Chapter 6, but now we need to know how net exports respond to the real interest rate.

In order to understand the impact of the real exchange rate on net exports, consider the effect on both imports and exports. A higher real exchange rate makes a country's exports more expensive and its imports less expensive. Thus, net exports are a negative function of the real exchange rate.

Next, we need to think a bit about capital inflow and outflow. Savers around the world are going to allocate their capital where the returns are the highest. We model the world real interest rate, r^w, as the average risk-adjusted real interest rate across countries. It is important to adjust for risk, as some countries may offer a high real interest not because their marginal products of capital are high on average, but because their marginal products are very uncertain. That means that if a domestic country is offering a real interest rate, r, that is higher than r^w, then the domestic economy will attract foreign savings. This influx of savings in turn pushes up the price of domestic goods and services, which means that the real exchange rate appreciates. Mathematically, we can write the real exchange rate as

$$\varepsilon_t = g(r_t - r_t^w), \qquad (4)$$

where we have now explicitly included the time dimension, denoted by the subscript t. The function g is positively related to the interest rate differential, $r_t - r_t^w$. Throughout this section, we will assume that the world real interest rate is exogenous. Figure 7.9 shows a graphical determination of the real exchange rate. Taking as given the equilibrium real interest rate, r_t^*, the equilibrium real exchange rate, ε_t^*, is determined at the intersection between the interest rate differential line and the function, $g(r_t - r_t^w)$.

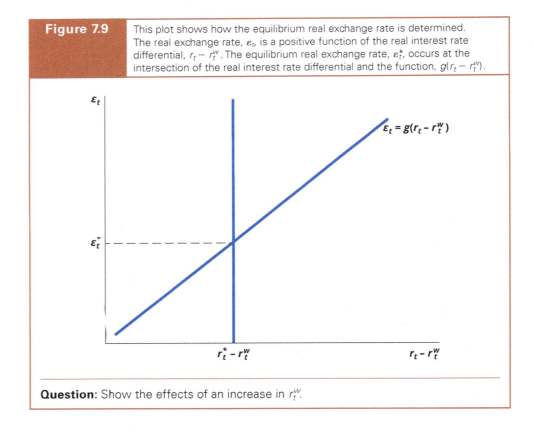

Figure 7.9 This plot shows how the equilibrium real exchange rate is determined. The real exchange rate, ε_t, is a positive function of the real interest rate differential, $r_t - r_t^w$. The equilibrium real exchange rate, ε_t^*, occurs at the intersection of the real interest rate differential and the function, $g(r_t - r_t^w)$.

Question: Show the effects of an increase in r_t^w.

Chapter 7 International Trade and the Macroeconomy **173**

Since net exports are a negative function of the real exchange rate, and the real exchange rate is a positive function of the real interest rate, we conclude that net exports are a negative function of the real interest rate. Thus, net exports can be written mathematically as

$$NX_t = NX(r_t, Q_t), \qquad (5)$$

where Q_t is an exogenous variable capturing the preference for domestically produced goods relative to foreign-produced goods. In the United States' case, perhaps the quality of GM vehicles increases relative to Honda's. This would be represented by Q_t increasing as U.S. and global consumers buy more GM vehicles and fewer Hondas. Thus, net exports are a positive function of Q_t.

Just as in Chapter 6, we assume that the government runs a balanced budget, so $G_t = T_t$. Combining Equations (5), (3), and the micro-founded consumption and investment demand functions of Chapter 6 gives

$$Y_t - C(Y_t - G_t, Y_{t+1} - G_{t+1}, r_t) - G_t - NX(r_t, Q_t) = I(r_t + f_t, A_{t+1}). \qquad (6)$$

The left-hand side is total savings or,

$$S_t = Y_t - C(Y_t - G_t, Y_{t+1} - G_{t+1}, r_t) - G_t - NX(r_t, Q_t). \qquad (7)$$

Note that total savings is the sum of domestic savings, $Y_t - C(Y_t - G_t, Y_{t+1} - G_{t+1}, r_t) - G_t$, and savings from abroad, $-NX(r_t, Q_t)$. The right-hand side is total investment or,

$$I_t = I(r_t + f_t, A_{t+1}). \qquad (8)$$

The intersection between investment demand and savings supply determines the equilibrium real interest rate. Then, using Equation (5), the real exchange rate can be determined. The model is summarized in Table 7.7.

Table 7.7	Summary of the Open-Economy Savings–Investment Model	
Endogenous variables		**Exogenous variables**
$S_t (I_t), r_t, \varepsilon_t$		$Y_t, Y_{t+1}, G_t, G_{t+1}, A_{t+1}, f_t, Q_t, r_t^w$
Key Equations:		
1. $I_t = I(r_t + f_t, A_{t+1})$		(Investment demand (Eq 8))
2. $S_t = Y_t - C(Y_t - G_t, Y_{t+1} - G_{t+1}, r_t) - G_t - NX(r_t, Q_t)$		(Savings supply Eq (7))
3. $\varepsilon_t = g(r_t - r_t^w)$		(Real exchange rate Eq (4))

Savings supply is a positive function of the real interest rate, and investment demand is a negative function of the real interest rate. Figure 7.10 shows that the real interest rate is determined at the intersection of supply and demand. The closed-economy savings line is also drawn for reference. Because net exports are a negative function of the real interest rate, savings supply is more interest-rate sensitive in the open economy than in the closed economy. This implies that the open-economy savings supply line is flatter. The next section discusses how changes in exogenous variables affect savings, investment, the real interest rate, and the real exchange rate.

7-3c Comparative Statics in the Open-Economy Savings–Investment Model

Just as in the closed-economy version of the model, we can analyze how changes to exogenous variables affect the endogenous variables. To start, suppose the current-period income, Y_t, increases. Consumers in the economy respond by consuming some of the extra income today and saving the rest for the future. The supply of savings shifts to the right. In equilibrium, savings and investment increase and the real interest rate decreases. This is shown in Figure 7.11.

Figure 7.10 This plots the savings supply and investment demand curves. The economy is in equilibrium when savings supply equals investment demand. The equilibrium real interest rate is r_t^* and the equilibrium quantity of investment (which is also the equilibrium quantity of savings) is I_t^*. The red line plots savings supply in the closed economy.

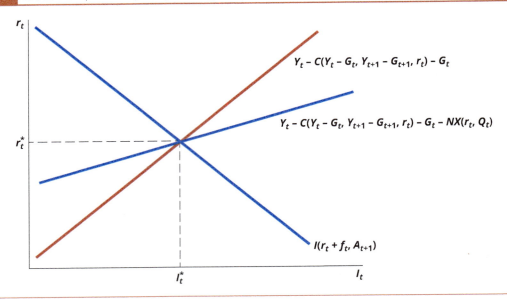

Question: What happens to the slope of the investment demand curve if investment is more sensitive to the real interest rate?

Figure 7.11 This graph plots the effect of an increase in current-period income. An increase in Y_t from $Y_{0,t}$ to $Y_{1,t}$ shifts the supply of savings to the right. In equilibrium, the real interest rate drops from $r_{0,t}^*$ to $r_{1,t}^*$ and investment increases from $I_{0,t}^*$ to $I_{1,t}^*$.

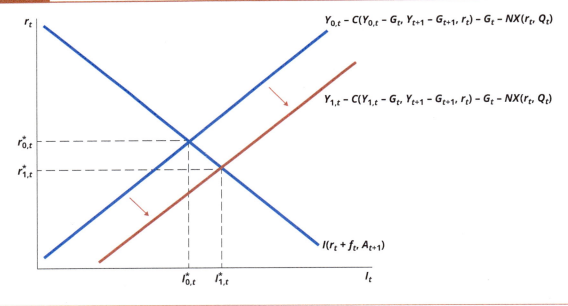

Question: Show the effects of a decrease in current-period income.

A decrease in the real interest rate causes savings to flow out of the domestic economy. As a result, the real exchange rate depreciates. Because the real exchange rate depreciates, net exports increase. From this, we infer that the increase in the equilibrium quantity of investment is smaller in the open economy than in the closed economy. The reason is that the decline in the real interest rate makes the domestic economy less attractive to international savers.

Next, consider an increase in current-period government spending, G_t. An increase in G_t reduces consumption, but less than one for one, as utility-maximizing consumers will smooth the loss of disposable income over multiple periods. This means that $Y_t - C_t - G_t$ declines, shifting the supply of savings to the left. As Figure 7.12 shows, the equilibrium real interest rate increases and the equilibrium quantity of investment declines. The increase in the real interest rate causes savings to flow in from abroad. The real exchange rate appreciates as a result.

Now let's consider changing the new exogenous variables specific to the case of the open economy. Suppose the world real interest rate, r_t^w, increases. This causes international savers to move their savings away from the domestic economy. As Figure 7.13 shows, the real exchange rate depreciates to $\tilde{\varepsilon}_t$. Note that this is the real exchange rate with an interest rate differential of $r_{0,t}^* - r_{1,t}^w$. We expect the domestic real interest rate to change in equilibrium, so $\tilde{\varepsilon}_t$ is not an equilibrium real exchange rate.

The initial depreciation of the real exchange rate causes net exports to increase. An increase in net exports shifts the savings supply curve to the left. This is shown in Figure 7.14. In equilibrium, the real interest rate increases and investment decreases. The increase in the real interest rate causes some savings to flow back into the economy and the equilibrium real exchange rate settles at $\varepsilon_{1,t}^*$ which is lower than the original. Thus, an increase the world's real interest rate increases the domestic real interest rate, but less than one for one. The real exchange rate depreciates as a result.

Figure 7.12

This graph plots the effect of an increase in current-period government spending. An increase in G_t from $G_{0,t}$ to $G_{1,t}$ shifts the supply of savings to the left. In equilibrium, the real interest rate increases from $r_{0,t}^*$ to $r_{1,t}^*$ and investment decreases from $I_{0,t}^*$ to $I_{1,t}^*$.

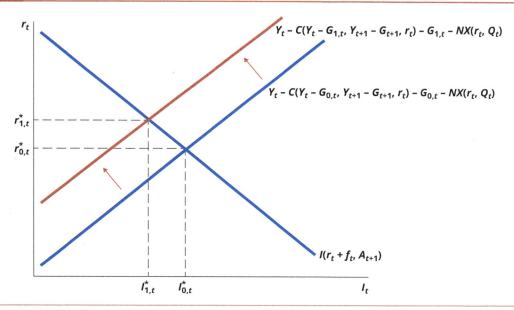

Question: Show the effects of a decrease in current-period government spending.

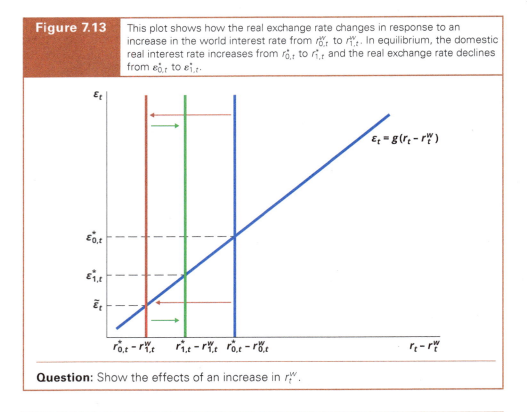

Figure 7.13 This plot shows how the real exchange rate changes in response to an increase in the world interest rate from $r_{0,t}^w$ to $r_{1,t}^w$. In equilibrium, the domestic real interest rate increases from $r_{0,t}^*$ to $r_{1,t}^*$ and the real exchange rate declines from $\varepsilon_{0,t}^*$ to $\varepsilon_{1,t}^*$.

Question: Show the effects of an increase in r_t^w.

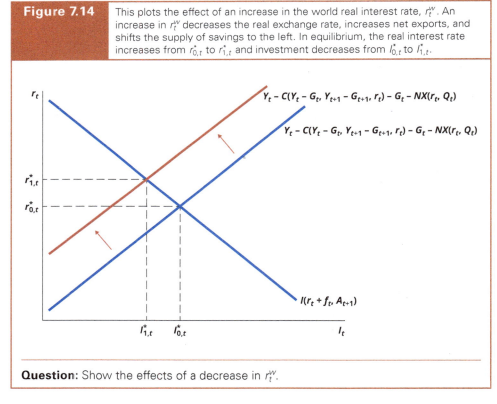

Figure 7.14 This plots the effect of an increase in the world real interest rate, r_t^w. An increase in r_t^w decreases the real exchange rate, increases net exports, and shifts the supply of savings to the left. In equilibrium, the real interest rate increases from $r_{0,t}^*$ to $r_{1,t}^*$ and investment decreases from $I_{0,t}^*$ to $I_{1,t}^*$.

Question: Show the effects of a decrease in r_t^w.

Finally, suppose that the quality of the domestic country's export goods increases. This is represented by an increase in Q_t. In the United States' case, an increase in Q_t could represent an increased preference for vacations in the United States compared to vacations outside of the country. The increase in Q_t increases net exports and shifts the supply of

Figure 7.15

This graph plots the effect of an increase in Q_t. An increase in Q_t increases net exports and shifts the supply of savings to the left. In equilibrium, the real interest rate increases from $r_{0,t}^*$ to $r_{1,t}^*$ and investment decreases from $I_{0,t}^*$ to $I_{1,t}^*$.

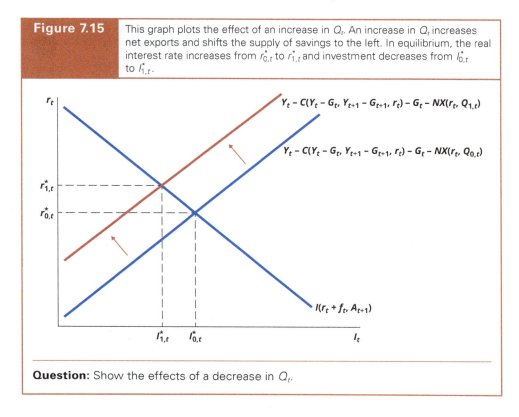

Question: Show the effects of a decrease in Q_t.

savings to the left, as shown in Figure 7.15. In equilibrium, the real interest rate increases and investment declines. The increase in the real interest rate causes savings to flow in from abroad, causing the real exchange rate to appreciate.

The open-economy version of the savings–investment model simultaneously determines equilibrium real interest rates, real exchange rates, and levels of investment and saving. All changes in exogenous variables that affect the real interest rate and investment in a closed economy also affect the real exchange rate in the open economy. A key thing to remember is that because international savings is mobile, the savings supply schedule is more sensitive to real interest rate changes.

Table 7.8 summarizes the comparative static results up to this point. The next knowledge check question and end-of-chapter problems ask you to work through other examples.

Table 7.8 Comparative Statics in the Open Economy Savings/Investment Model

Increase in:	Δr_t	$\Delta \varepsilon_t$	$\Delta I_t, \Delta S_t$
Y_t	−	−	+
G_t	+	+	−
r_t^w	+	−	−
Q_t	+	−	−

✓ Knowledge Check 7-5

Graphically depict the effects of an increase in f_t and describe what happens to the endogenous variables.

——————————————————— Answers are at the end of the chapter.

178   **Part 2** Classical Theory

Chapter Summary

- The nominal exchange rate is the rate at which two currencies trade for each other. The real exchange rate is the rate at which goods and services across countries trade for each other.

- The law of one price predicts that identical goods and services should trade at the same price in all countries. Reasons that the law of one price does not hold in reality include transportation costs and differences in tax rates across countries.

- Countries gain from trade by producing the good or service in which they have a comparative advantage: that is the good or service produced at a lower opportunity cost relative to other nations.

- Some arguments against completely free trade include specialization is risky; there is a possibility of bottlenecks in production; there is a desire to nurture infant industries; and free trade does not universally benefit the entire population.

- Countries where exports exceed imports run a trade surplus and experience a net capital outflow. Countries where imports

exceed exports run a trade deficit and experience a net capital inflow.

- Net exports are a decreasing function of the real exchange rate. As a country's real exchange rate appreciates, domestic goods become relatively more expensive than goods produced abroad.

- The real exchange rate in turn is an increasing function of the difference between the domestic real interest rate and the global real interest rate. If the domestic real interest rate exceeds the global real interest rate, capital flows into the domestic country, driving the real exchange rate up. The logic goes in reverse if the global real interest rate exceeds the domestic real interest rate.

- The equilibrium real interest rate is found where the economy's saving supply equals its investment demand. Relative to the closed economy, including foreign trade flattens the savings supply function, making it more sensitive to the real interest rate. The reason is that in addition to consumption, net exports also depend on the real interest rate.

Key Terms

Nominal exchange rate, 157
Real exchange rate, 158
Arbitrage, 159
Law of one price, 160
Absolute advantage, 161
Production possibilities frontier (PPF), 161

Autarky, 161
Terms of trade, 162
Comparative advantage, 164
Net exports, 169
Trade deficit, 169
Trade surplus, 169

Questions for Review

1. What is the difference between a real exchange rate and a nominal exchange rate?

2. Some services, like the medical care one receives from a doctor, aren't tradable across countries. Would you expect the law of one price to more closely hold for tradable services or non-tradable ones? Why?

3. Suppose country A is more efficient than country B at producing every single good and service. Are there still gains from trade? Explain.

4. Is a trade deficit always a sign of bad economic policy? Explain.

5. How does the real exchange rate depend on the difference between the domestic real interest rate and the global real interest rate?

Chapter 7 International Trade and the Macroeconomy **179**

Problems

7.1 Consider the following economic data:

Good	P_{US} (in dollars)	P_{Japan} (in yen)
10 ounces of honey	5	500
One pound of blueberries	4	700
One avocado	1	140
One pound of bacon	7	1,100

  a. Suppose the dollar-to-yen exchange rate is 120 yen per dollar. Where is each good the least expensive?

  b. Find the nominal exchange rate above which every good is less expensive in Japan.

7.2 In trade policy debates in the 1990s, a common refrain was that it is "better to make computer chips than potato chips."[7] Let's see if that is in fact true in the Ricardian model. Consider two countries, A and B, each with 1,000 workers. It takes 100 workers in A and 200 workers in B to produce 1.25 computers. A worker in A produces two pounds of potato chips. It takes two workers in B to produce a pound of potato chips. Assume the world starts in autarky and each country devotes half its labor force to computer production and the other half to the production of potato chips.

  a. Complete the rest of the table.

	$L_{Computer}$	L_{potato}	$Y_{computer}$	Y_{potato}	$C_{computer}$	C_{potato}
A	500	500				
B	500	500				
A+B	1,000	1,000				

  b. What is the cost of producing a computer in terms of potato chips in Country A? How about Country B?

  c. Suppose the countries specialize as follows.

	$L_{Computer}$	L_{potato}	$Y_{computer}$	Y_{potato}	$C_{computer}$	C_{potato}
A	300	700				
B	1,000	0				
A+B	1,300	700				

  Complete everything except the last two columns. What has happened to the global production of computers and potato chips?

  d. What is the lower and upper bound on the global price of computers such that both countries still benefit from trade?

  e. Suppose that the global price of a computer is 100 pounds of potato chips and that Country B purchases 300 pounds of potato chips from Country A. Fill in the rest of the table in part c.

  f. Assess the welfare gains from trade. Is it true that it is always better to produce computers than potato chips?

7.3 Complete the following table. In each case, describe if the country is experiencing a net capital inflow or outflow. All data are in trillions of dollars.

Y	$C + I + G$	NX	Capital inflow or outflow?
22.3	25.7	?	?
?	24	−6	?
27	?	4	?

7.4 Consider the open-economy savings–investment model. The savings supply function is given by

$$S_t = Y_t - C(Y_t - G_t, Y_{t+1} - G_{t+1}, r_t) - G_t - NX(r_t, Q_t).$$

The investment demand function is

$$I_t = I(r_t + f_t, A_{t+1}).$$

  a. Graphically depict the effects of an increase in future government spending, G_{t+1}. How are the endogenous variables affected?

  b. Graphically depict the effects of an increase in future government spending, G_{t+1}, in the closed economy.

  c. Assuming both the closed and open economies start at the same real interest rate, does the real interest rate change by more in the open economy or the closed economy? Explain the economic intuition behind these results.

7.5 Consider an algebraic version of the open-economy savings–investment model. The consumption function is given by

$$C_t = 0.7(Y_t - G_t) + 0.4(Y_{t+1} - G_{t+1}) - 100r_t.$$

The net exports function is given by

$$NX_t = Q_t - 50r_t.$$

  a. Derive the savings supply function.

  b. The investment demand function is given by

$$I_t = 10 - 100r_t.$$

  Derive the equilibrium real interest rate as a function of the exogenous variables.

  c. Suppose $Y_t = Y_{t+1} = 30, G_t = G_{t+1} = 10,$ and $Q_t = 4$. Solve for the equilibrium real interest rate and the equilibrium levels of investment, consumption, and net exports.

  d. Suppose Y_t increases to 40. Calculate the new equilibrium levels of the real interest rate, investment, consumption, and net exports. Are these results consistent with our qualitative analysis from this chapter?

  e. Find the level of Y_t such that trade is balanced.

---

[7]This is sometimes attributed to independent president candidate Ross Perot.

Knowledge Check 7-1 Answer

The euro-to-yen exchange rate can be found by dividing the dollar-to-yen exchange rate by the dollar-to-euro exchange rate:

$$e = \frac{134.32 \frac{yen}{\$}}{0.95 \frac{euro}{\$}}$$

$$= 141.39 \frac{yen}{euro}.$$

So the euro-to-yen exchange rate is 141.39. That is, 141.39 yen exchange for one euro. The yuan-to-peso exchange rate can similarly be calculated as

$$e = \frac{19.39 \frac{peso}{\$}}{7.02 \frac{yuan}{\$}}.$$

$$= 2.76 \frac{peso}{yuan}.$$

So the peso-to-yuan exchange rate is 2.76.

Knowledge Check 7-2 Answer

The real exchange rate between the United States and Germany is

$$\varepsilon = \frac{\$100}{80 \ euro} \times 0.9 \frac{euro}{\$}$$

$$= 1.125.$$

One U.S. Lego set exchanges for 1.125 German Lego sets. The real exchange rate between the United States and Mexico is

$$\varepsilon = \frac{\$100}{2{,}000 \ peso} \times 25 \frac{peso}{\$}$$

$$= 1.25.$$

One U.S. Lego set exchanges for 1.25 Mexican Lego sets. The real exchange rate between the United States and Japan is

$$\varepsilon = \frac{\$100}{32{,}000 \ yen} \times 140 \frac{yen}{\$}$$

$$= 0.44.$$

One U.S. Lego set exchanges for 0.44 Japanese Lego sets. Lego sets are least expensive in Mexico.

Country	e	P_F	ε
Germany	0.9 euros	80 euros	1.125
Mexico	25 pesos	2,000 pesos	1.25
Japan	140 yen	32,000 yen	0.44

Knowledge Check 7-3 Answer

Since 1.25 is below the autarky price of tofu in country A and above the autarky trade price in country B, trade will be beneficial as long as country A specializes in ice cream and B specializes in tofu. GDP in country A is 2,000 pints of ice cream. Country A spends half of this on ice cream, which means $C_{ice,A} = 1,000$. It trades the other 1,000 pints for tofu. Since the price of tofu is 1.25, 1,000 pints trades for 800 pounds of tofu. Thus, $C_{tofu,A} = 800$. Country B keeps 1,200 pounds of tofu for itself and gets 1,000 pints of ice cream through trade. The allocations are shown in the table below.

Table 7.3c	\multicolumn{6}{l}{Allocations with Free Trade (Relative Price Equals 1.25)}
	L_{tofu}	L_{ice}	Y_{tofu}	Y_{ice}	C_{tofu}	C_{ice}
A	0	1,000	0	2,000	800	1,000
B	1,000	0	2,000	0	1,200	1,000
A+B	1,000	1,000	2,000	2,000	2,000	2,000

Compared to the case where the relative price equals 1, country A loses. Its ice cream consumption is still 1,000, but its tofu consumption drops to 800. Country A's loss is B's gain. Country A is still better off compared to autarky.

 Knowledge Check 7-4 Answer

The results are shown in the table below. Country A exports 1,000 pints of ice cream in exchange for 1,000/1.8 = 555.5 pounds of tofu. With the higher international price of tofu, country A, the tofu importer, loses, while country B, the tofu exporter, gains.

	L_{tofu}	L_{ice}	Y_{tofu}	Y_{ice}	C_{tofu}	C_{ice}
A	0	1,000	0	2,000	555.5	1,000
B	800	200	1,600	600	1,044.5	1,600
A+B	1,000	1,000	1,600	2,600	1,600	2,600

 Knowledge Check 7-5 Answer

An increase in f_t increases the cost of investment and shifts the investment demand curve to the left. The equilibrium real interest rate rises and investment falls. This is shown in Figure 7.16. A higher real interest rate encourages savings to flow into the domestic economy, which increases the equilibrium real exchange rate.

182 Part 2 Classical Theory

Figure 7.16 This graph plots the effect of an increase in f_t. An increase in f_t from $f_{0,t}$ to $f_{1,t}$ shifts the demand for investment to the left. In equilibrium, the real interest rate drops from $r_{0,t}^*$ to $r_{1,t}^*$ and investment decreases from $I_{0,t}^*$ to $I_{1,t}^*$. The red line should be parallel to the downward sloping blue line. Add red arrows pointing to the left.

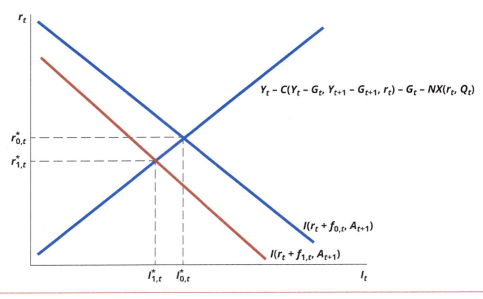

Question: Show the effects of a decrease in f_t.

Chapter 8
Labor Markets

Learning Objectives

8.1 Explain how statistical agencies in the United States calculate labor market variables, such as the rates of employment, unemployment, and labor force participation and hours per capita.

8.2 Describe the overall time-series trends in labor market variables and how the trends differ by demographic group.

8.3 Derive optimal quantities of work and leisure using the framework of indifference curves and budget lines.

8.4 Explain the connection between labor force participation and the reservation wage.

8.5 Solve for equilibrium unemployment in the search and matching model.

Chances are you will spend some of your life working, some of your life looking for work, and some of your life neither working, nor looking for work. Each of these situations presents a different set of economic incentives. If you are unemployed, you want to find a job that fits your interest and skill set. If you have a job, you need to decide how to allocate your time between working at your job, caring for family members, completing housework, sleeping, and watching Netflix. Then, at some point, you may decide to exit the labor force to go back to school or retire.

You are not alone. In the U.S. economy, millions of people enter and leave the labor force every month. Among those in the labor force, more than a million people every month transition from employment to unemployment even in good economic times. At the same time, people with steady jobs change how many hours per week they work in response to changes in their wage or demands outside of work, such as caring for children or other family members.

In this chapter, you will learn how statistical agencies in the United States measure different labor market variables, such as employment and unemployment. You will also learn about an economic model of labor force participation and the choice of hours worked among the employed. Finally, you will learn about a model that explains why some individuals who are willing to work nevertheless get stuck in unemployment.

8-1 The Data of the Labor Market

Labor is one of the most important inputs into production. But when we ask, "What is the state of the labor market?" there isn't a unique answer. Here is one way to think about it. Total hours worked in the economy equals the product of the number of people working and the average hours worked per worker. Mathematically,

$$N_t = E_t h_t, \tag{1}$$

where N_t is the total hours worked in the economy, E_t is the number of employed workers, and h_t is the number of hours per worker. The subscript t denotes the unit of time and is typically a month, quarter, or year. According to Equation (1), total hours go up if either the number of people working increase or the hours per worker increase.

Because the number of people working scales with the population, it is more informative to look at an economy's hours per capita. Divide both sides of Equation (1) by the population level, P_t, to get

$$\frac{N_t}{P_t} = \frac{E_t h_t}{P_t}$$

$$\Leftrightarrow n_t = e_t h_t. \qquad (1')$$

Employment–population ratio
The number of an economy's workers divided by its population.

In this equation, n_t is hours per capita and e_t is the proportion of the population that is working. The number of workers divided by the population is called the **employment–population ratio**.

Accurately understanding the level and evolution of hours per capita requires an appropriate measure of the population. Imagine, for instance, that the number of infants in the economy increased. If infants are included in our measure of the population, it will look like hours per capita and the employment-to-population ratio has declined even if the number of adults working stays constant. With this in mind, economists typically define the population as the **civilian, noninstitutionalized, 16 and over population**. This definition contains three important terms:

Civilian, noninstitutionalized, 16 and over population
A measure of the population that includes everyone 16 years and older who reside in the 50 states or the District of Columbia and are not on active duty in the military or an inmate of an institution, such as penal and mental facilities or a home for the aged.

1. *Civilian* means someone residing in one of the 50 states or the District of Columbia and not on active duty in the military.
2. *Noninstitutionalized* means someone who is not an inmate of an institution such as penal and mental facilities or a home for the aged.
3. People *16 and over* can legally join the labor market.

Using this definition of the population, annual hours per capita is shown in Figure 8.1. The gray lines of the plot indicate recessions. Although hours per capita fall during recessions, particularly the 2007–2009 recession, there is not a clear trend upward or downward in the series. The average American spent just over 1,100 hours at work in 1950 and just under

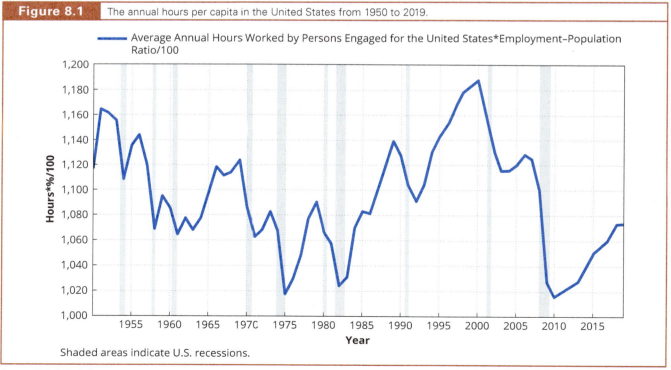

Figure 8.1 The annual hours per capita in the United States from 1950 to 2019.

Shaded areas indicate U.S. recessions.

Source: FRED, BLS, PWT.

1,100 hours of work in 2019. As the next two sections show, however, the relative constancy of hours per capita is the product of offsetting trends.

8-1a National Trends of the Extensive and Intensive Margins of the Labor Market

Hours per capita is the product of hours per worker and the employment–population ratio. Hours per capita can be roughly constant because either hours per worker and the employment–population ratio are both constant, or because these series trend in opposite and offsetting ways. Figure 8.2 shows that hours per worker experienced a long-run decline from about 2,000 hours in 1950 to 1,760 hours in 2019. In other words, employed people are working about 10 percent fewer hours in modern times compared to 1950.

At the same time, the fraction of the population who are working has increased. Figure 8.3 shows that the employment-to-population ratio was about 56 percent in 1950 and climbed to as high as 64 percent in 2000. By 2019, the employment-to-population ratio was about 61 percent before dropping during the Covid-19 pandemic. The increase in the fraction of the population employed combined with the decrease in hours per worker has produced relatively constant hours per capita.

The **labor force** is the sum of the number of people employed and the number of people **unemployed**. A person is unemployed if they are not working but looking for work. By this definition, neither a full-time student nor a retired person would be a part of the labor force. Upon graduating, the student would join the labor force as either someone who is employed or someone looking for work. The most common types of people out of the labor force include retirees, full-time students, stay-at-home parents, or people with disabilities that prevent them from working.

The **labor force participation rate** (**LFPR**) is the labor force divided by the civilian, noninstitutionalized population. The **unemployment rate** is the number of unemployed divided by the number in the labor force. Mathematically, these ratios are respectively given by

$$LEPR = \frac{\text{Labor force}}{\text{Population}}, \tag{2}$$

$$UR = \frac{\text{Unemployed}}{\text{Labor force}}. \tag{3}$$

Labor force
The sum of the number of employed individuals and unemployed individuals.

Unemployed
The state of being out of work but actively looking for work.

Labor force participation rate
The labor force divided by the population.

Unemployment rate
The number of unemployed individuals divided by the labor force.

Figure 8.2 The annual hours per worker in the United States from 1950 to 2019.

Shaded areas indicate U.S. recessions.

Source: https://fred.stlouisfed.org/series/AVHWPEUSA065NRUG

Figure 8.3 The employment–population ratio for the United States from 1950 to 2021.

Shaded areas indicate U.S. recessions.

Source: https://fred.stlouisfed.org/series/EMRATIO#

The labor force participation and unemployment rates for the United States are shown in Figures 8.4 and 8.5, respectively. The trend in the LFPR largely mirrors the trend in the employment–population ratio, rising from 1950 to 2000 and then declining since 2000.

The average unemployment rate is about 6 percent. Unlike the LFPR and employment–population ratio, there is no evident time trend in the unemployment rate. Instead, the

Figure 8.4 The labor force participation rate for the United States from 1950 to 2021.

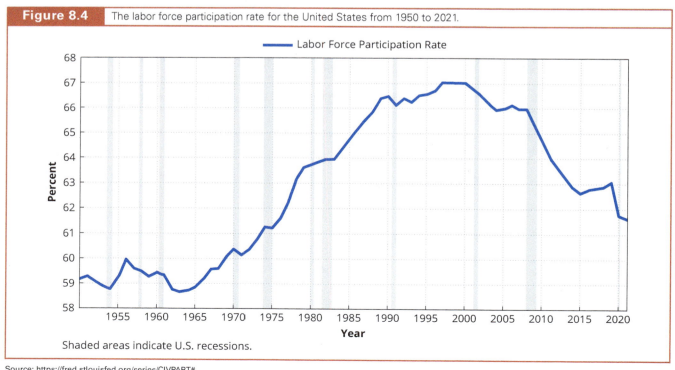

Shaded areas indicate U.S. recessions.

Source: https://fred.stlouisfed.org/series/CIVPART#

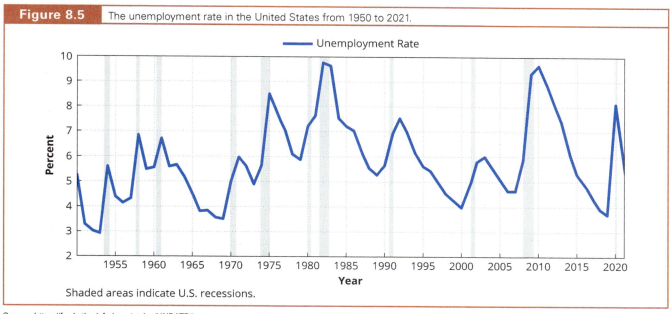

Figure 8.5 The unemployment rate in the United States from 1950 to 2021.

Shaded areas indicate U.S. recessions.

Source: https://fred.stlouisfed.org/series/UNRATE#

unemployment rate rises in recessions (as indicated by the gray bars) and falls when the economy recovers.

The time-series patterns of labor force participation and unemployment are interesting, but the aggregate data hide what is happening to various subgroups of the population. This is what we turn to next.

8-1b Labor Market Trends by Demographic Group

The trend in the labor force participation rate is driven by the rates moving in different directions for men and women. Figure 8.6 shows that the LFPR among American men was as high as 88 percent in 1950 and has declined to under 70 percent today. Women's LFPR started at just over 30 percent in the 1950s and climbed to as high as 60 percent by 2000.

Figure 8.6 The labor force participation rates of men and women in the United States from 1950 to 2021.

Shaded areas indicate U.S. recessions.

Source: https://fred.stlouisfed.org/series/LNS11300002#

The increase in women joining the labor market was bigger than the number of men leaving the labor market, which explains the overall trend in LFPR shown in Figure 8.4.

There are several complementary explanations for the increase in women's labor force participation. One is that the gap between the wages of men and women has decreased over time. In 1980, women earned about 40 percent less than men on average. By 2010, that gap had shrunk to 21 percent. Comparing women and men with similar levels of education, experience, and occupations shrinks the gap to about 8 percent.[1] Increasing wages has led to more married women joining the labor force.

Another explanation is that America has transitioned away from manufacturing industries to service industries. Historically, jobs in manufacturing required greater degrees of physical strength, for which men have a comparative advantage. Today, the service industry dominates, employing over 80 percent of the American work force. Two of the biggest service sectors are healthcare and education, where women vastly outnumber men. The shift away from jobs that required physical strength to jobs that prioritize intellect has drawn more women into the labor force.[2] Indeed, even manufacturing jobs have grown more cerebral as machines have replaced many types of manual labor.

A third reason behind the rise in women's LFPR has to do with changes in work around the home. Very few households had washers, dryers, and dishwashers in the 1950s. These became nearly universal household items over the next several decades. The diffusion of these appliances meant that households had to spend less time on household chores. Since household chores disproportionately fell on women, the adoption of time-saving durable goods allowed more married women to join the labor force.[3]

The economic mechanisms driving the decline in men's labor force participation are not as well understood. One thing we know is that the U.S. population is aging, so some of the decline can be attributed to an increase in retirees. Also, young adults, such as college-age students, spend more time in school compared to their counterparts in the 1950s and 1960s. This would further decrease men's labor force participation rates. However, as Figure 8.7 shows, the labor force participation rate has declined even among men between the ages of 25 and 54. By 25, most (but certainly not all!) people have completed their

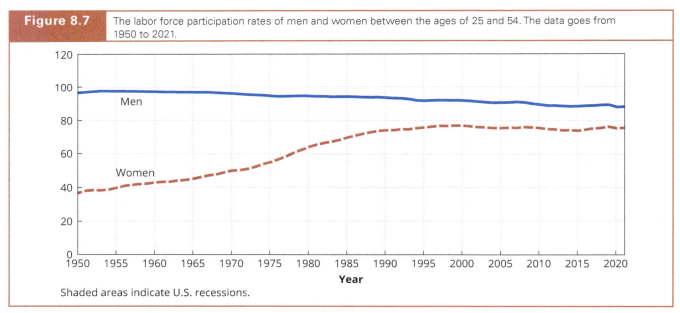

Figure 8.7 The labor force participation rates of men and women between the ages of 25 and 54. The data goes from 1950 to 2021.

Shaded areas indicate U.S. recessions.

Source: BLS, Current Population Survey (https://www.bls.gov/data/home.htm). I use the "one screen" mode for the CPS.

---

[1]Blau, Francine and Lawrence Kahn. 2017. "The Gender Wage Gap: Extent, Trends, and Explanations." *Journal of Economic Literature*, 55(3): 789–865.
[2]Rendall, Michelle. 2018. "Brain Versus Brawn: The Realization of Women's Comparative Advantage" [Working paper].
[3]Greenwood, Jeremy, Ananth Seshardi, and Mehmet Yorukoglu. 2005. "Engines of Liberation." *Review of Economic Studies*, 72: 109–133.

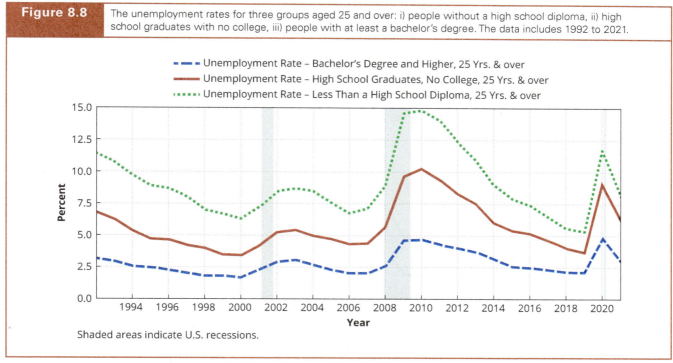

Figure 8.8 The unemployment rates for three groups aged 25 and over: i) people without a high school diploma, ii) high school graduates with no college, iii) people with at least a bachelor's degree. The data includes 1992 to 2021.

Source: Saint Louis Fred (https://fred.stlouisfed.org/series/LNS14027662#).

education, and 54 is well below the usual retirement age. The fact that men's labor force participation rates are declining in this age range suggests something else must be changing besides demographics and an increased preference for higher education.

People enter and exit the labor force for a variety of reasons; many of them, such as retirement or the birth of a child, are welfare improving. The same cannot be said about unemployment, which is usually unexpected and detrimental to a person's overall well-being. The risk of unemployment is unevenly spread throughout the United States. Figure 8.8 shows that people with higher education have lower unemployment rates than people with less education. Although all three unemployment rates tend to move together, college-educated individuals consistently have an unemployment rate that is at least two percentage points lower than those with only a high school degree. Those with a high school degree in turn consistently have an unemployment rate several percentage points lower than those who did not graduate from high school.

Unemployment is also distributed unevenly across race and ethnic groups in the United States. Figure 8.9 shows that the unemployment rate is consistently higher for African Americans than for Hispanic Americans. Hispanic Americans in turn have a higher unemployment rate than white Americans. Similar to the differences in education groups, however, the unemployment rates of different race and ethnic groups move up and down together.

The data analysis leads to several questions. First, among workers, what determines how much time they work versus engaged in leisure, sleep, and household activities? Second, what determines if someone joins the labor force? Third, among labor market participants, what determines if someone is employed versus unemployed? The next section tackles the first two questions, and Section 8.4 addresses the third question.

✓ Knowledge Check 8-1

Suppose the economy consists of a population of 100 million people, of whom 8 million are unemployed and 70 million are employed. Calculate the labor force participation rate and unemployment rate. Also, suppose that the average worker works 38 hours per week. Calculate hours per capita.

Answers are at the end of the chapter.

Figure 8.9
The unemployment rate among Black Americans, Hispanic or Latino Americans, and White Americans between 1974 and 2021.

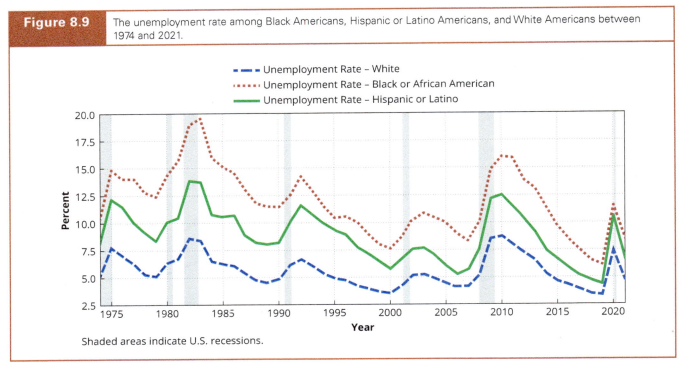

Shaded areas indicate U.S. recessions.

Source: Saint Louis FRED (https://fred.stlouisfed.org/series/LNU04000003#).

8-2 Labor–Leisure Model

The cost of many goods and services is explicit. A haircut might cost $30 and hiring a plumber for an hour might cost $100. How much does an hour of leisure cost? You might answer that it depends on what leisure activity you're doing. Playing miniature golf for an hour costs more than an hour reading in a public library. Usually, however, the biggest cost of an hour of leisure is implicit. An hour spent in the library or on a public beach may not have any monetary cost, but it does incur an opportunity cost. The opportunity cost of an hour of leisure is the foregone wages you could have earned by working that hour. A lower level of labor earnings implies a lower level of consumption. Thus, there is a trade-off between leisure and consumption. This section uses the indifference curve and budget constraint analysis from Chapter 6 to analyze the optimal choice of work and leisure. In particular, we analyze an individual's optimal choices of consumption, work, and leisure in a one-period model.

8-2a Budget Constraint and Preferences

We all wish there were more time in a day, but in reality, we have to make the best of our 24 hours. The labor–leisure model assumes that the 24 hours in a day are divided between work and leisure. You might think that this is a simplistic analysis, since time spent sleeping or brushing your teeth can't be classified as leisure. As you will see in the knowledge check, the assumption of 24 hours (rather than say 16 or 14) does not qualitatively affect the analysis. Mathematically, the time spent at work, N, plus leisure time, L, equals 24, or

$$L + N = 24. \qquad (4)$$

Equation (4) is usually referred to as a time constraint, as it specifies the feasible combinations of leisure and work. Note that because the model is one period, there are no time subscripts. There are two sources of income in the model. One is wage income, which is the hourly wage, w, multiplied by the number of hours the individual works, N. Total wage income is wN. Another source of income is nonwage income, d. Nonwage income might include things like dividends from owning stocks, interest income on a bank account, cash transfers from the government, or money from family members. In total, consumption, C, equals wage income plus nonwage income, or

$$C = wN + d. \tag{5}$$

Equation (5) is usually referred to as the budget constraint. In analyzing the model, it's useful to substitute the time constraint into the budget constraint:

$$C = w(24 - L) + d. \tag{6}$$

From Equation (6), it's clear that an additional hour of leisure lowers consumption by w. This formalizes what this section's introduction discussed, namely that the opportunity cost of an additional hour of leisure is w units of consumption.

Figure 8.10 depicts the budget constraint graphically. Consumption is plotted on the vertical axis and leisure on the horizontal axis. The horizontal intercept is 24 because leisure cannot exceed 24 hours in a day. Alternatively, if an individual spends all their time working, then consumption equals $24w + d$, which is the vertical intercept. If the individual chooses to spend all their time at leisure, then consumption equals nonwage income, d. The slope of the budget line is $-w$, as one additional hour of leisure costs w units of consumption.

Suppose the individual's nonwage income were to increase. This could be the result of a higher return on financial assets, a subsidy from the government, or a gift from grandparents. Figure 8.11 shows the effects. The increase in nonwage income shifts the budget line to the right. Since the opportunity cost of leisure is unaffected, the new budget line has a slope of $-w$, just like the initial budget line.

An increase in the wage makes the budget line steeper, while leaving the horizontal intercept the same. Intuitively, an increase in the wage increases the opportunity of leisure but does not change the total amount of time in a day. This is shown graphically in Figure 8.12, in which the wage increases from w_0 to w_1. With the higher wage, the individual can afford more consumption and leisure.

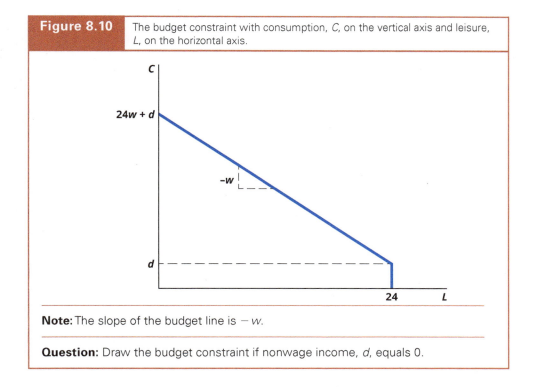

Figure 8.10 The budget constraint with consumption, C, on the vertical axis and leisure, L, on the horizontal axis.

Note: The slope of the budget line is $-w$.

Question: Draw the budget constraint if nonwage income, d, equals 0.

Figure 8.11 An increase in nonwage income from d_0 to d_1 shifts the budget line to the right.

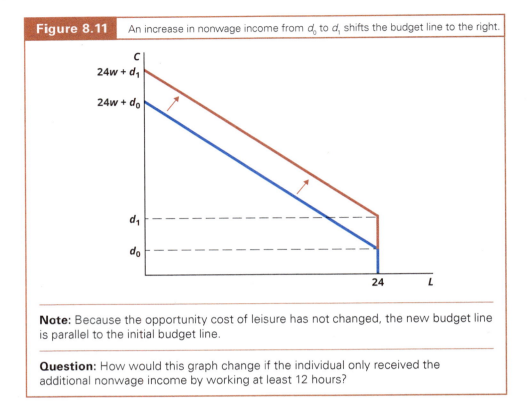

Note: Because the opportunity cost of leisure has not changed, the new budget line is parallel to the initial budget line.

Question: How would this graph change if the individual only received the additional nonwage income by working at least 12 hours?

Figure 8.12 An increase in the wage from w_0 to w_1 pivots the budget line to the right.

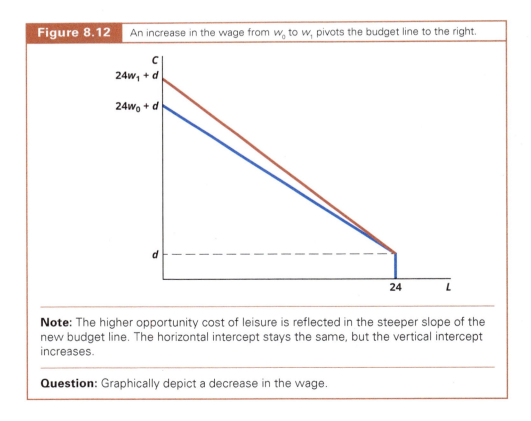

Note: The higher opportunity cost of leisure is reflected in the steeper slope of the new budget line. The horizontal intercept stays the same, but the vertical intercept increases.

Question: Graphically depict a decrease in the wage.

The graphical depiction of the budget constraint shows all the feasible combinations of consumption and leisure. Understanding the optimal choice of consumption and leisure requires information about the individual's preferences.

We assume that individuals derive utility from consumption and leisure. The utility function is given by

$$U = u(C, L). \tag{7}$$

Similar to Chapter 6, we assume that utility is increasing in both consumption and leisure. In other words, the marginal utilities of consumption and leisure are both positive. This is intuitive. Leaving consumption constant, one additional hour reading on the beach always increases the individual's utility. Similarly, leaving leisure constant, one additional plate of nachos always makes the individual better off.

We also assume that the marginal utilities of consumption and leisure are diminishing. If you are working 24 hours per day, you are probably exhausted, so the first hour of leisure is extremely valuable. But if you are only working two hours per day, an additional hour of leisure at best gets you another hour of scrolling through YouTube channels. Moving from zero to one hour of leisure raises utility more than by moving from 22 to 23 hours of leisure. A similar argument can be made for consumption. Consuming your first ice cream cone raises utility more than by going from 9 to 10 ice cream cones.

The left panel of Figure 8.13 shows how utility depends on consumption holding leisure constant. Additional consumption always increases utility because the marginal utility is always positive, but at a decreasing rate. The right panel shows the analogous graph for leisure.

Similar to the analysis in Chapter 6, we can draw indifference curves characterizing different combinations of consumption and leisure. Because the marginal utility of consumption and leisure is always positive, the indifference curves are downward sloping. If the individual takes more leisure, the only way to stay at the same level of utility is to reduce consumption. The indifference curves are also bowed in toward the origin because, with diminishing marginal utility, a balanced bundle of consumption and leisure is preferred to either extreme. Figure 8.14 shows two sample indifference curves with $U_2 > U_1$.

The marginal rate of substitution of leisure for consumption is the amount of consumption the individual is willing to give up for one additional hour of leisure while staying on the same indifference curve. The assumption of diminishing marginal utility guarantees

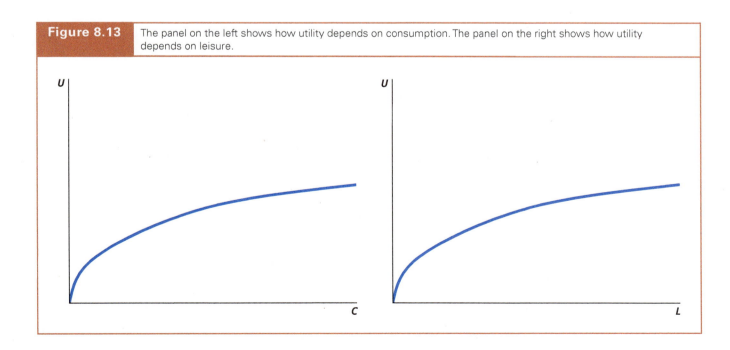

Figure 8.13 The panel on the left shows how utility depends on consumption. The panel on the right shows how utility depends on leisure.

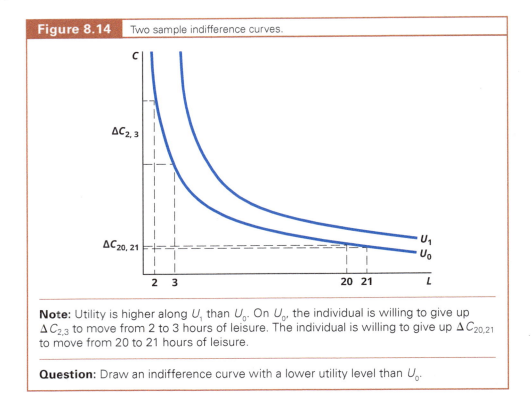

Figure 8.14 Two sample indifference curves.

Note: Utility is higher along U_1 than U_0. On U_0, the individual is willing to give up $\Delta C_{2,3}$ to move from 2 to 3 hours of leisure. The individual is willing to give up $\Delta C_{20,21}$ to move from 20 to 21 hours of leisure.

Question: Draw an indifference curve with a lower utility level than U_0.

that the marginal rate of substitution declines as leisure increases. To gain some intuition, consider a point like A in Figure 8.14, where the leisure equals two hours. At that point, the individual is willing to sacrifice a lot of consumption for one more hour of leisure. This makes sense. Two hours of leisure is hardly enough time for sleep and personal care, not to mention having some time for walking in a park or watching Netflix. At a point like B, the individual already has 20 hours of leisure and is willing to substitute only a little consumption for another hour of leisure. Again, this makes sense. With 20 hours of leisure, you probably have an adequate amount of sleep and would gain very little from watching another crime documentary on Netflix.

The next section shows how to use information on the budget constraint and indifference curves to solve for the optimal allocation of consumption and leisure.

✓ Knowledge Check 8-2

Suppose that the individual must spend T hours per day commuting to work. Graphically show how an increase in T from T_0 to T_1 affects the budget line.

Answers are at the end of the chapter.

8-2b Optimization and Comparative Statics

Having described preferences and the constraints facing the individual, we turn to the optimal choice of consumption, leisure, and work. The optimal bundle of consumption and leisure must lie on the budget line. Choosing any point inside the budget line is clearly suboptimal, as the individual could increase leisure without decreasing consumption, or the reverse. At point A in Figure 8.15, the marginal rate of substitution exceeds the slope of the budget line. In other words, the individual is willing to sacrifice more than w units of consumption for one more hour of leisure. Thus, at point A, the individual wants to take

Figure 8.15 The optimal choice of consumption and leisure.

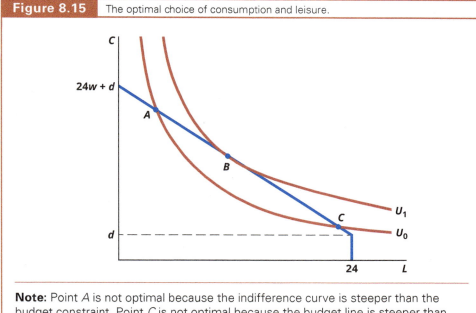

Note: Point A is not optimal because the indifference curve is steeper than the budget constraint. Point C is not optimal because the budget line is steeper than the indifference curve. The optimal point is B because the indifference curve and budget line have the same slope.

Question: Draw an indifference curve where the marginal rate of substitution is bigger than the slope of the budget line when leisure equals 24. What is the optimal solution for leisure in this case?

---

more leisure and less consumption. At a point like C, the slope of the budget line exceeds the marginal rate of substitution, which means the individual is willing to substitute less than w units of consumption for one more hour of leisure. At point C, the individual prefers less leisure and more consumption. These two examples can be generalized. As long as the marginal rate of substitution exceeds w, the individual prefers more leisure and less consumption. If the marginal rate of substitution is below w, then the individual prefers more consumption and less leisure. The optimal choice must be the bundle of consumption and leisure at which the marginal rate of substitution equals w. This is shown at point B, where the indifference curve is tangent to the budget line.

A slightly different way of describing the optimal bundle is as follows. The marginal rate of substitution reflects how the individual subjectively trades off consumption for leisure. If the individual is willing to give up more than w units of consumption for one more hour of leisure, then it is optimal to take more leisure. This decreases the marginal rate of substitution. Symmetric logic applies if the individual is willing to give up less than w units of consumption for one more hour of leisure. In that case, the individual finds it optimal to consume more and take less leisure, which increases the marginal rate of substitution. Thus, the best the individual can do is choose the bundle where the slope of the indifference curve equals the slope of the budget line.

We've seen how the budget constraint changes when model variables change. Now, let's see how changes to variables impact the optimal labor leisure choice as a whole. Suppose nonwage income increases from d_0 to d_1, as shown in Figure 8.16. The increase in nonwage income shifts the budget line up. Because the wage hasn't changed, the new budget line is parallel to the initial budget line. How does this affect the individual's optimal choice of consumption and leisure? In analyzing this, it is helpful to refer to the language of income and substitution effects from Chapter 6. Because the opportunity cost of leisure hasn't changed, the increase in nonwage income has only an income effect. Because consumption

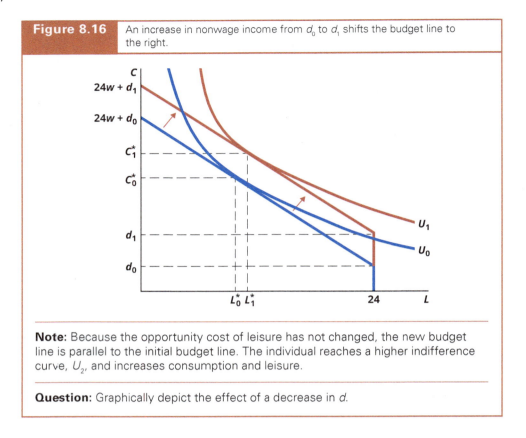

Figure 8.16 An increase in nonwage income from d_0 to d_1 shifts the budget line to the right.

Note: Because the opportunity cost of leisure has not changed, the new budget line is parallel to the initial budget line. The individual reaches a higher indifference curve, U_2, and increases consumption and leisure.

Question: Graphically depict the effect of a decrease in d.

and leisure are normal goods, an increase in income, leaving relative prices fixed, causes the individual to increase consumption and leisure. As leisure increases, time spent working decreases.

There are many real-world examples of changes in nonwage income affecting the allocation of labor and leisure. There is evidence that people close to retirement work more (and therefore take less leisure) when the stock market drops. With lower incomes coming from stock portfolios, people find it optimal to work more and take less leisure. There is also evidence that people who win lotteries decrease their labor supply.[4] With the lottery winnings, people can afford more consumption and leisure.

Now think about an increase in wages. You might intuitively think that an increase in wages should increase the quantity of labor supplied and decrease leisure. After all, don't supply curves always slope upward? The answer is no. And the reason is that an increase in the wage has two effects that move in opposite directions. First, an increase in the wage increases the price of leisure relative to consumption. Or, in other words, a higher wage increases the incentive to work. Remember from Chapter 6 that the substitution effect zeros in on the effects of a relative price change. In this case, the substitution effect says to reduce leisure and raise consumption. At the same time, an increase in the wage raises the individual's income. The income effect says to increase consumption and leisure. Thus, the change in leisure is theoretically ambiguous.

Figure 8.17 shows the effects of an increase in the wage from w_0 to w_1. The higher wage shifts the budget constraint to the right but leaves the horizontal intercept unchanged. The individual receives a higher utility, which is reflected by moving from the indifference curve labeled U_0 to U_1. Substitution and income effects both act to raise consumption, which, accordingly, is shown by the increase from C_0^* to C_1^*. The quantity of leisure decreases from L_0^* to L_1^*, which means that the substitution effect dominates the income effect.

---

[4]See, for instance, Cesarini, David, Erik Lindqvist, Matthew Notowidigdo, and Robert Ostling. 2017. "The Effect of Wealth on Individual and Household Labor Supply: Evidence from Swedish Lotteries." *American Economic Review*, 107(12): 3917–3946.

Figure 8.17 An increase in the wage from w_0 to w_1 pivots the budget line to the right.

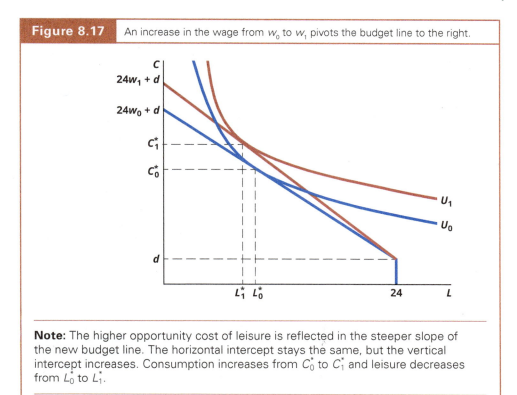

Note: The higher opportunity cost of leisure is reflected in the steeper slope of the new budget line. The horizontal intercept stays the same, but the vertical intercept increases. Consumption increases from C_0^* to C_1^* and leisure decreases from L_0^* to L_1^*.

Question: How would this graph look if the income effect dominated?

The comparative static exercises are summarized in Table 8.1. The thing to remember is that an increase in the wage has two effects that move in opposite directions for leisure. The income effect focuses on the fact that the individual is richer and acts to increase leisure (and decrease hours worked). The substitution effect focuses on the fact that the opportunity cost of leisure is higher and acts to decrease leisure (and increase hours worked). Thus, the effects of a change in the wage on the quantity of leisure and hours of work are theoretically ambiguous.

This section has exclusively focused on the optimal decisions of someone who is already working. However, as Section 8.1 noted, a big driver of the changes in hours per capita has occurred through people (especially married women) joining the labor force. The next section shows what the model has to say about labor force participation.

Table 8.1 Summarizing the Effects of an Increase in Wages

	C	L
Substitution effect	+	−
Income effect	+	+
Net effect	+	?

✓ Knowledge Check 8-3

Using the indifference curve and budget line analysis from this section, graphically depict a decrease in the wage, assuming the income effect dominates the substitution effect.

Answers are at the end of the chapter.

8-2c Labor Force Participation and the Reservation Wage

On a clear 80-degree day in the middle of your vacation, you would need a lot of consumption to compensate for even one lost hour of leisure. A case like this is depicted in Figure 8.18. The individual's indifference curves are very steep. This means that the individual would be willing to trade a lot of consumption for one more hour of leisure. In this case, there is not an indifference curve that is tangent to the budget line. Rather, the best the individual can do is to choose $L^* = 24$ and $C^* = d$. If the person is taking 24 hours of leisure, then the quantity of hours at work is zero. In other words, the person is out of the labor force. Note that the person is not *unemployed*. Given a market wage, they are choosing not to work. A situation in which $L^* = 24$ is called a **corner solution**. It differs from an interior solution for which the optimal bundle is found by equating the marginal rate of substitution to the slope of the budget line.

So, what draws this type of person to join the labor force? Figure 8.18 shows a hypothetical budget line with slope w_R that is tangent to the indifference curve when $L^* = 24$. Thus, applying our rule that the optimal bundle is found where the marginal rate of substitution equals the wage rate, we would get that leisure equals exactly 24 hours if the wage were w_R. This is called the **reservation wage**, or the wage above which a person joins the labor force.

This analysis implies that people out of the labor force have reservation wages that exceed the wages they could earn on the open market. A retiree, for instance, might find that they really enjoy spending time bird-watching. And they might enjoy bird-watching so much that the market wage isn't sufficient to draw them into the labor market. Or, perhaps, the retiree's skills depreciated so much as to decrease their market wage below their reservation wage.

An important corollary is that a person out of the labor force will join the labor force if wages get sufficiently high. From the perspective of someone out of the labor force, an increase in the wage has only a substitution effect. Since wage earnings are zero for someone out of the labor force, an increase in wages has no income effect. Thus, the labor supply model provides a cogent explanation for the patterns of hours per capita discussed in Section 8.1. Real wages have risen, albeit at different growth rates, between 1950 and today. The model predicts that increasing wages would draw people into the labor force. This is

Corner solution
In the context of the labor–leisure model, a situation in which an individual finds it optimal to spend all their time on leisure.

Reservation wage
The lowest wage at which an individual finds it optimal to join the labor force.

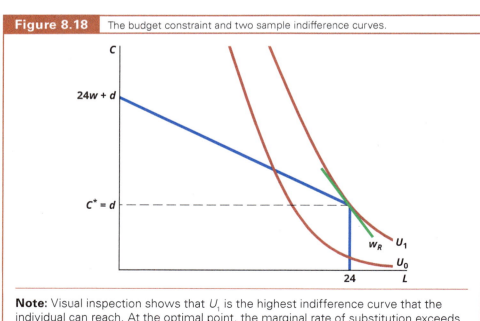

Figure 8.18 The budget constraint and two sample indifference curves.

Note: Visual inspection shows that U_1 is the highest indifference curve that the individual can reach. At the optimal point, the marginal rate of substitution exceeds the wage.

Chapter 8 Labor Markets **199**

particularly what we see for women. At the same time, the model can explain the decrease in hours per worker as long as the income effect dominates the substitution effect. Much applied economic research supports this conclusion.[5] Whether the income or substitution effect of a wage change dominates depends on the utility function and, in particular, on the slope of the utility function. This is the topic we turn to next.

✓ Knowledge Check 8-4

How does nonwage income affect the reservation wage? Explain the economic intuition.

Answers are at the end of the chapter.

8-2d Algebraically Solving for the Optimal Quantities of Labor, Leisure, and the Reservation Wage

The graphical analysis of the labor–leisure model provides indispensable economic intuition when thinking about the individual's optimal choices and comparative static exercises. However, it is sometimes useful to complement the graphical analysis with an algebraic one. Using algebra, we can show how endogenous variables respond to changes in exogenous variables quantitatively.

To start with, let's consider an interior solution. An interior solution requires that the consumption–leisure allocation be on the budget line and that the slope of the budget line equal the marginal rate of substitution. Mathematically, these two conditions are given by

$$C = w(24 - L) + d, \tag{8}$$

$$MRS = w. \tag{9}$$

The marginal rate of substitution is the slope of the indifference curve. Different indifference curves will have different slopes; however, given this information, the optimal quantities of consumption and leisure can be solved for. To take an example, suppose that the marginal rate of substitution is C/L. Equation (9) can be written as

$$\frac{C}{L} = w.$$

Note that the MRS is decreasing in leisure, which is consistent with the assumptions in Section 8.2a. There are two equations and two unknowns, C and L. Rearranging the new Equation (9), we have

$$C = wL.$$

Substitute this into Equation (8) to get

$$C = w(24 - L) + d$$

$$\Leftrightarrow wL = w(24 - L) + d$$

$$\Leftrightarrow 2wL = 24w + d$$

$$\Leftrightarrow L^* = 12 + \frac{d}{2w}.$$

---

[5]Although, to be fair, there is empirical work that finds the substitution effect dominates. A thorough literature review is beyond the scope of this book.

As predicted by theory, an increase in nonwage income, d, increases leisure. We also see that an increase in the wage decreases leisure, implying that the substitution effect dominates. Using the optimal quantity of leisure, we can back solve for consumption:

$$C^* = w(24 - L^*) + d$$

$$= w\left(24 - 12 - \frac{d}{2w}\right) + d$$

$$= 12w + \frac{d}{2}.$$

Consumption is increasing in both wage and nonwage income. Finally, the optimal quantity of leisure can be solved for using the time constraint:

$$N^* = 24 - L^*$$

$$= 24 - \left(12 + \frac{d}{2w}\right)$$

$$= 12 - \frac{d}{2w}.$$

An increase in the wage increases the quantity of hours worked. Thus, the labor supply curve is upward sloping. Notice from the last equation that if the wage is sufficiently low, or nonwage income is sufficiently high, then the optimal quantity of hours worked is negative. This, of course, is impossible. To complete the solution, we need to find the reservation wage, below which the optimal quantity of hours is zero. The reservation wage, w_R, is the wage that solves $N^* = 0$. Mathematically, this is given by

$$0 = 12 - \frac{d}{2w_R}$$

$$\Leftrightarrow \frac{d}{2w_R} = 12$$

$$\Leftrightarrow d = 24w_R$$

$$\Leftrightarrow w_R = \frac{d}{24}.$$

Just as we saw in the previous section, the reservation wage is increasing in nonwage income. The complete labor supply schedule can be summarized as

$$N^* = \begin{cases} 12 - \dfrac{d}{2w} & \text{if } w > w_R \\ 0 & \text{if } w \leq w_R. \end{cases} \tag{10}$$

Using Equation (10), the labor supply schedules for different levels of nonwage income are shown in Table 8.2. Three observations can be made about these labor supply schedules. First, the quantity of labor supplied is increasing in the wage. Second, the reservation wage increases with nonwage income. Third, an increase in nonwage income decreases labor supply. Application 8.1 discusses how the quality of leisure time affects labor force participation rates.

Table 8.2	Labor Supply Schedules for Different Levels of Nonwage Income		
	N^*		
w	$d = 48$	$d = 72$	$d = 96$
2	0	0	0
3	4	0	0
4	6	3	0
5	7.2	4.8	2.4
6	8	6	4
7	8.57	6.86	5.14

Knowledge Check 8-5

In the above example, solve for the optimal quantity of work, leisure, and the reservation wage if $d = 0$.

Answers are at the end of the chapter.

Application 8.1

Labor Force Participation and the Quality of Leisure Goods

Section 8.1 showed a decline in labor force participation among prime-aged men. Over the past 20 years, this trend is particularly pronounced among young men. Figure 8.19 shows that the fraction of nonemployed men between the ages of 21 and 30 rose from 7 percent in 2000 to 13 percent in 2018. In contrast, this fraction rose from 8 percent to 12 percent among men between the ages of 31 and 55. In other words, the fraction of nonemployed middle-aged men rose by about 50 percent, whereas the fraction of nonemployed young men rose by about 100 percent.

The labor–leisure model predicts that the fraction of nonemployed people rises when market wages fall or reservation wages increase. Although wage growth was slow between 2000 and 2018, real wages still rose by close to 10 percent during this period.[6] Alternatively, some economic research shows that in fact young men's indifference curves changed over this period.[7] And, in particular, their indifference curves became more oriented to leisure. With a higher preference for leisure, young men raised their reservation wage.

What possibly could have improved the quality of leisure time? In a recent research paper, a team of economists claim that the increase in video game quality on both computers and other gaming consoles over this period improved the quality of leisure and caused young men to retreat from work. The Xbox 360 and PlayStation 3, introduced in 2005 and 2006, respectively, allowed gamers to connect with each other online. These new gaming systems also had superior quality of graphics

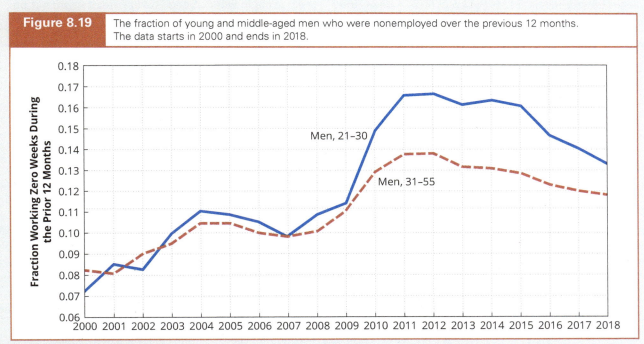

Figure 8.19 The fraction of young and middle-aged men who were nonemployed over the previous 12 months. The data starts in 2000 and ends in 2018.

Source: Aguiar, Mark, Mark Bils, Erik Hurst, and Kewin Charles. 2018. "Leisure Luxuries and the Labor Supply of Young Men." *Journal of Political Economy, 129*(2): 337–382.

[6] This figure uses the CPI to deflate nominal wages. As Application 5.1 shows, real wages grow by more if one deflates by the PCE.
[7] Aguiar, Mark, Mark Bils, Erik Hurst, and Kewin Charles. 2018. "Leisure Luxuries and the Labor Supply of Young Men." *Journal of Political Economy, 129*(2): 337–382.

Continues

202 **Part 2** Classical Theory

Application 8.1 (Continued)

Figure 8.20 The trend in leisure activities for young men between 2000 and 2017.

Leisure Activities for Men 21–30			
Activity	**2004–2007**	**2014–2017**	**Change**
Total Leisure	61.1	63.4	2.3 (0.9)
Recreational Computer	3.3	6.1	2.7 (0.4)
Video Game	2.1	3.9	1.8 (0.3)
ESP	24.3	26.0	1.7 (0.6)
TV/Movies/Netflix	17.4	15.8	−1.6 (0.5)
Socializing	7.8	7.6	−0.2 (0.4)
Other Leisure	8.3	8.9	−0.3 (0.4)

Source: Aguiar, Mark, Mark Bils, Erik Hurst, and Kewin Charles. 2018. "Leisure Luxuries and the Labor Supply of Young Men." Journal of Political Economy, 129(2): 337–382.

relative to previous consoles. As a consequence, video game revenue surged more than 50 percent between 2006 and 2009.

Using data from the American Time Use Survey, which tracks in detail how respondents spend every minute of their day, the four economists show that recreational gaming increased among young men. Figure 8.20 shows that the number of hours per week spent on computers (which includes video games) increased from 3.3 between 2000 and 2004 to 6.1 between 2014 and 2017, or 85 percent. In fact, the increased time spent on computers exceeds the increased amount of time spent on total leisure, implying that time spent in other categories of leisure must have gone down. Time spent on video games also increased by nearly 100 percent.

There is little doubt that video game quality has improved over the past 20 years. And this, in turn, has increased the quality of leisure time among video game players. At the same time, the decline in labor force participation is an equilibrium outcome. It depends on the supply side of the labor market and the demand side. While innovations to leisure activities probably explain some of the decline in work among young men, it might not be the whole story.

8-3 A Model of Unemployment

The labor–leisure model makes predictions about hours per worker and labor force participation but it is silent about unemployment. For any given wage, individuals can choose how much they want to work. In contrast, unemployed individuals, by definition, don't have a job but want to be working. This section uses a search and matching model to explain unemployment.

The model incorporates a real-world insight, namely that there are firms that post vacancies that go unfilled, and there are individuals who are actively looking for a job but can't find one. In other words, firms are actively searching for workers and workers are actively searching for jobs. This is where the "search and matching" model derives its name. The matching process between firms and workers is random. Some firms successfully find workers and some individuals are successfully matched to jobs, but this isn't true for everyone.

Frictional unemployment
Unemployment that comes from employees either voluntarily leaving their job or new workers looking for work.

Structural unemployment
Unemployment caused by a mismatch between the labor force's skills and what employers desire.

Cyclical unemployment
Unemployment caused by variations in the business cycle.

In your principles of macroeconomics class, you most likely learned about three types of unemployment. **Frictional unemployment** comes from employees either voluntarily leaving their job or new workers looking for work. The search and matching model in this chapter is best suited to address frictional unemployment. More complicated versions of the model can address **structural unemployment**, which is caused by a mismatch between the labor force's skills and what employers desire, and **cyclical unemployment**, which is caused by variations in the business cycle.

The model lasts for one period, which can be thought of as a week or a month, and assumes that an unemployed person and a firm match with some probability and then mutually decide on a wage. Once the match is formed, the worker–firm pair produces output, completing the period. At this point, all the matches separate and the economy is prepared to start the matching process all over again at the beginning of a new period. The next section describes how workers and firms match together.

8-3a Worker and Firm Behavior

The model lasts for one period, and we assume that all individuals start the period unemployed. To make the math easier, we will assume that the number of unemployed at the beginning of the period, U, equals 1. This means that the number of unemployed workers equals the fraction of the population unemployed. We also assume that each firm in the model can post one vacancy, v. The total number of vacancies is denoted by V. The probability, p, that an unemployed worker matches with a firm is given by

$$p = f(V). \tag{11}$$

Since p is a probability, it must be between zero and one, so $0 < f(V) < 1$. We assume that the probability a potential worker matches with a firm is increasing in V. Intuitively, it is a better job market for people looking for work when the number of vacancies is high. If a potential worker matches with a firm, they earn a wage, w. If the job search is unsuccessful, the individual remains unemployed and collects unemployment insurance, denoted by b. The expected value of searching for a job is given by

$$U = pw + (1 - p)b. \tag{12}$$

The expected value is the probability-weighted average of what the potential worker receives when the match is successful and when the match is unsuccessful.

Firms in the model are identical and perfectly competitive. The probability that a firm matches with a worker is given by

$$q = g(V). \tag{13}$$

Like p, q is a probability, so it must be between zero and one. We assume that $g(V)$ is declining in vacancies, V. Intuitively, the greater the number of firms that are posting vacancies, the harder it is for any one firm to successfully match with a worker. Posting a vacancy consumes resources. Not only is there a monetary cost to posting a vacancy on an online help-wanted index like Indeed, but there is a cost to reading job applications and interviewing candidates. We assume that all these costs are encapsulated in an exogenous variable, k. If the firm successfully matches with a worker, they produce z units of output. A firm's expected profits from posting a vacancy are therefore given by

$$\text{profit} = -k + q(z - w) + (1 - q) \times 0. \tag{14}$$

A firm that posts a vacancy incurs a cost of k even if they don't successfully match with a worker. With probability q, the match is successful and the firm gets to keep the difference between what is produced and what is paid in wages ($z - w$). With probability $1 - q$ the match is unsuccessful; nothing is produced and nothing is paid in wages.

8-3b Deriving the Equilibrium

Our goal is to solve for the equilibrium number of vacancies. Once we know how many vacancies are posted, we can determine the end-of-period unemployment rate.

Each firm faces the same decision: post a vacancy, or do nothing. A profit-maximizing firm operating in a perfectly competitive environment will post a vacancy as long as expected profit from posting a vacancy is greater than zero. As more firms post vacancies, the smaller the probability of filling a vacancy, hence the smaller the expected profit of

Part 2 Classical Theory

posting. This will continue to happen until expected profit is driven to zero. Thus, in equilibrium, Equation (14) can be written as

$$q = \frac{k}{z - w}. \tag{15}$$

Having established this equilibrium condition, we study how the model variables affect match probability. An increase in k raises the probability a firm successfully matches with a worker. Why does this make sense? If posting a vacancy becomes more expensive, fewer firms will post vacancies. Since $q = g(V)$ is declining in V, a reduction of the aggregate number of vacancies means that firms that do post a vacancy have a higher probability of success. Similarly, if $z - w$ goes up, the benefits to posting a vacancy are higher. More firms post vacancies, which drives the probability of successfully matching with a worker down.

Both k and z are exogenous, so Equation (15) contains two unknowns: q and w. In search models such as this one, it doesn't make sense for wages to be determined by supply and demand. The reason is that a successful match is between one worker and one firm. If they can't agree on a wage, they both get nothing. When wages, or any other price, are determined by supply and demand, there are a large number of buyers and sellers, which means that all buyers and sellers have to take prices as given. But price taking doesn't make sense in this context, because one worker and one firm are negotiating bilaterally.

Game theory

The branch of economics dealing with strategic interaction among market participants.

An example of bilateral bargaining such as this is covered in the branch of economics called **game theory**. Game theory analyzes the strategic interactions between decision makers in the market. For example, when Apple decides the price of an iPhone, they have to forecast how Samsung is going to price their smartphone. But Samsung's pricing decision depends on what they think the price of the iPhone will be. So, Apple's decision depends on what they think that Samsung thinks Apple will do. Game theory provides a way of approaching this problem that doesn't break our brain. There are many sophisticated ways to conceive of the bargaining process between the worker and firm, but here we will use a relatively standard and simple one. In particular, we assume that the **match surplus** or the total amount of output net of unemployment benefits, $z - b$, from a successful match is split evenly between workers and firms. For this to make sense, it must be assumed that match output exceeds unemployment benefits, or $z > b$. If this weren't the case, unemployed workers would be better off not searching for work.

Match surplus

The total amount of output net of unemployment benefits.

From the worker's perspective, the added value of matching with a firm relative to staying unemployed is $w - b$. Applying the rule that the match surplus is split evenly gives

$$\frac{z - b}{2} = w - b.$$

The left-hand side is one-half of the match surplus, and the right-hand side is the added value to matching. Solving for the wage gives

$$w = \frac{1}{2}(z + b). \tag{16}$$

In other words, the wage is the midpoint between what is produced with a successful match and unemployment benefits. Intuitively, if match productivity increases, workers are going to see some of the increase reflected in their wage. If unemployment benefits, b, increase, the value of being unemployed is higher and that allows workers to bargain for a higher wage.

Table 8.3 summarizes the endogenous variables, exogenous variables, and key equations of the model. There are four equations and four unknowns. However, using the free-entry condition in combination with the bargained wage allows us to determine the job-filling rate. From there, we can derive the equilibrium number of vacancies and job-finding rate. Finally, recalling that the fraction of unemployed people at the beginning of the period is 1, the end of period unemployment rate is the fraction of unemployed individuals who don't find a job, or $1 - p$.

Table 8.3	Summary of Search and Matching Model
Endogenous variables: V, q, p, w	**Exogenous Variables: z, b, k**
Key Equations:	
1. $q = g(V)$	(Job-filling rate)
2. $p = f(V)$	(Job-finding rate)
3. $q = \dfrac{k}{z - w}$	(Free-entry condition)
4. $w = \tfrac{1}{2}(z + b)$	(Bargained wage)

✓ Knowledge Check 8-6

We derived a reservation wage in the labor–leisure model. What is the reservation wage in the search and matching model?

Answers are at the end of the chapter.

8-3c Graphically Characterizing the Equilibrium

The search and matching model can be analyzed graphically. Figure 8.21 graphs the wage on the vertical axis and the job-filling rate, q, on the horizontal axis. From Equation (16), we see that the wage is independent of the job-finding rate. Therefore, the wage line is perfectly horizontal at $0.5(z + b)$. From Equation (15), we know that the job-filling rate is an increasing function of the wage. A higher wage, all else equal, means lower expected profits for firms. Fewer firms post vacancies, which drives up the job-filling rate and ensures that expected profits equal 0. The horizontal intercept is $\dfrac{k}{z}$. Note also that as w approaches z, the job-filling rate goes to infinity. Since q is a probability, it in fact is capped at one. The intersection of the free-entry line and the wage line determines the equilibrium wage, w^*, and job-filling rate, q^*.

We can use this graph to analyze several comparative static exercises. Figure 8.22 shows the effects of an increase in vacancy posting costs from k_1 to k_2. Vacancy posting costs do not affect the wage line, so the equilibrium wage is unaffected. But the increase in k shifts the free-entry line down and to the right. Higher vacancy posting costs, all else equal, reduce expected profits. In response to this, fewer firms post vacancies. This drives the job-filling

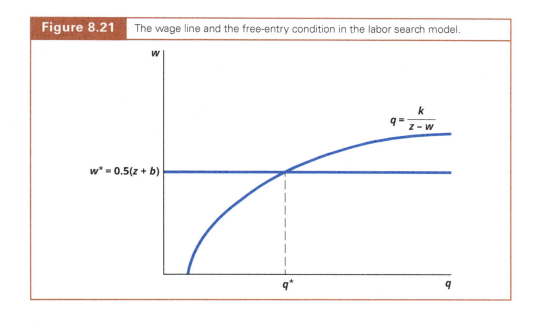

Figure 8.21 The wage line and the free-entry condition in the labor search model.

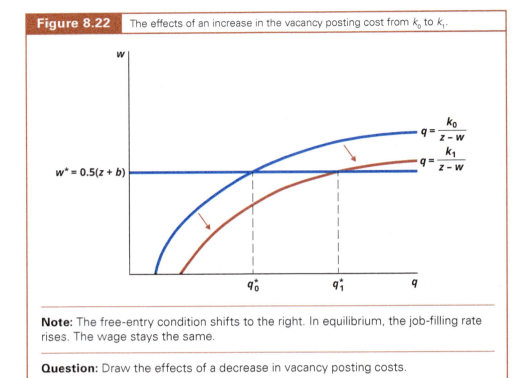

Figure 8.22 The effects of an increase in the vacancy posting cost from k_0 to k_1.

Note: The free-entry condition shifts to the right. In equilibrium, the job-filling rate rises. The wage stays the same.

Question: Draw the effects of a decrease in vacancy posting costs.

rate up from q_0^* to q_1^*. The lower number of vacancies implies a lower job-finding rate, p. Since the end-of-period unemployment rate is $1 - p$, the higher vacancy posting costs increase the unemployment rate.

Next, consider an increase in unemployment benefits from b_0 to b_1. Figure 8.23 shows that this shifts the wage line up. In equilibrium, the wage increases. The higher equilibrium wage, all else equal, reduces expected profits. Fewer firms post vacancies, and the job-filling rate increases from q_0^* to q_1^*. The lower number of vacancies implies a lower job-finding rate and a higher unemployment rate.

The conclusion that more generous unemployment benefits increase the unemployment rate is a familiar one. However, the economic mechanism driving the result in the search model is probably less familiar. If you ask someone outside of an economics classroom why more generous unemployment benefits increase the unemployment rate, they would likely say that the more generous benefits discourage unemployed people from looking for a job. While the common person's logic might be true empirically, this is not the economic mechanism in the model. Indeed, there is no decision about how intensely to search. In the model, higher unemployment benefits reduce the match surplus. Firms respond by posting fewer vacancies. A lower number of vacancies means a lower job-finding rate. And a lower job-finding rate means a higher unemployment rate.

Finally, an increase in match productivity from z_0 to z_1 shifts the wage line up, increasing the equilibrium wage. This is shown in Figure 8.24. The increase in productivity also shifts the free-entry line up and to the left. Note that the free-entry equation can be written as

$$q = \frac{k}{z - w}$$

$$= \frac{k}{z - 0.5(z + b)}$$

$$= \frac{k}{0.5(z - b)}.$$

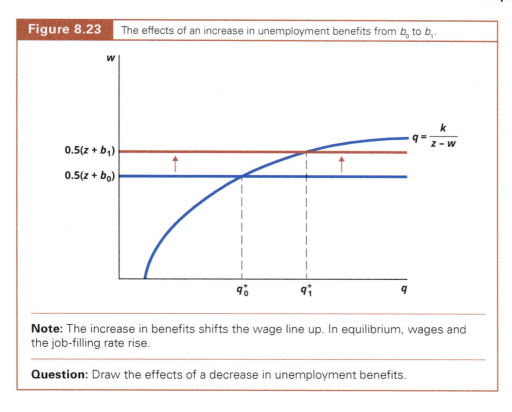

Figure 8.23 The effects of an increase in unemployment benefits from b_0 to b_1.

Note: The increase in benefits shifts the wage line up. In equilibrium, wages and the job-filling rate rise.

Question: Draw the effects of a decrease in unemployment benefits.

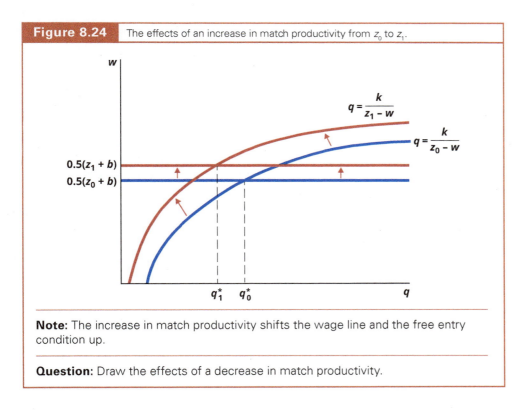

Figure 8.24 The effects of an increase in match productivity from z_0 to z_1.

Note: The increase in match productivity shifts the wage line and the free entry condition up.

Question: Draw the effects of a decrease in match productivity.

Thus, an increase in match productivity unambiguously decreases the job-filling rate. A lower job-filling rate means that more firms are posting vacancies. A higher number of vacancies means a higher job-finding rate and a lower end-of-period unemployment rate.

Table 8.4 Comparative Statics in the Search and Matching Model

		Increase in:		
		k	*b*	*z*
Wages	w	0	+	+
Job-filling rate	q	+	+	−
Vacancies	v	−	−	+
Job-finding rate	p	−	−	+
Unemployment rate	1 − p	+	+	−

Table 8.4 summarizes the comparative static exercises. The search and matching model provides a way to think about unemployment. Jobs are created when firms post vacancies and unemployed workers match with them. Because the matching process is random, it explains the real-world observation that at any given point in time there exist unfilled jobs and unemployed workers.

One issue that neither the labor–leisure model nor the search model addresses is how to treat **discouraged workers**. Discouraged workers are people who have not looked for work in the past four weeks but indicate some type of discouragement in their job prospects. Because these people have stopped looking for work, they are technically not "unemployed"; however, in some sense, they are still underutilized resources based on their own stated preferences. Application 8.2 discusses how statistical agencies in the United States treat discouraged workers and how quantitatively important they are.

Discouraged worker
A person who has not looked for work in the last four weeks but indicates some type of discouragement in their job prospects.

✓ Knowledge Check 8-7

Suppose workers receive only one-third of the total match surplus, $z - b$. Solve for the new equilibrium wage. Is it higher or lower than the wage in Equation (16)?

Answers are at the end of the chapter.

Application 8.2

Indicators of Labor Market Utilization

Unemployed workers are by definition underutilized resources. These are people who want to work and are looking for a job but, for whatever reason, can't find a job. For that reason, the unemployment rate—or the total number of unemployed divided by the labor force—would seem to be a good indicator of labor market utilization. There are, however, some qualifications to this conclusion.

The unemployment rate is calculated by the Bureau of Labor Statistics in the Current Population Survey (CPS). The CPS asks people if they are working or not working. If a survey respondent is not working, the CPS asks if the respondent has looked for a job in the past four weeks. If the answer is yes, that person counts as unemployed. If the answer is no, the person counts as out of the labor force. Most of the people answering "no" are truly not interested in working because they may be in school, retired, a stay-at-home parent, or disabled. However, some people who didn't look for work in the past four weeks may have looked for a job in previous months but didn't have any luck. Acknowledging this reality, the CPS computes a broader measure of labor market utilization that includes the unemployed and discouraged workers. Discouraged workers, again, are people who have not looked for work in the past four weeks but indicate some type of discouragement in their job prospects. The possible reasons that an individual may claim to be discouraged include a lack of training or education, no jobs for which they would qualify, or because they think employers discriminate against them. In the technical language of the CPS, this measure of underutilization is called U-4 and the traditional measure of unemployment is called U-3.

Figure 8.25 shows the time trends of U-3 and U-4 since 1994. The two series track each other very closely, indicating that the number of discouraged workers is small relative to the number of unemployed. The number of discouraged workers was the largest following the Great Recession of 2007–2009. The slow recovery of labor market utilization after the Great Recession is sometimes referred to as a *jobless recovery*. The unemployment rate was much quicker in coming down after the Covid-19 recession of 2020.

Continues

Application 8.2 (Continued)

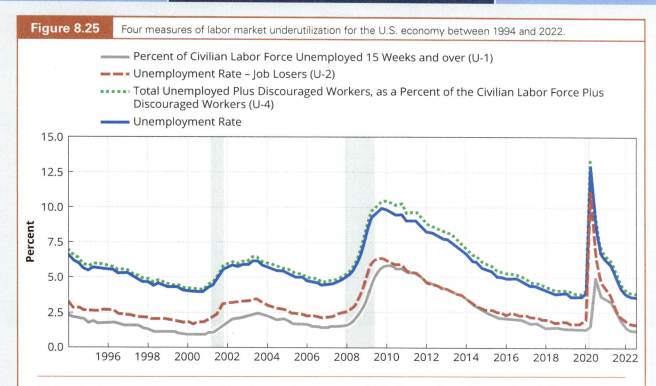

Figure 8.25 Four measures of labor market underutilization for the U.S. economy between 1994 and 2022.

Note: The four measures are: traditional unemployment rate (U3), the number of unemployed plus discouraged workers as a fraction of the labor force (U4), the number of job leavers as a fraction of the labor force (U-2), and the number of long-term unemployed as a fraction of the labor force (U-1).

Source: FRED.

While the existence of discouraged workers is a reason why the traditional measure of unemployment might give too optimistic a view of the labor market, there is also a reason why it might overestimate underutilized resources. Specifically, even a vibrant and healthy labor market will have people who are unemployed for a few weeks. If people quit their jobs to look for better opportunities in different industries or cities, that is part of the healthy churn in the labor market. To isolate this factor, economists sometimes look at the percent of the labor force that is long-term unemployed (unemployed for more than 15 weeks) versus short-term unemployed (unemployed for less than 15 weeks). Figure 8.28 shows that the long-term unemployed, or U-1 in the language of the CPS, is anywhere between one-third and half of the total unemployment rate. The share of long-term unemployed increased to over 50 percent in the wake of the Great Recession and remained there until 2013. Finally, U-2 includes the number of job losers as a fraction of the labor force. It is usually about half of the total unemployment rate. Table 8.5 summarizes the different measures of labor market underutilization used by the CPS.[8]

Different measures of the unemployment rate complement each other in diagnosing overall labor market health. Although you typically read about the unemployment rate, U-3, in the news media, a complete picture requires knowledge about the people who are not working. An economy with a 1 percent unemployment rate but millions of discouraged workers is a lot different from an economy with a 1 percent unemployment rate and no discouraged workers.

Table 8.5	Measures of Labor Market Underutilization
U-1	Persons unemployed 15 weeks or longer
U-2	Job losers and people who completed temporary jobs
U-3	Total unemployed
U-4	Total unemployed plus discouraged workers

[8]The CPS calculates two other measures, U-5 and U-6, that are not discussed in the application.

210 **Part 2** Classical Theory

Chapter Summary

- Hours per capita in the United States were relatively stable between 1950 and 2010. This stability was the product of an increase in the employment–population ratio, fueled largely by women joining the labor force and falling hours per worker.

- Some of the causes of the rise in women's labor force participation in the second half of the 20th century include rising wages for women relative to men, a shift toward services and away from manufacturing, and the widespread adoption of labor-saving durable goods in the household.

- Unemployment rates are higher for Black Americans than Hispanic Americans, which are in turn higher than the unemployment rates for White Americans. Also, unemployment rates are a decreasing function of educational attainment.

- In the labor–leisure model, individuals choose the optimal amounts of consumption, labor, and leisure subject to a budget constraint and a time constraint. At an optimal point, the marginal rate of substitution of consumption for leisure equals the wage rate.

- An increase in nonwage income only has an income effect and therefore increases consumption and leisure and decreases the quantity of hours worked.

- An increase in the wage increases income but makes leisure more expensive relative to consumption. On net, consumption increases, but the changes in work and leisure are ambiguous.

- In the labor–leisure model, an individual finds it optimal to join the labor force when the market wage exceeds the reservation wage.

- The search and matching model takes as given that the matching process between workers and firms is costly and random. Some individuals looking for work don't find jobs and some firms with job openings don't find workers.

- The equilibrium unemployment rate in the labor search model is a function of match productivity, unemployment benefits, and vacancy posting costs.

Key Terms

Employment–population ratio, 184
Civilian, noninstitutionalized, 16 and over population, 184
Labor force, 185
Unemployed, 185
Labor force participation rate, 185
Unemployment rate, 185
Corner solution, 198

Reservation wage, 198
Frictional unemployment, 202
Structural unemployment, 202
Cyclical unemployment, 202
Game theory, 204
Match surplus, 204
Discouraged worker, 208

Review Questions

1. Compare the trends in labor force participation rates for men and women over the past 70 years.

2. In some countries, hours of work increase with wages. Does this mean the substitution or income effect is dominant? Explain.

3. Labor force participation rates are lower among married women with young children compared to other demographic

groups in the same age range. What does this imply about their reservation wage?

4. Why do we assume vacancy posting is costly in the search and matching model?

5. Using the economics of the search and matching model, explain the effect an increase in unemployment benefits has on the unemployment rate.

Problems

8.1 Consider the following economic data. LFPR is labor force participation rate and UR is unemployment rate.

Category	Men	Women
Population (in millions)	100	115
Unemployed (in millions)	3	5
Employed	?	?
LFPR	80%	85%
UR	?	?

  a. Complete the missing values of the table.

  b. Calculate the LFPR and UR for the entire economy.

8.2 The budget constraint in the labor-leisure model is given by

$$C = w(24 - L).$$

The budget constraint says that consumption equals wage income.

  a. Assuming standard-looking indifference curves, graphically depict the optimal bundle of consumption and leisure.

  b. Suppose wage income is taxed at rate t, where $0 < t < 1$. How does this change the budget constraint?

  c. Suppose the marginal rate of substitution is given by $\frac{C}{L}$.

  Using the budget constraint in part b, solve for the optimal quantities of leisure, work, and consumption.

Chapter 8 Labor Markets **211**

d. Graphically depict a decrease in the tax rate. How does an increase in the tax rate affect the quantity of work and leisure?

e. One often hears that lowering tax rates leads to people increasing their hours at work. Based on your answers to the previous two parts, do you agree with this hypothesis? Explain the economic mechanisms at work.

8.3 The budget constraint in the labor-leisure model is given by

$$C = w(24 - L) + d.$$

The budget constraint says that consumption equals wage income plus nonwage income.

a. Assuming standard-looking indifference curves, graphically depict the optimal bundle of consumption and leisure.

b. Suppose the marginal rate of substitution is given by $\dfrac{kC}{L}$.

The parameter $k > 0$ can be interpreted as a person's disutility of work. The higher is k, the steeper are the indifference curves, meaning that the individual is willing to trade more consumption for one more hour of leisure. Using the budget constraint in part a, solve for the optimal quantities of leisure, work, and consumption. Assuming $k = 1$ and $d = 60$, solve for the reservation wage.

c. Assume there are three types of people in the economy each with the same marginal rate of substitution and nonwage income but different wages. In particular, assume $w_1 = 4$, $w_2 = 8$, and $w_3 = 12$. The economy's population consists of an equal number of all three types. What is the labor force participation rate in this economy?

d. During the first few months of the Covid-19 pandemic, people were reluctant to go to work for fear of being infected with the virus. From the perspective of the model, this can be viewed as an increase in k. Assuming k doubles from 1 to 2, calculate the new reservation wage. How does this affect the labor force participation rate in the economy?

8.4 A version of the labor search model can be solved for algebraically. To begin with, assume that the total number of hires, H, in the economy is given by

$$H = V^{0.5}U^{0.5}$$

where U is the number unemployed at the start of the period.

a. The job-finding rate is the probability a potential worker finds a job. This is given by $p = \dfrac{H}{U}$, or the total number of hires divided by the total number of unemployed. The job-filling rate is the probability a firm matches with a worker. This is given by $q = \dfrac{H}{V}$, or the total number of hires divided by the total number of vacancies. Assuming everyone starts the period as unemployed, i.e., $U = 1$, express the job-finding and job-filling rates as a function of V.

b. In the text, we assumed that the job-filling rate was a decreasing function of the number of vacancies and that the job-finding rate was an increasing function of the number of vacancies. Are your answers in the previous part consistent with these assumptions?

c. Assuming the equilibrium wage is $w = \dfrac{1}{2}(z + b)$ and that free entry drives expected profits to 0, calculate the equilibrium number of vacancies and end-of-period unemployment rate as a function of the exogenous variables, k, b, and z. Are the comparative statics consistent with our findings summarized in Table 8.4?

8.5 Suppose that an unemployed worker in the labor search model receives unemployment benefits of b but also gets some extra enjoyment from watching TV, tv. Employed workers don't get to enjoy TV, so the value of being unemployed is $b + tv$.

a. How does the introduction of TV change the match surplus between a firm and worker?

b. Solve for the new equilibrium wage, assuming workers and firms split the surplus 50–50.

c. Suppose the quality of daytime TV increases. In a graph similar to Figure 8.24, show how the increase in TV quality affects the equilibrium wage and job-filling rate.

d. How does the increase in TV quality affect the equilibrium number of vacancies and the unemployment rate?

✅ **Knowledge Check 8-1 Answer**

The labor force is the sum of the employed and unemployed, or $70 + 8 = 78$ million. The labor force participation rate, therefore, is 78 percent. The unemployment rate is

$$UR = \frac{8}{78} = 0.102,$$

or 10.2 percent.

Hours per capita is the product of the employment–population ratio and hours per worker: $n_t = e_t \times h_t$. In this example, hours per capita are given by

$$n = 0.7 \times 38 = 26.6.$$

So, hours per capita equal 26.6 hours per week.

Knowledge Check 8-2 Answer

The individual now divides time between, work, leisure, and commuting. The time constraint is therefore given by

$$N + L + T = 24.$$

This can be substituted into the budget constraint:

$$C = wN + d$$
$$= w(24 - L - T) + d.$$

Figure 8.26 shows the results of incorporating commute time. The horizontal intercept, or the maximum feasible hours for leisure, is $24 - T$. If the individual spends no time on leisure, then total consumption is $(24 - T)w + d$, which is the vertical intercept. Figure 8.26 also shows the effects of increasing commuting time from T_0 to T_1. The increase in commuting time shifts the budget line to the left. The horizontal intercept shifts in and the vertical intercept shifts down. Intuitively, an increase in commuting time means that the individual has less time for leisure and less time for work, which means less consumption. Because the change in commuting time does not affect the opportunity cost of leisure, the new budget line has the same slope as the initial budget line.

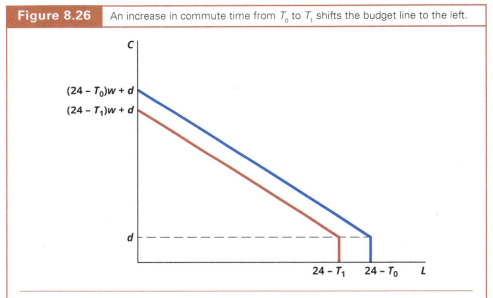

Figure 8.26 An increase in commute time from T_0 to T_1 shifts the budget line to the left.

Note: The individual can now afford less consumption and leisure. Because the opportunity cost of leisure is unaffected, the new budget line has the same slope as the initial budget line.

Knowledge Check 8-3 Answer

Figure 8.27 shows a decrease in the wage from w_0 to w_1. The lower wage pivots the budget constraint to the left. Because income and substitution effects work in the same way for consumption, we know that consumption must fall. This is reflected in that C_1 is lower than C_0. Because income has decreased, the income effect says to take less leisure and increase the quantity of work. Thus, the new quantity of leisure, L_1, is lower than the initial quantity, L_0.

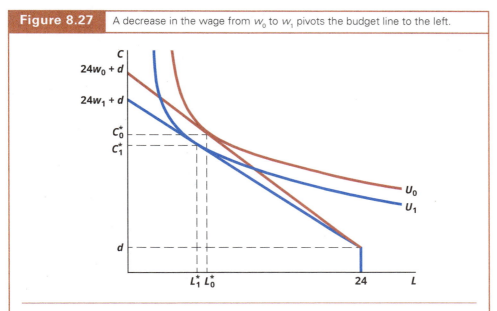

Figure 8.27 A decrease in the wage from w_0 to w_1 pivots the budget line to the left.

Note: The higher opportunity cost of leisure is reflected in the flatter slope of the new budget line. The horizontal intercept stays the same, but the vertical intercept increases. Consumption decreases from C_0^* to C_1^* and leisure increases from L_0^* to L_1^*.

Knowledge Check 8-4 Answer

Figure 8.28 shows an increase in nonwage income from d_0 to d_1. The increase in income allows the individual to reach a higher level of utility. The budget line touches the new indifference curve, U_1, at a steeper point. This means that the reservation wage increases, as seen by the steeper line marked $w_{1,r}$. Intuitively, a higher nonwage income increases desired leisure time. If the person is already at a corner solution, the wage required to draw that person into the labor market gets that much higher.

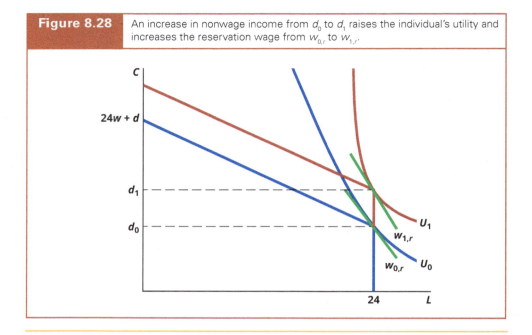

Figure 8.28 An increase in nonwage income from d_0 to d_1 raises the individual's utility and increases the reservation wage from $w_{0,r}$ to $w_{1,r}$.

✓ Knowledge Check 8-5 Answer

If $d = 0$, then $L^* = N^* = 12$. Since the time allocation doesn't depend on the wage, we infer that the substitution effect cancels with the income effect. Moreover, since the only way to get consumption is by working, the individual finds it optimal to work regardless of the wage. Thus, $w_R = 0$.

✓ Knowledge Check 8-6 Answer

From the worker's perspective, any job that pays more than the level of unemployment benefits, b, is worth accepting. Thus, b is the reservation wage.

✓ Knowledge Check 8-7 Answer

From the worker's perspective, the value of matching to the firm relative to unemployment is $w - b$. Setting this equal to one-third of the total match surplus gives

$$\frac{1}{3}(z - b) = w - b$$

$$\Leftrightarrow w = \frac{1}{3}z + \frac{2}{3}b.$$

Since $b < z$, the new wage is lower than the wage in Equation (16). This makes sense because workers receive a lower share of the surplus.

Chapter 9

Government Spending and the Macroeconomy

Learning Objectives

9.1 List the sources of government revenue and expenditure and explain how they have changed over the 20th and 21st centuries.

9.2 Incorporate taxes in the consumption–savings model.

9.3 Define the Ricardian equivalence theorem and the assumptions in the theorem.

9.4 Graphically show how different methods of government financing affect investment and the real interest rate in Ricardian and non-Ricardian economies.

9.5 Evaluate the economic effects of government debt in the United States.

Responding to the abrupt onset of the Covid-19 pandemic, the U.S. federal government nearly doubled its expenditure between the first and second quarters of 2020. With many sectors of the economy either partially or completely shut down, much of this expenditure went to individuals in the form of temporary relief checks or to businesses in the form of low interest, uncollateralized, forgivable loans. Federal contributions to unemployment insurance alone rose from about $28 billion dollars in 2019 to over $500 billion in 2020.[1] This was the third time this century when the federal government undertook massive stimulus. Both the Economic Stimulus Act of 2008 and the American Recovery and Reinvestment Act of 2009 injected billions of dollars into the economy.

This massive and unprecedented increase in government expenditure raises some economic questions. First, how does an increase in government transfer payments affect people's saving and consumption decisions? Does it matter if the government allocates the resources to transfer payments rather than to things like infrastructure investment or military spending? How does the type of government expenditure and the way it is financed affect investment and interest rates? Finally, the federal government's debt grew by nearly $3 trillion in 2020. How does the size of the government debt affect the economy's prospects moving forward? You learned in Chapter 6 how firms make investment decisions and how individuals make consumption and saving decisions, but we hardly analyzed the government sector in any detail. All of these questions will be addressed in this chapter.

9-1 A Primer on Government Spending and Revenue

Recall from Chapter 1 that the measure of government spending that is counted in GDP consists of government consumption and investment. Government consumption includes things like salary payments to teachers, military personnel, and federal judges. Government investment projects range from the construction of new elementary school buildings to repairing public roads to the purchase of new fighter jets for the military. The catch is that

---

[1]Bureau of Economic Analysis, bea.gov.

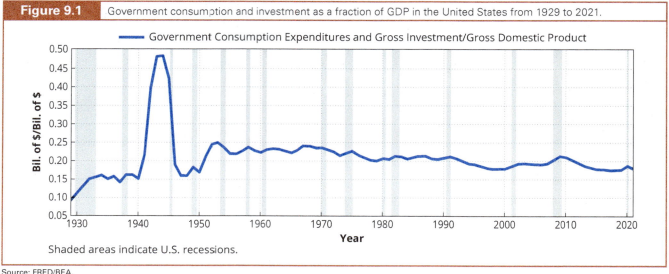

Figure 9.1 Government consumption and investment as a fraction of GDP in the United States from 1929 to 2021.

Shaded areas indicate U.S. recessions.

Source: FRED/BEA.

for government spending to be included in GDP, some good or service must actually be produced.

Figure 9.1 shows that after a very big spike in the early 1940s during World War II, government consumption and investment as a share of GDP has hovered at about 20 percent since 1970. At the same time, the government spends money on more categories than just those that are counted in GDP. The next section discusses these types of government spending before explaining how this spending is financed.

9-1a The Categories of Government Spending

Current government expenditures
The sum of consumption expenditures, transfer payments, interest payments, and subsidies.

Current government expenditures are the sum of consumption expenditures, transfer payments, interest payments, and subsidies. Transfer payments reallocate resources from one person to another person. Since nothing is produced in the exchange, transfer payments aren't included in GDP. The two biggest federal transfer programs in the United States are Social Security and Medicare. Social Security provides income support for retirees; the dollar value of retirement benefits is proportional to each retiree's lifetime labor earnings. Medicare provides medical insurance for retirees. Both programs are financed by taxes on labor earnings, half of which are paid by employers and the other half by employees.[2] Social Security and Medicare are good examples of why transfer payments aren't included in GDP. Both programs move resources from workers to retirees. Nothing is produced in the process. Another transfer program, Medicaid, provides healthcare to low-income Americans. It is financed through taxes at the federal and state level and administered by states. A final transfer program, unemployment insurance, was massively important during the 2020 recession. Unemployment insurance provides temporary benefits to unemployed workers; the level of benefits is proportional to each worker's past wages up to a certain cap.

Although transfer payments aren't included in GDP, that doesn't mean they are macroeconomically irrelevant. First, as Figure 9.2 shows, transfer payments are becoming increasingly quantitatively significant. They rose from about 1 percent of GDP in 1930 to close to 15 percent before the Covid-19 pandemic. The increase comes in part from the adoption of new programs, such as Medicare and Medicaid in 1965, and the increased generosity and coverage of existing programs. For instance, when the Social Security Act was passed

---

[2]The careful reader will note that the statutory incidence of the tax is different than the economic incidence. Most economists believe that workers end up paying all of the payroll tax through lower wages.

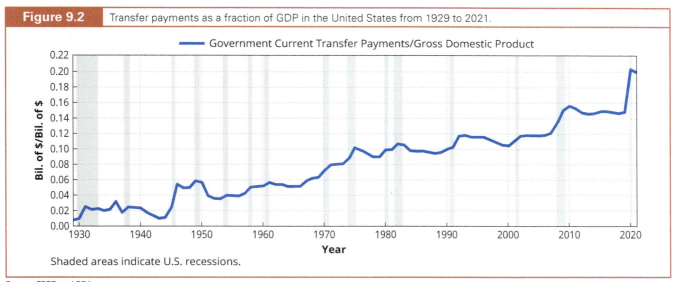

Figure 9.2 Transfer payments as a fraction of GDP in the United States from 1929 to 2021.

Shaded areas indicate U.S. recessions.

Source: FRED and BEA.

in 1935, the tax rate on wages was 1 percent and a large fraction of workers, notably the self-employed and those in agriculture, were excluded from the system.[3] Today, the tax rate is 6.2 percent and coverage is universal.

Second, transfer payments potentially influence the microeconomic behavior of individuals. If workers know that Social Security is waiting for them upon retirement, they will likely reduce their saving rate. Along similar lines, a temporary tax cut will affect consumption and savings decisions differently than a permanent tax cut. In a different context, you learned in Chapter 7 how unemployment insurance affects a firm's incentive to post vacancies, which ultimately determines the unemployment rate. Thus, despite not being counted in GDP, transfer payments can change economic behavior, which in turn affects the overall level of economic production.

The last two categories of current government expenditures are interest payments and subsidies. Neither is included in GDP. Interest payments go to bondholders of the government's debt. The magnitude of the interest payments is influenced by the size of the debt as well as the interest rate. The economic significance of government debt is something we return to in Section 9.4 of this chapter. Subsidies are government payments to individuals and businesses. In most years, the two biggest forms of subsidies in the United States go toward agriculture and housing. However, as Table 9.1 shows, subsidies unrelated to housing and agriculture spiked upward during the Covid-19 pandemic. Many of these subsidies went to small businesses in the form of PPP loans discussed in the introduction. Since these loans are forgivable—subject to certain stipulations—the Bureau of Economic Analysis treats them as subsidies.[4]

Table 9.1 Recipients of Subsidies in the United States from 2019 to 2021 (in Billions of Dollars)

Federal	2019	2020	2021
Housing	22.4	46.1	27.8
Agriculture	40.2	44.1	45.3
Air carriers	0.3	20.0	21.8
Other	9.4	546.5	383.9
State and local	**2019**	**2020**	**2021**
Total	0.6	0.6	3.1

Source: BEA, Table 3.13.

---

[3]This website contains a brief history of the Social Security Act: https://www.ssa.gov/history/50ed.html.
[4]For more information, check out the BEA's webpage: https://www.bea.gov/help/faq/1408.

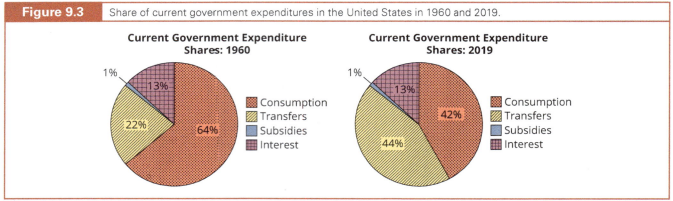

Figure 9.3 Share of current government expenditures in the United States in 1960 and 2019.

Source: BEA Table 3.1.

Figure 9.3 compares current government expenditures in 1960 and 2019. In each year, subsidies accounted for about 1 percent of current expenditures, whereas interest payments accounted for about 13 percent. The biggest change is that government transfers accounted for a much higher share in 2019 and consumption accounted for a much higher share in 1960.

Total government expenditures include current government expenditures and net investment, or gross investment minus the consumption of fixed capital, i.e., depreciation. Because investment projects like roads and schools are long-lived, the government separates them from current expenditures. Figure 9.4 shows that the gross government investment as a share of total government expenditures has declined from about 24 percent in 1960 to 8 percent in 2021. Like the stock of private capital, the stock of public capital, otherwise known as *infrastructure*, depreciates over time. The implication is that lower levels of government investment led to a lower stock of public capital.

A final stylized fact has to do with the jurisdiction of government spending. Relative to many of its European counterparts, the United States has historically had a more decentralized government. Indeed, as Figure 9.5 shows, government spending at the state and local levels has accounted for between 30 and 40 percent of total government expenditures since 1960. Conversely, spending at the sub-national level accounted for about 20 percent of total government spending in Great Britain and France in 2020.[5]

Total government expenditures
The sum of current government expenditures and net investment, or gross investment minus the consumption of fixed capital, i.e., depreciation.

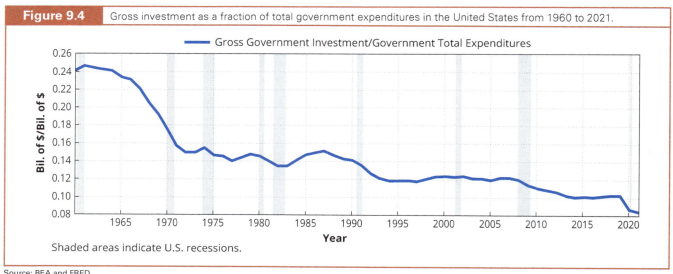

Figure 9.4 Gross investment as a fraction of total government expenditures in the United States from 1960 to 2021.

Shaded areas indicate U.S. recessions.

Source: BEA and FRED.

---

[5]OECD (2021), *Fiscal Federalism 2022: Making Decentralisation Work*, OECD Publishing, Paris, https://doi.org/10.1787/201c75b6-en.

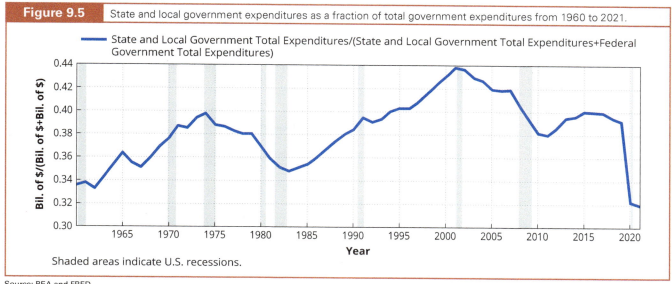

Figure 9.5 State and local government expenditures as a fraction of total government expenditures from 1960 to 2021.

Shaded areas indicate U.S. recessions.

Source: BEA and FRED.

9-1b The Sources of Government Revenue

The U.S. government at all levels collected $6.7 trillion in revenue in 2021. Table 9.2 lists the sources and their size. Two-thirds of government revenue come from current tax receipts. These are taxes on individuals, corporations, products, and imports. Taxes on individuals include the personal income tax as well as taxes on interest and realized capital gains. Taxes on corporate income include revenue that the government collects from taxing corporations. State and local sales taxes make up most of the tax revenue on products; however, some goods, like cigarettes, gasoline, and alcohol, face additional taxes that vary by state. Imported products, meanwhile, face custom duties and occasionally tariffs.

Figure 9.6 shows the revenue of each tax as a proportion of total tax receipts from 1960 to 2021. The revenue raised from corporate income taxes as a share of total taxes has declined from over 20 percent in 1960 to under 10 percent in 2021. The share of personal current taxes, meanwhile, has increased from 40 percent in 1960 to over 50 percent in 2021.

Contributions for government social insurance are the taxes the government collects from employers and employees to fund social insurance programs such as Social Security, Medicare, and unemployment insurance. These social insurance programs are administered almost entirely at the federal level. Figure 9.7 shows that contributions for government social insurance as a fraction of current federal receipts nearly tripled between 1947 and 2021.

Income receipts on assets consist of dividends, interest, and royalties from government-owned assets. Current transfer receipts include fines, fees, and deposit insurance premiums

Table 9.2 Sources of U.S. Government Revenue in 2021

Current receipts	Billions of dollars
Current tax receipts	$4,730.1
Contributions for government social insurance	$1,546.2
Income receipts on assets	$242.0
Current transfer receipts	$211.4
Current surplus of government enterprises	$2.1
Total receipts	
Current receipts	$6,731.8
Capital transfer receipts	$37.9

Source: BEA, Table 3.1.

Figure 9.6 Personal current taxes, taxes on production and imports, and corporate income taxes as a share of current tax receipts from 1960 to 2021.

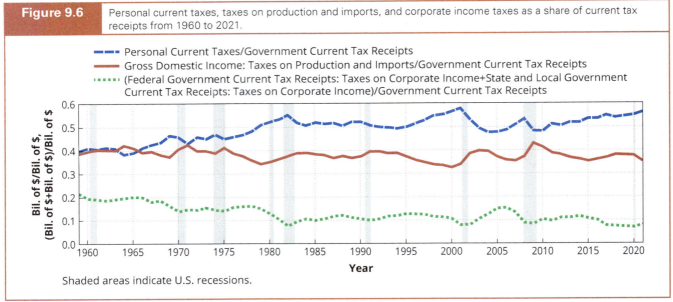

Shaded areas indicate U.S. recessions.

Source: BEA and FRED.

paid by banks, as well as a few other smaller items.[6] Current surplus of government enterprises is a profit-like measure for enterprises run by the government. At the federal level in 2021, the U.S. Federal Housing Administration earned a $6 billion surplus, while the U.S. Postal Service ran at a $3.1 billion loss. At the state and local level, water and sewerage facilities netted a $15.6 billion surplus and public transit ran at a $41.1 billion loss.[7] Although certain enterprises, like state-run liquor stores, always run at a profit[8] and others, like housing and urban renewal, always run at a loss, the aggregate surplus alternates between being positive and negative. Indeed, before 2021, 2004 was the last year the surplus was positive.

Figure 9.7 Contributions for government social insurance as a share of federal current receipts from 1947 to 2021.

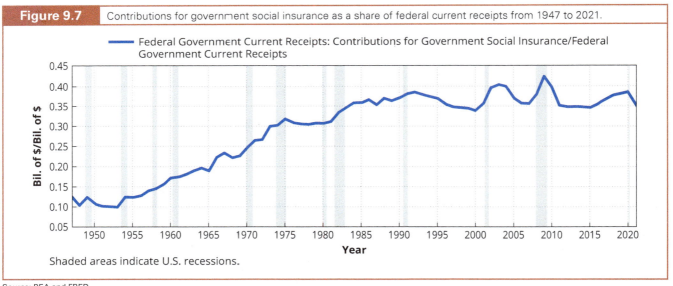

Shaded areas indicate U.S. recessions.

Source: BEA and FRED.

---

[6]This article is a good starting place for understanding the accounting procedures for government revenue and expenditure: https://www.bea.gov/resources/methodologies/primer-government-accounts.
[7]Figures are from BEA, Table 3.8.
[8]Not that one should think of patronizing a liquor store as fulfilling a patriotic duty.

Chapter 9 Government Spending and the Macroeconomy **221**

The sum of current tax receipts, contributions for government social insurance, income receipt on assets, current transfer receipts, and current surplus of government enterprises equals **current receipts**. Capital transfers include taxes collected on estates and gifts and the sales or purchases of assets. **Total receipts** are the sum of current receipts and capital transfer receipts.

It turns out that the difference between receipts and expenditures has been negative for more than 20 years. We return to the issue of government debt in the last section of this chapter.

Current receipts

The sum of current tax receipts, contributions for government social insurance, income receipt on assets, current transfer receipts, and current surplus of government enterprises.

Total receipts

The sum of current receipts and capital transfer receipts.

✓ Knowledge Check 9-1

Complete the table by finding out the values for contributions for government social insurance and interest payments.

Current receipts	Billions of dollars	Current expenditures	Billions of dollars
Current tax receipts	$4,061	Government consumption	$3,725
Contributions for government social insurance	?	Transfers	$3,162
Income receipts on assets	$214	Interest payments	?
Current transfer receipts	$190	Subsidies	$104
Current surplus of government enterprises	−$3		
Total	$6,327		$8,115

———————— Answers are at the end of the chapter.

9-2 Taxation in the Consumption–Savings Model

In Chapter 6, you learned how macroeconomists think about consumption and savings decisions. In particular, we assume that individuals are forward-looking lifetime utility maximizers. Taxes, of course, make up a significant part of the average American's budget, and you might (correctly) suspect that taxes influence an individual's consumption and savings decision. One of the lessons learned in Chapter 6 was that consumption today depends on lifetime income, not just current income. Does that logic carry through to taxes as well? That is, does an individual's consumption and saving plan depend not just on current taxes, but the taxes one expects to pay over a lifetime? This question has substantive implications for fiscal policy, as tax rates and tax credits frequently change over time.

9-2a Incorporating Taxes in the Lifetime Budget Constraint

We assume current and future taxes are unavoidable and do not depend on an individual's behavior. These are called **lump-sum taxes**. This, obviously, is a simplification. In the real world, the level of income taxes you pay depends on your income, which in turn depends on how many hours you work. This is also true for the payroll taxes that finance Social Security and Medicare. Taxes on interest income depend on the interest rate and how much you save. Despite all of this, lump-sum taxes are a useful simplification. In the context of income taxes, it may not even do much harm to reality, as labor supply responses to taxes are fairly small. Given the complexity of the macroeconomy, lump-sum taxes are not only useful but sometimes necessary to make progress in solving a macroeconomic model.

Lump-sum tax

A type of tax that is unavoidable and the size of which does not vary with individual behavior.

Let current-period taxes be denoted by T_t. Disposable income in the current period is the difference between total income, Y_t, and taxes. Just as in Chapter 6, we assume that individuals split income between consumption, C_t, and saving, S_t. It follows that the period t budget constraint is

$$C_t + S_t = Y_t - T_t. \tag{1}$$

Assuming a real interest rate of r_t, consumption in period $t + 1$ equals future disposable income, $Y_{t+1} - T_{t+1}$, plus $(1 + r_t)S_t$, or period t savings, S_t, plus the interest income $r_t S_t$. Mathematically, the period $t + 1$ budget constraint is given by

$$C_{t+1} = Y_{t+1} - T_{t+1} + (1 + r_t)S_t. \tag{2}$$

Remember, it is possible for S_t to be negative, which would mean that the individual borrows in the first period rather than saves. We can combine Equations (1) and (2) to get a lifetime budget constraint. Start by solving for S_t in Equation (2):

$$(1 + r_t)S_t = C_{t+1} - Y_{t+1} + T_{t+1}$$

$$\Leftrightarrow S_t = \frac{C_{t+1} - Y_{t+1} + T_{t+1}}{1 + r_t}.$$

Substitute this expression for savings into Equation (1):

$$C_t + S_t = Y_t - T_t$$

$$\Leftrightarrow C_t + \frac{C_{t+1} - Y_{t+1} + T_{t+1}}{1 + r_t} = Y_t - T_t$$

$$\Leftrightarrow C_t + \frac{C_{t+1}}{1 + r_t} = Y_t + \frac{Y_{t+1}}{1 + r_t} - \left(T_t + \frac{T_{t+1}}{1 + r_t} \right). \tag{3}$$

Equation (3) is the intertemporal budget constraint. It says that the present discounted value of consumption, $C_t + \dfrac{C_{t+1}}{1 + r_t}$, equals the present discounted value of income, $Y_t + \dfrac{Y_{t+1}}{1 + r_t}$, minus the present discounted value of taxes, $T_t + \dfrac{T_{t+1}}{1 + r_t}$. Or, in other words, the present discounted value of lifetime consumption equals the present discounted value of lifetime disposable income. Recall from Chapter 6 that the present discounted value takes values of future consumption, income, and taxes, and expresses them in period t prices. Deferring one unit of consumption in period t means that income goes up by $1 + r_t$ units in $t + 1$. Thus, the price of one additional unit of consumption today is $1 + r_t$. But $1 + r_t$ is a relative price—the price of period t consumption in terms of $t + 1$ consumption. It follows that the price of $t + 1$ consumption is $\dfrac{1}{1 + r_t}$ units of period t consumption. Dividing the future values of consumption, income, and taxes by $1 + r_t$ denominates all the variables in the same price.

Figure 9.8 plots the lifetime budget constraint. If the individual consumes all their lifetime resources in period t, then C_t equals $Y_t + \dfrac{Y_{t+1}}{1 + r_t} - T_t - \dfrac{T_{t+1}}{1 + r_t}$. Alternatively, if the individual defers all consumption until period $t + 1$, then C_{t+1} equals $(1 + r_t)(Y_t - T_t) + Y_{t+1} - T_{t+1}$. All the feasible pairs of C_t and C_{t+1} are connected by the budget line. Since one additional unit of period t consumption costs $1 + r_t$ units of period $t + 1$ consumption, the slope of the budget line is $-(1 + r_t)$.

Now consider an increase in period t taxes from $T_{0,t}$ to $T_{1,t}$. As Figure 9.9 shows, this shifts the budget line to the left. Since the relative price of consumption hasn't changed, the new budget line is parallel to the initial budget line. The individual has fewer lifetime resources with the new budget constraint compared to the old one. Since the relative price of consumption is the same, the change in policy does not have a substitution effect. This insight will be critical in our analysis of the optimal mix of consumption and savings.

| Figure 9.8 | Consumption in period t is plotted on the horizontal axis, and consumption in period $t+1$ is plotted on the vertical axis. The slope of the budget line is $-(1 + r_t)$. |

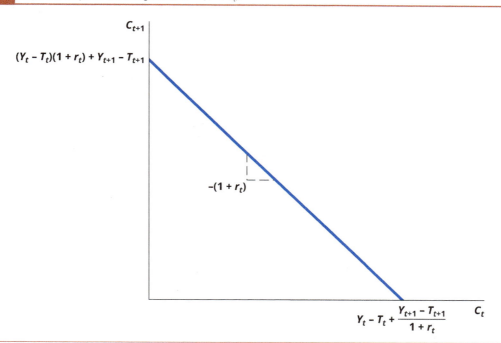

Question: Label the point on the budget constraint where savings equals zero.

| Figure 9.9 | An increase in period t taxes from $T_{0,t}$ to $T_{1,t}$ shifts the budget constraint to the left. The new budget line is parallel to the original budget line. |

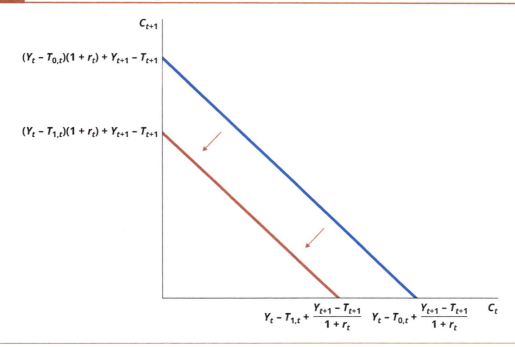

Question: Graphically depict a decrease in T_t.

Knowledge Check 9-2

Compute the present discounted value of lifetime disposable income given the following values of exogenous variables. How does an increase in the real interest rate affect your preferences to pay taxes in the present versus the future?

r_t	Y_t	T_t	Y_{t+1}	T_{t+1}	PDV income
0.1	10	2	8	0	
0.1	10	0	8	2.2	
0.2	10	2	8	0	
0.2	10	0	8	2.2	

Answers are at the end of the chapter.

9-2b Analyzing the Effects of Tax Changes on Consumption and Savings

Following the assumptions in Chapter 6, individuals derive utility over current and future consumption. The lifetime utility function is

$$U = u(C_t) + \beta u(C_{t+1}), \tag{4}$$

where $0 < \beta < 1$ is the subjective discount rate. Indifference curves are downward sloping and bowed in toward the origin. Recall that the marginal rate of substitution (MRS) is the rate at which the individual is willing to trade C_{t+1} for one more unit of C_t along an indifference curve.

Figure 9.10 graphically depicts some candidate points. Any consumption bundle that lies inside the budget constraint, such as A, is suboptimal, as the individual can afford more current and future consumption. At point B, the MRS exceeds the slope of the budget constraint, meaning that the consumer would be willing to give up more than $1 + r_t$ units of

Figure 9.10 This plot shows a budget line and indifference curve with four points of emphasis: A, B, C, and D. Point A is not optimal because the consumer could purchase more present and future consumption. The MRS exceeds $1 + r_t$ at point B and $1 + r_t$ exceeds the MRS at point C, making neither point optimal. The optimal point, D, is where the MRS equals $1 + r_t$.

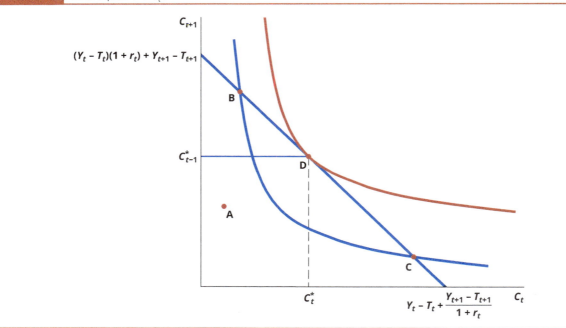

C_{t+1} for one more unit of C_t. So it would be optimal to consume more in the current period and less in the future. By similar logic, the slope of the budget constraint exceeds the MRS at point C, meaning that it would be optimal to consume more in the future and less in the present. The individual is satisfied with the consumption bundle only at point D, where the slope of the budget line equals the slope of the indifference curve. Given the present discounted value of lifetime resources, the consumer is optimizing with the consumption bundle (C_t^*, C_{t+1}^*).

Suppose that current-period taxes increase from $T_{0,t}$ to $T_{1,t}$. As Figure 9.9 showed, an increase in current-period taxes shifts the budget line in toward the origin. The present discounted value of lifetime income goes down with higher taxes, but the relative price of consumption isn't affected. Since C_t and C_{t+1} are normal goods, the income effect predicts that they will decrease when lifetime income falls. Accordingly, as Figure 9.11 shows, consumption falls in both periods.

Intuitively, the utility-maximizing individual likes to smooth consumption. Rather than take the entirety of the income hit from the tax hike today, the individual reduces consumption by some today and some in the future.

Suppose instead that future taxes, T_{t+1}, increase. This is shown in Figure 9.12. The increase in future taxes reduces lifetime income and shifts the budget constraint to the left. Again, since the relative price of consumption hasn't changed, meaning there is no substitution effect at work, the new budget line is parallel to the initial one. Current-period and future-period consumption both decrease because of the negative income effect. Another way of thinking about the comparative static is as follows. Being forward-looking, the individual perceives the increase in future taxes as a reduction in lifetime income. Since the individual likes to smooth consumption, it is optimal to reduce consumption by some today and some tomorrow.

Although these comparative statics may seem like somewhat mechanical extensions of what you learned in Chapter 6, they have deep implications for fiscal policy. First, not only do taxes today affect consumption and savings, but future taxes do, too. If people expect

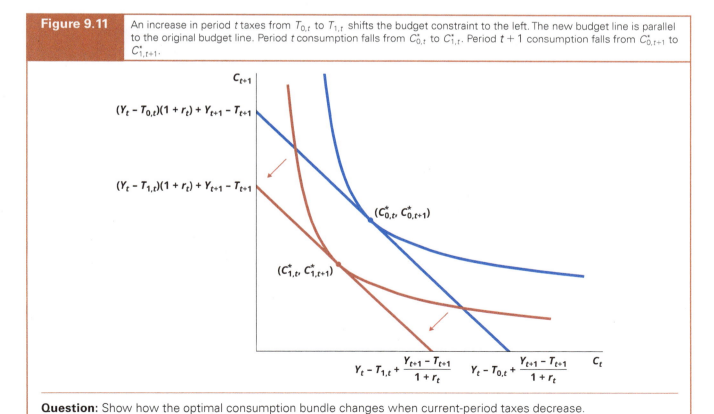

Figure 9.11 An increase in period t taxes from $T_{0,t}$ to $T_{1,t}$ shifts the budget constraint to the left. The new budget line is parallel to the original budget line. Period t consumption falls from $C_{0,t}^*$ to $C_{1,t}^*$. Period $t+1$ consumption falls from $C_{0,t+1}^*$ to $C_{1,t+1}^*$.

Question: Show how the optimal consumption bundle changes when current-period taxes decrease.

Figure 9.12

An increase in period $t+1$ taxes from $T_{0,t+1}$ to $T_{1,t+1}$ shifts the budget constraint to the left. The new budget line is parallel to the original budget line. Period t consumption falls from $C^*_{0,t}$ to $C^*_{1,t}$. Period $t+1$ consumption falls from $C^*_{0,t+1}$ to $C^*_{1,t+1}$.

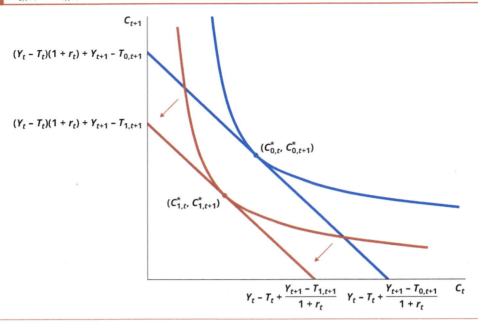

Question: Show how the optimal consumption bundle changes when current-period taxes decrease.

taxes to be high in the future, they will reduce their consumption today. This imposes a daunting challenge for fiscal policymakers in Congress. In addition to thinking about taxes today, they have to consider citizens' expectations over future taxes.

We can uncover another insight by recalling that the PDV of taxes is

$$T_t + \frac{T_{t+1}}{1 + r_t}.$$

A temporary tax change, that is a change in T_t holding T_{t+1} fixed, will affect consumption less than a permanent tax change. To clarify, consider the example where the individual's marginal rate of substitution is $\frac{C_{t+1}}{\beta C_t}$. Equating the marginal rate of substitution with the slope of the budget constraint gives

$$\frac{C_{t+1}}{\beta C_t} = 1 + r_t$$

$$\Leftrightarrow C_{t+1} = \beta(1 + r_t)C_t.$$

Substituting this last expression into the lifetime budget constraint allows us to solve for the period t consumption function:

$$C_t + \frac{C_{t+1}}{1 + r_t} = Y_t + \frac{Y_{t+1}}{1 + r_t} - T_t - \frac{T_{t+1}}{1 + r_t}$$

$$\Leftrightarrow C_t + \frac{\beta(1 + r_t)C_t}{1 + r_t} = Y_t + \frac{Y_{t+1}}{1 + r_t} - T_t - \frac{T_{t+1}}{1 + r_t}$$

$$\Leftrightarrow C_t(1 + \beta) = Y_t + \frac{Y_{t+1}}{1 + r_t} - T_t - \frac{T_{t+1}}{1 + r_t}$$

$$\Leftrightarrow C^*_t = \frac{1}{1 + \beta}\left[Y_t + \frac{Y_{t+1}}{1 + r_t} - T_t - \frac{T_{t+1}}{1 + r_t}\right].$$

Consumption today is a constant fraction, $\frac{1}{1+\beta}$, of lifetime income. If Congress enacts a temporary tax cut by reducing T_t by 1, then consumption increases by $\frac{1}{1+\beta} < 1$. That is, the marginal propensity to consume (MPC) out of the tax cut is less than one. Forward-looking individuals consume some of the tax cut and save the rest. Alternatively, if Congress cut taxes in all periods by 1, then the PDV of lifetime disposable income would increase by $\frac{1}{1+\beta}\left(1 + \frac{1}{1+r_t}\right) > \frac{1}{1+\beta}$. The implication is that permanent changes in taxes change consumption more than temporary tax cuts. This has significant implications for fiscal policy. It's not uncommon in recessions, for instance, for the government to cut taxes or issue tax rebates. Most recently, in responding to the Covid-19 pandemic, Congress passed the CARES Act in March 2020, which provided most adults with a $1,200 tax credit. The credit was widely understood to be a one-time measure, and we would expect consumption to act as such. Conversely, the reductions in income tax rates associated with the 2017 Tax Cuts and Jobs Act are in effect until 2025 and could possibly be made permanent. Our theory predicts that the MPC out of the Tax Cuts and Jobs Act is bigger than the MPC out of the CARES Act. While research on the CARES Act is still in its early stages, economists have researched the effects of prior tax rebates, such as the one during the 2008 financial crisis. This is discussed in the next application.

> ### ✓ Knowledge Check 9-3
>
> Suppose an individual faces the lifetime budget constraint
>
> $$C_t + \frac{C_{t+1}}{1+r_t} = Y_t + \frac{Y_{t+1}}{1+r_t} - T_t - \frac{T_{t+1}}{1+r_t}.$$
>
> Suppose that individual's marginal rate of substitution is $\frac{\sqrt{C_{t+1}}}{\beta\sqrt{C_t}} = 1 + r_t$. Solve for the period t consumption function. Also, assuming $\beta = \frac{1}{1+r_t} = 0.9$, compute the marginal propensity to consume out of a temporary tax cut, $\Delta T_t = -1, \Delta T_{t+1} = 0$, and a permanent tax cut, $\Delta T_t = \Delta T_{t+1} = -1$.[9]
>
> ——————————————————————————————— Answers are at the end of the chapter.

9-3 The Method of Government Financing and Macroeconomic Outcomes

Thus far, we have discussed how changes in taxes affect consumption. But does it matter how those taxes are spent? Moreover, how is consumption affected if the government finances its spending by issuing debt rather than increasing taxes? To begin to answer these questions, we must start with the government's budget constraint.

9-3a The Government's Intertemporal Budget Constraint

Continuing with the two-period model, assume that the government spends some resources in period t, G_t, and some resources in period $t + 1$, G_{t+1}. The government finances its expenditure in the first period through taxes, T_t, and borrowing, B_t. The government's budget constraint in period t is

$$G_t = T_t + B_t. \tag{5}$$

If spending exceeds taxes, $G_t - T_t > 0$, then the government runs a deficit, $B_t > 0$. If taxes exceed spending, $G_t - T_t < 0$, then the government runs a surplus, $B_t < 0$. In period $t + 1$,

---

[9] Recall that Δ, or "delta," is the mathematical operator for "change in."

the government must raise enough taxes to finance government spending and pay back its debt plus interest. Mathematically, the government's budget constraint in $t + 1$ is given by

$$G_{t+1} + (1 + r_t)B_t = T_{t+1}. \tag{6}$$

Of course, if the government runs a surplus in the first period, then they can use the surplus plus the interest income to finance its expenditures. We can combine Equations (5) and (6) to derive the government's intertemporal budget constraint. Start by solving for B_t in Equation (6):

$$(1 + r_t)B_t = T_{t+1} - G_{t+1}$$

$$\Leftrightarrow B_t = \frac{T_{t+1} - G_{t+1}}{1 + r_t}.$$

This last equation says that the government debt today equals the present discounted value of future surpluses. This is a theme we will return to in a few pages. Substitute this expression for government debt into Equation (5):

$$G_t = T_t + B_t$$

$$\Leftrightarrow G_t = T_t + \frac{T_{t+1} - G_{t+1}}{1 + r_t}$$

$$\Leftrightarrow G_t + \frac{G_{t+1}}{1 + r_t} = T_t + \frac{T_{t+1}}{1 + r_t}. \tag{7}$$

Equation (7) says the present discounted value of government spending must equal the present discounted value of taxes. Intuitively, the government may be able to run a deficit temporarily, but eventually any debt must be repaid with higher taxes. In other words, harkening back to your principles of microeconomics class, there is no free lunch.

As long as the government is not allowed to default, its lifetime budget constraint must hold.[10] This is independent of any particular economic theory and holds for any time horizon. In other words, the conclusion that the present discounted value of spending equals the present discounted value of taxes is widely applicable. However, even if Equation (7) must hold, does the timing of taxes matter?

9-3b The Ricardian Equivalence Theorem

Imagine that the government needs to spend $10 billion to repair the interstate highway system. Option A is to raise taxes by $10 billion this year. Option B is to issue $10 billion in bonds this year and repay the bonds (with interest) in the future. Taxpayers understand that deficit financing today means higher taxes in the future. Does the timing of taxation matter?

Table 9.3 evaluates the options in more detail. Under option A, current-period taxes increase by $10 billion. Because the government runs a balanced budget, there is no debt to pay off in period $t + 1$. Lifetime disposable income goes down by $10 billion.

Table 9.3	Comparing Methods of Government Financing	
	Option A	**Option B**
Period t		
ΔT_t	$10 billion	$0
ΔS_t	$0	$10 billion
Period $t + 1$		
ΔT_{t+1}	$0	$(1 + r_t)$10 billion
$(1 + r_t)\Delta S_t$	$0	$-(1 + r_t)$10 billion
Change in lifetime disposable income	$-$10 billion	$-$10 billion

---

[10]Ruling out default by assumption may be less appropriate for middle- and low-income countries, where defaults sometimes occur.

Chapter 9 Government Spending and the Macroeconomy   **229**

Under option B, current-period taxes stay constant, but the government issues $10 billion of bonds to the public. Household savings increase by $10 billion. In period $t + 1$, the government pays back what it borrowed plus interest. But, to pay back its debt, the government must raise taxes by the principal of the bonds plus interest. What the household receives as a return from holding the bonds in period $t + 1$, it pays back with higher taxes. So if the interest rate is 10 percent, the household receives $11 billion from holding government bonds but pays $11 billion in taxes. In summary, lifetime disposable income goes down by $10 billion.

The numerical example above suggests that the method of government financing is irrelevant from the perspective of the public. Recall from Equation (7) that the government's lifetime budget constraint is

$$G_t + \frac{G_{t+1}}{1 + r_t} = T_t + \frac{T_{t+1}}{1 + r_t}. \tag{7}$$

From Equation (3), the lifetime budget constraint for an individual is

$$C_t + \frac{C_{t+1}}{1 + r_t} = Y_t + \frac{Y_{t+1}}{1 + r_t} - T_t - \frac{T_{t+1}}{1 + r_t}. \tag{3}$$

If we assume that this lifetime budget constraint holds for the entire population, then we can combine Equations (3) and (7) to get

$$C_t + \frac{C_{t+1}}{1 + r_t} = Y_t + \frac{Y_{t+1}}{1 + r_t} - G_t - \frac{G_{t+1}}{1 + r_t}. \tag{8}$$

Equation (8) says that the present discounted value of lifetime consumption equals the present discounted value of income less the present discounted value of government spending. In other words, the timing of taxes has no impact on what is affordable. An increase in G_t has the same impact regardless of how it is financed.

This insight, first discovered by 18th-century economist David Ricardo and later formalized by Robert Barro in the 1970s, is called the **Ricardian equivalence theorem**. In brief, the theorem says that conditional on a time path of government expenditure, the timing of taxes is irrelevant. In the example in Table 9.3, it is the fact that the government spends $10 billion on infrastructure that changes disposable lifetime income, not the way that the infrastructure spending is financed.

Before moving on, it's important to make three distinctions between: 1) the valid implications coming from the Ricardian equivalence theorem, 2) the common confusions about the theorem, and 3) the assumptions necessary for the theorem to hold.

Start with the valid implications. First, it bears repeating, given particular values of current and future government spending, i.e., G_t and G_{t+1}, the timing of taxation is irrelevant. That is, macroeconomic variables, such as consumption, investment, GDP, inflation, interest rates, etc., are unaffected by the way the government finances its spending. Second, a tax cut today without a change in government spending, either now or in the future, will not affect macroeconomic variables. The reason is that individuals will perceive that a tax cut without an accompanying cut in spending will necessitate an increase in future taxes, leaving disposable lifetime resources unchanged. In Section 9.2, you learned that the desire to smooth consumption implies that the MPC from a current-period tax cut is less than one. Ricardian Equivalence says that without reductions in government spending, the MPC from a tax cut is zero. Third, without loss of generality, the Ricardian equivalence theorem allows us to assume that the government balances its budget in every period. Since it's the spending and not the timing of the financing that matters, we can assume that $T_t = G_t$ and $T_{t+1} = G_{t+1}$.

The Ricardian equivalence theorem does not say that government spending is irrelevant. You saw in Chapter 6 that a change in government spending affects savings, investment, and the real interest rate. Government spending, regardless of how it is financed, is very relevant for determining macroeconomic variables.

Finally, Ricardian equivalence relies on several critical assumptions, some of which we have yet to make explicit. First, the theorem assumes that taxes are lump sum. Recall that a lump-sum tax does not depend on individual behavior and there is nothing people can

Ricardian equivalence theorem
A theorem that says conditional on a time path of government spending, the method of financing is irrelevant.

230   **Part 2** Classical Theory

Distortionary tax

A tax that distorts the incentive to engage in an activity.

do to avoid it. Most taxes in the real world depend on the behavior of workers, consumers, and businesses and can at least partially be avoided. Taxes on labor earnings, for instance, depend on how many hours a person works and can be avoided entirely by exiting the labor force. A tax that distorts the incentive to engage in an activity is called a **distortionary tax**. If taxes are distortionary, then the theorem fails to hold. Second, it assumes that people are forward-looking. They correctly anticipate that higher levels of government borrowing today mean higher taxes tomorrow and adjust their consumption plans accordingly. Third, it assumes that the government and citizens in the economy borrow and save at the same interest rate. As an empirical matter, we know this to be false. The borrowing rate offered on a 1-year U.S. Treasury bill is much lower than a one-year credit card loan. The final assumption is that everyone in the economy is the same age and lives as long as the government. It was this assumption that allowed us to combine the lifetime budget constraint of the government with the household's lifetime budget constraint. This is self-evidently false. Indeed, one of the reasons people worry about government debt is that future generations will bear the consequences of the current generation's fiscal profligacy.

Why spend time discussing a theorem with at least four obviously wrong assumptions? Quite honestly, it's an unavoidable implication of the most basic intertemporal macroeconomic model. Avoiding the Ricardian conclusion requires complicating the model along some dimension. We could, for instance, add a financial market imperfection whereby the government finds it easier to borrow than households. Given that governments borrow at much lower interest rates than households and businesses, such an assumption is not unwarranted. Alternatively, we could build a model in which the government outlives its citizens. Every year, new citizens are born, and some die. If the government is going to outlive you, then, from your perspective, it may not matter if the government balances its intertemporal budget constraint or chooses to do so via increasing taxes in the distant future. Finally, we could assume that the government finances itself through distortionary taxes on labor and capital, as opposed to lump-sum taxes, which is consistent with the real world. These are all valid additions, but they force economists to be very careful in their modeling assumptions. Some of these additions are explored in the end-of-chapter problems.

Practically speaking, the Ricardian equivalence theorem gives us some theoretical justification for assuming the government balances its budget in every period as in Chapters 6 and 7 and, indeed, throughout most of the book. However, as we explore in the next section, the case of deficit-financed government expenditure when Ricardian equivalence does not apply has interesting implications.

9-3c Deficit Financing in the Savings–Investment Model

It is instructive to return to the savings–investment model of Chapter 6. The GDP expenditure equation in the closed economy is[11]

$$Y_t = C_t + I_t + G_t. \tag{9}$$

The expenditure equation can be rearranged to show that savings equals investment.

$$Y_t = C_t + I_t + G_t$$

$$\Leftrightarrow I_t = Y_t - C_t - G_t$$

$$\Leftrightarrow I_t = (Y_t - C_t - T_t) + (T_t - G_t). \tag{10}$$

The right-hand side is the sum of private savings, $Y_t - C_t - T_t$, and public savings, $T_t - G_t$. The investment demand equation depends on future productivity, A_{t+1}, and the cost of borrowing, $r_t + f_t$, where $f_t > 0$ is the risk premium. Mathematically, the investment demand equation is given by

$$I_t = I(r_t + f_t, A_{t+1}). \tag{11}$$

In Chapter 6, we assumed that the government ran a balanced budget, so that $G_t = T_t$. If Ricardian equivalence applies, then this assumption is completely innocuous. That is, the

---

[11]The results aren't qualitatively affected by the addition of foreign trade.

equilibrium real interest rate and levels of investment and saving do not change with the way government spending is financed. The consumption function is given by

$$C_t = C(Y_t - T_t, Y_{t+1} - T_{t+1}, r_t)$$
$$= C(Y_t - G_t, Y_{t+1} - G_{t+1}, r_t), \quad (12)$$

where the second line imposes Ricardian equivalence. From here, it is straightforward to analyze a change in government spending. An increase in current-period government spending from $G_{0,t}$ to $G_{1,t}$ shifts the savings supply curve to the left, as shown in Figure 9.13. The equilibrium interest rate rises as the equilibrium level of investment falls. Again, as long as Ricardian equivalence applies, the changes in equilibrium variables are the same regardless of how the government spending is financed.

Now, let's remove the Ricardian equivalence assumption. The easiest way to do this is to assume that consumption only depends on current disposable income:

$$C_t = C(Y_t - T_t). \quad (13)$$

At the individual level, someone might have this consumption function if they cannot access savings and credit institutions. Without access to these financial institutions, individuals are unable to smooth their consumption. We call these *non-Ricardian consumers*. In an economy with less-developed financial markets, more people will have the consumption function in Equation (13), and we call this a *non-Ricardian economy*. In this case, the savings supply curve is vertical. An increase in government spending financed through a deficit leaves T_t, and therefore consumption, unchanged. Figure 9.14 shows that the increase in government spending decreases the supply of savings in the economy, increases the equilibrium real interest rate, and decreases the equilibrium level of investment.

On the face of it, the results in the Ricardian and non-Ricardian economy look similar—interest rates increase and investment falls. Can we say more than this? Yes. In the non-Ricardian economy, consumption doesn't change. Because the resource constraint, $Y_t = C_t + I_t + G_t$, must hold, investment must drop by more in the non-Ricardian economy than in the Ricardian economy. Because the investment demand curve is the same

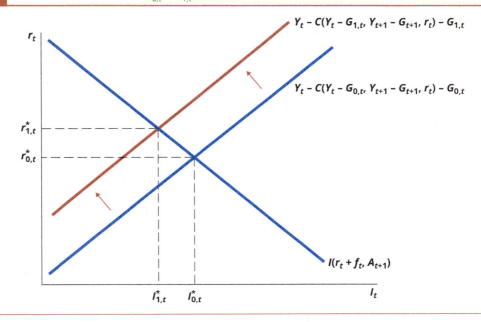

Figure 9.13 This graph plots the effect of an increase in current-period government expenditures. An increase in G_t from $G_{0,t}$ to $G_{1,t}$ shifts the supply of savings to the left. In equilibrium, the real interest rate increases from $r^*_{0,t}$ to $r^*_{1,t}$ and investment decreases from $I^*_{0,t}$ to $I^*_{1,t}$.

Question: Show the effects of a decrease in current-period government expenditures.

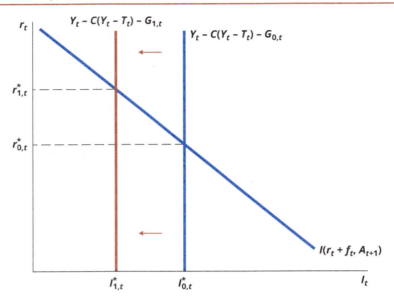

Figure 9.14 This graph plots the effect of an increase in current-period government expenditures. An increase in G_t from $G_{0,t}$ to $G_{1,t}$ shifts the supply of savings to the left. In equilibrium, the real interest rate increases from $r^*_{0,t}$ to $r^*_{1,t}$ and investment decreases from $I^*_{0,t}$ to $I^*_{1,t}$. Because consumption doesn't change, the reduction in investment equals the increase in government spending.

Question: Show the effects of a decrease in current-period government expenditures.

regardless of how government spending is financed, the equilibrium real interest rate must rise by more in the non-Ricardian economy.

How do we make sense of these results? Individuals who follow the more sophisticated consumption function in Equation (12) anticipate that debt-financed government expenditure will be met with higher future taxes. In anticipation of this, they save more today and that limits the extent to which aggregate savings (public plus private) go down. Individuals who follow the simple consumption function in Equation (13) don't change their consumption plans at all as long as disposable income stays fixed. Aggregate savings fall one-for-one with public savings. Since savings go down by more with non-Ricardian consumers, the real interest rate must rise by more.

There's an old adage in macroeconomics—that you perhaps learned in your principles class—that says government deficits crowd out private investment. In light of the preceding discussion, this needs to be qualified. *All* increases in current-period government spending raise interest rates and decrease investment. If Ricardian equivalence holds, then the actual changes in equilibrium interest rates and investment aren't affected by the way the government spending is financed. If Ricardian equivalence does not hold, then deficit financing raises the real interest rate and lowers investment by more than running a balanced budget. In this sense, it is true that deficit financing crowds out more investment.

✓ Knowledge Check 9-4

Assuming individuals have the simple consumption function, $C_t = C(Y_t - T_t)$, plot the effects of an increase in the risk premium, f_t. How do your results compare to the case when individuals have the more sophisticated consumption function, $C_t = C(Y_t - G_t, Y_{t+1} - G_{t+1}, r_t)$?

Answers are at the end of the chapter.

Chapter 9 Government Spending and the Macroeconomy

Application 9.1

Consumption Responses from Stimulus Checks

During recessions, governments commonly increase transfer payments, intending to ease the financial hardships faced by households and to stimulate the aggregate economy. One example of this is the Economic Stimulus Act of 2008. With the economy already in a recession, Congress passed, and President George W. Bush signed, an economic stimulus plan that sent between $300 and $600 to most individuals and between $600 and $1,200 to most married couples. The Act also sent an additional $300 per child to families with children.

The consumption–savings model combined with the Ricardian equivalence result makes strong predictions about the effects of government transfer payments, such as the 2008 stimulus. Ricardian equivalence predicts that households internalize the government budget constraint, thereby recognizing that a tax rebate today (without a corresponding decrease in spending) implies a tax increase in the future. Thus, if households are Ricardian, the marginal propensity to consume out of the tax rebate would be zero.

Even if households don't internalize the government budget constraint, the consumption–savings model makes predictions about how individuals react to a one-time financial windfall. In particular, the model predicts that individuals spend some fraction of a one-time transfer today and save the rest of it for the future. While the simple two-period model in Section 9.2 gets across that main point, quantitative predictions require a more realistic time horizon.

Imagine an individual lives for $T > 1$ periods. In each period, the individual gets some disposable income, $Y_{t+j} - T_{t+j}$, for $0 < j < T$. Assuming a constant real interest rate, r, the present discounted value of lifetime income is

$$Y_t - T_t + \frac{Y_{t+1} - T_{t+1}}{1+r} + \frac{Y_{t+2} - T_{t+2}}{(1+r)^2}$$
$$+ \cdots + \frac{Y_{t+T-1} - T_{t+T-1}}{(1+r)^{T-1}} + \frac{Y_{t+T} - T_{t+T}}{(1+r)^T}.$$

Income received j periods in the future is converted to period t prices by discounting by $(1+r)^j$. If $\beta = \frac{1}{1+r}$, meaning that the individual discounts future utility at the same rate at which the market discounts future income, then it can be shown that consumption in every period is equal to a constant fraction of the present discounted value (PDV) of lifetime income. Mathematically, consumption in period $t + j$ is

$$C_{t+j} = \overline{C} = \frac{1}{\sum_{j=0}^{T} \beta^j} (PDV \text{ lifetime income}).$$

You can verify this is true in the two-period model of Section 9.1, where $T = 1$. The marginal propensity of consumption from a tax rebate in period t is $\frac{1}{\sum_{j=0}^{T} \beta^j}$. As T gets bigger, the MPC declines. Also, note that the MPC doesn't depend on income. The model predicts that the MPC from a dollar of tax cuts is the same for a low-income and a high-income person.

To make this concrete, Table 9.4 compares the MPCs for different ages assuming that people expect to live to 80 and $\beta = 0.98$. Given the life expectancy is 80 years, T is the difference between 80 and the actual age. For a 40-year-old, $T = 80 - 40 = 40$. We can compute the MPC using the formula for exponential sum, which is $\sum_{j=0}^{T} \beta^j = \frac{1 - \beta^{T+1}}{1 - \beta}$. For $T = 40$, MPC $= \frac{1}{\sum_{j=0}^{T} \beta^j} = \frac{1 - \beta}{1 - \beta^{T+1}} = \frac{1 - 0.98}{1 - 0.98^{41}} = 3.6\%$. The following table shows that as predicted, the MPC is decreasing with T (or increasing with age).

Economists have used evidence from surveys to infer the consumption responses from tax refunds. The Michigan Survey of Consumers is a monthly survey that asks respondents about their expectations of the economy and their family's economic prospects. Several waves of the 2008 survey asked respondents how they planned on using their tax rebate.[12] About 20 percent of people said they planned to "mostly spend" their tax rebate, another 32 percent said they would "mostly save," and the remaining 48 percent said they would "pay off debt." Using these responses, the authors inferred that the average MPC was about 30 percent.

A few things about this result stand out. First, since the MPC is above 0, the Ricardian equivalence hypothesis can be easily rejected. Second, the result implies mixed success for the lifecycle consumption model. On the one hand, the personal savings rate in the United States is

Table 9.4	MPCs by Age	
Age	**T**	**MPC**
40	40	3.6%
50	30	4.3%
60	20	5.8%
70	10	10.0%

[12]Shapiro, Matthew D. and Joel Slemrod. 2009. "Did the 2008 Tax Rebates Stimulate Spending?" *American Economic Review, 99*(2): 374–379.

■ Continues

234 **Part 2** Classical Theory

Application 9.1 (Continued)

typically less than 10 percent, meaning people consume about 90 percent of their incomes. The fact that the average MPC of the rebate was 30 percent is evidence that people understood the one-time nature of the policy and smoothed their consumption accordingly. On the other hand, an MPC of 30 percent is much larger than the prediction of the lifecycle model for most ages. Using the analysis in Table 9.4, the MPC is only 30 percent or higher for those between the ages of 78 and 80. Finally, the MPCs increased with age, which is also consistent with the theory. Twice as many people 65 and older said they would "mostly spend" their tax rebate compared to the group in their thirties.

One omission from the standard lifecycle model that might be important is the absence of borrowing constraints. The model predicts that individuals can consume future income in the current period by borrowing at the real interest rate. In the real world, this isn't so easy. You typically need collateral for a loan or you need to use a credit card, which tends to come with high interest rates and strict credit limits. When someone faces a binding borrowing constraint and receives an increase in current-period income, they are likely to consume more of it then the standard model would predict. Intuitively, if someone

is expecting their income to grow over time, then their level of consumption with a borrowing constraint is lower than what it would be without a borrowing constraint. Consuming the entirety of an increase in current-period income gets their level of consumption with the borrowing constraint closer to the unconstrained optimum.

Assuming low-income households are more likely to be borrowing constrained, we would expect that they would have higher MPCs from the tax rebate. The evidence is mixed. Results from the aforementioned Michigan Survey of Consumers showed that the lowest income group actually planned to spend less of the rebate than any other income group. On the other hand, other economic research using different consumer surveys have shown that low-income groups spent more of their rebate.[13]

Here is what we can take away from the research on the 2008 tax rebate. First, the Ricardian equivalence hypothesis is strongly rejected. Second, there is some qualitative support for the lifecycle consumption model, but the quantitative magnitudes of the empirical MPCs were much higher than those predicted by theory. In Chapters 11 and 12, we will reexamine the effects of government spending and tax cuts in recessions.

[13]Johnson, David S., Robert McClelland, Jonathan A. Parker, and Nicholas S. Souleles. 2013. "Consumer Spending and he Economic Stimulus Payments of 2008." *American Economic Review, 103(6):* 2530–2553.

9-4 The Sustainability of U.S. Government Debt

Figure 9.15 shows that the federal debt-to-GDP ratio has increased to over 120 percent of GDP. This is quite high by historical standards, but is the high level of debt a cause for concern? Answering this question requires that we do some accounting up front.

9-4a The Government's Budget Constraint over the Very Long Run

We can generalize the analysis of the government's budget constraint in Section 9.3 past the two-period context. In any one period, the government's budget constraint is

$$G_t + (1 + r_{t-1})B_{t-1} = B_t + T_t. \tag{14}$$

In words, this equation says that government spending, G_t, plus the principal and interest on the national debt, $(1 + r_{t-1})B_{t-1}$, equals the level of debt taken into the next year, B_t, plus taxes, T_t. An equivalent way of expressing Equation (14) is

$$B_t - B_{t-1} = r_{t-1}B_{t-1} + G_t - T_t. \tag{14'}$$

New borrowing, $B_t - B_{t-1}$, equals the interest cost of the debt, $r_{t-1}B_{t-1}$, plus the **primary deficit**, $G_t - T_t$. Of course, it's possible that $B_t < B_{t-1}$, implying that the government

Primary deficit

The difference between government expenditure, excluding payments to service the debt, and taxes.

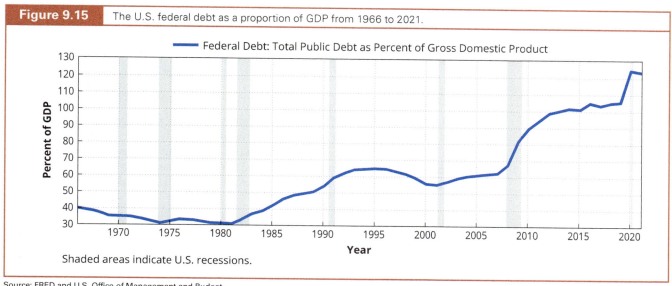

Figure 9.15 The U.S. federal debt as a proportion of GDP from 1966 to 2021.

Shaded areas indicate U.S. recessions.

Source: FRED and U.S. Office of Management and Budget.

decreases its debt. In Section 9.3, we imagined that the government effectively died after two periods. In that context, it makes sense to impose that the government not die in debt, which means $B_t = 0$. In the real world, there is no reason to expect the government to live for some known finite duration. Instead, economists usually think about the government living forever.

In beginning to conceptualize a government that lives forever, note that we can express Equation (14) in yet another way:

$$B_{t-1} = \frac{B_t + T_t - G_t}{1 + r}. \tag{14''}$$

To keep things as simple as possible, it is assumed that the real interest rate is a constant, r. We can write a version of Equation (14″) but for period $t + 1$:

$$B_t = \frac{B_{t+1} + T_{t+1} - G_{t+1}}{1 + r}. \tag{15}$$

Noting that B_t is common across periods, we can combine Equations (14″) and (15) to get

$$B_{t-1} = \frac{\frac{B_{t+1} + T_{t+1} - G_{t+1}}{1 + r} + T_t - G_t}{1 + r}$$

$$= \frac{B_{t+1} + T_{t+1} - G_{t+1}}{(1 + r)^2} + \frac{T_t - G_t}{1 + r}.$$

We can continue to iterate on these sequential budget constraints by going to periods $t + 2$, $t + 3$, and so forth all the way to period $t + T$, where T is an infinitely big number. If you crunch the numbers, you get[14]

$$B_{t-1} = \sum_{j=0}^{\infty} \frac{T_{t+j} - G_{t+j}}{(1 + r)^{j+1}}$$

$$= PDV \ (\textit{primary surpluses}). \tag{16}$$

---

[14]Technically, you need to impose that the PDV of the debt in the far-off future not explode. Economists call this a *transversality condition*.

That is, the level of debt today equals the present discounted value of all future primary surpluses. Intuitively, a government with some quantity of debt today must pay it back at some point in the future. Thus, in judging the ease at which a government might repay its debt, we have to forecast future revenues and expenditures.

9-4b Forecasting Government Revenue and Expenditure

The Congressional Budget Office (CBO) annually publishes a long-term budget analysis; its most recent one in 2021. In its long-term budget analysis, the CBO forecasts future government expenditure, government revenue, and the interest cost of servicing the debt. Equation (16) says that eventually the United States must start running a primary surplus. What are the prospects this will happen over the next several decades? The CBO predicts they are quite grim.

Figure 9.16 shows the CBO's forecast of primary surpluses/deficits, the total deficit, and net interest outlays as a fraction of GDP through 2052. The CBO projects that the government will run a primary deficit every year over the next three decades and that these deficits will get bigger over time, reaching 3.9 percent of GDP by 2052. As the federal debt grows as a fraction of GDP, the interest costs of servicing the debt also increase, reaching 7.2 percent of GDP by 2052.

What is behind the expected rise in deficits? The CBO actually projects that government revenue as a fraction of GDP will slightly increase from 18 percent in 2021 to 19 percent in 2022. But expenditure's share of GDP is expected to go up by six percentage points. A big reason for this is the rising cost of programs such as Social Security and Medicare. Figure 9.17 decomposes these changes. The aging population contributes to the rising expense of Social Security and Medicare. When a higher fraction of the population is retired and collecting benefits, expenditure on these programs goes up. Also, these retirees by definition don't work, so GDP goes down. Moreover, the costs of healthcare have been rising and this puts upward pressure on all government healthcare programs, not just Medicare.

Figure 9.16 This plot shows the historical values of the total deficit, primary deficit, and net interest outlays as a fraction of GDP from 1942 until 2021, followed by a forecast of each of these variables until 2052.

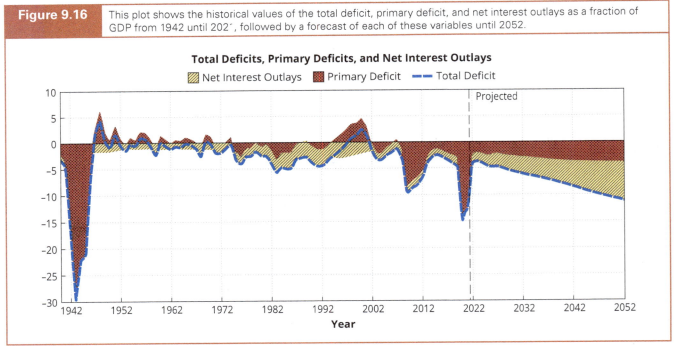

Source: CBO report: "The 2022 Long-Term Budget Outlook," Figure 1.1.

> **Figure 9.17** The costs of government contributions to healthcare programs and Social Security as a fraction of GDP in 2022 and 2052.

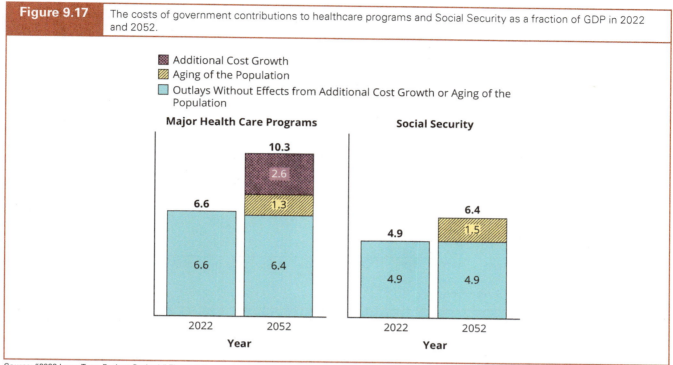

Source: "2022 Long-Term Budget Outlook," Figure 2-5.

9-4c Is It Possible to Grow Out of the Debt Problem?

All the CBO projections express debt, revenue, and expenditures as a fraction of GDP. This makes sense. A $10 million expenditure in an economy with a GDP of $100 million is a lot more important than if GDP were $100 billion. More formally, referring back to the government's flow budget constraint in Equation (14), defining real GDP growth as $1 + z_t = \frac{Y_t}{Y_{t-1}}$, and assuming a constant real interest rate, we see that

$$G_t + (1+r)B_{t-1} = B_t + T_t$$
$$\Leftrightarrow (1+r)B_{t-1} = B_t + T_t - G_t$$
$$\Leftrightarrow \frac{(1+r)B_{t-1}}{Y_t} = \frac{B_t + T_t - G_t}{Y_t}$$
$$\Leftrightarrow \frac{Y_{t-1}}{Y_{t-1}} \frac{(1+r)B_{t-1}}{Y_t} = \frac{B_t + T_t - G_t}{Y_t}$$
$$\Leftrightarrow \frac{(1+r)b_{t-1}}{(1+z_t)} = b_t + t_t - g_t$$
$$\Leftrightarrow b_t = \frac{(1+r)b_{t-1}}{(1+z_t)} - s_t. \tag{17}$$

Equation (17) is the law of motion for the debt-to-GDP ratio. Small letters in Equation (17) refer to a variable as a share of GDP, e.g., s_t is the primary surplus as a share of GDP. Equation (17) tells us it is possible for the government to shrink its debt to GDP ratio without ever running a primary surplus. As long as the growth rate of GDP exceeds the interest rate of servicing the debt, or $z_t > r$, then the government can roll over the debt forever. Intuitively, if the government runs a balanced budget, then the debt grows at rate r. If GDP grows faster than r, then the debt-to-GDP ratio shrinks over time. In fact, if economic growth is sufficiently rapid compared to interest rates, the government may be able to run primary deficits and still have the debt-to-GDP ratio shrink.

Part 2 Classical Theory

Figure 9.18 The real interest rate on one-year constant maturity treasury securities and the GDP growth rate from 1959 to 2021.

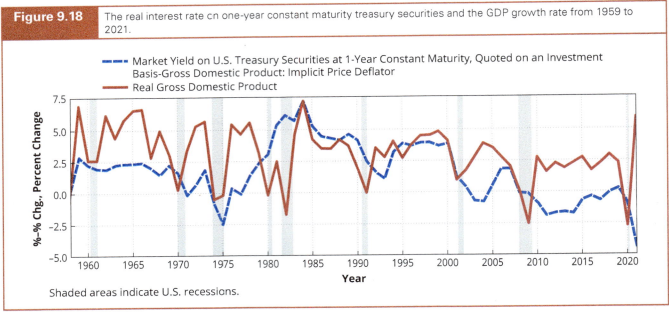

Shaded areas indicate U.S. recessions.

Source: FRED.

Figure 9.18 plots the real interest rate of one-year government treasuries against real GDP growth. More often than not, real GDP growth exceeds the real interest rate the federal government paid on its debt. Indeed, since 2009, the real interest rate has been consistently negative. Should $z_t > r$ continue in perpetuity, the government could get away without ever running a primary surplus.

Forecasting the growth rate of GDP and interest rates is not easy. However, the CBO makes some tentative projections. Real GDP growth is the sum of growth in output per worker and the growth in the labor force. Given the aging population, the growth in the labor force will decline over time. From 1992 to 2021, the labor force grew by about 1 percent per year. The CBO projects that this rate will decrease to less than half a percent a year in the ensuing decades. Growth in output per worker, meanwhile, has averaged about 1.5 percent over the last 30 years. If the real interest rate the government pays on its debt stays below 2 percent, then the perpetual rollover strategy could work.

There are two potential problems with this conclusion. First, perpetual debt turnover is risky, especially when the government issues bonds of short durations. If interest rates were to suddenly spike, then the government may need to either dramatically cut expenditures or increase taxes to service the debt. Second, while a high debt-to-GDP ratio may be feasible, it may not be desirable. To the extent that high levels of debt crowd out private investment, it may be preferable to pay off the debt more quickly and allow private capital to accumulate.

✓ Knowledge Check 9-5

The debt-to-GDP ratio currently stands at about 120 percent. Assuming a primary deficit of 2 percent per year, a real interest rate of −1 percent and a growth rate of real GDP of 2 percent, calculate the evolution of the debt-to-GDP ratio using the equation

$$b_t = \frac{(1 + r) b_{t-1}}{(1 + z_t)} + s_t.$$

Put the values you calculate into the table below.

Year	b_t
2021	1.2
2022	
2023	
2024	
2025	

Answers are at the end of the chapter.

9-4d Fiscal and Monetary Interactions with the Government's Debt

Up to this point, we have dealt entirely with real prices and quantities. The government finances its expenditures with a mix of taxes and borrowing. In principle, however, governments have a third option: printing money. With the introduction of money, we need to be careful about distinguishing real variables from nominal variables. Remember, real variables are denominated in constant dollars, whereas nominal variables are denominated in terms of current dollars.

Incorporating money in the government's budget constraint gives

$$P_t G_t + (1 + i_{t-1}) P_{t-1} B_{t-1} = P_t T_t + P_t B_t + M_t - M_{t-1}. \tag{18}$$

Equation (18) is the government's nominal budget constraint. For instance, $P_t G_t$ is nominal government expenditure, or the price level multiplied by the level of real government expenditure. The last term, $M_t - M_{t-1}$, is the change in the money supply. If there is \$100 billion in period $t - 1$ and the government creates another \$20 billion in period t, $M_t = \$120$ billion and the government can use \$20 billion to finance expenditure. The revenue the government earns through money creation is called **seigniorage**. Finally, note that bonds issued in period $t - 1$ are denominated in that period's prices.

Seigniorage
Government revenue from printing money.

We can write (18) in real terms by dividing both sides of the equation by P_t:

$$\frac{P_t G_t + (1 + i_{t-1}) P_{t-1} B_{t-1}}{P_t} = \frac{P_t T_t + P_t B_t + M_t - M_{t-1}}{P_t}$$

$$\Leftrightarrow G_t + \frac{1 + i_{t-1}}{1 + \pi_t} B_{t-1} = T_t + B_t + \frac{M_t - M_{t-1}}{P_t}$$

$$\Leftrightarrow G_t + (1 + r_{t-1}) B_{t-1} = T_t + B_t + \frac{M_t - M_{t-1}}{P_t}, \tag{19}$$

where the second line uses the fact that inflation equals the growth rate of the price level, $\pi_t = \frac{P_t}{P_{t-1}} - 1$, and the third line uses the Fisher equation first encountered in Chapter 5, $(1 + r_{t-1}) = \frac{1 + i_{t-1}}{1 + \pi_t}$. Comparing Equation (19) to (14), you see that that the only difference is the change in the money supply deflated by the price level. The real resources the government gets from printing money is the new money divided by the price level. Say the government wants to buy tanks, and each tank costs \$200,000. If the government prints \$10 million in currency, then it can afford to buy 50 tanks. Thus, the "real value" of newly created money is 50 tanks.

The budget constraint with money highlights some interesting interactions between fiscal and monetary policy. For instance, if the government consistently runs a primary deficit, it may choose to finance the deficit by printing money rather than issuing new debt. As the Quantity Equation from Chapter 5 tells us, higher rates of money growth eventually lead to higher prices. The implication is that a government may be able to get away with partially financing itself by printing money, but eventually the price level rises, which eats away at the purchasing power of the new money. If the price of tanks in the last example increases to \$400,000, then the government needs to print \$20 million in new currency to afford 50 tanks.

In many countries, fiscal policy is set by elected officials and monetary policy is set by an independent central bank. How fiscal policymakers choose to finance government spending may depend on just how independent their central bank is. For example, if the central bank credibly commits to grow the money supply slowly, fiscal policy makers are forced to finance expenditure through taxes or new borrowing. On the other hand, if the central bank lacks independence, fiscal policymakers may run up large deficits, knowing that monetary policymakers will eventually bail them out by printing money, thereby causing inflation.

240 **Part 2** Classical Theory

There is a way to express this more formally. We have already seen that provided $r > g$, the government can't roll over its debt forever. Thus, there must be some upper bound on debt. In an economy without money, there is no possibility of monetizing the debt. This places some discipline on fiscal policymakers in that, at some point in the future, they will have to run primary surpluses. With the possibility of monetizing the debt, the government knows that once it hits the upper bound on debt, borrowing is no longer an option. But once the upper bound is reached, the debt-to-GDP ratio might be too big to pay off by running a primary surplus. The only other way to satisfy the government budget constraint is through seigniorage.[15] Thus, government deficits, both now and in the future, contribute to inflation.

Thus, the Quantity Equation from Chapter 5 only gives part of the story. If the central bank doesn't have complete autonomy over the growth rate of the money supply, then inflation (even in the long run) will be determined by monetary *and* fiscal policy.

Application 9.2

The End of Four Big Inflations

In Chapter 5, we discussed the German hyperinflation after World War I. By the end of Germany's hyperinflation, the price level had gone up by a factor of about 1 trillion.[16] Hyperinflation, however, was not exclusive to Germany. Austria, Hungary, and Poland all experienced rapid price increases immediately after the war. Despite several years of rapidly rising prices and poor economic performance, inflation in each of these countries ended rapidly. Was there a common cause?

Economist and 2011 Nobel laureate Thomas Sargent said in a 1981 paper that the answer was yes. Sargent identified several commonalities between the countries in the years following World War I. The governments in all four countries ran large deficits while inflation was ongoing. The governments eventually took deliberate and drastic steps to deal with the hyperinflation. This was followed by an immediate stabilization of each country's price level and exchange rate, but the money supply continued to increase for a while even after the inflation ended.

The case of Austria is illustrative. Following the war's conclusion, the independent nation of Austria was formed as part of the dissolution of the Austro-Hungarian Empire. Austria faced food shortages, and a large portion of the country's population was unemployed. Since they were on the losing end of the war, they also owed reparation payments to Allied powers. Responding to the dire circumstances, the Austrian government ran large deficits from

1919 to 1922. As Table 9.5 shows, a large portion of these deficits was financed through money creation.

Between September 1921 and September 1922, the money supply rose by a factor of 285. Unsurprisingly, over the same time period, prices also rose by a factor of about 200. Then, as Table 9.6 shows, the price level stabilized abruptly. This happened in spite of continued increase in the money supply. Between September 1922 and September 1924, the money supply nearly quadrupled. So what happened? Why did prices stabilize despite the ongoing expansion in the money supply?

Sargent attributed the price level stabilization to radical changes in fiscal policy. In October 1922, the Council of the League of Nations charted an agreement between Austria and some of the Allied powers. One provision of the agreement was that the sovereignty of Austria would be respected. The second provision provided the terms of an international loan to Austria. In the third provision, Austria committed to establishing an independent central bank, to stop running large deficits, and limited the ability of the government to finance its deficit by selling bonds to the central bank. The central bank was instituted in January 1923, several months after prices had stabilized. By 1924, the Austrian government was running a surplus.

The combination of an independent central bank and responsible government budgeting crushed inflation. Prior to these economic reforms, the central bank's assets consisted of Austrian bonds. With expenditures consistently

[16]Sargent, Thomas J. 1981. "The End of Four Big Hyperinflations." In Inflation: *Causes and Consequences*, University of Chicago Press.

■ Continues

---

[15]The classic reference is Sargent, Thomas J. and Neil Wallace. 1981. "Some Unpleasant Monetarist Arithmetic." *Federal Reserve Bank of Minneapolis Quarterly Review, 531:* 1–15.

Chapter 9 Government Spending and the Macroeconomy **241**

Application 9.2 (Continued)

Table 9.5 Austrian Budgets, 1919–22 (in Millions of Paper Crowns)

	Receipts	Expenditures	Deficit	Percentage of expenditures covered by new issues of paper money
1 January–30 June 1919	1,339	4,043	2,704	67
1 July 1919–30 June 1920	6,295	16,873	10,578	63
1 July 1920–30 June 1921	29,483	70,601	41,118	58
1 January–31 December 1922	209,763	347,533	137,770	40

Source: Pasvolsky [25, p. 102].

Table 9.6 Austrian Retail Prices, 1921–24

		Retail price index, 52 commodities			Retail price index, 52 commodities
1921	January	100	1923	January	17,526
	February	114		February	17,851
	March	122		March	18.205
	April	116		April	19,428
	May	121		May	20,450
	June	150		June	20,482
	July	143		July	19,368
	August	167		August	18,511
	September	215		September	20,955
	October	333		October	21,166
	November	566		November	21,479
	December	942		December	21,849
1922	January	1,142	1924	January	22,941
	February	1,428		February	23,336
	March	1,457		March	23,336
	April	1,619		April	23,361
	May	2,028		May	23,797
	June	3,431		June	24,267
	July	4,830			
	August	11,046			
	September	20,090			
	October	18,567			
	November	17,681			
	December	17,409			

Source: Young [36, vol. 2, p. 293].

■Continues

242 **Part 2** Classical Theory

Application 9.2 (Continued)

outpacing revenues, the bonds had little value. That is, the Austrian government did not signal its commitment to raising revenue to pay off the debt. The reforms provided the commitment that any government deficit would be repaid with taxes rather than seigniorage and the currency stabilized as a result.

The cases of Germany, Hungary, and Poland are similar to Austria. The main lesson is that if a government wants to reduce inflation, it needs to be fiscally responsible. Fiscal responsibility means either running balanced budgets or credibly committing to paying off deficits with higher future taxes.

These historical episodes also have implications for today. It's often true that countries with hyperinflation have both high rates of growth in the money supply and very large government deficits. A credible commitment to responsible fiscal policy is key to bringing down the growth rates of the money supply and inflation.

Chapter Summary

- Current government expenditures are the sum of consumption expenditures, transfer payments, interest payments, and subsidies.

- Transfer payments as a share of current government expenditures have increased over the past 60 years, while the share of consumption expenditures has decreased.

- Current government receipts include current tax receipts, contributions to government social insurance, income receipt on assets, current transfer receipts, and current surplus of government enterprises.

- The intertemporal lifetime budget constraint in the consumption–savings model with lump-sum taxes equates the present discounted value of consumption with the present discounted value of income minus the present discounted value of taxes.

- Two key results from the consumption–savings model with lump-sum taxes are that 1) consumption responds to changes in current and future taxes and 2) consumption responds more strongly to a permanent tax change compared to a temporary tax change.

- Assuming no initial debt, the government budget constraint equates the present discounted value of government expenditure to the present discounted value of taxes.

- The Ricardian equivalence theorem says that households fully internalize the government's budget constraint. The result is

that, conditional on a time path of government expenditure, the way that it is financed is irrelevant.

- In Ricardian economies, an increase in government spending decreases consumption regardless of how the spending is financed. In non-Ricardian economies, deficit financing raises the real interest rate and reduces investment by more than running a balanced budget.

- Ricardian equivalence relies on several assumptions, including forward-looking individuals who have the same lifespan as the government, perfect financial markets, and lump-sum taxation.

- Provided the real interest rate exceeds the growth rate (i.e., $r > g$) shrinking the debt-to-GDP ratio requires running primary surpluses in the future. If $r < g$, then it is possible for the government to roll over the debt without ever running a primary surplus and shrink the debt-to-GDP ratio over time.

- The Congressional Budget Office projects that the United States will run primary deficits well into the next three decades and that, given forecasted real interest rates and GDP growth rates, the debt-to-GDP ratio will grow.

- A government may choose to pay off its debt by increasing the money supply. Moreover, if a central bank lacks independence, a government can potentially run persistent primary deficits and effectively compel the central bank to monetize the debt. This means fiscal policy can be a sustained cause of inflation.

Key Terms

Current government expenditures, 216
Total government expenditures, 218
Current receipts, 221
Total receipts, 221
Lump-sum tax, 221

Ricardian equivalence theorem, 229
Distortionary tax, 230
Primary deficit, 234
Seigniorage, 239

Chapter 9 Government Spending and the Macroeconomy **243**

Questions for Review

1. What are the biggest components of the government's budget? How has this changed over time?

2. The government spending-to-GDP ratio has not definitively trended up or down over the last 50 years. Over the same time period, the payroll tax rate (the tax that finances social security and Medicare) has increased substantially. Explain how this is possible.

3. Explain why transfer payments don't enter into the calculation of GDP. Because transfer payments don't enter GDP, are they still important for the macroeconomy? Explain.

4. The child tax credit gives money to parents based on the number of children they have. During the pandemic, the government raised the child tax credit from \$2,000 to \$3,600 per child. In 2022, the credit went back down to \$2,000. How would consumption of parents have changed if the tax credit were made permanent? How would consumption change for parents with an infant compared to parents with a teenager?

5. What assumptions go into the Ricardian equivalence theorem? Is the theorem likely to hold in reality?

6. How has the U.S. debt-to-GDP ratio evolved over time? Describe the CBO's forecasts for government revenue and expenditure over the next several decades.

Problems

9.1 Imagine you earn $Y_t - T_t$ in disposable income today and $Y_{t+1} - T_{t+1}$ in the future. Rather than pay T_t in period t, the tax authority allows you to defer the liability to period $t + 1$. If you defer paying T_t to the next period, the government also charges you a fine of F. Assuming you can borrow and save at a real interest rate of r_t, derive a condition on T_t, r_t, and F such that you prefer deferring taxes.

9.2 Assume that an individual's budget constraints are given by

$$C_t + S_t = Y_t - T_t,$$

$$C_{t+1} = (1 + r_t)S_t + Y_{t+1} - T_{t+1}.$$

Also assume that the individual cannot borrow, so $C_t \leq Y_t - T_t$.

a. If the marginal rate of substitution is $\dfrac{C_{t+1}}{0.9C_t}$ and $1 + r_t = \dfrac{1}{0.9}$, solve for the individual's period t consumption function.

b. If $Y_t = 30$ and $Y_{t+1} = 60$ and $T_t = T_{t+1} = 0$, solve for the optimal quantity of period t consumption.

c. Assume that the government spends $G_t = 20$. It can finance this spending by imposing a tax of $T_t = 20$ in period t or $T_{t+1} = 20(1 + r_t)$ in period $t + 1$. How does the timing of government taxes affect period t consumption? What can you say about Ricardian equivalence in this case?

9.3 **[Difficult]** One assumption driving the Ricardian equivalence theorem is that individuals have the same lifespan as the government. This example shows what happens when that assumption is removed. Suppose individuals live two periods, but the government lives forever. The individual earns 100 in income in both periods. In period t, a younger person has the budget constraint

$$C_{y,t} + S_t = 100 - T_t.$$

In words, the consumption of the younger person, $C_{y,t}$, plus savings, S_t, equals disposable income, $100 - T_t$. In period $t + 1$, the budget constraint is

$$C_{o,t+1} = (1 + r_t)S_t + 100.$$

The consumption of an older person $C_{o,t+1}$ equals the principal plus interest earnings on their savings plus income.

a. Suppose the government wants to consume 10 units of output in period t. Suppose they finance this consumption by raising taxes so $T_t = 10$. Because the government isn't borrowing, we can infer that the younger individual isn't saving, $S_t = 0$. Solve for the optimal levels of consumption directly from the budget constraints. Assuming that the marginal rate of substitution is $\dfrac{C_{o,t+1}}{0.9C_{y,t}}$, use the fact that the MRS equals $1 + r$ to solve for the equilibrium real interest rate.

b. Suppose instead that the government borrows the funds so that $S_t = 10$ and $T_t = 0$. In period $t + 1$, they raise taxes on the young. Calculate the new levels of $C_{y,t}$, $C_{o,t+1}$, and r_t. Does Ricardian equivalence hold?

c. Suppose that members of the older generation care about the welfare of the younger generation. In particular, the older generation feels guilty about leaving the younger generation with a tax liability. To compensate for this, the older generation leaves the younger generation a bequest, B, which changes the period $t + 1$ the budget constraint to

$$C_{o,t+1} = (1 + r_t)S_t + 100 - B.$$

Continuing to assume that the government borrows in period t and imposes taxes on the young in $t + 1$, calculate the bequest level such that the levels of consumption and real interest rate in part c are identical to part a. Explain the intuition of your findings.[17]

9.4 Assuming the government runs a balanced budget, the economy's aggregate supply of savings is

$$S_t = Y_t - C(Y_t - G_t, Y_{t+1} - G_{t+1}, r_t) - G_t.$$

The investment demand curve is

$$I_t = I(r_t + f_t, A_{t+1}).$$

a. Plot the effects of an increase in G_{t+1}. What happens to equilibrium consumption, investment, and real interest rates? Explain the economic intuition.

---

[17]For a formal treatment of this, see: Barro, Robert J. 1974. "Are Government Bonds Net Wealth?" *Journal of Political Economy*, 82(6): 1095–1117.

244   **Part 2** Classical Theory

b. Suppose that a portion of government spending is devoted to infrastructure and that an increase in infrastructure makes investment more productive. The new investment demand curve is

$$I_t = I(r_t + f_t, A_{t+1}, G_{t+1}).$$

Explain why investment demand depends on future infrastructure spending, G_{t+1}, rather than current infrastructure spending.

c. Plot the effects of an increase in G_{t+1}. Compare your results to part a.

9.5 Suppose the economy's investment demand curve is

$$I_t = I(r_t + f_t, A_{t+1}).$$

The economy's aggregate supply of savings is the sum of private savings and public savings, or

$$S_t = Y_t - C_t - T_t + T_t - G_t.$$

a. Assuming Ricardian equivalence holds and the consumption function is $C_t = C(Y_t - G_t, Y_{t+1} - G_{t+1}, r_t)$. What is the impact of a decrease in T_t assuming current and future government expenditures stay constant? Explain your answer.

b. Instead, assume the consumption function is $C_t = C(Y_t - T_t)$. Plot the effects on a decrease in T_t. What happens to the equilibrium real interest rate and level of investment?

c. Compare your results from parts a and b. Are they the same or different? What is the intuition behind your conclusions?

9.6 This is a quantitative version of the last question. Assume that

$$I_t = A_{t+1} - 100(r_t - f_t).$$

The consumption function is

$$C_t = a_0 + a_1(Y_t - T_t).$$

The marginal propensity to consume from disposable income is a_1. Savings supply is

$$S_t = Y_t - C_t - T_t + T_t - G_t.$$

Throughout this problem, assume $A_{t+1} = 25$, $Y_t = 100$, $f_t = 0.02$, $a_0 = 10$, and $a_1 = 0.7$.

a. Assume $G_t = T_t = 0$. Calculate the equilibrium real interest rate and level of investment.

b. Assume government expenditure increases to $G_t = 10$ and that it is financed by raising taxes in the current period, so $T_t = 10$. Calculate the new equilibrium real interest rate and level of investment.

c. Instead, suppose the government finances the spending by borrowing, so $G_t = 10$ and $T_t = 0$. Calculate the new equilibrium real interest rate and level of investment.

d. Does government spending crowd out investment? How does the magnitude of the crowding out depend on the method of financing? Would the method of financing matter in a version of the model with Ricardian equivalence?

9.7 The law of motion for the government's debt-to-GDP ratio is

$$b_t = \frac{(1 + r)b_{t-1}}{(1 + z_t)} - s_t.$$

where s_t is the primary deficit, b_t is the debt-to-GDP ratio in year t, z_t is the annual growth rate, and r is the real interest rate. The CBO projects that the average primary deficit will average 2.5 percent in 2023–2032, 3.4 percent in 2033–2042, and 4.8 percent in 2043–2052. Thus, over the first 10-year period, the cumulative deficit will be 25% = 2.5% × 10. Over the next 10 years, the cumulative deficit will be 34 percent and then 48 percent over the last 10 years.[18] If r is the annual interest rate, then the interest accumulated over 10 years is $(1 + r)^{10}$. Likewise, growth in GDP accumulated over 10 years is $(1 + z_t)^{10}$.

a. Assuming $z_t = r = 0.02$, complete the rest of the table. What happens to the debt-to-GDP ratio over time?

Year	b_{t-10}	s_t	b_t
2032	1.20	−0.025	
2042		−0.034	
2052		−0.048	

b. An optimistic projection for the government might be $z_t = 0.03$ and $r = 0$. Redo the table under these values. Comment on your findings.

c. A pessimistic projection for the government might be $z_t = 0.01$ and $r = 0.03$. Redo the table under these values. Comment on your findings.

d. Assuming the primary deficit stabilizes at $S = -0.05$ and r stabilizes at 0.02, find the value of z_t such that the debt-to-GDP ratio stays constant over time.

✔ Knowledge Check 9-1 Answer

Current receipts are the sum of the tax receipts, contributions for government social insurance, income receipts on assets, current transfer receipts, and current surplus of government enterprises. Since current receipts equal $6,327, we can solve for the unknown (social insurance):

$$\textit{Social insurance} = \$6,327 - \$4,061 - \$214 - \$190 - (-\$3) = \$2,065.$$

Current expenditures are the sum of government consumption, transfers, interest payments, and subsidies. Since current expenditures equal $8,115, we can solve for the unknown (interest payments):

$$\textit{Interest payments} = \$8,115 - \$3,725 - \$3,162 - \$104 = \$1,124.$$

---

[18]Technically, the future deficits should be discounted, but that depends on the values of r and z, so we ignore that.

The complete table is shown below.

Current receipts	Billions of dollars	Current expenditures	Billions of dollars
Current tax receipts	$4,061	Government consumption	$3,725
Contributions for government social insurance	$2,065	Transfers	$3,162
Income receipts on assets	$214	Interest payments	$1,124
Current transfer receipts	$190	Subsidies	$104
Current surplus of government enterprises	−$3		
Total	**$6,327**		**$8,115**

✓ Knowledge Check 9-2 Answer

The PDV of lifetime disposable income is

$$Y_t + \frac{Y_{t+1}}{1 + r_t} - T_t - \frac{T_{t+1}}{1 + r_t}.$$

Plugging in the values for each row of exogenous variables gives

$$10 + \frac{8}{1.1} + 2 + \frac{0}{1.1} = 15.27,$$

$$10 + \frac{8}{1.1} + 0 + \frac{2.2}{1.1} = 15.27,$$

$$10 + \frac{8}{1.2} + 2 + \frac{0}{1.2} = 14.67,$$

$$10 + \frac{8}{1.2} + 0 + \frac{2.2}{1.2} = 14.83.$$

A higher real interest rate lowers the present value of future tax liabilities. Thus, the higher the real interest rate, the stronger is one's preference for future versus current taxation.

r_t	Y_t	T_t	Y_{t+1}	T_{t+1}	PDV income
0.1	10	2	8	0	15.27
0.1	10	0	8	2.2	15.27
0.2	10	2	8	0	14.67
0.2	10	0	8	2.2	14.83

✓ Knowledge Check 9-3 Answer

Start by solving for future consumption in terms of current consumption:

$$\sqrt{C_{t+1}} = \beta(1 + r_t)\sqrt{C_t}$$

$$\Leftrightarrow C_{t+1} = (\beta(1 + r_t))^2 C_t.$$

Substitute this into the lifetime budget constraint.

$$C_t + \frac{C_{t+1}}{1 + r_t} = Y_t + \frac{Y_{t+1}}{1 + r_t} - T_t - \frac{T_{t+1}}{1 + r_t}$$

$$\Leftrightarrow C_t + \frac{(\beta(1 + r_t))^2 C_t}{1 + r_t} = Y_t + \frac{Y_{t+1}}{1 + r_t} - T_t - \frac{T_{t+1}}{1 + r_t}$$

$$\Leftrightarrow C_t(1 + \beta^2(1 + r_t)) = Y_t + \frac{Y_{t+1}}{1 + r_t} - T_t - \frac{T_{t+1}}{1 + r_t}$$

246 **Part 2** Classical Theory

$$\Leftrightarrow C_t^* = \frac{1}{1 + \beta^2(1 + r_t)}\left[Y_t + \frac{Y_{t+1}}{1 + r_t} - T_t - \frac{T_{t+1}}{1 + r_t}\right].$$

Imposing the simplifying assumption that $\beta = \frac{1}{1 + r_t} = 0.9$ gives

$$C_t^* = \frac{1}{1 + \beta^2(1 + r_t)}\left[Y_t + \frac{Y_{t+1}}{1 + r_t} - T_t - \frac{T_{t+1}}{1 + r_t}\right]$$

$$= \frac{1}{1 + \beta}\left[Y_t + \frac{Y_{t+1}}{1 + r_t} - T_t - \frac{T_{t+1}}{1 + r_t}\right]$$

$$= \frac{1}{1.9}[Y_t + 0.9Y_{t+1} - T_t - 0.9T_{t+1}].$$

If current-period taxes go down by 1, consumption increases by $\frac{1}{1.9} \approx 0.53$. If taxes go down by 1 in both periods, consumption increases by $\frac{1}{1.9}[1 + 0.9] = 1$. Thus, the MPC out of a current-period tax cut is about 0.53, and the MPC out of a permanent tax cut is 1.

✓ Knowledge Check 9-4 Answer

If consumption isn't a function of the real interest rate, then the savings supply curve is vertical. An increase in the risk premium increases the costs of investment and shifts the investment demand curve to the left. This is shown in Figure 9.19. The equilibrium real interest rate falls from $r_{0,t}^*$ to $r_{1,t}^*$. The equilibrium quantity of investment doesn't change. Intuitively, because savings supply isn't a function of the real interest rate, the real interest rate must fall sufficiently far so that the new quantity of investment demand equals the initial quantity. Since investment demand depends on total borrowing costs, $r_t + f_t$, we can infer that $r_{0,t}^* + f_{0,t} = r_{1,t}^* + f_{1,t}$. That is, the rise in the risk premium is offset with an equal change in the real interest rate, but in the opposite direction.

Figure 9.19 This plots the effect of an increase in the risk premium, f_t, from $f_{0,t}$ to $f_{1,t}$. The investment demand curve shifts to the left. In equilibrium, the real interest rate falls from $r_{0,t}^*$ to $r_{1,t}^*$. The equilibrium quantity of investment doesn't change.

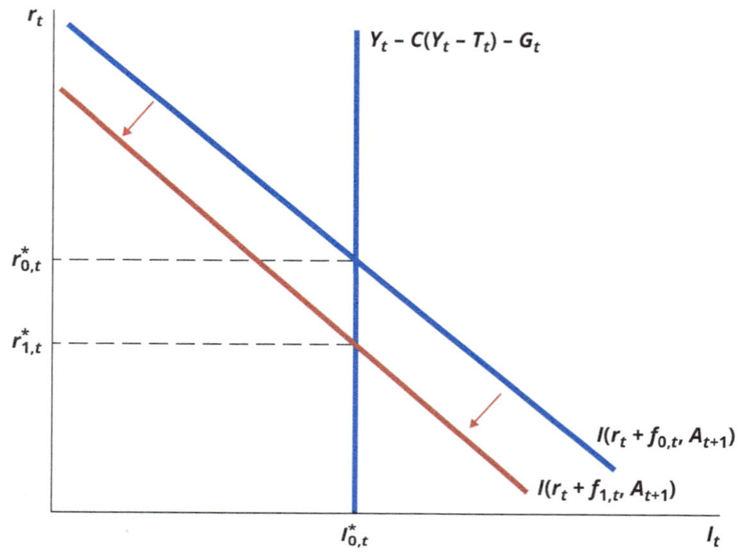

When savings supply is an upward function of the real interest rate, an increase in f_t shifts investment demand to the left, the equilibrium real interest rate falls, and the equilibrium quantity of investment goes down. We can infer that the real interest rate falls by less in this case.

Knowledge Check 9-5 Answer

The debt-to-GDP ratio in 2022 is given by

$$b_{2022} = \frac{(1+r)b_{2021}}{(1+z_t)} + s$$

$$= \frac{(1-.01)}{(1+.02)}1.2 - 0.02$$

$$= 1.185.$$

In 2023, the debt-to-GDP ratio is given by

$$b_{2023} = \frac{(1+r)b_{2022}}{(1+z_t)} + s$$

$$= \frac{(1-.01)}{(1+.02)}1.185 - 0.02$$

$$= 1.17.$$

The rest of the table is filled in below.

Year	b_t
2021	1.2
2022	1.19
2023	1.17
2024	1.16
2025	1.14

Chapter 10 Introduction to Business Cycles

Learning Objectives

10.1 Define business cycles and explain how economists measure them.

10.2 Explain the stylized facts of business cycles.

10.3 Compare and contrast trend output and potential output.

10.4 Explain the key elements of the real business cycle model.

10.5 Evaluate the strengths and weaknesses of the real business cycle model.

Between 1929 and 1933, consumption expenditures decreased more than 40 percent.[1] Over the same time period, the unemployment rate rose from less than 2 percent to more than 25 percent. Although these four years were the worst of it, the Great Depression lasted for more than a decade. It was the longest and most severe downturn in U.S. history. Contributing to the crisis was the lack of any sort of social safety net at the national level. The Social Security Act, which created nationwide unemployment insurance, wasn't passed until 1935. This was a period of excess unemployment, mass destruction of wealth, and general economic stagnation.

The 2008 financial crisis had a lot of similarities to the start of the Great Depression. Crashes in the housing market and then in the stock market fueled uncertainty. The failure of two prominent investment banks was a stark reminder of the commercial bank failures during the Great Depression. And yet GDP completely recovered its lost ground by 2010. Unemployment peaked at 10 percent, far lower than the catastrophically high rate of the Great Depression. Consumption expenditures in the 2008 crisis, meanwhile, decreased by a little more than 1 percent—a miniscule change compared to the Great Depression.

What explains the different economic trajectories of the United States in 1929 versus 2008? Why was the recession during the Covid-19 pandemic so brief?[2] The next several chapters cover models that economists have developed to explain business cycles and to guide policymakers. Throughout, we examine these historical episodes in more detail. Before developing the models, we must answer some preliminary questions: What exactly are business cycles, and how are they measured? How do quantities—like GDP, consumption, and unemployment—and prices, like wages, interest rates, and inflation—move together over time? In this chapter, you will learn how business cycles are measured, the stylized facts associated with them, and a preliminary theory that bridges the gap between economic growth and business cycle analysis.

---

[1] This is consumption in constant dollars.

[2] The economy was in a recession during the first quarter of 2020. All recession dates come from the National Bureau of Economic Research.

10-1 Measuring Business Cycles

The historical examples cited in the chapter's introduction were all recessions. The National Bureau of Economic Research defines a **recession** as a period in which "there is significant decline in economic activity that is spread across the economy and that lasts for a few months."[3] More generally, we are interested in studying the downturns and the upturns in the economy. **Business cycles** are the variation in GDP around the economy's trend. Figure 10.1 illustrates the idea. Time is plotted on the horizontal axis, and the value of some series, perhaps GDP or consumption, is plotted on the vertical axis. Each dot corresponds to the data value in that period. The linear blue line measures the trend. The distance between the dots and the trend line is the cyclical component of the data series.

Variables like GDP, consumption, and investment are all examples of **non-stationary data series**. Non-stationary data has a consistent trend up or down over time. A **stationary data series** does not have a consistent upward or downward trend. Figure 10.2 plots real GDP and the unemployment rate from 1950 through 2022. Real GDP, measured on the leftward vertical axis, trends upward over time. It is an example of a non-stationary series because there is a consistent upward trend. Unemployment is measured on the rightward axis. While there are periods of high unemployment and low unemployment, there is no consistent trend over time. Thus, unemployment is a stationary series.

Business cycle analysis deals with movements around the economy's trend, hence the word "cycle." As a first step, we need to remove trends from non-stationary series. It turns out we can decompose every non-stationary series into a trend component and a cyclical component. Using real GDP as an example, it is identically true that

$$GDP_t \equiv GDP_{t,trend} + GDP_{t,cycle}. \qquad (1)$$

To see this, imagine an economy that starts with a GDP per capita of $10,000 and expects to grow $200 annually, or $50 between quarters (there are four quarters in a year). Defining

Recession
A period in which there is significant decline in economic activity that is spread across the economy and that lasts more than a few months.

Business cycle
The variation in GDP around the economy's trend.

Non-stationary data series
A data series with a consistent trend up or down over time.

Stationary data series
A data series with no consistent trend up or down.

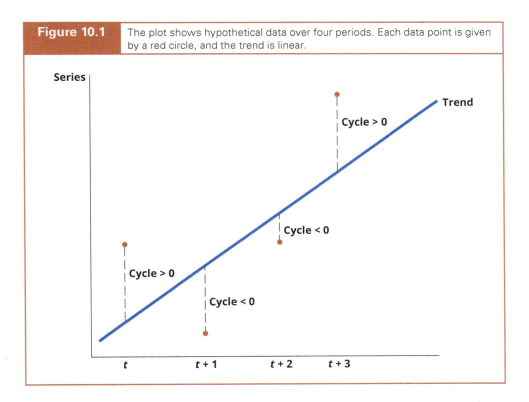

Figure 10.1 The plot shows hypothetical data over four periods. Each data point is given by a red circle, and the trend is linear.

---

[3]This is from the frequently asked questions in the "US Business Cycle Expansions and Contractions" compiled by the National Bureau of Economic Research, https://www.nber.org/research/business-cycle-dating/business-cycle-dating-procedure-frequently-asked-questions.

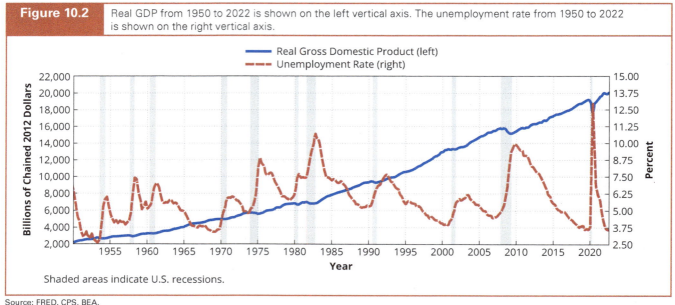

Figure 10.2 Real GDP from 1950 to 2022 is shown on the left vertical axis. The unemployment rate from 1950 to 2022 is shown on the right vertical axis.

Shaded areas indicate U.S. recessions.

Source: FRED, CPS, BEA.

each time period as a quarter, Table 10.1 shows hypothetical GDP data. Moving between period t and $t + 1$, the economy adds $30 in GDP per person. Since the economy on average adds $50 per person every quarter, the cyclical component of GDP is $10,030 − $10,050 = −$20. So, GDP is below trend. Likewise, between periods $t + 1$ and $t + 2$, trend GDP per person increases another $50 to $10,100. Since actual GDP per person is $10 below trend, the cyclical component of GDP is −$10.

Table 10.1 Trend and Cyclical GDP

Period	GDP	Trend	Cycle
t	$10,000	$10,000	0
$t + 1$	$10,030	$10,050	−$20
$t + 2$	$10,090	$10,100	−$10
$t + 3$	$10,160	$10,150	$10
$t + 4$	$10,240	$10,200	$40
$t + 5$	$10,240	$10,250	−$10

Table 10.1 provides the intuition for calculating the trend and cycle. In practice, computing the trend component of non-stationary series is a bit more challenging. This is not a statistical methods course, so we won't go into much further detail. It is useful, however, to briefly discuss two of the challenges. The first challenge is that non-stationary macroeconomic series grow exponentially rather than linearly. The second challenge is that many trends aren't constant.

✓ Knowledge Check 10-1

Assume that consumption per person grows at $100 per year on average. Assuming each time period, t, represents a quarter, fill in the missing values of the table.

Period	Consumption	Trend	Cycle
t	$5,000	$5,000	0
$t + 1$	$5,030		
$t + 2$			$10
$t + 3$	$5,090		
$t + 4$	$5,095		
$t + 5$			−$10

Answers are at the end of the chapter.

10-1a Measuring the Trend

There are two practical difficulties in measuring the trend of non-stationary macroeconomic series like GDP and consumption. First, they typically grow exponentially rather than linearly. In the last example, trend GDP grew linearly at $200 per year. But adding $200 to a base of $10,000 grows income by 2 percent, whereas adding $200 to a base of $100,000 grows income by 0.2 percent. When a data series increases linearly, the growth rate declines over time. Figure 10.3 shows that real GDP growth is not consistently declining over time, confirming that GDP growth is more exponential than linear.

To more easily visualize and measure data series with exponential growth, we typically take the natural log of them. It turns out that the natural log of an exponential function is linear. That is, given some function, $Y = e^{ax}$ with $a > 0$, $\ln(e^{ax}) = ax$. So the natural log transforms an exponential function into a linear one which, again, is easier to visualize. It's also true that, to a first approximation,

$$\ln(GDP_t) - \ln(GDP_{t-1}) \approx g_{GDP,t}. \qquad (2)$$

The difference between the natural log of GDP in adjacent periods equals the growth rate of GDP. When we plot the natural log of GDP over time, the vertical difference between two adjacent periods of GDP is the growth rate. If the growth rate is approximately constant through time, the natural log of a data series growing exponentially will be linear. Figure 10.4 shows how this works. The difference between the natural log of GDP in period t, $\ln(GDP_t)$, and in period $t-1$, $\ln(GDP_{t-1})$, is equal to the growth rate of GDP.

Given this property about natural logs embedded in Equation (2), we can express the cyclical component of GDP as percent deviations from trend. For instance, if GDP, on average, grows 1 percent between quarters and $\ln(GDP_t) - \ln(GDP_{t-1}) = 0.015$, then the cyclical component is 0.5 percent, or GDP is one half a percent above trend. If non-stationary series like GDP have roughly constant trend growth rates, then the trend can be measured by fitting a straight line through the natural log of the series (similar to Figure 10.1, but for natural logs).

This brings us to a second challenge, namely that many trends aren't constant themselves. Between 1950 and 1973, real GDP grew 4.3 percent per year on average. Over the next 24 years, from 1974 to 1997, GDP grew 3 percent per year on average. From 1998 to 2022, GDP grew 2.3 percent per year on average. GDP grows exponentially in all these periods; however, the growth rates are different, even over a large number of years. Fitting a straight line through the data would underestimate the trend in the early years and overestimate the trend in later years.

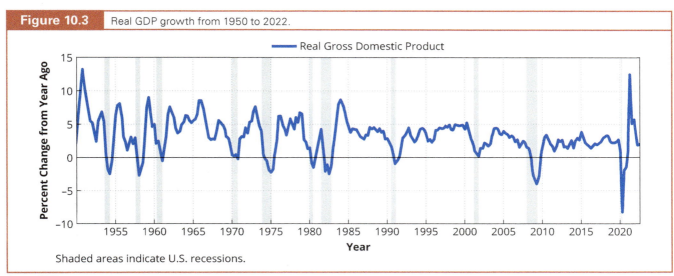

Figure 10.3 Real GDP growth from 1950 to 2022.

Shaded areas indicate U.S. recessions.

Source: FRED.

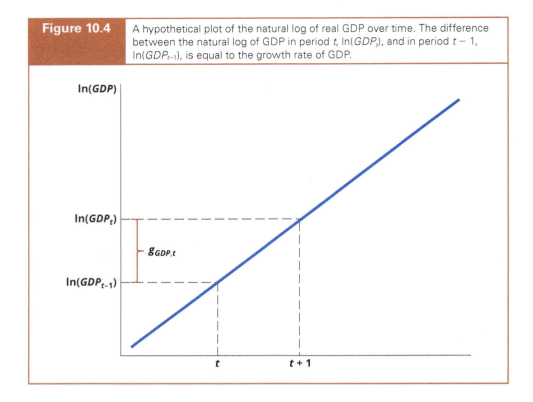

Figure 10.4 A hypothetical plot of the natural log of real GDP over time. The difference between the natural log of GDP in period t, $\ln(GDP_t)$, and in period $t-1$, $\ln(GDP_{t-1})$, is equal to the growth rate of GDP.

One way of dealing with this is to measure the trend by taking a moving average. The idea is to construct the trend in any given quarter by taking an average of GDP across a certain number of preceding quarters and a certain number of following quarters. For instance, let's say that we want to construct a 12-quarter moving average. The trend component in the first quarter of GDP in 2000 would be an average of GDP from 1997 through 2003. Mathematically, the trend component for a 12-quarter moving average of GDP in any period t is

$$\ln(GDP_{trend,t}) = \frac{1}{25} \sum_{j=-12}^{12} \ln(GDP_{t+j}). \qquad (3)$$

The moving average can be calculated in a spreadsheet program like Microsoft Excel. The cyclical component of GDP can then be calculated using the identity in Equation (1). Figure 10.5 shows the results. The trend component of GDP consistently moves up over time. This is capturing the long-run growth in the economy. The cyclical component, as you would expect, moves up and down. In recessions, the cyclical component is negative, as the economy is below trend. During the recession of the early 1980s, for instance, GDP falls about 5 percent below trend. You might notice that Figure 10.5 doesn't include the pandemic recession in the first quarter of 2020. The reason is that each trend point requires three years of data from the future to calculate. Since the most recent GDP data is from 2022, the **statistical decomposition**, or the separation of the trend from the cycle, stops in 2019.

With the decomposition method in hand, we can document several prominent facts about business cycles. There are a couple points to make by way of introduction. The **volatility** of a data series refers to the magnitude of its upward and downward swings. Statistically speaking, the volatility of a series can be captured by its standard deviation, which is discussed in the mathematical appendix. The **comovement** of a data series refers to how it correlates with the cyclical component of GDP. A series that is positively correlated with cyclical GDP is said to be procyclical. A series that is negatively correlated with cyclical GDP is said to be countercyclical. Statistically speaking, comovement is captured by the correlation coefficient, which is also discussed in the mathematical appendix.

Statistical decomposition
A statistical method separating the trend component of a data series from its cyclical component.

Volatility
The quantitative magnitude of the upward and downward swings in a data series.

Comovement
The way in which a data series correlates with the cyclical component of GDP.

Chapter 10 Introduction to Business Cycles 253

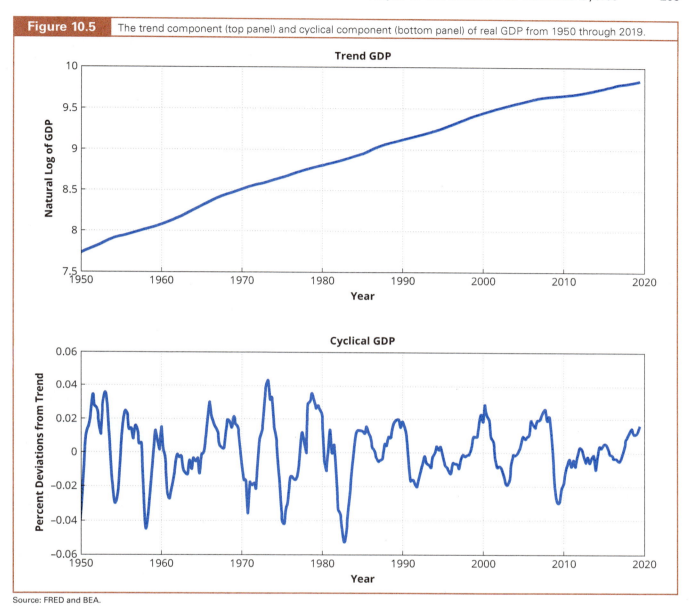

Figure 10.5 The trend component (top panel) and cyclical component (bottom panel) of real GDP from 1950 through 2019.

Source: FRED and BEA.

10-1b The Stylized Facts of Business Cycles

In this section, we discuss some stylized facts of business cycles.

1. **The Great Moderation:** After 2020, the idea that the economy is less volatile today than in decades past might sound like a naive idea. But this is consistent with the facts. An eyeball test of Figure 10.5 confirms that output became less volatile sometime in the mid-1980s. Quantitatively, the standard deviation of cyclical output from 1984 through 2019 was about 50 percent lower than the period from 1950 to 1983. Economists have referred to this decline in output volatility as the Great Moderation.

   The Great Moderation has been attributed to a combination of better policy and good luck.[4] On the policy front, the Federal Reserve improved its manage-

---
[4]The Federal Reserve offers a bit more on the history of the Great Moderation here: https://www.federalreservehistory.org/essays/great-moderation. They end the Great Moderation with the mid-2000s financial crisis. This is debatable. Although the financial crisis was a big shock, output quickly stabilized.

Stagflation
A simultaneous period of high inflation and low output.

ment of interest rates and the money supply. (This is discussed in Chapter 11.) In terms of luck, it took time for the economy to adjust to the postwar environment. Economic growth was high in the 1950s but also volatile. International conflict, albeit not the size and scope of World War II, persisted throughout the 1950s and 1960s, with the Korean and Vietnam Wars. The surge in oil prices in the 1970s increased inflation and sent the economy into a recession. A simultaneous period of high inflation and low output has come to be known as **stagflation**. By the mid-1980s, the Cold War had cooled down as the USSR was internally unraveling. Oil prices stabilized and didn't spike again until the mid-2000s. Although economic growth was lower in the Great Moderation period, it was also more stable.

It's debatable whether the Great Moderation ended in 2007 with the onset of the Great Recession. On the one hand, the Great Recession was quite severe, with output declining 3 percent from trend. On the other hand, the volatility in GDP between 2010 and the start of the Covid-19 pandemic was comparable to the rest of the Great Moderation period.

2. Output, consumption, and investment all move together, albeit with different volatilities: Figure 10.6 shows cyclical GDP, consumption, and investment. The first thing that stands out is strong positive comovement between the three series. The correlation coefficient between each of the two series is about 0.9. Also, investment is the most volatile series, and consumption is the least volatile series.

The model of real interest rate determination that you first saw in Chapter 6 can readily explain these facts. An unexpected increase in income causes forward-looking individuals to increase their consumption and savings, thereby smoothing the income gain over their lifecycle. This means that income, consumption, and investment all move together, just as in the data. Consumption smoothing also implies that consumption is less volatile than GDP, as individuals adjust their savings patterns in the face of a volatile income stream. This necessarily means that investment is the most volatile series of the three.

3. Unemployment is strongly negatively correlated with GDP, and wages aren't correlated with GDP: it's fairly intuitive that cyclical GDP and the unemployment rate are negatively correlated. After all, one often reads about high unemployment

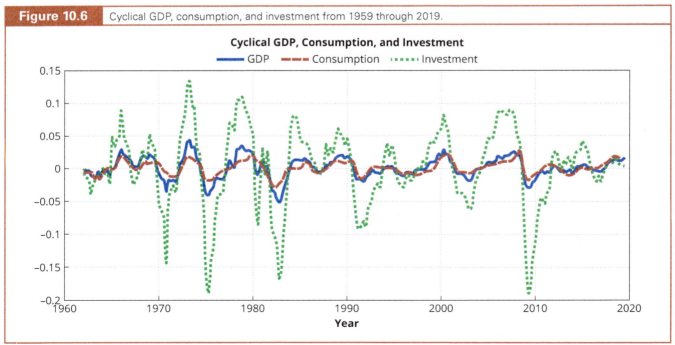

Figure 10.6 Cyclical GDP, consumption, and investment from 1959 through 2019.

Source: FRED, BEA, https://fred.stlouisfed.org/graph/?g=YpCg.

rates during recessions. The top panel of Figure 10.7 confirms that intuition. The vertical axis plots the deviation of the unemployment rate from its average, and the horizontal axis plots cyclical real GDP. The correlation is close to −0.7, implying a strong negative comovement between the unemployment rate and real GDP.

Less intuitive is the bottom panel. It shows essentially no correlation between cyclical real wages and cyclical GDP. The actual correlation is about 0.14, implying very weak comovement. You might expect real wages to decrease in recessions and increase in expansions, but that's not what the data show.

Before theorizing about the lack of correlation between wages and GDP, it's worthwhile to think more about measurement. The real wage series in Figure 10.7 comes from the Bureau of Labor Statistics. It's essentially a measure of the average wage among workers in the economy. In recessions, businesses and firms typically lay off more low-wage workers than high-wage workers. This means that even if the wages of everyone who remains employed stays constant, the average wage goes up. Thus, it looks like wages are negatively correlated with output when it's really the composition of the employed population that is changing.

Here is an example. Imagine three workers: Alex earns $20 per hour, Bea earns $30 per hour, and Curtis earns $40 per hour. The average wage between the three workers is $30 per hour. Now imagine that a recession comes around, and firms

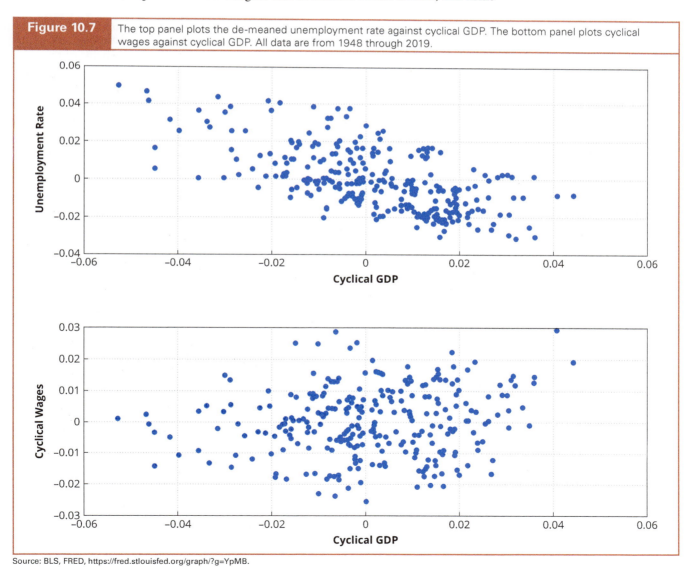

Figure 10.7 The top panel plots the de-meaned unemployment rate against cyclical GDP. The bottom panel plots cyclical wages against cyclical GDP. All data are from 1948 through 2019.

Source: BLS, FRED, https://fred.stlouisfed.org/graph/?g=YpMB.

find it optimal to fire Alex and retain the other two workers. The average wage during the recession rises to $35, making it look like wages are countercyclical. Even if Bea's and Curtis's wage go down 10 percent each, the average wage in the economy would be $\frac{\$27 + \$36}{2} = \$31.50$, a $1.50 increase compared to the economy when it's not in recession.

Economists have analyzed the quantitative significance of composition bias in the average wage series.[5] The punchline is that the correlation between cyclical wages and cyclical GDP after correcting for composition bias is much higher than the 0.14 we calculated above.

4. Automatic stabilizers rise in recessions: **Automatic stabilizers** are parts of the government's budget that vary with the business cycle and don't rely on passing new legislation. On the expenditure side of the government's ledger, unemployment insurance is an example of an automatic stabilizer. Unemployment insurance provides unemployed workers with a certain fraction of their employed income for a certain duration. Since the number of unemployed workers increases in recessions, spending on unemployment insurance mechanically increases. On the revenue side, tax revenue usually decreases during recessions. In recessions, people earn less income and businesses make less profit and, as a result, owe a lower tax bill to the government.

Figure 10.8 shows the quarter-by-quarter growth rate of unemployment insurance on the left axis and tax receipts on the right axis. In periods with gray bars, which indicate recessions, tax receipts go down and unemployment benefits go up.

The presence of these automatic stabilizers helps people smooth their consumption over business cycles. Recall that consumption dropped by over 40 percent during the height of the Great Depression. This was a time when the government offered little to no social insurance. Through the decades, the social safety net was strengthened. By the time the Great Recession of 2007–2009 hit, consumption only fell about 1 percent from its peak. One reason for this is the presence of automatic stabilizers.

Automatic stabilizer
Part of the government's budget that varies with the business cycle and doesn't rely on passing new legislation.

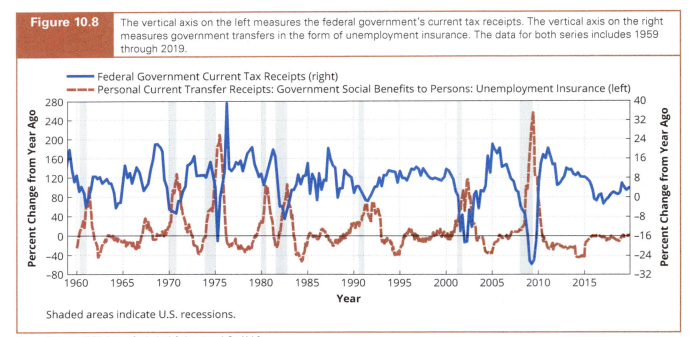

Figure 10.8 The vertical axis on the left measures the federal government's current tax receipts. The vertical axis on the right measures government transfers in the form of unemployment insurance. The data for both series includes 1959 through 2019.

Shaded areas indicate U.S. recessions.

Source: BEA and FRED, https://fred.stlouisfed.org/graph/?g=Ysh9.

---

[5]Barsky, Robert, Jonathan Parker, and Gary Salon. 1994. "Measuring the Cyclicality of Real Wages: How Important is Composition Bias?" *Quarterly Journal of Economics*, 109(1): 1–25.

10-1c Trend GDP Is Not the Same Thing as Potential GDP

Trend GDP is a statistical concept. It essentially tells us the average rate of GDP growth over a predetermined number of periods. **Potential GDP**, meanwhile, is the amount of output the economy could produce if all of the factors of production (such as labor, capital, and raw materials) were used efficiently.

Potential is not the same as trend. Here is one example: Between 2000 and 2019, GDP grew at about 1.5 percent per year. In the second quarter of 2020, which includes April, May, and June, GDP fell by 10 percent. So you could reasonably say that GDP was 11.5 percent below trend. Was GDP 11.5 percent below potential? Hardly. The onset of the Covid-19 pandemic in March 2020 led many businesses to temporarily shut their doors and workers to stay home. True, some of this was mandated by state governments; however, given the danger and highly contagious nature of the disease, people would have optimally stayed away from close working environments, and many people-facing services, such as nail painting, would have been curtailed. Thus, we can say with a high degree of certainty that potential GDP fell in the second quarter of 2020.

How much did potential GDP fall in 2020? That is a complicated question. Unlike trend GDP, which is a statistical construct, potential GDP is a theoretical construct. Only a theory can tell us the efficient levels of factors of production like labor and capital and therefore output. Again, use the pandemic as an example. The inference that potential output decreased relies on a theory that people wanted to avoid getting Covid-19; that is, people were willing to substitute wealth for health. The degree to which people wanted to make this substitution was a function of preferences, wages, the price of medical care, morbidity and mortality rates for the disease, and potentially a large number of other factors.

A theory comes from a model, which is a necessary simplification of reality. Economists have made some progress in modeling the economy and hence estimating potential output. But the estimates are still far from perfect and are subject to revision. This means that caution is called for when using real-time measures of output when conducting monetary and fiscal policy.

Before we get to macroeconomic policy, however, there is one specific theory that deserves attention. According to this theory, all fluctuations in actual GDP are fluctuations in potential GDP.

Potential GDP
The amount of output the economy could produce if all of the factors of production (such as labor, capital, and raw materials) were used efficiently.

10-2 Real Business Cycle Theory

Real business cycle (RBC) theory emerged in the early 1980s. RBC theorists made substantial methodological contributions to the study of business cycles.[6] While the discussion here focuses on the content of these models rather than the technical advancement they made to the field of economics, it's useful to explain why RBC models emerged in the first place.

From the time of John Maynard Keynes's publication of *The General Theory of Employment, Interest, and Money* in 1936 through the 1970s, "Keynesian macroeconomics" was the dominant theory in guiding economic policy. By the mid-1970s, the enterprise of Keynesian macroeconomics was failing on empirical and theoretical levels. On the empirical level, most Keynesian economists postulated a stable trade-off between inflation and the unemployment rate. According to this line of thinking, monetary policymakers could lower unemployment rates, perhaps even permanently, by accepting a higher rate of inflation. The top panel of Figure 10.9 shows the relationship between the unemployment rate and inflation rate from 1947 through 1970. Each dot on the graph represents a given year's inflation and unemployment rate, and you can see a clear, negative association between the two variables. The connection (both theoretical and empirical) between the inflation rate and unemployment rate came to be known as the **Phillips curve**.[7] The advice to monetary

Phillips curve
The relationship between the rates of unemployment and inflation.

---

[6]Fynn Kydland and Edward Prescott shared the 2004 Nobel Prize for having developed the RBC model.
[7]Named after economist A. W. Phillips.

258   Part 3 Business Cycles

Figure 10.9 Both panels show the relationship between the unemployment rate on the vertical axis and the inflation rate, as measured by the percent change in the GDP deflator, on the horizontal axis. The top panel is for the years between 1947 and 1970. The bottom panel is for the years between 1971 and 1980.

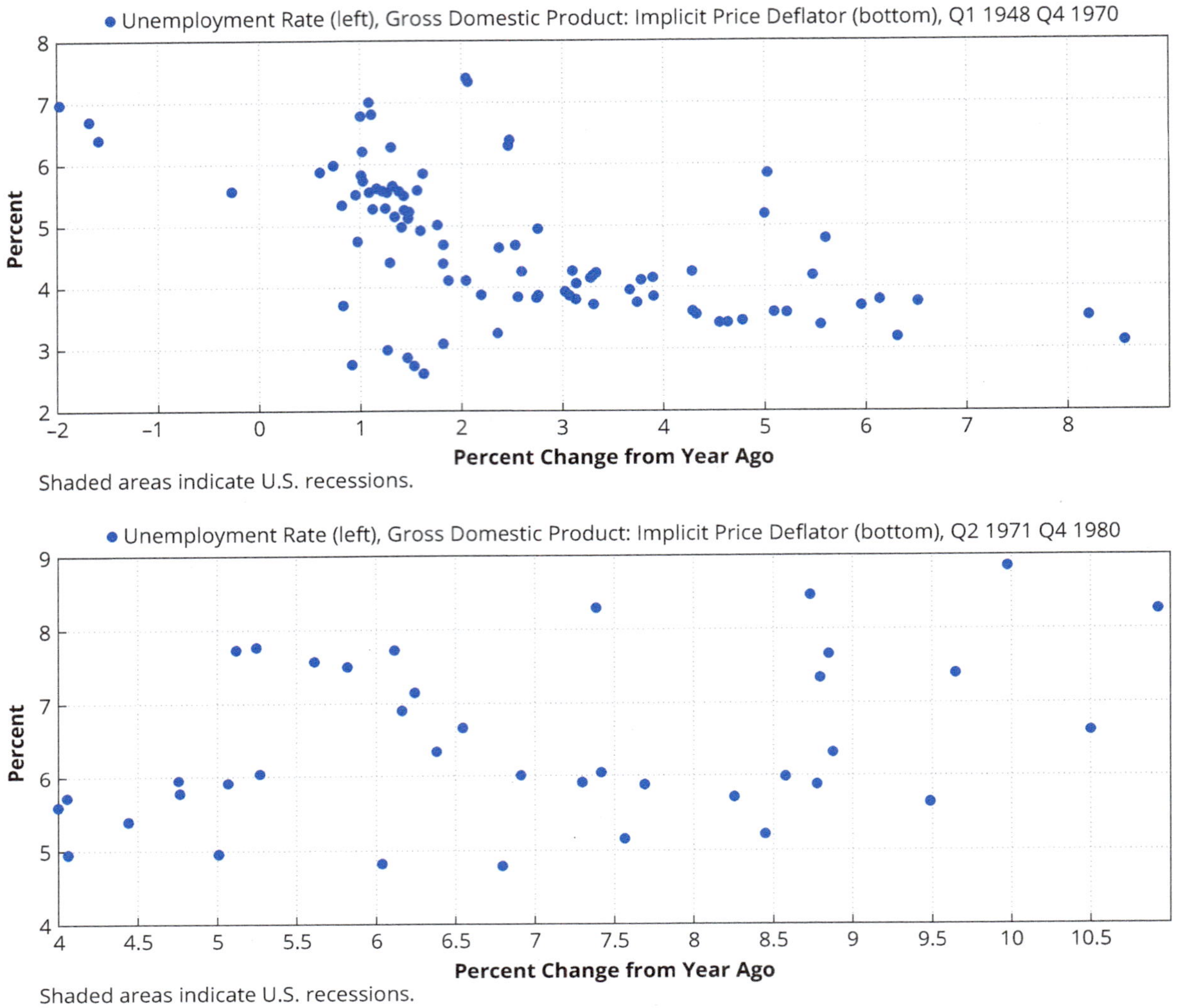

• Unemployment Rate (left), Gross Domestic Product: Implicit Price Deflator (bottom), Q1 1948 Q4 1970

Shaded areas indicate U.S. recessions.

• Unemployment Rate (left), Gross Domestic Product: Implicit Price Deflator (bottom), Q2 1971 Q4 1980

Shaded areas indicate U.S. recessions.

Source: FRED, BEA, BLS, https://fred.stlouisfed.org/graph/?g=Zup6.

policymakers was straightforward: the way to achieve a lower unemployment rate was by accepting higher inflation. If monetary policymakers found it desirable to lower inflation, the only way to do so was accepting a higher unemployment rate.

The bottom panel of Figure 10.9 shows that the negative relationship between the inflation rate and unemployment rate disappeared in the 1970s. The presence of simultaneously high unemployment and inflation during this decade caused many economists to question the stability of the Phillips curve and Keynesian macroeconomics more generally. Economists also recognized that their prevailing theories of business cycles were not always consistent with long-run growth theory (as embodied in something like the Solow model). The combination of the empirical breakdown of the Phillips curve relationship and the perceived theoretical shortcomings of Keynesian theory led economists of the early 1980s to real business cycle theory.

The benchmark **RBC model** assumes an economy with perfectly competitive markets. Individuals are forward-looking and use all available information in making their decisions. In this economy, the classical dichotomy holds. Recall from Chapter 5 that the classical dichotomy posits that real variables are determined independently of nominal variables.

RBC model

A business cycle model with perfectly competitive markets and forward-looking economic agents, where business cycles are the result of short-run variation in TFP and the classical dichotomy holds.

In an economy where the classical dichotomy holds, neither changes in nominal interest rates nor money supply affect output, even in the short run. Despite these arguably implausible assumptions, the early RBC theorists claimed that the model did a good job of explaining business cycle fluctuations. Next, we discuss the source of business cycles in the RBC model and then assess the model's performance against the data.

10-2a Total Factor Productivity as a Source of Business Cycle Variation

A big theme that emerged in Chapters 2 and 3 was that total factor productivity (TFP) explained the long-run economic performance across countries. RBC theorists ask to what extent do quarterly variations in TFP explain business cycles?

To answer this, recall from Chapter 2 that a production function turns inputs into output. Mathematically, this is given by

$$Y_t = A_t F(K_t, L_t), \qquad (4)$$

where K_t is capital, L_t, is labor, Y_t is GDP, and A_t is TFP. For a given level of inputs, higher levels of TFP raise GDP. Data on GDP, capital, and labor are all observable. So, conditional on a specific production function, TFP can be inferred from the other three variables. Solving for TFP in Equation (4) gives

$$A_t = \frac{Y_t}{F(K_t, L_t)}. \qquad (4')$$

If you read Chapter 2, you will recall that the most common production function used by economists is the Cobb–Douglas function, where $F(K_t, L_t) = K_t^a L_t^{1-a}$ and a is a parameter between 0 and 1 that describes how important capital is in the production process relative to labor. Assuming a value of a of 1/3, which is consistent with empirical estimates, we can infer quarterly values of TFP.

Figure 10.10 shows the time series of the growth rates in real GDP and TFP. The correlation between the series is quite high, at about 0.85. It appears that recessions are periods of low TFP growth and expansions are times of high TFP growth. This is broadly consistent with the RBC view that business cycles are caused by fluctuations in TFP.

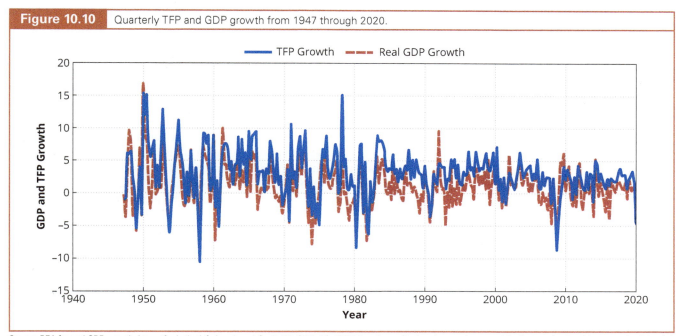

Figure 10.10 Quarterly TFP and GDP growth from 1947 through 2020.

Source: BEA for real GDP growth, https://fred.stlouisfed.org/graph/?g=Yd2B, SF Fed for TFP, https://www.frbsf.org/economic-research/indicators-data/total-factor-productivity-tfp/.

If the economy is well described by the RBC model, the implications are significant. First, since there are no market failures in the RBC model, the government need not intervene during recessions. Indeed, any intervention would make things worse. RBC theorists acknowledge that recessions aren't pleasant, but the government doesn't control TFP so there is nothing for them to do. Second, if the classical dichotomy holds, then monetary policy is irrelevant. Growth in the money supply would translate one-for-one to growth in prices, which all businesses and individuals would perfectly anticipate. According to the RBC model, it wouldn't matter if the Fed chair were Jerome Powell, Janet Yellen, or a random person, real quantities would be independent of nominal quantities.

These are provocative conclusions, and they are difficult to reconcile with economist's traditional thinking about business cycles. It turns out there are substantive critiques of the RBC model that call into question its conclusions. In the next several chapters, we will explore alternatives to the RBC model.

10-2b Critiques of the RBC Model

In Chapters 2, 3, and 4, we equated TFP with an economy's stock of ideas or technology. TFP tells us how efficiently the economy can transform inputs into output. Modern agriculture techniques and fertilizers have increased the output of crops per acre. Modern logistical techniques ensure prompt shipping of merchandise at minimal cost. Computers have increased in processing capability and memory, while their price has decreased. These are all examples of improvements in technology or in the stock of ideas.

Taken literally, RBC theory suggests that recessions are times when technology, or the stock of ideas, goes down. Is that plausible? Do people just forget how to make stuff during recessions? Likely not. If recessions were associated with declines in knowledge, we would probably read about it in the news. Thus, what we measure as declines in TFP may very well be capturing something besides a decline in technology or ideas.

The measurement issue also leads into another critique of the RBC model, namely that the effective quantity of capital and labor are difficult to measure at business cycle frequencies. An example might help. Suppose a construction company owns 10 bulldozers and uses all of them in producing output. In the next quarter, the company only uses seven bulldozers and output declines. From a measurement perspective, the number of bulldozers is the same in both quarters and output is lower in the second quarter. If that's all the information we had, we would infer that TFP declined. But that may not have happened. Perhaps mortgage rates shot up, causing people to demand fewer new homes and construction companies to build fewer. In this case, underutilization of capital (bulldozers) and the consecutive decline in output (new homes) would be coming from a spike in mortgage interest rates, not a decline in TFP.

Economists have made some progress toward measuring utilization-adjusted TFP.[8] The Federal Reserve Bank of San Francisco regularly updates the utilization-adjusted series, which goes back to 1948. Figure 10.11 shows that the correlation between real GDP growth and utilization-adjusted TFP growth is much weaker than the correlation between real GDP growth and standard TFP growth. This implies that the correlation between raw TFP growth and real GDP growth comes from mismeasurement of inputs rather than fluctuations in true technology.

Finally, even though economics is full of counterintuitive results (who would have guessed rent control can hurt renters!), the claim that recessions are caused by declines in technology is not plausible. Perhaps this was true historically. When a flood hit an agricultural economy, driving down crop output, it wouldn't be much of a stretch to equate "weather shocks" to "technology shocks." Or when competing civilizations would go to war, perhaps knowledge either written down or embodied in the minds of people who died in battle would cause sustained declines in the base of technological know-how. But it's hard to imagine that the Great Depression, with its massive number of bank failures and 25 percent unemployment, was caused by a decrease in technology. A more plausible theory would involve some sort of failure in financial intermediation and include a role for monetary policy. These mechanisms, by construction, are omitted from the RBC model.

---

[8]Basu, Susanto, John Fernald, and Miles Kimball. 2006. "Are Technology Improvements Contractionary?" *American Economic Review*, 96(5): 1418–1448.

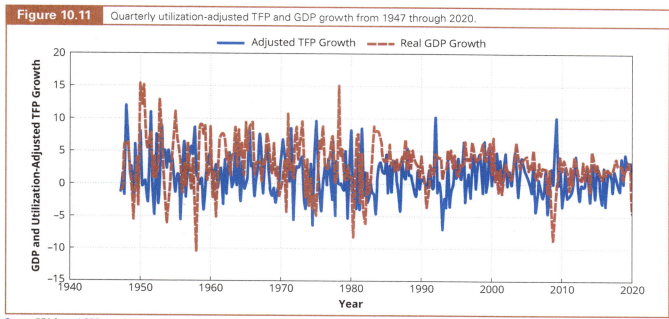

Figure 10.11 Quarterly utilization-adjusted TFP and GDP growth from 1947 through 2020.

Source: BEA for real GDP growth, https://fred.stlouisfed.org/graph/?g=Yd2B, SF Fed for TFP, https://www.frbsf.org/economic-research/indicators-data/total-factor-productivity-tfp/.

10-2c What Does the RBC Model Teach Us?

Even though the RBC model is not a good description of the economy in the short run, it does contain important lessons. First, RBC imposes consistency in the analysis of economic growth and business cycles. We learned in Chapters 2, 3, and 4 that economists study long-run economic performance through the lens of an aggregate production function. From the aggregate production function, we inferred that GDP differences across countries and over time are explained by differences in TFP. RBC theory takes the same aggregate production function and asks if TFP can explain business cycles. Even if the answer is no, a unified analysis of the economy in the short and long run is useful. Absent a unified analysis, economists must decide when to switch from the short-run model to the long-run model and how that transition would work exactly.

Second, by construction, there are no market failures in the RBC model. Through expansions and recessions, the levels of labor, capital, and output are all efficient. In other words, the level of output in the RBC model exactly matches our definition of potential output. Since we have good reason to believe that the actual economy is not always operating efficiently, monetary and fiscal policy can be used in such a way as to minimize the difference between actual and potential output. In this way, the RBC model is still useful for policy analysis.

✓ Knowledge Check 10-2

Suppose the aggregate production function is

$$Y_t = A_t(u_t K_t)^a L_t^{1-a},$$

where u_t is a measure of capital utilization. If you have data on GDP, capital, labor, and capital utilization, you can infer the correct level of TFP given by

$$A_t = \frac{Y_t}{(u_t K_t)^a L_t^{1-a}}.$$

However, without data on capital utilization, you would wrongly infer that TFP is

$$\widetilde{A}_t = \frac{Y_t}{K_t^a L_t^{1-a}}.$$

262 Part 3 Business Cycles

Assuming $a = \frac{1}{3}$, fill in the missing values of the following table and comment how true TFP and mismeasured TFP comove with GDP. What is driving the differences in comovement?

Y_t	K_t	L_t	u_t	A_t	$\widetilde{A}_t$
10	5	5	1		
12	5	5	2		
8	5	5	0.5		

Answers are at the end of the chapter.

Application 10.1

The Welfare Costs of Business Cycles

How costly are business cycles? Or, to rephrase, how much consumption would people be willing to sacrifice to eliminate all cyclical variations in GDP? Some economists have estimated that the number is trivially small, perhaps less than one-tenth of 1 percent of consumption.[9] The idea is that consumption at the aggregate level doesn't fall that much even during large recessions. Consumption only dropped about 1 percent during the Great Recession. The drop in consumption was more severe during the brief recession during the Covid-19 pandemic, but it quickly recovered. More generally, we have seen that the cyclical volatility of consumption is smaller than in GDP. Does it follow that the welfare costs of business cycles are that small?

One thing to keep in mind is that aggregate consumption is a function of fiscal and monetary policy. If fiscal and monetary policy reduces the volatility of output and consumption, then the welfare costs of business cycles absent these policies would be more severe. Referring again to the Great Depression, the money supply collapsed, and aggregate consumption fell by more than 40 percent. Could monetary policy have been conducted in such a way as to reduce the fall in GDP and consumption? Economic historians think so.[10] Thus, the lessons learned during the Great Depression have helped policy reduce the cost of business cycles.

It's also not clear if the volatility of aggregate consumption is a good measure of the welfare cost of business cycles for everyone in the economy. For instance, unemployment rates are more volatile for workers with fewer years of education, and that makes business cycles costlier for them. At the same time, many of the richest people in the economy derive a lot of their income from capital gains and dividends coming from investments in the stock market. To the extent that stock returns are positively correlated with cyclical GDP, business cycles will be costlier for wealthier people.

To summarize, in considering the welfare costs of business cycles, we need to recognize the large role already played by fiscal and monetary policy. Moreover, the costs of business cycles are distributed unevenly across the population, meaning that the welfare costs for the average person will not well represent the welfare cost for most people.

[9]Lucas, Robert E., Jr. 2003. "Macroeconomic Priorities." *American Economic Review*, 93(1): 1–14.
[10]Friedman, Milton and Anna Jacobson Schwartz. 2008. "The Great Contraction." *Princeton University Press*.

Chapter Summary

- Real GDP consistently trends up over time. The movements around GDP's trend is called the *business cycle*.

- Non-stationary data series have a consistent trend up or down over time. These series can be decomposed into a trend component and a cyclical component.

- Real GDP was significantly more volatile from 1947 through 1983 than after 1984. This later period has come to be known as the *Great Moderation*.

- Consumption and investment comove strongly with real GDP over the business cycle. Consumption is less volatile than real GDP and investment is more volatile.

- Unemployment is strongly negatively correlated with real GDP, meaning that recessions are usually times of high unemployment.

- Measured wages are weakly correlated with real GDP over the business cycle. Some of this is due to the fact that low-wage workers disproportionately leave employment during business cycle downturns, thereby changing the composition of the employed population.

- Potential GDP is the amount of output the economy could produce if all of the factors of production (such as labor, capital, and raw materials) were used efficiently. Potential GDP is a theoretical construct, which differentiates it from a statistical construct, like trend GDP. Potential GDP is notoriously difficult to measure.

- The real business cycle (RBC) model emerged after the stagflation period of the 1970s and the perceived theoretical shortcomings of conventional Keynesian macroeconomics.

Chapter 10 Introduction to Business Cycles 263

- The RBC model assumes that the economy always operates efficiently, meaning that GDP in the RBC model is a measure of potential GDP. The RBC model also assumes that people are forward looking and that variation in TFP is the source of business cycles.

- In the data, there is strong comovement between TFP and real GDP growth over the business cycle, which would seem to be a strength for the RBC model. However, a large part of this comovement can be attributed to mismeasurement of TFP. The correlation between real GDP growth and correctly measured TFP growth is significantly weaker, which casts doubt on the RBC model.

- Even though the RBC model does not give a good description of the economy in the short run, it is still useful in providing a unified framework for analyzing economic growth and business cycles. The RBC model also provides a measure of potential GDP which is useful in guiding economic policymakers.

Key Terms

Recession, 249
Business cycle, 249
Non-stationary data series, 249
Stationary data series, 249
Statistical decomposition, 252
Volatility, 252

Comovement, 252
Stagflation, 254
Automatic stabilizer, 256
Potential GDP, 257
Phillips curve, 257
RBC model, 258

Questions for Review

1. If one is interested in analyzing business cycles, why is it necessary to remove trends when dealing with non-stationary data?

2. What is the Great Moderation, and what do economists attribute it to?

3. Explain the difference between trend GDP and potential GDP.

4. Can recessions ever be efficient? Explain.

5. How do investment and consumption comove with real GDP over the business cycle? Are the movements consistent with consumption–savings theory?

6. What is the role for monetary policy in the real business cycle model?

7. Do cyclical movements in TFP explain cyclical movements in real GDP?

8. Is the RBC model useful for economic policy in the real world? Explain.

Problems

10.1 Suppose you are an economist at the Federal Reserve and your job is to calculate the output gap—defined as the difference between actual GDP and potential GDP. Assume that trend GDP increases at $250 billion per quarter. Fill in the missing table entries below.

Quarter	Actual	Potential	Trend	Cycle	Output gap
t	$1,000	$1,000	$1,000	$0	$0
$t+1$	$1,200	$1,100			
$t+2$	$1,475	$1,700			
$t+3$	$1,800	$2,000			

10.2 This question investigates composition bias more thoroughly. Imagine that there are two types of workers in the economy, low skilled and high skilled. The number of each workers for each skill type as well as their wage is shown below for periods t and $t+1$.

	High skill		Low skill	
	# Employees	Wage	# Employees	Wage
t	1,000	$50	3,000	$20
$t+1$	975	$45	1,500	$18

a. Compute the average wage in period t defined as follows:

$$w_t = \frac{E_{HS,t} w_{HS,t} + E_{LS,t} w_{LS,t}}{E_{HS,t} + E_{LS,t}},$$

where E_{HS} and E_{LS} are the employment levels of the high and low skilled. Also, w_{HS} and w_{LS} are the wages of the high and low skilled.

b. Suppose the economy falls into a recession during period $t+1$. Compute the average wage,

$$w_{t+1} = \frac{E_{HS,t+1} w_{HS,t+1} + E_{LS,t+1} w_{LS,t+1}}{E_{HS,t+1} + E_{LS,t+1}}.$$

How is it possible that the average wage increases despite the wage of each type of worker decreasing?

c. Now compute the average wage in period $t+1$, defined as

$$\widetilde{w}_{t+1} = \frac{E_{HS,t} w_{HS,t+1} + E_{LS,t} w_{LS,t+1}}{E_{HS,t} + E_{LS,t}}.$$

This measure of the average wage corrects for the role of compositional changes in the employment pool over the two periods. Discuss the role of composition bias in your answer from part b.

Knowledge Check 10-1 Answer

The first step is calculating the values for the trend column. Since consumption is expected to grow $100 per year, then it grows $25 per quarter on average. Therefore, trend consumption increases by $25 every quarter. The cyclical component in period $t + 1$ is

$$Consumption_{cycle, t+1} = Consumption_{t+1} - Consumption_{trend, t+1}$$
$$= \$5,030 - \$5,025 = \$5.$$

The trend component in period $t + 2$ is $5,050. Consumption is the sum of the trend and cyclical components, or

$$Consumption_{t+2} = Consumption_{trend, t+2} + Consumption_{cycle, t+2}$$
$$= \$5,050 + \$10 = \$5,060.$$

The rest of the table is filled out below.

Period	Consumption	Trend	Cycle
t	$5,000	$5,000	$0
$t + 1$	$5,030	$5,025	$5
$t + 2$	$5,060	$5,050	$10
$t + 3$	$5,090	$5,075	$15
$t + 4$	$5,095	$5,100	−$5
$t + 5$	$5,115	$5,125	−$10

Knowledge Check 10-2 Answer

Actual and mismeasured TFP in the first row is

$$A_t = \frac{10}{(1 \times 5)^{1/3} 5^{2/3}} = 2,$$

$$\tilde{A}_t = \frac{10}{5^{1/3} 5^{2/3}} = 2.$$

For the second row, actual and mismeasured TFP are

$$A_t = \frac{12}{(2 \times 5)^{1/3} 5^{2/3}} = 1.91,$$

$$\tilde{A}_t = \frac{10}{5^{1/3} 5^{2/3}} = 2.4.$$

For the third row, actual and mismeasured TFP are

$$A_t = \frac{8}{(0.5 \times 5)^{1/3} 5^{2/3}} = 2.02,$$

$$\tilde{A}_t = \frac{8}{5^{1/3} 5^{2/3}} = 1.6.$$

Actual TFP comoves negatively (albeit weakly) with output. Mismeasured TFP, which doesn't account for capital utilization, comoves positively with output. Utilization comoves positively with GDP. Omitting utilization from the TFP calculation makes it look like TFP and GDP move together when it's really utilization and GDP that move together.

Y_t	K_t	L_t	u_t	A_t	$\tilde{A}_t$
10	5	5	1	2	2
12	5	5	2	1.91	2.4
8	5	5	0.5	2.02	1.6

Chapter 11

The IS–MP Model

Learning Objectives

11.1 Define the IS and MP curves.

11.2 Derive the IS curve graphically and algebraically.

11.3 Compare and contrast an interest rate targeting rule to a money supply rule.

11.4 Perform comparative statics in the IS–MP model.

11.5 Use the IS–MP model to explain the 2007–2009 financial crisis and the Great Recession.

Every six weeks, the Federal Reserve Open Market Committee meets to discuss the state of the economy and whether to adjust the federal funds rate. Stock market traders, mortgage bankers, and economics journalists anxiously wait for the Fed's decision because an unexpected move in interest rates can cause large changes in wealth. The ritual of waiting for the Fed was probably at its most creative (or paranoid, depending on your perspective) with the "Greenspan Briefcase Indicator" invented in the late 1990s by CNBC.[1] The idea was that if Federal Reserve chairman Alan Greenspan physically carried a thick briefcase, then the Fed was more likely to change rates. If Greenspan traveled lightly (his briefcase looked thin), then the rate would not change much. Even in today's economy, Fed watchers scrutinize the Fed's statements and read over the minutes from the meetings to get clues about where monetary policy might be headed.

The classical dichotomy predicts that real variables are determined independently of nominal variables. Earlier in the book, you learned that most economists subscribe to the doctrine of the classical dichotomy in the long run. From this perspective, Fed policy might not matter much one way or the other over time. In the short run, however, Fed policy affects the level of real GDP and real interest rates. Chapters 11 and 12 deal with the simultaneous determination of output, interest rates, and inflation in the short run. This chapter discusses the demand side of the economy through the lens of the IS–MP model. IS stands for "investment–savings" and MP stands for "monetary policy." The model leverages what you learned about the market of savings and investment in Chapter 6 to determine equilibrium output and interest rates, taking expected inflation as given. In Chapter 12, we combine the IS–MP model with the economy's aggregate supply curve to simultaneously determine output, interest rates, and the inflation rate.

11-1 The IS Curve

We begin by studying the IS side of the model. Recall that, in a closed economy, one way of writing GDP is through the expenditure equation, or

$$Y_t = C_t + I_t + G_t, \tag{1}$$

---

[1] Jacob M. Schlesinger. "That Amazing Alan Greenspan: Moving Furniture, Moving Markets." *The Wall Street Journal*, November 5, 1998.

265

where Y_t is output, C_t is consumption, I_t is investment, and G_t is government spending. All these variables are expressed in real (constant) dollar terms. You learned the microeconomics behind the consumption and investment demand functions in Chapter 6. We start by reviewing those and then formally define the investment and savings curve, the so-called IS curve. The IS curve shows the relationship between the interest rate and the level of output in the market for goods and services.

11-1a The Components of the IS Curve

Recall from Chapter 6 that forward-looking individuals maximize their well-being by making consumption a function of lifetime disposable income. By and large, college students bank on a higher income in the future than when they are in school. Because of this, many college students borrow money to pay for college tuition as well as living expenses. Through borrowing, college students are essentially bringing some future income into the present. By similar logic, workers in the middle of their career save for retirement. They rationally anticipate a day when their income will be lower and plan accordingly. When retirement comes, a person's income will drop, but their consumption need not, provided they saved enough.

A typical consumption–income profile might look similar to Figure 11.1. Young college students earn little to no income for four years. Upon graduation, the person starts to earn income, and, because they continue to accumulate skills and experience, their income increases as they age. At age 65, the person retires and income goes to zero. While income changes over the lifecycle, consumption stays constant. The reason is that forward-looking people anticipate their future earnings. Since people prefer smooth consumption profiles to volatile ones: the person borrows during the early part of the lifecycle and then saves throughout most of their career. Once the person hits retirement, those savings get drawn down until age T, when the person dies.

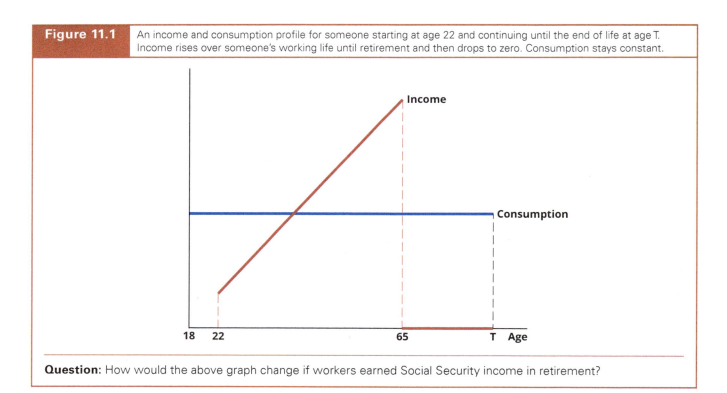

Figure 11.1 An income and consumption profile for someone starting at age 22 and continuing until the end of life at age T. Income rises over someone's working life until retirement and then drops to zero. Consumption stays constant.

Question: How would the above graph change if workers earned Social Security income in retirement?

There are many implications from the lifecycle consumption model. First, an increase in current-period income will cause consumption and savings to increase. In other words, the person will smooth the increase in income over their life cycle. A second implication is that an increase in future income will cause consumption to increase today. When future income goes up, lifetime income goes up. Since consumption is a function of lifetime income, an increase in future income causes consumption to go up. Third, consumption is more responsive to permanent changes in income than to one-time changes. A one-time increase in income, say of $1,000, will be smoothed over the entire lifecycle, whereas if income goes up by $1,000 every year, then annual consumption can rise by the full $1,000 this and every subsequent year.

In addition to current and future income, consumption also depends on the real interest rate. If the real interest rate rises from 5 percent to 10 percent, saving looks a lot more attractive and borrowing looks less attractive. Thus, an increase in real interest rates reduces consumption.

The consumption function is summarized mathematically by the equation

$$C_t = C(Y_t - T_t, Y_{t+1} - T_{t+1}, r_t). \tag{2}$$

Disposable income—that is, income minus taxes—in period t is given by $Y_t - T_t$. Future disposable income is $Y_{t+1} - T_{t+1}$, and the real interest rate is r_t. To simplify things, we assume that the government runs a balanced budget, meaning that $T_t = G_t$. Provided Ricardian equivalence (discussed in Chapter 9) holds, this assumption is without consequence. We can then write Equation (2) as

$$C_t = C(Y_t - G_t, Y_{t+1} - G_{t+1}, r_t). \tag{2'}$$

The investment demand curve comes from the profit maximizing decisions of firms. Because investment is a decision about the future stock of capital, it is inherently forward looking. A business deciding whether it is profitable to spend months retooling its software must think about future market conditions rather than current ones. We also assume that the investment demand curve is a negative function of the risk-adjusted real interest rate, $r_t + f_t$. The higher the interest rate, the more expensive it is for firms to borrow. The f_t variable can be thought of as a risk premium. Households save in a bank and get a return of r_t, and banks lend to businesses. Since lending to businesses is risky, banks are compensated for taking the risk. Mathematically, the investment demand curve is

$$I_t = I(r_t + f_t, A_{t+1}). \tag{3}$$

The A_{t+1} term represents future productivity or, more precisely, total factor productivity (TFP). Recall that TFP encapsulates how efficiently firms use capital and labor. Equation (3) embodies the assumption that firms are forward looking. Holding $r_t + f_t$ constant, if firms expect future productivity to be higher tomorrow, they will invest more today.

Finally, in Chapter 6, you learned that the resource constraint, Equation (1), could be rewritten as

$$Y_t - C_t - G_t = I_t. \tag{4}$$

The left-hand side, $Y_t - C_t - G_t$, is total savings. An equivalent way of writing Equation (4) is

$$(Y_t - C_t - T_t) + (T_t - G_t) = I_t, \tag{4'}$$

where T_t is taxes. Equation (4') shows that total savings is the sum of private savings, $(Y_t - C_t - T_t)$, and public savings, $(T_t - G_t)$. Because Equations (4) and (4') are equivalent, we will usually stick with Equation (4), as it is simpler, and only consider (4') in the case of deficit-financed government spending.

With these pieces in place, we are ready to formally define the IS curve. IS stands for *investment–savings,* so it's not surprising that the definition of the IS curve involves equilibrium in the market for savings and investment The **IS curve** is the set of (r_t, Y_t) pairs such that the savings and investment market is in equilibrium.

IS curve
The set of (r_t, Y_t) pairs such that the savings and investment market is in equilibrium.

11-1b Deriving the IS Curve Graphically

Figure 11.2 shows the market for savings and investment. The real interest rate is on the vertical axis and savings and investment are drawn on the horizontal axis. Since savings and investment are equal in equilibrium, we adopt the same convention as Chapter 6 and label the horizontal axis with only investment. Because consumption is a negative function of the real interest rate, the supply of savings slopes upward. Since investment demand is a negative function of the real interest rate, the investment demand curve slopes downward. Savings supply and investment demand cross at the equilibrium real interest rate, r_t^*.

To derive the IS curve, start with a certain level of income, $Y_{0,t}$. The equilibrium real interest rate must equate savings supply with investment demand, or

$$Y_{0,t} - C(Y_{0,t} - G_t, Y_{t+1} - G_{t+1}, r_t) - G_t = I(r_t + f_t, A_{t+1}).$$

Define the real interest rate that solves this equation, $r_{0,t}$. So $(r_{0,t}, Y_{0,t})$ is an equilibrium in the savings and investment market. Figure 11.3 shows two panels. The first panel is the savings and investment market. The savings supply curve with a level of income of $Y_{0,t}$ crosses the investment demand curve at $r_{0,t}$. Tracing over horizontally from $r_{0,t}$ to the panel on the right gives our first equilibrium pair of income and the real interest rate.

Now suppose the level of income rises to $Y_{1,t}$. The higher level of income raises consumption, but because individuals desire to smooth consumption over their lifetime, consumption does not rise as much as income. In other words, the desire to smooth consumption over the lifecycle implies that the **marginal propensity to consume (MPC)**, or the dollar increase in consumption per dollar increase in income, is less than one. Since income rises by more than consumption and government spending stays constant, the savings supply curve shifts to the right and the equilibrium real interest rates falls to $r_{1,t}$. Thus, the second equilibrium pair in the savings and investment market is $(r_{1,t}, Y_{1,t})$, which can be traced over to the panel on the right.

The symmetric logic applies for a level of income $Y_{2,t} < Y_{0,t}$. The decrease in income shifts savings supply to the left, raising the real interest rate to $r_{2,t}$. Connecting the three points in the panel on the right shows that the IS curve slopes downward. A higher level

Marginal propensity to consume (MPC)
The change in consumption per dollar change in current-period income.

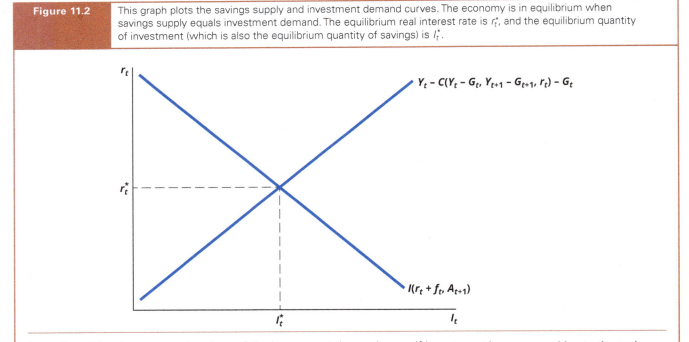

Figure 11.2 This graph plots the savings supply and investment demand curves. The economy is in equilibrium when savings supply equals investment demand. The equilibrium real interest rate is r_t^*, and the equilibrium quantity of investment (which is also the equilibrium quantity of savings) is I_t^*.

Question: What happens to the slope of the investment demand curve if investment is more sensitive to the real interest rate?

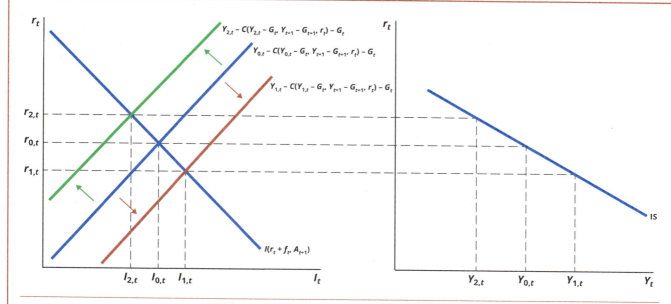

Figure 11.3 The derivation of the IS curve starts at a point $(r_{0,t}, Y_{0,t})$. An increase in income to $Y_{1,t}$ shifts savings supply to the right and lowers the equilibrium real interest rate to $r_{1,t}$. A decrease in income to $Y_{2,t}$ increases the equilibrium real interest rate to $r_{2,t}$. The set of (r_t, Y_t) pairs consistent with equilibrium in the market for savings and investment is drawn on the right.

Question: What happens to the slope of the IS curve as the MPC goes up?

of income is associated with a lower real interest rate. The economic mechanism can be summarized by:

$$\Uparrow \text{income} \Rightarrow \Uparrow \text{savings supply} \Rightarrow \Downarrow \text{real interest rate.}$$

Before discussing what shifts the IS curve, it's important to discuss what *doesn't* shift the IS curve. Recall from your principles of microeconomics class that a change in the price of a product causes a movement along the demand curve, not a shift in the demand curve. Similar logic applies to the IS curve. Changes in the real interest rate cause movements along the IS curve, rather than shifts in the IS curve.

✓ Knowledge Check 11-1

How does the MPC affect the slope of the IS curve? To answer this, derive one IS curve with a low MPC and another IS curve with a large MPC. Explain the economic intuition for the different slopes of the IS curve.

Answers are at the end of the chapter.

11-2 The Monetary Policy Rule

Responding to an unexpected surge in inflation coming out of the Covid-19 pandemic, the Federal Reserve increased the federal funds rate from effectively 0 percent in April of 2022 to 4 percent by year's end. How does the Fed decide to set interest rates, and what are the economic effects of these interest rate changes? To answer these questions, we combine the IS curve with the monetary policy curve, the so-called **MP curve**, which defines how monetary policy makers set interest rates.

MP curve
A graphical representation of how monetary policymakers set interest rates.

11-2a The MP Curve

There are many different interest rates in the world. You might pay one interest rate on a credit card, a different one on a student loan, and earn a third interest rate on money in a savings account. Before jumping into how the Fed chooses an interest rate, it helps to clarify which interest rate we are talking about.

The Fed targets the federal funds rate, or the rate banks charge to each other for overnight loans. The federal funds rate is what you read about in the newspaper when it is announced "The Fed lowers (or raises) interest rates." The federal funds rate is determined in the market for overnight bank lending, rather than set by decree by the Fed. To achieve the targeted federal funds rate, the Fed directly sets the interest rate on reserves that banks deposit at the Fed. Because the opportunity cost to a bank of lending to another bank is what they could get by depositing their reserves at the Fed, the interest rate on reserves and the federal funds rate track each other very closely, as shown in Figure 11.4. Chapter 14 discusses the Federal Reserve's balance sheet and market interventions in more detail.

The federal funds rate is a nominal interest rate. In Chapter 6, we distinguished between the real interest rate, which is the rate of return in terms of goods and services, and the nominal interest rate, which is the rate of return in dollars. Households and firms base their decisions on the real interest rate. The two interest rates are connected through the Fisher equation, which says that the real interest rate, r_t, equals the nominal interest rate, i_t, minus expected inflation, π^e. Mathematically, this is given by

$$r_t = i_t - \pi^e. \tag{5}$$

Think about the Fisher equation from the perspective of an individual saver. If the saver deposits $100 and the nominal interest rate is 5 percent, by the end of the year, the saver will have $105 with certainty. What is uncertain is inflation. If prices grow by 2 percent, then the real return is 3 percent. If prices grow by 6 percent, then the real return is −1 percent. In other words, if inflation exceeds the nominal interest rate, the real value of someone's savings—i.e., the real value of the purchasing power of that savings—declines over the course of the year. Again, it is the real interest rate that is relevant for the decision making of individuals and firms.

If the Fed controls a nominal interest rate, but the real interest rate is what people and firms use to make decisions, how does the Fed affect real GDP, unemployment, and so on? In answering this, it helps to distinguish the time horizon we are talking about. In Chapter 5, you learned that the classical dichotomy is a good approximation of the long-run

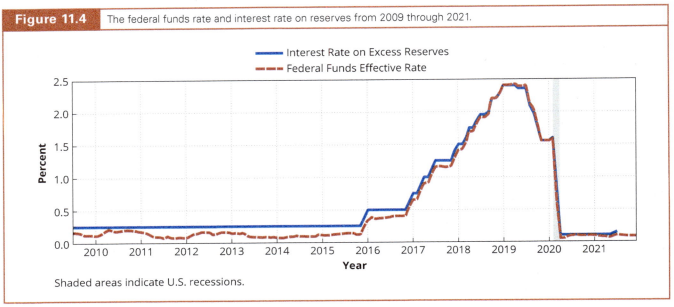

Figure 11.4 The federal funds rate and interest rate on reserves from 2009 through 2021.

Shaded areas indicate U.S. recessions.

Source: FRED and Federal Reserve Board of Governors https://fred.stlouisfed.org/graph/?g=YOdb.

economy. The classical dichotomy says that real variables are determined independently of nominal variables. In the long run, the real interest rate is determined by the economy's marginal product of capital, which is unrelated to the Fed's policies. Through its choice of the growth rate of the money supply (a nominal variable), the Fed can effectively set the economy's long-run inflation rate (another nominal variable).[2]

In the short run, which in practice means a few months, it is a reasonable approximation to assume that inflation expectations are exogenously fixed. It takes time for people, firms, and the Fed to incorporate new information in forming their expectations over the future price level. With inflation expectations fixed in the short run, the Fed effectively controls the real interest rate. Analyzing Equation (5), a one percentage point increase in nominal interest rates, holding expected inflation constant, increases real interest rates by one percentage point. The economic mechanism is summarized by the following:

$$\Uparrow \text{nominal interest rate} \Rightarrow \Uparrow \text{real interest rate}.$$

The MP rule is shown graphically in Figure 11.5. The real interest rate is measured on the vertical axis and real GDP is on the horizontal axis. When the Fed chooses a nominal interest rate, $i_{0,t}$, the real interest rate is given by $r_{0,t} = i_{0,t} - \pi^e$. Thus, the MP curve is a horizontal line at $r_{0,t}$. If the Fed chooses to raise nominal interest rates to $i_{1,t}$, then the real interest rate increases to $r_{1,t} = i_{1,t} - \pi^e$, which shifts the MP curve up.

It is now clear how the Fed influences real interest rates in the short run. A second question you might have is how an interest rate that banks pay each other for overnight lending affects the interest rate on your bank account or mortgage. The **term structure of interest rates** refers to the interest rates on liabilities of different maturities. So, you might compare a one-year U.S. government bond to a 5-year and a 10-year U.S. government bond. The **risk structure of interest rates** refers to the interest rates on liabilities with different risks. For example, U.S. government debt is viewed as less risky than mortgage debt, so interest rates on government debt tend to be lower. Since these riskier and longer-term loans are usually what matter for households and firms (think about taking out a mortgage or a firm issuing long-term debt), the Fed's goal is that these other interest rates change when the fed funds rate changes.

Term structure of interest rates
The pattern of interest rates on liabilities of different maturities.

Risk structure of interest rates
The pattern of interest rates on liabilities of different risks.

Figure 11.5 At MP_0, the Fed sets a nominal interest rate of $i_{0,t}$. The real interest rate is $r_{0,t} = i_{0,t} - \pi^e$. When the Fed moves the nominal interest rate up to $i_{1,t}$, the real interest rate increases to $r_{1,t} = i_{1,t} - \pi^e$. This is reflected by an upward shift in the MP curve.

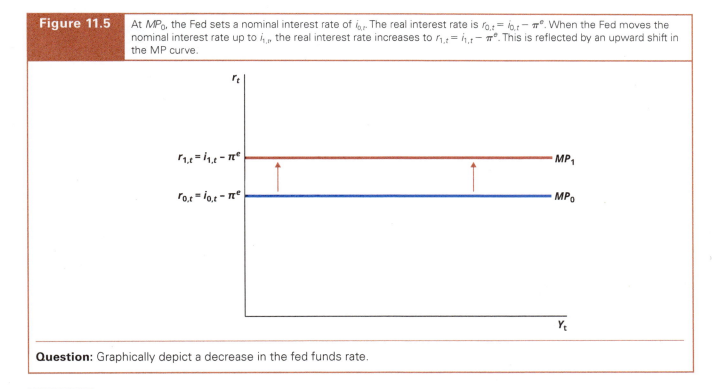

Question: Graphically depict a decrease in the fed funds rate.

---
[2]Even this is a simplification, in that it ignores the fiscal–monetary interactions discussed in Chapter 9.

Figure 11.6 shows that interest rates on bonds of different maturity lengths and risk factors tend to move with the fed funds rate. The top panel shows the fed funds rate along with the interest rates on 5-year and 10-year treasury securities. The bottom panel shows the fed funds rate along with the interest rates on Aaa corporate debt, which is perceived to be the least risky, and Baa corporate debt, which is perceived to be riskier. The interest rates on corporate debt tend to move with the fed funds rate. Also, note that the interest rate on the riskier bonds is higher than the interest rate on safer bonds. This makes sense because investors need to be compensated for the extra risk.

The mechanism through which a change in fed funds rate affects interest rates of different maturities and risk structures is discussed in greater detail in Chapter 15. However, we can explain some of the intuition now. First, note that the risk structure is already built into the savings–investment market. When individuals save, they earn a real return of r_t. When businesses borrow to invest, they pay $r_t + f_t$, with $f_t > 0$ being the risk spread. When

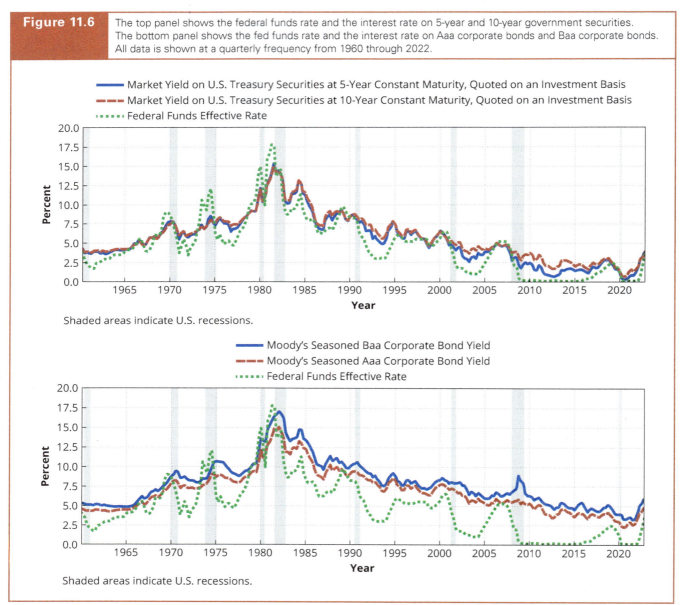

Figure 11.6 The top panel shows the federal funds rate and the interest rate on 5-year and 10-year government securities. The bottom panel shows the fed funds rate and the interest rate on Aaa corporate bonds and Baa corporate bonds. All data is shown at a quarterly frequency from 1960 through 2022.

Source: FRED https://fred.stlouisfed.org/graph/?g=ZdxL (bottom) https://fred.stlouisfed.org/graph/?g=Zdzt (top).

Chapter 11 The IS–MP Model **273**

the Fed lowers r_t, the rate firms borrow at also decreases. So, there is an assumed risk structure in the model. A more advanced model would make f_t endogenous.

While there are not loans of different maturities in the model, the connection between loans of different maturities can be explained as follows. Suppose you are thinking of an investment strategy to follow over the next two years. One option is to buy a bond that pays you back with interest at the end of two years. Another option is to buy a one-year bond that pays you back with interest at the end of the first year and then roll the principle and interest into another one-year bond. If you are to be indifferent between the options as an investor, then the annualized return on the two-year bond must equal the average return on the one-year bonds. So when the Fed lowers the interest rate on short-duration loans, the interest rates on longer-duration loans tend to also fall.

To recap, the Fed targets the federal funds rate, which is the nominal interest rate at which banks lend to each other over a short duration. By assuming that inflation expectations are exogenously fixed in the short run, the Fed effectively controls the real interest rate. Generalizing from the model to the real world shows that the Fed affects the interest rates faced by households, businesses, and the government through a term premium channel and a risk premium channel.

✓ Knowledge Check 11-2

Suppose the Fed follows the interest rate rule:

$$i_t = 3 + 2(\pi_t - 2),$$

where π_t is the realized rate of inflation (note that it is not inflation expectations). For each value of π_t, π^e, and f_t, compute the real interest rate at which households save and firms borrow. Compare how inflation affects the real interest rate versus how inflation expectations affect the real interest rate.

π^e	π_t	f_t	r_t	$r_t + f_t$
2	2	1		
2	3	1		
2	2	2		
3	2	1		
1	1	2		

———————————————————————————— Answers are at the end of the chapter.

11-2b Interest Rate Rules Versus Money Supply Rules

Until 2008, the Federal Reserve did not pay interest on reserves. Instead, the way the Fed targeted interest rates was by changing the money supply through open market operations. Back in Chapter 5, you learned a model of nominal interest rate determination in the money market. It's instructive to review that model in light of the MP rule just discussed. Recall that the demand for real money balances is given by

$$\frac{M_t}{P_t} = M^d(i_t, Y_t). \tag{6}$$

Because someone can hold wealth in the form of money or an interest-bearing asset, the nominal interest rate is the opportunity cost of holding money. We also assumed that the higher one's income, the more money they want to hold to facilitate transactions.

The supply of money is set exogenously by the Fed at $\overline{M}_t$ implying that the supply of real money balances is $\overline{M}_t/P_t$. The intersection between the supply and demand of real money balances determines the nominal interest rate.

Figure 11.7
Lowering the equilibrium nominal interest rate from $i^*_{0,t}$ to $i^*_{1,t}$ requires increasing the money supply from $\overline{M}_{0,t}$ to $\overline{M}_{1,t}$.

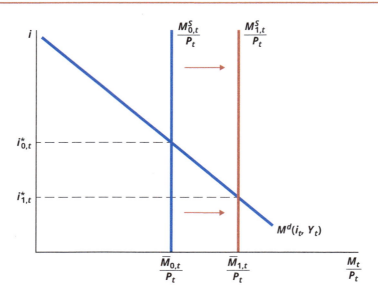

Question: How does an increase in income affect money demand? What has to happen to the money supply if the Fed wants to keep nominal interest rates constant?

Consider the situation depicted in Figure 11.7. The economy starts with an equilibrium nominal interest rate of $i^*_{0,t}$. Suppose that economists at the Federal Reserve come to believe that nominal interest rates need to fall to some new level, $i^*_{1,t}$. Since the Fed only controls the supply of money, rather than the demand, they can increase the supply of money to achieve the desired interest rate. The only way to entice people to hold the larger stock of money is for the nominal interest rate, that is the opportunity cost of holding money, to fall.

Figure 11.7 is an example of the Fed exogenously setting the money supply and allowing the nominal interest rate to adjust endogenously. Alternatively, and the approach we are taking with the MP rule, the Fed can exogenously set the nominal interest rate, and the money supply will adjust endogenously. The point of this discussion, though, is to show that the Fed can choose the money supply or the nominal interest rate, but not both. Application 11.1 discusses some of the factors that go into the Fed's choice of the fed funds rate.

✓ Knowledge Check 11-3

Suppose the money demand curve is

$$\frac{M_t}{P_t} = \frac{Y_t}{i_t}.$$

Assume $P_t = 1$ and $Y_t = 100$. What is the equilibrium level of money supply when the nominal interest rate is $i_t = 5$? Suppose the Fed decides to set it to $i_t = 10$. What is the new value of the money supply?

Answers are at the end of the chapter.

Application 11.1

Rules Versus Discretion and the Taylor Rule

The MP curve describes a monetary policy rule. The Fed gets to set the nominal interest rate. Conditional on exogenously given inflation expectations, the Fisher equation pins down the real interest rate. Although we have called this a "rule," the nominal interest rate is exogenous to the model, so the Fed (or the economics student working with the model) actually has a lot of discretion in setting Fed policy. In thinking about a monetary policy rule, what are some variables that the Fed may want to consider? Is there value of following a rule over discretion? And, finally, is there a rule that accurately predicts the behavior of the Fed?

The Fed has a dual mandate from Congress. One part of the mandate is to achieve price stability. To achieve sets a target inflation rate of 2 percent, the Fed carefully watches the inflation rate prevailing in the economy. Recall from Chapter 5 that there are many different ways to measure inflation, including the percent changes in the CPI, PCE, and GDP deflator. The Fed's preferred measure is the PCE. The Fed also considers at the "core" PCE, which excludes energy and food prices from the inflation calculation. The logic is that food and energy prices are more volatile than other prices so the core PCE is more informative about the persistent changes to inflation. The other part of the Fed's mandate is to promote maximum sustainable employment. In thinking about maximum sustainable employment, the Fed compares actual GDP to potential GDP which, as discussed in Chapter 10, is GDP when all inputs are used efficiently. Maximum sustainable employment is the level of employment consistent with potential GDP. The difference between actual and potential GDP is the output gap.

Given the Fed's dual mandate, you might expect that a monetary policy rule that relates the fed funds rate to inflation and the output gap. In a 1993 paper, Stanford economist John Taylor suggested just such a rule.[3] The aptly named **Taylor rule** specifies the federal funds rate as a linear function of the output gap and inflation:

$$ffr_t = 2 + \pi_t + 0.5(\pi_t - \overline{\pi}_t) + 0.5(Y_t - Y_t^p).$$

The difference between real GDP and potential real GDP, $(Y_t - Y_t^p)$, is the output gap and $\overline{\pi}_t$ is the target inflation rate.[4] The rule says that the Fed should raise the fed funds rate, ffr_t, when inflation is above its target or when output exceeds its potential. Taylor argued 30 years ago that his rule described actual Fed behavior quite well. Figure 11.8 compares the Taylor rule to the fed funds rate. The two series track each other quite closely, with an overall correlation coefficient of about 0.7.

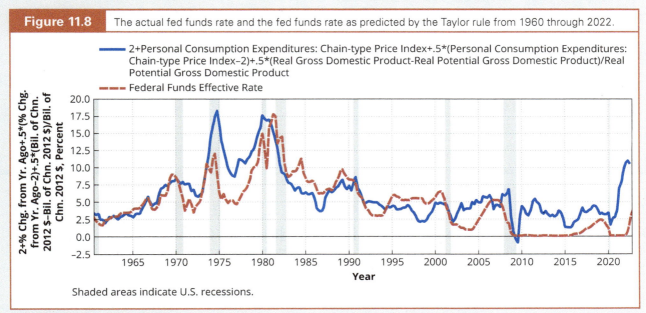

Figure 11.8 The actual fed funds rate and the fed funds rate as predicted by the Taylor rule from 1960 through 2022.

Shaded areas indicate U.S. recessions.

Source: FRED https://fred.stlouisfed.org/graph/?g=YVL2.

[3]Taylor, John. 1993. "Discretion Versus Policy Rules in Practice." *Carnegie-Rochester Conference Series on Public Policy*, 39: 195–214.
[4]Taylor measured potential output with a linear trend, so it was constant over time.

Continues

276 Part 3 Business Cycles

Application 11.1 (Continued)

Three historical episodes deserve special mention. First, the Taylor rule predicted a higher than realized fed funds rate in the mid-1970s. This was a time of high inflation somewhat driven by a surge in the price of oil. In hindsight, the Fed was probably too soft on inflation in the 1970s, and that set up the so-called Volker disinflation of the 1980s. Nominated by President Carter in 1979, Paul Volcker took the helm at the Fed with inflation running over 10 percent annually. Consistent with the Taylor rule, the Volcker Fed raised the fed funds rate to over 15 percent in the early 1980s. By the time Volcker left the Fed in 1987, the inflation rate had declined to under four percent, which is evidence in favor of the Taylor rule.

More recently, and discussed at the end of the next section, the Fed aggressively dropped rates in the mid 2000s in response to the 2007–2008 financial crisis. While the Fed kept the nominal interest rate at zero well past the conclusion of the recession, the Taylor rule predicted that the Fed would have raised the nominal interest rate.

And this gets to the heart of one of the perennial questions in monetary economics: Is the Taylor rule meant to be purely descriptive or also prescriptive? If the Taylor rule is only meant to be descriptive, then the Fed's policy in 2011–2016 could simply be explained by the Taylor Rule not accounting for the complexity of the economic situation during that time period. If the Taylor rule is meant to be prescriptive, then the Fed may have been too slow in raising the fed funds rate. The correct answer is probably nuanced. It's true that the Taylor rule has desirable welfare properties. It stimulates the economy when it is below potential and cools the economy off when it is above potential. At the same time, the period after the financial crisis was really complicated and the Fed was managing a number of new policies. In complicated situations like these, perhaps it is better to incorporate additional variables.

Indeed, in analyzing statements from their meetings, members of the Federal Reserve Open Market Committee almost certainly look at other factors. The statement from December 2022, for instance, cites that the FOMC will look at "public health, labor market conditions, inflation pressures and inflation expectations, and financial and international developments" in assessing the appropriate stance of monetary policy. At the same time, the FOMC says that they are "strongly committed to returning inflation to its 2 percent objective."[5] Based on their statements, it seems like the Fed is committed to a long-run inflation target but takes multiple factors into account when setting interest rates.

The value of looking at multiple factors seems obvious. Why omit potentially relevant information when setting interest rates? For example, if a member of the FOMC thinks that job postings in the leisure and hospitality industry is a leading indicator of overall economic activity, shouldn't that be considered? The downsides to following a strict monetary policy rule seem equally obvious. Rules can be too restrictive in that they ignore relevant information. Rules can be too rigid in that following them can be costly in certain economic conditions.

But rules also come with important benefits. First, if the MP rule is consistently followed, individuals and firms can more accurately form their expectations about policy, which gives them more confidence when making saving and investment decisions. Clearly communicated rules also keep central bankers accountable. If the Fed's *only* goal was to achieve a 2 percent inflation target, it would be easy enough to see if they were achieving it.

There are clearly benefits that come with rules and others that come with discretion. That's probably why the Fed follows a hybrid approach (i.e., selecting a firm rule for the inflation target, but taking in a variety of information when making its decisions). This allows the Fed to pursue less conventional policies during times of economic crisis while also anchoring the expectations about long-run price growth.

[5]Federal Reserve Press Release, December 14, 2002: https://www.federalreserve.gov/monetarypolicy/files/monetary20221214a1.pdf.

Taylor rule
A rule that expresses the federal funds rate as a linear function of the output gap and inflation.

11-3 Solving for Output and the Real Interest Rate in the IS–MP Model

We now have all the building blocks for the IS–MP model summarized by the two equations

$$\text{IS Curve:} \quad Y_t = C(Y_t - G_t, Y_{t+1} - G_{t+1}, r_t) + I(r_t + f_t, A_{t+1}) + G_t,$$

$$\text{MP Curve:} \quad r_t = i_t - \pi^e.$$

The IS curve summarizes the combinations of output and the real interest rate consistent with equilibrium in the market for savings and investment, and the MP curve pins down the Fed's target real interest rate. The intersection of the IS and MP curves, as shown in Figure 11.9, determines the economy's equilibrium real interest rate and GDP. Also, note

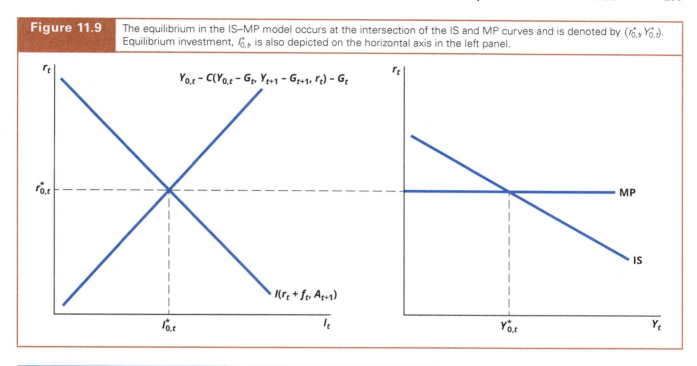

Figure 11.9 The equilibrium in the IS–MP model occurs at the intersection of the IS and MP curves and is denoted by $(r_{0,t}^*, Y_{0,t}^*)$. Equilibrium investment, $I_{0,t}^*$, is also depicted on the horizontal axis in the left panel.

Table 11.1 Summary of the IS–MP Model

Endogenous variables	Exogenous variables	Parameters
Y_t, r_t	$G_t, G_{t+1}, A_{t+1}, Y_{t+1}, f_t, i_t$	π^e

Key Equations:

$Y_t - C(Y_t - G_t, Y_{t+1} - G_{t+1}, r_t) - G_t = I(r_t + f_t, A_{t+1})$	(IS Curve, Eq (4))
$r_t = i_t - \pi^e$	(MP Curve, Eq (7))

that the intersection of savings supply and investment determines the equilibrium quantity of investment.

Table 11.1 contains the model's exogenous variables, endogenous variables, and the parameter π^e. At this point, inflation is an exogenous variable, but when we combine the demand and supply sides together in Chapter 12, inflation will be simultaneously determined with output and real interest rates.

11-3a Comparative Statics

Now that we have the components of the IS–MP model, we can put it to work by analyzing some comparative statics. Assume the economy begins with an equilibrium real interest rate, $r_{0,t}^*$, and real GDP, $Y_{0,t}^*$, and suppose current-period government spending, G_t, increases from $G_{0,t}$ to $G_{1,t}$. Because total savings is $Y_t - C_t - G_t$, an increase in government spending has the direct effect of reducing savings. The increase in government spending also reduces current-period disposable income, $Y_t - G_t$. Because the MPC out of disposable income is less than one, consumption falls, but by less than one-for-one with the rise in government spending. Taken together, we infer that the savings supply curve shifts to the left, as shown by the dotted red line in Figure 11.10. The new real interest rate associated with $Y_{0,t}^*$ is higher than $r_{0,t}^*$, which shifts the IS curve to the right.

Because the Fed hasn't changed nominal interest rates and inflation expectations are fixed, the new equilibrium real interest rate, $r_{1,t}^*$, is identical to the initial equilibrium real interest rate, $r_{1,t}^* = r_{0,t}^*$. The new IS curve intersects the MP curve at $Y_{1,t}^*$, meaning that output rises in equilibrium. This increase in output causes the savings supply curve to shift to the right, from the dotted red line back to the original dark blue line. We know that the final savings supply curve must be identical to the initial savings supply curve because the

For a level of government spending, $G_{0,t}$, the equilibrium in the IS–MP model is given by $(r_{0,t}^*, Y_{0,t}^*)$. When government spending increases to $G_{1,t}$, the savings supply curve shifts to the left. The new real interest rate associated with $Y_{0,t}^*$ is $\tilde{r}_t$. This means that the IS curve shifts to the right. Because the MP curve hasn't shifted, the equilibrium real interest rate stays the same. The new equilibrium is $(r_{1,t}^*, Y_{1,t}^*)$, and the savings supply curve shifts back to its original position.

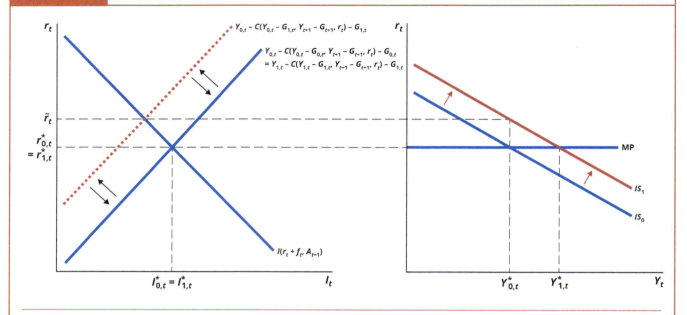

Question: Graphically depict a decrease in G_t.

equilibrium real interest rate hasn't changed. Because the real interest rate hasn't changed, investment doesn't change. Finally, because Y_t and G_t both increase, it looks as though the change in current-period disposable income is ambiguous, which would mean that the change in current-period consumption is ambiguous. It can be shown mathematically that, in equilibrium, Y_t increases one-for-one with G_t, so equilibrium consumption doesn't change.[6]

In summary, an increase in G_t initially shifts the savings supply curve to the left. At the initial level of equilibrium output, the real interest rate rises, shifting the IS curve to the right. Since the Fed keeps the nominal interest rate constant, the real interest rate also stays constant. Equilibrium output rises one-for-one with government spending, and the savings supply shifts back to its original position. Neither consumption nor investment changes.

Next, consider that people in the economy learn that the government plans to increase their spending in the future, G_{t+1}. At a given real interest rate, a higher G_{t+1} reduces future disposable income and causes consumption to fall. At the initial equilibrium level of output, $Y_{0,t}^*$, savings supply shifts to the right, as indicated by the dotted red line in Figure 11.11. The IS curve shifts to the left. Because the MP rule doesn't change, the equilibrium real interest rate stays constant at $r_{1,t}^* = r_{0,t}^*$ and output falls to $Y_{1,t}^*$. This shifts the savings supply line from the dotted red line back to the original. Since the equilibrium real interest rate doesn't change in equilibrium, neither does investment. Since disposable income in the current period and the future are lower, equilibrium consumption falls.

Next, suppose the risk premium, f_t, increases. An increase in the risk premium raises the cost of borrowing, which shifts the investment demand curve to the left. This is shown in the left panel of Figure 11.12. Starting at an initial equilibrium of $(r_{0,t}^*, Y_{0,t}^*)$, a leftward

---

[6] Writing the GDP equation as $Y_t = C(Y_t - G_t, Y_{t+1} - G_{t+1}, r_t) + I_t + G_t$ and taking the total derivative with respect to Y_t and r_t gives $dY_t = MPC \times (dY_t - dG_t) + dG_t$. Solving this equation for $\frac{dY_t}{dG_t}$ gives $\frac{dY_t}{dG_t} = 1$.

| Figure 11.11 | For a level of future government spending, $G_{0,t+1}$, the equilibrium in the IS–MP model is given by $(r^*_{0,t}, Y^*_{0,t})$. When future government spending increases to $G_{1,t+1}$, and holding output is fixed at $Y^*_{0,t}$, the savings supply curve shifts to the right. The new real interest rate associated with $Y^*_{0,t}$ is lower and the IS curve shifts to the left. Because the MP curve hasn't shifted, the equilibrium real interest rate stays the same. The new equilibrium is $(r^*_{1,t}, Y^*_{1,t})$, and the savings supply curve shifts back to its original position. |

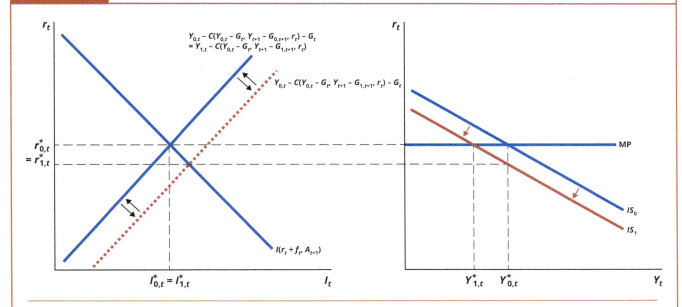

Question: Graphically depict a decrease in G_{t+1}.

| Figure 11.12 | At the initial credit spread, $f_{0,t}$, the equilibrium in the IS–MP model is given by $(r^*_{0,t}, Y^*_{0,t})$. When the credit spread increases to $f_{1,t}$, the investment demand curve shifts to the left. The new real interest rate associated with $Y^*_{0,t}$ is lower, and the IS curve shifts to the left. Since the MP curve hasn't shifted, the equilibrium real interest rate stays the same. Since output is lower, the savings supply curve shifts to the left. The new equilibrium is $(r^*_{1,t}, Y^*_{1,t})$. |

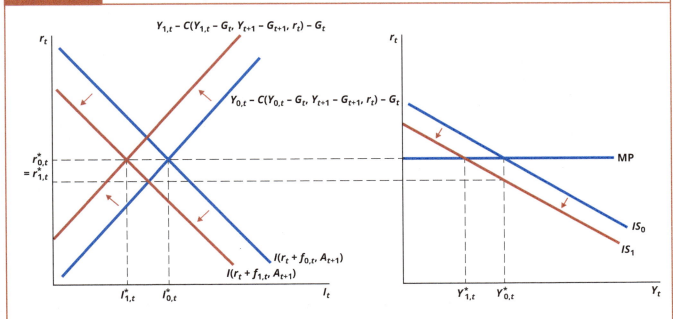

Question: Graphically depict a decrease in f_t.

shift of the investment demand curve causes the real interest rate associated with $Y^*_{0,t}$ to decline, which shifts the IS curve to the left. Since the Fed leaves nominal interest rates constant, the MP rule stays constant at $r^*_{0,t}$. The new equilibrium level of output, found at the intersection of the MP curve with the new IS curve, declines to $Y^*_{1,t}$. With a lower level of output, savings supply shifts left to the point where the new equilibrium real interest rate equals the initial one, $r^*_{1,t} = r^*_{0,t}$. The decline in equilibrium output causes consumption to fall. Although the real interest rate stays constant in equilibrium, the rate at which firms borrow, $r_t + f_t$, increases, which means investment decreases.

Finally, suppose the Fed decides to tighten monetary policy. This is reflected by an increase in the nominal interest rate from $i_{0,t}$ to $i_{1,t}$. Recall that the monetary policy rule comes from the Fisher equation, $r_t = i_t - \pi^e$. An increase in the nominal interest rate holding inflation expectations fixed raises the real interest rate, which shifts the MP curve up as shown in the right panel of Figure 11.13. Output declines from $Y^*_{0,t}$ to $Y^*_{1,t}$. The lower level of output shifts the savings supply curve to the left. Since the real interest rate is higher, equilibrium investment falls. Since disposable income is lower and the real interest rate is higher, consumption decreases.

Thus, contractionary monetary policy raises the real interest rate and lowers output, consumption, and investment. So, at least in the short run, the Fed can cause the economy to slow down. Through similar logic, you can see how the Fed might behave when they want to stimulate output (perhaps, say, in a recession). In that case, the Fed can lower nominal interest rates which transmit to the real side of the economy because inflation expectations are fixed. The real interest rate falls and output rises.

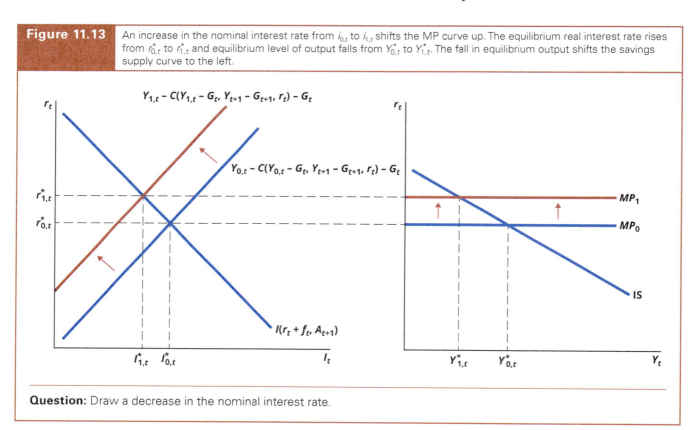

Figure 11.13 An increase in the nominal interest rate from $i_{0,t}$ to $i_{1,t}$ shifts the MP curve up. The equilibrium real interest rate rises from $r^*_{0,t}$ to $r^*_{1,t}$ and equilibrium level of output falls from $Y^*_{0,t}$ to $Y^*_{1,t}$. The fall in equilibrium output shifts the savings supply curve to the left.

Question: Draw a decrease in the nominal interest rate.

✓ Knowledge Check 11-4

Show how a decrease in π^e affects the IS-MP diagram. Describe how all the variables, including consumption and investment, change.

Answers are at the end of the chapter.

Chapter 11 The IS–MP Model · 281

11-3b Solving the IS–MP Model Algebraically

In addition to characterizing the equilibrium of the IS–MP model graphically, we can solve it algebraically, provided specific consumption and investment functions. The algebraic version of the model enables economists to make quantitative predictions about the effects of exogenous variables on endogenous variables. To keep things as simple as possible, assume that consumption and investment demand are linear functions:

$$C_t = a_1(Y_t - G_t) + a_2(Y_{t+1} - G_{t+1}) - a_3 r_t, \tag{7}$$

$$I_t = A_{t+1} - c(r_t + f_t). \tag{8}$$

Consistent with the assumptions of the consumption and investment demand curves, parameters, a_1, a_2, a_3, and c are all positive. Substituting Equations (7) and (8) into the GDP expenditure equation, Equation (1), gives

$$Y_t = a_1(Y_t - G_t) + a_2(Y_{t+1} - G_{t+1}) - a_3 r_t + A_{t+1} - c(r_t + f_t) + G_t.$$

Deriving the IS curve requires writing Y_t as a function of r_t:

$$Y_t(1 - a_1) = a_2(Y_{t+1} - G_{t+1}) - (a_3 + c)r_t + A_{t+1} - cf_t + (1 - a_1)G_t$$

$$\Leftrightarrow Y_t = G_t + \frac{a_2}{1 - a_1}(Y_{t+1} - G_{t+1}) - \frac{c}{1 - a_1}f_t + \frac{1}{1 - a_1}A_{t+1} - \frac{(a_3 + c)}{1 - a_1}r_t. \tag{9}$$

The slope of the IS curve is $-\dfrac{(a_3 + c)}{1 - a_1}r_t$. Increases in current-period government spending, G_t, future income, Y_{t+1}, or future productivity, A_{t+1} raise the level of GDP for any given interest rate. This means that the IS curve shifts to the right. Increases in future-period government spending, G_{t+1}, or the risk premium, f_t, shift the IS curve to the left.

The Fed chooses the nominal interest rate, which must be consistent with the Fisher equation:

$$i_t = r_t + \pi^e. \tag{10}$$

Substituting Equation (10) for r_t in Equation (9) gives

$$Y_t = G_t + \frac{a_2}{1 - a_1}(Y_{t+1} - G_{t+1}) - \frac{c}{1 - a_1}f_t + \frac{1}{1 - a_1}A_{t+1} - \frac{(a_3 + c)}{1 - a_1}r_t.$$

$$\Leftrightarrow Y_t = G_t + \frac{a_2}{1 - a_1}(Y_{t+1} - G_{t+1}) - \frac{c}{1 - a_1}f_t + \frac{1}{1 - a_1}A_{t+1} - \frac{(a_3 + c)}{1 - a_1}(i_t - \pi^e). \tag{11}$$

Everything on the right-hand side of the equation is exogenous or a parameter, meaning that it is determined outside the model. Consistent with the graphical analysis in 11.3a, equilibrium output is increasing in Y_{t+1}, G_t, A_{t+1}, and π^e. Equilibrium output is decreasing in f_t and i_t.

Conditional on values for the parameters, a_1, a_2, a_3, and c, Equation (11) predicts how output changes quantitatively with a change to an exogenous variable. For instance, if the Fed raises the nominal interest rate by one percentage point, Equation (11) predicts that output will decrease by $\dfrac{(a_3 + c)}{1 - a_1}$. A lot of macroeconomics research at the Federal Reserve and other institutions tries to estimate parameters in the IS curve. With precise estimates, monetary policymakers can better gauge the likely effects of monetary policy on output, consumption, and investment.

11-3c The IS–MP Model and the Great Recession

The period between the fourth quarter of 2007 and the second quarter of 2009 has come to be known as the Great Recession. In this section, we show how the events associated with the Great Recession can be mapped into the IS–MP model.

Many mark the waning housing market as the first sign of the Great Recession. Figure 11.14 shows the delinquency rate on mortgages measured on the right axis and the Case–Shiller home price index on the left axis. Home prices peaked in the third quarter of 2006, and shortly thereafter delinquency started to increase. By 2009, houses had dropped more than 20 percent from their peak and delinquency rates had tripled. How did the collapse in home prices affect homeowners? And how did the problems in the housing market spill over to the rest of the economy?

In about 2007, many macroeconomists didn't suspect that the fall in home prices would spill over to the rest of the economy. In their statement in March 2007, or about a year after the peak in housing prices, the Federal Reserve Open Market Committee acknowledged that "[r]ecent indicators have been mixed and the adjustment in the housing sector is ongoing." But they still arrived at the conclusion that "the economy seems likely to continue to expand at a moderate pace over the coming quarters." The Fed wasn't alone in thinking that a small decline in home prices would have small effects on the macroeconomy more broadly. Yet, developments in the financial market caused the softening of the housing market to spill over to the rest of the economy.

In the years preceding the crisis, it became popular for mortgage originators, that is the financial institutions that issue the mortgage, to sell the mortgage to another financial institution, such as a bigger bank. These bigger banks would pool together thousands of mortgages, split them into much smaller instruments, and then sell them to investors. Why would investors be interested in such questionable instruments? Here is the idea in brief. Let's say the interest rate on a mortgage is five percent. If you as an investor finance one mortgage, you could lose your entire investment if the borrower defaults. But if you buy 1/1000th of 1,000 mortgages and 10 homeowners default, you still make four percent on your investment. These **mortgage-backed securities**, or investment products that consist of a bundle of mortgages, are a way to connect investors to homebuyers. In theory, the propagation of these securities provided investors with a security that paid some interest with low risk and gave borrowers access to mortgages at lower interest rates.

With the housing market softening in 2007, the quality of the individual mortgages composing these securities began to be questioned. Over the ensuing months, it became clear that many mortgages were issued that really shouldn't have been. Applicants with low incomes and poor credit history were given loans with adjustable interest rates. Basically, these loans would obligate borrowers to pay a low interest rate in the first few years of the

Mortgage-backed security
An investment product consisting of bundled mortgages that connects investors to homebuyers.

Figure 11.14 The Case–Shiller home price index (left-hand axis) and mortgage delinquency rate (right-hand axis) from 2003 through 2015.

Shaded areas indicate U.S. recessions.

Source: Fred https://fred.stlouisfed.org/graph/?g=YSFO.

mortgage, and then the interest rate would shoot up. As long as home prices continued to rise, it wouldn't matter (from the perspective of the institutions that owned the mortgages) whether people paid or defaulted on their mortgages. If they paid their mortgages, the lenders received interest on their loans. If the homeowners defaulted, then the bank could recoup the cost of lending by foreclosing on a house that had increased in value. But as soon as home prices started to decrease, the banks and owners of the mortgaged-backed securities got burnt by defaults. The consequence was a wave of delinquent payments and defaults and a cratering in the value of mortgaged-back securities.

Dozens of books and thousands of articles have been written about the financial collapse behind the Great Recession, so condensing it into one change in one variable of one equation in one model might sound questionable, perhaps even irresponsible. So we will change two. For a lot of individuals, their house is their biggest asset. The value of their net worth rises and falls with the market value of their house. In the context of the IS–MP model, we can interpret a decrease in housing prices as a drop in future income, Y_{t+1}. Less income expected in the future causes households to cut back their consumption in the current period. The same is true for the economy as a whole at the aggregate level. The decrease in consumption (at given interest rates) causes savings supply to increase and shifts the IS curve to the left. Thus, the Great Recession started with a big shift in the IS curve to the left. That is, at every level of interest rates, people and businesses were forced to reduce their expenditure.

At the same time, the havoc in the financial markets can be represented by an increase in f_t. While an increase in f_t usually corresponds to a higher risk premium, we can think of it here as a general catchall for financial market frictions. Figure 11.15 shows the contraction of the IS curve coming from these shocks.

The Fed responded to deteriorating economic conditions by aggressively cutting interest rates starting in late 2007. By 2009, as Figure 11.16 shows, the fed funds rate hit zero and the inflation rate was negative.

As a nominal interest rate, the Federal funds rate can't go below zero. Remember that the nominal interest rate is the opportunity cost of holding cash. When nominal interest rates hit zero, there is no difference between holding your wealth in cash or depositing it in

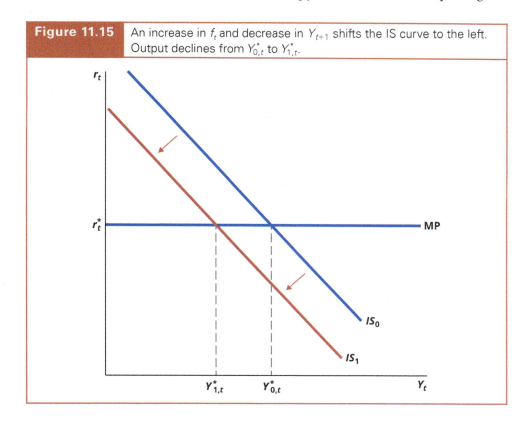

Figure 11.15 An increase in f_t and decrease in Y_{t+1} shifts the IS curve to the left. Output declines from $Y_{0,t}^*$ to $Y_{1,t}^*$.

284 Part 3 Business Cycles

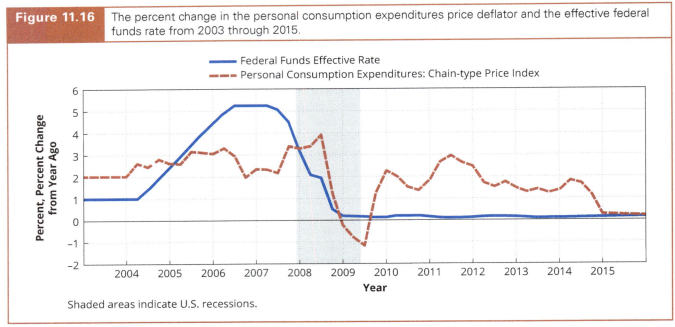

Figure 11.16 The percent change in the personal consumption expenditures price deflator and the effective federal funds rate from 2003 through 2015.

Shaded areas indicate U.S. recessions.

Source: FRED https://fred.stlouisfed.org/graph/?g=YSNM.

Zero–lower bound (ZLB)
A situation in which the nominal interest rate falls to zero.

an account that doesn't pay interest. Formally, the **zero–lower bound (ZLB)** of nominal interest rates is when $i_t = 0$. Using the Fisher equation, when the nominal interest rate is at the ZLB, the real interest rate is equal to $-\pi^e_{t+1}$. When the economy hits the ZLB, the Fed can no longer stimulate the economy by lowering interest rates.

With monetary policy proverbially "out of bullets," the United States turned to fiscal policy to stimulate the economy. President Obama signed the American Recovery and Reinvestment Act into law in February 2009. The act consisted of approximately $800 billion in government spending and tax cuts. Spending ranged on everything from extended unemployment insurance, to education, infrastructure, and healthcare. In the context of our model, the fiscal stimulus was a large increase in G_t and an expansion of the IS curve.

With conventional monetary policy rendered ineffective by the ZLB, the Fed attempted various unconventional monetary policy tools. Recall from Chapter 5 that when the Fed engages in open market operations, they exchange money for bonds. If the goal is to expand the money supply, they purchase bonds. The higher demand for bonds pushes their price up and interest rate down. Traditionally, the Fed purchased short-duration government bonds such as 3-month Treasury bills and relied on the fact that purchases of these short-duration securities usually influence the interest rates of longer duration maturities, such as 30-year mortgages. With interest rates of these short-duration maturities already at zero, the Fed began to purchase other assets, such as the mortgage-backed securities discussed earlier. Between 2009 and 2010, the Fed's holdings of MBS assets increased from zero to over $1 trillion. By 2015, as Figure 11.17 shows, the Fed held close to $2 trillion in MBS.

Forward guidance
A tool through which the Fed communicates with the public about its future course of action.

While constrained by the ZLB, the Fed also relied on **forward guidance**, a tool in which the Fed communicates with the public about its future course of action. Although the Fed couldn't drop the fed funds rate below zero, they conveyed an eagerness to do "whatever it took" to reestablish economic growth. The Fed was essentially promising not to raise the interest rate until the economy recovered. The goal was that promising a sustained period of low nominal interest rates would raise inflation expectations, π^e_{t+1}, and lower the real interest rate. The logic of the policy can best be described in the IS–MP diagram in Figure 11.18. If the Fed's forward guidance convinces people and businesses to increase their inflation expectations, the MP curve shifts down, causing the real interest rate to decrease and output to increase. We will have more to say about the formation of inflation expectations in Chapter 12.

Chapter 11 The IS–MP Model   285

Figure 11.17 — Mortgage-backed securities maturing over 10 years held by the Federal Reserve from 2003 through 2015.

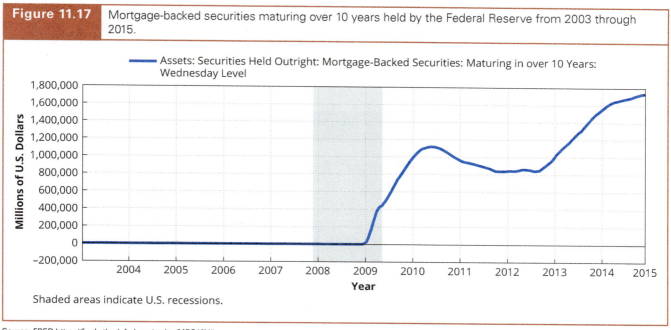

Shaded areas indicate U.S. recessions.

Source: FRED https://fred.stlouisfed.org/series/MBS10Y#.

The financial crisis and Great Recession of 2007–2009 presented many challenges to economic policymakers. The spillovers from the housing market took many people by surprise. Despite decisive action by fiscal and monetary policy, the economy went into a prolonged recession. And even after the recession officially concluded, economic growth was lackluster and unemployment remained high. All that being said, the last major financial

Figure 11.18 — At the zero–lower bound of nominal interest rates, the real interest rate is $-\pi^e$. An increase in inflation expectations shifts the MP curve down. Equilibrium output increases from $Y^*_{0,t}$ to $Y^*_{1,t}$.

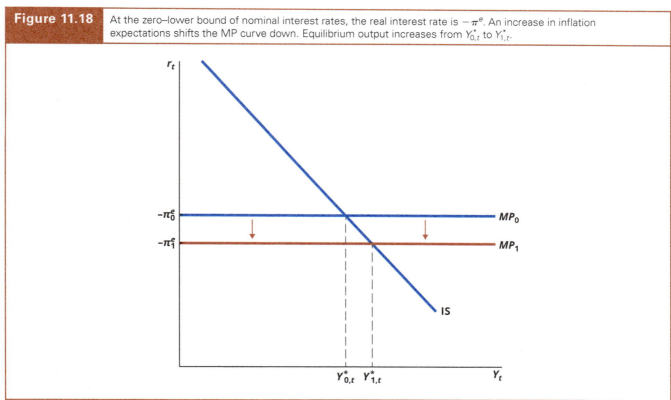

Source: FRED https://fred.stlouisfed.org/series/MBS10Y#.

Part 3 Business Cycles

crisis in the United States was the Great Depression of 1929–1939, which, as discussed in Chapter 10, was an unmitigated decade-long disaster. Thus, it is likely that both fiscal and monetary policy helped reduce the severity of the financial crisis. Perhaps it is no coincidence that Ben Bernanke, the chair of the Federal Reserve from 2006 through 2014, spent much of his academic career studying the Great Depression.

Application 11.2

Do Changes in Monetary Policy Affect Inequality?

The MP curve tells us that monetary policy affects the economy by changing real interest rates, which changes the optimal consumption and investment responses by individuals and firms. The IS–MP model analyzes the aggregate economy. It does not provide answers on the distributionary effects of monetary policy. When the Fed lowers the interest rate, how does that affect high-income versus low-income households, or older versus younger households, or households that have mortgages versus renters? While the IS–MP model is uninformative of these questions, a number of economic researchers have investigated these questions.

First, it helps to consider potential asymmetric effects of monetary policy. If the Fed raises the interest rate (hereafter referred to as a contractionary monetary shock), savers benefit because the interest income on their savings increases. Borrowers lose, because the cost of their borrowing increases. Even borrowers with a fixed-rate mortgage will lose in response to a contractionary monetary policy shock insofar as it reduces inflation. A lower inflation rate increases the real interest rate homeowners pay on their mortgages.

A second channel is through labor earnings. Low-wage earners face more volatility in their employment than high-wage earners. An increase in interest rates that lowers output and raises unemployment would, in theory, hurt those near the bottom of the income distribution.

Looking at the data, the effects of monetary policy on inequality aren't clear cut. Figure 11.19, taken from a 2017 paper, shows the effects of an unexpected one percentage point increase of the fed funds rate on income, earnings, expenditure, and consumption inequality.[7] In terms of definitions, earnings are what workers make in the labor market. Income includes earnings but also income from dividends, interest, business ownership, and transfers.

Consumption includes the purchase of nondurables; services; and some small durable goods, like dishwashers. Expenditures include consumption plus purchases of large durable goods, like cars. Inequality is measured as the 90–10 ratio. So, if annual consumption of households in the 90th percentile is $150,000 per year and consumption of households in the 10th percentile is $30,000 per year, the 90–10 ratio is 5 = $150,000/$30,000.

An unexpected rise in interest rates substantially raises consumption and expenditure inequality and has less of an effect on income and earnings inequality. The gray bars indicate the precision of the estimates. If the gray bars exclude 0, which they do for consumption and expenditure, we can be highly confident that monetary policy has some effect on inequality.[8] Since consumption is presumably forward looking and therefore takes account of all current and future forms of income, it is arguably the most comprehensive measure of economic welfare. Applying this logic and the results in Figure 11.19, it appears as though contractionary monetary policy increases economic inequality, whereas expansionary monetary policy (that is, interest rate cuts) reduces economic inequality.

According to the earnings panel of Figure 11.19, it doesn't look like the employment channel is that important for the transmission of monetary policy onto inequality. That is, changes in the fed funds rate have a very small effect on labor earnings inequality. How about the other channels? It turns out that an increase in consumption among mortgage holders and renters in response to an interest rate cut is significantly larger than among people who own their home outright.[9] To the extent that outright homeowners are the wealthiest group, this could explain the effects of monetary policy on consumption inequality. If an interest rate cut increases consumption by a lot among the least wealthy groups (mortgage holders and

---

[7]Coibion, Olivier, Yuriy Gorodnichenko, Lorenz Kueng, and John Silvia. 2017. "Innocent Bystanders? Monetary Policy and Inequality." *Journal of Monetary Economics, 88,* 70–89.

[8]Technically, these gray bars are "confidence intervals." If you have taken statistics, this is a term you probably recognize. If you haven't taken statistics, you should. It's almost as much fun as macroeconomics.

[9]Cloyne, James, Clodomiro Ferreira, and Paolo Surico. 2020. "Monetary Policy When Households Have Debt." *Review of Economic Studies, 87*(1): 102–129.

■ Continues

Application 11.2 (Continued)

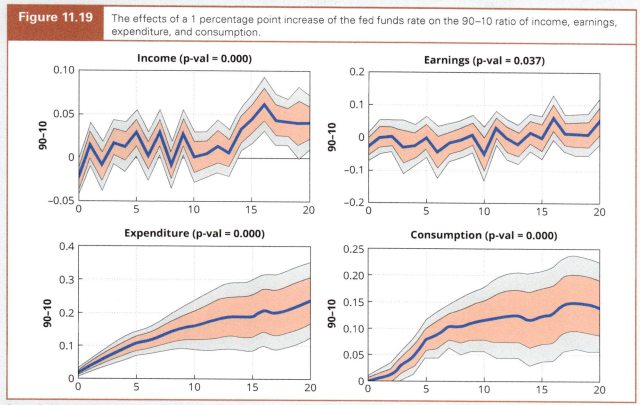

Figure 11.19 The effects of a 1 percentage point increase of the fed funds rate on the 90–10 ratio of income, earnings, expenditure, and consumption.

Source: Coibion et al. (2017).

renters) and by a little for the wealthiest group (outright homeowners), then an interest rate cut decreases consumption inequality and an interest rate hike increases consumption inequality.

Interestingly, as Figure 11.20 shows, the consumption responses to monetary policy changes in the United States and the UK are very similar. This is significant because UK mortgages are typically variable rate, whereas U.S. mortgages are typically fixed rate. When the Bank of England lowers interest rates, the nominal interest rate paid by existing mortgage holders comes down. When the Fed lowers interest rates, the nominal interest rate paid by existing mortgage holder stays fixed. So, one might expect the consumption responses to be bigger in the UK than the United States, but we don't see that.

There are a couple of possible explanations for the similarity of responses in the two countries. To the extent that a decrease in the fed funds rate raises inflation, the real interest rate paid by mortgage holders will decrease even though their nominal interest rate stays fixed. The lower real interest rate will increase consumption of mortgage holders in both countries. Second, the wealth of many mortgage holders is locked up in their house, meaning that it is illiquid. Given the present discounted value of their lifetime wealth, these mortgage holders may want to raise their consumption today through borrowing. But because their primary investment—their house—is illiquid, they can't easily access their wealth. An expansionary monetary policy shock that raises income will then cause a bigger increase in consumption among those liquidity-constrained households (the mortgage holders and renters) compared to outright homeowners, who have lots of liquid and illiquid wealth.

Economic research on the interaction between monetary policy on inequality is just getting started. If economists at the Fed and other central banks care about the distributionary effects of their policies, then the proliferation of this research may prove to be valuable. Finally, the research discussed above does not say how monetary policymakers should care about inequality. Without some kind of normative structure, we can't say whether the rise in inequality after a period of contractionary monetary policy is good or bad. It remains to be seen how, or even if, the FOMC will come to think about the effects of interest rate policy on inequality.

Continues

Application 11.2 (Continued)

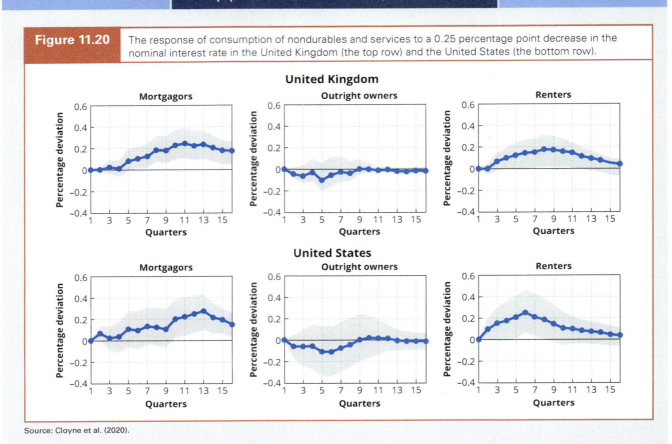

Figure 11.20 The response of consumption of nondurables and services to a 0.25 percentage point decrease in the nominal interest rate in the United Kingdom (the top row) and the United States (the bottom row).

Source: Cloyne et al. (2020).

Chapter Summary

- The IS curve is the set of (r_t, Y_t) such that the savings and investment market is in equilibrium.
- The IS curve is downward sloping because an increase in income shifts the savings supply curve to the right and lowers the real interest rate.
- Shifts in the IS curve include changes in current- or future-period government spending, future income, future TFP, or the credit spread.
- The monetary policy (MP) rule defines how monetary policy makers set the nominal interest rate.
- Inflation expectations are exogenously fixed in the short run. This means that monetary policymakers effectively set the real interest rate in the short run.
- The equilibrium nominal interest rate must be consistent with equilibrium in the money market. This means that the central bank can set the nominal interest rate and let the money supply adjust endogenously, or the central bank can set the money supply and let the nominal interest rate adjust endogenously. It can't choose the money supply and nominal interest rate independent of each other.
- A change to the nominal interest rate or inflation expectations changes the real interest rate and shifts the MP curve.
- The Taylor rule specifies the federal funds rate as a linear function of the output gap and inflation. The rule accurately predicts movements in the fed funds rate.
- The intersection between the IS and MP curves determines the economy's equilibrium real interest rate and output.
- The zero–lower bound occurs when the nominal interest rate hits zero. When the Fed hit the ZLB in 2009, it engaged in unconventional monetary policy such as the purchase of mortgaged-backed securities and forward guidance.

Chapter 11 The IS–MP Model   **289**

Key Terms

IS curve, 267
Marginal propensity to consume (MPC), 268
MP curve, 269
Term structure of interest rates, 271
Risk structure of interest rates, 271

Taylor rule, 276
Mortgage-backed security, 282
Zero–lower bound (ZLB), 284
Forward guidance, 284

Questions for Review

1. What elements of the IS curve are forward looking? Explain the economic logic for each of these.

2. The Fed controls a nominal interest rate, but economic decisions are governed by the real interest rate. How then does the Fed influence the real economy?

3. The fed funds rate is a very short-run (overnight) interest rate. The interest rates that affect people's decisions, such as car loans and mortgages, are typically over longer horizons.

How does the choice of the fed funds rate affect these longer-run interest rates?

4. Suppose the Fed decides to lower the fed funds rate. Explain how the money supply must adjust to ensure that the money market is in equilibrium.

5. Why is conventional monetary policy rendered ineffective at the ZLB? What alternatives are open to the central bank?

Problems

11.1 The investment demand curve, consumption function, and aggregate expenditure equation are respectively given by

$$I_t = I(r_t + f_t, A_{t+1}),$$

$$C_t = C(Y_t - G_t, Y_{t+1} - G_{t+1}, r_t),$$

$$Y_t = C_t + I_t + G_t.$$

a. Graphically derive the IS curve.

b. Draw the effects of an increase in current-period government spending.

c. Suppose instead that government spending increases in both periods by the same amount. Can you tell how the IS curve shifts now?

11.2 Suppose future TFP, A_{t+1}, increases.

a. How does an increase in future TFP affect consumption and investment? Explain the economic logic for each.

b. Show how an increase in future TFP shifts the IS curve.

c. Now assume consumption only depends on current income (rather than lifetime income). Redo part b under this new assumption. Compare the magnitude of the IS shift in part b to the IS shift in part c.

11.3 Suppose the investment demand function, consumption function, and aggregate expenditure equation are the same as in problem 11.1. Assume the MP curve is

$$r_t = i_t - \pi^e.$$

a. Show graphically how an increase in current-period government, G_t, spending affects equilibrium output and the real interest rate. How do consumption and investment change in equilibrium?

b. Now assume the consumption function is

$$C_t = C(Y_t - T_t, r_t).$$

Now consumption depends on current (rather than lifetime) disposable income. Under this consumption function, the individual does not internalize the government's intertemporal budget constraint. Redo part a assuming that the government runs a balanced budget. Compare your results to part a.

c. Continue to assume the same consumption function as part b, but now assume the government finances the increase in government spending through borrowing. Graphically show how this affects equilibrium output and the real interest rate. How do consumption and investment change in equilibrium? Compare the magnitude of the changes in the real interest rate, output, consumption, and investment in parts b and c. Does the method of government financing make a difference?

11.4 Assume the demand for real money balances takes the form

$$\frac{M_t}{P_t} = 10 - i_t + 0.5Y_t,$$

and that money demand depends negatively on the nominal interest rate, i_t, and positively on real income, Y_t.

a. Suppose $P_t = 1$, $Y_t = 12$, and $M_t = 10$. Solve for the equilibrium nominal interest rate.

b. If expected inflation equals 2 percent, what is the equilibrium real interest rate?

c. Suppose the Fed wants to achieve a 4 percent nominal interest rate. What level of the money supply is consistent with this?

d. At what level of the money supply is the economy at the zero–lower bound?

11.5 Suppose the consumption function and investment demand curve are given by

$$C_t = 0.8(Y_t - G_t) + 0.6(Y_{t+1} - G_{t+1}) - 0.1r_t,$$

$$I_t = A_{t+1} - 0.1(r_t + f_t).$$

a. Algebraically derive the IS curve.

b. Assume the MP curve is given by

$$r_t = i_t - \pi^e.$$

Derive expressions for the equilibrium real interest rate and equilibrium level of output.

c. Assume $Y_{t+1} - G_{t+1} = 70$, $G_t = 20$, $f_t = 0$, $A_{t+1} = 10$, $i_t = 4$, and $\pi^e = 2$. Solve for the equilibrium real interest rate and output.

d. Suppose G_t increases to 40. How does output change in equilibrium? What is the government spending multiplier?

e. Suppose G_t increases to 40. How must the Fed change the nominal interest rate to keep output at the same level as part d?

✓ Knowledge Check 11-1 Answer

Start at an equilibrium in the savings-investment market given by $(r_{0,t}, Y_{0,t})$ and increase income to $Y_{1,t}$. The larger is the MPC, the bigger is the increase in consumption. The larger the increase in consumption, the less savings supply shifts to the right and the smaller the decline in equilibrium real interest rates. Thus, for any given increase in income, the equilibrium real interest rate declines by less as the MPC goes up. Figure 11.21 shows that the slope of the IS curve is flatter when the MPC is bigger. Intuitively, a higher MPC makes consumption more sensitive to changes in income, which means savings is less sensitive to changes in income. Because the supply of savings doesn't increase by very much when income goes up, the real interest rate doesn't change by much. The resulting IS curve is flat.

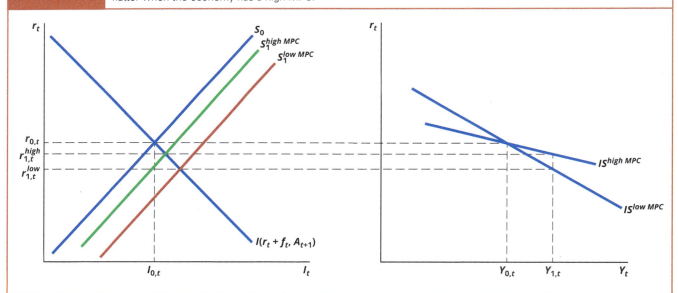

Figure 11.21 An increase in income from $Y_{0,t}$ to $Y_{1,t}$ shifts the savings supply curve from S_0 to $S_1^{high\ MPC}$ in the case of an economy with a high MPC or to $S_1^{low\ MPC}$ in the case of an economy with a low MPC. The equilibrium real interest rate falls by more in the economy with the low MPC. Tracing the real interest rates to the right panel shows that the IS curve is flatter when the economy has a high MPC.

✓ Knowledge Check 11-2 Answer

Plugging in the value of π_t into the interest rate rule gives

$$i_t = 3 + 2(\pi_t - 2)$$
$$= 3 + 2(2 - 2)$$
$$= 3.$$

Using the Fisher equation, $r_t = i_t - \pi^e$, we can infer the real interest rate

$$r_t = 3 - 2 = 1.$$

Finally, the rate at which firms borrow is the real interest rate plus the credit spread, $r_t + f_t$. Using the data from the first row,

$$r_t + f_t = 1 + 1 = 2.$$

We can follow the same steps for the second row of data. The nominal interest rate is given by

$$i_t = 3 + 2(\pi_t - 2)$$
$$= 3 + 2(3 - 2)$$
$$= 5.$$

The real interest rate is given by

$$r_t = i_t - \pi^e = 5 - 2 = 3.$$

The rate at which firms borrow is given by

$$r_t + f_t = 3 + 1 = 4.$$

The remaining rows can be completed by following the same steps. An increase in inflation expectations lowers the real interest rate, whereas an increase in inflation raises the real interest rate.

π^e	π_t	f_t	r_t	$r_t + f_t$
2	2	1	1	2
2	3	1	3	4
2	2	2	1	3
3	2	1	0	1
1	1	2	0	1

✓ Knowledge Check 11-3 Answer

When $i_t = 5$, the money supply is

$$M_t = \frac{Y_t}{i_t} = \frac{100}{5} = 20.$$

When the Fed raises the nominal interest rate to $i_t = 10$, the money supply is

$$M_t = \frac{Y_t}{i_t} = \frac{100}{10} = 10.$$

Thus, if the Fed raises the nominal interest rate, the money supply must decrease because people demand to hold less money when the opportunity cost of holding money is higher. Because money demand equals money supply in equilibrium, the money supply has to drop.

Knowledge Check 11-4 Answer

A decrease in π^e lowers the real interest rate through the Fisher equation, $r_t = i_t - \pi^e$. The MP curve shifts up causing the real interest rate to rise in equilibrium and output to fall. The fall in output causes the savings supply curve to shift to the left. The results are shown in Figure 11.22. The higher real interest rate causes investment to fall. The lower level of disposable income and higher real interest rate causes consumption to fall.

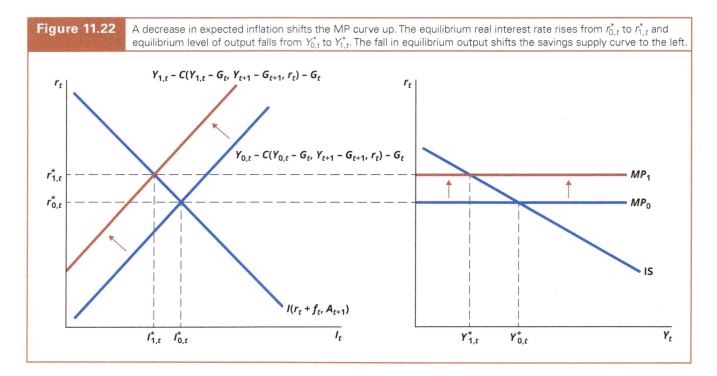

Figure 11.22 A decrease in expected inflation shifts the MP curve up. The equilibrium real interest rate rises from $r^*_{0,t}$ to $r^*_{1,t}$ and equilibrium level of output falls from $Y^*_{0,t}$ to $Y^*_{1,t}$. The fall in equilibrium output shifts the savings supply curve to the left.

Chapter 12
The IS–MP–AS Model

Learning Objectives

12.1 Explain the economic rationale for an upward-sloping aggregate supply (AS) curve.

12.2 Derive the AS curve under the assumption of flexible prices and wages and under the assumption of rigid nominal wages.

12.3 Perform comparative statics in the IS–MP–AS model graphically and algebraically.

12.4 Evaluate the predictions of the IS–MP–AS model against the business cycle facts in the data.

After remaining dormant for a decade, inflation suddenly spiked in the spring of 2021. CPI inflation surpassed 5 percent in June and went as high as 9 percent one year later. There are a number of potential factors that led to the spike in inflation. Various bottlenecks and supply chain disruptions during the Covid-19 pandemic had only partially resolved themselves by 2022 despite most national economies ending their lockdowns and economic activity increasing. The war in Ukraine, that began in February 2022, further added to global supply constraints. Even as vaccines were on their way and lockdowns were winding down, Congress passed and President Biden signed the American Rescue Plan Act in March of 2021, which committed $1.9 trillion in total spending. Later that year, the president signed the Infrastructure and Jobs Act, which planned to add $1 trillion in infrastructure investment over the coming decade. Finally, the Fed kept the federal funds rate at zero until the beginning of 2022.

With the benefit of hindsight, it's easy to read the last paragraph and conclude that of course inflation was inevitable. In real time, it wasn't so obvious. The high levels of government spending during the 2008 recession did not lead to discernably higher inflation. Neither did the Fed's having kept the nominal interest rate at zero between 2009 and 2016.

What explains the difference between the inflation episode of 2021–2022 and the lack of inflation in the previous decade? And how do changes in government spending, the Fed's interest rate policy, and the output gap affect inflation? These are issues addressed in this chapter through the lens of the IS–MP–AS model.

12-1 The Aggregate Supply Curve

The **aggregate supply curve** relates the economy's inflation rate to inflation expectations and the **output gap**, or the difference between the actual and potential level of output. Before jumping into the macro-level determination of inflation, output, and interest rates, it helps to think about the microeconomics underlying the aggregate supply curve.

Aggregate supply curve
The relationship between inflation and inflation expectations and the output gap.

Output gap
The difference between the actual and potential level of output.

293

294 **Part 3** Business Cycles

In Chapter 10, we defined potential output to be the amount of output the economy could produce if all factors of production (such as labor, capital, and raw materials) were used efficiently. There are all sorts of inefficiencies that could drag the economy below its potential level of output. High income taxes, for instance, could discourage workers from supplying their labor. Large firms may have market power, which allows them to restrict output and sell their products at a markup. Government licensing policies may restrict the number of qualified people from joining certain occupations, such as medicine, makeup artistry, and animal breeding.[1] There might be valid reasons for licensure and certification in some occupations (you probably don't want an economics professor as your dentist), but such barriers to entry add red tape and reduce output below its potential.

Nominal rigidities
The inability of prices to instantaneously adjust to economic fundamentals.

There are many other potential reasons why output may differ from its potential level. We focus on one reason: **nominal rigidities**, or the inability of prices to instantaneously adjust to economic fundamentals. Nominal rigidities can take the form of wage stickiness, which means nominal wages don't instantaneously adjust, or price stickiness, which means firms don't immediately change prices in the face of changing economic circumstances.

The reason for focusing on nominal rigidities is twofold. First, it's reasonable to expect that some prices and wages are sticky in the short run but flexible in the long run as employers and employees negotiate new wages and firms post new prices. Other market imperfections, such as distortionary taxes and the market power of large firms, are more of a long-run feature of the economy. Since business cycles deal with the economy in the short run, it makes sense to focus on nominal rigidities. Second, the Fed's interest rate policy affects inflation, and the inflation rate determines the degree to which nominal rigidities reduce efficiency in the economy.

Prior to analyzing the effects of nominal rigidities, it is helpful to think about an economy with completely flexible prices and wages. This provides a benchmark of economic efficiency and shows where the economy goes in the long run once all prices and wages can adjust. You can think about the economy with flexible prices and wages as one where the classical dichotomy holds. Recall from Chapter 5 that the classical dichotomy says that real variables are determined independently of nominal variables. The long-run economy is one where the classical dichotomy holds.

12-1a Completely Flexible Prices and Wages

Start by thinking about a simple economy. Workers produce one good—apples—and are paid in dollars. If the nominal wage is $12 per hour and the price of apples is $1, then the real wage is 12 apples $= \frac{\$12}{\$1}$ per hour. Since workers eat apples, not dollars, they care about the real wage. If the price of apples goes up to $2, but the nominal wage stays at $12, the real wage declines to $6. Workers are worse off even though their nominal wage remains constant.

Real wages are determined by the intersection of the supply and demand for labor. The demand for labor is downward sloping. As real wages increase, the quantity of labor demanded decreases. The supply of labor is upward sloping. As wages increase, more individuals are willing to join the labor force.[2] Figure 12.1 shows equilibrium in the labor market. The equilibrium real wage and quantity of labor are determined at the intersection of the labor supply and labor demand curves.

The equilibrium real wage, w_t^*, is the ratio of the nominal wage and price level, $\frac{W_t}{P_t}$. Again, employers and workers care about real variables, rather than nominal variables. Referring back to the apple example, if the equilibrium real wage is 12 apples per hour, workers and employers don't care if the nominal wage is $12 and each apple costs $1, or if

---

[1] Perhaps shockingly these last two are real-life examples. You can see for yourself here: https://ij.org/report/license-to-work-3/license-to-work-3-compare-states/.

[2] For those of you who covered Chapter 8, the following is relevant: casting this model in terms of the extensive margin (i.e., the number of people working) rather than the intensive margin (the number of hours worked by each worker) allows us to ignore the income effect of higher wages.

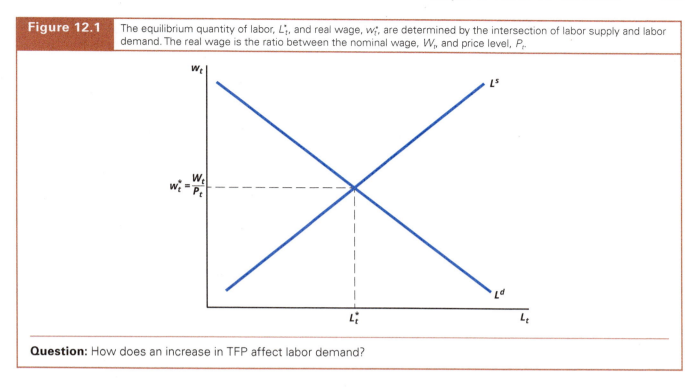

Figure 12.1 The equilibrium quantity of labor, L_t^*, and real wage, w_t^*, are determined by the intersection of labor supply and labor demand. The real wage is the ratio between the nominal wage, W_t, and price level, P_t.

Question: How does an increase in TFP affect labor demand?

the nominal wage is $24 and each apple costs $2. In either case, the real wage is 12 apples. Provided there are no shifts in the labor supply or demand curves, an increase in the price level leads to a proportionate increase in the nominal wage.

Recall from Chapter 10 that the standard neoclassical production function is given by

$$Y_t = A_t F(K_t, L_t). \tag{1}$$

The standard assumption is that output, Y_t, is increasing in capital, K_t, and labor, L_t, but at diminishing rates. For a constant capital stock, moving from one to two workers increases output more than moving from 11 to 12 workers. We also assume that the capital stock is taken as fixed. Although the capital stock was an endogenous variable in the chapters on economic growth, it's a harmless simplification to think of it as exogenous over business cycle frequencies. As you saw in Chapter 10, investment is quite volatile over the business cycle, but because annual investment is only about 6 percent of the capital stock, even a big change in investment in one quarter has a small effect on the capital stock. For instance, a 10 percent increase in investment would raise the capital stock by less than 1 percent.

With a fixed capital stock and an exogenous level of TFP, A_t, Figure 12.2 graphically depicts the equilibrium wage and levels of output and labor. Consistent with the assumption of a diminishing marginal product of labor, the production function gets flatter as labor increases.

A subtle implication of Figure 12.2 is that the level of output is independent of the price level. If the price level were to double, but neither labor supply nor labor demand changed, then nominal wages would double, leaving real wages constant. If the price level were to decrease by half, then nominal wages would decrease by half, again leaving real wages constant. The point is that the classical dichotomy holds: output is determined separately from the price level.

The relationship between output and the price level is shown in Figure 12.3. The top left panel determines labor market equilibrium. Taking the equilibrium level of labor, $L_{0,t}$, and tracing it down to the production function in the bottom left panel pins down the equilibrium level of output, $Y_{0,t}$. Next, we trace that level of output over to the 45-degree line in the bottom right panel to put output on the horizontal instead of the vertical axis. Finally, trace up to the top right panel, which shows that output is independent of the price level.

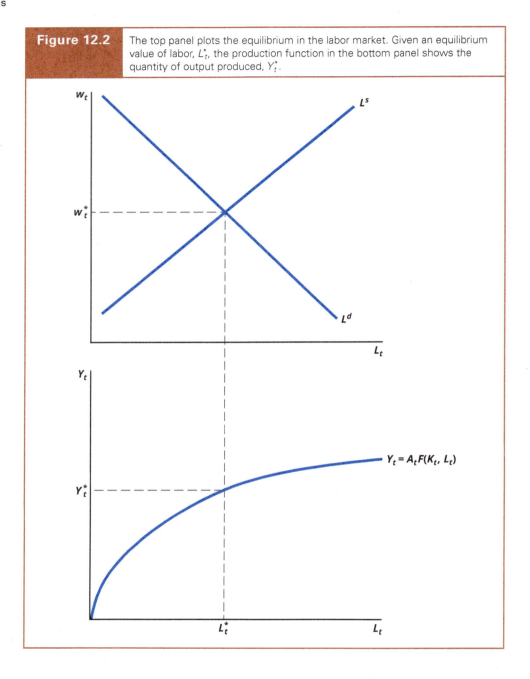

Figure 12.2 The top panel plots the equilibrium in the labor market. Given an equilibrium value of labor, L_t^*, the production function in the bottom panel shows the quantity of output produced, Y_t^*.

This is the aggregate supply curve consistent with flexible prices and wages. It doesn't matter how far the price level moves up or down, the level of output stays the same.

In Chapter 10, you learned about the real business cycle (RBC) model. The RBC model assumes that output always equals its potential level. Thus, the vertical aggregate supply curve is the aggregate supply curve in the RBC model. The RBC model also assumes that the source of business cycles is changes in TFP.

Figure 12.4 shows how a one-time increase in TFP affects labor market variables and output. The higher level of TFP causes firms to increase their hiring at any given wage rate, which shifts the labor demand curve to the right. Real wages and the equilibrium quantity of labor increase. Since more output is produced with any given amount of labor, the production function also shifts up. Thus, the real wage, labor, and output are all higher. Reflecting the new level of output on the 45-degree line and tracing up gives the new flexible price and wage AS curve. Output is higher at any given price level.

Chapter 12 The IS–MP–AS Model   **297**

Figure 12.3 | The top left panel depicts labor market equilibrium. Tracing the equilibrium labor supply to the bottom left panel gives the equilibrium level of output. Trace the equilibrium level of output over to the 45-degree line and then up to top right to end up with the flexible price/wage aggregate supply curve.

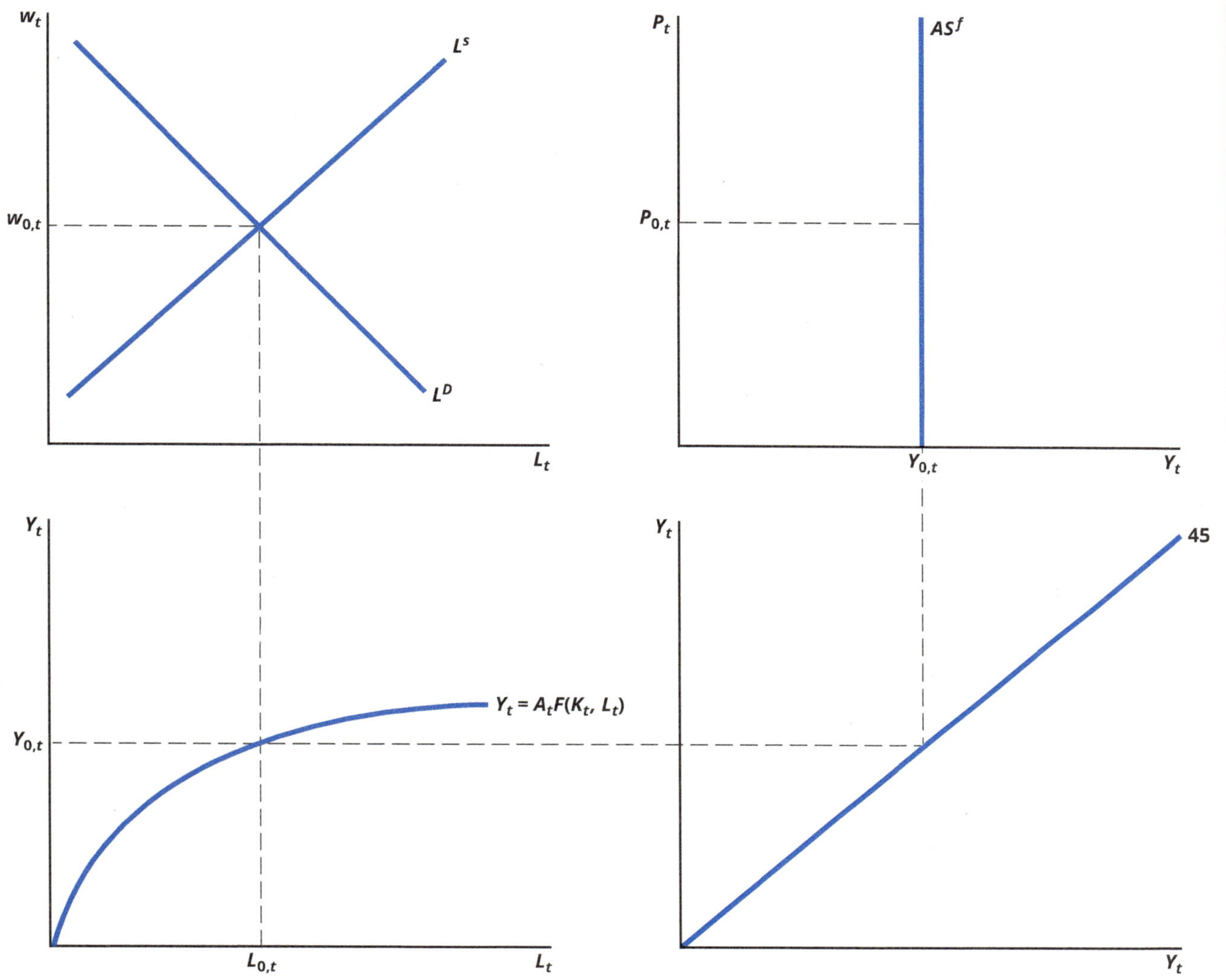

To reiterate the punch line from Chapter 10, the RBC model is probably not, on the whole, a good descriptor of business cycles in the U.S. economy. However, the RBC model provides a useful hypothetical. By tracing out the potential level of output, the RBC model gives us something to compare with the actual level of output (which is afflicted by nominal rigidities). This comparison shows us the efficiency losses due to these nominal rigidities, which the central bank attempts to minimize.

✓ **Knowledge Check 12-1**

Suppose an improvement in video game quality leads people to place a greater value on leisure. How does this affect the labor supply curve? Assuming wages and prices are perfectly flexible, how does it affect the AS curve?

———————————————————— Answers are at the end of the chapter.

Part 3 Business Cycles

Figure 12.4 An increase in TFP from $A_{0,t}$ to $A_{1,t}$ shifts the labor demand curve to the right and the production function up. Real wages, labor, and output rise. The aggregate supply curve shifts to the right.

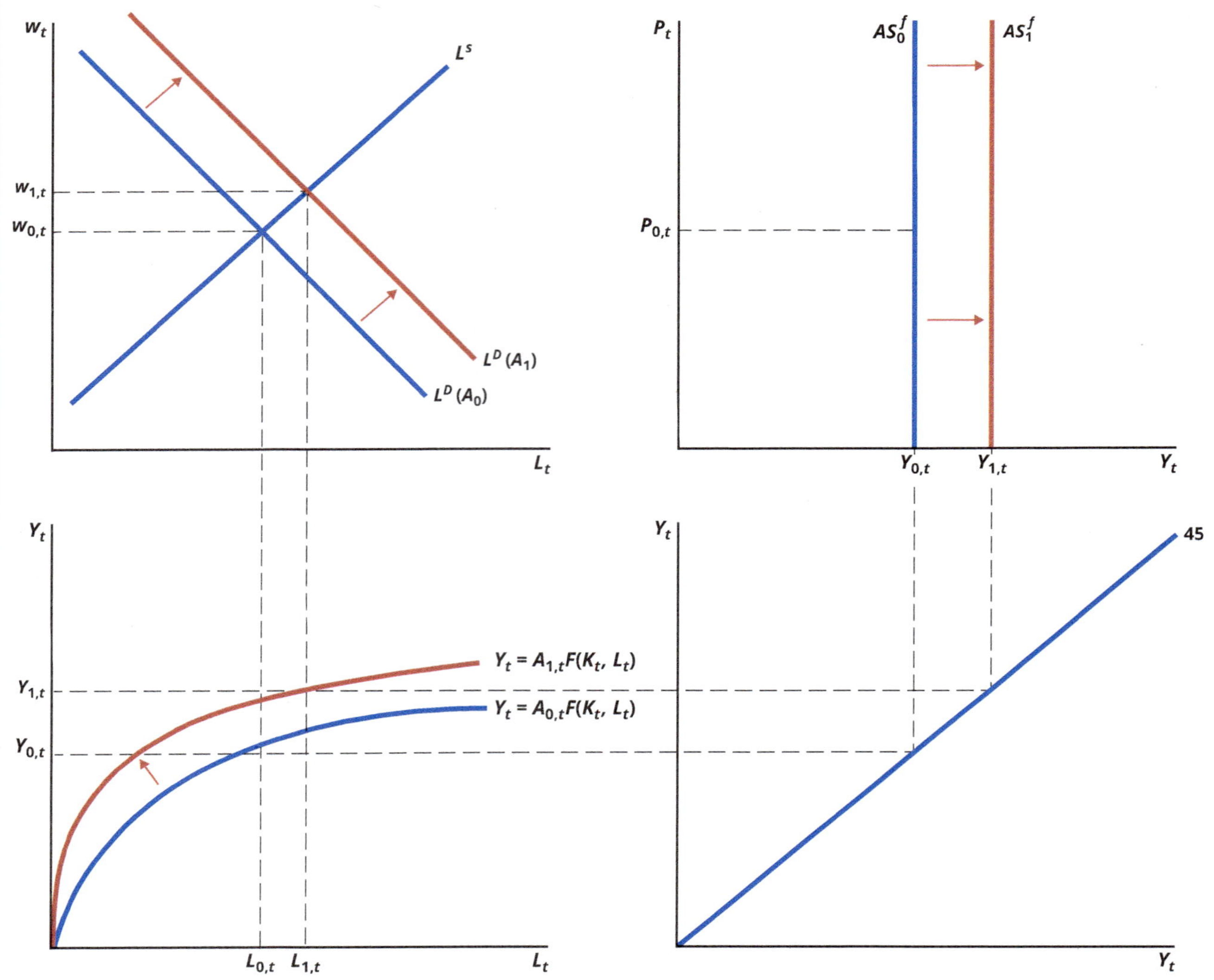

Question: Draw a decrease in TFP.

12-1b Sticky Nominal Wages

You might start your morning by scrolling through Twitter, or, if you're nostalgic, reading a newspaper.[3] If you flip to the economics section, you can read the latest news about inflation and real GDP. Imagine that one day, the first story you read says that the CPI rose by 5 percent last month even though economists predicted a 3 percent increase. After you curse the economic forecasters, how do you respond to this news? Perhaps you decide to hold less money (remember inflation is an implicit tax on money). One thing you probably don't do is demand an immediate increase in your wages.

The absence of a demand for higher nominal wages may sound intuitive, but it is hard to reconcile with the flexible-wage model of the last section. In a model with flexible nominal wages, the real wage is determined by labor supply and labor demand. If neither labor

---

[3]Probably reading the newspaper's app on your phone. After all, who is nostalgic enough to read a printed copy of a newspaper? Tip: Don't ask your professor this.

demand nor labor supply changes, then a 5 percent increase in the price level leads to a 5 percent increase in nominal wages. The fact that nominal wages don't universally and instantaneously adjust to changes in the price level means that we are omitting something critical from the simple labor supply and demand model from the last section.

Why might nominal wages be sticky? There are potentially many plausible reasons, but a popular one economists focus on is **transaction costs**, or the costs associated with negotiating a nominal wage. Typically, determining a new nominal wage depends on a lot of back and forth between an employer and an employee. The employee may even have to move jobs to secure the market-clearing nominal wage. To see this, imagine you work at an accounting firm and learn that a different accounting firm 1,000 miles away is willing to increase your pay by 5 percent. Would you accept the offer? The answer probably depends on how you and your family prefer the new city to the old city, the costs of moving, and how long you plan to stay at the new job. Would your answer change if the new firm were going to increase your pay by only 1 percent? Some people might answer yes, but others will answer no. And the fact that some people answer no implies that wages don't always equal their market-clearing levels.

Transaction costs The costs associated with negotiating a nominal wage.

To deal with transaction costs, a lot of companies change wages at the same time every year. That means that for some fraction of companies, nominal wages are effectively flexible for a brief period of the year and effectively sticky for the rest of the year. Since different companies change wages at different times of the year, nominal wages will be sticky for some segments of the economy and flexible for others.

Imagine it like this. There are four employers in the economy: Amazon, Walmart, UPS, and McDonald's. Amazon negotiates their wages in January through March, Walmart in April through June, UPS in July through September, and McDonald's in October through December.

Figure 12.5 shows that, at any given time, 75 percent of nominal wages are sticky. During the negotiation period, each company negotiates with their workers and both sides make forecasts about supply and demand conditions as well as the general price level in the nine months ahead. If the price level rises by more than expected, real wages go down. Employers gain and employees lose. If the price level rises by less than expected, real wages increase. Employers lose and employees gain.

How does the sticky nominal wage assumption affect the aggregate supply curve? Figure 12.6 shows the new derivation. The nominal wage is exogenously given by, $\overline{W}_t$. The real wage is $\frac{\overline{W}_t}{P_t}$ which changes with the price level. At a price level of $P_{0,t}$, labor supply equals labor demand. Tracing the equilibrium quantity of labor down to the production function shows that the equilibrium level of output is $Y_{0,t}$. Because the labor market is in equilibrium, $Y_{0,t}$ is equal to potential output, so the output gap is zero. Next, suppose the price level increases to $P_{1,t}$. Because the nominal wage is fixed, the real wage falls.

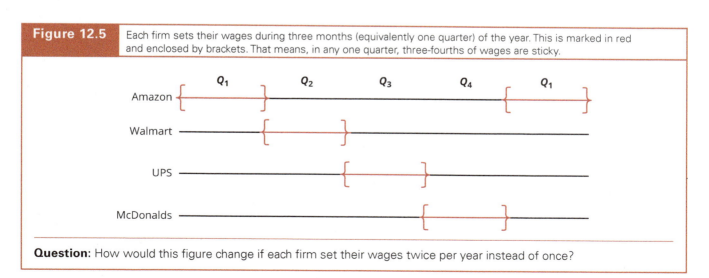

Figure 12.5 Each firm sets their wages during three months (equivalently one quarter) of the year. This is marked in red and enclosed by brackets. That means, in any one quarter, three-fourths of wages are sticky.

Question: How would this figure change if each firm set their wages twice per year instead of once?

With a lower real wage, firms hire more employees (or push their existing employees to work longer hours). The new level of labor, denoted by $L_{1,t}$ is consistent with a higher level of output, $Y_{1,t}$. Next, suppose the price level decreases to $P_{2,t} < P_{0,t}$. This lower price level raises the real wage and causes firms to reduce employment to $L_{2,t}$ and output declines. Connecting the three dots gives rise to an upward-sloping aggregate supply curve.

There are a few things to notice about the aggregate supply curve. First, if the quantity of labor supplied equals the quantity of labor demanded, then output is at potential. This occurs if the expected price level, which we can denote by P_t^e, equals the actual price level, $P_{0,t}$. Second, output equals its potential level when labor supplied equals labor demanded. When the price level is lower than anticipated, real wages are relatively high and the quantity of labor hired by firms drops. The lower level of labor implies a lower level of output. Because output is lower than its potential level, the output gap is negative. Analogous logic shows that the output gap is positive if prices exceed their expected level. Thus, one can write the aggregate supply curve as

$$P_t = P_t^e + k(Y_t - Y_t^p). \tag{2}$$

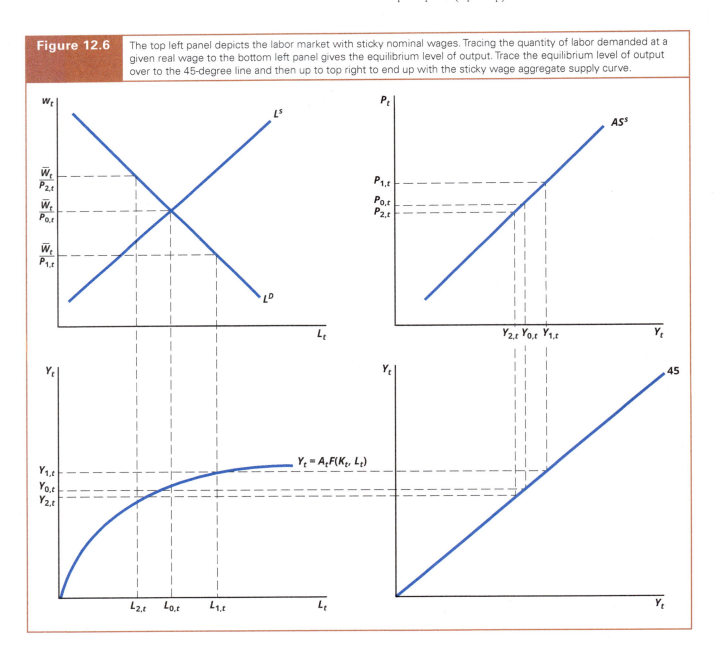

Figure 12.6 The top left panel depicts the labor market with sticky nominal wages. Tracing the quantity of labor demanded at a given real wage to the bottom left panel gives the equilibrium level of output. Trace the equilibrium level of output over to the 45-degree line and then up to top right to end up with the sticky wage aggregate supply curve.

The constant $k > 0$ measures the slope of the aggregate supply line. Because the price level trends up over time, it helps to write Equation (2) in terms of the change in prices, or inflation, rather than the price level. Taking this revision into account gives

$$\pi_t = \pi^e + k(Y_t - Y_t^p). \tag{2'}$$

The new version of the aggregate supply curve is shown in Figure 12.7. To get an intuitive understanding between the inflation rate and expected inflation, return to the overlapping contracts theory that we started the discussion with. If in January, Amazon and their employees expect prices to rise quickly over the year, workers will demand a higher nominal wage. Higher nominal wages mean higher labor costs for Amazon, which are passed on to consumers in the form of higher prices. Thus, the expectation of inflation becomes self-fulfilling.

The logic of self-fulfilling expectations causes monetary policy makers to carefully monitor expected inflation as measured in the data. If inflation expectations creep up, it might be in the best interest of the Fed to take immediate action. As Application 12.1 discusses, there are many different ways to measure expected inflation, and they don't always tell a consistent story.

Figure 12.8 shows the effects of an increase in potential output, possibly coming from an increase in TFP. An increase in Y_t^p shifts the AS curve to the right and lowers the inflation rate at any given level of output (or raises output at any level of inflation). This makes sense. An increase in technology allows firms to produce more efficiently. Some of this may be translated into higher levels of GDP, and the rest of it goes toward lower prices.

Finally, it makes sense to revisit our discussion of the Phillips curve from Chapter 10. Recall that the Phillips curve is the short-run relationship between unemployment and inflation that was identified in the data, at least up to the 1970s. Even when GDP is at its potential level, there will still be some unemployed workers. In Chapter 8, you learned that frictional unemployment comes when workers voluntarily leave their jobs or when people join the labor force. From this perspective, the existence of unemployed workers is not inconsistent with a healthy economy with a vibrant labor market. Thus, similar to the potential level of output, we can define the **natural rate of unemployment** as the

Natural rate of unemployment
The unemployment that would prevail absent of nominal rigidities.

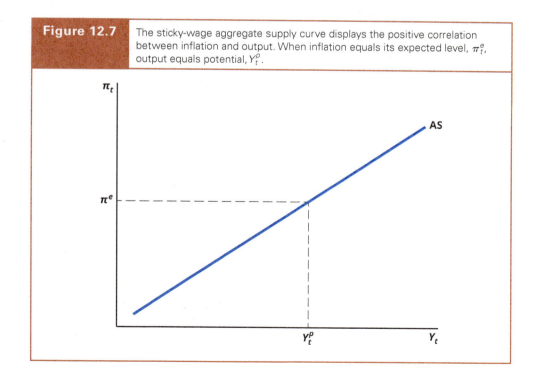

Figure 12.7 The sticky-wage aggregate supply curve displays the positive correlation between inflation and output. When inflation equals its expected level, π_t^e, output equals potential, Y_t^p.

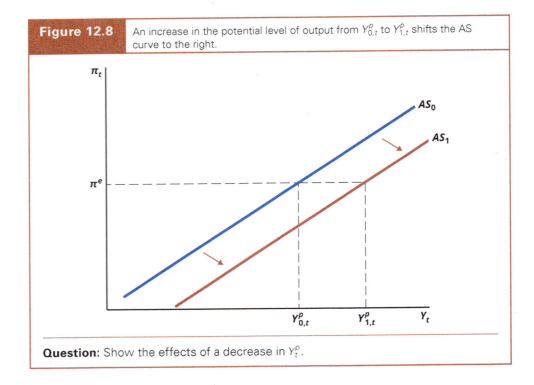

Figure 12.8 An increase in the potential level of output from $Y^p_{0,t}$ to $Y^p_{1,t}$ shifts the AS curve to the right.

Question: Show the effects of a decrease in Y^p_t.

unemployment that would prevail absent of nominal rigidities. If the price level is lower than expected, real wages are higher than expected and firms hire less labor and produce below potential. Fewer employees hired implies a higher unemployment rate. Thus, the unemployment rate is above the natural rate whenever output is below potential, and the unemployment rate is below the natural rate whenever output is above potential. Applying this insight, we can write the aggregate supply curve as

$$\pi_t = \pi^e + \kappa(u^*_t - u_t), \tag{3}$$

where u^*_t is the natural rate of unemployment and the Greek letter, κ (different from k in Equation (2)), is a constant. When inflation equals its expected level, unemployment equals its natural rate. Equation (3) is the theoretical version of the Phillips curve that, at least in certain decades, seemed to exist in the data. Equation (3) also suggests why the empirical relationship between inflation and the unemployment rate may have broken down in the late 1970s. High oil prices caused people and businesses to anticipate high levels of inflation despite the unemployment rate never being below 5 percent. From a certain perspective, stagflation, or the existence of high rates of inflation and unemployment, appeared to contradict the Phillips curve. Instead, our theoretical analysis shows that a properly specified Phillips curve must account for the natural rate of unemployment and inflation expectations. Neither of these are easily measured in the data. Application 12.1 discusses the measurement of inflation expectations.

✓ Knowledge Check 12-2

Assuming that nominal wages are sticky, graphically show how an increase in inflation expectations affects the aggregate supply curve.

Answers are at the end of the chapter.

Application 12.1

Measuring Inflation Expectations

Inflation expectations play a critical role in the aggregate supply curve. Higher inflation expectations for the future translate into a higher inflation rate or lower output today. But expectations can't be measured in the same way as a variable like labor force participation or GDP, which, although measured with some error, at least have objective definitions. When thinking about inflation expectations, we need to know whose expectations we are talking about. It's not obvious that households, businesses, and investors have uniform inflation forecasts. An accurate understanding of the range of inflation forecasts is important for the Fed when setting interest rates.

There are two notable surveys that ask participants to forecast inflation. One is the Michigan Survey of Consumers, which was discussed in Chapter 9. The survey calls a random sample of 600 cell phone numbers in the continental United States every month and asks respondents a range of questions about their personal financial situation and their forecasts of macroeconomic variables, such as GDP growth, the change in unemployment and interest rates, and inflation over the next one to five years. The Michigan Survey is one measure of inflation expectations from the perspective of consumers.

The second data source is the Survey of Professional Forecasters (SPF) conducted by the Federal Reserve Bank of Philadelphia. As the name would suggest, the survey participants are professional forecasters from various industries in the United States. The respondents are asked a range of questions, including their estimates of inflation over the next one to five years. Since these professionals are also likely providing forecasts to their own businesses, the SPF provides a measure of inflation expectations from the perspective of U.S. businesses.

Figure 12.9 shows the median forecast of inflation over the next 12 months in the Michigan survey and the SPF as well as the realized change in the CPI over that year. The series track each other closely with a correlation of just over 0.7. The professionals consistently forecasted a higher inflation rate through the mid-1990s than U.S. consumers. That pattern has completely reversed over the past 20 years, with consumers anticipating a higher rate of inflation. Both households and professional forecasters tend to underestimate big swings in the CPI. For instance, neither households nor professionals forecasted the deflation that occurred in the mid-2000s. They also missed the spike in inflation following the 2020 pandemic and, in look-

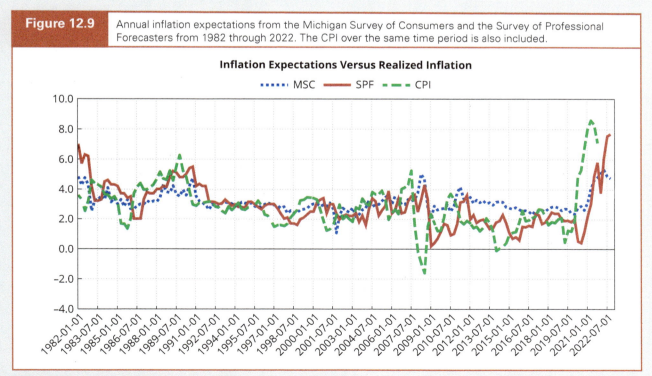

Figure 12.9 Annual inflation expectations from the Michigan Survey of Consumers and the Survey of Professional Forecasters from 1982 through 2022. The CPI over the same time period is also included.

Source: Federal Reserve Bank of Philadelphia, Michigan Survey of Consumers, and the BLS.

Continues

Application 12.1 (Continued)

ing at the data in 2022, the professional forecasters were more optimistic than consumers that inflation was going to come down. Although households sometimes make better forecasts than the professionals, and vice versa, the average of the absolute value deviation of inflation expectations from realized inflation averaged about one percentage point for both households and professionals.

As an alternative to measuring inflation expectations using surveys, it's possible to derive inflation expectations from the interest rates on different bonds. A typical treasury bond issued by the federal government promises to pay the bond holder a fixed nominal interest rate. If inflation is higher than expected, income is redistributed from the bondholder to the government. If inflation is lower than expected, income is redistributed from the government to bondholders. This is a particular example of the general lesson you learned in Chapter 5, namely that unexpected inflation redistributes income. There have been several historical episodes where this redistribution has been large. Following a large spike in inflation in the late 1970s and early 1980s, the interest rate on a 10-year constant maturity treasury was about 15 percent in 1981. But over the next two years, the Fed moved aggressively against inflation and, by 1983, inflation was under 4 percent. Thus, bond holders in the early 1980s received a massive windfall. The redistribution went the other direction if you purchased a treasury security in 2021, when the nominal interest rate on a 1-year bond was about 0.5% and 1.5% on a 10-year bond. When inflation spiked in 2022, income was redistributed to the bond issuer (the U.S. government) at the expense of bondholders.

To hedge against inflation risk, the U.S. government offers investors a **Treasury Inflation Protected Security (TIPS)**, which adjusts the interest rate by the CPI. If the CPI is higher than expected, the government pays more in interest. If the CPI is lower than expected, the government pays a lower interest rate. Thus, TIPS pay investors a constant real interest rate. With values of the nominal interest rate from the usual treasury securities, and values of the real interest rate from TIPS, inflation expectations can be inferred through the Fisher equation,

$$i_t - r_t = \pi^e.$$

Thus, the interest rate spread gives a measure of expected inflation over some time horizon. TIPS are issued with 5-, 10-, and 30-year maturities, so economists can use interest rate spreads to measure inflation expectations over a 5-, 10-, and 30-year time horizon. Figure 12.10 shows the results. The three series move together closely. Note in the most recent period of high inflation, the spring and summer of 2022, inflation expectations increased, but not nearly by as much as actual inflation. Evidently, bond

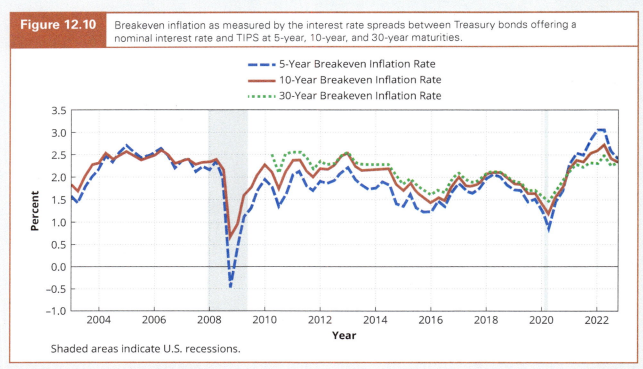

Figure 12.10 Breakeven inflation as measured by the interest rate spreads between Treasury bonds offering a nominal interest rate and TIPS at 5-year, 10-year, and 30-year maturities.

Shaded areas indicate U.S. recessions.

Source: FRED https://fred.stlouisfed.org/graph/?g=ZCxg.

Continues

Application 12.1 (Continued)

holders expect the Fed to get inflation under control. Also, note that inflation expectations rose more at the 5-year horizon than at the 10-year horizon, which in turn rose more than the 30-year horizon. This is a simple fact of averages. If investors expect inflation to be high (say at 5 percent) for another year before reverting to the Fed's target of 2 percent, the average rate of inflation would be $1/5 \times (5 + 2 + 2 + 2 + 2) = 2.6$. Over 10 years, the average rate of inflation would be 2.3 percent; over 30 years, the average rate of inflation would be 2.1 percent.

The Fed has many different sources of inflation expectations to draw from in making their decisions over monetary policy. Although the data are no doubt helpful, there are also complications. One big issue is that the expectations themselves depend on anticipated Fed policy. But the Fed uses the forecasts in making policy. This makes for some interesting interactions between the Fed and market participants in reality, and also has implications for how economists model monetary policy. This is something we turn to later in the chapter.

12-1c Alternatives to the Wage-Contracting Model

The upward-sloping aggregate supply curve (and associated Phillips curve) can be explained in a lot of different ways. One such explanation is that unanticipated inflation induces uncertainty among producers in an economy. Imagine a soybean farmer who observes that the price of soybeans increased 5 percent compared to last month. The farmer must forecast whether the price of soybeans increased relative to other commodities or that the general price level increased 5 percent. If the price of soybeans increased relative to other commodities, the farmer maximizes profits by producing more soybeans. Alternatively, the farmer would not want to raise production if there was an increase in the general price level. If the farmer is uncertain about the causes of the rise in soybean prices, they may choose to only produce a slightly higher quantity of soybeans.

Now imagine every producer in the economy making that same calculation. Some firms will mistake the increase in the general price level for an increased demand for their product. If enough firms make this mistake, then there will be an increase in aggregate output. Because the potential rate of output, by assumption, hasn't changed, there exists a positive relationship between inflation and the output gap.

Yet another explanation for the upward-sloping aggregate supply curve is the presence of menu costs. McDonald's introduced their dollar menu in 2002: it featured several prominent menu items for $1, such as McDoubles, McChickens, and apple pies. Despite the general price level increasing 25 percent between 2002 and 2013, McDonalds didn't change their dollar menu prices. In real terms, these items got cheaper over the decade, and the dollar menu was very popular with customers. Sadly, the dollar menu ended in 2013. Today, the McDouble costs about $3. That means the McDouble increased in price by about 200 percent between 2013 and 2023, while the general price level increased about 25 percent. In summary, the pricing pattern of the McDouble and similar items is nowhere close to replicating the trend in the general price level.

Provided the demand for McDonald's products was stable over the past 20 years and there wasn't some technological breakthrough in the production of hamburgers, you might expect the price of these products to scale with the general price level. The fact that they don't suggests that McDonald's faces costs in changing their prices. Adjusting the price of every product after the Bureau of Labor Statistics releases preliminary inflation numbers is unlikely to be an efficient use of resources. Moreover, businesses like McDonald's may lose customers if the customers perceive the increase in the price of a McDouble to be a relative price change rather than tracking the general price level. When businesses do change prices, they may find it optimal to increase their prices by more than the general price level would justify under the expectation that they won't get to make another adjustment for some time.

The costs that firms incur when changing prices are called **menu costs**. These can be tangible costs associated with changing prices, such as printing new menus, updating the website and barcodes, and doing market research to find the optimal price for each product.

Treasury Inflation Expected Security (TIPS)
Bonds issued by the U.S. government that index interest payments to the CPI.

Menu costs
The costs that firms incur when changing prices.

They can also be intangible, in that raising prices may hurt brand loyalty. Any kind of menu cost will cause firms to update their prices less frequently than would otherwise be justified by economic fundamentals. An implication is that an increase in the general price level, provided it isn't too large, won't cause all firms to update their prices proportionally and immediately. With relative prices lower, these firms will see an increase in the demand for their product and increase production. Thus, an increase in the general price level leads to a greater level of output. Because the natural rate of output hasn't changed, we again arrive at an upward-sloping aggregate supply curve.

To recap, there are several reasons for an upward-sloping supply curve, including contract frictions, information constraints, and menu costs. You may notice a similarity between this list and the costs of inflation in Chapter 5. Indeed, most of the costs of inflation come when inflation is *unexpected*. If the inflation rate is consistently stable, then producers and consumers don't mistake a change in a relative price level with a change in the general price level. We revisit the desirability of inflation targeting later in this chapter. Having described the aggregate supply curve, we proceed to combine it with the IS and MP curves from Chapter 11.

> ### ✓ Knowledge Check 12-3
>
> The CPI increased 8 percent between 2021 and 2022 and yet the Dollar Tree increased their standard price from $1 to $1.25, a 25 percent increase. How does the menu cost model explain this?
>
> ———————————————————————————— Answers are at the end of the chapter.

12-2 The IS–MP–AS Model

In Chapter 11, you learned about the simultaneous determination of output and real interest rates in the short run, where the short run is the time horizon at which inflation expectations are constant and the Fed effectively controls real interest rates. Is it reasonable to assume a constant rate of inflation expectations? A quick look back to Figures 12.9 and 12.10 would suggest not. Inflation expectations move up and down over time. On the other hand, inflation expectations do not instantaneously adjust to changes in economic fundamentals. The surge in inflation in 2022 was unanticipated, and even after several months of consistently high inflation in the data, expectations (both in the SPF and the Michigan survey) were slow to adjust. Thus, over a short duration, say a few months or a few quarters, it's reasonable to assume that inflation expectations are exogenously fixed.

Thus, a reasonable description of the economy in the short run are the three equations:

IS Curve:
$$Y_t = C(Y_t - G_t, Y_{t+1} - G_{t+1}, r_t) + I(r_t + f_t, A_{t+1}) + G_t, \tag{4}$$

MP Curve:
$$r_t = i_t - \pi^e, \tag{5}$$

AS Curve:
$$\pi_t = \pi^e + k(Y_t - Y_t^p). \tag{6}$$

The three endogenous variables are the real interest rate, r_t, real GDP, Y_t, and the level of inflation, π_t. Recall from Chapter 11 that the IS curve is the set of (r_t, Y_t) pairs such that the market for savings and investment is in equilibrium. Consumption is a positive function of current-period disposable income, $Y_t - G_t$, future-period disposable income, $Y_{t+1} - G_{t+1}$, and a negative function of the real interest rate, r_t. Investment is a negative function of the sum of the real interest rate and risk premium, $r_t + f_t$, and a positive function of future TFP, A_{t+1}. The MP curve graphically represents how monetary policy makers choose the interest rate. We assume that the Fed sets the nominal interest rate, i_t, and that, given exogenous inflation expectations, the Fisher equation, $r_t = i_t - \pi^e$, determines the real interest rate. The next section graphically depicts the model and defines the objective of monetary policy.

12-2a Graphing the IS–MP–AS Model

Just as in Chapter 11, we can graph the IS and MP curves with the real interest rate on the vertical axis, and output on the horizontal axis. This is shown in the top panel of Figure 12.11. To conserve space, we do not graph the market for savings and investment, although that market is still in equilibrium in the background (remember how we derived the IS curve in Chapter 11). The bottom panel depicts the relationship between output and inflation as embodied in the upward-sloping aggregate supply curve. As drawn, GDP is equal to its potential level and actual inflation equals expected inflation.

Although there are three equations and three endogenous variables, solving for an equilibrium graphically, and even algebraically, is fairly straightforward. The solution also highlights some of the economic mechanisms in the model. You can think about it in three steps.

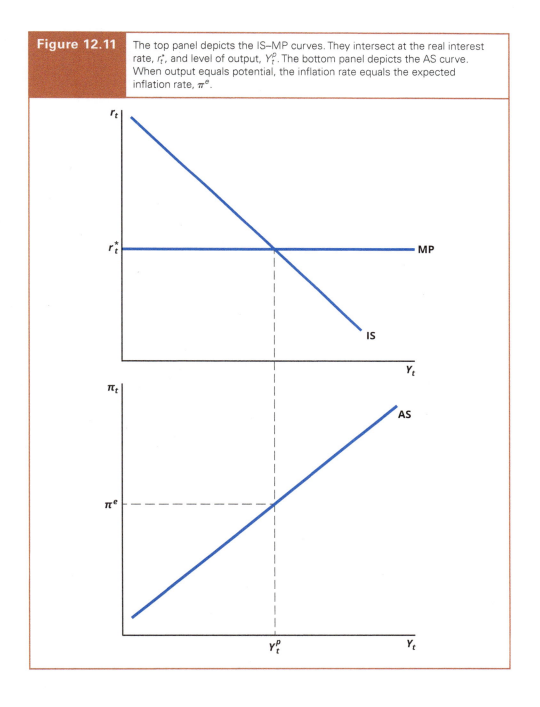

Figure 12.11 The top panel depicts the IS–MP curves. They intersect at the real interest rate, r_t^*, and level of output, Y_t^p. The bottom panel depicts the AS curve. When output equals potential, the inflation rate equals the expected inflation rate, π^e.

1. The Fed chooses a nominal interest rate that, because expected inflation is exogenously fixed, pins down the equilibrium real interest rate.

2. Given the real interest rate from step 1, the IS curve determines the equilibrium quantity of output. That is, given the real interest rate effectively chosen by the Fed, the equilibrium in the market for savings and investment determines the level of output consistent with that real interest rate.

3. Given an equilibrium quantity of output in step 2, the inflation rate is pinned down by the aggregate supply curve.

Or, more concisely, the model is summarized by

$$\text{Fed picks } r_t \Rightarrow \text{IS curve pins down } Y_t \Rightarrow \text{AS curve pins down } \pi_t.$$

The model's key equations, endogenous variables, exogenous variables, and parameters are summarized in Table 12.1.

Table 12.1	Summarizing the IS–MP–AS Model	
Endogenous variables	**Exogenous variables**	**Parameters**
Y_t, r_t, π_t	$G_t, G_{t+1}, A_{t+1}, Y_{t+1}, f_t, i_t, Y_t^p$	π^e, k
Key equations:		
$Y_t - C(Y_t - G_t, Y_{t+1} - G_{t+1}, r_t) - G_t = I(r_t + f_t, A_{t+1})$	(IS Curve, Eq (4))	
$r_t = i_t - \pi^e$	(MP Curve, Eq (5))	
$\pi_t = \pi^e + k(Y_t - Y_t^p)$	(AS Curve, Eq (6))	

Before discussing comparative static exercises, it's useful to compare the model with a sticky-wage AS curve to one with a flexible price and wage AS curve as discussed in Section 12.1. Remember, the presence of sticky nominal wages can cause output to deviate from its potential level, whereas output, by definition, equals its potential level when wages are flexible. As the AS curve gets steeper, price changes become more sensitive to deviations of output from its potential level. This means that the more flexible prices and wages are, the steeper the AS curve. The goal of monetary policy is to minimize the output gap. Indeed, the flexible price AS curve is actually a special case of Equation (6) with $k = \infty$.

Figure 12.12 shows how this works. At the original equilibrium, the output gap is negative, meaning that the economy is underproducing relative to potential. To minimize the output gap, the Fed lowers nominal rate which, because expected inflation is fixed, lowers the real interest rate. As the real interest rate goes down, output increases. The Fed continues to do this until output equals potential.

It's easy enough to see why the Fed would want to raise output when it is below potential, but the reverse isn't so obvious. That is, why would the Fed want to reduce output when it is above potential? There are two reasons. First, when the economy operates above its potential GDP, inflation is relatively high. From Chapter 5, you know that inflation imposes microeconomic costs. Indeed, the existence of contracting frictions, which is our rationale for the upward-sloping aggregate supply curve, are exacerbated when inflation is unexpectedly high. A higher level of inflation lowers real wages and causes firms to employ more labor. Firms hiring more labor may sound like a good thing, but that's not always true. At any time, it's optimal for some people to be unemployed and looking for work. If people always accepted their first job offer, then a lot of better matches will never be formed. Imagine if you sent out 20 applications to 20 employers and one of them calls you back the very next day and offers a minimum wage salary. Would it be optimal for you to take it? Probably not. It would be better to endure a temporary unemployment spell and hope for a better job. The same is true for the macroeconomy. It's not efficient for every single person in the labor force to be employed. Neither is it efficient for every person who is employed to work 24 hours per day. Full employment of capital and labor does not mean maximizing

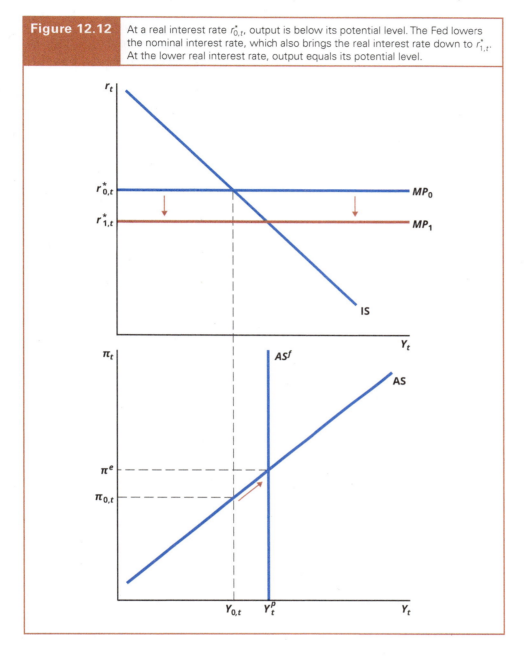

Figure 12.12 At a real interest rate $r_{0,t}^*$, output is below its potential level. The Fed lowers the nominal interest rate, which also brings the real interest rate down to $r_{1,t}^*$. At the lower real interest rate, output equals its potential level.

their utilization. That means, in any given period, there is a cap to potential output and it's possible for the economy to be operating above potential. For these reasons, the Fed wants to minimize the output gap in either direction.

With this framework in place, we can think about how changes to exogenous variables affect the economy and also derive the optimal response of monetary policy to any changes.

✓ Knowledge Check 12-4

How does the AS curve look when $k = 0$? Graphically depict an increase in inflation expectations.

Answers are at the end of the chapter.

12-2b Comparative Statics in the IS–MP–AS Model

You learned in the Chapter 11 how changes to the IS and MP curves affect the real interest rate and output in the short run. We will combine those changes with the sticky-wage AS curve to determine what happens to output, the real interest rate, and inflation absent a change in monetary policy. Then, we will ask what the optimal monetary policy action would be. To make things easier to analyze, we begin all of these comparative statics at a common reference point, which is where output equals potential output and inflation equals inflation expectations.

Begin with an increase in government spending, G_t. For a fixed level of output, $Y^*_{0,t}$, an increase in government spending reduces the supply of savings, raising the equilibrium real interest rate associated with $Y^*_{0,t}$, in the savings–investment market, thereby shifting the IS curve to the right. This is shown in Figure 12.13. If the Fed holds nominal interest rates constant, the equilibrium real interest rate stays at $r^*_{0,t}$, which means equilibrium output increases to $Y^*_{1,t}$. From there, we trace the new equilibrium level of output down to the aggregate supply curve and find that inflation rises from $\pi^*_{0,t}$ to $\pi^*_{1,t}$.

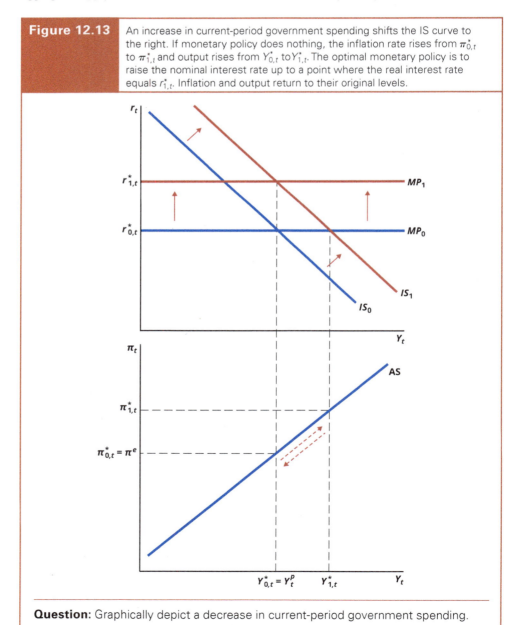

Figure 12.13 An increase in current-period government spending shifts the IS curve to the right. If monetary policy does nothing, the inflation rate rises from $\pi^*_{0,t}$ to $\pi^*_{1,t}$ and output rises from $Y^*_{0,t}$ to $Y^*_{1,t}$. The optimal monetary policy is to raise the nominal interest rate up to a point where the real interest rate equals $r^*_{1,t}$. Inflation and output return to their original levels.

Question: Graphically depict a decrease in current-period government spending.

Chapter 12 The IS–MP–AS Model   **311**

The emergence of a positive output gap tells us that this is a suboptimal equilibrium. The potential level of output is unaffected by a change in government spending. The reason government spending increased actual output is because of contracting frictions in the labor market. Can monetary policy restore the efficient equilibrium? Yes. Since output is higher than potential, the Fed can raise nominal interest rates which, through the Fisher equation, raise real interest rates and reduce output as the economy moves along the IS curve. The Fed continues to raise the nominal interest rate until the real interest rate is high enough to bring output back to potential, which occurs at $r_{1,t}^*$.

It may be strange to think about the Fed effectively undoing the effects of an increase in government spending, but this is the efficient response. Here is why. Suppose state governments collectively decide to raise the pay of elementary school teachers, raising government spending in the aggregate. Raising the pay of teachers may in fact be good public policy and, in the mind of some voters and politicians, be well deserved. If higher pay attracts better teachers, then future GDP may increase as the students of today become the workers of tomorrow. But that doesn't change the fact that potential output today hasn't changed. If the Fed adopts **passive monetary policy** and does not raise the nominal interest rate, then output goes up because people work more than what is optimal from the perspective of when they set their contracts. Instead, the Fed should raise the real interest rate to reflect that savings supply has indeed decreased. The economy shifts to a higher level of government spending and a lower level of consumption and investment. The optimal mix of government spending, consumption, and investment is a different question that is beyond the scope of this chapter. All the Fed needs to know (and all you need to know) is that potential output has not changed.

> **Passive monetary policy**
> A monetary policy rule characterized by the central bank holding the nominal interest rate constant after a change in another exogenous variable.

One important caveat to the previous discussion is that the economy starts at the efficient level of output when government spending increases. Large increases in government spending, particularly during recessions, are often justified because output is below its efficient level and monetary policy is constrained by the zero-lower bound (ZLB). Recall that the ZLB occurs when the nominal interest rate hits zero. If the nominal interest rate is zero and output is below potential, the Fed can't lower the nominal interest rate to a level that restores efficiency. In that case, the right level of expansionary fiscal policy, as shown in Figure 12.14, can get the economy back to the efficient level of output.

Next, suppose that the potential level of output increases. An increase in the potential level of output shifts the sticky price/wage AS curve to the right, as shown in Figure 12.15. The flexible price/wage AS curve, drawn here for reference, also shifts to the right as the potential level of output increases from $Y_{0,t}^P$ to $Y_{1,t}^P$. If monetary policy holds constant the nominal interest rate, then the real interest rate also stays constant. But if the real interest rate stays constant, then, from the IS curve, output does not change. Because the economy is on the new AS curve and output doesn't change, the inflation rate drops from $\pi_{0,t}^*$ to $\pi_{1,t}^*$.

The fact that a higher level of potential output doesn't lead to a higher level of actual output is paradoxical. What is the economic mechanism at work? An increase in potential output, perhaps coming from an increase in TFP, puts downward pressure on prices. But if prices are lower and nominal wages are fixed, real wages go up. On the one hand, an increase in TFP should lead to higher real wages, as workers have a higher marginal product. But what our graphical analysis shows is that real wages rise by even more than would be justified by an increase in TFP with flexible nominal wages. Firms end up hiring less labor, despite using labor more efficiently, and, on balance, output does not change.

Because it is desirable for actual output to track potential output as much as possible, we know that passive monetary policy is inefficient. Monetary policy can improve the situation by lowering the nominal interest rate. A lower nominal interest rate leads to a lower real interest rate, which shifts the MP curve down. The Fed continues to lower the nominal interest rate until the real interest rate reaches the point on the IS curve where output equals its potential level. This is shown in Figure 12.16. The final equilibrium has the new level of output, $Y_{1,t}$ equaling its new potential level, $Y_{1,t}^P$, and inflation moving back to π^e. In summary, comparing the initial equilibrium to the final equilibrium with optimal monetary policy, we see that the real interest rate falls and output rises. These two changes imply that consumption and investment must also be higher.

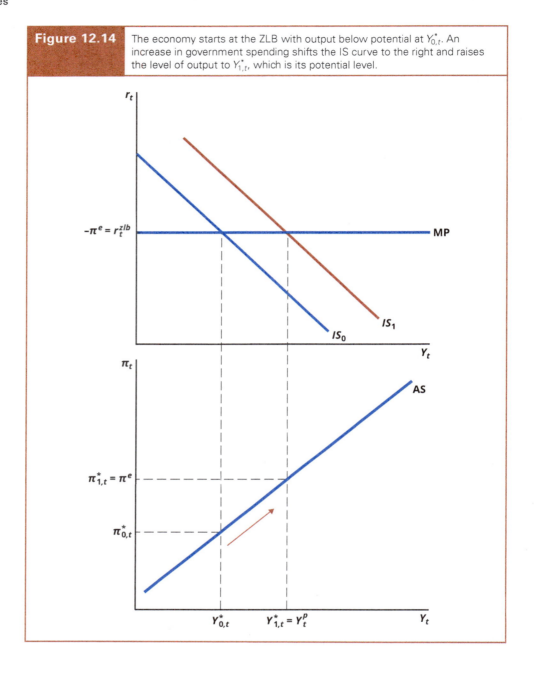

Figure 12.14 The economy starts at the ZLB with output below potential at $Y^*_{0,t}$. An increase in government spending shifts the IS curve to the right and raises the level of output to $Y^*_{1,t}$, which is its potential level.

Finally, consider an increase in inflation expectations. If such an increase is permanent, this could come from a change in the Fed's inflation target. An increase in inflation expectations lowers the real interest rate, which shifts the MP curve down and the AS curve to the left. Since the new MP curve intersects the IS curve at a lower real interest rate, output increases. Tracing the level of output down to the new AS curve shows that inflation increases from $\pi^*_{0,t}$ to $\pi^*_{1,t}$. Because the potential level of output is not affected by the change in inflation expectations, the output gap, absent a change in monetary policy, is positive. To close the output gap, the Fed raises the nominal interest rate to a point where the MP curve goes back to the original. In the end, the increase in inflation expectations increases inflation but leaves the real interest rate and output the same. This makes sense in light of what you learned in Chapter 5. An increase in the Fed's inflation target raises inflation expectations and equilibrium inflation rate but does not affect real variables, namely the real interest rate and output.

Figure 12.15 An increase in potential output from $Y^p_{0,t}$ to $Y^p_{1,t}$ shifts the AS curve to the right. The flexible price/wage AS curve also shifts to the right. If monetary policy keeps the nominal interest rate fixed, inflation falls to $\pi^*_{1,t}$ and output stays fixed at $Y^*_{0,t}$. The optimal monetary policy shifts the MP curve down until the real interest rate is $r^*_{1,t}$ and output equals its new potential level.

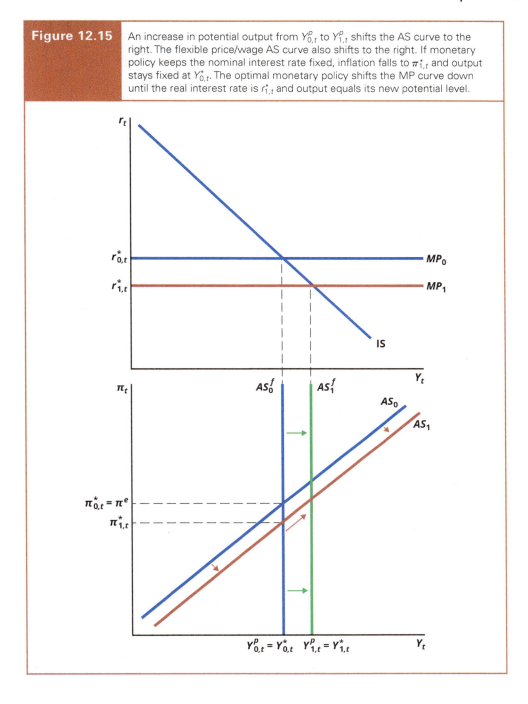

As you saw in Chapter 11, managing inflation expectations through forward guidance, where the Fed not only explains their current policy but gives hints about their future policy, can be especially effective at the ZLB. The recovery after 2007–2009 recession is an illustrative case study. Despite the recession ending in the fourth quarter of 2009, the unemployment rate remained above its pre-recession level until 2015. The Fed, having run into the ZLB by 2008, was looking for alternative mechanisms to achieve its dual mandate of price stability and full employment. Forward guidance was one such tool. In statements following their meetings, the Fed provided concrete details on the time path of future policy. For instance, after their August 2011 meeting, the Federal Reserve Open Market Committee (FOMC) statement read, "The Committee currently anticipates that economic conditions—including low rates of resource utilization and a subdued outlook

314 **Part 3** Business Cycles

Figure 12.16 An increase in inflation expectations shifts the AS curve to the left. If monetary policy leaves the nominal interest rate unchanged, the MP curve shifts down. Equilibrium output rises to $Y_{1,t}^*$ and inflation rises to $\pi_{1,t}^*$. Optimal monetary policy entails raising the nominal interest rate to the point where the MP curve goes back to MP_0. Output goes back to potential.

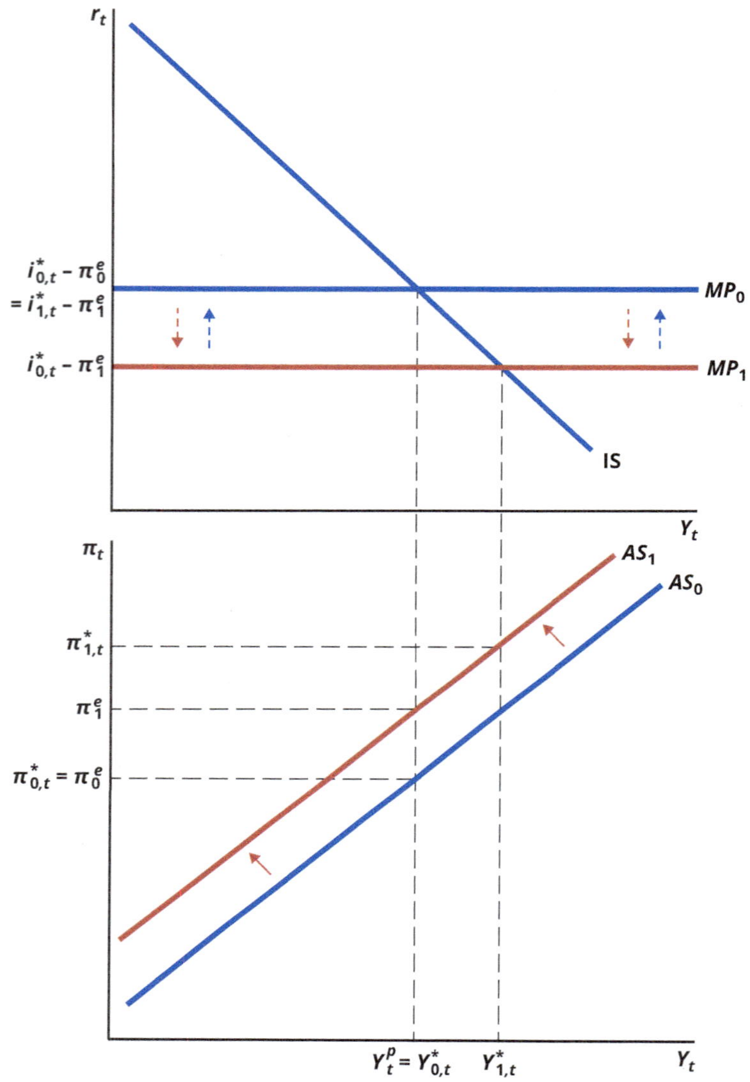

Question: Graphically depict a decrease in inflation expectations.

for inflation over the medium run—are likely to warrant exceptionally low levels for the federal funds rate at least through mid-2013."[4] By providing hints about future policy, the Fed was hoping to affect the real interest rate and aggregate supply curve by anchoring inflation expectations. Evidence on the success of forward guidance is mixed, but it is one more tool at the Fed's disposal.[5]

---

[4]FOMC statement, August 2011: https://www.federalreserve.gov/newsevents/pressreleases/monetary20110809a.htm.
[5]Becker, Thealexa and Andrew Lee Smith. 2015. "Has Forward Guidance Been Effective?" *Economic Review Federal Reserve Bank of Kansas City*, issue Q III: 57–78.

Chapter 12 The IS–MP–AS Model **315**

✓ Knowledge Check 12-5

Graphically depict an increase in f_t. Also depict optimal monetary policy.

Answers are at the end of the chapter.

12-2c Does the IS–MP–AS Model Explain Business Cycle Facts?

You learned in Chapter 10 that output, consumption, and investment move together over the business cycle. You also learned that unemployment is strongly countercyclical and real wages are mildly procyclical (where the degree of procyclicality depends on issues like correcting for composition bias). Is the IS–MP–AS model consistent with these facts?

This is a nuanced question for two reasons. First, there are numerous potential sources of shocks in the model. Some of these shocks shift the IS curve, while others shift the AS curve. The time path of investment, consumption, and other economic variables will depend on what shock is driving the business cycle. The second reason is that effects of any given shock depends on the actions of monetary policy. To see this, return to the effects of an increase in current-period government spending in Figure 12.13. If the Fed does nothing, an increase in government spending increases output. If the Fed implements optimal monetary policy, then output doesn't change. Thus, if two economies are hit with identical shocks, but have different monetary policies, the time path of economic variables will be different.

With these nuances in mind, let's summarize the effects of shocks to the AS and IS curves under completely passive optimal monetary policy versus optimal monetary policy. Figure 12.15 showed the effects of a shock to potential output, which could plausibly come from an increase in TFP. Table 12.2 summarizes the effects on five endogenous variables under the assumptions of passive versus optimal monetary policy.

Table 12.2	Summarizing the Effects of an Increase in Potential Output	
	Passive MP	**Optimal MP**
Y_t	0	+
C_t	0	+
I_t	0	+
u_t	+	−
w_t	+	+

An increase in potential output does not affect actual output if the Fed follows a passive monetary policy, so it can't be the case that the business cycle is driven by supply shocks under passive monetary policy. If, on the other hand, the Fed implements optimal monetary policy, then shocks to the AS curve are a possible source of business cycles. In response to an increase in potential output, the Fed lowers nominal interest rates which, through the Fisher equation, lower real interest rates. Lower real interest rates and a higher level of output imply that consumption and investment will both increase. Using the connection between the Phillips curve and the AS curve, an increase in the potential and actual levels of output implies a reduction in the natural rate and actual rate of unemployment. Finally, with a stable inflation rate and an increased demand for workers, it is likely that real wages will increase at least to a small degree. The reason is that even if a large fraction of the workforce has a contract for a fixed nominal wage (for reasons discussed in Section 12.2b), the fraction of workers resetting their wages in the period potential output increases will negotiate higher wages.

Although shocks to potential output under optimal monetary policy are a possible source of business cycle variation, are they a plausible one? Chapter 10 discussed why one might be dubious about such claims. Random and recurring reductions in the economy's technology level are difficult to motivate in real life. Moreover, properly measured TFP, that is, one that corrects for varying rates of capital and labor utilization, is significantly less correlated with output. Finally, while many economists think that the operation of monetary policy has improved in recent years, it is unlikely that the Fed is implementing optimal monetary policy all the time. We return to monetary policy in practice later in this chapter. It's more likely that the Fed moves the nominal interest rate in the right direction following a shock to potential output, which would induce the same correlations as shown in the third column of Table 12.2. So shocks to potential output probably explain some, but not all, of business cycles.

Next, let's think about shocks to the IS curve. Government spending at the local, state, and federal levels does change over time, but it probably isn't realistic to think of them as a persistent source of business cycles. Nondiscretionary spending is legislated and takes months or even years to change. Discretionary spending, some of which changes with the business cycle, if anything, responds to economic booms and recessions rather than causing them. For instance, the increase in unemployment benefits during the Covid-19 recession was in response to economic circumstances. While it is true that government spending can affect the persistence of business cycles (more generous unemployment insurance may cause the unemployment rate to remain high, for instance), the government spending itself, at least in isolation, will not explain the business cycles in the data.

So that leaves two candidates: f_t, the credit spread, and A_{t+1}, future TFP, although future income, Y_{t+1}, is affected through A_{t+1}. Persistent changes in f_t could come from changing credit market conditions. If the riskiness of lending to businesses frequently changes, say because of the profitability of the underlying projects being financed, changes in f_t, may be a likely source of business cycles in the data. Many economists, including former Fed chairman Ben Bernanke, have pointed to credit frictions as a source of business cycles.

Likewise, because consumption and investment are forward looking, changes in expectations over future productivity can change output today. John Maynard Keynes emphasized these "animal spirits," or the changes in optimism and pessimism by businesses and individuals, in his book *The General Theory of Employment, Interest, and Money*. In modern terminology, animal spirits are often referred to as consumer and business confidence. The Michigan Survey of Consumers, which you first encountered in Application 12.1, has reported a monthly index of consumer sentiment since 1982. Figure 12.17 shows that consumer sentiment falls during recessions, which is not all that surprising. More interesting is

Figure 12.17 The index of consumer sentiment as measured by the Michigan Survey of Consumers from 1982 through 2022.

Shaded areas indicate U.S. recessions.

Source: FRED and Michigan Survey of Consumers https://fred.stlouisfed.org/graph/?g=ZRpw.

Chapter 12 The IS–MP–AS Model **317**

the fact that declines in consumer confidence, with the exception of the Covid-19 recession, precede actual recessions. This is consistent with the Keynesian idea that a wave of pessimism may cause consumers to cut back on their spending and firms to reduce investment. These expectations fulfill themselves as less consumption and less investment imply lower levels of output.

A decrease in f_t or an increase in A_{t+1} shifts the IS curve to the right. If monetary policy keeps the nominal interest rate constant, the MP curve stays fixed and output increases. A positive output gap leads to rising inflation. With output today (and tomorrow in the case of an increase in A_{t+1}) being higher, consumers increase spending. With either the decrease in f_t or the increase in A_{t+1}, firms increase investment. Thus, output, consumption, and investment all move together. Since output is higher and current-period TFP is the same, we can infer that unemployment is lower. The upward pressure on inflation, combined with sticky nominal wages, leads to a falling real wage. This is summarized in the second column of Table 12.3.

Table 12.3	Effects of a Demand Shock with Optimal and Passive Monetary Policy	
	Passive MP	**Optimal MP**
Y_t	+	0
C_t	+	?
I_t	+	?
u_t	−	0
w_t	−	0

Because the potential rate of output is unaffected by an increase in A_{t+1} or a decrease in f_t, optimal monetary policy entails moving the nominal interest rate so that actual output stays the same in equilibrium. This means that the Fed raises the nominal interest rate, shifting the MP curve up to a point where output doesn't change. Since output doesn't change, neither does the unemployment rate. If the unemployment rate is the same, then so are real wages. Although output stays constant, the composition of output, between consumption and investment, will change. If the real interest rate increase follows a decrease in f_t, consumption falls and investment rises. If the real interest rate increase follows an increase in A_{t+1}, then the real interest rate and future income is higher, which has offsetting effects on consumption. There are also offsetting effects on investment. Thus, we can't be sure how consumption and investment change, but we know the sum of their changes must be zero.

Provided the Fed follows a passive monetary policy, changes in the credit spread and consumer and business sentiment are viable sources of business cycles. The only wrong prediction is real wages being negatively correlated with output. To reiterate from our discussion on supply shocks, while it is unlikely the Fed implements optimal monetary policy, they are explicit about trying to neutralize the effects of IS shocks, which the Fed sometimes refers to as demand shocks. The Taylor rule, which you learned about in the last chapter, predicts that the Fed raises the nominal interest rate when inflation is above its target rate and output is above potential, which are both true following an IS shock. Since the Taylor rule is an accurate predictor of Fed policy, we can be confident that the Fed moves the nominal interest rate in the right direction following an IS shock.

Where does this leave us? Fed policy has improved over time, but it is doubtful that monetary policymakers have the information necessary to implement optimal monetary policy. Even if they had all the relevant information and all of it was accurate, the Fed only meets every six weeks, and there is no reason to think that variables like consumer sentiment stay constant over that six-week period. Thus, monetary policy in the United States might be described as reasonably effective, but not optimal. That leaves room for changes to potential output, credit market conditions, and consumer and business sentiment to all play a role in driving business cycles.

Although the Fed may not have an accurate and real-time measure of potential output, the Fed might be able to get closer to optimal monetary policy by following a simpler strategy. In the case of either supply shocks or demand shocks, optimal policy entails stabi-

318 **Part 3** Business Cycles

Divine coincidence
The result that inflation targeting stabilizes inflation and minimizes the output gap.

Friedman rule
The result suggesting that a central bank should set the long-run inflation rate to achieve a nominal interest rate of zero.

lizing inflation. Even if the Fed can't measure potential output, it can implement monetary policy through a strict inflation target. We mentioned the Fed's dual mandate earlier in the chapter. Namely, the Fed is supposed to act in a way to achieve price stability and full employment. If we take full employment to mean minimizing the output gap, then the Fed is supposed to stabilize inflation and minimize the output gap. Inflation targeting achieves both objectives. This has come to be known as the **divine coincidence**.[6] Given the divine coincidence, it is not surprising that many central banks have adopted a firm inflation target. This is discussed in Application 12.2.

Application 12.2

Inflation Targeting Is a Good Idea: What Should the Target Be?

There are three unambiguous benefits to inflation targeting. The first benefit is that it avoids hyperinflation. From chapter 5 you know that hyperinflation, or a very high inflation rate, is very economically costly. When currency loses much of its value over the course of a day or month, decisions over how much money to carry, when to deposit money into the bank, and how frequently to adjust prices are critically important. Constantly changing prices or making frequent deposits and withdrawals at the bank consumes time and other resources that could, absent the hyperinflation, be put to better use. A central bank that adopts a firm inflation target and sticks to it avoids the catastrophic consequences of hyperinflation.

Recalling from Chapter 9 that one way to finance government budget deficits is through printing money, standing by an inflation target requires some degree of central bank independence. In other words, the demands of fiscal policy cannot dictate the decisions of the central bank. A strong commitment to an inflation target also then imposes discipline on fiscal policymakers. If the legislature knows that its spending can't be financed by monetizing the debt, it will have to carefully budget revenue and expenditure. Imposing some degree of fiscal discipline is another benefit of inflation targeting and is one reason why many developing countries have adopted an inflation target.

The third benefit is that a strong commitment to an inflation target anchors expectations. From the aggregate supply curve, you know that the actual rate of inflation depends on expected inflation. A credible commitment to stable price growth stabilizes inflation expectations and makes business cycles easier to manage. Applying this logic, the Fed adopted an explicit 2 percent inflation target in 2012. And, indeed, inflation expectations were less volatile in the United States in the decade following this policy. (You can see this by looking at Figure 12.9.) Analyzing recent FOMC statements, you will see the sentence,

"The Committee seeks to achieve maximum employment and inflation at the rate of 2 percent over the longer run." The Fed sets nominal interest rates in accordance with this objective. So, when inflation rose in the spring of 2022, the Fed immediately raised interest rates.

The benefits to inflation targeting are so clear that many countries have adopted it. The International Monetary Fund distinguishes between "full-fledged inflation targeters" that explicitly commit to keeping inflation at a certain value, from other central banks that have other objectives in addition to price stability.[7] The Federal Reserve in the United States would fall into the second category, as the Fed also tries to achieve full employment. As Figure 12.18 shows, many other countries fall into the first category. The figure shows the year each country adopted its inflation target and the target range of inflation. Both low- and high-income countries are represented among inflation-targeting countries. At the same time, the target inflation rate is different across countries, ranging from a low of 2 percent (in Japan) to a high of 8 percent (in Ghana). If inflation targeting is good monetary policy, what should the target be?

Because holding money provides social benefits, such as serving as a medium of exchange, and the social costs to printing money are almost zero, one theory is to equate the private costs of holding money with the social costs. The opportunity cost of holding cash is the nominal interest rate. So, using this logic, the central bank shock should set the nominal interest rate to zero. This is known as the **Friedman rule**, named after economist Milton Freidman. From the Fisher equation, a nominal interest rate of zero implies

$$i_t = r_t + \pi^e$$
$$\Leftrightarrow 0 = r_t + \pi^e$$
$$\Leftrightarrow \pi^e = -r_t$$
$$\Leftrightarrow \overline{\pi} = -\overline{r},$$

[7]Jahan, Sarwat. (n.d.). "Inflation Targeting: Holding the Line." International Money Fund: https://www.imf.org/external/pubs/ft/fandd/basics/72-inflation-targeting.htm.

■ Continues

---

[6]Blanchard, Oliver and Jordi Gali. 2007. "Real Wage Rigidities and the New Keynesian Model." *Journal of Money, Credit, and Banking, 39*(1): 35–65.

Chapter 12 The IS–MP–AS Model

Application 12.2 (Continued)

where the last line evaluates expected inflation and the real interest rate at their long-run values. Given a long-run real interest rate of about 1 percent, the Friedman rule says that central banks should set an inflation target of −1 percent.

Although the Friedman rule has appealing logic, there are a variety of circumstances where it isn't optimal.[8] As we've seen, if the nominal interest is zero then the Fed is at the ZLB and doesn't have room to cut the nominal interest rate. If we want the Fed to be able to fight recessions, the target inflation rate should be much higher than zero. Also, because a large fraction of U.S. currency is held abroad, inflation is a tax borne in part by foreign investors.

This means that some portion of U.S. government expenditure can be financed by a tax on non-U.S. citizens, which the government should generally view as a good bargain. Overall, then, there are good reasons to maintain a positive inflation target.

In practice, the Fed's 2 percent target may be a reasonable compromise between the slight deflation implied by the Friedman rule and some of the other considerations discussed in the last paragraph. More broadly, by strongly committing to a 2 percent inflation target, the Fed hopes to anchor inflation expectations and make it easier to manage the business cycle.

Figure 12.18 | Inflation targets across countries.

TARGETING INFLATION
Countries across the world have adopted inflation targeting irrespective of their income level.

Country	Inflation targeting adoption date	Target Inflation Rate at time of Adoption	Country	Inflation targeting adoption date	Target inflation rate at time of adoption
New Zealand	1990	1−3	Philippines	2002	4+/−1
Canada	1991	2+/−1	Guatemala	2005	5+/−1
United Kingdom	1992	2 (point target)	Indonesia	2005	5+/−1
Australia	1993	2−3	Romania	2005	3+/−1
Sweden	1993	2 (point target)	Serbia, Republic of	2006	4−8
Czech Republic	1997	3+/−1	Turkey	2006	5.5+/−2
Israel	1997	2+/−1	Armenia	2006	4.5 +/−1.5
Poland	1998	2.5+/−1	Ghana	2007	8.5+/−2
Brazil	1999	4.5+/−2	Uruguay[1]	2007	3−7
Chile	1999	3+/−1	Albania	2009	3+/−1
Colombia	1999	2−4	Georgia	2009	3
South Africa	2000	3−6	Paraguay	2011	4.5
Thailand	2000	0.5−3	Uganda	2011	5
Hungary	2001	3+/−1	Dominican Republic	2012	3−5
Mexico	2001	3+/−1	Japan	2013	2
Iceland	2001	2.5 +/−1.5	Moldova	2013	3.5−6.5
Korea, Republic of	2001	3+/−1	India	2015	2−6
Norway	2001	2.5+/−1	Kazakhstan	2015	4
Peru	2002	2+/−1	Russia	2015	4

Sources: Hammond 2011; Roger 2010; and IMF staff calculations.
Note: Countries are classified as inflation targeters based on the IMF's Annual Report on Exchange Arrangements and Exchange Restrictions (AREAER) database.
[1]Adoption date is based on the starting point when the interest rate became the main monetary policy instrument.

Source: https://www.imf.org/external/pubs/ft/fandd/basics/72-inflation-targeting.htm.

[8]Schmitt-Grohe, Stephanie and Martin Uribe. 2010. "The Optimal Rate of Inflation." *Handbook of Monetary Economics, 3*: 653–722.

320 **Part 3** Business Cycles

Chapter Summary

- The aggregate supply curve relates current inflation to inflation expectations and the output gap.

- With completely flexible prices and wages, potential output equals actual output, meaning that the output gap is zero. The flexible price/wage aggregate supply curve is vertical.

- Nominal wage rigidities are often the result of costs associated with negotiating a new wage. Workers and employers will often find it optimal to negotiate periodically. This means that, at any given time, nominal wages for many workers are fixed.

- With sticky nominal wages, a higher price level reduces the real wage, which increases the quantity of labor demanded and output. Thus, there is a positive relationship between output and the price level. In a dynamic context, this can be generalized to a positive relationship between output and inflation.

- Another way of expressing the aggregate supply curve is through the Phillips curve, which relates inflation to expected inflation and the deviation of unemployment from its natural rate.

- The upward sloping aggregate supply curve can also be motivated by menu costs associated with changing prices or information constraints, which cause firms to mistake increases in the general price level for changes in the relative price of their product.

- The IS–MP–AS model determines the real interest rate, inflation rate, and level of output in the economy.

- The objective of monetary policy is to minimize the output gap. It does this by changing the nominal interest rate, which, through the Fisher equation, changes the MP curve.

- By minimizing the output gap, the Fed also minimizes inflation volatility. This is called the *divine coincidence* and coincides well with the Fed's dual mandate to achieve maximum employment and price stability.

- An economy driven by a mix of shocks to aggregate supply and the IS curve can explain the comovement of output, consumption, and investment, provided monetary policy moves in the right direction but isn't quite optimal.

Key Terms

Aggregate supply curve, 293
Output gap, 293
Nominal rigidities, 294
Transaction costs, 299
Natural rate of unemployment, 301

Treasury Inflation Expected Security (TIPS), 305
Menu costs, 305
Passive monetary policy, 311
Divine coincidence, 318
Friedman rule, 318

Questions for Review

1. Explain the economic rationale for sticky nominal wages.

2. How do inflation expectations influence the AS curve? Why does that make sense?

3. How should monetary policy move the nominal interest rate in response to a decrease in the IS curve? Relative to the case of monetary policy inaction, what happens to the real interest rate and level of output?

4. How should monetary policy optimally move the nominal interest rate in response to a decrease in the potential level of

output? What happens to the real interest rate and level of output? How does this differ from the case of passive monetary policy?

5. To what extent does the IS–MP–AS model explain such business cycle facts as the positive comovement of output, consumption, and investment and the negative relationship between cyclical output and unemployment?

Problems

12.1 This question investigates the effects of TFP shocks on the flexible price/wage AS curve and the sticky wage AS curve.

    a. Using the four-part graph of Figure 12.3, show how an increase in TFP affects the flexible price/wage AS curve.

    b. Using the four-part graph of Figure 12.6, show how an increase in TFP affects the sticky wage AS curve.

    c. Does the flexible price/wage AS curve shift by more or less than the sticky wage AS curve? Explain the economic intuition.

12.2 Suppose the labor demand, labor supply, and production function are respectively given by

$$N_t^d = 20 - w_t,$$

$$N_t^s = 4 + w_t,$$

$$Y_t = A_t N_t^{0.5} K_t^{0.5}.$$

Assume $K_t = 1$ and $A_t = 1$. Note that, to simplify the problem, we are assuming the labor demand curve doesn't depend on TFP.

Chapter 12 The IS–MP–AS Model **321**

a. Using the supply and demand curves, solve for the equilibrium quantity of labor and real wage.

b. Using the production function, solve for the equilibrium quantity of output.

c. The real wage, w_t, is the nominal wage, W_t, divided by the price level, P_t. When nominal wages are sticky, the nominal wage is given by $\overline{W}_t$ and labor demand need not equal labor supply. The labor demand and production function are the same, but the labor supply equation is replaced by

$$w_t = \frac{\overline{W}_t}{P_t}.$$

Assuming $\overline{W}_t = 12$, solve for the real wage and the level of labor and output for the price levels shown in the table below. How does output depend on the price level? Is this consistent with our graphical analysis of the sticky price AS curve?

P_t	w_t	N_t	Y_t
1			
1.5			
2			
3			

d. Suppose that $\overline{W}_t$ increases to 16. Redo the table in Part c. How does an increase in the nominal wage affect the AS curve?

12.3 This question investigates how expectations over future policy affect the real interest rate, output, and inflation.

a. Suppose individuals and businesses come to learn that the government plans to increase government spending, G_{t+1}. Assuming the Fed keeps nominal interest rates constant, show what happens to output, inflation, and the real interest rate in the IS–MP–AS graphs. How are consumption, investment, and unemployment affected?

b. What is optimal monetary policy in this case?

c. Suppose instead that individuals and businesses come to learn that the government plans to deregulate certain sectors of the economy, which are expected to raise future productivity, A_{t+1}. Assuming the Fed keeps nominal interest rates constant, show what happens to output, inflation, and the real interest rate in the IS–MP–AS graph. How are consumption, investment, and unemployment affected?

d. What is optimal monetary policy in this case?

12.4 The chapter's introduction discussed the increase in inflation following the pandemic. This question investigates the inflation in light of the IS–MP–AS model.

a. Fiscal policy expanded a great deal in 2021, which can be represented by an increase in G_t. Assuming a constant nominal interest rate, show what happens to output, inflation, and the real interest rate in the IS–MP–AS graphs. Is the increase in government spending inflationary?

b. Various supply chain disruptions also continued to afflict the economy through 2021. If we think of a supply chain disruption as a decrease in potential output, and assuming a constant nominal interest rate, show what happens to output, inflation, and the real interest rate in the IS–MP–AS graphs. Is the decrease in potential output inflationary?

c. Despite the supply chain disruptions, the United States has (as of 2023) avoided a second recession. Are your results in part b consistent with that?

12.5 In your principles of macroeconomics class, you may have seen the aggregate demand (AD) curve. With a slight change to the MP rule, we can also derive the AD curve. Continue to assume that inflation expectations, π^e are taken as exogenous. Assume that the real interest rate is set according to the equation

$$r_t = \overline{r} + b_\pi(\pi_t - \overline{\pi}).$$

The long-run real interest rate is $\overline{r}$ and $\overline{\pi}$ is the Fed's inflation target. The parameter, b_π governs how sensitive the real interest rate is to deviations in inflation from target.

a. Assume $\pi_t = \overline{\pi}$. Graphically depict the MP curve. Does it look any different than the regular MP curve from this and the previous chapter?

b. Suppose inflation increases so $\pi_t > \overline{\pi}$. Show how this affects the MP curve. What happens to output?

c. Suppose inflation decreases so $\pi_t < \overline{\pi}$. Show how this affects the MP curve. What happens to output?

d. Generalizing your findings from parts b and c, graph the relationship between output and the inflation rate. This is the AD curve. Put the AS curve in the same graph.

e. Suppose a change in an exogenous variable shifts the IS curve to the right. Show how this affects the IS–MP and AD–AS diagrams (it helps to stack them vertically).

Knowledge Check 12-1 Answer

If people value leisure more, the labor supply curve shifts to the left. The real wage increases, and the equilibrium quantity of work goes down. The new equilibrium quantity of labor is traced down to the production function (which hasn't changed). Fewer workers means less output at every given price level. Thus, the aggregate supply curve shifts to the left. This is shown in Figure 12.19.

Figure 12.19 An increased preference for leisure shifts the labor supply curve to the left from L_0^s to L_1^s. The real wage increases and the quantity of labor decreases. Tracing the new quantity of labor down to the production function shows that output decreases from $Y_{0,t}$ to $Y_{1,t}$. Reflecting this off the 45-degree line shows that the aggregate supply curve shifts to the left from AS_0^f to AS_1^f.

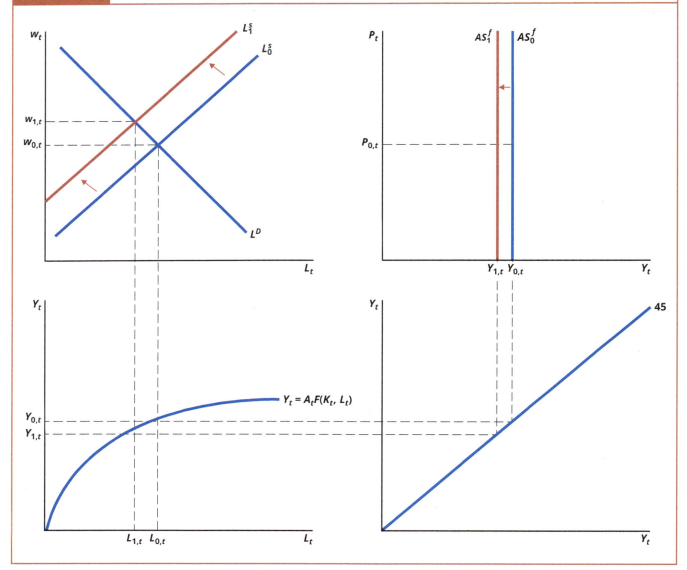

✓ Knowledge Check 12-2 Answer

An increase in inflation expectations shifts the aggregate supply curve to the left. Inflation increases at any given level of output. This is shown in Figure 12.20.

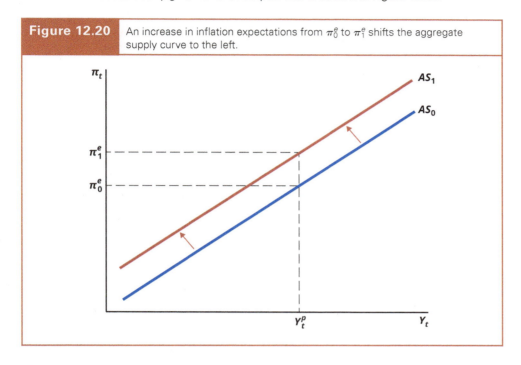

Figure 12.20 An increase in inflation expectations from π_0^e to π_1^e shifts the aggregate supply curve to the left.

✓ Knowledge Check 12-3 Answer

With the existence of menu costs, firms anticipate that they will not change prices again for some time. So, although prices increased by 8 percent between 2021 and 2022, the Dollar Tree may want to avoid paying the menu costs of changing their prices again so soon.

✓ Knowledge Check 12-4 Answer

When $k = 0$ the AS curve is flat. Figure 12.21 shows the effects of an increase in inflation expectations. An increase in inflation expectations shifts the AS curve up.

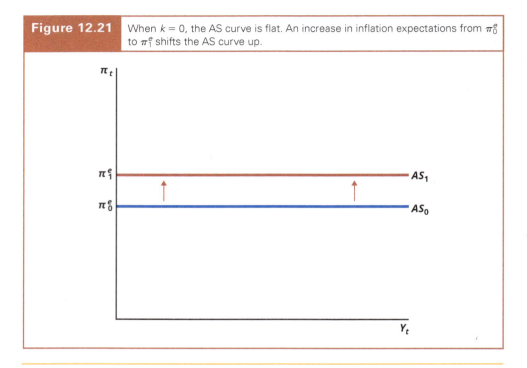

Figure 12.21 When $k = 0$, the AS curve is flat. An increase in inflation expectations from π_0^e to π_1^e shifts the AS curve up.

✓ Knowledge Check 12-5 Answer

An increase in f_t raises a firm's borrowing costs and shifts the IS curve to the left. If the Fed leaves nominal interest rates unchanged, then output and inflation both fall. Since the potential level of output is unaffected, optimal monetary policy entails a reduction in the nominal interest rate. This shifts the MP curve down as the real interest rate falls. The MP curve continues to decrease until output returns to potential. This is shown in Figure 12.22.

Figure 12.22 An increase in f_t shifts the IS curve to the left. Leaving the nominal interest rate constant, output declines to $Y^*_{1,t}$ and inflation declines to $\pi^*_{1,t}$. Optimal monetary policy entails reducing the nominal interest rate, which shifts the MP curve down. The real interest rate declines to $r^*_{1,t}$ and output returns to potential.

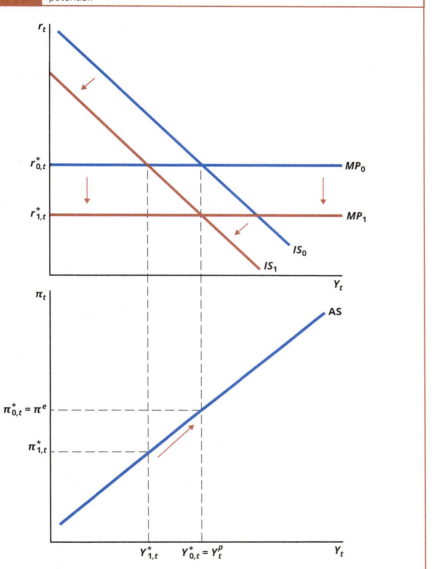

Chapter 13

IS–MP–AS in the Open Economy

Learning Objectives

13.1 Derive the open economy IS curve.

13.2 Simultaneously determine output, inflation, and the real exchange rate using the open-economy IS–MP–AS model.

13.3 Analyze comparative statics in the open-economy IS–MP–AS model under passive and optimal monetary policy.

13.4 Distinguish between a fixed and floating exchange rate regime.

13.5 Explain the impossible trinity.

13.6 Evaluate the costs and benefits of a currency union.

Coming on the heels of the 2007–2009 financial crisis, the Greek government was running persistent deficits on the order of 10 percent of GDP. While they could finance the deficit by selling bonds to domestic and foreign investors, interest rates on government bonds started to increase in 2010, with the 10-year bond reaching 12 percent by year-end. With tax revenues still low because of the lingering recession and the government either unable or unwilling to cut pension obligations and other forms of nondiscretionary spending, the country was headed for sovereign default.

A similar, yet significantly less severe, situation played out in the United States. The federal government's deficit exceeded 9 percent of GDP in 2009 as the unemployment rate peaked at 10 percent. And yet, the U.S. government's defaulting on their debt was never seriously on the table. At the same time as the interest rate on Greek 10-year bonds reached 12 percent, the comparable yield on U.S. Treasury securities was about 3 percent. Just like the Greek government, the U.S. government faced large quantities of nondiscretionary spending and the American tax base was eroded by the recession. What explains the difference between Greece and the United States?

While a comprehensive explanation is beyond the scope of this chapter, the United States had one tool Greece didn't: independent monetary policy. The Federal Reserve sets the nominal interest rate so as to achieve price stability and maximum employment. As a member of the eurozone, Greece surrendered its ability to independently set monetary policy. Rather, the European Central Bank sets monetary policy to achieve a 2 percent inflation target for the entire eurozone. This means that what is the optimal monetary policy for Greece may not be optimal monetary policy for Germany. With independent monetary policy off the table, Greece had to rely on loans from the European Central Bank and International Monetary Fund to avoid default. The lenders tied conditions to the loans to Greece that included cuts to government spending and reductions in public-sector employment. These austerity measures caused a national strike and protests throughout Greece. Despite the economic pain, Greece continued to implement austerity policies through 2017 to remain fiscally solvent.

Given the apparent costs to joining a currency union like the eurozone, you might wonder why a country would find it in its best interest to adopt the euro to begin with. Additionally, how does the inclusion of the international sector affect our analysis of the

Chapter 13 IS–MP–AS in the Open Economy   **327**

IS–MP–AS model discussed in the previous two chapters? In this chapter, we develop an international version of the IS–MP–AS model and discuss the trade-offs inherent in a fixed exchange rate regime or currency union.

13-1 The Open Economy IS–MP–AS model

The closed economy version of the IS–MP–AS model does not include a role for international trade and capital flows. With only one country it's also impossible to analyze movements in the exchange rate. We begin this chapter by adding an open economy component to our IS-MP-AS model from Chapter 12.

13-1a The Open Economy IS Curve

Recall that the GDP expenditure equation is given by

$$Y_t = C_t + I_t + G_t + NX_t. \tag{1}$$

As discussed in Chapter 7, a country with $NX_t > 0$ runs a trade surplus. If a country is running a trade surplus, then exports exceed imports. When exports exceed imports, domestic citizens hold a surplus of foreign currency. Because these domestic citizens didn't find it optimal to spend the currency on foreign goods and services, they will instead use the currency to invest either in foreign stocks or bonds or deposit it at a foreign bank. Thus, a trade surplus is matched with a net capital outflow. Alternatively, in the case of a trade deficit, foreigners hold excess domestic currency that they invest in the domestic country. This means that a trade deficit is matched with a net capital inflow.

At any given time, it must always be true that net exports equal net capital outflow, or

$$NX = CO - CI = NCF, \tag{2}$$

where CO is capital outflow, and CI is capital inflow. The difference between capital outflow and capital inflow is defined as **net capital outflow**. The real exchange rate, ε_t, is the price of domestic goods and services relative to foreign goods and services. An increase in the real exchange rate raises the price of domestic goods relative to foreign goods causing net exports to drop. As in Chapter 7, we assume that net exports are also a function of an exogenous variable, Q_t, which captures the preference for domestic relative to international goods. For instance, if people around the world develop a taste for Hershey's Chocolate relative to Lindt Chocolate (which is Swiss), then Q_t increases. Additionally, changes in trade policy can be captured through Q_t. An increase in U.S. tariffs, for instance, which raise the price of goods and services produced abroad relative to goods and services produced in the United States, can be represented by an increase in Q_t.[1] The net export function can be summarized by

> **Net capital outflow**
> The difference between capital outflow and capital inflow.

$$NX_t = NX(\varepsilon_t, Q_t). \tag{3}$$

Net capital outflow depends on the difference between the domestic real interest rate, r_t, and the global real interest rate, r_t^w. You can think of the global real interest rate as an average of real interest rates from across the world. The bigger is $r_t - r_t^w$, the more attractive it is to invest in domestic companies. The more attractive it is to invest in the domestic country, the more capital will flow in from abroad and the less domestic capital will flow to foreign countries. Thus, the net capital outflow equation can be summarized as

$$NCF_t = NCF(r_t - r_t^w). \tag{4}$$

A higher domestic interest rate, all else constant, decreases net capital outflow.

---

[1] Any inefficiency caused by the tariff could possibly be represented by a decrease in aggregate supply.

The consumption and investment demand functions are identical to what we used in Chapter 11. In particular, consumption is a positive function of disposable income today, $Y_t - G_t$, future disposable income, $Y_{t+1} - G_{t+1}$, and a negative function of the domestic real interest rate. Mathematically, this is summarized by

$$C_t = C(Y_t - G_t, Y_{t+1} - G_{t+1}, r_t). \tag{5}$$

Note that it is assumed the government runs a balanced budget (or that Ricardian equivalence holds). Investment is a negative function of the real interest rate plus the credit spread, $r_t + f_t$, and a positive function of future productivity, A_{t+1}. The investment demand equation is therefore given by

$$I_t = I(r_t + f_t, A_{t+1}). \tag{6}$$

Using Equations (2) through (6), we can rewrite Equation (1) as

$$Y_t - C(Y_t - G_t, Y_{t+1} - G_{t+1}, r_t) - G_t - NCF(r_t - r_t^w) = I(r_t + f_t, A_{t+1}). \tag{7}$$

Defining domestic savings as $Y_t - C_t - G_t$, Equation (7) says that domestic savings minus net capital outflow equals investment. Because the negative of net capital outflow is equivalent to net capital inflow, another way to interpret Equation (7) is that the sum of domestic savings and net capital inflow equals investment. Intuitively, domestic investment must be financed by either domestic savings or savings from abroad. Because domestic savings and net capital inflow are positive functions of the real interest rate, the savings supply curve in the open economy is more sensitive to the real interest rate than the savings supply curve in the closed economy. Equilibrium in the savings and investment market is depicted in Figure 13.1. The dashed red line shows a hypothetical savings supply curve in the closed economy.

The open economy IS curve is the set of (r_t, Y_t) pairs at which the market for savings and investment is in equilibrium (i.e., Equation (7) holds). Just as in Chapter 11, we can derive the IS curve by changing Y_t and finding the new equilibrium value of r_t. Figure 13.2 shows how this works. The panel on the left shows the market for savings and investment.

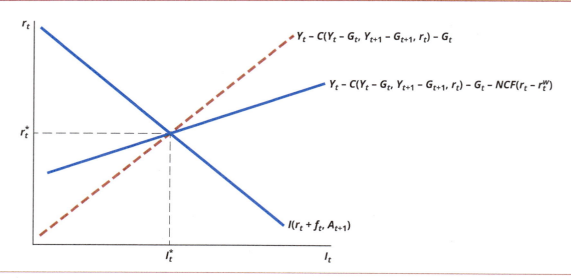

Figure 13.1 This graph plots the savings supply and investment demand curves. The dotted red line is the savings supply curve in the closed economy. The economy is in equilibrium when savings supply equals investment demand. The equilibrium real interest rate is r_t^* and the equilibrium quantity of investment (which is also the equilibrium quantity of savings) is I_t^*.

Question: What happens to the slope of the investment demand curve if investment is more sensitive to the real interest rate?

> **Figure 13.2** The derivation of the IS curve starts at a point $(r_{0,t}, Y_{0,t})$. An increase in income to $Y_{1,t}$ shifts savings supply to the right and lowers the equilibrium real interest rate to $r_{1,t}$. The hypothetical closed-economy savings supply curve (denoted by the dashed red line) also shifts to the right by the same amount and the equilibrium real interest rate falls by more than in the open economy. Tracing these interest rates to the panel on the left shows that the open-economy IS curve is flatter than the closed economy IS curve.

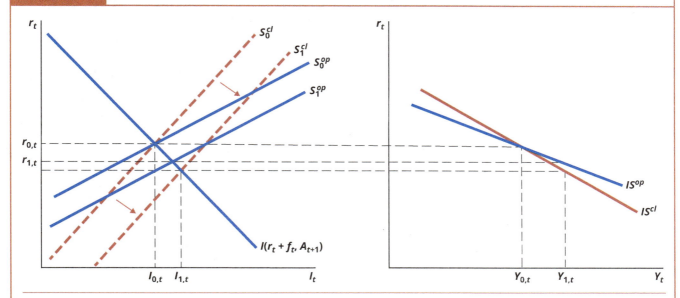

> **Question:** How does the sensitivity of net capital outflow to the real interest rate affect the slope of the savings supply curve?

For reference, both the closed-economy and open-economy savings supply curves are drawn. Starting at $Y_{0,t}$, the equilibrium real interest rate in the savings and investment market is $r_{0,t}$. Tracing this over to the panel on the right gives the first equilibrium pair, $(r_{0,t}, Y_{0,t})$.

Suppose income increases to $Y_{1,t} > Y_{0,t}$. The increase in income shifts both the open-economy and closed-economy savings supply curves to the right by the same amount. Since the open-economy supply curve is flatter, the equilibrium real interest rate falls by less than it would in the closed economy. Intuitively, when the real interest rate falls, net capital outflow increases, which causes equilibrium investment to rise by less than it would in the closed economy. Tracing the equilibrium real interest rates to the panel on the right shows that the open-economy IS curve is flatter. That means output is more sensitive to changes in the real interest rate in the open economy.

Having derived the IS curve, we next discuss the determination of the real interest rate, real exchange rate, and level of output.

✓ Knowledge Check 13-1

Graphically show how an increase in G_t affects the IS curve.

Answers are at the end of the chapter.

13-1b The MP Curve and Determination of Real Exchange Rates

Just as in the closed economy, we assume that the Fed chooses the fed funds rate, which is a nominal interest rate. Recall that a nominal interest rate is the rate of return in terms of dollars. Assuming that expected inflation, π^e, is fixed and exogenous, the real interest rate, or the rate of return net of inflation, is determined through the Fisher equation:

$$r_t = i_t - \pi^e. \tag{8}$$

Equation (8) summarizes the MP rule. Through its choice of the nominal interest rate, i_t, the Fed effectively controls the real interest rate in the short run.

Once the equilibrium real interest rate is determined by the MP rule, net capital outflow can be determined by Equation (4). Finally, because net capital outflow must equal net exports, and net exports are a negative function of the real exchange rate, the equilibrium level of net exports pins down the equilibrium real exchange rate.

Figure 13.3 shows how this works. The panel in the top left graphically depicts the IS and MP curves. Just as in Chapter 11, the equilibrium real interest rate and level of output are determined by the intersection of the IS and MP curves. The top right panel shows the relationship between net capital outflow and the real interest rate. As explained in the previous section, an increase in the real interest rate causes capital to flow into the domestic economy, which reduces net capital outflow. Thus, the net capital outflow line slopes down. Tracing the equilibrium real interest rate, r_t^*, to the NCF line in the top right panel determines the equilibrium quantity of net capital outflow. The bottom right panel shows the inverse relationship between the net exports and the real exchange rate. A higher real exchange rate makes domestic goods more expensive relative to foreign goods, which reduces net exports. Because net exports equal net capital outflow, we can trace the equilibrium quantity of net capital outflow down to the net exports line. The equilibrium real exchange rate, ε_t^*, is the real exchange rate consistent with the equilibrium quantity of net exports.

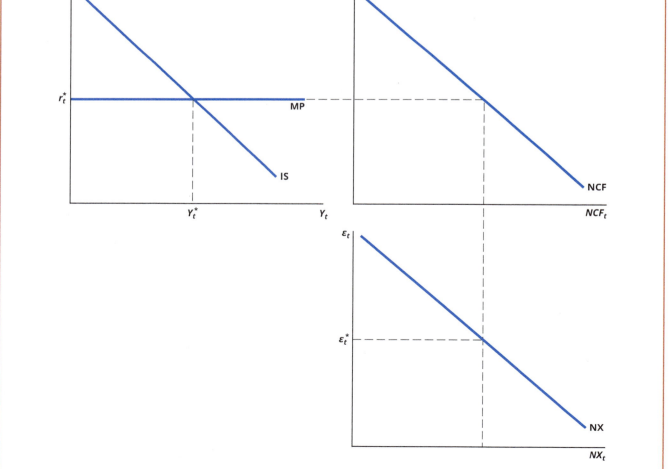

Figure 13.3 The plot in the top left shows that the equilibrium real interest rate and output are determined by the intersection of the IS and MP curves. Given an equilibrium real interest rate, r_t^*, equilibrium net capital outflow is determined in the top right panel. Because net capital outflow equals net exports, once NCF is determined, the equilibrium real exchange rate can be determined. This is shown in the bottom right panel.

With this framework in place, we can conduct comparative static exercises. Suppose that the Fed raises the fed funds rate. Through the Fisher equation, an increase in the nominal interest rate raises the real interest rate, which shifts the MP line up. This is shown in the top left panel of Figure 13.4. An increase in the real interest rate lowers the equilibrium quantity of output. The higher real interest rate encourages capital to flow in from abroad and reduces net capital outflow, which can be seen by tracing the new equilibrium real interest rate, $r^*_{1,t}$, to the NCF line in the top right panel. The capital inflow causes the price of domestic goods and services to be bid up, thereby increasing the real exchange rate, as shown in the bottom right panel. In summary, an increase in the fed funds rate raises the real interest rate and real exchange rate and reduces output and net exports. The higher real interest rate reduces the equilibrium level of investment and consumption.

The above analysis is useful in determining the effects of monetary policy as well as other changes to exogenous variables. However, we do not know the conditions under which monetary policymakers would find it optimal to raise or lower interest rates. Discerning this requires that we compare the actual level of output to the potential level of output. In the next section, we combine the IS–MP graph with the AS curve from Chapter 12.

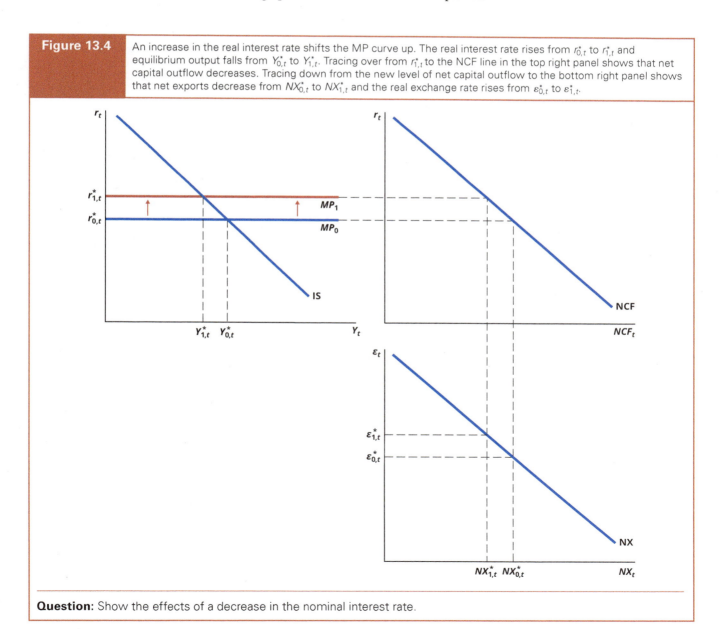

Figure 13.4 An increase in the real interest rate shifts the MP curve up. The real interest rate rises from $r^*_{0,t}$ to $r^*_{1,t}$ and equilibrium output falls from $Y^*_{0,t}$ to $Y^*_{1,t}$. Tracing over from $r^*_{1,t}$ to the NCF line in the top right panel shows that net capital outflow decreases. Tracing down from the new level of net capital outflow to the bottom right panel shows that net exports decrease from $NX^*_{0,t}$ to $NX^*_{1,t}$ and the real exchange rate rises from $\varepsilon^*_{0,t}$ to $\varepsilon^*_{1,t}$.

Question: Show the effects of a decrease in the nominal interest rate.

13-1c The Complete IS–MP–AS Diagram

The IS–MP analysis in the open-economy setting can be combined with the same aggregate supply curve from the closed economy in Chapter 12. The AS curve is given by

$$\pi_t = \pi^e + k(Y_t - Y_t^p). \tag{9}$$

Just as in Chapter 12, Y_t^p is the potential level of output, or the level of output absent nominal rigidities. The difference between actual output and the potential level of output, $Y_t - Y_t^p$, is the output gap. When the output gap is zero, inflation equals expected inflation.

The parameter k is the slope of the AS curve. As k gets bigger, the AS curve gets steeper and nominal rigidities become less important. In the limit, as k goes to infinity, actual output must equal expected output implying that prices and wages are perfectly flexible, and inflation equals expected inflation. The flexible-price and sticky-price AS curve are shown in the bottom left panel of Figure 13.5.

Figure 13.5 The plot in the top left shows that the equilibrium real interest rate and output are determined by the intersection of the IS and MP curves. Tracing the equilibrium level of output down to the AS curve in the bottom right panel determines the economy's inflation rate of π^e. Starting again from the intersection of the IS–MP curves and tracing the equilibrium real interest rate, r_t^*, over to the NCF curve in the top right panel shows the equilibrium level of net capital outflow. Tracing the equilibrium level of net capital outflow down to the net exports curve in the bottom right panel determines the equilibrium exchange rate, ε_t^*.

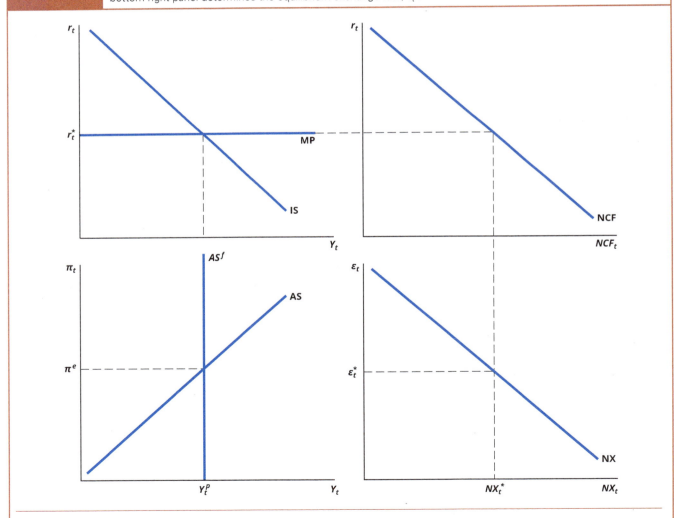

Question: Draw the AS curve when $k = 0$.

The IS–MP diagram in the top left panel determines the equilibrium real interest rate and level of output. Starting from the level of equilibrium output determined by the intersection of the IS and MP curves in the top left panel and tracing down to the AS curve in the bottom left panel determines the inflation rate. Returning to the equilibrium real interest rate determined by the intersection of the IS and MP curves in the top left panel and tracing over to the NCF curve in the top right panel determines the equilibrium level of net capital outflow. Finally, tracing the equilibrium level of net capital outflow down to the net exports line in the bottom right panel determines the equilibrium real exchange rate.

The complete model is summarized in Table 13.1. Besides the addition of net exports and the determination of the real exchange rate, the main difference between the closed and open economy is that output is more sensitive to real interest rate changes in the open economy. A change in the real interest rate triggers a net capital inflow or outflow, which is a mechanism that is absent in the closed-economy model.

Table 13.1	Open-Economy IS–MP–AS Model	
Endogenous variables	**Exogenous variables**	**Parameters**
$Y_t, r_t, \pi_t, \varepsilon_t$	$G_t, G_{t+1}, A_{t+1}, Y_{t+1}, f_t, i_t, Y_t^p, r_t^w, Q_t$	π^e, k
Key equations:		
$NX_t = NX(\varepsilon_t, Q_t)$	(Net exports, Eq (3))	
$Y_t - C(Y_t - G_t, Y_{t+1} - G_{t+1}, r_t) - G_t - NCF(r_t - r_t^w) = I(r_t + f_t, A_{t+1})$	(IS Curve, Eq (7))	
$r_t = i_t - \pi^e$	(MP Curve, Eq (8))	
$\pi_t = \pi^e + k(Y_t - Y_t^p)$	(AS Curve, Eq (9))	

✓ **Knowledge Check 13-2**

When output equals its potential level, actual inflation equals expected inflation. We can define the real interest rate consistent with an output gap of 0 as r_t^f. Similarly, the real exchange rate consistent with an output gap of 0 is ε_t^f. If the output gap is positive, what must be true about the real exchange rate relative to ε_t^f?

Answers are at the end of the chapter.

13-2 Comparative Statics in the Open-Economy IS–MP–AS Model

Just as in Chapter 12, we will conduct each comparative static exercise by first assuming monetary policy does nothing, or is passive, and then by assuming monetary policy behaves optimally by moving the nominal interest rate in a way that minimizes the output gap.

13-2a Shift in the IS Curve

Begin with a shift in the IS curve, such as a decrease in G_t. A decrease in G_t has the direct effect of increasing savings. However, because a decrease in G_t increases current-period disposable income, consumption also increases. Because the marginal propensity to consume out of current-period disposable income is less than one, we know that the decrease in government spending is bigger than the increase in consumption. Consequently, the savings supply schedule shifts right and the IS curve shifts to the left. Because the nominal interest rate stays constant, the real interest rate also stays constant. Given the negative shock to the IS curve and the constant MP curve, output declines from $Y_{0,t}^*$ to $Y_{1,t}^*$. This is shown in the upper-left panel of Figure 13.6.

Tracing the new level of equilibrium output down to the aggregate supply curve in the bottom-left panel shows that equilibrium inflation falls below expected inflation. Because

334 Part 3 Business Cycles

Figure 13.6 A decrease in G_t shifts the IS curve to the left. Under passive monetary policy, the real interest rate stays constant. Output declines from $Y^*_{0,t}$ to $Y^*_{1,t}$. Tracing down from the intersection of the MP curve and IS_1 to the AS curve in the bottom right panel shows that inflation declines from $\pi^*_{0,t}$ to $\pi^*_{1,t}$. Under optimal monetary policy, the real interest rate decreases from $r^*_{0,t}$ to $r^*_{1,t}$. Output and inflation return to their original levels. Tracing over from $r^*_{1,t}$ to the NCF curve in the top right panel determines the new level of net capital outflow. Tracing the new level of net capital outflow down to the bottom right panel shows that the lower level of government spending combined with optimal monetary policy raises net exports from $NX^*_{0,t}$ to $NX^*_{1,t}$, and the real exchange rate decreases from $\varepsilon^*_{0,t}$ to $\varepsilon^*_{1,t}$.

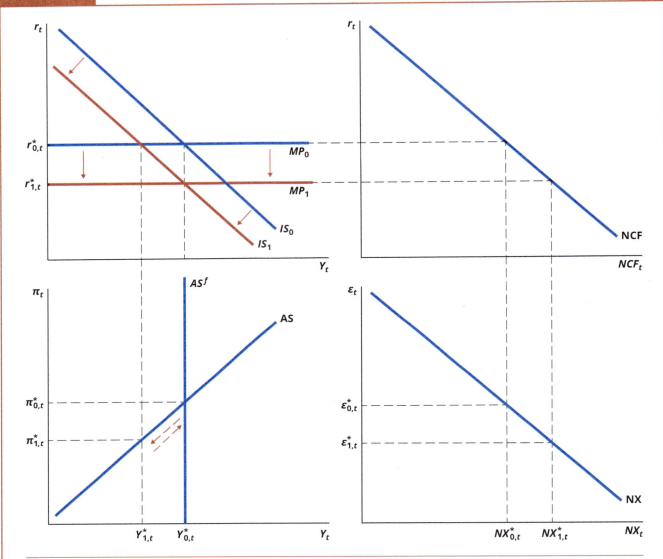

Question: Plot an increase in government spending under passive and optimal monetary policies.

the real interest rate remains constant, neither net exports nor the real exchange rate change. Also, the constant real interest rate implies that equilibrium investment stays the same. Finally, since government spending and output go down, it looks like the change in current-period disposable income, $Y_t - G_t$, is ambiguous. As in Chapter 11, it can be shown that output decreases one-for-one with government spending. Thus, consumption doesn't change.

What is the optimal monetary policy in response to the decline in government spending? Because the potential level of output isn't affected by a change in government spending, optimal monetary policy entails reducing the nominal interest rate. The reduction of the nominal interest rate, through the Fisher equation, reduces the real interest rate and shifts

Chapter 13 IS–MP–AS in the Open Economy   **335**

the MP line down from MP_0 to MP_1. The nominal interest rate should be lowered until output returns to potential. This occurs at a real interest rate of $r_{1,t}^*$. With output returning to its potential level, actual inflation again equals expected inflation. Shifting to the panels on the right, the reduction in the real interest rate encourages capital to flow abroad, which reduces the real exchange rate and stimulates net exports. Thus, net exports rise and the real exchange rate falls. Finally, the decline in the real interest rate implies an increase in equilibrium investment and consumption.

Table 13.2 summarizes the effects of a decrease in government spending under passive and optimal monetary policy. Absent optimal monetary policy, a sufficiently large reduction in government spending can induce a recession. Returning to the chapter opener, this is one reason why the Greek economy fared so poorly over the last decade. In the face of a historically large deficit and high-risk premiums attached to bonds issued by the Greek government, Greece had to borrow from the European Central Bank, International Monetary Fund, and other European countries. One condition for accepting the loans was to decrease government spending. Since the monetary policy for Greece—as with other countries in the eurozone—is set by the ECB, Greece was unable to conduct monetary policy that was optimal for the Greek economy. As you just read, the optimal monetary policy is expansionary in response to cuts in government spending. The inability to set independent monetary policy likely contributed to the depth and duration of Greece's recession.

Table 13.2	Summarizing the Effects of a Decrease in G_t	
	Passive MP	**Optimal MP**
Y_t	↓	0
r_t	0	↓
π_t	↓	0
ε_t	0	↓
NX_t	0	↑
C_t	0	↑
I_t	↓	↑

The case of Greece is one downside to joining a **currency union**, or a collection of countries with a single currency and monetary policy. We will have more to say about currency unions and fixed exchange rates in the next section, but for now it's sufficient to know that Greece would have preferred a more accommodating monetary policy than other members of the eurozone.

Currency union
A collection of countries with a common currency and monetary policy.

13-2b Shift in the AS Curve

Next, consider an increase in potential output, perhaps originating from an increase in TFP. An increase in potential output shifts the AS curve to the right. For reference, the hypothetical flexible-price AS curve also shifts to the right. Under passive monetary policy, the real interest rate doesn't change. Because the real interest rate is constant, output and the real exchange rate stay constant. Since the economy must be on the new AS curve, inflation drops from $\pi_{0,t}^*$ to $\pi_{1,t}^*$. This is shown in Figure 13.7.

Because the level of potential output increases, optimal monetary policy is expansionary. In particular, optimal monetary policy entails reducing the nominal interest rate. Through the Fisher equation, the real interest rate falls and the MP curve shifts down. The Fed continues to lower the nominal interest rate until the real interest rate falls to $r_{1,t}^*$. At $r_{1,t}^*$, actual output equals the new level of potential output, $Y_{1,t}^P$. The lower real interest rate also causes capital outflow, which reduces the real exchange rate and increases net exports. Finally, the lower real interest rate raises equilibrium investment, and the combination of the lower real interest rate and higher level of output raises consumption. Table 13.3 summarizes the effects of an increase in potential output under passive and optimal monetary policy.

336 Part 3 Business Cycles

Figure 13.7 An increase in potential output shifts the AS curve (and the flexible-price AS curve) to the right. Under passive monetary policy, inflation declines from π^e to $\pi^*_{1,t}$. No other endogenous variable changes. Under optimal monetary policy, the MP curve shifts down. The real interest rate falls from $r^*_{0,t}$ to $r^*_{1,t}$. Output rises from $Y^p_{0,t}$ to $Y^p_{1,t}$. Tracing down from the new level of output in the top right panel down to the AS curve in the bottom right panel shows that inflation returns to π^e. Starting from $r^*_{1,t}$ in the top left panel and tracing over to the NCF line in the top right panel shows that net capital outflow increases. Tracing down from the new level of net capital outflow to the net exports curve in the bottom right panel shows that the increase in TFP combined with optimal monetary policy raises net exports from $NX^*_{0,t}$ to $NX^*_{1,t}$ and the real exchange rate declines from $\varepsilon^*_{0,t}$ to $\varepsilon^*_{1,t}$.

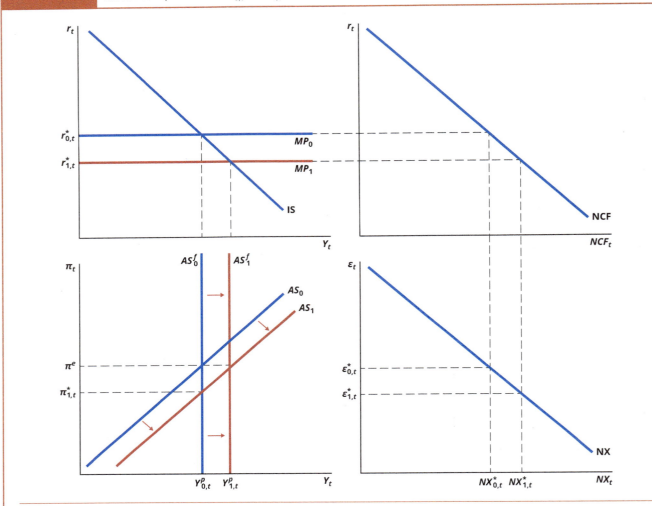

Question: Plot a decrease in potential output under passive monetary policy and under optimal monetary policy.

Table 13.3 Summarizing the Effects of an Increase in Y^p_t

	Passive MP	Optimal MP
Y_t	0	↑
r_t	0	↓
π_t	↓	0
ε_t	0	↓
NX_t	0	↑
C_t	0	↑
I_t	0	↑

13-2c Changes to r_t^w and Q_t

In addition to the changes in exogenous variables in the closed economy, we can consider changes to the new exogenous variables. First, suppose that the global real interest rate, r_t^w, increases. This shifts the NCF curve to the right. This is shown in Figure 13.8. Under passive monetary policy, the domestic real interest rate stays constant. Because the global real interest rate increases relative to the domestic real interest rate, foreign and domestic investors can get a higher return from investing outside the domestic economy. This causes an increase in net capital outflow and depreciates the real exchange rate, which raises net exports.

Figure 13.8 An increase in r_t^w shifts the IS and NCF curves to the right. Under passive monetary policy, the MP curve stays fixed. Starting in the top left panel, the intersection of the new IS_1 curve and MP_0 curve shows that output increases from Y_t^p to $Y_{1,t}^*$. Tracing down from the new level of output to the AS curve in the bottom right panel shows that inflation rises from π^e to $\pi_{1,t}^*$. Returning to the top right panel and tracing over from $r_{0,t}^*$ to NCF_1 in the top right panel shows that the level of net capital outflow increases. Tracing down from the NCF_1 line to the NX line in the bottom right panel shows that net exports increase from $NX_{0,t}^*$ to $NX_{1,t}^*$ and the real exchange rate falls from $\varepsilon_{0,t}^*$ to $\varepsilon_{1,t}^*$. Under optimal monetary policy, the MP curve shifts up to MP_1. The real interest rate increases from $r_{0,t}^*$ to $r_{1,t}^*$. Output falls back to Y_t^p. The real exchange rate settles at $\varepsilon_{2,t}^*$.

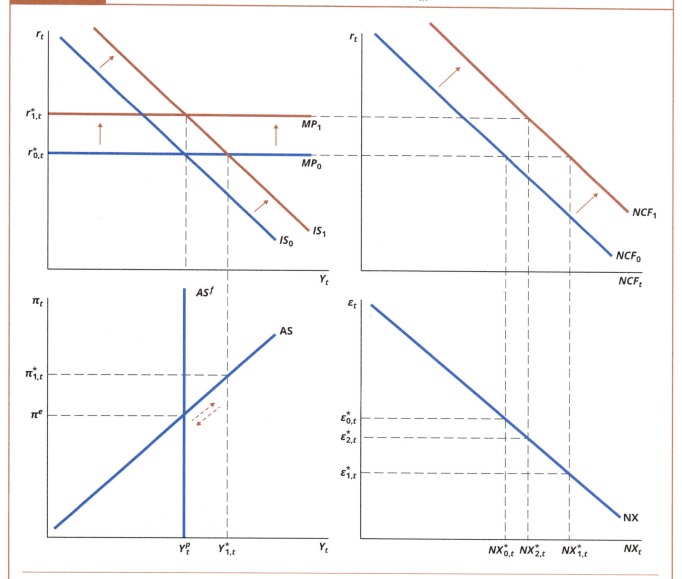

Question: Plot a decrease in r_t^w under passive monetary policy and under optimal monetary policy.

338 **Part 3** Business Cycles

At the same time, the increase in net capital outflow decreases the domestic supply of savings, which shifts the IS curve to the right. Under passive monetary policy, the real interest rate stays constant. The rightward shift in the IS curve with a constant real interest rate implies that output increases and inflation rises above expected inflation. Since the real interest rate stays constant, investment stays constant. However, because the level of output increases, consumption also increases.

The flexible price AS curve is not a function of the global real interest rate. Therefore, the potential level of output is not affected by the increase in r_t^w. Because actual output exceeds potential output, the Fed implements optimal monetary policy by raising the nominal interest rate, which, through the Fisher equation, raises the real interest rate and shifts the MP line up. The MP line continues to shift up until output is back to potential. Output returning to potential means the inflation rate returns to the expected inflation rate. The higher real interest rate means that consumption and investment both decrease. Since government spending remains constant and the GDP expenditure equation, $Y_t = C_t + I_t + G_t + NX_t$, has to hold, net exports must increase. Because net exports equal net capital outflow, net capital outflow must increase in equilibrium even under optimal monetary policy. The only way for net exports to increase in equilibrium is for the real exchange rate to depreciate. Under optimal monetary policy, the real exchange rate falls to $\varepsilon_{2,t}^*$. Table 13.4 summarizes the results of an increase in r_t^w under passive and optimal monetary policy.

Table 13.4	Summarizing the Effects of an Increase in r_t^w	
	Passive MP	**Optimal MP**
Y_t	↑	0
r_t	0	↑
π_t	↑	0
ε_t	↓	↓
NX_t	↑	↑
C_t	↑	↓
I_t	0	↓

Finally, suppose that Q_t increases. This could originate from an increased preference for domestic goods relative to foreign goods, or because of some sort of trade policy. A U.S. tariff on foreign goods, for instance, would increase the cost of foreign goods relative to U.S. goods, which could be captured by an increase in Q_t. The increase in Q_t increases net exports at any given real exchange rate. This is represented by a rightward shift of the net exports line in the bottom right panel of Figure 13.9. Because the MP curve hasn't changed, the real interest rate stays constant, which means that net capital outflow stays constant. Since net capital outflow equals net exports, net exports also remain constant. The only way this is possible is for the real exchange rate to appreciate to the point where net exports are back to their original level. Thus, despite the increase in Q_t, net exports do not change in equilibrium. Since the real interest rate doesn't change, neither output nor any of the components to output are affected. The potential level of output also remains fixed, which means optimal monetary policy coincides with passive monetary policy.

The results displayed in Figure 13.9 may be counterintuitive in that one might expect an increase in the desirability of domestic goods relative to foreign goods to lead to an increase in net exports. To make sense of this, it's important to distinguish between the effects of Q_t all else equal and the equilibrium effects of Q_t. Analyzing the net export equation, $NX_t = NX(\varepsilon_t, Q_t)$, shows that an increase in Q_t holding the exchange rate fixed increases net exports. But it's also true that in equilibrium, net exports must equal net capital outflow. And as neither domestic nor global real interest rates have changed, net capital outflow remains constant. The only way for net exports to equal net capital outflow after the increase in Q_t is for the real exchange rate to appreciate sufficiently. Thus, the increase in demand for net exports gets translated into higher domestic (relative to foreign) prices.

Chapter 13 IS–MP–AS in the Open Economy   **339**

> **Figure 13.9** An increase in preference for domestic goods relative to foreign goods, Q_t, raises net exports at any given real exchange rate shifting the net exports line from NX_0 to NX_1 in the bottom right panel. Since the NCF curve doesn't shift, the real exchange rate increases from $\varepsilon_{0,t}^*$ to $\varepsilon_{1,t}^*$ and net exports don't change. No other endogenous variable changes.

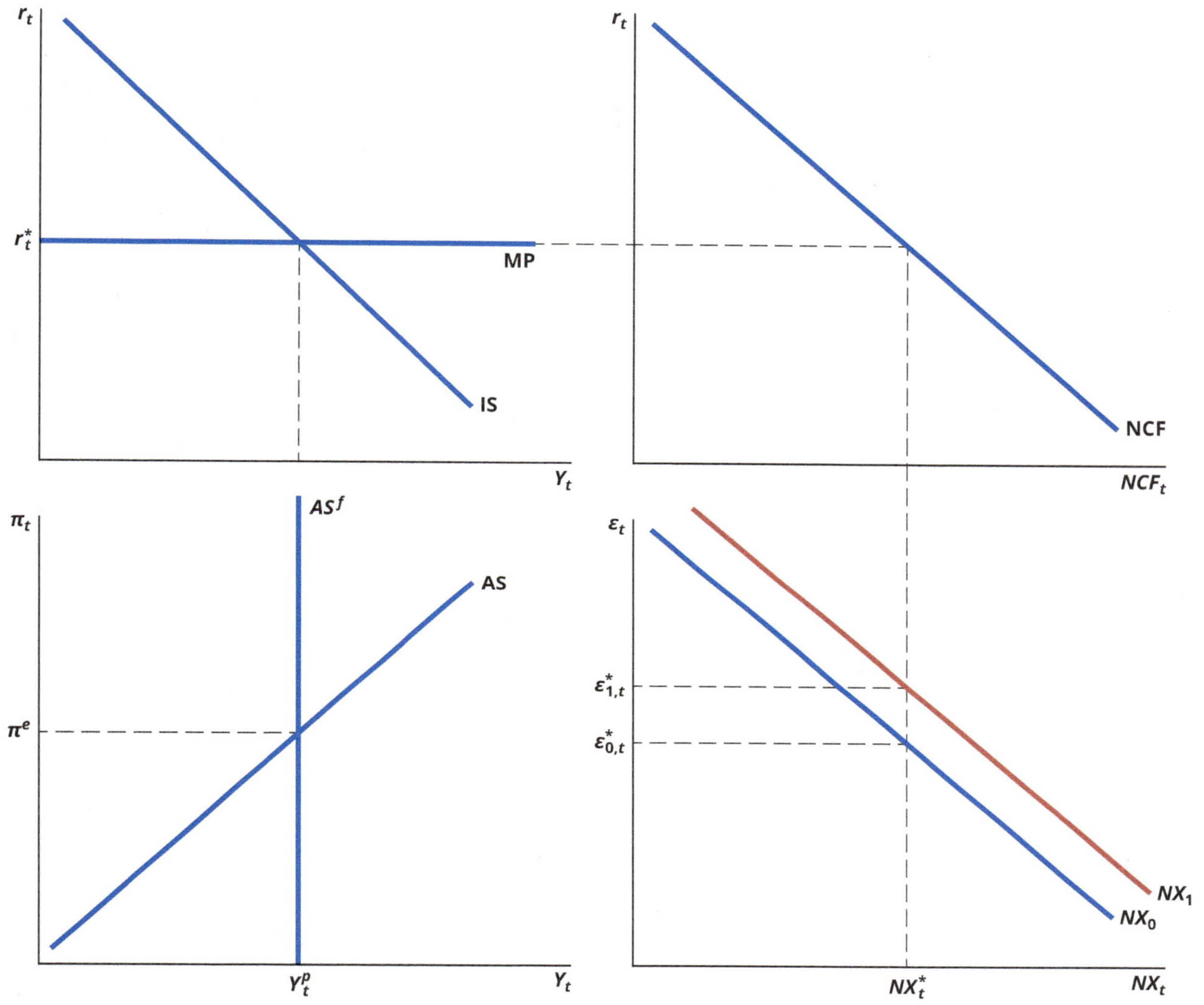

Question: Draw a decrease in Q_t.

Finally, note that one characteristic of optimal monetary policy summarized in Tables 13.2 through 13.4 is that inflation remains constant. This means that an inflation targeting central bank achieves optimal monetary policy that is identical to the lesson in Chapter 12. In reality, a central bank may choose to target the exchange rate instead of the inflation rate. The next section discusses why some central banks around the world prefer exchange rate targeting to inflation targeting.

✓ Knowledge Check 13-3

Graphically show the effects of an increase in G_{t+1} under passive and optimal monetary policy.

—————————————————————————— Answers are at the end of the chapter.

Part 3 Business Cycles

13-3 Exchange Rate Regimes

In the first two sections, we allowed the real exchange rate to change in response to changes in exogenous variables and monetary policy. A policy that allows for the exchange rate to continually adjust according to supply and demand is called a **floating exchange rate regime**. This is in contrast to a **fixed exchange rate regime**, where the government or central bank explicitly targets an exchange rate and, when necessary, intervenes in the currency market to maintain the target. For instance, until 1971, the U.S. government allowed people to convert $35 for one ounce of gold. Many other countries between the end of World War II and 1971 pegged their exchange rate to the U.S. dollar. While most of the world's high-income countries follow floating exchange rate regimes today, many low- and middle-income countries have fixed exchange rate regimes.

A fixed exchange rate compels a country's central bank to hold a sufficient quantity of the reserve currency to ensure redemption. For instance, Denmark pegs their currency, the krone, to the euro. At the time of this book's writing, the exchange rate is about 7 krone per euro. To preserve the fixed exchange rate, the Danish central bank must be willing to trade krone for euro at the pegged rate. Some countries go so far as to adopt a foreign currency as their own. Since 2000, Ecuador has adopted the U.S. dollar as its own currency. As of 2023, 54 countries have either a conventional exchange rate peg (like Denmark) or have no separate legal tender (like Ecuador).[2] Why would a country choose to adopt a fixed exchange rate regime instead of a floating regime? And how does the analysis of the preceding two sections change under fixed exchange rates? We discuss these questions in turn.

13-3a Benefits and Disadvantages of Fixed Exchange Rates

The first major benefit to a fixed exchange rate is that it eliminates exchange rate volatility. This is beneficial for a number of reasons. Exchange rate volatility introduces a lot of uncertainty into business contracts. Imagine an American businessperson entering a contract in Canada in which an investment of 1,000 Canadian dollars today promises a return of 2,000 Canadian dollars a year from now. On the face of it, this looks like the investor stands to make a 100 percent return. But that's before taking exchange rate uncertainty into account.

Suppose at the time of the investment, one U.S. dollar trades for one Canadian dollar. If one year from now, the Canadian dollar depreciates so that 1 U.S. dollar trades for 2 Canadian dollars, then the 2,000 Canadian dollars at the end of the year is worth only 1,000 American dollars. Thus, what was a 100 percent return turns into a 0 percent return.

The general lesson is that if a country is heavily reliant on foreign investment and its exchange rate (when floating) tends to be volatile, then pegging its exchange rate to a more stable currency reduces the uncertainty faced by foreign investors. Reducing uncertainty in turn attracts foreign investment and grows a country's capital stock. Moreover, small countries with lower volumes of total currency tend to face more volatility because of currency speculation by financial institutions (such as hedge funds). This financial market speculation leads to even more movement in exchange rates than would be justified by economic fundamentals. Highly volatile exchange rates and heavy reliance on foreign investment are typical in low and middle-income countries, which is one reason why they are more likely to adopt a fixed exchange rate.

Beyond investment opportunities, there are other costs to a volatile exchange rate. A country that relies heavily on tourism, like Cuba does from the United States, may

---

Floating exchange rate regime

A system in which a country's exchange rate is determined by supply and demand.

Fixed exchange rate regime

A system in which a country's government explicitly targets the exchange rate and allows people to exchange the domestic currency for the foreign currency at the statutory exchange rate.

---

[2]For a complete list, visit the Wikipedia page: https://en.wikipedia.org/wiki/List_of_countries_by_exchange_rate_regime.

Chapter 13 IS–MP–AS in the Open Economy 341

want to peg its exchange rate so that travelers can more easily plan for expenditures on their trip.

Second, countries may choose to fix their exchange rates to encourage exports. Throughout the 1990s and early 2000s, China maintained an exchange rate of about 8 yuan per dollar. At the same time, exports from China to the United States surged (as discussed in Chapter 7). Over this period, the Chinese central bank accumulated vast reserves of U.S. dollars, which indicated the yuan was undervalued relative to the dollar.

Finally, a fixed exchange rate imposes some degree of discipline on monetary policy. Suppose the central bank wants to lower the real interest rate. From the last section, you know that in a floating exchange rate system, a lower real interest rate causes net capital outflow to increase and the currency to depreciate. Functionally, capital outflow would entail domestic citizens trying to trade their local currency for foreign currency. To defend the peg, the central bank needs to hold sufficient levels of reserves in the foreign currency. If the central bank runs out of foreign currency, they can no longer defend the peg. Anticipating this problem in advance limits the central bank's ability to engage in expansionary monetary policy. If citizens of a country are worried that the central bank may, perhaps due to external political influence, choose to expand the money supply, the fixed exchange rate constrains the central bank from an unlimited monetary expansion. Application 13.1 discusses a historical case study of a country forced to abandon their peg.

Because the benefit of greater monetary discipline comes with the cost of a loss of central bank autonomy, each country has to weigh the pros and cons of fixing the exchange rate. A country with a history of a strongly independent central bank may choose to keep central bank independence and let its exchange rate float. Countries in which maintaining central bank independence is more difficult may find that pegging their exchange rate is worth the cost.

Application 13.1

Speculative Attacks

One downside of a fixed exchange rate is that it requires the central bank to hold sufficient levels of international currency as reserves. If the central bank fears that it will run out of reserves, it has to devalue their currency or even abandon the fixed exchange rate regime altogether. Worse yet, if investors expect that a country's currency is overvalued, that leaves them vulnerable to a speculative attack.

Let's first think about how investors stand to make a profit through a speculative attack. If investors come to believe that a domestic currency is overvalued, they can borrow in that currency in the hopes of paying back the loan in devalued currency. To see how this works, return to the Canadian and U.S. dollar example in the last section. Suppose the Canadian central bank pegs its currency at one-for-one with the U.S. dollar. If investors (either in Canada or the rest of the world) believe that

the Canadian dollar is overvalued and a devaluation is imminent, they can take out a short-term loan of, say, 1,000 Canadian dollars that they have to pay back in a week and convert it to 1,000 U.S. dollars. If, during that week the Canadian central bank devalues its currency to 2 Canadian dollars per U.S. dollar, then it only takes 500 U.S. dollars to repay the loan, meaning that the investor makes a $500 = $1,000 − $500 profit.[3]

This example gets at the "speculative" aspect of the speculative attack, in that investors can gain by betting on the devaluation of a currency. But the "attack" aspect comes from the fact that currency devaluation isn't a random event. If investors suspect that a domestic country's currency is overvalued and that the central bank is running low on the foreign reserve currency, they will sell the domestic currency to the central bank in exchange

[3] The investor would also pay back some interest on the loan, which would reduce profits.

■ Continues

Application 13.1 (Continued)

for the foreign currency. If the attack is swift enough, then the central bank must abandon the peg.

One historical case study of a speculative attack comes from Mexico in 1994. The Mexican central bank pegged the peso to the U.S. dollar at a rate of about 3 pesos per dollar in the early 1990s. Technically, the central bank set a lower bound and upper bound for the exchange rate and adjusted reserves and the money supply accordingly. Figure 13.10 shows the rates of inflation and GDP per capita growth in Mexico between 1980 and 2000. After suffering a major recession during the 1980s, the Mexican economy was relatively strong in the early 1990s, with growth in GDP per capita averaging about 2 percent annually between 1990 and 1994. Inflation, which exceeded 100 percent just several years before, decreased to about 20 percent in the early 1990s.

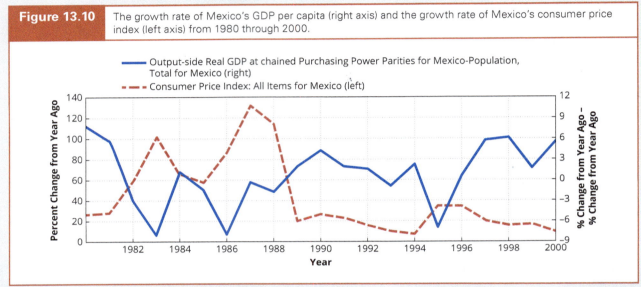

Figure 13.10 The growth rate of Mexico's GDP per capita (right axis) and the growth rate of Mexico's consumer price index (left axis) from 1980 through 2000.

Source: Penn World Table 10.1 and FRED https://fred.stlouisfed.org/graph/?g=10Tcg.

Moreover, in 1994, Mexico joined Canada and the United States in the North American Free Trade Agreement, which significantly reduced trade barriers between the three countries. Certainly, most signs seemed to be pointing up for the Mexican economy.

At about the same time, Mexico was running persistent trade deficits. On the one hand, this was a signal of the strong investment opportunities in Mexico, as trade deficits are associated with capital inflow. On the other hand, some economists speculated at the time that the peso was overvalued. The overvaluation concerns were tempered, in part, because the Mexican central bank appeared to have ample dollar reserves. In March 1994, Luis Donaldo Colosio, the leading candidate for the Mexican presidency, was assassinated. This caused a massive capital outflow. As Figure 13.11 shows, between March and April alone, the Mexican central bank decreased dollar reserves by more than $10 billion.[4]

The ensuing months witnessed more political turmoil, including another assassination and additional capital flight from Mexico. By the time the Mexican central bank decided to depreciate the peso by 15 percent, it had to abandon the peg entirely. Between November 1994 and January 1995, the peso depreciated from 3.4 pesos per dollar to 5.6 pesos per dollar over the next year, Mexican GDP per capita declined by close to 7 percent.

While it's true that investors who borrowed short term in pesos gained as a result of Mexico having abandoned its exchange rate peg, it's not as if they caused it. That is, while capital flight and depletion of dollar reserves were the functional causes of the peso devaluation, there were also fundamental reasons behind the depreciation, such as the rise in political instability and a concerning trade deficit. If the economic and political reality made the depreciation certain, then the speculative attack just accelerated the inevitable. Finally, the Mexican example shows that if a central bank wants to defend a certain exchange rate peg, then the targeted exchange rate should align with economic fundamentals as much as possible.

[4]Whitt Jr., Joseph. 1996. "The Mexican Peso Crisis." *Economic Review, Federal Reserve Bank of Atlanta*, 81: 1–20.

Continues

Application 13.1 (Continued)

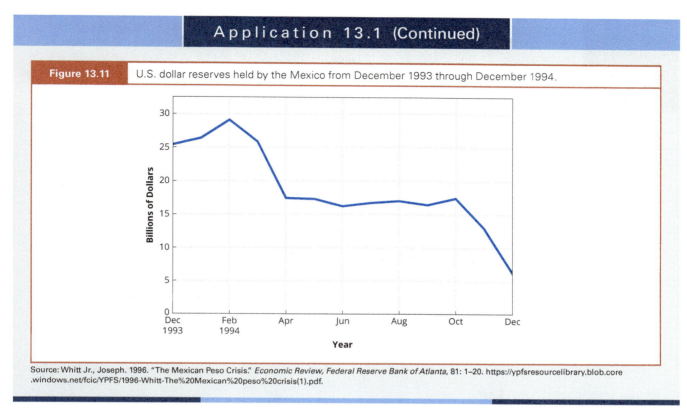

Figure 13.11 U.S. dollar reserves held by the Mexico from December 1993 through December 1994.

Source: Whitt Jr., Joseph. 1996. "The Mexican Peso Crisis." *Economic Review*, Federal Reserve Bank of Atlanta, 81: 1–20. https://ypfsresourcelibrary.blob.core.windows.net/fcic/YPFS/1996-Whitt-The%20Mexican%20peso%20crisis(1).pdf.

13-3b Exchange Rate Targeting in IS–MP–AS Model

We can use the open-economy IS–MP–AS model to analyze the effects of exchange rate targeting. Suppose that the central bank chooses to target a real exchange rate of $\varepsilon_t = \bar{\varepsilon}_t$.[5] The first observation, which you can verify in the next knowledge check, is that an exchange rate peg essentially implements passive monetary policy in the case of a shift in either the AS curve or (with one exception) the IS curve. The reason is that passive monetary policy keeps the nominal interest rate fixed which, through the Fisher equation, keeps the real interest rate fixed in the short run. Provided the global real interest rate doesn't change, then net capital outflow and the real exchange rate stay constant.

The one exception is in the case of a change in the global real interest rate, r_t^w. Figure 13.12 shows the results of an increase in r_t^w under a fixed exchange rate. An increase in the global real interest rate implies superior investment opportunities outside the domestic economy. This causes the net capital outflow line in Figure 13.12 to shift to the right. Because the central bank pegs the exchange rate at $\bar{\varepsilon}_t$, net exports stay fixed. Since net exports equal net capital outflow in equilibrium, net capital outflow can't change either. But the only way net capital outflow doesn't change is if the domestic real interest rate rises one-for-one with the global real interest rate so that $r_t - r_t^w$ remains constant. Thus, implementing a fixed exchange rate requires the central bank to follow a contractionary monetary policy.

We can draw even stronger conclusions than that. Recall from our analysis in Figure 13.8 that optimal monetary policy entailed increasing real interest rates following an increase in r_t^w when the exchange rate was floating. However, domestic real interest rates rose less than one-for-one in the case of optimal monetary policy. We know this because net capital outflow increases in equilibrium with floating exchange rates under optimal monetary policy. This means that the increase in the real interest rate under fixed exchange rates is big enough to reduce output in equilibrium. The increase in the real interest rate causes investment and consumption to decline. The consequences of an increase in r_t^w under fixed and floating exchange rates are summarized in Table 13.5. Note that the first two columns repeat Table 13.4.

---

[5] In reality, central banks target nominal exchange rates. Provided the domestic relative to the foreign price level doesn't change too much in any given period, real and nominal exchange rates move in the same direction.

344 Part 3 Business Cycles

Figure 13.12 An increase in r_t^w shifts the NCF line in the top right panel to the right. If the central bank pegs the exchange rate at $\bar{\varepsilon}_t$, then net exports don't change in equilibrium. Since net exports don't change, net capital outflow doesn't change which requires that the real interest rate rises from $r_{0,t}$ to $r_{1,t}$, shifting the MP curve up in the top left panel. The intersection between MP_1 and IS_1 shows that output declines. Tracing down from the lower level of output in the top left panel to the AS curve in the bottom right panel shows that inflation declines from π^e to $\pi_{1,t}$ and the new level of equilibrium output is $Y_{1,t}^*$.

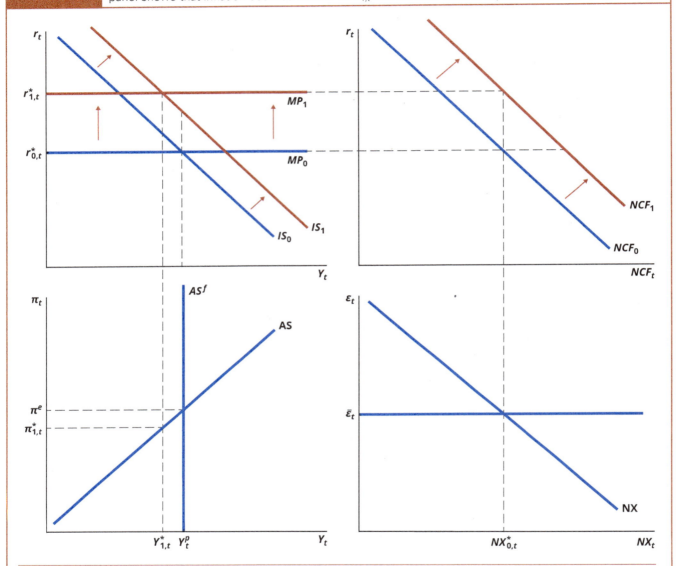

Question: Plot a decrease in r_t^w assuming the central bank pegs the real exchange rate.

Table 13.5 Summarizing the Effects of an Increase in r_t^w Under Fixed and Floating Exchange Rates

	Flexible exchange rate		Fixed exchange rate
	Passive MP	Optimal MP	
Y_t	↑	0	↓
r_t	0	↑	↑
π_t	↑	0	↓
ε_t	↓	↓	0
NX_t	↑	↑	0
C_t	↑	↓	↓
I_t	0	↓	↓

Chapter 13 IS–MP–AS in the Open Economy   345

> **Figure 13.13** An increase in Q_t shifts the net exports line in the bottom right panel from NX_0 to NX_1. Under an exchange rate, peg raises net exports from $NX^*_{0,t}$ to $NX^*_{1,t}$. Tracing up from the bottom right panel to the NCF line shows that net capital outflow increases and the real interest rate falls from $r^*_{0,t}$ to $r^*_{1,t}$. The fall in the real interest rate is consistent with a downward shift in the MP curve shown in the top left panel. The intersection of the IS curve and MP_1 shows that output increases. Tracing down to the AS curve in the bottom right panel shows that inflation increases from π^e to $\pi^*_{1,t}$ and the new level of equilibrium output is $Y^*_{1,t}$.

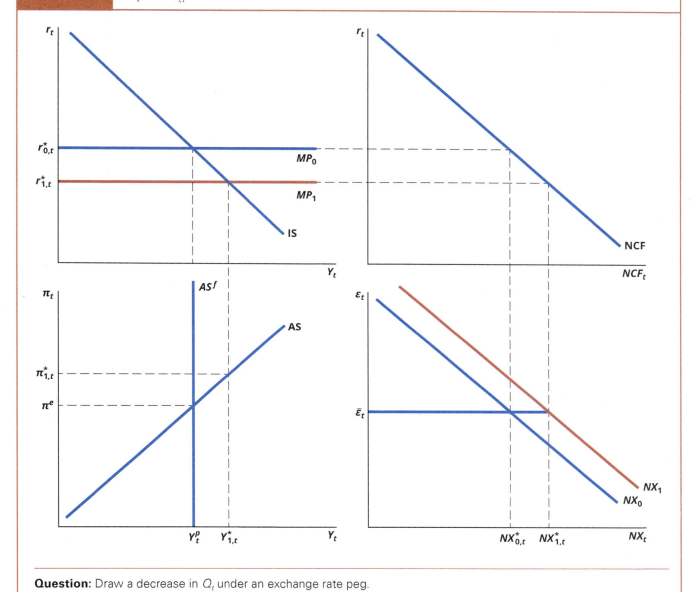

Question: Draw a decrease in Q_t under an exchange rate peg.

Next, consider an increase in Q_t as shown in Figure 13.13. The increase in Q_t shifts the net exports line to the right. Given that the exchange rate is pegged at $\bar{\varepsilon}_t$, net exports increase. Because net exports must equal net capital flow, the real interest rate must decrease so as to encourage capital to leave the domestic economy. To accommodate the increase in net capital outflow, the central bank lowers the nominal interest rate, which shifts the MP curve down. Output rises above its potential level and inflation increases. Finally, the lower real interest rate raises equilibrium investment and the combination of the lower real interest rate and higher level of output raises consumption.

346 **Part 3** Business Cycles

One thing is clear from Figures 13.12 and 13.13. A real exchange rate peg fails to implement optimal monetary policy. That is, within the context of the IS–MP–AS model, it is better for the central bank to set monetary policy independently under a floating exchange rate rather than peg the exchange rate. Furthermore, if the central bank must choose an intermediate macroeconomic variable to target, it's much better to choose the inflation rate than the real exchange rate.

You should draw a red line under the "within the context of the model" qualifier in the last paragraph. The potential benefits to fixed exchange rates enumerated in the previous section aren't accounted for in the model. For instance, if policymakers want to achieve export-led growth, then weighing the costs and benefits of such a policy falls outside the scope of the IS–MP–AS model. Or if the central bank believes that a fixed exchange rate will give international investors more confidence in the domestic economy, then a fixed exchange rate may be preferred to a floating exchange rate. The choice of which exchange rate regime to adopt requires careful consideration of all these factors.

> ### ✓ Knowledge Check 13-4
>
> How does a fixed exchange rate system accommodate an increase in potential output? How does such a system accommodate an expansionary shift in the IS curve that doesn't come from r_t^w?
>
> ———————— Answers are at the end of the chapter.

13-3c Capital Controls and the Impossible Trinity

You have learned that a country that fixes its exchange rate eventually cedes independent monetary policy. If a government pegs its country's exchange rate and the central bank lowers interest rates, capital will flow out of the country and put downward pressure on the exchange rate. People will try to exchange the domestic currency for the foreign reserve currency at banks for the fixed exchange rate. Eventually, the central bank will run out of reserves and the peg will have to be abandoned. Thus, a fixed exchange rate imposes stark limits on independent monetary policy.

The argument in the preceding paragraph relies on a connection between interest rates and capital flow. As long as investors are permitted to move capital in and out of countries in search of the highest return, this makes sense. Investors, however, don't always have that permission. Indeed, some governments limit the extent to which capital can flow in and out of their countries. Limits on capital inflow and outflow are called **capital controls**.

Capital controls
Limits on a country's capital inflow or capital outflow.

The presence of capital controls allows a government to peg its exchange rate and the central bank to set independent monetary policy. In the preceding example, if the government has instituted effective capital controls, then it can prohibit capital outflow following expansionary monetary policy. The prohibition of capital outflow stops the exchange rate from depreciating. Thus, the combination of a fixed exchange rate, independent monetary policy, and capital controls is feasible.

Alternatively, a country can choose to let its exchange rate float, conduct independent monetary policy, and allow the free flow of capital, which is basically what we covered in the first section of this chapter. Or the country can fix its exchange rate, allow the free flow of capital, and effectively surrender independent monetary policy. This is what we just covered in 13-3b. In essence, there are three ingredients: a fixed exchange rate, independent monetary policy, and free capital flow. Every country gets to choose two of the three but forgo the third. This has come to be known as the **impossible trinity**, which is illustrated in Figure 13.14.

Impossible trinity
The idea that it is impossible for a country to simultaneously achieve independent monetary policy, maintain a fixed exchange rate, and allow the free flow of capital across borders.

We have discussed reasons why independent monetary policy is desirable as well as some of the reasons for a fixed exchange rate, but why is free capital flow desirable? Chapter 7 reviewed the microeconomic case for free trade. A similar argument can be made for the free movement of capital. Allowing capital to freely flow into and out of countries maximizes economic efficiency. In a highly globalized and technologically advanced world, it is

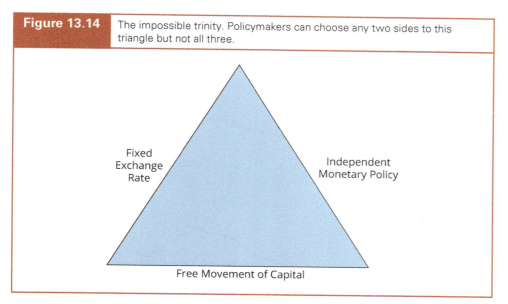

Figure 13.14 The impossible trinity. Policymakers can choose any two sides to this triangle but not all three.

also the most practical. Now that bank deposits, stock and bond transactions, and transfers between individuals can all be done with a smartphone, it has become more difficult for countries to regulate capital flows.

Capital controls were more common during the **Bretton–Woods system**, which lasted several decades after World War II. After the war, many of the major economies agreed that economic coordination was the best path toward prosperity. This meant that countries pegged their exchange rates to the U.S. dollar, making competitive devaluations (i.e., devaluations meant to spur exports) impossible. The dollar was, in turn, pegged to the price of gold. Countries could keep some degree of independent monetary policy by implementing capital controls. For instance, throughout the 1960s, the United States limited foreign investment and bank lending abroad.[6] In 1971, President Richard Nixon suspended the ability of foreign governments to trade their dollars for gold, which effectively ended the Bretton–Woods system. In response, during the 1970s and 1980s, high-income countries removed restrictions on international capital flow.

Today, capital controls are more prominent among low-income countries. Figure 13.15 shows the Chinn–Ito index (labeled KA Open in the graph), which ranks countries on the openness of their capital account. A higher number means a more liberalized capital account, or fewer limitations on the movement of capital. Industrial countries significantly expanded their openness between 1970 and 2000. Emerging economies and less-developed (which essentially means low-income) countries have more capital account regulations.

High-income countries, such as the United States, have, for the most part, converged on autonomous monetary policy, a floating exchange rate, and free capital flows. The abandonment of fixed exchange rate regimes does not imply that there is no coordination between countries or even between states in the United States. The next section discusses one such coordinated effort.

Bretton–Woods system
The system of fixed exchange rates among high-income nations that prevailed for several decades after World War II.

13-3d Currency Unions

As mentioned in Section 13.2a, a currency union is an agreement among countries to share a common currency. The most notable currency union today is the eurozone, consisting of 20 member countries who all share the euro as a common currency. Being part of the

---

[6]For more information, see the Federal Reserve's history of this period: https://www.federalreservehistory.org/essays/bretton-woods-launched.

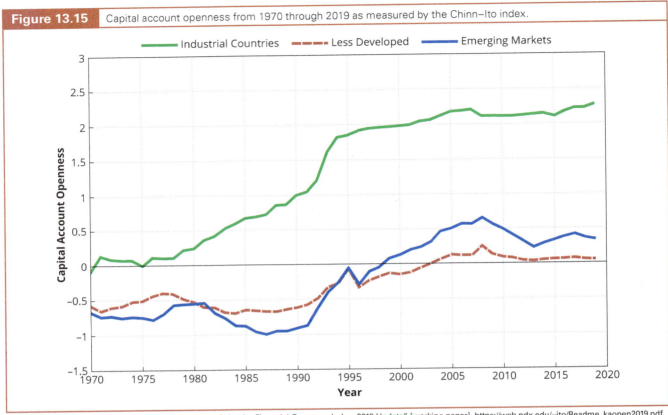

Figure 13.15 Capital account openness from 1970 through 2019 as measured by the Chinn–Ito index.

Source: Ito, Hiro and Menzie Chinn. 2019. "Notes on the Chinn-Ito Financial Openness Index, 2019 Update" [working paper]. https://web.pdx.edu/~ito/Readme_kaopen2019.pdf.

currency union means that one euro in one member country (Italy, for example) trades for one euro in another member country (France, for example).

A currency union creates a number of advantages for its members. First, by eliminating the need of currency conversion, the currency union makes trade easier among nations. Since trade flows are high across countries in Europe, this is a significant benefit. Currency unions are also more conducive to travel. When I drive to New Hampshire from Maine, I don't have to worry about converting my Maine currency to a distinct currency in New Hampshire. Similarly, people traveling between Germany and France in the 1990s had to exchange marks for francs, but now no such conversion is needed.

Currency unions tend to work better when business cycles are well synchronized across countries. If all countries were hit with a common shock, then they would all agree on optimal monetary policy. If one country in a currency union was hit by a shock and another country wasn't, then that could cause problems. Returning to the chapter's introduction, the lack of synchronization between Greece and some of the other eurozone countries is one reason why the Greek recession was so severe. Or, to take a hypothetical example, let's say potential output increases in Germany but stays constant in France. Optimal monetary policy in Germany would be expansionary. That is, Germany would want to lower the nominal interest rate to accommodate the supply shock. But, since nothing changed in France, optimal monetary policy from the French perspective would be to keep the nominal interest rate constant. To the extent business cycles across member countries differ, a currency union will not perform as well.

Business cycles across U.S. states are far more synchronized than business cycles in the European Union. Moreover, because states share a common language (in addition to a common currency), it is easier for people to move across regions in the United States than it is to move across countries in Europe. Despite these advantages, there have been times in U.S. history where preferences over monetary policy differed across U.S. regions. Application 13.2 discusses just such an instance.

Chapter 13 IS–MP–AS in the Open Economy   349

Application 13.2

The Free Silver Movement

After a rapid increase in prices during the Civil War, the price level fell substantially between 1870 and 1890. At the same time, real income per capita more than doubled.[7] Despite the high rate of income growth, all was not well in the American economy at the close of the 19th century. Farm prices declined faster than the general price level, affecting farmers, particularly in the southern and western parts of the country. These farmers were hurt not only by the fall in the relative price of agricultural commodities but also by their high levels of indebtedness. Moreover, by 1894, the U.S. economy was in recession, with the unemployment rate reaching 18 percent. Overall, there was a desire for economic reform, especially among American farmers.

Their primary target of reform was the gold standard. Under the gold standard, the U.S. government promised to exchange an ounce of gold for $20.67. In practice, this tied the U.S. money supply to the stock of gold. If there were a large increase in the quantity of gold, the money supply would increase. If gold flowed from the United States to the rest of the world, the money supply would decrease. Critics of the gold standard believed that the United States would be better served by a bimetallic standard, with both gold and silver serving as currency. These critical voices reached their apex in the 1890s as impoverished farmers recognized that circulating silver would raise the money supply and alleviate the effects of the recession. The advocacy of the bimetallic system became known as the *free silver movement*.

Perhaps the most prominent critic of the gold standard was 1896 presidential candidate William Jennings Bryan. As a congressman in Nebraska, Bryan saw the devastating effects of the recession on farmers and realized that circulating silver would raise inflation, thereby reducing the debt burden of farmers. During his speech to the Democratic National Convention in 1896, Bryan concluded with the warning, "You shall not crucify mankind on the cross of gold."[8]

William McKinley, the Republican nominee for president, sided with his supporters in the Northeast who opposed the free silver movement. Unlike the farmers who supported free silver, those who supported a strict gold standard were more likely to be creditors. Recognizing that the adoption of silver would be inflationary, creditors were rightly concerned that the real value of debt would be eroded by inflation. McKinley ended up winning a close and bitterly contested election. McKinley and Bryan would meet again in 1900; however, by that time, the economy had recovered and McKinley won by a bigger margin, which effectively ended the free silver movement.

The push for a bimetallic system highlights the tensions in a currency union. Lenders in the Northeast favored tight monetary policy with a low growth rate of money supply in order to keep inflation low and real interest rates on their loans high. Farmers in the Midwest preferred higher rates of money growth and inflation as a way to alleviate their debt burden. But, as part of a currency union, all the states had to share a common currency and therefore a common monetary policy. The gold standard favored some geographic locations of the country and hurt others.

In some sense, the free silver movement can be interpreted as a populist uprising that pitted lower-income farmers in the "heartland" against creditors from more industrialized states. And cultural observers at the time noted as much. Indeed, it has been argued that L. Frank Baum's 1900 novel, *The Wonderful Wizard of Oz*, was a monetary allegory in which William McKinley played the role of the Wicked Witch of the West and the yellow brick road symbolized the gold standard.[9] Although the populists may have made crude arguments in favor of silver, they were also ahead of their time in arguing for active monetary policy during recessions.

[7]All figures are from Rockoff, Hugh. 1990. "The 'Wizard of Oz' as a Monetary Allegory." *Journal of Political Economy*, 98(4): 739–760.
[8]https://en.wikipedia.org/wiki/Cross_of_Gold_speech.
[9]This is Rockoff's argument in the paper cited in footnote 7.

Chapter Summary

- In the open economy, net exports equal net capital outflow, or the difference between capital outflow and capital inflow.

- Net exports are a negative function of the real exchange rate. Net capital outflow is a negative function of the difference between the domestic and global real interest rates.

- Compared to the closed economy, output is more sensitive to real interest rate changes in the open economy, implying a flatter IS curve.

- A floating exchange rate regime allows the exchange rate to be adjusted according to supply and demand. In a fixed exchange

350   **Part 3** Business Cycles

rate regime, the government intervenes in the currency market to ensure the exchange rate stays fixed.

- A fixed exchange rate reduces exchange rate volatility and imposes discipline on monetary policy. To the extent the exchange rate is undervalued, it also promotes exports.

- A country that pegs its exchange rate surrenders independent monetary policy.

- In the context of the open-economy IS–MP–AS model, a system of a floating exchange rate and an independent central bank is preferred to a fixed exchange rate.

- It is possible to peg the exchange rate and maintain independent monetary policy. Capital controls, however, come with efficiency costs and are difficult to enforce.

- In general, a country can choose up to two of the following three options: independent monetary policy, a fixed exchange rate, and free capital flows. They can't have all three. This is known as the impossible trinity.

- A currency union is an agreement among countries to share a common currency. The eurozone is one example of a currency union.

- By eliminating the need for currency conversion, currency unions promote international trade and make it easier to travel between countries. On the other hand, currency unions impose a one-size-fits-all monetary policy among members. This can be especially costly if business cycles aren't well synchronized across member countries.

Key Terms

Net capital outflow, 327
Currency union, 335
Floating exchange rate regime, 340
Fixed exchange rate regime, 340

Capital controls, 346
Impossible trinity, 346
Bretton–Woods system, 347

Questions for Review

1. Explain why net capital outflow is a negative function of the difference between the domestic and global real interest rates.

2. Is the open-economy IS curve steeper or flatter than the closed economy? Explain.

3. How does a rise in the nominal interest rate affect the real exchange rate? Does this increase or decrease net exports?

4. Explain why unlimited monetary policy expansion makes it impossible to maintain a fixed exchange rate without capital controls. How does the inclusion of capital controls affect your analysis?

5. What is the impossible trinity? What makes it impossible?

6. Compare the costs and benefits of a fixed exchange system.

Problems

13.1 Suppose current-period government spending increases in a country with a floating exchange rate.

    a. If the central bank follows passive monetary policy, does output change by more or less in the open economy compared to the closed economy? How about inflation?

    b. If the central bank wants to implement optimal monetary policy, how does the magnitude of the interest rate change differ in the open versus the closed economy?

13.2 Suppose a central bank wants to attract capital inflow into their country.

    a. How must the central bank change the nominal interest rate? Show what happens in the IS–MP–AS graph. What happens to the real exchange rate?

    b. Historically, some countries adopted an exchange rate band within which they would conduct monetary policy so that the exchange rate stayed between a lower bound and an upper bound. If a country's exchange rate is nearing the lower bound, argue that a central bank can achieve a higher exchange rate by engineering a recession.

13.3 One element of the 1990s crisis in Mexico was an increase in the risk premium, which in our model is given by f_t.

    a. Show how an increase in f_t affects the IS–MP–AS diagram under a fixed exchange rate.

    b. Show how an increase in f_t affects the IS–MP–AS diagram under a flexible exchange rate and passive monetary policy.

    c. Show how an increase in f_t affects the IS–MP–AS diagram under a flexible exchange rate and optimal monetary policy.

13.4 Suppose that a loss in consumer confidence causes a deep recession in Italy.

    a. What exogenous variable is affected by the loss in consumer confidence?

    b. Suppose the European Central Bank sets the nominal interest rate to achieve optimal monetary policy from the perspective of the Italian economy. How should they change the nominal interest rate?

    c. If the German economy does not suffer a loss in consumer confidence, show how the ECB's policy affects the German economy in the IS–MP–AS diagram. Is the optimal policy for Italy also the optimal policy for Germany?

13.5 Suppose that a country's net export function is given by
$$NX_t = Q_t - \varepsilon_t.$$
Their net capital outflow is given by
$$NCF_t = 10 - (r_t - r_t^w).$$

a. Solve for the real exchange rate as a function of Q_t, r_t, and r_t^w.

b. How does the real exchange rate change in response to the three variables in part a? Are these results consistent with the graphical analysis in the chapter?

✓ Knowledge Check 13-1 Answer

An increase in G_t shifts the savings supply curve to the left. At any given level of income, the real interest rate goes up, which shifts the IS curve to the right. This is shown in Figure 13.16.

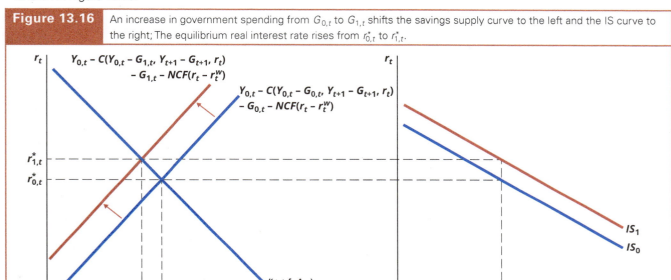

Figure 13.16 An increase in government spending from $G_{0,t}$ to $G_{1,t}$ shifts the savings supply curve to the left and the IS curve to the right; The equilibrium real interest rate rises from $r_{0,t}^*$ to $r_{1,t}^*$.

✓ Knowledge Check 13-2 Answer

If $Y_t > Y_t^p$, then the real interest rate is lower than r_t^f. A lower real interest rate encourages capital to flow out of the domestic economy, pushing net capital outflow up and the real exchange rate down. Thus, the real exchange rate is lower than ε_t^f. This is shown in Figure 13.17.

352 **Part 3** Business Cycles

Figure 13.17 Starting with a positive output gap, $Y_t > Y_t^p$, means that the real interest rate is lower than r_t^f. A lower real interest rate raises net capital outflow and decreases the real exchange rate.

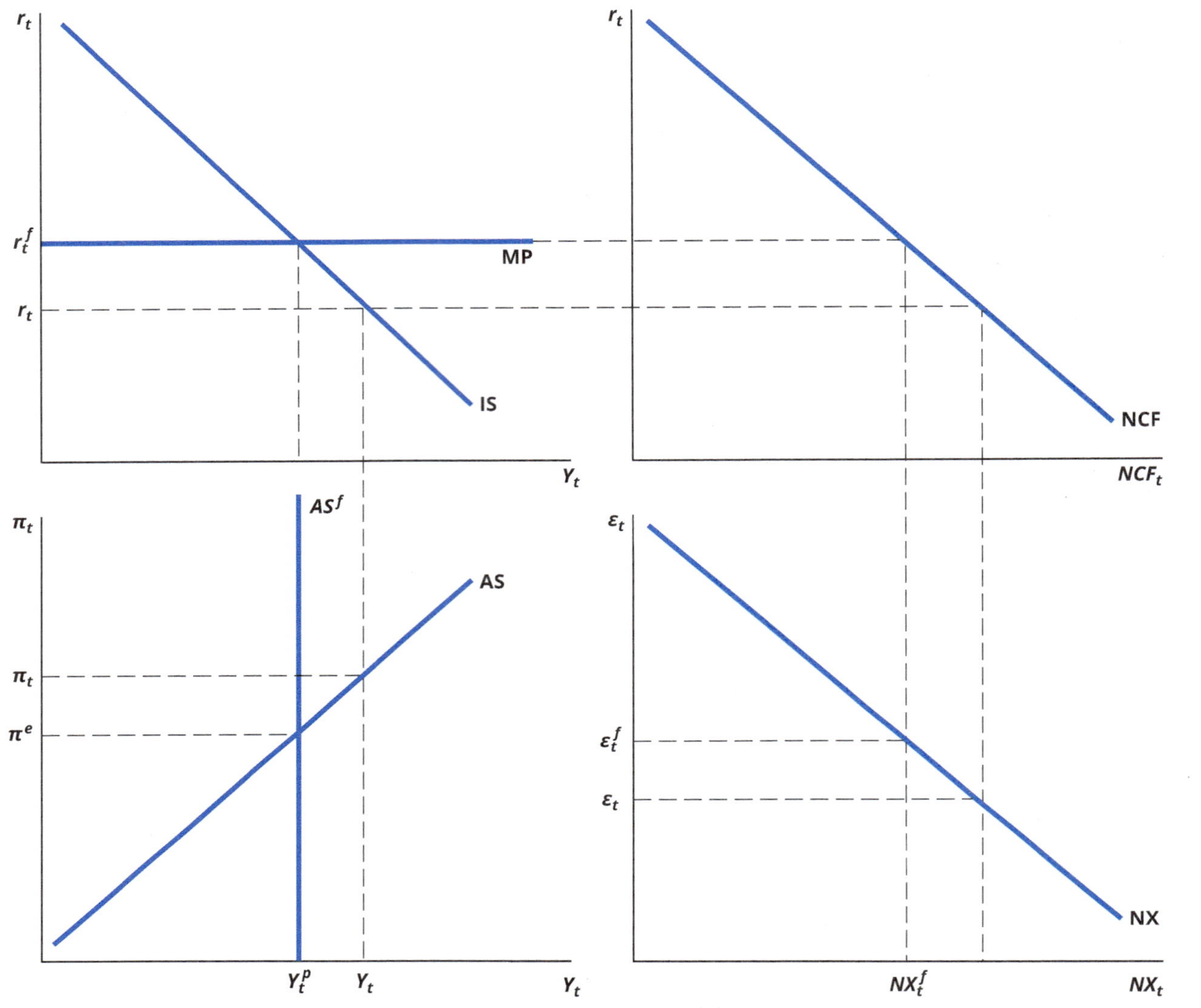

✓ Knowledge Check 13-3 Answer

An increase in G_{t+1} reduces future disposable income, which causes consumers to cut back their spending today. The IS curve shifts to the left. Absent a change in monetary policy, the real interest rate stays fixed and equilibrium output declines. Inflation falls below expectations. Given that the real interest rate stays fixed, investment, net capital outflow, and the real exchange rate stay constant. This is depicted in Figure 13.18.

Chapter 13 IS–MP–AS in the Open Economy 353

Figure 13.18 An increase in G_{t+1} shifts the IS curve to the left. Under passive monetary policy, output declines to $Y_{1,t}^*$ and inflation declines to $\pi_{1,t}^*$. Under optimal monetary policy, the MP curve shifts down. The real interest rate declines from $r_{0,t}^*$ to $r_{1,t}^*$ and output returns to Y_t^p. The real exchange rate depreciates from $\varepsilon_{0,t}^*$ to $\varepsilon_{1,t}^*$ and net exports increase from $NX_{0,t}^*$ to $NX_{1,t}^*$.

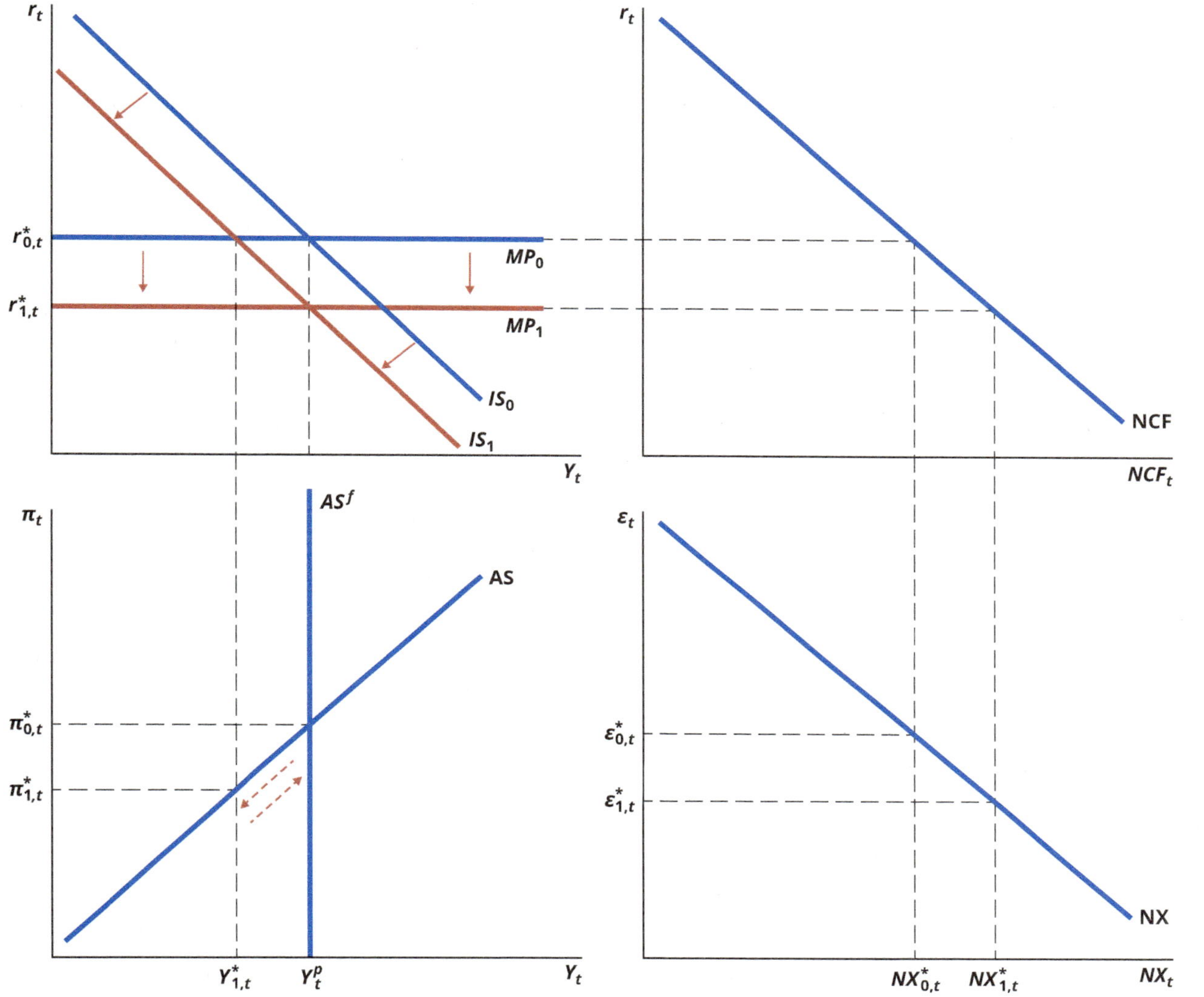

Because potential output hasn't changed, optimal monetary policy entails reducing the nominal interest rate, which in turn shifts the MP curve down and lowers the real interest rate. Output returns to its potential level and the inflation rate returns to its expected level. The lower real interest rate increases net capital outflow. Capital flowing out of the domestic economy causes the real exchange rate to depreciate and net exports to increase. The lower real interest rate also causes investment to increase. Finally, because the GDP expenditure equation, $Y_t = C_t + I_t + G_t + NX_t$, must hold and output is back at Y_t^p while investment and net exports have increased, consumption must decline.

Knowledge Check 13-4 Answer

Figure 13.6 shows an expansionary shift in the IS curve. Under passive monetary policy, the real exchange rate doesn't change. Thus, a fixed exchange rate essentially implements passive monetary policy. The analysis is similar in response to an increase in potential output. Such an increase is depicted in Figure 13.7. Under passive monetary policy, the real exchange rate stays fixed, meaning that a fixed exchange rate essentially implements passive monetary policy.

Chapter 14

Banking and the Macroeconomy

Learning Objectives

14.1 Explain why banks exist in terms of maturity transformation, diversification of risk, and asymmetric information.

14.2 Using a bank's balance sheet, calculate the reserve ratio, leverage ratio, return on equity, and return on assets.

14.3 Compare and contrast liquidity risk and solvency risk.

14.4 Evaluate the strengths and weaknesses associated with policies designed to limit bank runs.

The late 1970s and early 1980s had higher interest rates and inflation rates than any other time over the past 100 years. The Fed funds rate peaked at about 18.5 percent in 1981, and inflation topped 10 percent. To make matters worse, businesses and workers were stung by a brief but painful recession in 1980. Perhaps no one had it harder over this period than banks, and savings-and-loan banks in particular.

Unlike commercial banks, which loan to a variety of individuals and businesses, savings and loan banks (S&Ls) specialize in residential home mortgages. In the years following World War II, high rates of economic growth and the baby boom increased the demand for housing and S&Ls became more prominent. S&Ls attract deposits by offering interest on savings accounts and then use these deposits to fund mortgages.

The problem, as the 1970s and 1980s brutally illustrated, is that mortgages are long commitments, whereas depositors can withdraw their deposits at any time. In the mid-1970s, S&Ls issued mortgages at rates between 8 and 9 percent. That meant that when inflation rose to 10 percent, S&Ls earned a negative real return on their mortgages. To make matters worse, depositors were demanding higher interest rates on their savings accounts to keep pace with inflation. S&Ls responded to the higher demand by issuing high-risk loans that paid the S&Ls more in interest but were also more likely to default.

The defaults on the risky loans eventually caught up with the S&Ls, driving many of them to *insolvency*, or a situation in which net worth is negative. Between 1986 and 1995, the number of S&Ls declined from 3,234 to 1,645.[1]

The S&L crisis illustrates some of the classic points in banking, such as how banks minimize (or fail to minimize) risk. It also illustrates trade-offs associated with the regulation of banks. The depositors at S&Ls were completely bailed out by deposit insurance. That is, despite the failure of the bank, depositors recouped their funds. While depositors were put at ease with the insurance payouts, the payouts themselves were funded by taxpayers. How should the government think about such a transfer, and how might the existence of deposit insurance change the incentives of depositors to monitor the loans made by banks? All of these questions are addressed in this chapter.

---

[1]Curry, Stephen and Lynn Shibut. 2000. "The Cost of the Savings and Loan Crisis: Truth and Consequences." *FDIC Banking Review, 13*(2): 26–35.

14-1 Why Do Banks Exist?

In the 1950s, 1960s, and 1970s, it was sometimes said that bankers lived by a "3-6-3" rule.[2] According to the rule, bankers would gather deposits at 3 percent, issue loans at 6 percent, and play golf at 3 o'clock in the afternoon. Although this is a bit of a caricature, it was meant to describe the perceived lack of competitiveness in the banking industry. Various forms of banking deregulation in the 1980s, such as the removal of prohibitions on interstate banking, made the industry much more competitive in the subsequent decades. However, the 3-6-3 rule has a more basic question: Why would depositors accept a lower rate of interest on their deposits than they could get from lending directly? That is, why would depositors allow the bank to pocket the 3 percent interest rate spread when they could make the loan themselves?

An example illustrates the point. Suppose Maria has $10,000 in savings and would like to accumulate interest on it. Ahmed would like to borrow $10,000 to start a food truck business. In an economy with banks, Maria would deposit $10,000 and earn 3 percent interest, or $300 in income over the course of the year. Ahmed would borrow $10,000 at 6 percent, and pay the bank the $10,000 in principal plus $600 in interest. By matching the supply of Maria's savings with Ahmed's demand to borrow, the bank earns $300.

But what if Maria and Ahmed talk with each other instead of going to a bank? Ahmed could agree to pay Maria more than $300, but less than $600 in interest income. Perhaps they settle on $500. Then Maria earns 5 percent on her deposits, and Ahmed pays an interest rate of 5 percent on his loan. They are both better off by contracting directly with each other rather than having the transaction mediated through a bank.

The direct contracting method may seem appealing, but economic frictions in the real world make direct contracting difficult to achieve in practice. In other words, while some of the interest rate spread may have historically been due to imperfect competition, banks perform costly but valuable services. The next several sections discuss economic frictions in the savings and loan market that make direct contracting difficult, if not impossible, and explains how banks reduce those frictions.

14-1a Maturity Transformation

In the example of Maria and Ahmed, Maria wants to deposit $10,000 and leave it alone for one year. Ahmed wants to take out a loan and pay it back in one year. In reality, depositors often want access to their funds at any given moment. You might deposit your paycheck at the beginning of the month in your checking account but then use your debit card to purchase groceries or transportation or pay rent. You are probably not as patient as Maria is, waiting one year before withdrawing her deposits.

At the same time, Ahmed has an unusually short duration for a loan. Typically, repayments for small business loans are spread out over several years. Moreover, Ahmed would probably be unable to quickly repay the loan if Maria suddenly wanted to redeem her deposits.

In general, there is a maturity mismatch problem between depositors and borrowers. People who deposit their money in banks want quick and easy access to their funds. Deposits are highly liquid in that they can easily be transformed into cash. Borrowers, on the other hand, turn their bank loan into an illiquid project. Ahmed, for instance, uses the loan to purchase a food truck and the equipment necessary to operate his business. With some effort, the truck and equipment can be sold and converted into cash, but probably at a loss.

Banks collect liquid deposits—many of them in small quantities that people want to be able to redeem on demand—and turn them into illiquid loans that take years to repay. This process is called **maturity transformation**. To see how it works, imagine that the bank collects $1,000 from 11 depositors and issues a $10,000 loan to Ahmed. The bank keeps

Maturity transformation
The process of turning liquid deposits into illiquid loans.

---

[2]Walter, John. 2006. "The 3-6-3 Rule: An Urban Myth?" Federal Reserve Bank of Richmond. *Economic Quarterly*, 92(1): 51–78.

Chapter 14 Banking and the Macroeconomy **357**

the extra $1,000 as its **cash reserves**. Provided that depositors don't withdraw more than $1,000 at any given time, the bank can accommodate the withdrawal requests. As people with checking accounts at the bank continue to deposit their paychecks there, holding 1/11th of the deposits as reserves might be sufficient. Even if withdrawal demand exceeds cash reserves, the bank can borrow in the short term to meet demand. In practice, banks can borrow from each other and from the Fed to meet a temporary increase in the demand for withdrawals.

In summary, banks turn liquid deposits into illiquid loans. Given the time preferences of depositors and borrowers, this would be difficult to achieve by bargaining between individuals. This is not the only source of value provided by banks. We assumed that Ahmed would repay his loan. The reality, as the defaults in the S&L crisis illustrate, is much more complicated. The next section discusses how a successfully operating bank minimizes the risk to depositors.

Cash reserves
Assets that a bank holds as cash or deposits at the Federal Reserve.

14-1b Diversification of Risk

For the moment, let's assume there is no maturity mismatch problem and ask what else might go wrong with direct contracting between savers and borrowers. The last section assumed that Ahmed repays his loan with certainty. But what if there is a 1 percent chance he defaults and loses the entire investment? In answering this question, we need to be clear about what happens in the event Ahmed goes out of business. In the United States, businesses are typically protected by **limited liability**: if the business fails, then the individuals aren't personally responsible for making good on the loan. If Maria lends Ahmed $10,000 and the interest rate on the loan is 5 percent, then 99 times out of 100, Maria earns $500. One time out of 100 she loses the entire $10,000. Maria's expected return is $0.99 \times \$500 + 0.01 \times (-\$10,000) = \$395$, equivalent to a 3.95 percent interest rate.

The positive expected return may be enough of an incentive for Maria to invest in Ahmed's business. On the other hand, if the $10,000 is a significant fraction of Maria's net worth, she may be **risk averse** in that she would prefer scenarios with low uncertainty to outcomes of high uncertainty. With the uncertain investment, Maria does okay on average, but faces a financial catastrophe 1 percent of the time. Maria might prefer to avoid the catastrophe and hold onto her money rather than invest it. Thus, Ahmed's project fails to get funding, despite it having a positive expected return.

Banks can minimize risk faced by depositors by pooling together multiple investment projects. Imagine that there 100 depositors like Maria with $10,000 to deposit and that there are 100 food trucks that require a loan. Like Ahmed's, each food truck requires $10,000 to start its business. Each food truck stands a 1/100 chance of failing completely, but the other 99 will survive and pay the bank back 5 percent interest. On average, the bank earns 3.95 percent back in interest. Importantly, because the bank spreads their funds over 100 food trucks, the bank earns a positive revenue if no more than four food trucks fail, which, given the assumptions over success and failure, happens less than 0.5 percent of the time.[3] The bank can afford to pay depositors an interest rate of 2 percent per year and earn a profit with more than a 90 percent probability.

Table 14.1 runs through the numbers. No food trucks fail about 36.6 percent of the time.[4] With a 5 percent interest rate, the bank earns $500 per loan. If they pay 2 percent to each depositor, then banks end up with $\$500 - 0.02 \times \$10,000 = \$300$ in profit per loan. Exactly one food truck fails with a probability of 37 percent.[5] In that case, bank profit per loan is given by

$$(0.99)\$500 - (0.01)\$10,000 - (0.02)\$10,000 = \$195.$$

Limited liability
A legal protection in which a business owner's personal assets aren't at risk if the business fails.

Risk averse
A preference for projects with low uncertainty to outcomes of high uncertainty.

---

[3]The distribution of food truck variables is binomial. The probability of less than five food trucks failing can be evaluated using the cumulative distribution function of the binomial distribution.

[4]The chance that no food trucks fail is the product of the probabilities that each individual food truck succeeds, or 0.99^{100}.

[5]The chance that exactly one food truck fails is $1,000.99^{99}0.01^{1}$.

358 **Part 4** Banking and Financial Markets

The total return to the bank is the weighted average of the returns on the food trucks that succeed and the ones that fail, $(0.99)\$500 - (0.01)\$10,000$, minus what the bank pays to depositors, $(0.02)\$10,000$. The remaining rows are filled in analogously.

Table 14.1	Returns to the Bank and Depositors		
Number of failures	**Probability**	**Return on deposits**	**Bank profit (per loan)**
0	36.6%	2%	$300
1	37.0%	2%	$195
2	18.5%	2%	$90
3	6.1%	2%	−$15
4	1.5%	2%	−$120

Now even risk-averse depositors will feel comfortable depositing their money in the bank. True, 2 percent interest is less than the 3.95 percent interest they would expect to earn on average by directly investing in the project, but depositing in the bank carries much less risk. Banks add value by pooling deposits from risk-averse depositors and lending them to a diversified set of investment opportunities. While the investment opportunities might individually be quite risky, collectively they are much safer. This is a general lesson in finance: risk is reduced through diversification. In sum, valuable investment projects receive funding, deposits earn risk-free interest, and banks earn profit from diversifying risk.

✓ **Knowledge Check 14-1**

Consider an identical table to 14.1, but now assume the bank charges each food truck a 6 percent interest rate. Complete the last column. With what probability does the bank earn negative profit?

Number of failures	Probability	Return on deposits	Bank profit (per loan)
0	36.6%	2%	?
1	37.0%	2%	?
2	18.5%	2%	?
3	6.1%	2%	?
4	1.5%	2%	?

——— Answers are at the end of the chapter.

14-1c Adverse Selection and Screening

We showed how banks can effectively diversify risk by investing in a large number of projects. There were two critical assumptions in that analysis. First, all the food trucks were equally risky; second, depositors and banks accurately assessed the likelihood of success of each project. In the real world, investment projects are likely to have different expected returns and the potential entrepreneurs know more about the viability of their projects than lenders do.

To understand this, let's return to the example of Maria and Ahmed. To simplify things, we will assume that Maria is **risk neutral** in that she only cares about the expected returns of the project, rather than its riskiness. Suppose that if Ahmed borrows the $10,000 from Maria, he is certain to make a 10 percent, or $1,000 return on investment. This implies that Ahmed would be willing to pay up to 10 percent for a loan of one year. If the borrowing rate ends up being 5 percent, then Ahmed makes $1,000 − $500 = $500 in profit. Assuming Maria has no better investment options for her savings of $10,000, she is better off making the loan at any positive interest rate. Thus, as long as the interest rate on the loan is between 0 and 10 percent, both Maria and Ahmed gain by Ahmed borrowing from Maria.

Risk neutral

A preference for projects with the highest expected value, regardless of the riskiness.

Now suppose that there is another potential borrower, Elena, who also wants to borrow $10,000. Unlike Ahmed's low-risk investment, the prospects for Elena's investment are uncertain. In particular, Elena expects that there is a 50-50 chance her business will be successful. If her business is successful, then there is a 50 percent return on investment, for a total return of $5,000. If her business fails, then she loses all $10,000. Given these prospects, would there be a mutually beneficial transaction between Elena and Maria?

Assume Elena has limited liability so that if she goes out of business, it is the lender that bears the $10,000 cost of the failure, not Elena. Given these assumptions, Elena would find it beneficial to borrow provided that the interest rate is less than 50 percent. If the business fails, then she loses nothing. If the business is successful, then she earns $5,000 − $10,000$r$. As long as r is less than 0.5, then she is profitable.

If Maria lends to Elena, then Maria faces a 50 percent chance of losing $10,000. At Elena's breakeven interest rate of 50 percent, the expected value for Maria is

$$0.5(-\$10,000) + 0.5(0.5)(\$10,000) = -\$2,500.$$

Even at the highest possible interest rate that Elena would accept, Maria loses money on average. Therefore, Maria would not find it optimal to lend to Elena.

As long as Maria can distinguish Elena from Ahmed, the analysis can stop there. Maria will lend to Ahmed, but not Elena. But, in making this distinction, Maria needs to know how different factors influence the expected return of each business. Maybe Elena plans to operate in an area heavily reliant on tourism where demand is unpredictable, while Ahmed plans to operate in the business district where he will have many regular customers. Or maybe Elena's menu includes a lot of exotic fish that don't store well, and Ahmed sells corndogs which can be stored in the freezer for 10 years. In principle, Maria could weigh these factors in assessing the viability of each food truck. But if Maria isn't an expert in the food truck industry, then this isn't so likely.

What happens if Maria wants to invest her $10,000 but can't distinguish Ahmed's projects from Elena's? She knows there is a 50 percent chance of being matched with Elena and a 50 percent chance of being matched with Ahmed. At an interest rate of r, the return to lending conditional on being matched with Ahmed is $10,000$r$. The expected return conditional on being matched with Elena is $0.5(-\$10,000) + 0.5(\$10,000r)$. Because there is 50-50 chance of being matched with Ahmed or Elena, the expected value to making the loan is

$$0.5(\$10,000r) + 0.5(0.5(-\$10,000) + 0.5(\$10,000r)) = \$7,500r - \$2,500.$$

As long as $r > 1/3$, it is profitable for Maria to make the loan. For instance, if $r = 0.4$ or 40 percent, Maria expects to earn $500 on average. However, at an interest rate of 40 percent, it's not profitable for Ahmed to take out the loan. But if Ahmed drops out of the market, then only Elena wants to take out the loan at $r = 0.4$. But, if Maria lends to Elena at a 40 percent interest rate, she expects to lose $3,000. Anticipating this outcome, Maria doesn't lend at all and neither Ahmed nor Elena's project receives funding.

This is an example of **adverse selection**, or a situation in which borrowers have hidden information. In this case, Elena and Ahmed know more about their business prospects than Maria. Because of this, the market for lending breaks down and Ahmed's project, despite having a positive return on investment, doesn't receive funding.

Banks understand the adverse selection problem and take steps to minimize it. To begin with, a prospective business loan applicant, such as Elena or Ahmed, would need to provide a business plan with projections on income, expenses, and forecasts on business growth. They would also need to provide information on their own credit, employment, and income history. Using all this information, as well as any knowledge about the restaurant industry, experts at the bank would make a call about each project's viability. Through this process of screening, the bank hopes to fund projects with positive expected values like Ahmed's and weed out projects like Elena's.

Collecting information, analyzing it, and screening loan applicants may be feasible for a bank, but it wouldn't be feasible for an individual depositor. In practice, banks have entire

Adverse selection
A situation in which borrowers have more information about the quality of their project than lenders.

360 **Part 4** Banking and Financial Markets

divisions that screen business and personal loan applications. They add value by minimizing the adverse selection problem. Depositors, meanwhile, sacrifice some of the upside, but avoid the costly acquisition of information. Unfortunately, asymmetric information doesn't begin and end at the lending stage. Once the funds are obtained, borrowers might use them in riskier ways than lenders would like. The consequences of this are discussed in the next section.

✓ Knowledge Check 14-2

Using the concept of adverse selection, are cautious or reckless drivers more likely to take out car insurance? How might car insurers screen insurance applications?

——————————————— Answers are at the end of the chapter.

14-1d Moral Hazard and Monitoring

Moral hazard

A situation in which borrowers take an action that is difficult for lenders to observe.

Returning one last time to our example with Maria and Ahmed, let's assume that Ahmed's $10,000 food truck investment will earn a 10 percent return on investment with certainty, so he and Maria might settle for a 5 percent interest rate on a loan for one year. Furthermore, assume that there is no hidden information. Maria knows what Ahmed's food truck is capable of producing. Despite these assumptions, there still may be asymmetric information in that Ahmed could divert the loan to riskier ventures behind Maria's back. This type of action is called a **moral hazard**.

To specify, Ahmed may take the $10,000 and gamble on sports. In an extreme case, suppose he bets on the Detroit Lions to win the Super Bowl which, as of the time of this writing, has about 30–1 odds. If the Lions win the Super Bowl, Ahmed wins $300,000 minus the $500 in interest he has to pay Maria. If the Lions don't win the Super Bowl, then, because of limited liability, he loses nothing.[6] Ahmed's expected profit from betting on the Lions is $299,500/30 = $9,983.33, significantly higher than the $500 from running the food truck. Ahmed wants to accept more risk, because he gets all the upside and none of the downside.

The situation is reversed for Maria. She gets none of the upside when Ahmed wins a big bet but bears all the downside if Ahmed goes out of business. Maria may realize upfront that Ahmed has an incentive to divert funds to riskier projects and this causes her not to lend in the first place. Just as in the case of adverse selection, asymmetric information causes the lending market to break down, but this time by hidden action rather than hidden information.

Banks have an incentive to not only analyze loan applications, but then also continually monitor how the loan funds are being directed. Banks may, for instance, ask for periodic profit-and-loss statements or balance sheets to verify the business is doing what it says it is. The business, anticipating that it will be monitored, likely behaves well even prior to the audit. When businesses use loans responsibly, they are more likely to meet interest payments which is also good for depositors. Thus, another way a bank can add value is by reducing moral hazard.

✓ Knowledge Check 14-3

Suppose a person takes out a loan for a home mortgage but then uses the home as an Airbnb rental instead of a residence for themselves. Why might this concern the lending bank? What steps might the bank take to protect its investment?

——————————————— Answers are at the end of the chapter.

———————

[6]Despite generally being cautious in forecasting, we can be almost certain the Lions won't win the Super Bowl.

Chapter 14 Banking and the Macroeconomy **361**

14-2 The Bank's Balance Sheet

Accounting, as we know it today, was discovered in the late 1400s by Italian mathematician, Luca Pacioli.[7] Key to Pacioli's analysis was the **balance sheet**, which is an accounting device that keeps track of an entity's **assets**, **liabilities**, and **equity**. Every entity, whether it be a household, business, bank, or government, owns some things and owes other things. The things an entity owns are called assets. The things an entity owes are called liabilities. For instance, if you own a house valued at $300,000, that is an asset. If you have $200,000 left on a mortgage, that is a liability. The difference between assets and liabilities is equity.

In the last example, the equity is the difference between the home value and the value of the mortgage, $300,000 − $200,000 = $100,000. Table 14.2 shows how this appears on a balance sheet. The left-hand side shows the value of assets, which in this example is the $300,000 house. Every dollar that appears on the left-hand side as an asset must be fully offset by either a liability or equity on the right-hand side. The only liability is the $200,000 mortgage and the equity is $100,000. Another way to think about equity is the amount that would remain if a household sold all of its assets and paid all of its debts. In other words, equity is a measure of net worth. If the household sold its only asset (for $300,000) and paid its only debt (for $200,000), what would be left over is the $100,000 in equity. A foundational principle of double-entry accounting is that both sides of the balance sheet must balance. That is, assets equal the sum of liabilities and equity. Each time an entity acquires an asset, the asset's value must be divided between liabilities and equity.

Balance sheet
An accounting device that keeps track of an entity's assets, liabilities, and equity.

Assets
Things an entity owns.

Liabilities
Things an entity owes.

Equity
The difference in value between assets and liabilities.

Table 14.2	Household Balance Sheet	
Assets		**Liabilities**
Home = $300,000		Mortgage = $200,000
		Equity = $100,000

Pacioli's discovery vastly improved the accuracy and efficiency of businesses in 15th-century Europe and continues to be used today. The remainder of this section focuses on the balance sheet of one particular entity—a bank.

14-2a Assets and Liabilities of a Bank

Suppose you have $10,000 in cash and deposit it in a checking account at your local bank. The $10,000 is your asset, but it is the bank's liability. By depositing the $10,000 in your checking account, you've provided the bank with an interest-free loan that can be redeemed by you on demand. In fact, the most common form of liabilities for banks is deposits. Because they can be redeemed whenever the depositor wants, they are called **demand deposits**. This example illustrates another principle of double-entry bookkeeping, namely one entity's liability is another entity's asset. Banks take their liabilities and invest them in assets.

Demand deposit
Deposits that can be redeemed on the demand of the depositors.

Banks may have many different types of assets. The most common are loans made to households (typically in the form of mortgages) and businesses. If you owe $200,000 on a home mortgage, that is a liability for you but an asset for the bank you borrowed from. The same is true of a business loan. When Ahmed takes out a loan of $10,000 for his food truck, that is a liability for him but an asset for the bank.

A second type of asset includes securities purchased by the bank. For instance, a bank might own U.S. Treasury securities or bonds issued by other countries. The bank might also own corporate bonds or mortgage-backed securities. One feature of all these securities is that they pay interest. Another feature is that they can all fluctuate in value. U.S. government and corporate bond prices fluctuate all the time, and banks bear the upside and downside risk on their balance sheets.

---

[7]Smith, Murphy. 2018. "Luca Pacioli: The Father of Accounting" [working paper].

Unlike loans (which may or may not be repaid) and securities (which fluctuate in value), a bank may choose to hold a fraction of deposits in cash. Cash reserves can be physically held in the bank vault but are more commonly held electronically at the Federal Reserve. Specifically, each bank has an account at the Federal Reserve where it can deposit cash. Thus, the Fed is to a bank as a bank is to a household. The household deposits cash in a bank, and a bank can deposit its cash into their account at the Fed. This is why the Fed is sometimes referred to as the "banker's bank."

Cash reserves that banks deposit at the Fed pay interest, but at a lower interest rate than the bank could get by issuing a loan, such as a mortgage. Figure 14.1 shows the interest rate on bank reserves and the 30-year mortgage rate. Although both interest rates have risen with inflation between 2021 and 2023, the mortgage interest rate is consistently higher than the interest rate on reserves. Despite the opportunity cost of foregone interest, banks choose to hold some of their assets in cash because it is a lower risk than making a loan.

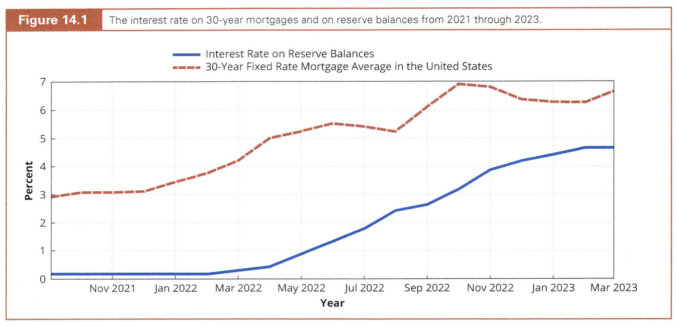

Figure 14.1 The interest rate on 30-year mortgages and on reserve balances from 2021 through 2023.

Source: Board of Governors of the Federal Reserve https://fred.stlouisfed.org/graph/?g=11xzG.

Capital
The differences between the value of assets and liabilities.

Finally, the difference between a bank's assets and its liabilities is its equity. In banking especially, equity usually goes by the name of **capital**, or "bank capital." Table 14.3 shows an example of a bank's balance sheet. The bank owns $100 million in mortgages, $30 million in treasuries, and $20 million in cash reserves for a total of $150 million in assets. It holds $110 in deposits, which means its equity is $150 − $110 = $40 million.

Table 14.3 Example of a Bank's Balance Sheet

Assets	Liabilities
Mortgages = $100 million	Deposits = $110 million
U.S. Treasuries = $30 million	**Equity** = $40 million
Cash Reserves = $20 million	

Given the nature of double-entry bookkeeping, any change to one side of the balance sheet affects the other. For instance, suppose depositors withdraw $5 million in deposits from the bank. To immediately meet the withdrawal request, banks take $5 million out of their cash reserves. On net, and as displayed in Table 14.4, both assets and liabilities decrease by $5 million.

Chapter 14 Banking and the Macroeconomy **363**

Table 14.4	Effects of a Decrease in Deposits	
Assets		**Liabilities**
Mortgages = $100 million		Deposits = $110 million − $5 million
U.S. Treasuries = $30 million		**Equity** = $40 million
Cash Reserves = $20 million − $5 million		

Alternatively, suppose that the value of U.S. Treasury securities increases by 10 percent, which raises the bank's assets by $3 million. Because deposits haven't changed, the increase in the value of the bank's assets raises their equity by $3 million. This is shown in Table 14.5.

Table 14.5	Effects of an Increase in Asset Values	
Assets		**Liabilities**
Mortgages = $100 million		Deposits = $110 million
U.S. Treasuries = $30 million + $3 million		**Equity** = $40 million + $3 million
Cash Reserves = $20 million		

Changes originating on either side of the bank's balance sheet affect the financial health of the bank. For instance, if depositors want to withdraw more than $20 million, then banks wouldn't be able to meet the demand without selling assets or taking out a loan. We will investigate issues surrounding the financial health of a bank in Section 14.3 but first it is helpful to define a few key concepts in the bank's balance sheet.

✔ Knowledge Check 14-4

Suppose many of the mortgages that the bank issued end up in default. Specifically, suppose that the value of mortgages declines by $10 million. Starting from the balance sheet in Table 14.3, show how the decline in mortgage values affects the bank's balance sheet.

——————————————————————————— Answers are at the end of the chapter.

14-2b Balance Sheet Concepts

There are a variety of ways to assess a bank's financial health. These are not only internally useful for banks and their shareholders, but also for bank regulators, such as those at the Fed. The following concepts are used when analyzing the state of a bank's balance sheet:

1. Bank liquidity: Recall from Chapter 5 that liquidity is defined as the ease with which assets can be used in exchange. Cash is the most liquid asset, as it is "payable for all debts private and public." Because banks are required to meet withdrawal requests from depositors on demand, they want to have enough liquidity. Accordingly, the **liquidity ratio** is defined as the ratio of cash reserves to total assets. In Table 14.3, cash reserves equal $20 million and total assets equal $150 million, implying a liquidity ratio of $20/$150 = 0.13, or 13 percent. Similarly, a bank's **reserve ratio** is the fraction of ratio of cash reserves to total deposits, which in the example is equal to $20/$110 = 0.18, or 18 percent.

   Prior to March 2020, banks were required to hold some fraction of their deposits in reserves, but with the onset of the global pandemic, the Fed removed the requirement altogether. This isn't as abrupt of a change as one might think. The Fed has been paying interest on reserves since 2008 and banks have found it optimal to hold reserves well in excess of the required level. Figure 14.2 shows that the ratio

Liquidity ratio
The ratio of a bank's cash reserves to its total assets.

Reserve ratio
The ratio of a bank's cash reserves to its deposits.

Figure 14.2 The ratio of reserves to deposits of commercial banks from 1973 through 2023.

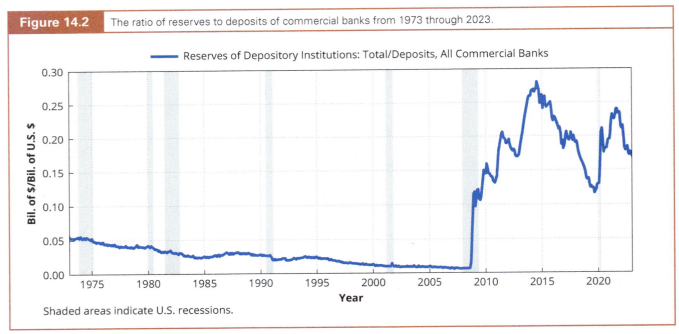

Shaded areas indicate U.S. recessions.

Source: https://fred.stlouisfed.org/graph/?g=11Bd7 Federal Reserve Board of Governors.

of reserves to deposits rose from less than 5 percent in 2008 to over 25 percent by 2015. Moreover, even without abundant cash reserves, a bank's balance sheet can still be fairly liquid. U.S. Treasury securities can be bought or sold in a very short period of time, so the $30 million in Treasuries from our imaginary bank are almost as liquid as cash.

2. **Bank profitability**: The balance sheet is a static concept, displaying a bank's assets and liabilities at a point in time. A bank's objective, however, is to maximize profit, or the return to its shareholders. Banks achieve this by lending at higher rates than what they pay depositors. Returning to the example in Table 14.3, suppose that mortgages return an average of 5 percent per year, Treasuries return 2 percent per year, and cash reserves return nothing. Furthermore, assume that depositors earn 1 percent interest on their checking and savings accounts. The bank's profit is the difference between the interest on its assets and liabilities, which in this case is

$$\text{profit} = 0.05(\$100) + 0.02(\$20) - 0.01(\$110) = \$4.3.$$

So, the bank's profit is $4.3 million. Realistically, the bank needs to pay employees, purchase computers, and rent a building to operate in. The $4.3 million is therefore an upper-bound of bank profits.

The **return on assets** (ROA) is a bank's profit divided by the total value of its assets. In this example, the ROA would be $4.3/$150 = 0.029, or 2.9%. The bank's **return on equity** (ROE) is profit divided by the bank's equity, which in this case would be $4.3/$40 = 0.108, or 10.8%. The ROA and ROE are a way to express the bank's profitability while accounting for its size. A bank with $1 million in profits and $10 million in assets performs significantly better than a bank with $1 million in profits and $10 billion in assets.

Return on assets
A bank's profits divided by its assets.

Return on equity
A bank's profits divided by its equity.

3. **Bank leverage**: Imagine that you buy a house valued at $100,000 with a down payment of $10,000 and a mortgage of $90,000. If the house increases in value to $110,000, then your mortgage stays fixed, and your equity goes up to $20,000. Remember that equity is a measure of net worth, so even though the house's value increases by only 10 percent, the homeowner's net worth doubles—an increase of 100 percent. Alternatively, suppose the house was purchased with a $5,000 down

Chapter 14 Banking and the Macroeconomy · **365**

payment. Then, a $10,000 increase in the home's value raises the homeowner's equity to $15,000—a 200 percent increase in net worth.

This example generalizes. Because debt stays fixed, an increase in asset values increases equity one-for-one. Following an increase in asset prices, equity goes up by more in percentage terms when starting from a lower value. In the example of the homeowner, an increase in the home's value of $10,000 leaves debt constant and raises equity by $10,000. But the *percent* by which equity increases depends on the initial value of equity. The smaller the initial value, the more equity increases in percentage terms.

Now think about it from the bank's perspective. Consider two banks with balance sheets shown in the top and bottom panels of Table 14.6. The asset side of each balance sheet is the same, with loans equaling $100 million, securities equaling $30 million and cash reserves equaling $20 million. The methods through which the banks finance their assets are different. The bank in the top panel has $100 million in deposits and $50 million in equity. The **leverage ratio** is defined as the bank's liabilities divided by its equity. The bank in the top panel has a leverage ratio of 2. The bank in the bottom panel has $140 million in deposits and $10 million in equity, meaning that their leverage ratio is 14.

Leverage ratio
A bank's liabilities divided by its equity.

Table 14.6	Banks with Different Leverage Ratios

Panel A	
Assets	**Liabilities**
Mortgages = $100 million	Deposits = $100 million
Securities = $30 million	**Equity** = $50 million
Cash Reserves = $20 million	

Panel B	
Assets	**Liabilities**
Mortgages = $100 million	Deposits = $140 million
Securities = $30 million	**Equity** = $10 million
Cash Reserves = $20 million	

Suppose that over the course of the year, the value of securities increases by $10 million, which counts toward each bank's profit. Despite profit increasing by the same amount for each bank, the ROE for the bank in Panel A is $10/$50 = 0.2, or 20%, while it is $10/$10 = 1, or 100% for the bank in Panel B. In general, the higher the bank's leverage ratio is, the greater its return on equity.

Why is this relevant to banks? All banks have owners. Banks that are smaller and geographically concentrated tend to be owned privately, whereas larger banks (e.g., Wells Fargo or U.S. Bank) are traded publicly and have thousands of shareholders. These owners, whether in a private group or shareholders of a public company, want to direct their capital to investment opportunities offering the highest returns, which are the banks with the highest ROEs.

If banks with high ROEs are the most profitable, why don't they maximize their leverage ratios? To understand this, it's helpful to return to the example of an individual homebuyer that we began this discussion with. If the homebuyer purchases a home for $100,000 with a $10,000 down payment, and the house increases in value by $10,000, then the net worth of the homebuyer doubles. If the home is purchased with a $20,000 down payment, then net worth increases by only 50 percent. However, if, instead of increasing by $10,000, the value of the home drops to $90,000, then the person who put $10,000 down has a net worth of zero, whereas net worth for the person who put $20,000 down only declines by 50 percent. Thus, higher leverage carries the potential for higher returns, but also entails more risk. This is just as true for banks as it is for homebuyers. The next section discusses some of the major risks banks confront.

Knowledge Check 14-5

For the following bank balance sheet, compute the reserve ratio, liquidity ratio, and leverage ratio. Assuming the bank earned $25 million in profit, also compute the ROA and ROE.

Assets	Liabilities
Mortgages = $120 million	Deposits = $100 million
Securities = $10 million	**Equity** = $70 million
Cash Reserves = $40 million	

Answers are at the end of the chapter.

14-3 Bank Risks, Runs, and Regulations

Banks face several kinds of risk. Recognizing the potential of bank failure means that banks are susceptible to depositors trying to withdraw all their money simultaneously. Banks face several different types of regulations to protect depositors and minimize imprudent risk taking. This section begins by discussing bank risk.

14-3a Liquidity Versus Solvency Risk

One of the perils of owning an old car is that it sometimes requires unexpected repairs. Suppose that you own an old car valued at $8,000 and have $2,000 in cash, for a total of $10,000 in assets. If your car suddenly requires $1,500 in repairs, you can pay for the cars immediately with your cash savings. Alternatively, suppose you own the same car, but instead of having $2,000 in cash, you have a baseball card collection valued at $2,000. While you still have $10,000 in assets, paying for the car repairs won't be as easy. You will have to sell your baseball card set, which means finding a buyer and paying any sort of transaction costs associated with the sale. Instead of paying for the repairs immediately, you may have to wait days or even weeks before the sale is finalized.

Despite having $10,000 in assets in both scenarios, the liquidity of the assets is very different. It isn't straightforward to turn a baseball card collection into cash, and that has consequences for how easily you can pay for a big repair. Similarly, banks face varying degrees of **liquidity risk** depending on the liquidity composition of their assets. To see this, imagine that a bank has $80 million in deposits and $10 million in cash reserves, $30 million in securities, and $100 million in commercial and residential loans. The bank can easily meet the withdrawal requests for the first $10 million of deposits. But if depositors collectively want to withdraw $25 million from the bank, then the bank will have to sell some of its securities. The market for U.S. government and corporate debt is quite large, so the bank could easily make the necessary sales if that's what they invested in. If the withdrawal requests exceed $40 million, however, the bank gets in trouble. Commercial and residential loans have long durations and it's not like banks can ask mortgage holders to pay off the rest of their balance all at once. Moreover, it is unlikely that banks could sell off their assets for 100 percent on the dollar. The reason is that the financial institution purchasing the assets (perhaps another bank) will be uncertain about the quality of the loans the bank is selling. If the bank is expected to sell its worst quality of loans first, then that will lower their price. This is another example of adverse selection in financial markets.

Banks can deal with liquidity risk in a couple of different ways. First, rather than sell off their illiquid assets, banks can borrow from other banks using their illiquid assets as **collateral**. In the event the borrowing bank defaults on its loan, the lending bank can seize the collateral. Additionally, banks can borrow from the Federal Reserve through the **discount window**. The discount window was critically important during the financial crisis of 2007–2008 and, more recently, in March 2023, following the failure of Silicon Valley Bank. To reduce the stigma of using the discount window, the Fed does not release the identities of the borrowing institutions for two years.

Liquidity risk
The risk that a bank's liquid assets run so low that they can't meet withdrawal requests.

Collateral
Assets that a borrower puts up that the lender can seize if the borrower defaults.

Discount window
The lending program in which banks can borrow from the Fed on a short-term basis.

Although banks might have to sell illiquid assets in a hurry and at a discount, it has been assumed that the bank remains **solvent**, or that its assets exceed its liabilities. **Solvency risk** is the risk that a bank's assets depreciate in value so much that they become insolvent. For example, if the value of a bank's mortgages declines because of a wave of missed payments, then the value of its assets could drop to the point where liabilities exceed assets. At a point of insolvency, if a bank sells off all their assets, they still won't have enough to pay back depositors.

Table 14.7 shows a sample bank balance sheet. The bank's total assets initially consist of $100 million in mortgages, $70 million in securities, and $30 million in reserves. The bank's liabilities include $180 in demand deposits, meaning that it has $20 million in equity.

Solvent
A situation in which assets exceed liabilities.

Solvency risk
The risk that a bank's assets depreciate in value so much that they become insolvent.

Table 14.7 Solvency Risk on a Bank's Balance Sheet

Assets	Liabilities
Mortgages = $100 million − $20 million	Deposits = $180 million
U.S. Treasuries = $70 million	**Equity** = $20 million − $20 million
Cash Reserves = $30 million	

If the value of mortgages drops by $20 million, then the value of assets and equity decreases by $20 million. Because there are no withdrawals by assumption, deposits don't change. With an equity value of zero, the bank is on the edge of insolvency. If asset values drop by another dollar, then the bank is insolvent.

Banks can reduce insolvency risk in a couple of different ways. First, they can invest in safer assets or hold a greater portion of their assets as cash reserves. By investing in safer assets, the bank is less likely to experience a big drop in asset values. Safer assets, however, do not pay as high of a return as riskier assets, so safety comes at the cost of higher expected returns. Second, the bank could fund itself with a greater fraction of capital and a lower fraction of deposits. The bank in Table 14.7 initially has a leverage ratio equal to 9. The higher the leverage ratio is, the more vulnerable the bank is to a fall in asset values. A lower leverage ratio, however, means a lower return on equity. Again, we see that bank safety comes at the expense of higher returns for the owners of the bank. The risk/return tradeoff and the role of government policy are topics we return to in Section 14.3c.

The topic of bank failures might bring to mind the Great Depression or even the financial crisis of 2007–2008 and, indeed, thousands of banks failed during the first few years of the depression. The creation of the Federal Reserve in 1913 was inspired by a bank panic in 1907. Banks can fail, however, even outside of recessions. Figure 14.3 shows that the biggest

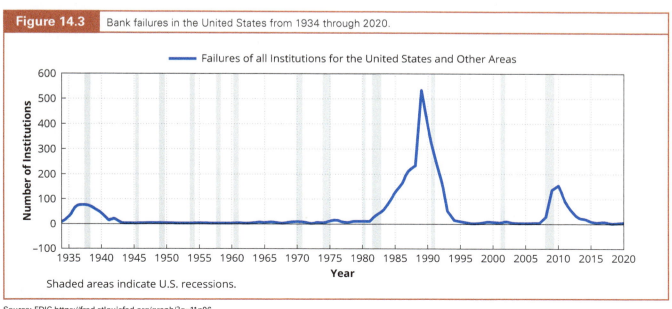

Figure 14.3 Bank failures in the United States from 1934 through 2020.

Shaded areas indicate U.S. recessions.

Source: FDIC https://fred.stlouisfed.org/graph/?g=11n96.

Part 4 Banking and Financial Markets

wave of bank failures occurred during the period discussed in the chapter's introduction, namely the savings and loan crisis of the 1980s. The situation facing many of the S&Ls was similar to the one depicted in Table 14.7. In the face of rising interest rates, S&Ls made risky loans, many of which ended up in default. The deterioration of the assets of the S&Ls also reduced equity to the point of insolvency. More recently, Silicon Valley Bank failed in 2023. Rather than defaulting on loans, the failure of Silicon Valley Bank had more to do with the declining value of the securities in which they invested. Application 14.1 discusses the case study in more detail.

Application 14.1

Bank Failures and the Case of Silicon Valley Bank

The Federal Reserve and Federal Deposit Insurance Corporation (FDIC) try to carefully monitor the financial health of banks. As discussed in the last section, however, bank failures sometimes happen. Banks fail when they can no longer meet their obligations to depositors. In the event of a bank failure, the FDIC acts as the receiver of the bank. That is, the FDIC is responsible for paying out insured depositors up to $250,000, paying the bank's debts and collecting on its assets such as mortgage and commercial loans. Ideally, the FDIC looks to sell some or all of the assets of the failed bank to a healthy institution that also assumes some or all of the failed bank's liabilities. The FDIC is responsible for collecting on any of the assets that they don't sell to another institution.

A recent example of a bank failure is Silicon Valley Bank (SVB), which failed in March 2023. Based in Santa Clara, California, SVB, from its founding in 1983, catered to start-ups in the technology and life science industries. Indeed, as late as 2022, more than half of its loans were to venture capital or private equity firms and nearly a quarter of its loans were to various technology and healthcare companies.[8] Given its location, many of its depositors also hailed from the technology industry.

Besides its tech-heavy clientele, SVB's balance sheet had two other distinctive characteristics. First, it was heavily invested in long-duration securities, mostly U.S. government debt. In 2022, banks with over $1 billion in assets held, on average, 6 percent of their debt portfolio in long-duration securities, while the figure was 75 percent for SVB.[9] You may recall from your principles of macroeconomics class that bond prices and interest rates move in opposite directions. When the Fed raised interest rates in 2022, bond prices went down, and the prices of the longest duration bonds were the most affected. So,

if a bank wanted to sell a 30-year U.S. Treasury security, it would do so at a loss. At the same time, if the bank could hold onto the security for the entire 30 years or sell it once prices rebounded, then it wouldn't realize a loss.

The composition of a bank's loan portfolio is something depositors don't typically worry about.[10] But the other distinctive element of SVB was that, due to its tech-savvy and highly affluent clientele, 94 percent of its deposits were uninsured, or above the $250,000 threshold.[11] According to one report, SVB had a higher ratio of uninsured deposits to total deposits than any bank with more than $50 billion in assets. JP Morgan Chase and U.S. Bank, for instance, have just over half of their deposits uninsured.

As the tech industry softened in 2022 and laid off workers, SVB's customers started to withdraw their money. When SVB sold some of its longer-duration bonds for a loss, the depositors with big checking accounts took notice. On a Wednesday in March, the bank announced that it had lost nearly $2 billion in bond sales. Depositors rushed to withdraw their funds, and by Friday morning, trading of the company's stock was halted and the FDIC took control of the bank.

As the bank was collapsing, the U.S. government promised that all depositors, regardless of whether they exceeded the $250,000 threshold, would be repaid in full. The expressed motivation was to quell the possibility of other bank runs, but critics referred to the action as a bailout. Bank bailouts are discussed in greater detail in the next application. As for SVB, its managers were fired, its equity holders wiped out, and just two weeks after the FDIC's intervention, another bank, First Citizens BancShares, purchased SVB's deposits and assets at a discounted price. SVB was the second-largest bank failure in U.S. history and serves as a cautionary tale of balance sheet risk.

---

[8]Kokalitcheva, Kia. (2023, March 11). "The Rise and Stunning Fall of Silicon Valley Bank." *Axios.* https://www.axios.com/2023/03/11/silicon-valley-bank-rip.

[9]Farrell, Maureen. (2023, March 14). "Inside the Collapse of Silicon Valley Bank." *New York Times.* https://www.nytimes.com/2023/03/14/business/silicon-valley-bank-gregory-becker.html?searchResultPosition=22.

[10]Do you know (without looking) what fraction of your personal bank's assets are in the form of mortgages versus commercial loans? If so, you are more impressive than I.

[11]Hayes, David. (2023, March 14). "SVB, Signature, Racked Up Some High Rates of Uninsured Deposits." *S&P Global Market Intelligence.* https://www.spglobal.com/marketintelligence/en/news-insights/latest-news-headlines/svb-signature-racked-up-some-high-rates-of-uninsured-deposits-74747639.

14-3b Bank Runs

In addition to setting an impossibly high standard for childcare, the 1964 movie *Mary Poppins* also provides a lesson on **bank runs**, or a situation in which a large number of a bank's depositors simultaneously demand to withdraw their money. In the relevant scene, the children in the story visit a bank. A banker encourages Michael, one of the children, to invest his money in the bank. After some back and forth, the banker physically seizes Michael's coin, causing Michael to yell, "Give me back my money." Hearing this, the bank's other customers run to the teller windows demanding to withdraw their deposits. Chaos temporarily ensues, but the children escape and sing another delightful song with Mary Poppins in the next scene.

Although apocryphal, *Mary Poppins* carries a fundamental insight on bank runs, namely, that they can theoretically occur in banks with good financial health. That is, a bank can have a lot of equity and sound asset values, but still face the possibility of a bank run. Suppose a bank has $50 million in cash reserves, $100 million in mortgages, $100 million in demand deposits, and $50 million in equity. If I have money deposited in the bank and expect other people to withdraw more than $50 million in deposits, then it is in my best interest to try to withdraw my deposits first. If $50 million in deposits is withdrawn by other customers before I get to the bank, the bank's cash reserves will be depleted and I will have to wait for the bank to sell or borrow against some of its illiquid mortgages. All the other depositors have the same incentive that I do. If they expect other customers to withdraw their deposits, then they should "run to the bank" and be the first to withdraw. This is an example of self-fulfilling expectations, in that the expectation of the bank run causes the actual bank run. Despite there being nothing fundamentally wrong with the bank, they won't be able to pay out all of their depositors.

Bank runs may also occur because depositors suspect that the bank is, or soon will be, insolvent. If a bank has negative equity, then its deposits exceed its assets. This means that the bank won't be able to repay all of its depositors. Recognizing this reality, depositors run to the bank to withdraw their deposits. This is what happened to some banks during the Great Depression. Regional economic shocks and declining asset values deteriorated bank balance sheets to the point of insolvency. Depositors ran on their banks, which accelerated the process.

The distinction between bank runs driven by illiquidity versus insolvency raises a number of important questions. First, to the extent that the quality of a bank's assets is privately known only to the bank, how might the insolvency of one bank affect the financial health of other banks? For example, if an economy has four banks and depositors expect one of them to be insolvent, the response might be to run on all the banks. How should economic policy be designed to minimize these informational asymmetries? Finally, is there a way to regulate banks that protects depositors, but also induces responsible behavior by banks? The next section discusses issues regarding regulation and policy.

> **Bank runs**
> A situation in which a large number of a bank's depositors simultaneously demand to withdraw their money.

14-3c Bank Regulation and Policy

To deal with the possibility of depositors losing their savings during bank runs, the Glass–Steagall Act of 1933 established the Federal Deposit Insurance Corporation, which insures deposits up to a certain amount ($250,000 as of the time this book was written).[12] All banks eligible for **FDIC insurance** are required to pay premiums for the coverage. When a depositor puts their money, up to the limit, into an insured bank, they do not have to worry about the possibility of bank failure. Not only does FDIC insurance reduce the risks confronted by depositors, but it is also designed to reduce the number of bank failures. If each bank customer knows that their deposits are covered, then there is no reason to run on the bank.

While deposit insurance minimizes the risk faced by depositors, it, in isolation, distorts a bank's incentives. It's helpful to see why through the context of another example. The American company General Motors (GM) finances itself through a mix of debt and equity.

> **FDIC insurance**
> Insurance that banks can purchase from the Federal Deposit Insurance Corporation, which insures up to $250,000 in deposits per customer.

---

[12]The Glass–Steagall Act was repealed in 1999, but the FDIC remained.

Part 4 Banking and Financial Markets

That is, GM has bondholders, who are promised a certain return on their investment, and stockholders who receive no such promise, but get the upside if the value of the stock increases. A bondholder might pay $100 for a bond that promises to pay $103 in a year. If GM's share price doubles, bondholders still get the $3. If GM's share price falls by half, bondholders still get the $3. If GM becomes insolvent and goes into bankruptcy, its stock is worthless, so the equity holders are wiped out. Because its liabilities exceed its assets, some bondholders don't get their promised 3 percent return on investment. The lesson is this: the owners of the firm get the upside and the downside of an investment. The bondholders only get the downside. Therefore, the owners of a firm will be more accepting of risk than the firm's creditors. It is the equity holder's job to encourage risk taking and innovation; it is the creditor's job to exercise prudence.

A bank's creditors are its depositors. Because depositors get all their deposits insured, they have no incentive to exercise prudence. That is, I don't care if my bank invests in 1-month U.S. Treasury bills (which are very low risk) or in a shopping mall near an active volcano. All I care about is the safety of my deposits. And if I'm investing in a bank that is FDIC insured, then my deposits are safe. Thus, absent any countervailing regulations, deposit insurance creates moral hazard among banks. Banks would like to invest in riskier projects to maximize their expected return on equity, knowing that depositors won't care if the bank fails.

To deal with the moral hazard issue, the government imposes a number of regulations on banks. The regulations essentially come in two forms: one form regulates the composition of assets, and another regulates how the assets are financed. On the asset side of the balance sheet, banks were traditionally required to hold a certain fraction of their assets as cash reserves. That reduced liquidity risk for the bank and also ensured that a fraction of its assets was very safe. Since the Fed began paying interest on reserves in 2008, banks have optimally chosen to hold reserves in excess of what is required. In March 2020, the Fed eliminated the reserve requirement altogether.

Capital requirements
Regulations that ensure that a certain portion of a bank's risk-weighted assets are financed with capital rather than debt.

Capital requirements ensure that a certain portion of a bank's risk-weighted assets are financed with capital rather than debt. Assets that are perceived to be of lower risk (such as short-duration U.S. Treasury securities) can be financed with a lower fraction of capital compared to riskier assets (such as commercial loans). Requiring banks to maintain a certain level of capital gives them a buffer to withstand losses on their balance sheet. Additionally, large banks face additional capital requirements because of their systematic importance to the economy. Systematic importance is just a way of saying that the general macroeconomy is affected by the health of the bank. For instance, if a local bank with $250 million in assets fails, it might be painful to the owners of the bank. But if a bank of $250 *billion* in assets fails, it might disrupt other parts of the macroeconomy. The issue of systemic importance was a key element in the 2007–2008 financial crisis. This is discussed in Application 14.2.

Application 14.2

Too Big to Fail

Imagine that you lend your little brother $100 to start a lemonade stand. Your brother buys lemons, sugar, cups and even hires one of his friends to help out. Moreover, to assure you that your investment is safe, your brother gives you his rock collection as collateral. In the event he defaults, you get to keep the rock collection.

When the big weekend comes, it's raining, and your brother earns only $25 in revenue. After paying his friend, you get $15, or a −85 percent return on investment. With

your brother in default, you rush to the pawn store to sell the rock collection for a meager $30. With a total loss of $55, you go to your parents and ask for a bailout. Initially, they gently chide you on the importance of doing due diligence and that market discipline requires that they allow you to take your losses. But then you tell them that if you don't recover your full $100, you won't be able to pay your sister back for the money she lent you for ice skates. And if your sister doesn't get her money, she won't be able to

■ Continues

Chapter 14 Banking and the Macroeconomy **371**

Application 14.2 (Continued)

repay your cousin for buying concert tickets. Essentially, allowing you to fail exposes your counterparties to losses, and the disruption to the market of familial harmony would be too catastrophic to endure.

Do you think your parents would be persuaded? At the risk of drawing an imperfect analogy, this is pretty close to the arguments some large financial institutions made during the 2007–2008 financial crisis. As discussed in Chapter 11, financial institutions invested heavily in mortgage-backed securities that fell in value when home values dropped, and default rates increased. Because these financial institutions were heavily leveraged, even small losses in the MBS market left them vulnerable to insolvency. The defunct investment bank, Bear Stearns, had a leverage ratio of over 30 and was heavily invested in MBS before its collapse in March 2008.[13] Regulators, particularly at the Federal Reserve, were concerned that if Bear Stearns collapsed, there would be adverse effects on their counterparties. In light of this, the Federal Reserve Bank of New York purchased $30 billion in Bear Stearns's assets and engineered its sale to JPMorgan Chase.

Whether this constituted a "bail out" needs some clarification. Bear Stearns stockholders were ultimately paid $10 per share. While that isn't a total wipeout, the stock was trading at over $100 a year earlier. So, stockholders were significantly hurt. At the same time, Bear Stearns's creditors (that is its bondholders and financial institutions it borrowed from) did not suffer losses. That is, their counterparties were bailed out and this, at least temporarily, stopped the cascade of deleveraging and defaults that the Fed was worried about.

The Fed faced criticism from two angles at the time. First, Lehman Brothers, a financial institution in a similar position, was allowed to fail five months later. The rescue of Bear Stearns but failure of Lehman Brothers signaled that the Fed didn't have clear criteria for which institutions would be saved and which would be allowed to fail. Second, it could be argued that the Fed's purchase of assets to sweeten the deal for JPMorgan and protect Bear Stearns's counterparties encouraged moral hazard by other financial institutions. If creditors know they will be bailed out, the firm's management will make riskier investments and finance them with greater levels of debt. While the moral hazard concern was recognized by the Fed at the time, they concluded that Bear Stearns was too systematically important and that the costs of its failure would exceed the downside of encouraging moral hazard by other financial institutions in the future.

The Dodd–Frank Wall Street Reform and Consumer Protection Act of 2010 attempted to increase transparency and the orderly liquidation of financial institutions. The Federal Reserve now subjects banks to "stress tests," where they evaluate how banks would withstand hypothetical adverse shocks to their balance sheets. Banks who don't perform well on their stress tests or are classified as systematically important are subject to higher capital requirements. Despite these regulations and policies, it's not clear that the moral hazard problem has been solved. If creditors think they will be bailed out, they will take excessive risk. And neither the U.S. government nor the Fed has taken a firm and unequivocal stand against bailouts. We may have to wait until the next financial crisis to tell how serious economic regulators are about imposing market discipline.

[13]Boyd, Roddy. (2008, March 31). "The Last Days of Bear Stearns." *Fortune*. https://web.archive.org/web/20080919002944/https://money.cnn.com/2008/03/28/magazines/fortune/boyd_bear.fortune/.

Chapter Summary

- Banks turn liquid deposits into illiquid loans through a process called maturity transformation.

- By investing in many different projects, banks minimize risk faced by their depositors.

- Banks provide value by screening the credit worthiness of loan applicants and then monitoring the loans once they are made.

- A bank's assets typically consist of loans made to households and businesses, cash reserves, and securities such as U.S. government bonds.

- Banks fund their asset purchases through a mix of liabilities and equity. Liabilities for a bank consist mostly of deposits.

- The more easily that a bank can convert its assets to cash, the more liquid its balance sheet is.

- A bank's profitability depends on the difference between the return on its assets and the interest it pays to its depositors.

- The leverage ratio is the ratio of liabilities to assets. The higher a bank's leverage ratio is, the higher its return on equity. However, the higher the leverage ratio, the less a bank can withstand a drop in the value of its assets.

- Banks face liquidity risk in that depositors can suddenly demand to withdraw their deposits in excess of a bank's cash reserves. Banks manage liquidity risk by holding a sufficient

372 **Part 4** Banking and Financial Markets

fraction of their deposits in cash reserves and through short-term borrowing from the Fed or other banks.

- Banks face solvency risk in that the value of their assets could drop so far as to render them insolvent. Banks manage solvency risk by investing in assets with lower risk profiles and funding their acquisition of assets through capital rather than debt.

- Bank runs may occur even in banks that have low solvency risk if some bank customers think that other bank customers are withdrawing their deposits. Alternatively, depositors may withdraw their money if they question the value of a bank's assets.

- To reduce the risk of bank runs, banks can invest in deposit insurance, whereby $250,000 in deposits are insured. This means that if the bank fails depositors with less than $250,000 in deposits, they get their money back.

- Deposit insurance creates incentives for banks to invest in riskier assets with high levels of leverage. Therefore, the U.S. government mandates a certain level of capital requirements for banks.

Key Terms

Maturity transformation, 356
Cash reserves, 357
Limited liability, 357
Risk averse, 357
Risk neutral, 358
Adverse selection, 359
Moral hazard, 360
Balance sheet, 361
Assets, 361
Liabilities, 361
Equity, 361
Demand deposit, 361
Capital, 362

Liquidity ratio, 363
Reserve ratio, 363
Return on assets, 364
Return on equity, 364
Leverage ratio, 365
Liquidity risk, 366
Collateral, 366
Discount window, 366
Solvent, 367
Solvency risk, 367
Bank runs, 369
FDIC insurance, 369
Capital requirements, 370

Questions for Review

1. How do banks engage in maturity transformation?
2. Why is it less risky for a saver to deposit their money in a bank rather than invest in a particular investment project?
3. How do banks limit the effects of adverse selection?
4. What categories of assets do banks invest in? How do they finance these assets?
5. Explain the connection between bank profitability and its leverage ratio.
6. Compare and contrast liquidity risk with solvency risk.
7. Why might a solvent bank face a bank run?
8. How does deposit insurance promote moral hazard?

Problems

14.1 Suppose a person is looking to invest $50,000 in savings.

    a. An entrepreneur has a project that requires $50,000 in start-up capital. Suppose the entrepreneur takes out a $50,000 loan and pays it back in one year with 10 percent interest. What is the saver's return in dollars?

    b. Suppose that the entrepreneur defaults 1 percent of the time and loses the entire $50,000. What is the saver's expected return in dollars?

    c. Suppose that the entrepreneur defaults 1 percent of the time but loses only $25,000. What is the saver's expected return in dollars?

    d. Suppose a bank offers the saver a 5 percent return with certainty. Would a risk neutral saver prefer the 5 percent return with certainty, or the uncertain return in part b?

Can you say which investment a risk averse person would prefer?

14.2 Suppose a person is looking to invest $100 in savings. The person is willing to invest in any project that pays a positive expected return.

    a. Wei, an entrepreneur, can take the $100 and in one year earn $110 with certainty, or a $10 return. What range of interest rates would be acceptable to Wei and the saver?

    b. A different entrepreneur, Ali, can invest in a risky project. 75 percent of the time, the project earns $130, or a $30 return. The other 25 percent of the time, the project earns $0, or a $-100 return. Assuming Ali has limited liability, what is the maximum interest rate at which they would be willing to borrow?

Chapter 14 Banking and the Macroeconomy · **373**

c. Would the saver be willing to lend to Ali at the interest rate you calculated in part b? Show your work.

d. Suppose the saver can't distinguish between Wei and Ali. If there is a 50 percent chance of meeting Wei and a 50 percent chance of meeting Ali, is there an interest rate where the saver finds it optimal to save and either Wei or Ali (or both) finds it optimal to borrow?

e. How can a bank remedy the situation in part d?

14.3 Suppose a person purchases a $300,000 home with a $60,000 down payment and $240,000 in mortgage.

a. If the house value increases by 10 percent and the person sells the house, what is their return on investment?

b. If the house decreases by 10 percent and the person sells the house, can they pay off the mortgage without some other source of savings?

c. Suppose instead the person purchases the home with a $20,000 down payment and a $280,000 mortgage. If the home increases by 10 percent and the person sells the house, what is their return on investment?

d. Continue to assume that the person puts $20,000 down. If the house decreases by 10 percent and the person sells the house, can they pay off the mortgage without some other source of savings?

e. Comparing your results in a and c, would a borrower prefer to put a higher or lower down payment on a home?

f. As you learned in the chapter, banks screen loan applicants for their credit worthiness. Considering your results in parts b and d, should banks direct more of their screening effort to borrowers with low down payments or borrowers with high down payments?

14.4 Consider the following bank balance sheet:

Assets	Liabilities
Mortgages = $200 million	Deposits = $200 million
Securities = $50 million	**Equity** = $100 million
Cash Reserves = $50 million	

a. Calculate the reserve ratio, liquidity ratio, and leverage ratio.

b. Assuming the bank earns 5 percent on its mortgages, 3 percent on its securities, 1 percent on its cash reserves, and pays 3 percent on its deposits, calculate its return on assets and return on equity.

14.5 Consider two banks with balance sheets given respectively by:

Bank A		
Assets		**Liabilities**
Mortgages = $150 million		Deposits = $120 million
Cash Reserves = $0		**Equity** = $30 million

Bank B		
Assets		**Liabilities**
Mortgages = $70 million		Deposits = $110 million
Cash Reserves = $30 million		**Equity** = −$10 million

a. Which bank faces a liquidity problem, and which bank faces a solvency problem?

b. Would the Fed want to lend to Bank A or Bank B? Explain.

✅ Knowledge Check 14-1 Answer

If there are no failures, then the bank earns $600 in interest income minus the $200 it pays depositors, for a total of $400. If there is one failure, bank profit is given by

$$(0.99)\$600 - (0.01)\$10,000 - (0.02)\$10,000 = \$294.$$

If there are two failures, bank profit is given by

$$(0.98)\$600 - (0.02)\$10,000 - (0.02)\$10,000 = \$188.$$

If there are three failures, bank profit is given by

$$(0.97)\$600 - (0.03)\$10,000 - (0.02)\$10,000 = \$82.$$

If there are four failures, bank profit is given by

$$(0.96)\$600 - (0.04)\$10,000 - (0.02)\$10,000 = -\$24.$$

The probability the bank makes a profit is

$$36.6\% + 37\% + 18.5\% + 6.1\% = 98.2\%.$$

Number of failures	Probability	Return on deposits	Bank profit (per loan)
0	36.6%	2%	$400
1	37.0%	2%	$294
2	18.5%	2%	$188
3	6.1%	2%	$82
4	1.5%	2%	−$24

Knowledge Check 14-2 Answer

If reckless drivers can hide the fact that they are reckless, then they will be more likely to take out insurance. To screen applicants, insurers might ask for accident reports, traffic violations, and a history of claims filed with previous insurers.

Knowledge Check 14-3 Answer

The bank might be worried that travelers renting the Airbnb will not take as good of care of the house as the borrower would if they were living there. Moreover, if the market for vacation rentals is weak, the borrower might not be able to repay their loan. The bank may request that the borrower send them periodic income statements on the property and also require that the borrower purchase more insurance on the property to cover potential damage from the tenants.

Knowledge Check 14-4 Answer

A decline in the value of mortgages by $10 million reduces the value of assets by $10 million. Because deposits haven't changed, equity decreases by $10 million.

Assets	Liabilities
Mortgages = $100 million − $10 million	Deposits = $110 million
U.S. Treasuries = $30 million	**Equity** = $40 million − $10 million
Cash Reserves = $20 million	

Knowledge Check 14-5 Answer

The three ratios, ROA, and ROE are given by

$$\text{Reserve ratio} = \frac{\$40 \text{ million}}{\$100 \text{ million}} = 0.4,$$

$$\text{Liquidity ratio} = \frac{\$40 \text{ million}}{\$170 \text{ million}} = 0.24,$$

$$\text{Leverage ratio} = \frac{\$100 \text{ million}}{\$70 \text{ million}} = 1.43,$$

$$\text{ROA} = \frac{\$25 \text{ million}}{\$170 \text{ million}} = 0.147,$$

$$\text{ROE} = \frac{\$25 \text{ million}}{\$70 \text{ million}} = 0.356.$$

Chapter 15 Bonds, Stocks, and Monetary Policy

Learning Objectives

15.1 Calculate the prices, rates of return, and yields to maturity of bonds with different durations.

15.2 Explain the term structure and risk structure of interest rates.

15.3 Compare traditional monetary policy tools for affecting the yield curve versus current policy tools.

15.4 Calculate the price of stocks.

15.5 Evaluate the pros and cons of monetary policy attempting to deflate asset price bubbles.

When you tell a non-economist what your college major is, they will likely have two questions: What is going to happen with interest rates, and where is the stock market headed? The usual response from an economist is that if they knew what direction interest rates were going or which way the stock market were headed, they'd be living on a private island, not studying economics. Indeed, one of the key lessons in financial economics is that the expectations over future movements in interest rates and prices are already included in the prices of bonds and stocks today. If everyone expects the price of a certain stock to be higher tomorrow, they will bid up the price today.

Even though economics doesn't provide a fool-proof "get rich quick scheme," we can still make some predictions about the way bond and stock prices are determined. More relevant to macroeconomics, we can make predictions about how the actions of monetary policymakers affect interest rates and stock prices. This chapter shows how to calculate prices of bonds and stocks and how interest rates of various bonds are related. Remember that monetary policy only sets the overnight interest rate on reserves deposited at the central bank. But because interest rates are related to each other, the overnight interest rate on reserves affects all the other interest rates in the economy.

Monetary policy also affects equity prices. It's not uncommon for the stock market to jump after the Fed decides to change the short-run nominal interest rate. Every jump in the stock market causes a significant transfer of wealth, so monetary policymakers may be interested in understanding the connection between stock prices and interest rate changes. Monetary policymakers also monitor the stock market for signs of a bubble and adjust the interest rate to manage the bubble.

15-1 Bond Prices and Interest Rates

There is no single interest rate. We have referenced data from the Saint Louis FRED (which stands for Federal Reserve Economic Data) throughout this book. On the FRED's website alone there are over 440 interest rates, ranging from everything from reserves to deposits by banks at the Fed, to mortgages, automobiles, treasury securities, and corporate bonds.

376 **Part 4** Banking and Financial Markets

In all these transactions, individuals and institutions are borrowing and lending. For instance, with mortgages, the home buyer is the borrower and the bank is the lender. For corporate bonds, the corporation is the borrower and the bondholder is the lender. Before we discuss the connection between all these interest rates, we need to discuss how bond prices are determined.

15-1a Bonds: Definitions, Types, and Pricing

Bonds come in several different varieties and can be issued by governments or businesses. Despite the varieties, they share some common terms. Bonds are all debt instruments. The issuer of the bond promises to pay the holder of the bond a certain amount of money over a certain time horizon. The **maturity** of a bond is the length of time it takes for the issuer to pay the buyer of the bond. The **face value** of the bond is what the issuer pays the bondholder at maturity. This is also called the *principal*. So, if you purchase a $100 30-day Treasury bill, the government will pay you $100 in 30 days. Bonds may also pay **coupons**, which are regular payments from the bond issuer to the bondholder. For instance, if you buy a 10-year Treasury security, the U.S. government will pay you a coupon every six months until maturity.

A **discount bond** offers no coupon payments (and is what we focus on for the duration of this chapter).[1] Instead, the issuer promises to pay the buyer the face value at some predetermined date. A Treasury bill is an example of a discount bond. Treasury bills are issued by the U.S. government with maturities ranging from three weeks to one year. Let's say you buy a 1-year $100 U.S. Treasury bill. You pay a certain amount upfront, and the U.S. government promises to pay you $100 in one year. What is the price of the bond?

To answer this, we need to return to the concept of present discounted value first discussed in Chapter 6. In general, $100 one year from now is worth less than $100 today. The reason is that the $100 today can be invested and earn interest. If the annual nominal interest rate is 3 percent, then the present value of $100 one year from now is $100/(1 + 0.03) = $97.09. By analogy, the price, P, of a 1-year $100 U.S. Treasury bill is

$$P = \frac{FV}{1 + i}, \tag{1}$$

where FV is the face value and i is the nominal interest rate. In other words, the price of a discount bond is the present discounted value of the principal. Note that the price of the bond and the interest rate move in opposite directions. A higher interest rate reduces the price of the bond. Intuitively, if interest rates rise, then a bondholder can earn a higher return by investing elsewhere. The only way for the bond to remain attractive is for the price to drop sufficiently.

The interest rate, i, is sometimes referred to as the **yield to maturity** (YTM). It is the (annual) interest that a bondholder earns by holding the bond to maturity. Rewriting Equation (1) shows this clearly:

$$i = \frac{FV}{P} - 1. \tag{1'}$$

The YTM is closely related to the **rate of return** an investor earns from selling a bond. Mathematically, the rate of return, denoted by R, is the percent return that an investor earns over a specified time period. In the case of a 1-year discount bond, if the investor holds the bond the entire year, then the YTM and rate of return are identical. If, however, the investor sells the bond before maturity, this may not be true. We return to this later in the section.

It is often more convenient to compare bonds in terms of their YTM. The reason is that bonds differ in their face values, time to maturities, and prices. The YTM puts bonds on an even playing field.

Maturity
The length of time it takes an issuer of the bond to repay the holder of the bond.

Face value
The principal payment that a bond issuer pays the bondholder at maturity.

Coupon
Regular payment from the bond issuer to the bondholder.

Discount bond
A bond that offers no coupon payments. The price of a discount bond is the present discounted value of the principal.

Yield to maturity
The (annual) interest that a bondholder earns by holding the bond to maturity.

Rate of return
The percent return that an investor earns over a specified time period.

---

[1]Textbooks on money, banking, and finance provide a more thorough treatment of coupon bonds.

Here is an example. Suppose there is a discount bond with a yield to maturity of five years and a face value of $200, selling at a price of $170. To price the face value payable in five years, you must discount by a factor of 5. To see this, investing $1 today allows you to earn $1(1 + i)$ in one year. Over the course of two years, the $1 invested today earns $1(1 + i)(1 + i)$. Generalizing this idea, $1 invested today is worth $1(1 + i)^N$, N years in the future. The bond-pricing equation is

$$P = \frac{FV}{(1 + i)^5}$$

$$\Leftrightarrow \$170 = \frac{\$200}{(1 + i)^5}$$

$$\Leftrightarrow (1 + i)^5 = \frac{\$200}{\$170}$$

$$\Leftrightarrow i = \sqrt[5]{\frac{\$200}{\$170}} - 1 = 0.033.$$

Thus, the yield to maturity of this bond is about 3.3 percent. Recall that the $100 bond selling for $97.09 with a time to maturity of one year had a YTM of 3 percent. If you plan to hold each bond to maturity, then the one with a 3.3 percent YTM offers a better deal. In general, the YTM for an N-year discount bond must satisfy the equation

$$i = \sqrt[N]{\frac{FV}{P}} - 1. \tag{2}$$

There is an important caveat in the last paragraph. The bond paying a YTM of 3.3 percent is a better deal than the one paying 3 percent, provided you hold both bonds to maturity. But what if you plan to sell the five-year bond prior to the maturity date? Suppose you sell the bond after one year for $175.64. Because you paid $170 for the bond, the rate of return, R, is

$$R = \frac{\$175.64 - \$170}{\$170} = 0.033.$$

Thus, the rate of return is the same as the yield to maturity. Why might this be the case? When you sell a bond with a time to maturity of five years in one year, it's equivalent to selling a bond with a time to maturity of four years. A bond with a time to maturity of four years must satisfy the bond-pricing equation

$$P = \frac{\$200}{(1 + i)^4}.$$

If the YTM on the four-year bond is also 3.3 percent, then

$$P = \frac{\$200}{(1 + 0.033)^4} = \$175.64.$$

Thus, provided that the interest rate doesn't change, the rate of return to selling the bond early equals the YTM. Suppose that the interest rate rises to 6 percent and you sell the bond in one year. Then the price is

$$P = \frac{\$200}{(1 + 0.06)^4} = \$158.42.$$

The rate of return is

$$R = \frac{\$158.42 - \$170}{\$170} = -0.068,$$

or -6.8 percent. Suppose instead that over the course of the year, the interest rate falls from 3.3 to 1 percent. The price of the bond is now

$$P = \frac{\$200}{(1 + 0.01)^4} = \$192.20.$$

The rate of return is

$$R = \frac{\$192.20 - \$170}{\$170} = 0.131,$$

or 13.1 percent. There are several insights from this example. First, leaving the interest rate constant, the price of a bond increases as the time to maturity decreases. Figure 15.1 shows this in the case of the bond in the last example with a face value of $200 and a YTM of 3.3 percent. The reason is that as time to maturity shrinks, the present discounted value of the bond's principal increases. Again, remember that $1 today is worth more than $1 in the future. And $1 one year from now is worth more than $1 five years from now.

Figure 15.1 The relationship between the price of a bond and its time to maturity, assuming a face value equal to $200 and a yield to maturity of 3.3 percent.

Second, holding the bond to maturity equates the rate of return with the YTM. This follows from the definition of YTM. Third, the return from selling a bond early equals the yield to maturity, provided the interest rate doesn't change. If the interest rate rises, bond prices go down, so the bondholder sells at a loss. If the interest rate decreases, bond prices go up, so the bondholder gains. Thus, there is a negative relationship between interest rates and the rate of return. This is another example of the inverse relationship between interest rates and bond prices that we learned in the case of the one-period discount bond. In general, increases in the interest rate are bad for bondholders, while decreases in the interest rate are good for bondholders. Table 15.1 summarizes the relationship between bond prices, YTM, and returns.

Table 15.1 The Relationship Between Bond Prices, YTM, and Returns

	Percentage Change in Price (%ΔP)	Return
Interest rates stay constant	%ΔP = YTM	R = YTM
Interest rates increase	%ΔP < YTM	R < YTM
Interest rates decrease	%ΔP > YTM	R > YTM

Having discussed the connection between bond prices and interest rates, we can now think about how interest rates on different bonds are related to one another. Remember that although the Fed only controls the interest rate on bank reserves, its ultimate goal is to affect interest rates that influence the decisions of firms and households.

Knowledge Check 15-1

Suppose you purchase a discount bond with a time to maturity of 10 years and a face value of $1,000 for $875. Calculate the YTM. Instead of holding the bond to maturity, suppose you sell it in one year for $900. Calculate the rate of return.

Answers are at the end of the chapter.

15-1b The Term Structure

Recall from Chapter 11 that the term structure of interest rates is the yield to maturity of bonds of different durations. Figure 15.2 shows the term structure on U.S. Treasury securities with the times to maturity between 1 year and 30 years during 1983, 1993, 2003, 2013, and 2022. In four out of the five years, the yield curve is upward sloping, meaning that bonds with longer times to maturity pay an interest rate premium.

The premium associated with longer duration bonds is called the **term premium**, which is a general feature of corporate as well as government debt. Even in household finances, it is most often the case that 30-year mortgages have higher interest rates than 15-year and 10-year mortgages.

Can the term premium be rationalized in the asset pricing framework from the previous section? Consider an individual investor with $1,000 and a time horizon of five years considering two investment options. The first option is to buy a 5-year discount bond, offering a YTM of $i_{t,5}$ where the t is a time subscript, meaning it's from the perspective of today, and the 5 subscript denotes a 5-year bond. At the end of five years, the investor earns

$$\$1{,}000(1 + i_{t,5})^5.$$

The second option is to buy a bond with a time to maturity of one year and then reinvest the interest and principal into another 1-year bond in year $t + 1$. At the end of year $t + 1$, the principal and interest could be invested in yet another 1-year bond. The YTM of the 1-year bond in period t is $i_{t,1}$. From the perspective of period t, the investor doesn't know what the

Term premium
The higher yield to maturity associated with longer duration bonds compared to shorter duration bonds.

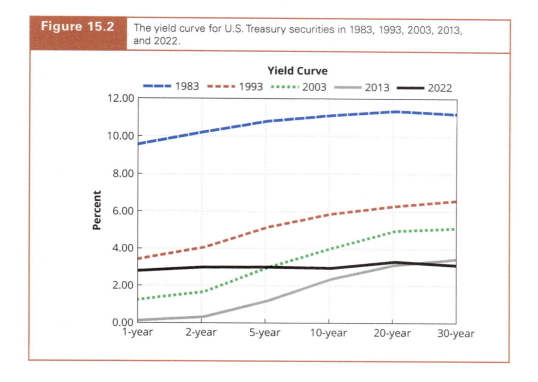

Figure 15.2 The yield curve for U.S. Treasury securities in 1983, 1993, 2003, 2013, and 2022.

Part 4 Banking and Financial Markets

YTM on a 1-year bond in $t + 1$ will be but can make a forecast of it. The expectation of the 1-year bond rate in $t + 1$ from the perspective of period t is $i^e_{t+1,1}$. Similarly, the expectation of the 1-year bond rate in $t + 2$ from the perspective of period t is $i^e_{t+2,1}$. At the end of five years, the investor earns

$$\$1,000(1 + i_{t,1})(1 + i^e_{t+1,1})(1 + i^e_{t+2,1})(1 + i^e_{t+3,1})(1 + i^e_{t+4,1}).$$

If the 5-year bond offered a higher return on investment, you would expect investors to put their money into 5-year bonds, driving the price of the bonds up and interest rates down. Alternatively, if 1-year bonds offered a higher return on investment, you would expect investors to put their money in 1-year bonds, driving those interest rates down. Investors would continue this selective investment pattern as long as the expected returns differed from each other. This is an example of **financial arbitrage**, or the process through which risk-adjusted returns are equalized through the buying and selling patterns of profit-maximizing investors.

Using the principle of financial arbitrage, we would expect that the return from investing in the 5-year bond should equal the return of investing in the sequence of 1-year bonds. From the previous two equations, that means

$$(1 + i_{t,5})^5 = (1 + i_{t,1})(1 + i^e_{t+1,1})(1 + i^e_{t+2,1})(1 + i^e_{t+3,1})(1 + i^e_{t+4,1}).$$

Provided the nominal interest rate is less than 10 percent, the following approximation holds:[2]

$$i_{t,5} = \frac{1}{5}(i_{t,1} + i^e_{t+1,1} + i^e_{t+2,1} + i^e_{t+3,1} + i^e_{t+4,1}).$$

That is, the YTM on the bond with the duration of five years is the average of the expected one-year interest rates. If the YTM on the bond with a time to maturity of five years exceeds the expected YTMs of a sequence of five 1-year bonds, investors would pour money into 5-year bonds, driving $i_{t,5}$ down. Financial arbitrage ensures that the 5-year rate is equal to the average of the expected 1-year rates over the next five years. The **expectations hypothesis** predicts that the interest rate on a bond with a time to maturity of N years is the average expected interest rate on 1-year bonds over the next N years. Mathematically, the expectations hypothesis is given by

$$i_{t,N} = \frac{1}{N}\sum_{i=0}^{N-1} i^e_{t+i,1}. \tag{3}$$

The expectations hypothesis can be used to predict future short-term interest rates. For instance, suppose that the current interest rate is 4 percent on a 1-year bond and 6 percent on a 5-year bond. For Equation (3) to hold, the average 1-year rate over the next four years must exceed 6 percent. That means that short-term rates are expected to rise in the future.

Although the expectations hypothesis is a good starting point for explaining the connection between interest rates on debt of different maturities, it is an insufficient explanation for the term structure. Figure 15.2 showed that the yield curve is usually upward sloping, meaning that interest rates tend to rise with time to maturity. The expectations hypothesis predicts that this is possible only if short-term interest rates are expected to continuously rise. Figure 15.3 shows that this is definitively not the case. There are periods when the 3-month Treasury bill has increased, but it has not been sustained. Instead, short-term interest rates have temporary movements up and down. Thus, the expectations hypothesis, by itself, can't explain the upward sloping yield curve.

Financial arbitrage
The process through which risk-adjusted returns are equalized through the buying and selling patterns of profit-maximizing investors.

Expectations hypothesis
A theory that predicts that the interest rate on a bond with more than one year to maturity is the average expected interest rate on 1-year bonds over the same time horizon.

---

[2]Taking natural logs of both sides gives:

$$5\ln(1 + i_{t,5}) = \sum_{i=0}^{4} \ln(1 + i^e_{1,t+i}).$$

Provided $i < 0.1$, $\ln(1 + i) \approx i$, it follows that

$$5i_{t,5} = i_{1,t} + i^e_{1,t+1} + i^e_{1,t+2} + i^e_{1,t+3} + i^e_{1,t+4}.$$

Chapter 15 Bonds, Stocks, and Monetary Policy

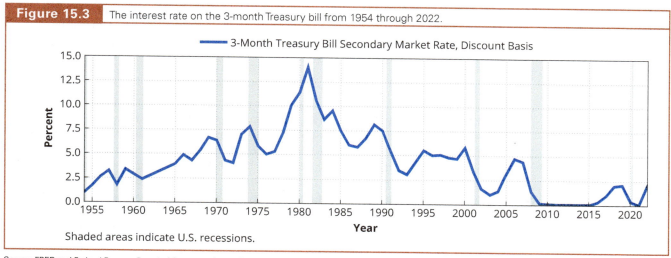

Figure 15.3 The interest rate on the 3-month Treasury bill from 1954 through 2022.

Shaded areas indicate U.S. recessions.

Source: FRED and Federal Reserve Board of Governors https://fred.stlouisfed.org/graph/?g=12BWx.

What might explain the term premium then? The expectations hypothesis assumes that investors only care about expected returns. Financial arbitrage drives the interest rate on longer-maturity debt to equal the average of expected short-term rates. But, in real life, investors not only care about expected returns of an investment, but also its riskiness. Imagine that you can invest in one of two projects. The first one returns 10 percent in one year with certainty and the second one returns -10 percent half the time and 30 percent the other half of the time. The expected value of the second project is 10 percent, as $0.5 \times (-10) + 0.5(30) = 10$. Despite both projects having the same expected return, chances are you prefer the first. And you wouldn't be alone. Faced with two investments with equal expected returns but different levels of riskiness, investors tend to prefer the less risky option. This is an application of risk aversion, which you saw in the last chapter.

The prices of longer duration bonds are more susceptible to interest rate changes than bonds with a shorter duration. If an investor is thinking about selling a bond before it matures, then holding a longer duration bond is riskier. Here is an example. Suppose an investor purchases two bonds, each with a YTM of 4 percent and a face value of $1,000. One has a time to maturity of 2 years and the other has a time to maturity of 30 years. The prices of the 2-year and 30-year bonds are respectively given by

$$P_2 = \frac{\$1,000}{1.04^2} = \$924.56,$$

$$P_{30} = \frac{\$1,000}{1.04^{30}} = \$308.32.$$

If the economy's inflation rate goes up by one percentage point, then (according to the Fisher equation) all nominal interest rates go up by one percentage point. Say that the investor decides to sell each bond at the end of the first year. At the point of sale, the investor holds a bond with a time to maturity of 1 year and another bond with a time to maturity of 29 years. Their prices are respectively given by

$$P_1 = \frac{\$1,000}{1.05} = \$952.38,$$

$$P_{29} = \frac{\$1,000}{1.05^{29}} = \$242.95.$$

The return on the shorter duration bond is

$$R = \frac{\$952.56 - \$924.56}{\$942.56} = 0.030.$$

382 **Part 4** Banking and Financial Markets

In other words, the increase in the nominal interest rate lowers the return relative to the YTM (3 percent versus 4 percent), but the investor still earns a positive return. Alternatively, the return on the longer duration bond is

$$R = \frac{\$242.95 - \$308.42}{\$308.42} = -0.212,$$

or a return of -21.2 percent. Because interest rate changes are compounded over time, the prices of longer duration bonds are more sensitive to interest rate changes. This means that any macroeconomic shock that affects the economy's interest rates will change the prices of longer duration bonds more than shorter duration bonds. Recognizing this, investors demand a **risk premium** for holding the longer duration bond. A risk premium is the difference in returns between a riskier investment and a safer investment.

Risk premium

The difference in returns between a riskier investment and a safer investment.

Under the assumption that investors are risk averse and must therefore receive a risk premium for holding bonds with longer times to maturity, we can modify the expectations hypothesis to include the risk premium. Suppose that investors demand an additional rp in yield to hold a 5-year bond versus a sequence of five 1-year bonds. Then the yield on the 5-year bond must satisfy the equation

$$i_{t,5} = rp + \frac{1}{5}(i_t + i_{t+1}^e + i_{t+2}^e + i_{t+3}^e + i_{t+4}^e).$$

Because the level of riskiness rises with time to maturity, the risk premium will be larger for bonds with longer times to maturity. This is why the yield curve is upward sloping most of the time.

The "most of the time" qualifier is important. If future short-term interest rates are expected to decline significantly, then the yield curve could be flat or even downward sloping. Figure 15.2 showed that the yield curve was basically flat in 2022, and there have been times in recent history where the yield curve was inverted. Economic forecasters and policymakers pay special attention to the slope of the yield curve because it contains expectations of where the economy is headed. Application 15.1 discusses this in more detail.

✓ Knowledge Check 15-2

Suppose the expected sequence of 1-year bond prices over the next six years is given by the following table. If the risk premium for holding a bond with a time to maturity of three years is 0.5 percent and the risk premium for holding a bond with a time to maturity of six years is 1 percent, calculate the yield of a 3-year bond and a 6-year bond. Is the yield curve upward sloping?

Year	Interest Rate (Percent)
t	3
$t + 1$	3
$t + 2$	4
$t + 3$	4.5
$t + 4$	5
$t + 5$	5

Answers are at the end of the chapter.

Application 15.1

Does an Inverted Yield Curve Predict Recessions?

As discussed in the previous section, longer duration bonds tend to pay higher interest rates than shorter duration bonds, which gives rise to an upward sloping yield curve. At least this is the case most of the time. But as Figure 15.4 shows, there are exceptions. Figure 15.4 shows the difference between the interest rate on 5-year and 1-year U.S. Treasury securities. As theory would predict, the 5-year rate generally exceeds the 1-year rate. However, there are times, such as the recent period of 2022–2023, when the 1-year rate is higher. Since the term structure captures expectations over the future path of interest rates, what can we learn about times when the yield curve is inverted?

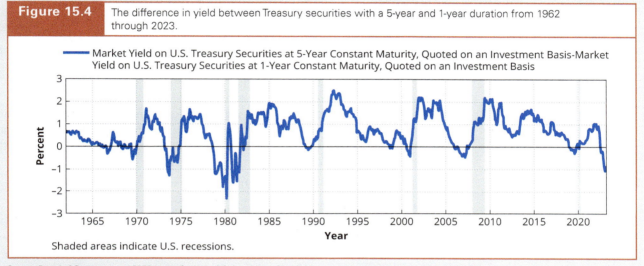

Figure 15.4 The difference in yield between Treasury securities with a 5-year and 1-year duration from 1962 through 2023.

Shaded areas indicate U.S. recessions.

Source: Board of Governors and FRED https://fred.stlouisfed.org/graph/?g=12L1N.

The gray bars in Figure 15.4 denote recessions. Analyzing the starting dates of the last three recessions in 2020, 2007, and 2001, we see that the slope of the yield curve becomes negative within a year of the recession. This pattern has resulted in economic forecasters using the inverted yield curve as a warning sign of a recession. And this pattern isn't arbitrary. That is, an inverted yield curve can be explained by economic theory. You may recall from Chapters 11 and 12 that the Fed lowers interest rates when the economy goes into a recession.[3] If investors anticipate a recession and expect the Fed to lower the short-run nominal interest rate in response to the recession, then the future short-term rate would be lower than the current short-term rate. If future interest rates are expected to fall sufficiently far for a sufficiently long time, then the yield curve would invert. Thus, it seems like the inverted yield curve predicts a recession both empirically and theoretically.

Looking outside the window of 2000–2020, however, the answer isn't as clear-cut. One issue is that even if all recessions are preceded by an inverted yield curve, it doesn't follow that all yield curve inversions are followed by a recession. The late 1970s are a case in point. The slope of the yield curve went negative in 1978 and stayed negative through half of the recession in 1980. More recently, the yield curve has been inverted since the summer of 2022 and there hasn't been a recession. What might explain these events?

The late 1970s and the 2022–2023 period were characterized by high inflation rates. Recall that the Fisher equation says that the nominal interest rate in any given year is the sum of the real interest rate and the expected annual inflation rate. If investors expect inflation to be transitory (as it was in the late 1970s and as it may be in the more recent period), then short-term interest rates could exceed long-term interest rates. For example, if investors expect the inflation rate to be 10 percent next year but 2 percent thereafter, and the real interest rate on bonds maturing in one and two years is 2 percent, then the one-year rate in the first year would be 12% = 10% + 2% and expected to be 4% = 2% + 2% in the second year. The expectations hypothesis predicts that the two-year rate (ignoring the risk premium) should be ½(12% + 4%) = 8%. Thus, if investors predict that inflation will be lower in the future than in the present, the yield curve could be inverted.

Although the yield curve isn't a perfect predictor of recessions, it may be a useful one when combined with other economic metrics. Policymakers at the Fed use different measures of the yield curve as well as other financial market and labor market data in assessing the future path of the economy.

[3]Technically, this is only true after an adverse shock to the IS curve, or a recession coming from the demand side. If potential output fell, the Fed would raise interest rates, which would close the output gap and induce a recession.

15-1c The Risk Structure of Interest Rates

We assumed in the previous two sections that bond issuers always pay back the face value. But, in reality, there are many historical examples of companies and countries defaulting on their debt. Issuers of riskier bonds need to pay investors a higher rate of interest to compensate them for bearing the risk. Figure 15.5, for instance, shows that Moody's Aaa-rated bonds have lower yields than Baa-rated bonds. Since Aaa-rated bonds are safer, this pattern makes sense. Recall from Chapter 11 that the risk structure of interest rates is the pattern of interest rates on liabilities with different risks. This section shows how different probabilities of default risk across bonds with identical maturities implies a risk structure of interest rates.

Begin by considering a discount bond with a time to maturity of one year and a face value of $100. The pricing equation for this bond must satisfy

$$P = \frac{\$100}{1+i}.$$

If the yield to maturity on one-year bonds happens to be 3 percent, then the price of the bond is $P = \frac{\$100}{1.03} = \$97.09$. Paying the price of $97.09 entitles the bondholder to $100 one year from now: a 3 percent return on investment.

Now suppose that there is a 5 percent chance the company goes into bankruptcy and defaults on their bond payment. In the case of default, assume that the company pays nothing to the bondholder. Because investors recover the face value only 95 percent of the time, the pricing equation becomes

$$P = 0.95 \frac{\$100}{1+i} + 0.05 \frac{\$0}{1+i}.$$

There are two observations about the price of the bond with default risk. First, the risky bond will trade at a lower price relative to the riskless bond. Intuitively, the higher the probability is that a company will default, the less investors are willing to pay for their bonds. Second, the face values in the risky and riskless bond are discounted by the same interest rate, i. In both cases, we are valuing $100 one year from now in the present. The fact that a company may default on their debt doesn't change how we discount the face value.

Continuing to assume $i = 3\%$, the price of the risky bond is

$$P = 0.95 \frac{\$100}{1+0.03} + 0.05 \frac{\$0}{1+0.03} = \$92.23,$$

which confirms that the price of the risky bond trades at a discount relative to the riskless bond. Importantly, in the case of the riskless bond, the discount rate equals the yield to maturity. That is, the interest the investor earns from purchasing the bond equals the rate at

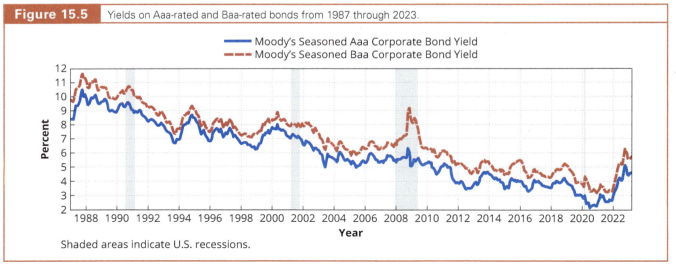

Figure 15.5 Yields on Aaa-rated and Baa-rated bonds from 1987 through 2023.

Shaded areas indicate U.S. recessions.

Source: Moody's and FRED https://fred.stlouisfed.org/graph/?g=12SrB.

which future cashflows are discounted. Since the price of the risky bond is lower, the YTM will necessarily be higher. In particular, the YTM of the risky bond is

$$i = \frac{FV}{P} - 1 = \frac{\$100}{\$91.35} - 1 = 0.084.$$

That is, the YTM for the risky bond is 8.4 percent. To calculate the bondholder's expected return, recognize that 95 percent of the time, the bondholder earns 8.4 percent. The other 5 percent of the time, the bondholder loses their entire investment, for a return of -100 percent. Therefore, the expected return is

$$0.95(0.084) + 0.05(-1) = 0.03,$$

which is identical to certain return with the riskless asset. While the YTM of the risky bond is higher than the safe bond, their expected returns are the same. This is yet another example of financial arbitrage. If the expected return of investing in the risky bond exceeds the certain return of the safe bond, investors will put more money into risky bonds, driving their prices up and yields down. Because investors in the real world may be risk averse, bonds with uncertain payouts offer investors higher expected returns as compensation for taking the additional risk. Similar to the term structure model of the last section, we could add a risk premium onto the risky bonds to produce a higher rate of expected return. Section 15.2 covers how stock prices are formed. Because stocks—like bonds with a possibility of default—are risky investments, we incorporate a risk premium from the start.

> ### ✓ Knowledge Check 15-3
>
> Suppose a bond with a face value of $500 and time to maturity of one year has a 10 percent default risk. In the event of default, the bond issuer pays the bondholder $100. Assume that the yield to maturity on a one-year risk-free bond is 5 percent. Calculate the price and the yield to maturity of the risky bond.
>
> ———————————————————————————— Answers are at the end of the chapter.

15-1d Monetary Policy and the Term and Risk Structure of Interest Rates

As discussed in Chapter 11, the traditional way monetary policy affects interest rates on debt with longer durations and different risk profiles is by adjusting the short-run interest rate. In particular, the Fed targets the federal funds rate, which is the interest rate that banks charge each other for overnight borrowing. When the Fed lowers the short-term interest rate, the expectations hypothesis predicts that longer-term interest rates also move down.

The Fed also influences the term structure through forward guidance, which was discussed in Chapter 11. Recall that with forward guidance, the Fed signals its commitment to future interest rate changes. Provided these signals are credible, investors update their expectations over future short-term interest rates. The change in expected future short-term interest rates changes the interest rate on longer maturity debt today.

In the early 2010s, the Fed began to purchase greater quantities of longer-maturity debt. Figure 15.6 shows the Fed's holdings of U.S. Treasury securities maturing in over 10 years. The series essentially stayed flat from 2002 through 2010 and then steadily rose. The Fed was motivated by the tepid recovery from the Great Recession, which officially ended in 2009. The unemployment rate was higher than 8 percent at the beginning of 2012, compared to 4.5 percent before the start of the recession. With short-run interest rates already constrained by the zero-lower bound, the Fed attempted to influence the yield curve directly by purchasing debt with longer maturities. By 2015, the Fed's purchase of longer duration bonds leveled off as short-term interest rates began to rise. However, the purchase of these bonds accelerated once again during the Covid-19 recession in 2020.

Figure 15.6
Holdings by the Federal Reserve from 2002 through 2023 of U.S. Treasury securities maturing in over 10 years.

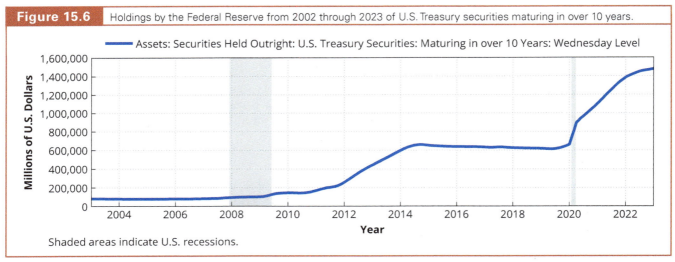

Shaded areas indicate U.S. recessions.

Source: Board of Governors and FRED, https://fred.stlouisfed.org/graph/?g=12L04.

The Fed's actions also affect the risk-structure of interest rates. Because banks face little risk in borrowing and lending to each other overnight, the federal funds rate is a good measure of the risk-free interest rate. The analysis in Section 15.1c implies that interest rates on riskier debt fall when the risk-free interest rate falls. This, traditionally, was how the Fed affected the interest rate on everything from car loans to mortgages. Beginning in 2009, the Fed began to take a more direct approach to targeting interest rates on riskier debt by purchasing mortgage-backed securities. As discussed in Chapter 11, mortgage-backed securities are investment products consisting of a bundle of mortgages. The added demand for these securities coming from the Fed drove their prices up and interest rates down. Figure 15.7 shows that as of 2023, the Fed owns more than $2 trillion of these assets.

Monetary policy, both through its traditional tool of lowering the short-term interest rate, and its more recent practices of forward guidance and purchasing longer duration and riskier securities, affects interest rates on debt of various maturities and risk profiles. Changes in the interest rate not only affect the bond market, but also the stock market. The next section shows this connection in more detail.

Figure 15.7
Mortgaged-backed securities maturing in over 10 years held by the Fed from 2002 through 2023.

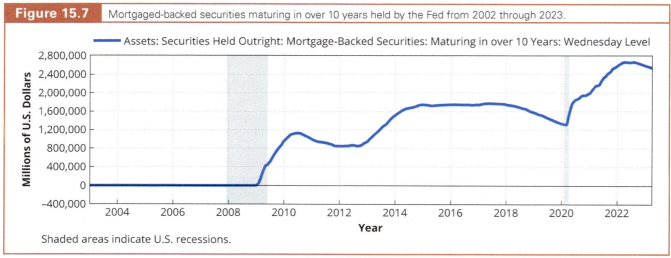

Shaded areas indicate U.S. recessions.

Source: FRED and Board of Governors https://fred.stlouisfed.org/graph/?g=13nQ9.

15-2 The Stock Market and Monetary Policy

Although both bonds and stocks may appear in any one person's investment portfolio, they are fundamentally different financial instruments. Bonds are debt instruments. They require that the bond issuer pay the bondholder certain amounts at certain times. Stocks, meanwhile, are ownership claims in a firm. So, if a company is valued at $1 billion and has 10 million shares, then the price of each share is $1 billion/10 million = $100.

Owners of the firm are **residual claimants** in that they get paid only after all expenses and debt payments are made. That means that bondholders are paid before stockholders. Investing in stocks is risky because owners are not entitled to anything. At the same time, investing in stocks usually carries more upside, since if a company performs better than expected, stockholders benefit, whereas the bondholders receive the same payments they were promised.

Residual claimants
The owners of a firm. They get paid only after all debt payments and other expenses have been paid.

This section discusses how stocks are priced and how monetary policy affects the stock market.

15-2a Pricing Stocks

Suppose you are considering the purchase of a share of stock from some company at a price of p_t. As the owner of the stock, you are entitled to any **dividend** payments made by the firm. Dividend payments are distributed profits from the firm to its stockholders. Firms do not have to distribute all of their profit as dividends. Indeed, some firms, particularly young ones, prefer to reinvest their profits back into the company. This reinvestment might improve the company's future prospects.

Dividend
Distributed profits made by the firm to its stockholders.

Picking up with the last example, suppose in the first year of owning the stock, you are promised a dividend payout of $10. Also, suppose that in one year, you think you can sell the stock for the expected price, p_{t+1}^e, where the superscript e denotes expected value. Like bonds, stock prices must satisfy an asset-pricing formula. In particular, the cost of buying a share of stock, p_t, must equal the expected benefits. There are two sources of benefits: one is the dividend that the firm might pay, D_t, and the other is what you expect you can sell the stock for at the end of the year, p_{t+1}^e. Because the sale of the stock is in the future, the sale price must be discounted to put into present value terms.

Our earlier model of investment from Chapter 6 incorporated the fact that investing in private companies is risky. The way we captured that added risk in earlier parts of the book was to assume that investing in private companies pays a total real interest rate of $r_t + f_t$, where r_t is the risk-free real interest rate and f_t is the risk premium. Discounting future cash flows by a higher interest rate lowers prices and increases expected returns. To maintain consistency with the discussion on bond pricing, we will express the discount rate in nominal terms. The nominal interest rate is related to the real interest rate through the Fisher equation, $i_t = r_t + \pi^e$. Financial arbitrage equates the price of the stock to the expected benefits of owning the stock, or

$$p_t = D_t + \frac{p_{t+1}^e}{1 + i_t + f_t}. \tag{4}$$

Intuitively, if investors expect that the price of the stock will be higher one year from now, they will be willing to pay more for the stock today. Thus, a higher expected future price raises the price today. Likewise, if a company pays out a higher dividend, then that will increase what investors are willing to pay for the stock. Meanwhile, if investing in stock is perceived to be riskier, which is reflected through an increase in f_t, then the stock price goes down.

Equation (4) begs the question of where does the expected future price, p_{t+1}^e, come from? From the perspective of $t + 1$, the price of the stock must satisfy the same version of Equation (4) but with a one-year lead, or

$$p_{t+1} = D_{t+1} + \frac{p_{t+2}^e}{1 + i_{t+1} + f_{t+1}}. \tag{4'}$$

388 Part 4 Banking and Financial Markets

The cost of purchasing a share of stock in year $t + 1$ is p_{t+1} and the benefit of purchasing the stock is the dividend, D_{t+1}, plus the discounted expected future share price, $\dfrac{p^e_{t+2}}{1 + i_{t+1} + f_{t+1}}$.

If we assume a constant discount factor, $i + f$, to make the math easier, we can combine Equations (4) and (4') and end up with

$$p_t = D_t + \frac{p^e_{t+1}}{1 + i + f}$$

$$= D_t + \frac{D^e_{t+1} + \dfrac{p^e_{t+2}}{1 + i + f}}{1 + i + f}$$

$$= D_t + \frac{D^e_{t+1}}{1 + i + f} + \frac{p^e_{t+2}}{(1 + i + f)^2}.$$

The price of the stock in period t is the present discounted value of dividends over the next two years, $D_t + \dfrac{D^e_{t+1}}{i + f}$, plus the discounted expected sale price two years in the future, $\dfrac{p^e_{t+2}}{(i + f)^2}$. Note that from the perspective of year t, the dividends in $t + 1$ are uncertain, which is why next year's dividends are marked with an e superscript. Continuing to apply Equation (4) iteratively results in

$$p_t = D_t + \frac{D^e_{t+1}}{1 + i + f} + \cdots + \frac{D^e_{t+T-1}}{(1 + i + f)^{T-1}} + \frac{p^e_{t+T}}{(1 + i + f)^T}$$

$$= \sum_{j=0}^{T-1} \frac{D^e_{t+j}}{(1 + i + f)^j} + \frac{p^e_{t+T}}{(1 + i + f)^T}. \tag{5}$$

In other words, the price of a stock today is the present discounted value of future dividends plus the present discounted value of the terminal price, p^e_{t+T}. Unlike bonds, stocks do not necessarily have a finite duration. Although companies occasionally go bankrupt or merge with other companies, those possibilities are not known with certainty from the perspective of the present. Thus, any possibility of bankruptcy will be factored into the risk premium, f.

Bubble term
The difference between the price of a stock and the present discounted value of its expected dividends.

The term $\dfrac{p^e_{t+T}}{(1 + i + f)^T}$ is referred to as the **bubble term**, or the part of the stock price that is in excess of the PDV of dividends. Evaluating Equation (5) as T goes to infinity requires that the stock price of the company not explode. In practice, this is a weak assumption. Even high growth companies like Google and Amazon in the early 2000s, and Tesla more recently, have high, but finite, prices. As long as p^e_{t+T} doesn't explode, $\dfrac{p^e_{t+T}}{(1 + i + f)^T}$ converges to 0 as T goes to infinity. Equation (5) can be rewritten as

$$p_t = \sum_{j=0}^{\infty} \frac{D^e_{t+j}}{(1 + i + f)^j}. \tag{5'}$$

Equation (5') says that the price of a stock increases when expected dividends go up or when the discount factor goes down.

One often hears about stock market bubbles and, indeed, it's something we address in the next section. But what is the economic rationale for ruling out the bubble term? Remember that a share of a company's stock is a claim to their future and current dividends. If someone pays a higher price for a stock than the expected PDV of dividends would justify, you have to ask what exactly are they paying for? An investor might believe, for instance, that while a certain stock may be overpriced relative to its fundamental value, the stock can be sold at a later time for even more money.

To make this concrete, suppose that a company, Dog Leash, Inc., is trading at $12 per share even though smart investors know that the PDV of expected dividends justifies a price of only $10 per share. If the smart investors expect the mispricing to widen, then it

Chapter 15 Bonds, Stocks, and Monetary Policy   **389**

is smart to buy shares of Dog Leash, Inc., and sell it later at a profit. To a smart investor, it doesn't matter that Dog Leash, Inc., is overpriced. What matters is that it will be even more overpriced in the future. While a market correction might send the price of Dog Leash, Inc., back to its fundamental value, investors can profit in the interim.

What might cause a stock to be mispriced? One possibility is that it is difficult to form expectations over events that happen in the far-off future. Perhaps most people have incomplete information about Dog Leash, Inc. Or perhaps all the information is there, but most people don't process it in the right way, which leads to the stock being overvalued. These reasons suggest that bubbles are a short-term phenomenon. When all the relevant information comes to light and is framed in the right way, the stock price adjusts to its fundamental value. In other words, the bubble pops.

Finally, we can make additional progress by assuming that dividends grow at a constant rate of $g > 0$ per year. Provided $g < i + f$, one can show that the price of the stock is

$$p_t = \frac{(1 + g)D_t}{i + f - g}. \tag{6}$$

The stock price is increasing in the growth rate of dividends. Intuitively, companies that expect to grow faster trade at a higher share price.

The assumption of constant dividend growth is made more for analytic convenience rather than capturing an empirical reality. A lot of companies start by paying no dividends at all in their first few years as they reinvest all their profits. Indeed, Amazon still doesn't pay dividends. Despite not capturing the behavior of all individual stocks, the model makes several sensible predictions. First, companies with higher dividends and higher rates of dividend growth should, all else equal, have higher stock prices. Second, the riskier a company's prospects are, the lower its stock price will be.

The stock pricing equation is useful when thinking about the prospects of an individual stock in someone's investment portfolio. But can we say anything about the value of the stock market in its entirety? Moreover, how might monetary policy affect stock market performance?

✓ Knowledge Check 15-4

Suppose a company pays a dividend per share of $4 and that the current share price is $40. If $i + f = 0.06$, what is the expected price of the stock next year? Suppose the actual price next year happens to be $41. If the annual return is defined as

$$R = \frac{p_{t+1} + D_t - p_t}{p_t},$$

calculate the return.

——————————————————————— Answers are at the end of the chapter.

15-2b Stock Market Performance and Valuation

The **Standard and Poor's 500 (S&P 500)** is the stock price index of 500 of the largest publicly traded companies in America. The performance of the S&P 500 is a common metric in assessing the performance of the stock market as a whole. In fact, modern investment funds allow investors to effectively buy shares of the S&P rather than individual companies. Figure 15.8 shows that the index, after adjusting for inflation, rose by a factor of 38 between 1871 and 2023. In other words, $1 invested in the S&P in 1871 would be worth about $38 today.

While S&P returns over 150 years provide some historical perspective, they aren't that relevant for the individual investor who is deciding how to allocate funds for personal finance decisions, such as retirement. To shed more light on this, let's think about a worker who is investing some money in the stock market now and plans to withdraw it at retirement 30 years from now. Investing $1,000 today results in $1,000(1 + g)^{30}$ in 30 years where g is the average annual growth rate. For example, the real value of the S&P 500 index was about 4,100 at the beginning of 2023, versus about 920 at the beginning of 1993. The total

Standard and Poor's 500 (S&P 500)

A stock price index of 500 of the largest publicly traded companies in America.

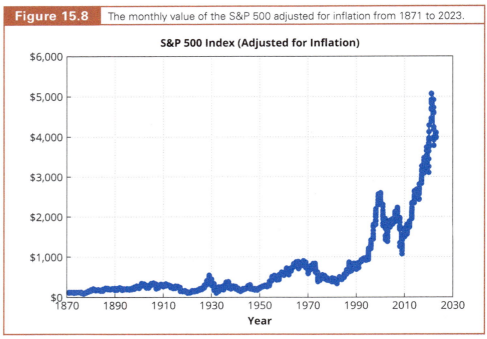

Figure 15.8 The monthly value of the S&P 500 adjusted for inflation from 1871 to 2023.

Source: Robert Shiller's webpage http://www.econ.yale.edu/~shiller/data.htm.

cumulative growth over that 30-year stretch was about 340 percent, implying a g of about 0.051. A person who invested $1,000 in 1993 would have $1,000(1.05)^{30} = \$4,447$ by 2023.

Figure 15.7 shows how much $1,000 would be worth at the end of a 30-year interval starting in 1960. As you can see, the returns vary substantially. The $1,000 invested in 1960 would have only been worth about $1,500 in 1990, whereas $1,000 invested in 1990 would have been worth about $6,000 in 2020. One often hears that the average annual return of the stock market is quite high. And, indeed, it is. The average annual return adjusted for inflation is more than 6 percent since 1870. However, as Figure 15.9 shows, *when* you start investing matters.

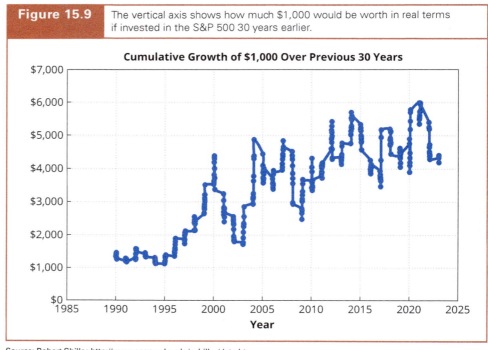

Figure 15.9 The vertical axis shows how much $1,000 would be worth in real terms if invested in the S&P 500 30 years earlier.

Source: Robert Shiller http://www.econ.yale.edu/~shiller/data.htm.

Moving beyond personal finance, is it possible to say the value of the stock market is "too high" or "too low" relative to fundamentals, such as the market risk premium and average dividends? The stock-pricing formula from the previous section gives us a clue how one might make that judgment. Recall that the price of an individual stock is the present discounted value of its dividends. If dividends grow at a constant rate, then the stock price (from Equation (6)) is

$$p_t = \frac{(1+g)D_t}{i+f-g}.$$

Or, if we want to adjust for the size of the company, we can write this in terms of the **price–dividend ratio**, or

$$\frac{p_t}{D_t} = \frac{(1+g)}{i+f-g}. \qquad (7)$$

Price–dividend ratio
The price of a company's stock divided by its dividend per share.

Companies that are expected to grow quickly will have higher price–dividend ratios than other companies. This makes sense. Young companies typically pay very low dividends but are expected to grow quickly over time, whereas more established and older companies typically pay more in dividends but have slower rates of growth. According to Equation (7), if $\frac{p_t}{D_t} > \frac{(1+g)}{i+f-g}$, the stock price would be overvalued, meaning that the price of the stock would exceed what is justified by its fundamentals. In the language of the previous section, there would be a positive bubble term. Unless investors thought that they could sell an overvalued stock for an even higher price in the future, they want to avoid purchasing overvalued stocks. The logic goes in reverse for stocks with $\frac{p_t}{D_t} < \frac{(1+g)}{i+f-g}$. They are undervalued relative to fundamentals, and investors would like to purchase them.

Closely related to the price–dividend ratio is the **price–earnings** (PE) ratio. The PE ratio is the price of a company's stock divided by its earnings per share. The difference between the price–dividend ratio and the PE ratio is that not all earnings are paid out as dividends. Remember, companies can also choose to reinvest earnings into the firm. Conceptually, however, the PE ratio can potentially tell us if an individual stock is overvalued. If a stock has a high PE ratio, the company could either be overvalued or investors are expecting that earnings will increase over time. This is why young high-growth companies tend to have higher PE ratios. The high price is justified by high levels of future potential earnings.

Price–earnings ratio
The price of a company's stock divided by its earnings per share.

A PE ratio can also be calculated for an entire stock market index, such as the S&P 500. Just as in the case of individual stocks, a high PE ratio for the entire market could be a signal of high expected earnings growth or a signal that the stock market as a whole is overvalued. One difficulty, whether examining the fortunes of an individual company or the entire market, is that earnings are very volatile. Profits tend to rise during business cycle expansions and fall in recessions. The swings of the business cycle add volatility to the PE ratio that is unrelated to the fundamentals driving profitability.

To remove business cycle effects, some forecasters, investors, and economic policymakers prefer to look at the **Shiller PE ratio** (also called the cyclically adjusted price-to-earnings ratio, or the CAPE ratio). The Shiller PE ratio, popularized by economist, Robert Shiller, uses a 10-year average of inflation adjusted earnings in the denominator of the PE ratio. Averaging earnings over 10 years removes the ups and downs of the business cycle. Moreover, averaging over 10 years may remove some of the PE ratio that is due to expectations of higher or lower earnings in the future. That is, a high PE ratio may be due to expectations of higher earnings in the next year or two, but taking the average over 10 years should smooth out those expectations. The result is a PE ratio that gives a better indication as to whether the stock market as a whole is over- or undervalued.

Shiller PE ratio
A PE ratio that uses a 10-year inflation adjusted average of earnings.

Figure 15.10 shows the Shiller PE ratio between 1871 and 2023 as well as a measure of the long-run interest rate. Several notable dates are labeled, including the large drop in the stock market in 1929 that preceded the Great Depression. In the last three months of 1929, the S&P dropped more than 30 percent in real terms. The year 2000 is also of

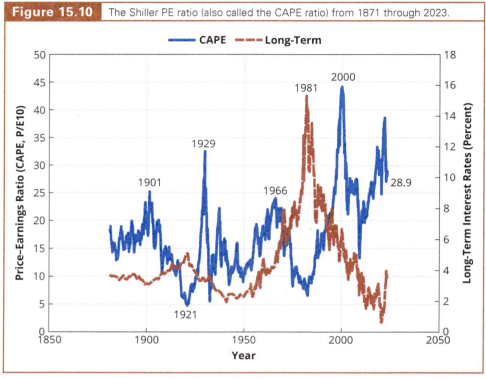

Figure 15.10 The Shiller PE ratio (also called the CAPE ratio) from 1871 through 2023.

Source: Shiller.

interest because that's widely associated with the end of the "dot-com" bubble. The mid-1990s featured a number of e-commerce companies exploding onto the stage. Their stock prices were bid up by investors to extraordinarily high PE ratios, until the subsequent drop in stock prices starting in 2000. Although the fall in the stock market wasn't as abrupt as it was in the Great Depression, the S&P lost 40 percent of its value between 2000 and 2003.

The takeaway is that large increases in the Shiller PE ratio appear to predict subsequent drops in the stock market. Thus, this supports the view that a high Shiller PE ratio is a good indicator of the stock market being overvalued. Also note from Figure 15.10 that the Shiller PE ratio is negatively correlated with the long-run (nominal) interest rate. Since monetary policy influences the long-run interest rate, one might wonder how monetary policy influences stock prices and what (if anything) monetary policymakers should do when they suspect there may be an asset price bubble. This is what we turn to next.

15-2c Monetary Policy and the Value of the Stock Market

Return once again to Equation (6), which expresses the price of a stock in terms of its current dividend, dividend growth, and interest rate:

$$p_t = \frac{(1+g)D_t}{i+f-g}.$$

As argued in this and previous chapters, monetary policy controls the short-run nominal interest rate. Through the term-structure of interest rates, changes in monetary policy affect longer-run interest rates. According to Equation (6), if monetary policymakers raise the interest rate, the price of stocks drops. The reason is that a higher nominal interest rate lowers the PDV of future dividends, which decreases stock prices today. Conversely, if monetary policy decreases the nominal interest rate, stock prices increase today. Since stock prices are forward looking and earnings (either in the current year, or the 10-year retrospective average) are static, interest rates and the PE ratio will tend to move in different directions. This, in part, explains the correlation in Figure 15.10.

Chapter 15 Bonds, Stocks, and Monetary Policy   393

If stock market values are a function of monetary policy, should monetary policymakers think about this relationship when setting the short-run interest rate? The Fed's dual mandate from Congress is to ensure stable prices and maximize sustainable employment. It's not immediately clear how stock market prices affect either of these. On the one hand, the biggest stock market bubbles in 1929 and 2000 (as defined by high Shiller PE ratios) were followed by recessions. Because the unemployment rate spikes in recessions, the Fed perhaps should be concerned about bubbles. If the Fed identifies a PE ratio that is high by historical standards, then it might make sense to raise the interest rate and deflate the bubble. On the other hand, there were plenty of times the PE ratio was high by historical norms, but the economy didn't fall into a recession. This occurred most recently in 2021.

There are other practical difficulties besides popping bubbles that don't turn into a recession. First, although a high Shiller PE ratio predicts lower subsequent returns, it's not clear when the stock market is done rising. That is, even if the Fed could pop the bubble, it's unclear when they should start to deflate the balloon. The Shiller PE ratio reached a historical high in 1997, but the S&P rose for three more years before finally crashing. Had the Fed raised rates in 1997, three years of stock market gains may have been erased.

Finally, if the Fed is concerned about bubbles, then why should they only care about the stock market? Some forecasters and economists (including Shiller) warned that housing prices were excessively high during the mid-2000s.[4] Housing prices then contracted during the 2007–2008 financial crisis and subsequent recession. In theory, the Fed could have raised the nominal interest rate in the mid-2000s, which would have raised mortgage rates and cooled off housing prices. Perhaps the Great Recession would have been shorter and less severe had the Fed intervened earlier.

In summary, the extent to which the Fed should pay attention to asset prices in various markets depends on its ability to overcome the theoretical challenges (i.e., identifying when prices are high because of a bubble rather than fundamentals) and the practical challenges (i.e., what asset market should it be looking at). Fifteen years after the Great Recession, this continues to be a topic of debate among economists. The next application discusses the housing market in more detail.

Application 15.2

Bubble Watching in the U.S. Housing Market

Like stocks and bonds, the price of real estate properties can be modeled with an asset pricing equation. Consider a single-family home. Instead of the home paying dividends every year, like a stock would, the home is valuable because it can earn rent. Sometimes the property owner rents the house to tenants, but other times the owner lives in the house and implicitly pays rent to themselves. In either case, and analogous to the case of stocks, the price of a house should equal the rent today plus the present discounted value of the future price, or

$$P_t = R_t + \frac{P_{t+1}^e}{1 + i}.$$

Home prices can increase because rents, R_t, increase, the nominal interest rate decreases, or the expected future price increases. To varying degrees, all of these factors were present in the mid-2000s when some commentators and economists started to worry about a housing bubble.

Figure 15.11 shows the Fed funds rate decreased from over 6 percent in 2000 to under 2 percent between 2001 and 2004. At the same time, the ratio of the price of shelter to the overall consumer prices increased modestly. Price expectations are more difficult to measure, but the Case and Shiller paper cited in the previous footnote describes a survey from 2003 in which recent homebuyers expressed remarkably optimistic expectations over future home price growth. In particular, these homeowners expected a rate of growth of over 10 percent per year.

■ Continues

---

[4]Case, Karl E. and Robert J. Shiller. 2003. "Is There a Bubble in the Housing Market?" *Brookings Paper on Economic Activity*, 2003, no. 2, 299–362.

Application 15.2 (Continued)

Figure 15.11 The consumer price index for shelter relative to the entire consumer price index (shown on the vertical axis on the right) and the effective fed funds rate (shown on the axis on the left) from 2000 through 2023.

Shaded areas indicate U.S. recessions.

Source: BLS and Fred https://fred.stlouisfed.org/graph/?g=12Tcu.

Figure 15.12 shows that these homeowners actually had the correct expectations for the next two years, as home prices grew by 12.5 and 14.2 percent in 2004 and 2005, respectively. Home price growth slowed in 2006 and by 2007 it was negative. Although the housing market crash may not have been perceived as inevitable from the perspective of 2003, it was also clear that people were buying houses with very optimistic expectations over future price growth. The Fed didn't start moving interest rates up until late 2004. Should it have moved sooner?

Again, bubbles are easier to spot in hindsight than anticipate in advance. The Case–Shiller home price index increased cumulatively by more than 40 percent between 2003 and 2006. If the Fed increased interest rates more aggressively, perhaps home price growth would have been suppressed, but it's no guarantee the Great Recession would have been avoided. Moreover, by 2017, home prices completely regained all the ground they lost between 2006 and 2011. To claim that the housing market was in a bubble in the early 2000s would require that home prices in the early 2000s were not justified by fundamentals, but the same home prices in 2017 were. Given changes in demographics, income, and constraints on housing supply, this justification may be possible, but it isn't self-evident.

Understanding the possibility of bubbles in the housing market isn't just a matter of historical significance. Figure 15.12 shows that home prices increased dramatically between 2020 and 2023. And despite higher interest rates, home prices, as of the writing of this book, have not cooled off. Whether a steep decline in housing prices is coming remains to be seen.

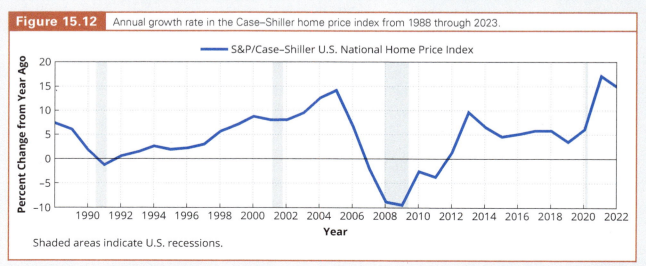

Figure 15.12 Annual growth rate in the Case–Shiller home price index from 1988 through 2023.

Shaded areas indicate U.S. recessions.

Source: FRED https://fred.stlouisfed.org/graph/?g=12Thx.

Chapter Summary

- Bonds are debt instruments and can be issued by governments or private businesses. Bonds differ by their maturity, face value, level of riskiness, and coupon payments.

- The price of a bond equals the present discounted value of its expected future payments.

- The yield to maturity is the interest rate that equates the price of a bond to the present discounted value of its expected future payments.

- Bond prices and interest rates move in different directions. Intuitively, if interest rates rise, then a bondholder can earn a higher return by investing elsewhere. The only way for the bond to remain attractive in the face of rising interest rates is for the price to drop sufficiently.

- The rate of return from holding a bond is the percent return an investor earns from the investment over a specified time period. If the investor holds the bond to maturity, the rate of return equals the YTM.

- When interest rates fall, bondholders can sell their bonds and earn a return in excess of the yield to maturity. When interest rates rise and bondholders sell their bonds prior to their maturity date, the return is less than the yield to maturity.

- The yield curve plots the yield to maturities of bonds with different durations. Typically, the yield curve is upward sloping, implying that bonds with longer times to maturity pay higher interest rates.

- The prices of longer duration bonds are more sensitive to changes in the interest rate. Because investors are risk averse, longer duration bonds must pay a risk premium.

- Bonds with a risk of default trade at a lower price and offer a higher yield than riskless bonds with the same maturities. Despite the higher yields, financial arbitrage leads to equal rates of expected return between risky and riskless assets.

- Traditionally, monetary policy affected interest rates on longer duration debt through a term-structure channel. Since long interest rates are a function of current and expected short-run interest rates, the Fed can lower the long run rates by changing the short-run rate today.

- More recently, the Fed has affected longer-run interest rates by promising to keep short-run rates low for some duration (forward guidance) and buy directly purchasing longer maturity debt.

- Monetary policy traditionally affected interest rates on riskier bonds by changing the risk-free interest rate. Since 2009, the Fed has purchased mortgaged-backed securities in an attempt to lower interest rates on riskier debt directly.

- The price of a stock equals the present discounted value of its expected dividends. The discount rate for stocks is higher than risk-free assets because of the risk premium.

- If the price of a stock exceeds the present discounted value of its dividends, there is a bubble in that the price of the stock is not justified by its fundamentals.

- A high PE ratio may indicate that investors expect the company to have high growth in future earnings. It may also indicate that the stock is overvalued. The same analysis for an individual company can be done for the stock market as a whole.

- Because earnings are sensitive to the ups and downs of the business cycle, the Shiller PE ratio uses a 10-year inflation adjusted average of earnings.

- The stock market performs worse by historical standards following periods when the Shiller PE ratio is high.

Key Terms

Maturity, 376
Face value, 376
Coupon, 376
Discount bond, 376
Yield to maturity, 376
Rate of return, 376
Term premium, 379
Financial arbitrage, 380
Expectations hypothesis, 380

Risk premium, 382
Residual claimants, 387
Dividend, 387
Bubble term, 388
Standard and Poor's 500 (S&P 500), 389
Price–dividend ratio, 391
Price–earnings ratio, 391
Shiller PE ratio, 391

Questions for Review

1. Explain why discount bonds trade for less than their face value.

2. How can the expectations hypothesis explain the upward sloping yield curve? Is this consistent with historical data?

3. Compare and contrast the way the Fed has traditionally affected long-term interest rates versus their more recent policies.

4. Why might a high PE ratio be suggestive of a bubble? Must a high PE ratio necessarily imply a bubble? Explain.

5. What advantage does the Shiller PE ratio have over traditional PE ratios?

Problems

15.1 Consider the following bond-pricing questions.

a. The price of a bond with a face value of $100 and a time to maturity of one year is $96. Calculate the yield to maturity.

b. Suppose a bond has a time to maturity of two years and a face value and YTM that is identical to part a. Calculate the price of the bond. Comment on how the price of the bond is related to the time to maturity.

c. Assume that an investor purchases a two-year bond for the price you calculated in part b, but sells the bond at the end of the first year. If the YTM of a bond with a time to maturity of one year is the same as what you found in part a, calculate the investor's rate of return. Comment on the relationship between the bond's rate of return and the YTM.

15.2 Suppose a bond with a time to maturity of five years has a face value of $500 and sells at $450.

a. Calculate the yield to maturity for this bond.

b. One year from now, suppose that bonds with a time to maturity of four years have a YTM of 4 percent. If the bond from part a is sold in a year, what is the return?

c. Is the return in part b higher or lower than the YTM in part a? Why?

15.3 Suppose that the YTM on a discount bond maturing in three years is 7 percent.

a. The sequence of expected one-year rates is shown in the table below.

Year	Expected Interest Rate
1	5%
2	4%
3	?

What, according to the expectations hypothesis, must the expected one-year interest rate be in year 3?

b. Suppose that the 3-year bond carries a risk premium of 2 percent. What is the minimum expected one-year interest rate in year 3 that is consistent with an upward sloping yield curve?

15.4 Bonds issues by the U.S. government are widely perceived to have an extremely low risk of default. We are going to compare the price of U.S. bonds to bonds issued by other countries.

a. At the time this book is being written, the yield on a 10-year constant maturity Treasury bond is 3.5 percent. Assuming this is a 10-year discount bond, what is the price of a Treasury bond with a face value of $1,000?[5]

b. The yield on an equivalent bond issued by the Colombian government is about 13 percent. Assuming that bonds issued by the U.S. are riskless and that investors recover nothing in the case of default by the Colombian government, calculate the implied probability of default by the Colombian government.

c. Instead, assume that, in the case of default, the Colombian government pays bondholders $200. Calculate the implied probability of default by the Colombian government.

d. Discuss why understanding the value of bonds conditional on default is important for forecasting the probability of default.

15.5 Suppose that a stock pays $4 per share in dividends and that the dividend growth rate is 5 percent. Assume that the nominal interest rate, i, is 4 percent and the risk premium, f, is 3 percent.

a. Calculate the price of this stock.

b. Suppose that the risk premium increases to 5 percent. Calculate the price of the stock. Comment on how an increase in the risk premium affects the value of the stock.

c. Suppose that the risk premium goes back to 3 percent, but the dividend growth rate falls to 4 percent. Calculate the price of the stock. Comment on how a decrease in the dividend growth rate affects the value of the stock.

✓ Knowledge Check 15-1 Answer

The YTM is

$$i = \sqrt[10]{\frac{\$1,000}{\$875}} - 1 = 0.013,$$

or 1.3 percent. If the price of the bond rises to $900 in one year, the rate of return is

$$R = \frac{\$900 - \$875}{\$875} = 0.029,$$

or 2.9 percent.

---

[5] In reality, Treasury securities make coupon payments. We are ignoring those payments to keep things simple.

Knowledge Check 15-2 Answer

The yield of the bond with a yield to maturity of three years is

$$i_{t,3} = 0.5 + \frac{1}{3}(3 + 3 + 4) = 3.83\%.$$

The yield of the bond with a yield to maturity of six years is

$$i_{t,3} = 1 + \frac{1}{6}(3 + 3 + 4 + 4.5 + 5 + 5) = 5.08\%.$$

Because the yield on the 6-year bond is higher than the 3-year bond, which is in turn higher than the 1-year bond, the yield curve is upward sloping.

Knowledge Check 15-3 Answer

The pricing equation is

$$P = 0.9\frac{\$500}{1.05} + 0.1\frac{\$100}{1.05} = \$438.09.$$

The YTM is

$$YTM = \frac{\$500}{\$438.09} - 1 = 0.143,$$

or 14.3 percent.

Knowledge Check 15-4 Answer

According to Equation (4), we have

$$p_t = D_t + \frac{p^e_{t+1}}{1 + i + f}$$

$$= \$4 + \frac{p^e_{t+1}}{1 + 0.06}.$$

Substituting $p_t = \$40$ and solving for p^e_{t+1} gives $p^e_{t+1} = \$38.16$. If the price next year happens to be $41, the annual rate of return is

$$R = \frac{\$41 + \$4 - \$40}{\$40} = 0.125,$$

or 12.5 percent.

Appendix

Mathematical Appendix

Throughout the book, we use concepts from mathematics and statistics. This mathematical appendix provides a concise review of relevant topics as well as examples and applications to the macroeconomy.

A-1 A Word on Notation

The book commonly denotes variables that change over time with a subscript, t. For instance, if we are looking at GDP, then GDP_t would be the value of GDP in time period t. The time period interval usually depends on the model being studied. Models of economic growth, such as those in Chapters 3 and 4, use a year as a reference time period. So GDP_t would be GDP in the year t, or current GDP, and GDP_{t-1} would be GDP in the previous year. In business cycle models, such as those discussed in Chapters 10 through 13, a time period of a quarter (which is three months) is more common.

A-2 Exponents and Logs

Many macroeconomic variables, such as GDP and consumption, get very big over time. More precisely, GDP and consumption have grown more in recent years compared to the distant past. Figure A.1 shows nominal GDP from 1929 through 2022. Between 1936 and 1937, GDP rose by about $9 billion. Between 1996 and 1997, GDP rose by about $500 billion. Because the slope of GDP gets bigger through the years, GDP is not well approximated by linear growth.

Figure A.1 Nominal gross domestic product for the United States from 1929 through 2022.

Shaded areas indicate U.S. recessions.

Source: FRED and BEA https://fred.stlouisfed.org/graph/?g=12dZp.

Instead, GDP is better approximated by exponential growth. If a variable, x_t, is growing at constant rate, $g > 0$, then it satisfies the following after equation

$$x_t = x_0(1 + g)^t. \tag{1}$$

398

The number, x_0, is a constant. To calculate the growth rate of x_t, divide both sides of Equation (1) by the value of x in the previous period, or $x_{t-1} = x_0(1 + g)^{t-1}$:

$$\frac{x_t}{x_{t-1}} = \frac{x_0(1 + g)^t}{x_0(1 + g)^{t-1}}$$

$$= 1 + g.$$

Hence, the growth rate between periods $t - 1$ and t is g.

In addition to GDP, many macroeconomic variables grow exponentially through time. One difficulty in using an exponential function is that year-to-year changes are difficult to read from the graph. Referring to Figure A.1, the year-to-year movements in GDP are barely discernable before the 1970s. To deal with this, it is often useful to graph the natural log of a data series. It turns out that if a variable is growing exponentially, like x_t in Equation (1), then the natural log of x_t grows linearly. To see this, take the natural log of both sides of Equation (1):

$$\ln x_t = \ln(x_0(1 + g)^t)$$

$$= \ln x_0 + \ln((1 + g)^t)$$

$$= \ln x_0 + t\ln(1 + g)$$

$$\approx \ln x_0 + gt. \tag{1'}$$

Equation (1') says that the natural log of x_t grows linearly with time with a slope of g. The last line is an approximation. It turns out to be true that $\ln(1 + g) \approx g$ provided $g < 0.1$. So, for growth rates that are less than 10 percent, this is a good approximation. Moving from line to line to derive Equation (1') requires algebraic rules that apply to natural logs, a summary of which is provided in Table A.1.

Table A.1	Rules Governing the Natural Log Function
1. $\ln(x_t y_t) = \ln(x_t) + \ln(y_t)$	
2. $\ln\left(\dfrac{x_t}{y_t}\right) = \ln(x_t) - \ln(y_t)$	
3. $\ln(x_t^a) = a\ln(x_t)$	
4. $\ln(1 + g) \approx g$	
5. $\ln(1) = 0$	

The top panel of Figure A.2 shows the relationship between x_t and time, assuming that $x_0 = 1$ and $g = 0.02$ for 100 time periods. It is evident that the per-year changes in x_t get bigger over time. The bottom panel, meanwhile, plots the $\ln(x_t)$. The plot starts at $\ln(x_0) = \ln(1) = 0$ and grows at a rate of 0.02 every period.

Note that the difference between the natural log of x_t in period t and period $t + n$ is given by

$$\ln(x_{t+n}) - \ln(x_t) = \ln x_0 + g(t + n) - \ln x_0 + gt = gn.$$

Thus, the vertical difference between the natural log of x_t in period $t + n$ and t is the cumulative growth in the n periods.

Oftentimes, the growth rate of a variable itself changes. For instance, perhaps GDP grows quickly in one decade and then slowly in another decade. The growth rate of a variable x_t can be computed across any two periods by taking differences in the natural log across the two periods:

$$\ln(x_t) - \ln(x_{t-1}) = \ln\left(\frac{x_t}{x_{t-1}}\right)$$

$$= \ln(1 + g_{x,t}) \approx g_{x,t}. \tag{2}$$

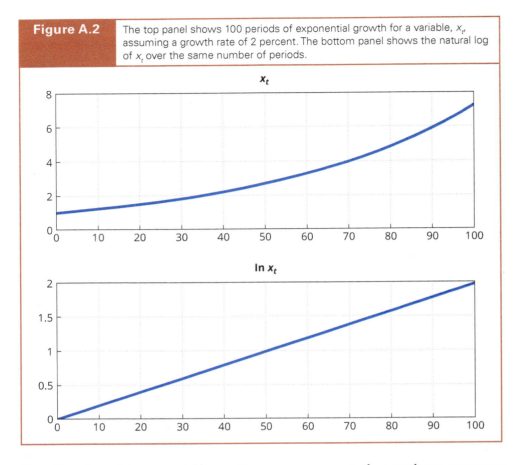

Figure A.2 The top panel shows 100 periods of exponential growth for a variable, x_t, assuming a growth rate of 2 percent. The bottom panel shows the natural log of x_t over the same number of periods.

Thus, if you have data on a variable over time, you can compute the growth rate across any two periods by taking the difference in natural logs.

This result is useful in a variety of circumstances. For instance, suppose you want to calculate the growth rate of a product. To make this concrete, let's return to the example of nominal GDP. Nominal GDP, $NGDP_t$, is the product of real GDP, $RGDP_t$, and the price level, P_t. Mathematically, this is given by

$$NGDP_t = RGDP_t \times P_t.$$

Rule 1 in Table A.1 says that the natural log of a product is the sum of the natural log of each variable, or

$$\ln(NGDP_t) = \ln(RGDP_t \times P_t)$$
$$= \ln(RGDP_t) + \ln(P_t).$$

Subtracting nominal GDP in period $t - 1$ gives

$$\ln(NGDP_t) - \ln(NGDP_{t-1}) = \ln(RGDP_t) + \ln(P_t) - (\ln(RGDP_{t-1}) + \ln(P_{t-1}))$$
$$\Leftrightarrow g_{NGDP,t} = g_{RGDP,t} + g_{P,t}.$$

Thus, the growth rate of nominal GDP is the sum of the growth rate of real GDP and the growth rate of prices. The growth rate of prices is the inflation rate, so you can also interpret this as inflation equals the difference between nominal GDP growth and real GDP growth.

We can also review a useful application for natural log rule 2, namely that the growth rate of a quotient is the difference in growth rates of the numerator and denominator. For instance, hours per worker, h_t, equals the total number of hours worked in an economy H_t, divided by the number of workers in the economy, E_t. Or, mathematically,

$$h_t = \frac{H_t}{E_t}.$$

Applying Rule 2,

$$\ln(h_t) = \ln\left(\frac{H_t}{E_t}\right)$$
$$= \ln(H_t) - \ln(E_t).$$

Subtracting hours per worker in period $t - 1$ gives the following equation:

$$\ln(h_t) - \ln(h_{t-1}) = \ln(H_t) - \ln(E_t) - (\ln(H_{t-1}) - \ln(E_{t-1}))$$
$$\Leftrightarrow g_{h,t} = g_{H,t} - g_{E,t}.$$

In other words, the growth rate of hours per worker is the growth rate of total hours worked minus the growth rate of the total number of workers employed.

Finally, macroeconomists are often interested in finding the growth rate of a product of variables each raised to a power. The Cobb–Douglas production function, used throughout the book, is an important case. The Cobb–Douglas production function is

$$Y_t = A_t K_t^a L_t^{1-a}.$$

The production function says that real GDP, Y_t, is a function of TFP, A_t, capital, K_t, and labor, L_t. The parameter, a, is between 0 and 1. Using rules 1 and 3 from Table A.1, we can write the natural log of the production function as

$$\ln(Y_t) = \ln(A_t K_t^a L_t^{1-a})$$
$$= \ln(A_t) + \ln(K_t^a) + \ln(L_t^{1-a})$$
$$= \ln(A_t) + a\ln(K_t) + (1 - a)\ln(L_t).$$

Taking the difference between the natural log of Y_t and the natural log of Y_{t-1} gives

$$\ln(Y_t) - \ln(Y_{t-1}) = \ln(A_t) + a\ln(K_t) + (1 - a)\ln(L_t) - (\ln(A_t) + a\ln(K_t)$$
$$+ (1 - a)\ln(L_t))$$
$$\Leftrightarrow g_{Y,t} = g_{A,t} + ag_{K,t} + (1 - a)g_{L,t}.$$

In other words, the growth rate of real GDP is the sum of the growth rate of TFP and the weighted growth rate of the inputs, capital and labor.

A-3 Summary Statistics

Summary statistics are quantitative summaries of data series. We frequently depict data series graphically in the book; however, quantitative measurements are occasionally helpful.

Suppose you have a data series in which observations are given by x_i. The subscript "i" indexes the data so x_1 is a different value from x_2 which is a different value from x_3 and so on. The mean of the data is the average value of the observations. Mathematically, the mean is given by

$$\bar{x} = \frac{1}{N}\sum_{i=1}^{N} x_i, \tag{3}$$

where N is the number of observations. Equation (3) says that the mean, $\bar{x}$, is the sum of the observations divided by the number of observations. As an example, Table A.2 contains data on the unemployment rate from seven different U.S. cities in 2023.[1]

The mean unemployment rate across the seven cities is given by

$$\bar{x} = \frac{1}{7}(4.4 + 2.9 + 3.7 + 4.9 + 3.2 + 4.0 + 2.4) = 3.6.$$

---

[1]Technically, these are unemployment rates from "metropolitan statistical areas" (MSA) rather than cities, but there is typically one large city in each MSA. For instance, Chicago is part of the Chicago–Naperville–Elgin MSA.

402 **Appendix**

Table A.2	Unemployment Rates in Seven U.S. Cities
City	**2023 Unemployment Rate (in percent)**
Chicago	4.4
Phoenix	2.9
San Diego	3.7
Cleveland	4.9
Atlanta	3.2
Baltimore	4.0
Iowa City	2.4

In other words, the average unemployment rate across these seven cities is 3.6 percent. Another summary statistic is the median. The median is the data value such that half the observations are below the value and other half of the observations are above the value. We can compute the median by first sorting the data from the lowest value to the highest value:

$$2.4, 2.9, 3.2, 3.7, 4.0, 4.4, 4.9.$$

The median unemployment rate is 3.7, because half of the observations are below 3.7 and half of the observations are above 3.7. We often denote the median by x_{50}, because half of the observations are below x_{50} and half are above x_{50}. This can be generalized. In particular, the median is an example of a percentile. The pth percentile of a data series, x_p, is the value such that p percent of the observations lie below x_p. In the case of the median, $p = 50$. The 90th percentile, x_{90}, would be the value of x such that 90 percent of the observations lie below x_{90}. Because we have only seven values in Table A.2, this isn't applicable; however, it is for data series with more observations.

The mean and median are measures of centralized tendency, or a value that is most representative of an entire data series. In addition to knowing about the average value, we may also want to know how dispersed the variable is. The primary way of measuring dispersion is the standard deviation. The standard deviation measures how spread out (on average) a variable is from its mean. Formally, the standard deviation is given by

$$s = \sqrt{\frac{\sum_{i=1}^{N}(x_i - \bar{x})^2}{N}}. \tag{4}$$

The further the x_i terms are from the mean, the bigger is the standard deviation. The standard deviation can be computed in steps. The unemployment data in Table A.2 demonstrates this. The average unemployment rate is 3.6 percent. The difference between the average unemployment rate and the unemployment rate in Chicago is $4.4 - 3.6 = 0.8$. Squaring it gives $0.8^2 = 0.64$. We can apply the same approach to all the other cities as well. The results are displayed in Table A.3.

Table A.3	Calculating Standard Deviation		
City	**2023 Unemployment Rate (in percent)**	$x_i - \bar{x}$	$(x_i - \bar{x})^2$
Chicago	4.4	0.8	0.64
Phoenix	2.9	-0.7	0.49
San Diego	3.7	0.1	0.01
Cleveland	4.9	1.3	1.69
Atlanta	3.2	-0.4	0.16
Baltimore	4.0	0.4	0.16
Iowa City	2.4	-1.2	1.44

With the squared differences calculated, we can sum them together to get 4.59. The standard deviation is given by

$$s = \sqrt{\frac{\sum_{i=1}^{N}(x_i - \bar{x})^2}{N}}$$

$$= \sqrt{\frac{4.59}{7}} = 0.81.$$

Relative to the mean of 3.6, a one standard deviation increase in the unemployment rate is about 4.4.

Finally, consider relationships between two variables. For instance, suppose you want to find the correlation between a city's unemployment rate, indexed by x_i, and its level of per capita income, indexed by y_i. The data series are shown in Table A.4.

Table A.4	Unemployment Rates and Incomes per Capita in Seven U.S. Cities	
City	2023 Unemployment Rate (in percent)	2023 Income
Chicago	4.4	$71,912
Phoenix	2.9	$58,308
San Diego	3.7	$72,637
Cleveland	4.9	$61,948
Atlanta	3.2	$63,219
Baltimore	4.0	$58,556
Iowa City	2.4	$60,316

The correlation coefficient measures how strongly (either positively or negatively) two variables move together. Formally, the correlation coefficient between two data series, x and y, is given by the equation

$$r = \frac{\sum_{i=1}^{N}(x_i - \bar{x})(y_i - \bar{y})}{N s_x s_y}. \tag{5}$$

Mathematically, it must always be true that $-1 < r < 1$. The closer r is to 1, the stronger the positive correlation. The closer r is to -1, the stronger the negative correlation. A correlation coefficient close to 0 means that the variables are neither positively nor negatively correlated with each other.

We previously calculated the mean and standard deviation for the unemployment rates. Calculating the same statistics for per capita income yields

$$\bar{y} = \$63,842,$$
$$s_y = \$5,574.$$

Finally, we need to calculate the numerator of Equation (5). Table A.5 shows the results. Summing all the rows in the last column together gives $11,113. Dividing this value by $N s_x s_y$, gives a correlation coefficient is 0.35. In summary, there is a weak positive relationship between a city's unemployment rate and its per capita income.

Many macroeconomic variables are more strongly correlated (either positively or negatively) than the two from the last example. Figure A.3 shows the strong positive correlation between the growth rate of quarterly real GDP and real investment. The correlation coefficient is about 0.8, meaning that quarters with high GDP growth correspond to quarters with high growth in investment.

Table A.5

City	2023 Unemployment Rate	2023 Income	$x_i - \bar{x}$	$y_i - \bar{y}$	$(x_i - \bar{x})(y_i - \bar{y})$
Chicago	4.4	$71,912	0.8	$8,070	$6,110
Phoenix	2.9	$58,308	−0.7	−$5,534	$4,111
San Diego	3.7	$72,637	0.1	$8,795	$503
Cleveland	4.9	$61,948	1.3	−$1,894	−$2,381
Atlanta	3.2	$63,219	−0.4	−$623	$276
Baltimore	4.0	$58,556	0.4	−$5,286	−$1,888
Iowa City	2.4	$60,316	−1.2	−$3,526	$4,382

Figure A.3 Real GDP growth (vertical axis) and real investment growth (horizontal axis) at a quarterly frequency from 1960 through 2020.

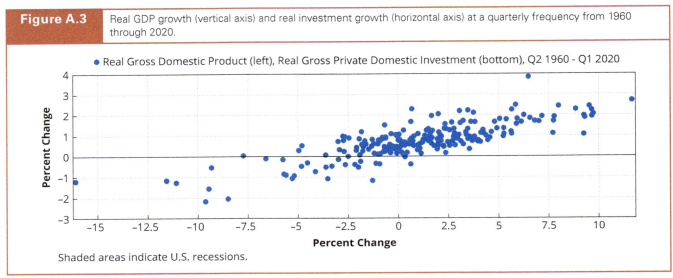

Shaded areas indicate U.S. recessions.

Source: FRED and BEA https://fred.stlouisfed.org/graph/?g=135CL.

Meanwhile, Figure A.4 shows the strong negative relationship between the unemployment rate and job posting rate. In weak labor markets, firms post fewer jobs and the unemployment rate is higher. The correlation coefficient is approximately −0.88.

Figure A.4 The hiring rate (vertical axis) and unemployment rate (horizontal axis) at a monthly frequency between 2001 and 2020.

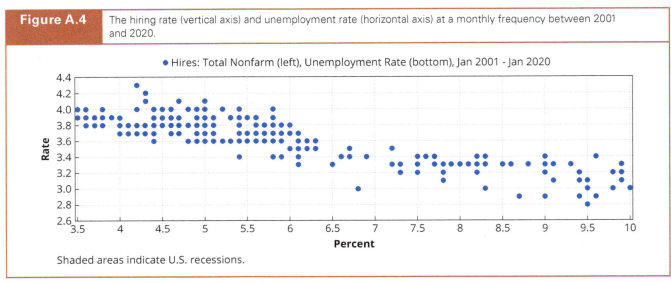

Shaded areas indicate U.S. recessions.

Source: JOLTS, BLS, FRED, https://fred.stlouisfed.org/graph/?g=135G7.

Scatter plots such as those in Figures A.3 and A.4 are useful in depicting the correlation between two variables.

Solutions

To Odd-Numbered Problems

This section contains solutions to all of the odd-numbered problems in the text. Solutions to all of the text problems are contained in the Instructor's Manual.

Chapter 1 Solutions

Questions for Review

1. Consider two alternatives: you take your car to the carwash or you wash the car in your driveway. Do either, neither, or both of these alternatives contribute to GDP? Explain.

    Solution: Taking your car to the carwash is a service that is counted in GDP. Washing your car by yourself is also a service, but it is not recorded in GDP. The reason is that no transaction is recorded.

3. Suppose nominal GDP grew by 12 percent last year. Provide two reasons why this cannot be interpreted as a 12 percent increase in the purchasing power of the average citizen.

    Solution: The first reason is that prices may have increased over the last year. This would raise nominal GDP but not affect living standards. The second reason is that population may have increased. A bigger population would produce more output, but leave output per person the same.

5. Is real GDP per capita a good measure of living standards? Explain.

    Solution: Real GDP per capita is highly correlated with other metrics of living standards such as consumption and life expectancy. Some forms of pollution are higher in countries with high per capita GDP. By and large, GDP per capita is a good measure of living standards.

Problems

1. Consider the following economic data.

Year	Price of avocados	Quantity of avocados	Price of bell peppers	Quantity of bell peppers
2021	$0.90	2,500	$1.40	3,000
2022	$1.05	2,750	$1.45	3,400
2023	$1.20	2,800	$1.70	3,600

    a. Calculate nominal GDP, real GDP, and the GDP deflator using 2022 as the base year.

    Solution:

    $$NGDP_{2021} = p_{avocado,21} q_{avocado,21} + p_{peppers,21} q_{peppers,21}$$
    $$= \$0.90 \times 2{,}500 + \$1.40 \times 3{,}000$$
    $$= \$6{,}450$$

    $$NGDP_{2022} = p_{avocado,22} q_{avocado,22} + p_{peppers,22} q_{peppers,22}$$
    $$= \$1.05 \times 2{,}750 + \$1.45 \times 3{,}400$$
    $$= \$7{,}8157.50$$

    $$NGDP_{2023} = p_{avocado,23} q_{avocado,23} + p_{peppers,23} q_{peppers,23}$$
    $$= \$1.20 \times 2{,}800 + \$1.70 \times 3{,}600$$
    $$= \$9{,}480$$

$$RGDP_{2021} = p_{avocado,22}q_{avocado,21} + p_{peppers,22}q_{peppers,21}$$
$$= \$1.05 \times 2{,}500 + \$1.45 \times 3{,}000$$
$$= \$6{,}975$$

$$RGDP_{2022} = p_{avocado,22}q_{avocado,22} + p_{peppers,22}q_{peppers,22}$$
$$= \$1.05 \times 2{,}750 + \$1.45 \times 3{,}400$$
$$= \$7{,}8157.50$$

$$RGDP_{2023} = p_{avocado,22}q_{avocado,23} + p_{peppers,22}q_{peppers,23}$$
$$= \$1.05 \times 2{,}800 + \$1.45 \times 3{,}600$$
$$= \$8{,}160$$

$$GDP\,Deflator_{2021} = \frac{NGDP_{2021}}{RGDP_{2021}} \times 100$$
$$= 92.47$$

$$GDP\,Deflator_{2022} = \frac{NGDP_{2022}}{RGDP_{2022}} \times 100$$
$$= 100$$

$$GDP\,Deflator_{2023} = \frac{NGDP_{2023}}{RGDP_{2023}} \times 100$$
$$= 116.18$$

b. Compute the percent change in nominal GDP, real GDP, and the GDP deflator between 2021 and 2022.

Solution: The percent change in nominal GDP is 21.20 percent. The percent change in real GDP is 12.08 percent. The percent change in the GDP deflator is 8.14 percent.

c. Assuming the population level stayed constant in all three years, did economic well-being rise by more in 2022 or 2023? Explain.

Solution: Real GDP growth between 2022 and 2023 was 4.38 percent. Because population is constant across all three years, we can infer that GDP per capita increased by more (both in percent terms and in total) in 2022. If you believe GDP per capita is a good measure of economic well-being, then well-being increased more in 2022.

3. When a realtor helps with a property transaction, they are compensated by taking a certain percentage of the sales price of the property.

	Quantity (in thousands)	Average price (in thousands)	Realtor fees
New residential houses	25	$400	2%
Old residential houses	150	$250	5%
New factories	20	$1,500	1%
Old factories	30	$800	2%

Calculate the increase in GDP due to the sales of new and old houses and factories. Which of these sales get counted as residential fixed investment and which get counted as nonresidential fixed investment?

Solution: The sale of new residential houses counts as residential fixed investment. The sale of new factories counts as nonresidential fixed investment. The contribution of new residential houses to GDP is $25{,}000 \times \$400{,}000 = \$10{,}000{,}000{,}000$. The contribution of new factories to GDP is $20{,}000 \times \$1{,}500{,}000 = \$30{,}000{,}000{,}000$. The realtor fees for the old houses and factories get counted toward GDP. The contribution is $25{,}000 \times \$8{,}000 = \$200{,}000{,}000$ for residential houses and $20{,}000 \times \$15{,}000 = \$300{,}000{,}000$. Note that the realtor fees for the new houses and factories do **not** count towards GDP because that would be double counting.

5. GDP deflators can be calculated for various industries as well as for the entire economy. Consider the following economic data from 2022 and 2023. Gross output, intermediate inputs, and value added are in billions.

Construction	2022	2023
Gross output	$712	$760
Intermediate inputs	$204	$226
Value added	?	?
Industry deflator	105	107
Manufacturing		
Gross output	$1,240	$1,310
Intermediate inputs	?	?
Value added	$980	$1,002
Industry deflator	103	99

a. Fill in the missing values of the table.

Solution: Value added is the difference between gross output and intermediate inputs.

Construction	2022	2023
Gross output	$712	$760
Intermediate inputs	$204	$226
Value added	$508	$534
Industry deflator	105	107
Manufacturing		
Gross output	$1,240	$1,310
Intermediate inputs	$260	$308
Value added	$980	$1,002
Industry deflator	103	99

b. If the economy only consists of these two sectors, compute real GDP for both years.

Solution: Real GDP for construction and manufacturing in 2022 is $508/1.05 = $484 and $980/1.03 = $951, respectively. Real GDP for the economy in 2022 is $1,435. Real GDP for construction and manufacturing in 2023 is $534/1.07 = $499 and $1,002/99 = $1,012, respectively. Real GDP for the economy in 2023 is $1,511.

Chapter 2 Solutions

Questions for Review

1. Explain how TFP is different from the inputs in a production function.

   Solution: Instead of being a distinct input, TFP captures how efficiently the economy uses its inputs.

3. Do differences in TFP or capital per worker explain most of the variation in cross-country income?

   Solution: For plausible choices of the labor share parameter, TFP explains most of the differences.

5. Intuitively explain why the demand curves for labor and capital slope down.

   Solution: The labor demand curve is the marginal product of labor. As the wage increases, firms hire less labor, which increases the MPL.

Problems

1. For each of the following production functions list which (if any) of the four assumptions from Section 2-1b are violated.

   Solution: Recall the four assumptions: i) output requires both inputs, ii) positive marginal products, iii) diminishing marginal products, iv) constant returns to scale.

   a. $Y = L + K$

   Solution: The first assumption is clearly violated. If labor or capital increase, output increases, so the second assumption is satisfied. Output is linear in labor and capital, so the third assumption is violated. To test returns to scale, double both labor and capital: $2L + 2K = 2(L + K) = 2Y$. The fourth assumption is satisfied.

b. $Y = KL$

Solution: The first assumption is satisfied. If you fix labor and increase capital, output goes up. If you fix capital and increase labor, output goes up. So, the second assumption is satisfied. If you fix one input, the production function is linear in the other. So, the third assumption is violated. To test returns to scale, double both labor and capital: $(2K)(2L) = 4KL = 4Y$. Output is increasing returns to scale, so the fourth assumption is violated.

c. $Y = \min[K, L]$ where, for example, $Y = \min[3, 4] = 3$

Solution: The first assumption is satisfied because, $\min[0, L] = 0$ and $\min[K, 0] = 0$. If you increase one input and leave the other fixed, output stays fixed. So the second assumption is violated. Since the marginal product is zero, the third assumption is also violated. To test returns to scale, double both labor and capital: $\min[2K, 2L] = 2\min[K, L] = 2Y$. So output is constant returns to scale.

3. Depict how each of the following changes affects the level of wages or the rental rate.

   a. A plague kills 25 percent of a country's population.

   Solution: This shifts the labor supply curve to the left. Wages increase.

   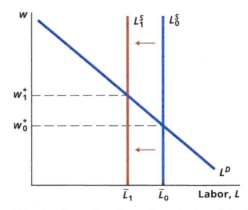

   This plot shows the effects of a reduction of the labor force.

   b. A new regulation makes it less efficient for firms to hire capital and labor.

   Solution: A regulation that makes firms less efficient can be thought of as a reduction in TFP. This shifts the demand for capital and labor inward. Wages and rental rates decline.

   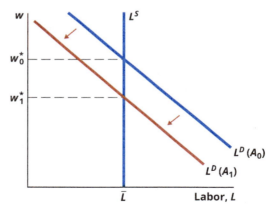

   This plot shows how an efficiency-reducing regulation affects the labor demand curve.

   c. Congress implements a law that taxes revenue at rate $0 < t < 1$. The revenue for the firm is now $(1 - t)AF(K, L)$.

   Solution: Implementing the tax has the same effects qualitatively as a reduction in TFP.

   d. Congress implements a law that taxes profit at rate $0 < t < 1$.

   Solution: Recall that profits are

   $$AF(K, L) - wL - rK.$$

Solution: With the usual production function, hours per worker are absorbed into TFP. Since hours per worker are negatively correlated with income per worker, that would make TFP differences with the new production function bigger than TFP differences in the original.

After tax profits are

$$(1 - t)(AF(K, L) - wL - rK).$$

Since revenue and costs are proportionally scaled down, it is still is optimal to equate marginal products to factor prices. Therefore, the labor and capital demand curves are unaffected by this policy.

5. Suppose the aggregate production function is given by

$$Y = AK^a(hL)^{1-a},$$

where L is the number of workers and h is the hours worked per worker in a year. The average US worker in 2019 for instance worked close to 1,800 hours over the course of the year.

a. Algebraically transform this production function into per-worker form.

Solution: Divide both sides by L:

$$
\begin{aligned}
y &= \frac{Y}{L} \\
&= \frac{AK^a(hL)^{1-a}}{L} \\
&= \frac{AK^a(hL)^{1-a}}{L^a L^{1-a}} \\
&= Ak^a h^{1-a}.
\end{aligned}
$$

b. The Penn World Tables discussed in Section 2.3 has data on h for each country. Since the PWT also has data on GDP, capital, and the number of workers, do you have enough information to infer TFP? If so, use the production function to solve for TFP as a function of these variables.

Solution: Yes. If we have data on GDP, capital, the number of workers, and hours of work, there is only one unknown in the production function. Solving for TFP gives

$$A = \frac{Y}{K^a(hL)^{1-a}}.$$

c. Output per worker and hours per worker are negatively correlated across countries. That is, workers in richer countries tend to work less than workers in poorer countries. Would this make TFP differences across countries bigger or smaller compared to the production function that omitted hours per worker (discussed in Section 2.3b)?

Solution: With the usual production function, hours per worker are absorbed into TFP. Since hours per worker are negatively correlated with income per worker, that would make TFP differences with the new production function bigger than TFP differences in the original.

Chapter 3 Solutions

Questions for Review

1. Argue that $k_t = 0$ is a steady state in the Solow Model. Do you think it is a realistic outcome given the dynamics of the model? Explain.

Solution: The capital accumulation equation is $k_{t+1} = \dfrac{1}{1 + n} \times [(1 - d)k_t + sy_t]$. If $k_t = 0$, then the entire right-hand side is 0. This means k_{t+1} is 0. This is not a realistic steady state. The reason is that if the economy starts with just a little more capital than 0, it converges to the steady state with positive capital.

3. Explain why one-time increases in the savings rate and level of TFP lead to permanently higher levels in GDP per worker, but not to permanently higher growth rates in GDP per worker.

Solution: Both of these changes increase steady-state GDP per worker. There is positive economic growth moving from the lower steady state to the higher one, but the growth ends once the economy is at the new steady state.

5. Explain the difference between unconditional and conditional convergence. Which does the Solow model predict? Which is supported by the data?

Solution: Unconditional convergence predicts initially poor countries grow faster than initially rich countries until all countries converge to the same level of income. Conditional convergence says this is only true if the economies have the same steady states. The Solow model predicts conditional convergence.

Problems

1. Suppose you have an economy with a production function and capital accumulation equation given respectively by

$$Y_t = A_t K_t^a L_t^{1-a},$$
$$K_{t+1} = (1-d)K_t + sY_t.$$

Assume the labor force grows at rate $n > 0$.

a. Convert the production function and capital accumulation equation into per-worker terms.

   Solution: Output per worker is given by

   $$y_t = \frac{A_t K_t^a L_t^{1-a}}{L_t}$$
   $$= \frac{A_t K_t^a L_t^{1-a}}{L_t^a L_t^{1-a}}$$
   $$= A_t k_t^a.$$

   The accumulation equation can be written as

   $$\frac{K_{t+1}}{L_t} = (1-d)\frac{K_t}{L_t} + s\frac{Y_t}{L_t}$$
   $$\Leftrightarrow \frac{K_{t+1}}{L_t}\frac{L_{t+1}}{L_{t+1}} = (1-d)k_t + sy_t$$
   $$\Leftrightarrow k_{t+1}(1+n) = (1-d)k_t + sy_t$$
   $$\Leftrightarrow k_{t+1} = \frac{1}{1+n}[(1-d)k_t + sy_t].$$

b. Graph the per-worker capital accumulation equation and show that the economy converges to a steady state, $k^{ss} > 0$.

   Solution: See below.

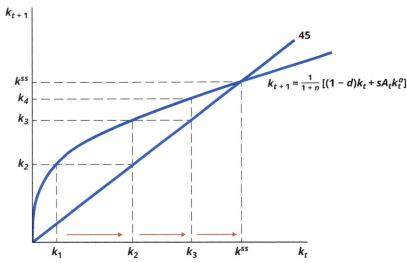

Starting at k_1 in the first year, the accumulation equation implies a capital level of k_2 next year. Tracing that over to the 45-degree line gives the capital stock in year two, k_2. Tracing up to the accumulation equation shows that the capital stock is k_3 in the third year. Repeating this process shows that the capital per worker converges to k^{ss}.

c. Show the effects on the capital accumulation line of a one-time permanent increase in the depreciation rate, d. Also plot the transition dynamics of capital per worker and output per worker.

   Solution: The effects are shown below. An increase in the depreciation rate shifts the capital accumulation line down.

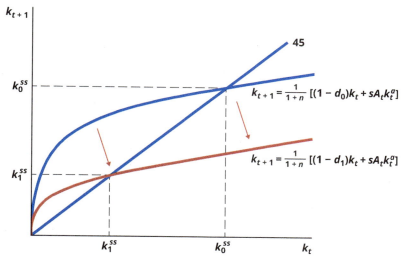

An increase in the depreciation rate shifts the capital accumulation line down. Steady-state capital per worker declines from k_0^{ss} to k_1^{ss}.

The per-worker capital stock declines until a new steady state is reached. The transition dynamics are shown below.

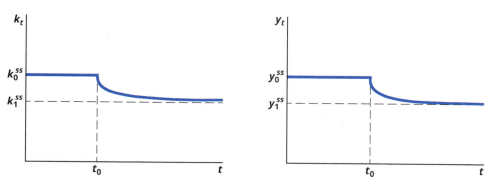

At time t_0 the depreciation rate increases from d_0 to d_1. The left panel shows the transition dynamics of capital per worker and the right panel shows the transition dynamics of output per worker.

d. Algebraically solve for the steady state of output per worker, y^{ss}, and capital per worker, k^{ss}. Solve for numeric values of these variables if $a = 1/3$, $s = 0.2$, $A_t = 1$, $d = 0.1$, and $n = 0.01$.

Solution: The equation for steady-state per worker capital is

$$k_{ss} = \left(\frac{sA_t}{d+n}\right)^{\frac{1}{1-a}}.$$

Substituting in the parameters, we get $k_{ss} = 2.45$. The equation for steady-state output per worker is

$$y_{ss} = A_t\left(\frac{sA_t}{d+n}\right)^{\frac{a}{1-a}}.$$

Substituting in the parameters, we get $y_{ss} = 1.35$.

e. If d increases to 0.15 by what percent does output per worker fall in the long run?

Solution: Steady-state output per worker is $y_{ss} = 1.12$ which is a decline of about 17 percent.

3. Suppose you have an economy with a Cobb-Douglas aggregate production function with $a = 1/3$.

a. What is the golden-rule savings rate for this economy?

Solution: 1/3.

b. Suppose the economy starts in a steady state with $s = 0.2$ and then it experiences a one-time permanent change in its savings rate to 0.3. Draw the transition dynamics of consumption per worker.

Solution: Consumption initially decreases, but as per-worker output grows over time, consumption per worker eventually exceeds its initial level.

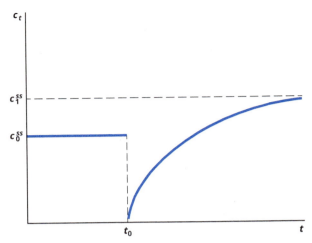

At time t_0 the savings rate increases from $s = 0.2$ to $s = 0.3$.

c. Suppose the economy starts in a steady state with $s = 0.4$ and then it experiences a one-time permanent change in its savings rate to 0.5. Draw the transition dynamics of consumption per worker.

Solution: Consumption per worker jumps down on impact, but it increases as output per worker grows. Since the savings rate exceeds the golden-rule level, consumption per-worker settles on a lower level then it was initially.

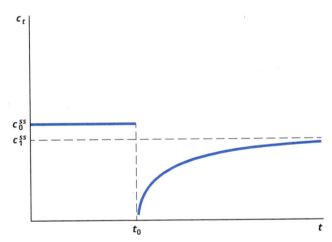

At time t_0 the savings rate increases from $s = 0.4$ to $s = 0.5$.

d. Based on your answers to parts b and c, should economic policy always look to increase a country's savings rate?

Solution: No. If a country's savings rate exceeds the golden rule, then increasing the savings rate further lowers per-worker consumption of the current and future generations.

5. Suppose an economy has the following Cobb-Douglas aggregate production function:

$$Y_t = A_t K_t^a (h_t L_t)^{1-a}$$

where h_t is the economy's human capital. You can think of human capital as the knowledge workers attain through experience and education. The capital accumulation equation is standard and population grows at rate n.

a. Convert the production function and capital accumulation equation into per-worker terms.

Solution: Output per worker is given by

$$y_t = \frac{A_t K_t^a h_t^{1-a} L_t^{1-a}}{L_t}$$

$$= \frac{A_t K_t^a h_t^{1-a} L_t^{1-a}}{L_t^a L_t^{1-a}}$$

$$= A_t h_t^{1-a} k_t^a.$$

The accumulation equation can be written as

$$\frac{K_{t+1}}{L_t} = (1-d)\frac{K_t}{L_t} + s\frac{Y_t}{L_t}$$

$$\Leftrightarrow \frac{K_{t+1}}{L_t}\frac{L_{t+1}}{L_{t+1}} = (1-d)k_t + sy_t$$

$$\Leftrightarrow k_{t+1}(1+n) = (1-d)k_t + sy_t$$

$$\Leftrightarrow k_{t+1} = \frac{1}{1+n}\big[(1-d)k_t + sy_t\big].$$

b. Algebraically solve for steady-state output per worker and capital per worker.

Solution: Impose the steady state in the accumulation equation:

$$k_{ss} = \frac{1}{1+n}\big[(1-d)k_{ss} + sy_{ss}\big]$$

$$\Leftrightarrow (n+d)k_{ss} = sA_t h_t^{1-a}k_{ss}^{1-a}$$

$$\Leftrightarrow k_{ss} = \left(\frac{A_t h_t^{1-a}s}{n+d}\right)^{\frac{1}{1-a}}.$$

Steady-state output per worker is given by

$$y_{ss} = A_t h_t^{1-a}\left(\frac{A_t h_t^{1-a}s}{n+d}\right)^{\frac{a}{1-a}}.$$

c. How does a one-time increase in h_t affect output per worker in the long run?

Solution: An increase in human capital increases output per worker in the long run. Human capital makes the economy more efficient at using the existing capital stock and it also causes the economy to accumulate more capital.

d. Human capital is a function of an economy's education level. In particular, economists conventionally write the function as an exponential function,

$$h_t = e^{bu_t}.$$

Here, u_t is the number of years of education for an average person in the economy and $b > 0$ is a parameter that represents the quality of a country's schooling. Describe two ways economic policy makers can increase an economy's human capital. What are the tradeoffs associated with each?

Solution: Economic policy could either aim to increase the average number of school years for its citizens or improve the quality of schooling. Both of these have the potential to raise output per worker in the long run. On the other hand, they both have opportunity costs. If people stay in school longer they will have fewer years to produce output on the labor market. And more resources devoted to improving school quality means that fewer resources get devoted to things like health care.

Chapter 4 Solutions

Questions for Review

1. What distinguishes an idea from other economic inputs?

   Solution: An idea is non-rival which means that one person's use does not diminish the ability of someone else to use the same idea. This is in contrast to other types of economic inputs, e.g., only one person can use a given hammer.

3. Why is the capital-to-output ratio instead of capital by itself included in growth accounting exercises?

   Solution: The economy accumulates more capital when TFP increases. If we included capital by itself, some of the credit that should go to TFP gets misattributed to capital.

5. Compare and contrast the traditional "endogenous" growth model to the "semi-endogenous" growth model.

   Solution: In traditional endogenous growth models, an increase in the number of scientists permanently raises the growth rate of output per worker. In semi-endogenous growth models, an increase in the number of scientists permanently increases the level of output per capita, but not the growth rate.

414 **Solutions**

Problems

1. Suppose the aggregate production function is

$$Y_t = A_t K_t^a (e_t P_t)^{1-a},$$

where P_t is the adult population and e_t is the fraction of the adult population that is employed. The number of employed people is $L_t = e_t P_t$.

a. Define output per capita as $y_t = \dfrac{Y_t}{P_t}$. Show that you can write output per capita as

$$y_t = A_t^{\frac{1}{1-a}} \left(\frac{K_t}{Y_t}\right)^{\frac{a}{1-a}} e_t.$$

Solution:

$$\frac{Y_t}{Y_t^a} = \frac{A_t K_t^a (e_t P_t)^{1-a}}{Y_t^a}$$

$$\Leftrightarrow Y_t^{1-a} = A_t \left(\frac{K_t}{Y_t}\right)^a (e_t P_t)^{1-a}$$

$$\Leftrightarrow Y_t = A_t^{\frac{1}{1-a}} \left(\frac{K_t}{Y_t}\right)^{\frac{a}{1-a}} e_t P_t$$

$$\Leftrightarrow y_t = A_t^{\frac{1}{1-a}} \left(\frac{K_t}{Y_t}\right)^{\frac{a}{1-a}} e_t.$$

b. Using the same change of variables as in Equation (5), show that the growth in output per capita is

$$g_y = g_a + g_k + g_e,$$

where g_y is the growth rate of output per capita, g_a is the growth rate of the TFP component, g_k is the growth of the capital to output ratio component, and g_e is the growth rate of the employment rate.

Solution: Let $\tilde{A}_t = A_t^{\frac{1}{1-a}}$ and $\tilde{k}_t = \left(\dfrac{K_t}{Y_t}\right)^{\frac{a}{1-a}}$. Then we have

$$y_t = \tilde{A}_t \tilde{k}_t e_t.$$

Then it follows that

$$g_y = g_a + g_k + g_e.$$

c. Between 1950 and 1990 the employment rate in the US rose from about 57 percent to 63 percent as more married women entered the labor force. Would omitting the employment rate from the growth accounting equation raise or lower the contribution attributed to TFP? Explain.

Solution: Omitting the employment rate increases the TFP component. The credit that should be going to employment goes to TFP instead.

3. An alternative endogenous growth model is to assume new ideas are created by R&D spending and not by scientists. The concept is that the economy allocates some GDP to consumption and the rest of it to R&D spending, perhaps on lab equipment. The production function is

$$Y_t = A_t L_t.$$

Assume that population grows at rate $n > 0$. The idea accumulation equation is

$$A_{t+1} - A_t = A_t^b R_t.$$

The economy allocates a constant fraction, s_R, to R&D spending so $R_t = s_R Y_t$.

a. Calculate TFP growth at any point in time.

Solution: Divide both sides by A_t:

$$\frac{A_{t+1} - A_t}{A_t} = \frac{A_t^b R_t}{A_t}$$

$$= \frac{R_t}{A_t^{1-b}}.$$

b. What parameter restriction must be placed on b for a balanced growth path to exist?

Solution: A BGP requires the growth rate of TFP to be constant. This requires R_t to grow at the same rate as A_t^{1-b}. Substituting the R&D equation in for R_t gives

$$\frac{A_{t+1} - A_t}{A_t} = \frac{R_t}{A_t^{1-b}}$$
$$= \frac{s_R A_t L_t}{A_t^{1-b}}$$
$$= \frac{s_R L_t}{A_t^{-b}}.$$

The only way to achieve a balanced growth path is for L_t to grow at the same rate as A_t^{-b}. This requires $b < 0$.

c. Assume $b = -1$. Calculate the growth rate of TFP and output per worker on a balanced growth path.

Solution: The growth rate of TFP is

$$\frac{A_{t+1} - A_t}{A_t} = \frac{s_R L_t}{A_t}.$$

The labor force and TFP must grow at the same rate on the BGP. So TFP grows at rate n on a BGP.

d. Suppose there is a one-time permanent increase in s_R. Describe what happens to the stock of ideas and the growth rate of ideas in the short run and the long run. Hint: You might want to use something like Figure 4.10.

Solution: TFP growth increases in the short run, but declines to the original rate, n, in the long run. The stock of ideas is permanently higher.

5. Suppose the United States government considers a massive one-time expansion in high-skilled immigration, with particular emphasis on foreign workers with a graduate degree in a STEM field. You are going to analyze this in the endogenous growth model.

a. What variable does this policy affect?

Solution: This would increase the number of research scientists, $L_{R,t}$.

b. Suppose the idea accumulation equation is identical to Section 3, namely,

$$A_{t+1} - A_t = L_{R,t} A_t^b.$$

Graphically analyze the effects of this policy. What are the short and long-run implications on the stock of ideas and idea growth **assuming $b = 0$**.

Solution: An increase in the number of research scientists increases the ratio of research scientists to TFP. The growth rate of TFP temporarily exceeds the population growth rate. Over time, the economy reverts to the initial balanced growth path.

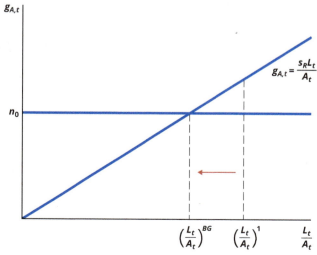

An increase in the number of research scientists increases the ratio of research scientists to TFP ratio. The growth rate of TFP temporarily exceeds the population growth rate. Over time, the economy reverts to the initial balanced growth path.

416   **Solutions**

c. Suppose instead the idea accumulation equation is

$$A_{t+1} - A_t = L_{R,t} A_t.$$

What are the short and long-run implications of this policy on the stock of ideas and idea growth?

Solution: The growth rate of TFP is

$$\frac{A_{t+1} - A_t}{A_t} = L_{R,t}.$$

A permanent increase in the number of research scientists permanently increases the growth rate of TFP.

Chapter 5 Solutions

Questions for Review

1. Describe some of the shortcomings of the CPI.

   Solution: By using a fixed consumption basket, the CPI does not account for the tendency of consumers to substitute away from more expensive items towards cheaper items. The statisticians responsible for the CPI also face a difficulty in adjusting for quality differences. For example, if the price of a car goes up 10 percent between one year and the next, is that because the car got more expensive or did its quality improve?

3. What are the strengths and weaknesses of a fiat money system?

   Solution: Unlike a commodity money system, fiat money is intrinsically worthless. The price of commodities varies based on supply and demand. Also, many commodities do not store well. Third, there are quality differences between different units of the same commodity. Finally, many commodities are imperfectly divisible. Fiat money is uniform, easily divisible, durable, and, in most economies, has its supply set by a central bank. These are strengths relative to the commodity system. On the other hand, fiat money only retains its value insofar as people believe that other people and the government will accept it. Also, fiat money is easy to print and governments may find it optimal to pay off their debts by printing money. This causes inflation.

5. What are the costs of inflation?

   Solution: Several of them include: i) inflation acts as a tax, ii) inflation imposes shoe leather costs, iii) unexpected income redistributes income, and iv) inflation can distort relative prices.

Problems

1. Suppose an economy produces tomatoes and X-ray machines. Consumers import sauerkraut from Germany.

Year	Tomatoes (in pounds)		German sauerkraut (in pounds)		X-ray machines	
	Quantity	Price	Quantity	Price	Quantity	Price
2022	8,000	$3	6,000	$4	10	$4,000
2023	10,000	$3.25	5,500	$7	12	$3,800
2024	11,000	$3.40	6,000	$5	13	$3,700

a. Compute the economy's inflation rate for 2023 and 2024 using the CPI and 2022 as a base year.

   Solution: Since x-rays are an investment good, they are not included in the CPI. The CPI in 2023 is

   $$\begin{aligned} CPI_{23} &= \frac{q_{tom,22} P_{tom,23} + q_{sauer,22} P_{sauer,23}}{q_{tom,22} P_{tom,22} + q_{sauer,22} P_{sauer,22}} \times 100 \\ &= \frac{8,000 \times \$3.25 + 6,000 \times \$7}{8,000 \times \$3 + 6,000 \times \$4} \times 100 \\ &= 141.67. \end{aligned}$$

   The CPI in 2024 is

   $$\begin{aligned} CPI_{24} &= \frac{q_{tom,22} P_{tom,24} + q_{sauer,22} P_{sauer,24}}{q_{tom,22} P_{tom,22} + q_{sauer,22} P_{sauer,22}} \times 100 \\ &= \frac{8,000 \times \$3.40 + 6,000 \times \$5}{8,000 \times \$3 + 6,000 \times \$4} \times 100 \\ &= 119.17. \end{aligned}$$

The inflation rate in 2023 was 41.67 percent. The inflation rate in 2024 was -15.88 percent.

b. Compute the economy's inflation rate for 2023 and 2024 using the CPI and 2023 as a base year. Does the choice of the base year make a difference?

Solution: The CPI in 2023 is 100 by construction. The CPI in 2022 is

$$
\begin{aligned}
CPI_{22} &= \frac{q_{tom,23}P_{tom,22} + q_{sauer,23}P_{sauer,22}}{q_{tom,23}P_{tom,23} + q_{sauer,23}P_{sauer,23}} \times 100 \\
&= \frac{10{,}000 \times \$3 + 5{,}500 \times \$4}{10{,}000 \times \$3.25 + 5{,}500 \times \$7} \times 100 \\
&= 73.2
\end{aligned}
$$

The CPI in 2024 is

$$
\begin{aligned}
CPI_{24} &= \frac{q_{tom,23}P_{tom,24} + q_{sauer,23}P_{sauer,24}}{q_{tom,23}P_{tom,23} + q_{sauer,23}P_{sauer,23}} \times 100 \\
&= \frac{10{,}000 \times \$3.40 + 5{,}500 \times \$5}{10{,}000 \times \$3.25 + 5{,}500 \times \$7} \times 100 \\
&= 86.62
\end{aligned}
$$

The inflation rate in 2023 was 36.54 percent. The inflation rate in 2024 was -36.56 percent. Yes, the choice of base year makes a difference.

c. Compute the economy's inflation rate for 2023 and 2024 using the GDP deflator and 2022 as a base year. Does using the GDP deflator make a difference?

Solution: X-rays are included in the deflator, but sauerkraut isn't because it's an import. The GDP deflator in 2023 is

$$
\begin{aligned}
Def_{23} &= \frac{q_{tom,23}P_{tom,22} + q_{ray,23}P_{ray,22}}{q_{tom,22}P_{tom,22} + q_{ray,22}P_{ray,22}} \times 100 \\
&= \frac{10{,}000 \times \$3 + 12 \times \$4{,}000}{8{,}000 \times \$3 + 10 \times \$4{,}000} \times 100 \\
&= 121.89.
\end{aligned}
$$

The GDP deflator in 2024 is

$$
\begin{aligned}
Def_{24} &= \frac{q_{tom,24}P_{tom,22} + q_{ray,24}P_{ray,22}}{q_{tom,22}P_{tom,22} + q_{ray,22}P_{ray,22}} \times 100 \\
&= \frac{11{,}000 \times \$3 + 13 \times \$4{,}000}{8{,}000 \times \$3 + 10 \times \$4{,}000} \times 100 \\
&= 132.81.
\end{aligned}
$$

The inflation rate in 2023 was 21.89 percent. The inflation rate in 2024 was 8.96 percent. Inflation under the GDP deflator is different from inflation under the CPI.

3. Consider the money demand equation:

$$
\frac{M}{P} = Yi^{-b},
$$

where $b > 0$.

a. Show that this equation is identical to the quantity equation of money, Equation (1) in the text, if velocity is equal to i^b.

Solution: The money demand equation can be rewritten as

$$
Mi^b = PY.
$$

The quantity equation is

$$
MV = PY.
$$

These last two equations are identical if $V = i^b$.

418   **Solutions**

b. How does velocity depend on the nominal interest rate? Explain the economic intuition for this.

Solution: Velocity depends positively on the nominal interest rate. A higher nominal interest rate means that the opportunity cost of money is higher. A higher opportunity cost causes people to hold less money. For a fixed nominal supply of money, people holding less money means that each unit of money must turn over faster.

5. Section 5.4d discussed why some firms do not immediately adjust their prices in response to a change in the aggregate price level. Economists have studied this formally using menu-cost models. The idea behind the menu-cost model is that there are fixed costs to updating prices. In a literal sense, there are costs to reprinting menus (even if an employee has to update the website and QR code). This question walks through a simple menu-cost model.

a. Suppose profit for a firm is given by

$$profit = N(p - c).$$

Here, N is the number of units sold, p is the price per unit, and c is the cost per unit. Under what condition does the firm make a positive profit?

Solution: $p > c$.

b. Now suppose the economy's inflation rate is $\pi > 0$. The firm does not have control over its costs, which adjust automatically with inflation, but it does set its price. If the firm chooses to update its price, it must pay a fixed cost of F. This is the menu cost. If the firm chooses not to update its price, profit is given by

$$profit = N(p - c(1 + \pi)).$$

If the firm chooses to update its price, profit is given by

$$profit = N(p(1 + \pi) - c(1 + \pi)) - F.$$

Derive a condition under which the firm chooses to update its price. How does it depend on $N, \pi, p, c,$ and F? Comment on the economic intuition.

Solution: A firm will choose to update its price if the profits from updating exceed the profits from not updating. In math,

$$N(p(1 + \pi) - c(1 + \pi)) - F > N(p - c(1 + \pi))$$
$$\Leftrightarrow Np(1 + \pi) - F > Np$$
$$\Leftrightarrow Np\pi > F.$$

A firm chooses to update its price the lower is F and the higher are $N, p,$ and π. A higher fixed cost makes changing prices costlier. A higher inflation rate makes it more attractive to change prices since costs automatically scale with inflation. An increase in (real) revenue, Np, also makes it more attractive to update prices since a given percent increase in the price level increases the level of revenues by more. For instance, if the inflation rate is 10 percent and revenue is $100, then updating prices means that revenue would increase by $10. If revenue is $200, updating prices means that revenue would increase by $20.

c. At any given time, some firms will find it optimal to raise their prices and others will find it optimal to wait. What will happen to the demand for the firms that don't update their prices?

Solution: Firms that don't update will have lower prices than firms that do. This will raise the demand for firms selling the cheaper products. This makes the analysis in parts a and b more complicated as N would be an endogenous variable in this case.

Chapter 6 Solutions

Questions for Review

1. Suppose person A's income decreases because they retire from the labor force. Person B's income decreases because they unexpectedly lose their job and enter unemployment. What will happen to the consumption levels of A and B?

Solution: Retirement is predictable, so we would expect forward-looking consumers to plan for retirement and smooth their consumption accordingly. A surprise unemployment spell is, by definition, unanticipated. This surprise decrease in income will cause consumption to fall. Therefore, we would expect person A to not change their consumption at all, whereas person B's consumption would be expected to decrease.

3. How is the income effect coming from an increase in the real interest rate different for borrowers and savers?

Solution: Savers experience a positive income effect since the interest income on their savings, i.e., $r_t S_t$, increases. Since $S_t < 0$ for borrowers, the income effect of an increase in the real interest rate is negative.

5. Suppose people come to expect government expenditures to increase in the future. How does that affect the equilibrium real interest rate and quantity of investment? Describe the economic intuition.

   Solution: An expected increase in future government spending causes expected future disposable income to decline. Since consumers are forward looking, they decrease consumption and increase savings. This shifts the savings supply curve to the right, lowering the equilibrium real interest rate and raising the equilibrium quantity of investment.

Problems

1. Suppose a person has sequential budget constraints given by
$$C_t + S_t = Y_t,$$
$$C_{t+1} = Y_{t+1} + S_t(1 + r_t).$$

   a. Algebraically derive the lifetime budget constraint.

   Solution: Solve for S_t in the second equation.
   $$S_t(1 + r_t) = C_{t+1} - Y_{t+1}$$
   $$\Leftrightarrow S_t = \frac{C_{t+1} - Y_{t+1}}{1 + r_t}.$$

   Substitute this into the period t budget constraint.
   $$C_t + S_t = Y_t,$$
   $$\Leftrightarrow C_t + \frac{C_{t+1} - Y_{t+1}}{1 + r_t} = Y_t$$
   $$\Leftrightarrow C_t + \frac{C_{t+1}}{1 + r_t} = Y_t + \frac{Y_{t+1}}{1 + r_t}.$$

   b. Graphically depict the lifetime budget constraint. Make sure you label the intercepts and slope.

   Solution: Shown in Figure 6.24

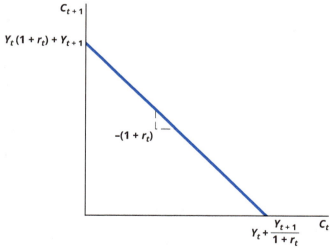

   Consumption in period t is plotted on the horizontal axis and consumption in period $t + 1$ is plotted on the vertical axis. The slope of the budget line is $-(1+r_t)$.

   c. In reality, borrowers often pay a higher rate of interest than savers receive. This can be formalized by assuming $r_b > r_s$, where r_b is the real interest rate paid by borrowers and r_s is the real interest rate received by lenders. Graphically show how this affects the budget constraint. Clearly label the point at which the person is neither a borrower nor a saver.

   Solution: If $C_t < Y_t$ then the person is a saver and subject to the interest rate $r_{s,t}$. If $C_t > Y_t$ then the person is a borrower and subject to the interest rate $r_{b,t}$. If current consumption equals current income, $C_t = Y_t$, then the person is neither a borrower nor a saver. This is shown in the following figure.

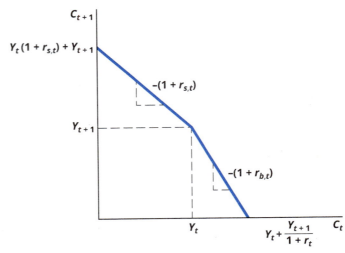

Consumption in period t is plotted on the horizontal axis and consumption in period $t+1$ is plotted on the vertical axis. If $C_t < Y_t$ then the person is a saver and subject to the interest rate $r_{s,t}$. If $C_t > Y_t$ then the person is a borrower and subject to the interest rate $r_{b,t}$.

3. Suppose a person has a marginal rate of substitution of $\dfrac{C_{t+1}}{\beta C_t}$ and a standard lifetime budget constraint.

   a. Derive the period t consumption function.

   Solution: The MRS equals price ratio condition is
   $$\frac{C_{t+1}}{\beta C_t} = 1 + r_t.$$

   Solving for C_{t+1} in terms of C_t gives $C_{t+1} = \beta(1 + r_t)C_t$. Substituting this into the lifetime budget constraint gives

   $$C_t + \frac{C_{t+1}}{1 + r_t} = Y_t + \frac{Y_{t+1}}{1 + r_t}$$

   $$\Leftrightarrow C_t + \frac{\beta(1 + r_t)C_t}{1 + r_t} = Y_t + \frac{Y_{t+1}}{1 + r_t}$$

   $$\Leftrightarrow (1 + \beta)C_t = Y_t + \frac{Y_{t+1}}{1 + r_t}$$

   $$\Leftrightarrow C_t = \frac{1}{1 + \beta}\left[Y_t + \frac{Y_{t+1}}{1 + r_t}\right].$$

   b. Assume $\beta = 0.9, r_t = 0.1, Y_t = 5$ and $Y_{t+1} = 10$. Solve for the optimal quantity of period t consumption. Is the person a saver or a borrower?

   Solution: Plugging in these parameters gives
   $$C_t = \frac{1}{1 + 0.9}\left[5 + \frac{10}{1 + 0.1}\right] = 7.42.$$

   Since $C_t > Y_t$, the person is a borrower.

   c. Derive the marginal propensity of consumption if Y_t increases from 5 to 6. How can you tell that the person is smoothing consumption across time?

   Solution: The new level of consumption is
   $$C_t = \frac{1}{1 + 0.9}\left[6 + \frac{10}{1 + 0.1}\right] = 7.94.$$

   The MPC is $7.94 - 7.42 = 0.52$. Since the MPC is less than one, we know that the person is smoothing consumption across time.

   d. Suppose the person is not allowed to borrow. Formally, $C_t \leq Y_t$. Show how this changes the graphical representation of the lifetime budget constraint.

   Solution: This is shown in the following figure. Since the consumer is not allowed to borrow, the maximum amount of period t consumption is Y_t.

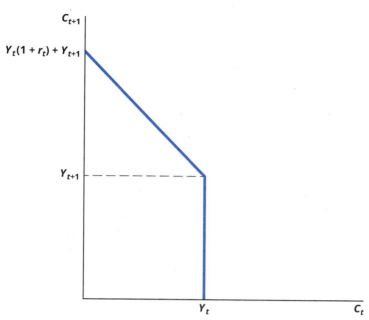

Consumption in period t is plotted on the horizontal axis and consumption in period $t + 1$ is plotted on the vertical axis. The borrowing constraint is reflected in that $C_t \leq Y_t$.

e. If $\beta = 0.9, Y_t = 5, r_t = 0.1$, and $Y_{t+1} = 10$, argue that the optimal quantity of consumption you solved for in part b is no longer feasible. What is the new optimal level of consumption?

Solution: The optimal level of consumption in the absence of the borrowing constraint is $C_t = 7.42$. But that would imply the consumer is a borrower which is not allowed once there is a borrowing constraint. Thus, the best the consumer can do is consume all of the current period income today, i.e., $C_t = 5$.

f. Derive the marginal propensity of consumption if Y_t increases from 5 to 6. Is the person smoothing consumption? What explains the difference with part c?

Solution: Again, absent the borrowing constraint, the optimal level of current-period consumption is $C_t = 7.94$. Since $7.94 > 6$ and borrowing isn't possible, the best the consumer can do is consume all of the current period income today, i.e., $C_t = 6$. This means that the marginal propensity to consume is 1. A binding borrowing constraint causes the consumer to consume all the extra income today.

g. Economic researchers have found that the marginal propensity to consume out of one-time tax cuts is highest for people who face borrowing constraints. Are your results in part f consistent with this?

Solution: Yes. If consumers don't face borrowing constraints, then we would expect that they smooth the value of their tax cut.

5. Consider a quantitative version of Question 4. The savings supply equation is given by

$$S_t = Y_t - (a_1(Y_t - G_t) + a_2(Y_{t+1} - G_{t+1}) - a_3 r_t) - G_t,$$

where a_1, a_2, and a_3 are positive constants. The investment demand equation is given by

$$I_t = b_1 A_{t+1} - b_2(r_t + f_t)$$

where b_1 and b_2 are positive constants.

a. How is the slope of the savings supply curve affected by a_3? How is the slope of the investment demand curve affected by b_2?

Solution: An increase in a_3 makes the quantity of savings supplied more sensitive to the real interest rate. This flattens the savings supply curve. By similar logic, an increase in b_2 makes the quantity of investment demanded more sensitive to the real interest rate. This flattens the investment demand curve.

422   Solutions

b. Solve for the equilibrium real interest rate.

Solution: We can find the equilibrium interest rate by setting the savings supply equal to investment demand:

$$Y_t - (a_1(Y_t - G_t) + a_2(Y_{t+1} - G_{t+1}) - a_3 r_t) - G_t = b_1 A_{t+1} - b_2(r_t + f_t)$$
$$\Leftrightarrow (a_3 + b_2) r_t = b_1 A_{t+1} - (1 - a_1)(Y_t - G_t) + a_2(Y_{t+1} - G_{t+1}) - b_2 f_t$$
$$\Leftrightarrow r_t = \frac{b_1 A_{t+1} - (1 - a_1)(Y_t - G_t) + a_2(Y_{t+1} - G_{t+1}) - b_2 f_t}{a_3 + b_2}.$$

c. How does the equilibrium real interest rate react in response to a one percentage point increase in f_t?

Solution: A one percentage point increase in f_t reduces the real interest rate by $\dfrac{b_2}{a_3 + b_2}$.

Chapter 7 Solutions

Questions for Review

1. What is the difference between a real exchange rate and a nominal exchange rate?

   Solution: The nominal interest rate is the rate at which two currencies trade for each other. The real exchange rate is the rate at which goods and services in one country trade for goods and services in another country.

3. Suppose country A is more efficient than country B at producing every single good and service. Are there still gains from trade? Explain.

   Solution: Yes, as long as there are differences in relative productivities across countries, both countries can gain by specializing in their comparative advantage.

5. How does the real exchange rate depend on the difference between the domestic real interest rate and the global real interest rate?

   Solution: If the domestic real interest rate exceeds the global real interest rate, foreign savings flows into the domestic economy which bids up the price of domestically produced goods and services, thereby appreciating the real exchange rate. The logic goes in reverse if the global real interest rate exceeds the domestic real interest rate.

Problems

1. Consider the following economic data:

Good	P_{US} (in dollars)	P_{Japan} (in yen)
10 ounces of honey	5	500
One pound of blueberries	4	700
One avocado	1	140
One pound of bacon	7	1,100

a. Suppose the dollar-to-yen exchange rate is 120 yen per dollar. Where is each good the least expensive?

   Solution: The price of US honey in yen is

   $$\$5 \times \frac{120\,yen}{\$} = 700\,yen.$$

   The price of US blueberries in yen is

   $$\$4 \times \frac{120\,yen}{\$} = 480\,yen.$$

   The price of US avocados in yen is

   $$\$1 \times \frac{120\,yen}{\$} = 120\,yen$$

The price of US bacon is

$$\$7 \times \frac{120\,yen}{\$} = 840\,yen.$$

Honey is cheaper in Japan. The other three goods are cheaper in the US.

b. Find the nominal exchange rate above which every good is less expensive in Japan.

Solution: Relative to the US, blueberries are the most expensive good in Japan. The nominal exchange rate that equates the price of blueberries in the US to the price in Japan is

$$\$4e = 700\,yen$$
$$\Leftrightarrow e = \frac{175\,yen}{\$}.$$

3. Complete the following table. In each case describe if the country is experiencing a net capital inflow or outflow. All data are in trillions of dollars.

Y	C + I + G	NX	Capital inflow or outflow?
22.3	25.7	?	?
?	24	−6	?
27	?	4	?

Solution:

Y	C + I + G	NX	Capital inflow or outflow?
22.3	25.7	−2.4	inflow
18	24	−6	inflow
27	23	4	outflow

5. Consider an algebraic version of the open-economy savings-investment model. The consumption function is given by

$$C_t = 0.7(Y_t - G_t) + 0.4(Y_{t+1} - G_{t+1}) - 100r_t.$$

The net exports function is given by

$$NX_t = Q_t - 50r_t.$$

a. Derive the savings supply function.

Solution: The savings supply function is given by

$$S_t = Y_t - C_t - G_t - NX_t.$$

Substituting in the functional forms of consumption and net exports gives

$$S_t = Y_t - (0.7(Y_t - G_t) + 0.4(Y_{t+1} - G_{t+1}) - 100r_t) - G_t - (Q_t - 50r_t)$$
$$= 0.3(Y_t - G_t) - 0.4(Y_{t+1} - G_{t+1}) - Q_t + 150r_t.$$

b. The investment demand function is given by

$$I_t = 10 - 100r_t.$$

Derive the equilibrium real interest rate as a function of the exogenous variables.

Solution: Equating investment demand with savings supply gives

$$10 - 100r_t = 0.3(Y_t - G_t) - 0.4(Y_{t+1} - G_{t+1}) - Q_t + 150r_t.$$

Solving for r_t gives

$$10 - 0.3(Y_t - G_t) + 0.4(Y_{t+1} - G_{t+1}) + Q_t = 250r_t$$
$$\Leftrightarrow r_t^* = \frac{10 - 0.3(Y_t - G_t) + 0.4(Y_{t+1} - G_{t+1}) + Q_t}{250}.$$

This is the equilibrium real interest rate, r_t^*

424   Solutions

c. Suppose $Y_t = Y_{t+1} = 30, G_t = G_{t+1} = 10$, and $Q_t = 4$. Solve for the equilibrium real interest rate and the equilibrium levels of investment, consumption, and net exports.

Solution:

$$r_t^* = \frac{10 - 0.3(Y_t - G_t) + 0.4(Y_{t+1} - G_{t+1}) + Q_t}{250}$$

$$= \frac{10 - 0.3(30 - 10) + 0.4(30 - 10) + 4}{250}$$

$$= 0.064.$$

The equilibrium real interest rate is 6.4 percent. Investment is given by

$$I_t^* = 10 - 100r_t^* = 3.6.$$

Consumption is given by

$$C_t^* = 0.7(Y_t - G_t) + 0.4(Y_{t+1} - G_{t+1}) - 100r_t^*$$

$$= 0.7(20) + 0.4(20) - 6.4 = 15.6.$$

Net exports are given by

$$NX_t^* = Q_t - 50r_t^*$$

$$= 4 - 50(0.064) = 0.8.$$

d. Suppose Y_t increases to 40. Calculate the new equilibrium levels of the real interest rate, investment, consumption, and net exports. Are these results consistent with our qualitative analysis from this chapter?

Solution: Substituting in the new values of exogenous variables gives

$$r_t^* = 0.052,$$
$$I_t^* = 4.8,$$
$$C_t^* = 23.8,$$
$$NX_t = 1.4.$$

These findings are consistent with the qualitative analysis. An increase in current-period income shifts savings supply to the right. Equilibrium investment rises and the equilibrium real interest rate falls. A fall in the equilibrium real interest rate causes the real exchange rate to depreciate and net exports to rise. Since current-period income went up and the real interest rate went down, consumption also goes up.

e. Find the level of Y_t such that trade is balanced.

Solution: Trade is balanced when $NX_t = 0$. This will only happen if

$$4 - 50r_t = 0,$$

or $r_t^* = 0.08$. That is, net exports are equal to zero when the real interest rate equals 8 percent. Substitute this equilibrium real interest rate into the savings equals investment equation:

$$10 - 100r_t = 0.3(Y_t - G_t) - 0.4(Y_{t+1} - G_{t+1}) - Q_t + 150r_t.$$

Substitute in everything we know:

$$10 - 0.3(Y_t - 10) + 0.4(20) + 4 = 250(0.08)$$
$$\Leftrightarrow 22 - 0.3(Y_t - 10) = 20$$
$$\Leftrightarrow 2 = 0.3(Y_t - 10)$$
$$\Leftrightarrow Y_t = 16.67$$

Chapter 8 Solutions

Questions for Review

1. Compare the trends in labor force participation rates for men and women over the last 70 years.

   Solution: Women's labor force participation rate increased from about 30 percent in 1950 to 60 percent in 2000. Men's labor force participation rate declined from about 88 percent in 1950 to 70 percent in 2023.

3. Labor force participation rates are lower among married women with young children compared to other demographic groups in the same age range. What does this imply about their reservation wage?

Solution: This implies that married women with young children have higher reservation wages compared to the rest of the population. This makes sense because caring for young children is an important and time-consuming obligation that increases the opportunity cost of market work.

5. Using the economics of the search and matching model, explain the effect an increase in unemployment benefits has on the unemployment rate.

   Solution: An increase in unemployment benefits increases wages and decreases the expected profits from posting a vacancy. In equilibrium, fewer vacancies are posted, the job finding rate falls, and the unemployment rate rises.

Problems

1. Consider the following economic data. LFPR is labor force participation rate and UR is unemployment rate.

Category	Men	Women
Population (in millions)	100	115
Unemployed (in millions)	3	5
Employed	?	?
LFPR	80%	85%
UR	?	?

   a. Complete the missing values of the table.

   Solution: Starting with men, if the population is 100 million and the LFPR is 80 percent, then 80 million men are in the labor force. Since 3 million of them are unemployed, 77 million men are employed. The unemployment rate is

   $$UR_{men} = \frac{3}{80} = 0.038,$$

   or 3.75 percent. Likewise for women, if there are 115 million women in the economy and 85 percent of them are in the labor force, then the number of women in the labor force is 115×0.85 or 97.75 million. If 5 million women are unemployed, then 92.75 women are employed. The unemployment rate is

   $$UR_{men} = \frac{5}{97.75} = 0.051,$$

   or 5.1 percent. The completed table is shown below.

Category	Men	Women
Population (in millions)	100	115
Unemployed (in millions)	3	5
Employed	77	92.75
LFPR	80%	85%
UR	3.8%	5.1%

   b. Calculate the LFPR and UR for the entire economy.

   Solution: There are 80 million men and 97.75 million women in the labor force. So the total size of the labor force is 177.75 million. The LFPR is

   $$LFPR = \frac{177.75}{215} = 0.827,$$

   or 82.7 percent. The unemployment rate is

   $$UR = \frac{8}{177.75} = 0.045,$$

   or 4.5 percent.

3. The budget constraint in the labor-leisure model is given by
$$C = w(24 - L) + d.$$
The budget constraint says that consumption equals wage income plus nonwage income.

a. Assuming standard-looking indifference curves, graphically depict the optimal bundle of consumption and leisure.

Solution: Shown in the following figure.

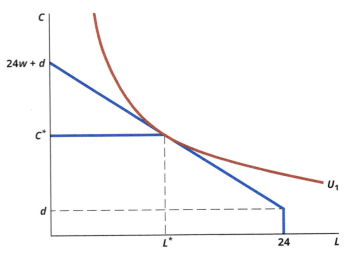

This plots the optimal amount of leisure, L^*, and consumption, C^*. The optimal allocation of consumption and leisure is found where the indifference curve is tangent to the budget constraint.

b. Suppose the marginal rate of substitution is given by kC/L. The parameter $k > 0$ can be interpreted as a person's disutility of work. The higher is k, the steeper are the indifference curves meaning that the individual is willing to trade more consumption for one more hour of leisure. Using the budget constraint given above, solve for the optimal quantities of leisure, work, and consumption. Assuming $k = 1$ and $d = 60$, solve for the reservation wage.

Solution: With $k = 1$, the MRS equals wage condition is
$$\frac{C}{L} = w.$$
This can be written as $C = wL$. Substituting this into the budget constraint gives
$$C = w(24 - L) + 60$$
$$\Leftrightarrow wL = w(24 - L) + 60$$
$$\Leftrightarrow 2wL = 24w + 60$$
$$\Leftrightarrow L^* = 12 + \frac{30}{w}.$$
Solving for consumption and work gives
$$N^* = 24 - L^* = 12 - \frac{30}{w},$$
$$C^* = wL^* = 12w + 30.$$

The reservation wage is when the optimal quantity of hours worked is 0. Solving for the reservation wage gives

$$0 = 12 - \frac{60}{2w_r},$$

or $w_r = 2.5$.

c. Assume there are three types of people in the economy each with the same marginal rate of substitution and non-wage income, but different wages. In particular, assume $w_1 = 4, w_2 = 8$, and $w_3 = 12$. The economy's population consists of an equal number of all three types. What is the labor force participation rate in this economy?

Solution: Since the wages for each type of worker exceed the reservation wage, the LFPR is 100 percent.

d. During the first few months of the COVID-19 pandemic people were reluctant to go to work for fear of being infected with the virus. From the perspective of the model, this can be viewed as an increase in k. Assuming k doubles from 1 to 2, calculate the new reservation wage. How does this affect the labor force participation rate in the economy?

Solution: The new MRS equals wage equation is

$$\frac{2C}{L} = w.$$

Substituting this into the budget constraint gives

$$C = w(24 - L) + 60$$
$$\Leftrightarrow \frac{wL}{2} = w(24 - L) + 60$$
$$\Leftrightarrow 1.5wL = 24w + 60$$
$$\Leftrightarrow L^* = 16 + \frac{40}{w}.$$

Hours worked equals $N^* = 24 - 16 - \frac{40}{w} = 8 - \frac{40}{w}$. Imposing $N^* = 0$ and solving for the reservation wage gives

$$0 = 8 - \frac{40}{w_r},$$

or $w_r = 5$. Since one-third of the population has a wage of 4 which is below the reservation wage, the LFPR is 66.7 percent.

5. Suppose that an unemployed worker in the labor search model receives unemployment benefits of b, but also gets some extra enjoyment from watching TV, tv. Employed workers don't get to enjoy TV, so the value of being unemployed is $b + tv$.

a. How does the introduction of TV change the match surplus between a firm and worker?

Solution: Match surplus is the value of output net of the value of being unemployed, or $z - b - tv$.

b. Solve for the new equilibrium wage assuming workers and firms split the surplus 50-50.

Solution: The value to the worker of being employed is $w - b - tv$. Assuming that the worker captures half of the surplus gives

$$w - b - tv = \frac{z - b - tv}{2}$$
$$\Leftrightarrow w = 0.5(w + b + tv).$$

c. Suppose the quality of daytime TV increases. In a graph similar to Figure 8.24 show how the increase in TV quality affects the equilibrium wage and job-filling rate.

Solution: The following figure shows that the equilibrium wage increases as does the job-filling rate.

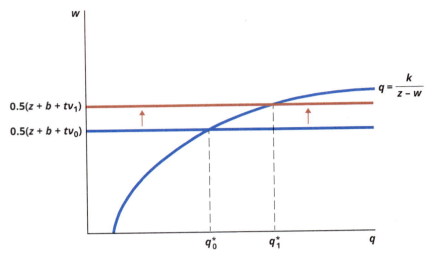

This plots an increase in TV quality from tv_0 to tv_1. The equilibrium wage rises from $0.5(z + b + tv_0)$ to $0.5(z + b + tv_1)$. The job-filling rate rises from q_0^* to q_1^*.

d. How does the increase in TV quality affect the equilibrium number of vacancies and the unemployment rate?

Solution: Since the job-filling rate goes up, the equilibrium number of vacancies goes down. A lower number of vacancies means a lower job-finding rate and a higher end-of-period unemployment rate. Effectively, an increase in TV quality is qualitatively identical to an increase in unemployment benefits.

Chapter 9 Solutions

Questions for Review

1. What are the biggest components of the government's budget? How has this changed over time?

   Solution: Consumption and transfers are the biggest components, jointly accounting for over 80 percent of current expenditure. However, consumption's share has declined over time whereas the share spent on transfers has risen.

3. Explain why transfer payments don't enter into the calculation of GDP. Since transfer payments don't enter GDP, are they still important for the macroeconomy? Explain.

   Solution: A transfer moves resources from one person to a different person. Nothing is produced. Since GDP is a measure of domestic production, transfers aren't included. Transfers are still important for the macroeconomy because they affect people's decisions. For instance, social security, which taxes you while you are young and provides a pension when you are retired influences labor supply.

5. What assumptions go into the Ricardian Equivalence Theorem? Is the Theorem likely to hold in reality?

   Solution: The theorem assumes that households are forward looking, borrow and save at the same rate as the government, and have the same lifespan as the government. It also assumes that taxes are lump sum rather than distortionary. The first assumption is questionable and none of the last three hold in the real world.

Problems

1. Imagine you earn $Y_t - T_t$ in disposable income today and $Y_{t+1} - T_{t+1}$ in the future. Rather than pay T_t in period t the tax authority allows you to defer the liability to period $t + 1$. If you defer paying T_t to the next period, the government also charges you a fine of F. Assuming you can borrow and save at a real interest rate of r_t, derive a condition on $T_t, r_t,$ and F such that you prefer deferring taxes.

Solution: If you pay the period t taxes in period t the present discounted value of lifetime income is

$$Y_t - T_t + \frac{Y_{t+1} - T_{t+1}}{1 + r_t}.$$

If you pay the period t taxes in period $t + 1$ the present discounted value of lifetime income is

$$Y_t + \frac{Y_{t+1} - T_{t+1} - T_t - F}{1 + r_t}.$$

You prefer deferring taxes if

$$Y_t - T_t + \frac{Y_{t+1} - T_{t+1}}{1 + r_t} < Y_t + \frac{Y_{t+1} - T_{t+1} - T_t - F}{1 + r_t}$$

$$\Leftrightarrow -T_t < -\frac{(T_t + F)}{1 + r_t}$$

$$\Leftrightarrow T_t(1 + r_t) - T_t > F$$

$$\Leftrightarrow T_t r_t > F.$$

Holding all else constant, you prefer deferring taxes if the penalty is small, the real interest rate is big, or the period t tax liability is big.

3. **[Difficult]** One assumption driving the Ricardian Equivalence Theorem is that individuals have the same lifespan as the government. This example shows what happens when that assumption is removed. Suppose individuals live two periods, but the government lives forever. The individual earns 100 in income in both periods. In period t, a younger person has the budget constraint

$$C_{y,t} + S_t = 100 - T_t.$$

In words, the consumption of the younger person, $C_{y,t}$, plus savings, S_t, equals disposable income, $100 - T_t$. In period $t + 1$ the budget constraint is

$$C_{o,t+1} = (1 + r_t)S_t + 100.$$

The consumption of an older person $C_{o,t+1}$ equals the principal plus interest earnings on their savings plus income.

a. Suppose the government wants to consume 10 units of output in period t. Suppose they finance this consumption by raising taxes so $T_t = 10$. Since the government isn't borrowing, we can infer that the younger individual isn't saving, $S_t = 0$. Solve for the optimal levels of consumption directly from the budget constraints. Assuming that the marginal rate of substitution is $\dfrac{C_{o,t+1}}{0.9 C_{y,t}}$, use the fact that the MRS equals $1 + r$ to solve for the equilibrium real interest rate.

   Solution: If $T_t = 10$ and $S_t = 0$ it must be the case that $C_{y,t} = 100 - 10 = 90$ and $C_{o,t+1} = 100$. Using the fact that the marginal rate of substitution must equal $1 + r_t$ we get

   $$\frac{100}{0.9(90)} = 1.23.$$

   Thus, the equilibrium real interest rate is 0.23 or 23 percent.

b. Suppose instead that the government borrows the funds so that $S_t = 10$ and $T_t = 0$. In period $t + 1$ they raise taxes on the young. Calculate the new levels of $C_{y,t}, C_{o,t+1}$, and r_t. Does Ricardian Equivalence hold?

   Solution: If $S_t = 10$ and $T_t = 0$ then $C_{y,t} = 90$. Consumption for the older person in $t + 1$ is given by the equation

   $$C_{o,t+1} = (1 + r_t)S_t + 100$$
   $$= (1 + r_t)10 + 100.$$

430 Solutions

There are two unknowns in this equation, r_t and $C_{o,t+1}$. From the MRS equals price ratio condition we get

$$\frac{C_{o,t+1}}{0.9C_{y,t}} = 1 + r_t$$
$$\Leftrightarrow C_{o,t+1} = 0.9(90)(1 + r_t).$$

Substitute this into the $t + 1$ budget constraint for the older person:

$$C_{o,t+1} = (1 + r_t)10 + 100$$
$$\Leftrightarrow 81(1 + r_t) = (1 + r_t)10 + 100$$
$$\Leftrightarrow 71(1 + r_t) = 100$$
$$\Leftrightarrow 1 + r_t = \frac{100}{71}.$$

Thus, $1 + r_t = 1.41$. Finally, consumption for the older person in $t + 1$ is

$$C_{o,t+1} = 0.9(90)(1 + r_t) = 114.08.$$

Comparing the solutions to parts a and b, it's clear that Ricardian Equivalence does not hold. The interest rate is higher in part b and so is the consumption of the older person in $t + 1$. Intuitively, under deficit financing, the young person in period t understands that that tax will be paid by next period's young. Thus, the young person today does not internalize the government's budget constraint. This is what people are talking about when they say we are "saddling the next generation with debt".

c. Suppose that members of the older generation care about the welfare of the younger generation. In particular, the older generation feels guilty about leaving the younger generation with a tax liability. To compensate for this, the older generation leaves the younger generation a bequest, B, which changes the period $t + 1$ the budget constraint to

$$C_{o,t+1} = (1 + r_t)S_t + 100 - B.$$

Continuing to assume that the government borrows in period t and imposes taxes on the young in $t + 1$, calculate the bequest level such that the levels of consumption and real interest rate in part c are identical to part a. Explain the intuition of your findings.[1]

Solution: The real interest rate must be 23 percent and consumption of the older generation in $t + 1$ must equal 100. Substituting these values into the $t + 1$ budget constraint for the older generation gives

$$C_{o,t+1} = (1 + r_t)S_t + 100 - B$$
$$\Leftrightarrow 100 = 1.23(10) + 100 - B$$
$$\Leftrightarrow B = 12.3.$$

Thus, the level of bequests must equal 12.3. Intuitively, the generation in period t effectively internalizes the government's budget constraint by leaving bequests to the next generation. The generation born in $t + 1$ has to pay the government's debt, but they also get an equal and offsetting bequest from the previous generation. Thus, if people are altruistic across generations, the Ricardian Equivalence theorem can still hold.

5. Suppose the economy's investment demand curve is

$$I_t = I(r_t + f_t, A_{t+1}).$$

The economy's aggregate supply of savings is the sum of private savings and public savings, or

$$S_t = Y_t - C_t - T_t + T_t - G_t.$$

a. Assuming Ricardian Equivalence holds and the consumption function is $C_t = C(Y_t - G_t, Y_{t+1} - G_{t+1}, r_t)$. What is the impact of a decrease in T_t assuming current and future government expenditures stay constant? Explain your answer.

Solution: A decrease in T_t without a decrease in current or future government spending implies that taxes must rise by an equal amount (in present discounted value terms) in the future period. Consumption doesn't change, neither does equilibrium investment or the real interest rate.

---

[1]For a formal treatment of this, see: Barro, Robert J. 1974. "Are Government Bonds Net Wealth?" *Journal of Political Economy*, 82(6): 1095–1117.

b. Instead, assume the consumption function is $C_t = C(Y_t - T_t)$. Plot the effects on a decrease in T_t. What happens to the equilibrium real interest rate and level of investment?

Solution: A decrease in taxes causes consumption to increase and savings supply to shift to the left. Equilibrium investment declines and the real interest rate increases. This is shown in the following figure.

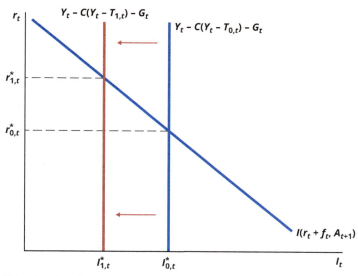

This plots the effect of a decrease in current-period taxes. An increase in T_t from $T_{0,t}$ to $T_{1,t}$ shifts the supply of savings to the left. In equilibrium, the real interest rate increases from $r^*_{0,t}$ to $r^*_{1,t}$ and investment decreases from $I^*_{0,t}$ to $I^*_{1,t}$.

c. Compare your results from parts a and b. Are they the same or different? What is the intuition behind your conclusions.

Solution: They are different. In part a, the consumer anticipates the increase in future taxes and the equilibrium is unaffected by the timing in taxes. In part b, the consumer only responds to changes in current disposable income, so an increase in current disposable income affects consumption, savings, and the real interest rate.

7. The law of motion for the government's debt-to-GDP ratio is

$$b_t = \frac{(1+r)b_{t-1}}{(1+z_t)} - s_t.$$

The CBO projects that the average primary deficit will average 2.5 percent in 2023–2032, 3.4 percent in 2033–2042, and 4.8 percent in 2043–2052. If r is the annual interest rate, then the interest accumulated over 10 years is $(1+r)^{10}$. Likewise, growth in GDP accumulated over 10 years is $(1+z_t)^{10}$.

a. Assuming $z_t = r = 0.02$ complete the rest of the table. Note that deficit over each ten-year period has been summed.[2] What happens to the debt-to-GDP ratio over time?

Year	b_{t-10}	s_t	b_t
2032	1.20	−0.25	
2042		−0.34	
2052		−0.48	

Solution: If $r = z_t$, the rest of the table is

Year	b_{t-10}	s_t	b_t
2032	1.20	−0.25	1.45
2042	1.45	−0.34	1.79
2052	1.79	−0.48	2.27

---

[2] Technically, the future deficits should be discounted, but that depends on the values of r and z, so we ignore that.

432   **Solutions**

b. An optimistic projection for the government might be $z_t = 0.03$ and $r = 0$. Redo the table under these values. Comment on your findings.

Solution: The rest of the table is

Year	b_{t-10}	s_t	b_t
2032	1.20	−0.25	0.92
2042	1.14	−0.34	1.19
2052	1.19	−0.48	1.37

The debt goes down in the first ten years before expanding in the next two decades. Relative to part a, debt accumulation is slower.

c. A pessimistic projection for the government might be $z_t = 0.01$ and $r = 0.03$. Redo the table under these values. Comment on your findings.

Solution: The rest of the table is

Year	b_{t-10}	s_t	b_t
2032	1.20	−0.25	1.71
2042	1.71	−0.34	2.42
2052	2.42	−0.48	3.42

The debt accumulates much faster than in part a.

d. Assuming the primary deficit stabilizes at $s = -0.05$ and r stabilizes at 0.02, find the value of z_t such that the debt-to-GDP ratio stays constant over time.

Solution: The value of the debt-to-GDP ratio must solve

$$1.2 = \frac{(1+r)1.2}{(1+z_t)} - s_t$$

$$\Leftrightarrow 1.2\left(1 - \frac{1.02}{1+z_t}\right) = 0.05$$

$$\Leftrightarrow z_t = 0.064$$

In other words, the economy must grow at 6.4 percent.

Chapter 10 Solutions

Questions for Review

1. If one is interested in analyzing business cycles, why is it necessary to remove trends when dealing with non-stationary data?

Solution: Non-stationary data such as GDP trends up over time. Simply looking at the raw data series wouldn't allow one to isolate the trend component from the cyclical component. To isolate the cyclical component of the series, it is necessary to remove the trend.

3. Explain the difference between trend GDP and potential GDP.

Solution: Trend GDP is a statistical concept. It essentially tells us the average rate of GDP growth over a predetermined number of periods. Potential GDP is a theoretical concept. It tells us the amount of output the economy could produce if all of the factors of production (such as labor, capital, and raw materials) were used efficiently.

5. How do investment and consumption comove with real GDP over the business cycle? Are the movements consistent with consumption–savings theory?

Solution: Investment, output, and real GDP are positively correlated with each other. Consumption is less volatile then real GDP and investment is more volatile. These features are consistent with consumption-savings theory. In the face of a volatile income stream, individuals smooth their consumption, so when income rises (falls), consumption rises (falls), but by a lower magnitude. Since consumption is less volatile than real GDP savings/investment is more volatile.

7. Do cyclical movements in TFP explain cyclical movements in real GDP?

Solution: The answer in part depends on how TFP is measured. If variable utilization isn't considered, then TFP and GDP are highly correlated which is consistent with the view that variation in TFP explains cyclical movements in real GDP. However, accounting for variable utilization significantly reduces the correlation between cyclical real GDP and TFP. Since accounting for variable utilization is a better measure of TFP, the variation in TFP as measured in the data likely doesn't explain a quantitatively large fraction of cyclical variation in real GDP.

Problems

1. Suppose you are an economist at the Federal Reserve and your job is to calculate the output gap—defined as the difference between actual GDP and potential GDP. Assume that trend GDP increases at $250 billion per quarter. Fill in the missing table entries below.

Quarter	Actual	Potential	Trend	Cycle	Output gap
t	$1,000	$1,000	$1,000	$0	$0
$t+1$	$1,200	$1,100			
$t+2$	$1,475	$1,700			
$t+3$	$1,800	$2,000			

Solution:

Quarter	Actual	Potential	Trend	Cycle	Output gap
t	$1,000	$1,000	$1,000	$0	$0
$t+1$	$1,200	$1,100	$1,250	−$50	$100
$t+2$	$1,475	$1,700	$1,500	−$25	−$225
$t+3$	$1,800	$2,000	$1,750	$50	−$200

Chapter 11 Solutions

Questions for Review

1. What elements of the IS curve are forward looking? Explain the economic logic for each of these.

   Solution: Consumption is forward looking because consumption is a function of lifetime income. Investment is also forward looking because investment in the current period goes towards capital that will be used in the next period.

3. The fed funds rate is a very short-run (overnight) interest rate. The interest rates that affect people's decisions, such as car loans and mortgages, are typically over longer horizons. How does the choice of the fed funds rate affect these longer-run interest rates?

   Solution: The Fed's choice of the short-run interest rate influences interest rates over longer horizons through a term structure channel in which interest rates on loans of longer horizons are functions of the expected sequence of short-run interest rates.

5. Why is conventional monetary policy rendered ineffective at the ZLB? What alternatives are open to the central bank?

   Solution: One alternative is forward guidance in which the central bank makes promises about interest rates in the future. Another option is to purchase bonds with longer maturities or bonds that originated in the private sector such as mortgages.

Problems

1. The investment demand curve, consumption function, and aggregate expenditure equation are respectively given by

$$I_t = I(r_t + f_t, A_{t+1}),$$
$$C_t = C(Y_t - G_t, Y_{t+1} - G_{t+1}, r_t),$$
$$Y_t = C_t + I_t + G_t.$$

a. Graphically derive the IS curve.

   Solution:

The derivation of the IS curve starts at a point $(r_{0,t}, Y_{0,t})$. An increase in income to $Y_{1,t}$ shifts savings supply to the right and lowers the equilibrium real interest rate to $r_{1,t}$. A decrease in income to $Y_{2,t}$ increases the equilibrium real interest rate to $r_{2,t}$. The set of (r_t, Y_t) pairs consistent with equilibrium in the market for savings and investment is drawn on the right.

b. Draw the effects of an increase in current-period government spending.

   Solution:

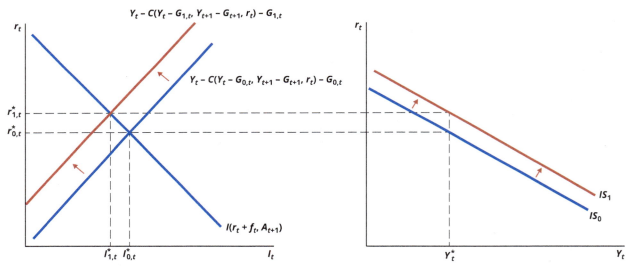

An increase in the level of government spending from $G_{0,t}$ to $G_{1,t}$ shifts the savings supply curve to the left and shifts the IS curve to the right.

c. Suppose instead that government spending increases in both periods by the same amount. Can you tell how the IS curve shifts now?

   Solution: One can't tell which direction the IS curve moves. An increase in current-period spending alone shifts the IS curve to the right (as shown in the solution to part b). An increase in future-period government spending shifts the IS curve to the left.

3. Suppose the investment demand function, consumption function, and aggregate expenditure equation are the same as in problem 1. Assume the MP curve is

$$r_t = i_t - \pi^e.$$

   a. Show graphically how an increase in current-period government, G_t, spending affects equilibrium output and the real interest rate. How do consumption and investment change in equilibrium?

   Solution: This was shown in Figure 11.11. The increase in current-period government spending shifts the IS curve to the right. Equilibrium output increases and the real interest rate stays the same. Equilibrium investment does not change. It looks as though the change in $Y_t - G_t$, and therefore the change in consumption, is ambiguous. But, as mentioned in the chapter, it can be shown that output rises one-for-one with government spending so consumption does not change.

   b. Now assume the consumption function is

$$C_t = C(Y_t - T_t, r_t).$$

   Now consumption depends on current (rather than lifetime) disposable income. Under this consumption function, the individual does not internalize the government's intertemporal budget constraint. Redo part a assuming that the government runs a balanced budget. Compare your results to part a.

   Solution: The following figure combines parts b and c. When the government finances its spending through current-period taxes, the results are identical to part a. The increase in government spending shifts savings supply to the left which shifts the IS curve to the right. The new IS curve is labeled "BB" for balanced budget. Equilibrium output increases, neither consumption nor investment change.

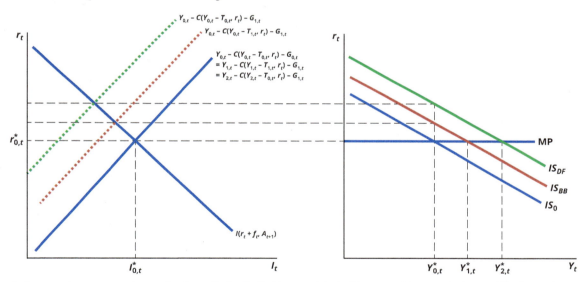

   An increase in government spending from $G_{0,t}$ to $G_{1,t}$ that is associated with an equal increase in taxes shifts the savings supply curve to the left, which in turn shifts the IS curve to the right. The new IS curve is denoted by IS_{BB} where "BB" is for balanced budget. If the same increase in government spending is financed by running a deficit, then the savings supply curve shifts even further to the left and the IS curve shifts to IS_{DF} where "DF" is for deficit financing. Equilibrium output rises to $Y^*_{1,t}$ under a balanced budget and $Y^*_{2,t}$ with deficit financing.

   c. Continue to assume the same consumption function as part b, but now assume the government finances the increase in government spending through borrowing. Graphically show how this affects equilibrium output and the real interest rate. How do consumption and investment change in equilibrium? Compare the magnitude of the changes in the real interest rate, output, consumption, and investment in parts b and c. Does the method of government financing make a difference?

   Solution: Yes, the method of financing makes a difference. An increase in government spending that is deficit financed reduces the supply of savings by more than the balanced budget scenario. The new IS curve is denoted with a "DF" for deficit financed. Equilibrium output rises by more under deficit financing. Since the real interest rate doesn't change, investment continues to remain constant. Since output increased by more in part c than part b, consumption must rise under deficit financing. This makes sense, because current-period disposable income has gone up.

436   **Solutions**

5. Suppose the consumption function and investment demand curve are given by

$$C_t = 0.8(Y_t - G_t) + 0.6(Y_{t+1} - G_{t+1}) - 5r_t,$$

$$I_t = A_{t+1} - (r_t + f_t).$$

a. Algebraically derive the IS curve.

Solution: The IS curve is

$$Y_t = 0.8(Y_t - G_t) + 0.6(Y_{t+1} - G_{t+1}) - 5r_t + A_{t+1} - (r_t + f_t) + G_t$$

$$\Leftrightarrow Y_t = G_t + 3(Y_{t+1} - G_{t+1}) - 25r_t + 5A_{t+1} - 5(r_t + f_t).$$

b. Assume the MP curve is given by

$$r_t = i_t - \pi^e.$$

Derive expressions for the equilibrium real interest rate and equilibrium level of output.

Solution: Substituting the MP curve into the IS curve gives

$$Y_t = G_t + 3(Y_{t+1} - G_{t+1}) - 25(i_t - \pi^e) + 5A_{t+1} - 5(i_t - \pi^e + f_t).$$

c. Assume $Y_{t+1} - G_{t+1} = 70$, $G_t = 20$, $f_t = 0$, $A_{t+1} = 10$, $i_t = 4$, and $\pi^e = 2$. Solve for the equilibrium real interest rate and output.

Solution: The equilibrium real interest rate is $4 - 2 = 2$. The equilibrium level of output is

$$Y_t = 20 + 3(70) - 25(2) + 5(10) - 5(2) = 220.$$

d. Suppose G_t increases to 40. How does output change in equilibrium? What is the government spending multiplier?

Solution: The new equilibrium level of output is

$$Y_t = 40 + 3(70) - 25(2) + 5(10) - 5(2) = 240.$$

An increase of government spending by 20, increases output by 20. Thus, the government spending multiplier is 1.

e. Suppose G_t increases to 40. How must the Fed change the nominal interest rate to keep output at the same level as part c?

Solution: The real interest rate that keeps output at 220 can be found by solving the equation

$$220 = 40 + 3(70) - 25r_t + 5(10) - 5r_t.$$

Solving for r_t gives 2.67 percent. So the Fed must raise the nominal interest rate from 4 percent to 4.67 percent.

Chapter 12 Solutions

Questions for Review

1. Explain the economic rationale for sticky nominal wages.

Solution: Wage negotiation is a costly process. Because of this, employers and employees often agree to negotiate wages during certain periods of the year. Wages are sticky during the periods they aren't negotiated.

3. How should monetary policy move the nominal interest rate in response to a decrease in the IS curve? Relative to the case of monetary policy inaction, what happens to the real interest rate and level of output?

Solution: A decrease in the IS curve moves output below its potential level. Monetary policy should cut the nominal interest rate which, through the Fisher equation, will lower the real interest rate and shift the MP curve down. Monetary policy should continue to cut the nominal interest rate until output is back at potential.

5. To what extent does the IS-MP-AS model explain business cycle facts such as the positive comovement of output, consumption, and investment and the negative relationship between cyclical output and unemployment?

Solution: If business cycles are caused by changes to potential output and the central bank behaves optimally, then consumption, investment, and output comove together. Output and employment would also be positively correlated. If business cycles are caused by changes to demand-side variables such as future productivity and the risk premium, then the model can explain the data if the central bank behaves passively. On net, it's likely that a central bank like the Fed behaves somewhere between passive and optimal monetary policy and the economy is hit with a mix of supply-side and demand-side shocks.

Problems

1. This question investigates the effects of TFP shocks on the flexible price/wage AS curve and the sticky wage AS curve.

   a. Using the four-part graph of Figure 12.3 show how an increase in TFP affects the flexible price/wage AS curve.

   Solution: This is shown in the following figure. An increase in TFP shifts labor demand to the right and the production function up. The flexible price/wage AS curve shifts to the right.

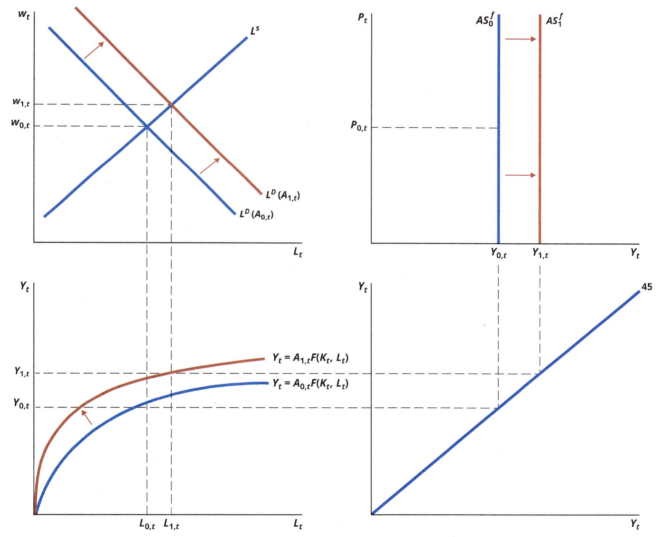

An increase in TFP from $A_{0,t}$ to $A_{1,t}$ shifts the labor demand curve to the right and the production function up. Real wages, labor, and output rise. The aggregate supply curve shifts to the right.

   b. Using the four-part graph of the following figure show how an increase in TFP affects the sticky wage AS curve.

   Solution: This is shown in the following figure. An increase in TFP shifts labor demand to the right. At the given price level of $P_{0,t}$, firms hire $L_{1,t}$ units of labor. Note that the quantity of labor hired by firms is more than the quantity supplied. This represents unemployment decreasing.

438   Solutions

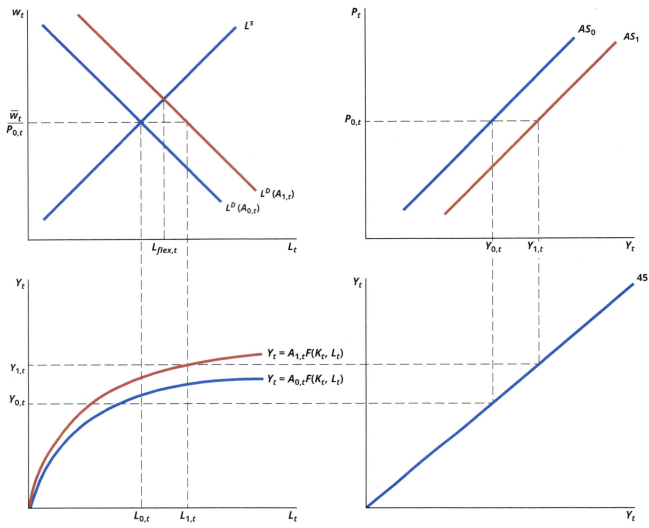

The increase in TFP from $A_{0,t}$ to $A_{1,t}$ shifts the labor demand curve to the right. Firms increase their hiring from $L_{0,t}$ to $L_{1,t}$ and the AS curve shifts to the right. For reference, $L_{flex,t}$ is the quantity of labor hired if nominal wages are flexible.

    c. Does the flexible price/wage AS curve shift by more or less than the sticky wage AS curve? Explain the economic intuition.

    Solution: The sticky wage AS curve shifts by more. The reason is that real wages don't rise in the sticky wage case so firms find it optimal to hire more workers than in the flexible price/wage case.

3. This question investigates how expectations over future policy affect the real interest rate, output, and inflation.

    a. Suppose individuals and businesses come to learn that the government plans to increase government spending, G_{t+1}. Assuming the Fed keeps nominal interest rates constant, show what happens to output, inflation, and the real interest rate in the IS-MP-AS graphs. How are consumption, investment, and unemployment affected?

    Solution: An increase in future-period government spending causes households to cut back on their consumption today which shifts the IS curve to the left. Equilibrium output and inflation fall. Because the Fed follows a passive monetary policy, the real interest rate stays constant. This is shown in the following figure. The lower level of output today and the expected reduction in future disposable income reduce consumption. Investment doesn't change. Since output goes down, but TFP stays fixed, unemployment goes up.

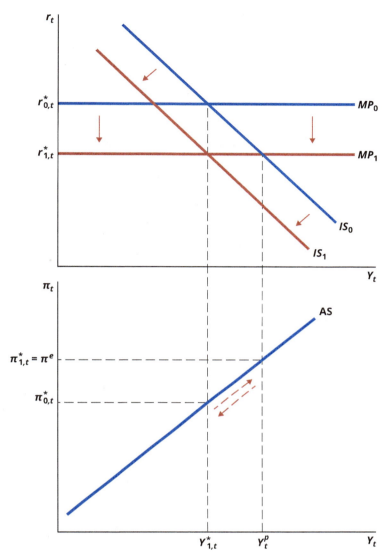

An increase in future-period government spending shifts the IS curve to the left. If monetary policy does nothing, the inflation rate falls from $\pi^*_{0,t}$ to $\pi^*_{1,t}$ and output falls from Y^p_t to $Y^*_{1,t}$. The optimal monetary policy is to lower the nominal interest rate up to the point where the real interest rate equals $r^*_{1,t}$. Inflation and output return to their original levels.

b. What is optimal monetary policy in this case?

Solution: Optimal monetary policy is expansionary. In particular, the Fed would lower the nominal interest rate which, through the Fisher equation, would lower the real interest rate until output is back at potential.

c. Suppose instead that individuals and businesses come to learn that the government plans to deregulate certain sectors of the economy which are expected to raise future productivity, A_{t+1}. Assuming the Fed keeps nominal interest rates constant, show what happens to output, inflation, and the real interest rate in the IS-MP-AS graph. How are consumption, investment, and unemployment affected?

Solution: An increase in future productivity increases investment. To the extent it raises future income, forward-looking consumers also increase their consumption. Together these shift the IS curve to the right which increases equilibrium output and inflation. This is shown in the following figure. Consumption and investment both go up in equilibrium and unemployment falls.

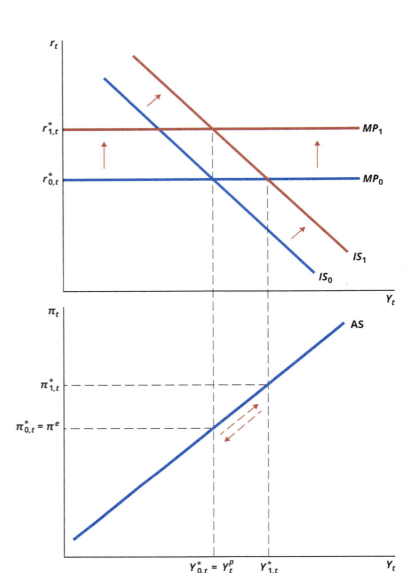

An increase in future-period TFP shifts the IS curve to the right. If monetary policy does nothing, the inflation rate rises from $\pi^*_{0,t}$ to $\pi^*_{1,t}$ and output rises from Y^p_t to $Y^*_{1,t}$. The optimal monetary policy is to raise the nominal interest rate up to the point where the real interest rate equals $r^*_{1,t}$. Inflation and output return to their original levels.

d. What is optimal monetary policy in this case?

Solution: Optimal monetary policy is contractionary. In particular, the Fed would raise the nominal interest rate which, through the Fisher equation, would increase the real interest rate until output is back at potential.

5. In your principles of macroeconomics class, you may have seen the aggregate demand (AD) curve. With a slight change to the MP rule, we can also derive the AD curve. Continue to assume that inflation expectations, π^e are taken as exogenous. Assume that the real interest rate is set according to the equation

$$r_t = \bar{r} + b_\pi(\pi_t - \bar{\pi}).$$

The long-run real interest rate is $\bar{r}$ and $\bar{\pi}$ is the Fed's inflation target. The parameter, b_π governs how sensitive the real interest rate is to deviations in inflation from target.

a. Assume $\pi_t = \bar{\pi}$. Graphically depict the MP curve. Does it look any different than the regular MP curve from this and the previous chapter?

Solution: The MP curve looks the same since the MP rule isn't a function of output.

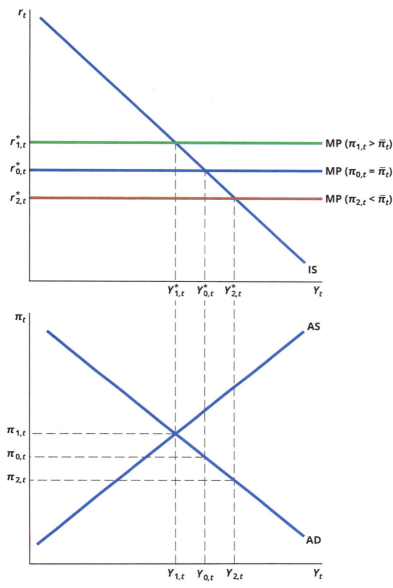

The top panel depicts the IS-MP curves. The bottom panel shows the AS-AD diagram. An increase in inflation causes the real interest rate to increase according to the MP rule, which causes output to go down.

b. Suppose inflation increases so $\pi_t > \bar{\pi}$. Show how this affects the MP curve. What happens to output?

Solution: This is shown in the previous figure. An increase in the inflation rate from $\pi_{0,t}$ to $\pi_{1,t}$ causes the real interest rate to increase via the MP rule. Output declines.

c. Suppose inflation decreases so $\pi_t < \bar{\pi}$. Show how this affects the MP curve. What happens to output?

Solution: This is shown in the previous figure. A decrease in the inflation rate from $\pi_{0,t}$ to $\pi_{2,t}$ causes the real interest rate to decrease via the MP rule. Output increases.

d. Generalizing your findings from parts b and c, graph the relationship between output and the inflation rate. This is the AD curve. Put the AS curve in the same graph.

Solution: This is shown in the bottom panel of the previous figure.

e. Suppose a change in an exogenous variable shifts the IS curve to the right. Show how this affects the IS-MP and AD-AS diagrams (it helps to stack them vertically).

Solution: A shift in the IS curve to the right raises output at every given level of inflation which shifts the AD curve to the right. Equilibrium inflation and output increase. The higher inflation rate raises the real interest rate which shifts the MP curve up. This is shown in the following figure.

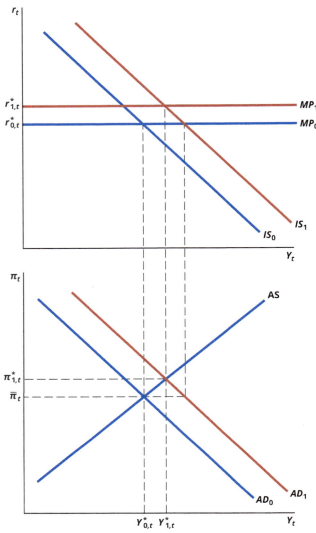

The top panel depicts the IS-MP curves. The bottom panel shows the AS-AD diagram. A shift in the IS curve to the right shifts the AD curve to the right. Inflation increases from $\bar{\pi}_t$ to $\pi^*_{1,t}$ and output increases from $Y^*_{0,t}$ to $Y^*_{1,t}$. The higher inflation rate shifts the MP curve up and the real interest rate rises from $r^*_{0,t}$ to $r^*_{1,t}$.

Chapter 13 Solutions

Questions for Review

1. Explain why net capital outflow is a negative function of the difference between the domestic and global real interest rates.

   Solution: If the domestic interest rate is higher than the global interest rate then it is more attractive for investors to invest in the domestic economy compared to the global economy. This causes capital to flow into the domestic economy, thereby decreasing net capital outflow.

3. How does a rise in the nominal interest rate affect the real exchange rate? Does this increase or decrease net exports?

   Solution: A rise in the nominal interest rate raises the real interest rate through the Fisher equation. This causes capital to flow into the economy driving up the real exchange rate. A higher real exchange rate causes net exports to fall.

5. What is the impossible trinity? What makes it impossible?

   Solution: The impossible trinity says that it is impossible to simultaneously maintain free capital flows, independent monetary policy, and a fixed exchange rate. Question for Review 4 explained why a fixed exchange rate and independent monetary policy require capital controls.

If the country wants to allow the free flow of capital into and out of their economy, then either the fixed exchange rate or independent monetary policy must be abandoned.

Problems

1. Suppose current-period government spending increases in a country with a floating exchange rate.

   a. If the central bank follows passive monetary policy, does output change by more or less in the open economy compared to the closed economy? How about inflation?

   Solution: The open-economy IS curve is flatter than the closed-economy IS curve. An increase in government spending shifts the IS curve to the right by the same magnitude. This means that output rises by the same amount in both economies. This is shown in the following figure.

   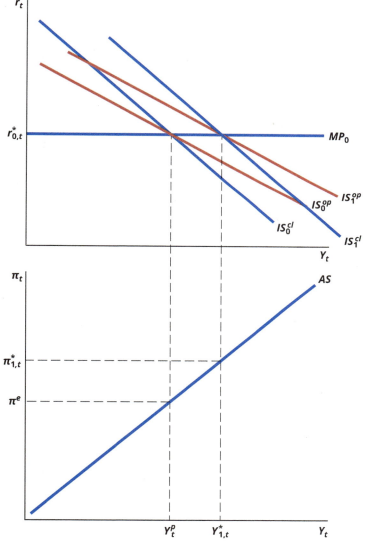

   An increase in government spending shifts the open-economy and closed-economy IS curves to the right. Under passive monetary policy, output rises from Y_t^p to $Y_{1,t}$. Inflation rises from π^e to $\pi_{1,t}^*$. Optimal monetary policy entails raising the real interest rate. The interest rate must rise by more in the closed economy than in the open economy.

   b. If the central bank wants to implement optimal monetary policy, how does the magnitude of the interest rate change differ in the open versus the closed economy?

   Solution: Optimal monetary policy entails raising the nominal interest rate, which, through the Fisher equation, raises the real interest rate and shifts the MP curve up. The MP curve should shift up until output equals Y_t^p. This means that the real interest rate must rise by more in the closed economy.

444 Solutions

3. One element of the 1990s crisis in Mexico was an increase in the risk premium, which in our model is given by f_t.

   a. Show how an increase in f_t affects the IS-MP-AS diagram under a fixed exchange rate.

   Solution: An increase in f_t shifts the IS curve to the left. Maintaining a constant real exchange rate requires that monetary policy be conducted in such a way as to leave real interest rates constant. This means that the MP curve doesn't move. In equilibrium, output and inflation fall. This is shown in the following figure.

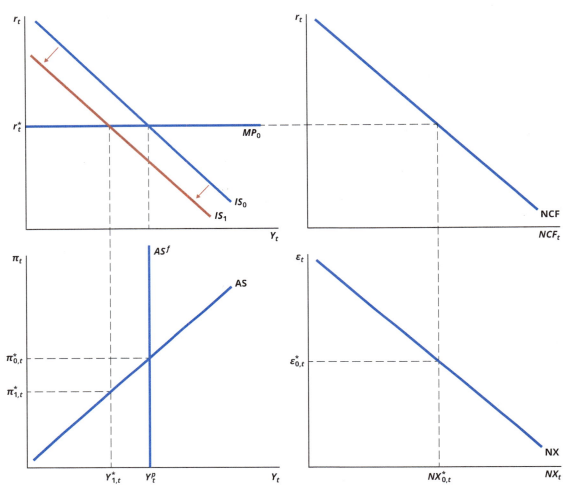

An increase in f_t shifts the IS curve to the left. Under passive monetary policy, the real interest rate stays constant. Output declines from $Y^*_{0,t}$ to $Y^*_{1,t}$. Tracing down from the intersection of the MP curve and IS_1 to the AS curve in the bottom left panel shows that inflation declines from $\pi^*_{0,t}$ to $\pi^*_{1,t}$. Because net capital outflow stays constant, the real exchange rate also stays constant. Thus, the results under a fixed exchange rate system are identical to a floating exchange rate system with passive monetary policy.

   b. Show how an increase in f_t affects the IS-MP-AS diagram under a flexible exchange rate and passive monetary policy.

   Solution: The results are identical to the previous figure. The reason is that passive monetary policy leaves the real interest rate constant.

   c. Show how an increase in f_t affects the IS-MP-AS diagram under a flexible exchange rate and optimal monetary policy.

   Solution: Optimal monetary policy entails reducing the nominal interest rate, which, through the Fisher equation, reduces the real interest rate. Graphically, the MP curve shifts down from MP_0 to MP_1. Output moves back to its potential level, the real exchange rate depreciates, and net exports increase. This is shown in the following figure.

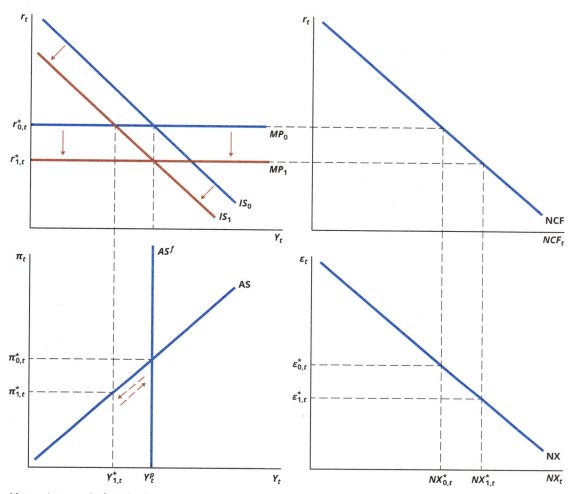

After an increase in f_t, optimal monetary policy entails reducing the nominal interest rate which shifts the MP curve down. The equilibrium real interest rate falls from $r_{0,t}^*$ to $r_{1,t}^*$. Equilibrium output returns to Y_t^p. The reduction in real interest rate increases net capital outflow, which in turn reduces the real exchange rate from $\varepsilon_{0,t}^*$ to $\varepsilon_{1,t}^*$ and increases net exports from $NX_{0,t}^*$ to $NX_{1,t}^*$.

5. Suppose that a country's net export function is given by

$$NX_t = Q_t - \varepsilon_t.$$

Their net capital outflow is given by

$$NCF_t = 10 - (r_t - r_t^w).$$

a. Solve for the real exchange rate as a function of $Q_t, r_t,$ and r_t^w.

   Solution: It must be the case that net capital outflow equals the real exchange rate. Imposing this equality and solving for the real exchange rate gives

   $$Q_t - \varepsilon_t = 10 - (r_t - r_t^w)$$
   $$\Leftrightarrow \varepsilon_t = Q_t - 10 + (r_t - r_t^w).$$

b. How does the real exchange rate change in response to the three variables in part a? Are these results consistent with the graphical analysis in the chapter?

   Solution: The real exchange rate is a positive function of Q_t and r_t and a negative function of r_t^w. These results are consistent with the graphical analysis.

446 **Solutions**

Chapter 14 Solutions

Questions for Review

1. How do banks engage in maturity transformation?

   Solution: Banks pool deposits from a large number of depositors to fund illiquid investment projects. Although all depositors want access to their deposits on demand, it's unlikely (absent a bank run) that all the depositors would want to withdraw their deposits simultaneously. This allows the bank to turn highly liquid deposits that are available on demand into illiquid investment projects.

3. How do banks limit the effects of adverse selection?

   Solution: Banks screen borrowers before they issue a loan. The hope is that the screening process weeds out investment projects that have too low of an expected return.

5. Explain the connection between bank profitability and its leverage ratio.

   Solution: The higher is a bank's leverage ratio, the higher is its return on equity (profits as a proportion of equity). A higher leverage ratio also comes with more risk, since it takes a smaller decline in asset values to make the bank insolvent.

7. Why might a solvent bank face a bank run?

   Solution: Banks only hold a fraction of their deposits as cash reserves. If depositors think that other customers are withdrawing their money, then it is in their best interest to withdraw first. If every depositor is thinking like this, you get a bank run. This is true regardless of the bank's solvency status.

Problems

1. Suppose a person is looking to invest \$50,000 in savings.

   a. An entrepreneur has a project that requires \$50,000 in startup capital. Suppose the entrepreneur takes out a \$50,000 loan and pays it back in one year with 10 percent interest. What is the saver's return in dollars?

   Solution: The return is $0.10(\$50{,}000) = \$5{,}000$.

   b. Suppose that the entrepreneur defaults 1 percent of the time and loses the entire \$50,000. What is the saver's expected return in dollars?

   Solution: The expected return is $0.99(0.10)\,\$50{,}000 + 0.01(-\$50{,}000) = \$4{,}450$.

   c. Suppose that the entrepreneur defaults 1 percent of the time, but loses only \$25,000. What is the saver's expected return in dollars?

   Solution: The expected return is $0.99(0.10)\,\$50{,}000 + 0.01(-\$25{,}000) = \$4{,}700$.

   d. Suppose a bank offers the saver a 5 percent return with certainty. Would a risk neutral saver prefer the 5 percent return with certainty, or the uncertain return in part b? Can you say which investment a risk averse person would prefer?

   Solution: A 5 percent return in dollars is $0.05(\$50{,}000) = \$2{,}500$. A risk neutral person prefers the investment in part b because it has a higher expected payout. We can't say for sure what a risk averse person would prefer.

3. Suppose a person purchases a \$300,000 home with a \$60,000 down payment and \$240,000 in mortgage.

   a. If the house value increases by 10 percent and the person sells the house, what is their return on investment?

   Solution: The home's value increases to \$330,000. If the person sells the home, they earn \$30,000. Since \$60,000 was the size of the initial investment, the ROI is $\$30{,}000/\$60{,}000 = 0.5$, or 50 percent.

   b. If the house decreases by 10 percent and the person sells the house, can they pay off the mortgage without some other source of savings?

   Solution: If the home's value falls by 10 percent, then it is worth \$270,000. If they sell the house, they can pay off the \$240,000 mortgage.

   c. Suppose instead the person purchases the home with a \$20,000 down payment and a \$280,000 mortgage. If the home increases by 10 percent and the person sells the house, what is their return on investment?

   Solution: The home's value increases to \$330,000. If the person sells the home then they earn \$30,000. Since \$20,000 was the size of the initial investment, the ROI is $\$30{,}000/\$20{,}000 = 1.5$ or 150 percent.

d. Continue to assume that the person puts $20,000 down. If the house decreases by 10 percent and the person sells the house, can they pay off the mortgage without some other source of savings?

Solution: If the home's value falls by 10 percent, then it is worth $270,000. The value of the mortgage is $280,000, so if they sell the house they can't pay off the mortgage without some other source of savings.

e. Comparing your results in parts a and c, would a borrower prefer to put a higher or lower down payment on a home?

Solution: Provided the person wants to maximize their return on investment, then they want to put a lower down payment on the home.

f. As you learned in the chapter, banks screen loan applicants for their credit worthiness. Considering your results in parts b and d, should banks direct more of their screening effort to borrowers with low down payments or borrowers with high down payments?

Solution: Banks should direct their efforts to screening low down payment borrowers. In the event of a sale, people with high down payments will be able to pay back the mortgage to the bank. People with low down payments may not be able to pay back their mortgage. Thus, banks will want to make sure people with low down payments have stable sources of income.

5. Consider two banks with balance sheets given respectively by

Bank A	
Assets	**Liabilities**
Mortgages = $150 million	Deposits = $120 million
Cash Reserves = $0	**Equity** = $30 million

Bank B	
Assets	**Liabilities**
Mortgages = $70 million	Deposits = $110 million
Cash Reserves = $30 million	**Equity** = −$10 million

a. Which bank faces a liquidity problem and which bank faces a solvency problem?

Solution: Bank B has negative equity and is insolvent. Bank A has positive equity and is therefore solvent but faces a liquidity problem since they have no cash reserves to fulfill demands from depositors.

b. Would the Fed want to lend to Bank A or Bank B? Explain.

Solution: The Fed would want to lend to Bank A, which faces a liquidity problem. Since Bank A has no cash reserves, it will not be able to meet withdrawal requests by depositors. Bank A can take out a loan (from the Fed) and pay the loan back as it makes money from its mortgages or it sells the mortgages to a different bank.

Chapter 15 Solutions

Questions for Review

1. Explain why discount bonds trade for less than their face value.

Solution: Bond holders receive the face value of the bond in the future. Because a given quantity of dollars is worth more in the present than the future, discount bonds trade for less than their face value.

3. Compare and contrast the way the Fed traditionally affected long-term interest rates versus their more recent policies.

Solution: Traditionally monetary policy only targeted the short-term interest rate which, through the term structure, affects longer-term interest rates. More recently, the Fed has used forward guidance and purchases of longer-duration bonds to affect long-term interest rates.

5. What advantage does the Shiller PE ratio have over traditional PE ratios?

Solution: The Shiller PE ratio uses an average of 10 years of earnings. Averaging over 10 years removes the effects of the business cycle on earnings. The 10-year average also dampens the effects of year-to-year fluctuations in expected earnings. Both of these are advantages over a traditional PE ratio.

448 **Solutions**

Problems

1. Consider the following bond-pricing questions.

   a. The price of a bond with a face value of $100 and a time to maturity of one year is $96. Calculate the yield to maturity.

   Solution: The bond pricing equation is

   $$\$96 = \frac{\$100}{1 + i}.$$

   Thus, the yield to maturity is $i = 0.42$ or 4.2 percent.

   b. Suppose the face value and YTM with a time to maturity of two years is identical to part a. Calculate the price of the bond. Comment on how the price of the bond is related to the time to maturity.

   Solution: The bond pricing equation is

   $$P = \frac{\$100}{1.042^2} = \$92.16.$$

   Given the same face value and YTM, as the time to maturity increases, the price of the bond decreases.

   c. Assume that an investor purchases a two-year bond for the price you calculated in part b, but sells the bond at the end of the first year. If the YTM of a bond with a time to maturity of one year is the same as what you found in part a, calculate the investor's rate of return. Comment on the relationship between the bond's rate of return and the YTM.

   Solution: The price of a bond with a face value of $100, a YTM of 4.2 percent, and a time to maturity of one year is $96. The rate of return is

   $$R = \frac{\$96 - \$92.16}{\$92.16} = 0.042.$$

   The rate of return is identical to the YTM.

3. Suppose that the YTM on a discount bond maturing in 3 years is 7 percent.

   a. The sequence of expected one-year rates is shown in the table below.

Year	Expected interest rate
1	5
2	4
3	?

   What, according to the expectations hypothesis, must the expected one-year interest rate be in year 3?

   Solution: The expectations hypothesis predicts that the long-term interest rate today is the average of expected short-term rates:

   $$7 = \frac{1}{3}(5 + 4 + i^e_{t+2,1}).$$

   Solving for $i^e_{t+2,1}$ gives

   $$i_{t,3} = \frac{1}{3}(i_{t,1} + i^e_{t+1,1} + i^e_{t+2,1})$$

   $$\Leftrightarrow 7 = \frac{1}{3}(5 + 4 + i^e_{t+2,1})$$

   $$\Leftrightarrow 21 = 9 + i^e_{t+2,1}$$

   $$\Leftrightarrow i^e_{t+2,1} = 12.$$

   So the one-year rate in $t + 2$ is predicted to be 12 percent.

b. Suppose that the three-year bond carries a risk premium of 2 percent. What is the minimum expected one-ear interest rate in year 3 that is consistent with an upward sloping yield curve?

Solution: The condition for an upward sloping yield curve is that $i_{t,3} > i_{t,1}$. Adjusting the expectations hypothesis equation to include the risk premium gives

$$i_{t,3} = \frac{1}{3}(i_{t,1} + i^e_{t+1,1} + i^e_{t+2,1}) + rp > i_{t,1}$$

$$\Leftrightarrow \frac{1}{3}(5 + 4 + i^e_{t+2,1}) + 2 > 5$$

$$\Leftrightarrow \frac{1}{3}(5 + 4 + i^e_{t+2,1}) > 3$$

$$\Leftrightarrow i^e_{t+2,1} > 0.$$

Provided $i^e_{t+2,1}$ exceeds 0 percent, the yield curve is upward sloping.

5. Suppose that a stock pays \$4 per share in dividends and that the dividend growth rate is 5 percent. Assume that the nominal interest rate, i, is 4 percent and the risk premium, f, is 3 percent.

a. Calculate the price of this stock.

Solution: The price of the stock is

$$p_t = \frac{(1 + 0.05)D_t}{i + f - g}$$

$$= \frac{(1 + 0.05)\$4}{0.04 + 0.03 - 0.05}$$

$$= \$210.$$

b. Suppose that the risk premium increases to 5 percent. Calculate the price of the stock. Comment on how an increase in the risk premium affects the value of the stock.

Solution:

$$p_t = \frac{(1 + g)D_t}{i + f - g}$$

$$= \frac{(1 + 0.05)\$4}{0.04 + 0.05 - 0.05}$$

$$= \$105.$$

An increase in the risk premium reduces the stock price.

c. Suppose that the risk premium goes back to 3 percent, but the dividend growth rate falls to 4 percent. Calculate the price of the stock. Comment on how a decrease in the dividend growth rate affects the value of the stock.

Solution:

$$p_t = \frac{(1 + g)D_t}{i + f - g}$$

$$= \frac{(1 + 0.04)\$4}{0.04 + 0.03 - 0.05}$$

$$= \$208.$$

A decrease in the dividend growth rate reduces the price of the stock.

Glossary

A

Absolute advantage   The good or service that an economy produces more efficiently than another economy.

Adverse selection   A situation in which borrowers have more information about the quality of their project than lenders.

Aggregate production function   A production function describing the entire economy.

Aggregate supply curve   The relationship between inflation and inflation expectations and the output gap.

Arbitrage   The process of exploiting cross-country price differences of an identical product.

Assets   Things an entity owns.

Asymmetric information   A situation in which two people are engaged in a transaction and one person knows more than the other person.

Autarky   A situation in which no countries trade with each other.

Automatic stabilizer   Part of the government's budget that varies with the business cycle and doesn't rely on passing new legislation.

B

Balance sheet   An accounting device that keeps track of an entity's assets, liabilities, and equity.

Balanced growth path   A situation in which all of an economy's variables are growing at a constant, although not necessarily the same, rate.

Bank runs   A situation in which a large number of a bank's depositors simultaneously demand to withdraw their money.

Bretton–Woods system   The system of fixed exchange rates among high-income nations that prevailed for several decades after World War II.

Bubble term   The difference between the price of a stock and the present discounted value of its expected dividends.

Business cycle   The variation in GDP around the economy's trend.

C

Capital   The structures, equipment, and intellectual property that go into producing output.

Capital controls   Limits on a country's capital inflow or capital outflow.

Capital good   A machine, piece of equipment, or physical operating space used by a business.

Capital requirements   Regulations that ensure that a certain portion of a bank's risk-weighted assets are financed with capital rather than debt.

Cash reserves   Assets that a bank holds as cash or deposits at the Federal Reserve.

Civilian, noninstitutionalized, 16 and over population   A measure of the population that includes everyone 16 years and older who reside in the 50 states or the District of Columbia and are not on active duty in the military or an inmate of an institution, such as penal and mental facilities or a home for the aged.

Classical dichotomy   A theory that predicts that real variables are determined independently of nominal variables.

Collateral   Assets that a borrower puts up that the lender can seize if the borrower defaults.

Commodity money   A type of money with intrinsic value.

Comovement   The way in which a data series correlates with the cyclical component of GDP.

Comparative advantage   The good or service that an economy produces at a lower opportunity cost than another economy.

Conditional convergence   A prediction that all countries with identical savings rates, population growth rates, and levels of TFP will eventually have the same level of real GDP per worker.

Consumer price index   The average price of a basket of goods and services purchased by urban consumers.

Corner solution   In the context of the labor–leisure model, a situation in which an individual finds it optimal to spend all their time on leisure.

Coupons   Regular payments from the bond issuer to the bond holder.

Crowding out   The reduction in investment by private firms that occurs when additional government spending raises real interest rates.

Currency union   A collection of countries with a common currency and monetary policy.

Current government expenditures   The sum of consumption expenditures, transfer payments, interest payments, and subsidies.

Current receipts   The sum of current tax receipts, contributions for government social insurance, income receipt on assets, current transfer receipts, and current surplus of government enterprises.

Cyclical unemployment   Unemployment caused by variations in the business cycle.

Glossary   451

D

Demand deposit   Deposits that can be redeemed on the demand of the depositors.

Depreciation   The decline in value of capital goods associated with physical deterioration and obsolescence.

Depreciation rate   The rate at which capital that is used up during the course of production.

Discount bond   A bond that offers no coupon payments. The price of a discount bond is the present discounted value of the principal.

Discount window   The lending program in which banks can borrow from the Fed on a short-term basis.

Discouraged worker   A person who has not looked for work in the last four weeks but indicates some type of discouragement in their job prospects.

Disposable income   Income minus taxes.

Distortion   Anything that reduces economic efficiency. Examples include taxes and subsidies imposed by the government, monopoly power held by firms, and externalities like pollution.

Distortionary tax   A tax that distorts the incentive to engage in an activity.

Dividend   Distributed profits made by the firm to its stockholders.

Divine coincidence   The result that inflation targeting stabilizes inflation and minimizes the output gap.

Durable good   A good that physically persists despite being used. The BEA defines a durable good as a good with an average useful life of at least three years.

Dynamic inefficiency   A situation in which an economy's savings rate is above the golden-rule savings rate.

E

Employment–population ratio   The number of an economy's workers divided by its population.

Equity   The difference in value between assets and liabilities.

Expectations hypothesis   A theory that predicts that the interest rate on a bond with more than one year to maturity is the average expected interest rate on one-year bonds over the same time horizon.

F

Face value   The principal payment that a bond issuer pays the bond holder at maturity.

FDIC insurance   Insurance that banks can purchase from the Federal Deposit Insurance Corporation, which insures up to $250,000 in deposits per customer.

Federal funds rate   The nominal interest rate banks charge each other for overnight loans.

Fiat money   A type of money with no intrinsic value.

Financial arbitrage   The process through which risk-adjusted returns are equalized through the buying and selling patterns of profit-maximizing investors.

Financial intermediary   An institution that matches people who want to save with people who want to borrow.

Firm   A unit that hires capital and labor to produce output.

Fisher equation   An equation that shows that the real interest rate equals the nominal interest rate minus expected inflation.

Fixed exchange rate regime   A system in which a country's government explicitly targets the exchange rate and allows people to exchange the domestic currency for the foreign currency at the statutory exchange rate.

Floating exchange rate regime   A system in which a country's exchange rate is determined by supply and demand.

Forward guidance   A tool through which the Fed communicates with the public about its future course of action.

Frictional unemployment   Unemployment that comes from employees either voluntarily leaving their job or new workers looking for work.

Friedman rule   The result suggesting that a central bank should set the long-run inflation rate to achieve a nominal interest rate of zero.

G

Game theory   The branch of economics dealing with strategic interaction among market participants.

GDP deflator   A country's nominal GDP divided by its real GDP.

GDP per capita   GDP divided by a country's population.

GDP per worker   GDP divided by a country's workforce.

Golden-rule savings rate   The savings rate that maximizes long-run consumption.

Gross domestic product (GDP)   The current dollar value of all final goods and services produced in a country in a year.

Gross national income (GNI)   The sum of all forms of income earned by a nation's citizens.

Growth accounting   The procedure of dividing GDP growth into the share that is attributable to TFP and what is attributed to all other factors.

H

Household   A unit that supplies capital and labor and consumes output.

I

Idea   Anything that has the potential to increase output for any given level of inputs.

Impossible trinity   The idea that it is impossible for a country to simultaneously achieve independent monetary policy, maintain a fixed exchange rate, and allow the free flow of capital across borders.

Income effect   The change in the optimal quantities of consumption coming from a change in income that leaves prices constant.

Indifference curve   All pairs of current and future consumption, (C_t, C_{t+1}), that provide the same level of utility.

Inflation   An increase in the average price level.

Inflation rate   The percent change in the average level of prices.

Intermediate good   A good that is not yet ready for final consumption or investment.

Investment   New capital created by the fraction of household income used as savings.

IS curve   The set of (r_t, Y_t) pairs such that the savings and investment market is in equilibrium.

452 Glossary

L

Labor force The sum of the number of employed individuals and unemployed individuals.

Labor force participation rate The labor force divided by the population.

Law of one price The theory that identical goods and services should trade for the same price, regardless of the location.

Leverage ratio A bank's liabilities divided by its equity.

Liabilities Things an entity owes.

Limited liability A legal protection in which a business owner's personal assets aren't at risk if the business fails.

Liquidity The ease with which assets can be used in exchange.

Liquidity ratio The ratio of a bank's cash reserves to its total assets.

Liquidity risk The risk that a bank's liquid assets run so low that they can't meet withdrawal requests.

Lump-sum tax A type of tax that is unavoidable and the size of which does not vary with individual behavior.

M

Marginal product of capital The amount that output changes per unit change of capital.

Marginal product of labor The amount that output changes per unit change of labor.

Marginal propensity to consume (MPC) The change in consumption per dollar change in current-period income.

Marginal rate of substitution The quantity of future consumption, C_{t+1}, the individual must give up for one additional unit of current consumption, C_t, to stay on the same indifference curve.

Marginal utility The increase in utility that comes with a small increase in consumption.

Match surplus The total amount of output net of unemployment benefits.

Maturity The length of time it takes an issuer of the bond to repay the holder of the bond.

Maturity transformation The process of turning liquid deposits into illiquid loans.

Medium of exchange Anything that can be used to trade for goods and services.

Menu costs The costs that firms incur when changing prices.

Moral hazard A situation in which borrowers take an action that is difficult for lenders to observe.

Mortgage-backed security An investment product consisting of bundled mortgages that connects investors to homebuyers.

MP curve A graphical representation of how monetary policymakers set interest rates.

N

Natural rate of unemployment The unemployment that would prevail absent of nominal rigidities.

Net capital outflow The difference between capital outflow and capital inflow.

Net exports Exports minus imports.

Nominal exchange rate The rate at which two currencies trade for each other.

Nominal GDP A country's GDP calculated using current-year prices.

Nominal interest rate The percentage return in dollars one gets from investing.

Nominal rigidities The inability of prices to instantaneously adjust to economic fundamentals.

Non-stationary data series A data series with a consistent trend up or down over time.

O

Output gap The difference between the actual and potential level of output.

P

Passive monetary policy A monetary policy rule characterized by the central bank holding the nominal interest rate constant after a change in another exogenous variable.

Phillips curve The relationship between the rates of unemployment and inflation.

Potential GDP The amount of output the economy could produce if all of the factors of production (such as labor, capital, and raw materials) were used efficiently.

Present discounted value The denomination of future goods and services in terms of present goods and services.

Price-dividend ratio The price of a company's stock divided by its dividend per share.

Price-earnings ratio The price of a company's stock divided by its earnings per share.

Primary deficit The difference between government expenditure, excluding payments to service the debt, and taxes.

Production function A mathematical function that describes how inputs are turned into output.

Production possibilities frontier (PPF) A graph showing all the combinations of two goods produced in a country given its technology levels and the size of its labor force.

Purchasing power parity exchange rate Exchange rate that corrects for differences in price levels across countries.

R

Rate of Return The percent return that an investor earns over a specified time period.

RBC model A business cycle model with perfectly competitive markets and forward-looking economic agents, where business cycles are the result of short-run variation in TFP and the classical dichotomy holds.

Real exchange rate The rate at which goods and services in one country trade for goods and services in another country.

Real GDP A country's GDP calculated using constant prices.

Real interest rate The rate of return in terms of goods and services.

Recession A period in which there is significant decline in economic activity that is spread across the economy and that lasts more than a few months.

Rental rate The price at which households supply their capital.

Representative firm The stand-in firm for the entire economy.

Glossary **453**

Representative household   The stand-in household for the entire economy.

Reservation wage   The lowest wage at which an individual finds it optimal to join the labor force.

Reserve ratio   The ratio of a bank's cash reserves to its deposits.

Residual claimants   The owners of a firm. They get paid only after all debt payments and other expenses have been paid.

Return on assets   A bank's profits divided by its assets.

Return on equity   A bank's profits divided by its equity.

Returns to scale   The factor by which output increases when all inputs double.

Ricardian equivalence theorem   A theorem that says conditional on a time path of government spending, the method of financing is irrelevant.

Risk averse   A preference for projects with low uncertainty to outcomes of high uncertainty.

Risk neutral   A preference for projects with the highest expected value, regardless of the riskiness.

Risk premium   The added risk of investing in capital relative to the return from a savings account.

Risk structure of interest rates   The pattern of interest rates on liabilities of different risks.

Rival good   A good characterized by the property that one person's use of it diminishes the potential of other people to use the good.

Rule of 70   An equation used to determine how long it takes an economy to double its income per capita.

S

Seigniorage   Government revenue from printing money.

Shiller PE ratio   A PE ratio that uses a 10-year inflation adjusted average of earnings.

Solvency risk   The risk that a bank's assets depreciate in value so much that they become insolvent.

Solvent   A situation in which assets exceed liabilities.

Stagflation   A simultaneous period of high inflation and low output.

Standard and Poor's 500 (S&P 500)   A stock price index of 500 of the largest publicly traded companies in America.

Stationary data series   A data series with no consistent trend up or down.

Statistical decomposition   A statistical method separating the trend component of a data series from its cyclical component.

Steady state   A situation in which an economic variable is not growing or shrinking over time.

Store of value   An asset that preserves at least some of its value over time.

Structural unemployment   Unemployment caused by a mismatch between the labor force's skills and what employers desire.

Substitution bias   The error that results from the CPI not accounting for the tendency of consumers to substitute away from expensive goods toward cheaper goods.

Substitution effect   The change in the optimal quantities of consumption resulting from a change in the relative price, leaving the level of utility fixed.

T

Taylor rule   A rule that expresses the federal funds rate as a linear function of the output gap and inflation.

Term premium   The higher yield to maturity associated with longer duration bonds compared to shorter duration bonds.

Term structure of interest rates   The pattern of interest rates on liabilities of different maturities.

Terms of trade   A country's export price divided by its import price.

Total factor productivity (TFP)   A term that describes how efficiently inputs are used in producing output.

Total government expenditures   The sum of current government expenditures and net investment, or gross investment minus the consumption of fixed capital, i.e., depreciation.

Total receipts   The sum of current receipts and capital transfer receipts.

Trade deficit   A situation in which imports exceed exports.

Trade surplus   A situation in which exports exceed imports.

Transaction costs   The costs associated with negotiating a nominal wage.

Transfer payment   Moving money or resources from one person to another without anything being produced.

Treasury Inflation Expected Security (TIPS)   Bonds issued by the U.S. government that index interest payments to the CPI.

U

Unconditional convergence   A prediction that all countries will eventually have the same levels of real GDP per worker regardless of any differences in exogenous variables or parameters.

Unemployed   The state of being out of work but actively looking for work.

Unemployment rate   The number of unemployed individuals divided by the labor force.

Unit of account   Anything that can be used to quote the prices of goods and services.

Utility   A term used to describe a consumer's overall level of happiness.

V

Velocity   The number of times the average unit of money turns over.

Volatility   The quantitative magnitude of the upward and downward swings in a data series.

W

Wage rate   The price at which households supply their labor.

Y

Yield to maturity   The (annual) interest that a bond holder earns by holding the bond to maturity.

Z

Zero–lower bound (ZLB)   A situation in which the nominal interest rate falls to zero.

Index

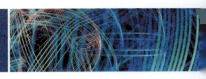

A

Absolute advantage, 161
Accounting, for imports and exports in GDP equation, 166–177
Adverse selection, 359
Aggregate production function
    definition, 27
    mathematical representation, 28
    shape of, 28–30
Aggregate supply curve
    alternatives of wage-contracting model, 305–306
    completely flexible prices and wages, 294–298
    nominal wages, 298–302
Aguiar, Mark, 142
American Time Use Survey (ATUS), 4
Annual real interest, 149
Arbitrage, 159
AS curve, shift in, 335–336
Assets, of bank, 361–363
Asymmetric information, 81
Australia
    average annual growth in GDP per worker by decade, 84
    evolution of output per worker, 83, 84
Austria
    budgets and retail prices, 241
    hyperinflation, 240
Autarky, 161
Automatic stabilizers, 256

B

Balanced growth path (BGP), 52
Balance sheet
    assets and liabilities, 361–363
    concepts, 363–365
    household, 361
Bank failures, 368
Bank leverage, 364–365
Bank liquidity, 363–364
Bank profitability, 364
Bank runs, 369
Banks
    adverse selection and screening, 358–360
    balance sheet, 361–365
    diversification of risk, 357–358
    liquidity vs. solvency risk, 366–368
    maturity transformation, 356–357
    moral hazard and monitoring, 360
    regulation and policy, 369–370
Barro, Robert, 229
Barter economy, 108
Baum, L. Frank, 349
Bell, Alexander Graham, 1
Bernanke, Ben, 286, 316
Biden, Joe, 293
Big Mac index, 16, 17
Bitcoin, 109
Bond prices and interest rates, 375–386
Bonds
    definitions, types, and pricing, 376–378
    term structure, 379
Bretton-Woods system, 347
Bryan, William Jennings, 349
Bubble term, 388
Budget constraint, 127–130, 234–236
    government's intertemporal, 227–228
Budget line and indifference curve, 135, 136
Bureau of Economic Analysis (BEA), 7
Bureau of Labor Statistics (BLS), 101
Bush, George W., 233
Business cycles
    measurements, 249–257
    stylized facts of, 253–256
    welfare costs of, 262

C

Capital, 27, 31, 362
    controls, 346
    demand for, 32–34
    goods, 7
    requirements, 370
    share, 40
    supply of, 31
CARES Act, 227
Case, Karl E., 393
Case–Shiller home price index, 282, 394
Cash reserves, 357, 362
Change in private inventories, 10
China
    establishment size distribution, 78
    exports from, 341
    savings rates, 62, 150
    share of gross capital formation for, 62
    trade with, 167–168
Civilian, noninstitutionalized, 16 and over population, 184
Classical dichotomy, 111
Cobb, Charles, 38
Cobb–Douglas aggregate production function, 49
Cobb–Douglas production function, 38–42, 75, 76, 77, 82, 86, 87, 401
Collateral assets, 366
Colosio, Luis Donaldo, 342
Commodity money, 108
Commuting zones (CZs), 167
Comovement, 252
Comparative advantage, 164–165
Conditional convergence, 66
Congressional Budget Office (CBO), 236
Consumer price index (CPI), 101–102, 115, 394
    calculation challenges, 102–104
    vs. GDP deflator, 104–105
Consumer Protection Act of 2010, 371
Consumption
    expenditures, 248
    of fixed capital, 7
    tax change effects on, 224–227
Consumption–savings model, 233
    taxation in, 221–227
Consumption-savings theory
    budget constraints, 127–130
    consumption function, 140–141
    current and future consumption, preferences for, 131–134
    optimal consumption bundle, characterization of, 135–140
Corner solution, 198–199
Costs of inflation, 115
Coupons, 376

Index   **455**

COVID-19 pandemic, 215, 217, 227, 248, 262
  employment-to-population ratio, 185
  inflation rate during, 15
  money supply during, 110
Crowding out, 148
Cryptocurrencies, 108. *See also* Bitcoin
Currency, 110
Currency union, 335, 347–348
Current government expenditures, 216
Current-period government expenditures, 231, 232
Current-period income, 136, 137
Current Population Survey (CPS), 208
Current receipts, 221
Cyclical unemployment, 202

D

Debt-to-GDP ratio, 237
Demand
  combining supply and, 34–36
  deposit, 361
  for labor and capital, 32–34
Depreciation, 7
Depreciation rate, 49
Discount bond, 376
Discount window, 366
Discouraged workers, 208
Disposable income, 145
Distortionary tax, 230
Distortions, 76
Dividend, 387
Divine coincidence, 318
Dodd–Frank Wall Street Reform, 371
Dollar value, current, 2
Domestic and foreign goods, 338–339
Douglas, Paul, 38
Durable goods, 9
Dynamic inefficiency, 61

E

Economic Stimulus Act of 2008, 233
The Economist, 16
Economy's price level measurement
  consumer price index, 101–105
  costs of inflation, 113–115
  money, 107–112, 116–117
  nominal interest rate determination, 117–119
Ehrlich, Paul, 92
Employee compensation, 7, 8
Employment–population ratio, 184
Equilibrium real interest rate determination, 144
  government spending, 145
  graphical determination of, 145–146
  private savings, 145
  public savings, 145
  savings–investment model, 145–149

Equilibrium wage determination, in labor market, 34, 35
Equity, 361
Ex-ante real interest rate, 125
Exchange rates
  law of one price, 160
  nominal, 157–158
  real, 158–159
Excise tax, 7
Expectations hypothesis, 380
Expenditure approach, GDP calculation, 8–13
Exponents and logs, 398–401
Export, 11
Ex-post real interest rate, 125

F

Face value, of bond, 376
Federal Deposit Insurance Corporation (FDIC), 368
  insurance, 369
Federal funds rate, 116
  and interest rates, 270, 272
Federal Reserve Open Market Committee, 265
Fiat money, 108
Financial arbitrage, 380
Financial intermediary, 79
Firm, 31
Fiscal interactions, with government's debt, 239–240
Fiscal policy, in Solow model, 59–60
Fisher equation, 125–127
Fixed exchange rate
  benefits and disadvantages of, 340–341
  regimes, 340
Floating exchange rate regimes, 340
Food consumption, and age, 141–142
Food expenditure, and age, 141–142
Forward guidance, 284
France, 100
  average annual growth in GDP per worker by decade, 84
  evolution of output per worker, 83, 84
Free silver movement, 349
Free trade, 160
  limits to, 165–166
  Ricardian model, 161–165
Frictional unemployment, 202
Friedman, Milton, 318
Friedman rule, 318

G

Game theory, 204
GDP deflator, 15
GDP per capita, 18
  and consumption per capita, 21

vs. consumption per capita, 21, 22
  facts of, 18–20
  and infant mortality rate, 21
  and living standards, 20–22
  vs. per capita CO_2 emissions, 21, 22
  for Singapore, Thailand, Hong Kong, and South Korea, 19
GDP per worker, 18
The General Theory of Employment, Interest, and Money (Keynes), 111, 257
Germany, 100
  hyperinflation, 240
  real GDP per capita for, 66
GNI. *See* Gross national income (GNI)
Golden-rule savings rate, 60
Government consumption, 215, 216
Government financing, method of, 227–232
Government investment projects, 215
Government revenue
  and expenditure forecast, 236, 237
  sources of, 219–221
Government's intertemporal budget constraint, 227–228
Government spending, 10–11
  categories of, 216–221
Great Moderation, 253–254
Greece, 326
Greenspan, Alan, 265
Gross domestic product (GDP), 1, 248
  accounting for imports and exports in GDP equation, 166–177
  calculating
    expenditure approach, 8–13
    income approach, 6–8, 13
    at industry level, 5
    value-added approach, 6, 13
  definition, 2–3
  global imports plus exports as share of, 160
  inequality and, 22–23
  share of labor compensation in, 42
  tracking price changes
    across countries, 16–17
    within a country, 14–16
  transfer payments as a fraction of, 216, 217
  trend and cyclical, 250
  valuing nonmarket work, 3–4
Gross national income (GNI), 6, 7, 8
Growth accounting
  in action, 83–84
  framework, 82–83

H

Hamilton, Alexander, 166
Hong Kong, GDP per capita for, 19
Household, 31

456 Index

Hsieh, Chang-Tai, 78, 79
Hungary, hyperinflation, 240
Hurst, Erik, 142

I

Ideas, 85, 90–92
Immigration effects on wages, 37
Import, 11
Impossible trinity, 346, 347
Income approach, GDP calculation, 6–8, 13
Income effect, 137
India, establishment size distribution, 78
Indifference curve, 132
Inflation, 15
    benefits to inflation targeting, 318–319
    expectations, 303–305
    price distortion, 115
    shoe leather costs, 113–114
    tax, 113
    unexpected, 114–115
Inflation rates, 101
    vs. nominal interest rates, 126
Interest rates, 124
    bond prices and, 375–386
    equilibrium real interest rate
        determination, 144–149
    federal funds rate and, 270, 272
    vs. money supply rules, 273–274
    term and risk structure of, 384–385
    on 3-month Treasury bill, 380, 381
Intermediate good, 2
International macroeconomics, 157
International trade, 169
Intertemporal budget constraint, 128
Investment, 49
Investment demand curve, 267
Investment demand rule, 144
Investment model, 143–144
IS curve, 265, 327–329
    components of, 266–267
    graphical derivation of, 268–269
    shift in, 333–335
IS–MP–AS model
    aggregate supply curve, 293–306
    business cycle facts, 315–318
    comparative statics in, 310–314
    graphing, 307–309
    in open economy (*See* Open economy
        IS–MP–AS model)
IS–MP model, 265
    algebraic solution, 281
    comparative statics, 277–280
    endogenous variables, 277
    equilibrium in, 276, 277
    exogenous variables, 277
    and Great Recession, 281–286
    IS curve, 265–269
    monetary policy rule, 269–276
    parameters, 277

J

James, LeBron, 114
Japan
    average annual growth in GDP per
        worker by decade, 84
    evolution of output per worker, 83, 84
    real GDP per capita for, 66
    savings rate for, 62
    share of gross capital formation
        for, 62

K

Karabarbounis, Loukas, 42
Kennedy, Robert F., 20
Keynesian macroeconomics, 257
Keynes, John Maynard, 111, 257, 316
Klenow, Peter, 78, 79
Kuznets, Simon, 1

L

Labor
    demand for, 32–34
    optimal quantity of, 199–200
    supply of, 31
Labor demand curves, for economies
        with and without distortions, 77
Labor force, 185
    participation among prime-aged men,
        201
Labor force participation rate (LFPR), 185
Labor–leisure model
    budget constraint and preferences,
        190–194
    graphical analysis of, 199
    labor force participation, 198–199
    optimization and comparative statics,
        194–197
    reservation wage, 198
Labor markets
    data of, 183–190
    labor–leisure model, 190–200
    national trends of extensive and
        intensive margins of, 185–187
    trends by demographic group,
        187–190
    utilization, indicators of, 208–209
Law of one price, 160
Leisure
    activities for young men, 202
    goods, quality of, 201–202
    optimal quantity of, 199–200
Leverage ratios, 365
Liabilities, of bank, 361–363
Lifetime budget constraint, tax
        incorporation in, 221–223
Lifetime utility, 131
Limited liability, 357
Liquidity, 110
Liquidity ratio, 363

Liquidity risk, 366
Lump-sum taxes, 221

M

Macroeconomic impossibility theorem,
    85–86
Macroeconomics, 232
Mahomes, Patrick, 164
Marginal product of capital (MPK), 28,
    143
Marginal product of labor, 28
Marginal propensity to consume (MPC),
    137, 227, 233, 234, 268
Marginal rate of substitution (MRS), 134,
    224
Marginal utility, 131, 132
Match surplus, 204
Mathematical appendix
    exponents and logs, 398–401
    notation, 398
    summary statistics, 401–404
Maturity, of a bond, 376
Maturity transformation, 356–357
McKinley, William, 349
Medicaid, 216
Medicare, 219, 236
Medium of exchange, 108
Menu costs, 305
Mexico, GDP per capita growth rate, 342
Michigan Survey of Consumers, 303
Misallocation theories, of TFP, 76–78
Monetary interactions, with
    government's debt, 239–240
Monetary policy, 286–288, 375, 385, 386
    rule
        interest rate *vs.* money supply rules,
        273–274
        MP curve, 269–273
    stock market and, 387–394
Money
    growth *vs.* inflation, 112
    quantity theory of, 111–112
    roles of, 107–108
    supply
        and demand of, 116–118
        vs. interest rate rules, 273–274
        measurement, 109–110
Moral hazard, 360
Mortgage-backed securities, 282, 285,
    371, 386
MP curve, 269–273, 275, 329–331

N

National income and product accounts
    (NIPA), 1
Natural rate of unemployment, 301–302
Neiman, Brent, 42
Net capital outflow, 327, 330
Net exports, 159, 169

Index 457

Net operating surplus, 7
Nixon, Richard, 347
Nominal exchange rates, 157
   calculation, 158
Nominal GDP, 14, 111
Nominal interest rate, 116
   graphical derivation of, 117–119
Nominal interest rates, 125–127
Nominal rigidities, 294
Nonresidential fixed investment, 10
Non-Ricardian consumers, 231
Non-Ricardian economy, 231
Non-stationary data series, 249
Nonwage income, 190–191
   labor supply schedules for different
      levels, 200
Nordhaus, William, 68, 69
North American Industry Classification
   System (NAICS), 5

O

Obama, Barack, 284
Open economy
   real interest rate determination in,
      172–173
   savings and investment in, 169, 170
Open economy IS–MP–AS model
   Bretton–Woods system, 347
   capital controls, 346
   comparative statics in, 333–339
   complete diagram, 332–333
   currency unions, 347–348
   exchange rate regimes, 340–349
   exchange rate targeting, 343–346
   impossible trinity, 346, 347
   IS curve, 327–329
   MP curve, 329–331
   real exchange rate determination,
      329–331
Open-economy savings–investment
   model, 173–177
Output gap, 293

P

Passive monetary policy, 311
Penn World Table, 39, 42
Personal consumption expenditures
   (PCE) price index, 106
Phillips curve, 257, 301–302
Poland, hyperinflation, 240
Potential GDP, 257
Present discounted value, 128
Price–dividend ratio, 391
Price–earnings (PE) ratio, 391
Primary deficit, 234
Private investment, 9
Production function
   aggregate, 27–30
   assumptions, 28–30

cross-country income differences,
   38–41
definition, 27
Production possibilities frontier (PPF),
   161
Profit, definition, 32
Property rights, 81
Purchasing power parity (PPP)
   exchange rates, 17
   tracking price changes across
      countries, 16–17

Q

Quantity theory of money, 111–112

R

Radford, R. A., 107
Rate of return, 376
RBC model, 258
   critiques of, 260, 261
Real business cycle (RBC) model, 296,
   297
Real business cycle (RBC) theory, 257
Real exchange rates, 158–159
   open economy IS–MP–AS model,
      329–331
Real GDP, 14–15, 249, 250
Real interest rate, 125–127
   declining, 149–151
   determination in open economy,
      172–173
   of one-year government treasuries *vs.*
      real GDP growth, 238
Real-world distortions, 78–79
Recession, 249
Rental rate, 31
Representative firm, 31
Representative household, 31
Reservation wage, 198
   optimal quantity of, 199–200
Reserve ratio, 363
Residential fixed investment, 9–10
Residual claimants, 387
Return on assets (ROA), 364
Return on equity (ROE), 364
Returns to scale, 29
Ricardian equivalence theorem,
   228–230
Ricardian model, 161–164
   with comparative advantage, 164–165
Ricardo, David, 161, 229
Risk averse, 357
Risk neutral, 358
Risk premium, 143, 382
Risk structure of interest rates, 271
Rival good, 85
Robert, J. Shiller, 393
Romer model of endogenous growth
   graphical analysis, 92–94

macroeconomic impossibility theorem,
   85–86
preliminaries of, 86–87
solving, 88–89, 92
Rule of 70, 20

S

Sargent, Thomas, 240
Savings and loan banks (S&Ls), 355
Savings–investment model, 145
   comparative statics in, 146–149
   deficit financing in, 230–232
Savings, tax change effects on, 224–227
Screening, 359–360
Seigniorage, 239
Semi-endogenous growth model, 88, 91
Shiller PE ratio, 391–393
Silicon Valley Bank (SVB), 366, 368
Singapore, GDP per capita for, 19
Social Security, 216, 219, 236
Solow model of economic growth
   algebraically solving, 53–54
   basic ingredients of, 49–52
   and climate change, 68–69
   dynamic efficiency, 60–62
   fiscal policy, 59–60
   graphical characterization, 52–53
   limitation of, 68
   long-run predictions of, 62–65
   macroeconomy, 60–62
   predictions of
      increase in population growth rate,
         56
      increase in savings rate, 54–56
      increase in total factor productivity,
         56–57, 58
   transition dynamics in model and data,
      65–67
   variables and key equations of, 50
Solow, Robert, 48
Solvency risk, 367
Solvent, 367
South Korea, GDP per capita for, 19
Stagflation, 254
Standard and Poor's 500 (S&P 500), 389
Standard deviation, 402
State-owned enterprises (SOEs), 78
Stationary data series, 249
Statistical Abstract of the United States, 1
Statistical decomposition, 252
Steady state, 52
Stock market
   performance and valuation, 389–392
   value and monetary policy, 392–393
Stock pricing, 387–389
Store of value, 108
Structural unemployment, 202
Substitution bias, 102
Substitution effect, 139

458 Index

Summary statistics, 401–404
Supply
    combining demand and, 34–36
    of labor and capital, 31
Survey of Professional Forecasters (SPF), 303

T

Tax
    incorporation in lifetime budget constraint, 221–223
    on production and imports less subsidies, 7
Taxation, in consumption–savings model, 221–227
Taylor, John, 275
Taylor rule, 275–276, 317
Term premium, 379
Terms of trade, 162
Term structure of interest rates, 271
TFP. *See* Total factor productivity (TFP)
Thailand GDP per capita for, 19
3-6-3 rule, 355
Total factor productivity (TFP), 28, 35, 74, 143, 267
    cross-country TFP differences, 75–76
    financial constraints, 79–81
    misallocation theories, 76–78
    as source of business cycle variation, 259–260
Total government expenditures
    gross investment as fraction of, 218
    state and local government expenditures as fraction of, 218, 219
Total receipts, 221
Trade deficit, 169
Trade surplus, 169
Transaction costs, 299
Transfer payments, 10

Treasury inflation-protected securities (TIPS), 115, 304
Trend GDP, 257

U

Unconditional convergence, 66
Unemployed, 185
Unemployment, 249, 254–256
    rates, 185, 189, 190
Unemployment model
    equilibrium
        deriving, 203–205
        graphical characterization, 205–208
    worker and firm behavior, 203
United States, 100, 157, 326
    annual hours per capita in, 184
    average annual growth in GDP per worker by decade, 84
    bank failures in, 367
    cross-country TFP distribution, 75
    dollar reserves, 343
    dollar value, 2
    employment–population ratio for, 185, 186
    establishment size distribution, 78
    evolution of output per worker, 83, 84
    expenditure shares, 11, 12
    federal transfer programs in, 216
    and GDP, 1
    government debt, sustainability of, 234–240
    Housing Market, 393–394
    inflation rate, 15, 16
    labor force participation rate, 186
    median worker, earnings of, 106
    and Mexico, trade between, 169
    net exports or exports minus imports in, 11, 12
    real GDP per capita for, 66
    recipients of subsidies in, 217

    retail sector, 76
    savings rate for, 62
    share of current government expenditures, 218
    share of gross capital formation for, 62
    statistical agencies in, 7
    total factor productivity growth in, 150
    trade deficit, 170–171
    unemployment rate, 186, 187
Unit of account, 108
The U.S. Department of Commerce, 1
Utility, 131

V

Value-added approach, GDP calculation, 6, 13
Velocity of money, 111
Volatility, 252

W

Wage, 106–107
    immigration effects on, 37
    and salary income, 8
Wage-contracting model, alternatives of, 305–306
Wage income, 190
Wage rate, 31
Welfare costs of business cycles, 262
World Development Indicators, 21

Y

Yield curve
    inverted, 383
    for U.S. Treasury securities, 379
Yield to maturity (YTM), 376–378

Z

Zero–lower bound (ZLB), 284, 285